PHILOSOPHICAL GROUNDS
OF RATIONALITY

Philosophical Grounds
of Rationality

INTENTIONS, CATEGORIES, ENDS

EDITED BY

RICHARD E. GRANDY

AND

RICHARD WARNER

CLARENDON PRESS · OXFORD
1986

Oxford University Press, Walton Street, Oxford OX2 6DP

Oxford New York Toronto
Delhi Bombay Calcutta Madras Karachi
Kuala Lumpur Singapore Hong Kong Tokyo
Nairobi Dar es Salaam Cape Town
Melbourne Auckland

and associated companies in
Beirut Berlin Ibadan Nicosia

Oxford is a trade mark of Oxford University Press

Published in the United States
by Oxford University Press, New York

© Oxford University Press 1986

British Library Cataloguing in Publication Data
Philosophical grounds of rationality: intentions,
categories, ends.
1. Grice, H. P.
I. Grandy, Richard E.   II. Warner, Richard
149'.94'0924   B1641.G7
ISBN 0-19-824747-8

Library of Congress Cataloging in Publication Data
Main entry under title:
Philosophical grounds of rationality.
"The Publications of H. P. Grice": p.
Includes index.
1. Grice, H. P. (H. Paul)—Addresses, essays, lectures.
I. Grandy, Richard E.   II. Warner, Richard, 1946–
B1641.G484P48 1985   192   85-5134
ISBN 0-19-824747-8

Typeset by Joshua Associates Limited, Oxford
Printed in Great Britain by
The Alden Press Ltd.
Oxford

CONTENTS

METAPHYSICS

ETHICS

PAUL GRICE: A VIEW OF HIS WORK

RICHARD E. GRANDY AND RICHARD WARNER

Paul Grice is a systematic philosopher with a highly original and important vision of extremely wide range. However, the systematic nature of his work is little recognized—perhaps because Grice has not published the bulk of it. Our goal is to exhibit the connections among Grice's various projects. We will not discuss all of the various projects, and some of those discussed receive only brief attention. We focus on Grice's work on meaning, reasoning, psychological explanation, metaphysics, and ethics. Our picture is painted with a far larger brush than Grice customarily uses; we sacrifice the intricate subtlety characteristic of his work to highlight the interwoven themes.

1. MEANING: THE FIRST TWO STAGES

The most striking feature of Grice's work on meaning is his claim that semantic notions can be explicated, non-circularly, and without semantic remainder, in terms of psychological notions. A less striking but equally important feature is his view of communication as a reason-governed activity. As Grice has shown in many ways and places, a variety of aspects of our communicative activity can be explained by seeing it as a purposive reason-governed endeavour. Grice's views about how to carry out this programme have evolved over the years, and we distinguish three stages in this evolution. Identifying and characterizing these stages provides a brief but illuminating picture of Grice's thought about meaning.

The first stage: 'Meaning', 1957. In 'Meaning', Grice distinguished between (what he will later call) utterer's meaning and utterance-type meaning. Utterer's meaning is the concept involved in such assertions as: 'By uttering "I'm blue" Jones meant that he was sad.' The [1957] suggestion is:

by uttering 'I'm blue' Jones means that he is sad if and only if Jones utters 'I'm blue' intending:

(1) that his audience believes that he is sad;
(2) that the audience recognize his intention (1);
(3) that this recognition be part of the audience's reason for believing that he is sad.[1]

We call such an intention an M-intention. The first stage account of utterer's meaning can be put this way: an utterer U means that p by uttering x if and only if U M-intends that p by uttering x.

We should clarify two points here. First, the utterance need not be a sound or mark or anything linguistic at all. Taking 'utter' in an extended sense, a gesture might be an utterance. One can M-intend by gesture, grunts, and groans. Second, M-intending must be understood more broadly to include imperative utterances. The intention to get one's audience to perform an action is a possible content for an M-intention. We will return to this point later as the second stage of the theory includes an account of the possible forms M-intentions may take.

We move next to the concept of utterance-type meaning. An utterance-type is virtually any type of thing since (tokens of) almost anything can be 'uttered' in the artificially extended sense of 'utter'. In what follows we will focus on sentences. The concept of utterance-type meaning is the concept involved in assertions such as: the sentence, 'Grass is green' means (has as one of its meanings) that grass is green.

In 'Meaning', Grice suggests that the claim that a sentence x means that p 'might as a first shot be equated with some statement or disjunction of statements about what "people" (vague) intend (with qualifications about "recognition") to effect by x.' The idea is to explicate utterance-type meaning in terms of M-intentions—in terms of utterer's meaning. This is the first stage of Grice's claim that semantic notions can be explicated in terms of psychological notions.

The first stage version is vague, with talk of 'some statement or disjunction of statements'. What is the relevant condition? Grice is frequently taken to answer this question by offering a *convention-based* account of meaning.[2] This answer has been proposed, *not by Grice*, but by Stephen Schiffer who develops this answer in great detail in *Meaning*.[3] Grice's own answer forms the heart of his 1968 article, 'Utterer's Meaning, Sentence Meaning, and Word Meaning,' an article which represents the second stage in his thought about meaning.

---

[1] This way of presenting the 1957 account is taken from Stephen Schiffer, *Meaning*, Oxford, 1972.

[2] We have encountered this interpretation almost universally in conversation.

[3] Stephen Schiffer, op. cit., chapters 5 and 6.

Second stage: The 1968 article offers an outline of a more systematic, comprehensive, and ambitious approach to meaning than the 1957 article. As Grice says:

My aim in this paper is to throw light on the connection between (a) a notion of meaning which I want to regard as basic, viz., that notion which is involved in saying of someone that by (when) doing such-and-such he meant that so-and-so . . . , and (b) notions of meaning involved in saying (i) that a given sentence means 'so-and-so' (ii) that a given word or phrase means 'so-and-so' . . . This enterprise forms part of a wider programme . . .

The wider programme . . . arises out of a distinction which . . . I wish to make within the total signification of a remark: a distinction between what the speaker has *said* (in a certain favored, and maybe in some degree artificial sense of 'said'), and what he has 'implicated' (e.g. implied, indicated, suggested, etc.) . . . The programme is directed toward an explication of the favored sense of 'say' and a clarification of its relation to the notion of conventional meaning. [1968, p. 225.]

It is worth noting in passing that Grice makes important use of the distinction between what is said and what is implicated in, for example, his defence of the causal theory of perception [1961]; but our concern here is not with the programme's applications, but with the programme itself.

Grice begins by offering a revised version of his 1957 account of utterer's Meaning.

He writes,

In the earlier [1957] account I took the view that the M-intended effect is, in the case of indicative-type utterance, that the hearer should *believe* something, and, in the case of imperative-type utterances, that the hearer should *do* something. I wish for present purposes to make two changes here.

(1) I wish to represent the M-intended effect of imperative-type utterances as being that the hearer should *intend* to do something (with, of course, the ulterior intention on the part of the utterer that the hearer go on to do the act in question).

(2) I wish to regard the M-intended effect common to indicative-type utterances as being, not that the hearer should believe something (though there will frequently be an ulterior intention to that effect), but that the hearer should *think that the utterer believes* something. [1968, p. 230.]

Grammatical moods—moods in the sense, for example, of the subjunctive mood—figure explicitly in the revised account; and this, it

will turn out, is an especially important feature of that account—
a feature Grice exploits not only in his discussion of sentence meaning
but also later in his treatment of practical reasoning and ethics.

To make the revised account perspicuous, we need to consider the
role of moods in specifying meaning. Suppose U utters 'It is' in response
to being asked whether the door is closed. U means by uttering 'It is'
that the door is closed. Again, suppose U, who wants A to close the
door, utters 'Close the door'. U means that A should close the door.
The point to emphasize is that, in specifying what U means, we have,
in each case, used a sentence in a certain grammatical mood. The
sentence 'It is' is in the indicative mood; 'A should close the door', in
the subjunctive mood. Grice's idea is that the mood of a sentence
plays an essential and systematic role in the specification of what
U means.

In his revised account of utterer's meaning, Grice employs a notation that represents separately that aspect of meaning which is specified
by grammatical mood. To motivate this notation, note that there is a
common content to what U means in each of the above two examples.
In each case U is concerned with the proposition that the door is
closed. But in the first case, U wants A to think U *thinks* the door is
closed; in the second, to think U *intends* that A make it true that the
door is closed.

In Grice's notation we say that, in the first case, U means that $\vdash$ (the
door is closed); in the second, that U means that ! (the door is closed).
We explain this notation contextually:

    (i) U means that $\vdash (p)$ by uttering x if and only if U utters x
        M-intending A to think U *thinks* that p;

    (ii) U means ! (p) if and only if U utters x M-intending (a) A to
        think U *intends* (to bring it about) that p; and (b) A to *intend*
        that p—having, as part of his reason U's intention (a).

The symbols '$\vdash$' and '!' are mood operators; we may regard them as
technical devices used in the specification of what someone means. We
may, of course, need more than two operators to handle the full range
of things utterers may mean. But we do not need a complete list to
fomulate the revised account of meaning. Given a function from
pscyhological states onto mood operators, if ψ is a psychological state
and * the associated mood operator, U means that *(p) by uttering
x if and only if U utters x M-intending:

(i) that A should think U to ψ that p; and (in some cases only), depending on *,

(ii) that A should via fulfilment of (i), himself ψ that p.[4]

Grice further refines this definition in his 1969 article, 'Utterer's Meaning and Intention.' While this article raises some very interesting issues, we will not pursue them here although we should note that in a later paper, 'Meaning Revisited' [1982], Grice suggests that the [1969] account should be understood in the light of a certain ideal notion of utter's meaning, an ideal that is never realized in practice. This suggestion is grounded in Grice's view about psychological explanation, which we will treat later. The import of the suggestion can be understood only against the background of those views.

Utterance-type meaning: We are now ready to return to the concept of utterance-type meaning. Grice offers an explication of utterance-type meaning in terms of the notion of *having a procedure in one's repertoire*. Grice takes this notion more or less for granted. As he says,

This idea seems to me to be intuitively fairly intelligible and to have application outside the realm of linguistic, or otherwise communicative, performances, though it could hardly be denied that it requires further explication. A faintly eccentric lecturer might have in his repertoire the following procedure: if he sees an attractive girl in his audience, to pause for half a minute and then take a sedative. His having in his repertoire this procedure would not be incompatible with his also having two further procedures: (a) if he sees an attractive girl, to put on a pair of dark spectacles (instead of pausing to take a sedative); (b) to pause to take a sedative when he sees in his audience not an attractive girl, but a particularly distinguished colleague. [1969, p. 233.]

Grice first uses this notion to explicate meaning for *unstructured* utterance-types. These are nonsentential items, like flag signals. For example, in yacht racing, a blue flag means that there are ten minutes to the start. The flag has no syntactic structure and no components that themselves have a meaning that contribute to the meaning of the whole. What is it for such an unstructured utterance-type to mean something?

Grice answers this question by considering a group[5] of utterers, each of whom has in his repertoire the procedure of making a certain gesture—call it H-W (for handwave)—if he wants his audience to think

---

[4] We have departed slightly from the notation of the 1968 article: Grice uses '*' for the *function* that maps psychological states into mood operators.

[5] Actually Grice first considers a single speaker and then turns to groups; we are simplifying for ease of exposition.

he knows the route. (The utterers might also have other procedures such as uttering, 'I know the route'.) Suppose an utterer U produces H-W with the intention that his audience A thinks that U knows the route. U can have such an intention only if he thinks that there is some chance of getting A to think that U knows the route. But U is justified in supposing that uttering H-W has a chance of success only if he has reason to think that A will take *this particular utterance* of H-W to be an instance of U's procedure for getting an audience to think that U knows the route. That is, U must produce H-W expecting that A will realize that U uttered H-W intending that A think that U knows the route. It is this realization that U counts on, in fact, as giving A a reason to think that U does indeed know the route. A is to think: 'Why, in these circumstances, would U want me to think this if it weren't true?' So U must utter H-W intending: (1) that A believe that U knows the route; (2) that A recognize U's intention (1); (3) that this recognition be part of A's reason for believing that U knows the route. That is, U means that—M-intends that—U knows the route.

So if the utterers in the group have the H-W procedure in their repertoires, then—given that they all know this[6]—H-W is a particularly efficacious way of meaning that the utterer knows the route. In such a case, Grice suggests that H-W means (in the sense of utterance-type meaning) that the utterer knows the route.

But what of *sentences*? Sentences are *structured* utterance-types. The meaning of the whole is consequent (in ways determined by syntactic structure) on the meaning of the parts. Moreover, there are infinitely many sentences. If an utterer is to associate a procedure with each sentence of his language he must have infinitely many procedures. If he has to acquire them one by one, it will take him an infinite amount of time. These considerations lead Grice to

the notion of a 'resultant procedure': as a first approximation, one might say that a procedure for an utterance-type X will be a resultant procedure if it is determined by (its existence is inferrable from) a knowledge of procedures (a) for particular utterance-types which are elements in X, and (b) for any sequence of utterance-types which exemplifies a particular ordering of syntactic categories (a particular syntactic form). [1968, p. 235.]

The idea is that an utterer has a finite stock of *basic procedures*; these generate an infinite set of resultant procedures—including at least one

[6] And *perhaps* know that they all know this, and so on.

procedure for each sentence of the utterer's language. So, for example, if U is an English speaker, U will have the resultant procedure of uttering 'Snow is white' if U wants his audience to think that snow is white.

Grice introduces a general canonical form for the specification of resultant procedures. To describe this form we must note a syntactic thesis that Grice advances. He holds that the mood of a sentence is separately and distinctly represented in the underlying syntactic structure of that sentence. More exactly, he sees the sentence 'Close the door', for example, as having roughly the following structure:

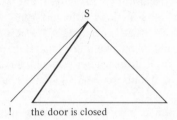

In English, this structure becomes 'Close the door'. '!' represents the imperative mood, while the string 'the door is closed' is to be read 'moodlessly' (just as one might read it tenselessly). Grice calls 'the door is closed' a *radical* (by analogy with a radical in chemistry) since it also appears in other structures, for example:

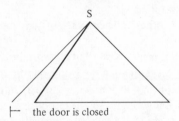

this structure becomes the *indicative* sentence. 'The door is closed'. In general, we are to think of a sentence as consisting of a mood-operator, plus a sentence radical, R. In drawing this distinction between mood-operators and radicals, Grice is to some extent following Hare[7] and Stenius.[8]

There is one more preliminary point. Let us—for the moment—assume as a given relation Σ between sentences and propositions.

[7] Richard Hare, *The Language of Morals*, Oxford, 1952.
[8] Eric Stenius, *Wittgenstein's Tractatus*, Oxford, 1960.

Let $\Sigma(*+R)$ be the set of all propositions associated with any sentence with the structure $(* + R)$.[9]

Now, where $p \in \Sigma(* + R)$, a resultant procedure for $* + R$ takes one of two forms: U has the resultant procedure of:

(1) uttering $* + R$ if U wants A to ψ that p; or
(2) uttering $* + R$ if U wants A to think U to ψ that p.

A complete theory of sentence meaning would specify such procedures. Such a theory would consist of a finite stock of basic procedures from which one could derive infinitely many resultant procedures.

As a definition of structured utterance-type meaning we can say (provisionally, at least) that, where $p \in \Sigma(* + R)$, $* + R$ means p in a group G if and only if members of G have the resultant procedure either of uttering $* + R$ if the utterer wants his audience to ψ that p, or of uttering $* + R$ if the utterer wants his audience to think the utterer to ψ that p.

Qualifications will, of course, be necessary to handle 'audienceless' cases. And we have also suppressed the difficult question of the knowledge of resultant procedures. If resultant procedures play a role in reasoning, members of G must know members of G have them. But must members of G know members of G know members of G have them, and so on? Stephen Schiffer has argued that the answer is *yes* for any number of iterations of 'know'. This is an interesting and important issue, but we will put it aside.

There are two other difficulties—or apparent difficulties—on which we will focus.

First, what does it mean to say that a person has a certain procedure? These procedures are supposed to guide one in speaking and understanding. Is one explicitly or implicitly guided? Surely not the former. Suppose U says, I know the route'. In response, A forms the belief that U knows the route. He forms this belief virtually immediately, without deliberation. A does not explicitly call up any procedure before his mind and infer therefrom that he should believe that U knows the route. Similarly, U just straight away utters, 'I know the route'. U does not first formulate or review procedures. So if utterers and audience are guided by procedures, they must be implicitly guided by them. What is it to be *implicitly* guided in this way?

We can formulate the second problem as a question: in the

---

[9] Grice does *not* proceed in this way; he does not use the notion of a proposition in formulating resultant procedures.

explication of utterance-type meaning, what does the variable '*p*' take as values? The values of '*p*' are the objects of meaning, intention, and belief—propositions, to call them by their traditional name. But isn't one of the most central tasks of a theory of meaning to give an account of what propositions are? Such an account forms the heart of Frege's philosophy of language.[10] This conception is one of Wittgenstein's stalking-horses in the *Tractatus*; Wittgenstein locates the fundamental difference between his position and Frege's in their differing conceptions of what a proposition is.[11] Much of the recent history of philosophy of language consists of attacks on or defences of various conceptions of what a proposition is, for the fundamental issue involved here is the relation of thought and language to reality. How can Grice offer an explication of utterance-type meaning that simply takes the notion of a proposition more or less for granted?

Grice's recent work contains answers to these difficulties; in particular his John Locke lectures on reasons and reasoning contain material which bears importantly on the first difficulty. This recent work, in so far as it bears on meaning, constitutes the third stage of Grice's theory of meaning.

2. REASONING

Grice begins by considering the suggestion that reasoning consists in the entertainment (and often acceptance) in thought or in speech of a set of initial ideas (propositions), together with a sequence of ideas each of which is derivable by an acceptable principle of inference from its predecessors in the set, [Locke, Kant]. Grice shows that it is scarcely plausible to suppose that reasoning always involves the entertainment or acceptance of a sequence of ideas—the steps in the reasoning— each of which is derivable (or taken by the reasoner to be derivable) from its predecessors. Grice makes this point in the course of a detailed and illuminating discussion of reasoning; we abstract only three points from this discussion. Consider the following example.

Suppose Jill reasons (in thought or speech) as follows: 'Jack broke his crown, but he is an Englishman; therefore, he will be brave.' It is natural to suggest that Jill thinks that all Englishmen are brave. But this suggestion overlooks two possibilities.

[10] See Hans Sluga, *Gottlob Frege*, Routledge and Kegan Paul, 1980, esp. chapter 5.
[11] See H. O. Mounce, *Wittgenstein's Tractatus*, University of Chicago, 1981.

First, Jill might be employing a different 'suppressed premiss'. She might think: 'Englishmen are normally brave', or 'Englishmen are brave when they break their crowns', or 'People of Jack's age and description are brave provided that they are also Englishmen', and so on.

The second possibility is that Jill does not employ *any* 'suppressed premiss'. She *merely* thinks: 'But he is an Englishman; therefore, he will be brave'. Imagine this thought occurring to her in a way that carries conviction with it. She thinks the thought while *taking and intending* the inference signalled by 'therefore' to be valid, but she does not—even implicitly—think *any* 'suppressed premiss' that would —as a matter of formal validity—allow the move from 'He is an Englishman' to 'He is brave'.

We should emphasize the point about *intention*. Grice argues that it is a necessary condition of reasoning from A to B that one *intend* that there be a formally valid (and non-trivial) argument from A to B. One can have such an intention without entertaining or accepting, even implicitly, any of the 'suppressed premisses' needed to secure formal validity. This is what we are supposing Jill does. She has the intention without entertaining the relevant premisses, the premisses that would render her inference formally valid.

A word about formal validity. Following Grice, we have taken the notion of formal validity for granted. Although we use the expression 'the notion of formal validity', there are at least two relations which are relevant: deductive validity and inductive acceptability.[12] Grice assumes that he may appeal to these notions in discussing reasoning, for reasoning, not formal validity, is the topic.

Returning to Jill, suppose we point out to her that her reasoning is not formally valid and requires an extra premiss if it is to be so. Jill might supply us with one. She might offer, 'all Englishmen are brave', or 'Englishmen are brave when they break their crowns', or any of the alternatives. In proposing one of these alternatives, Jill is not *reporting* her 'suppressed premiss'; she cannot be since she did not, even implicitly, think any such premiss. She is *constructing* a premiss—advancing a premiss she is willing to put forward *now* as what she would—or, perhaps, should—have thought or said *then* if the question of formal validity had been raised. And here Jill is not confined to just one premiss. She might advance a variety of different premisses as what she

---

[12] We are *not* suggesting that inductive acceptability can be fully characterized by a set of formal rules.

would, or should, have said—e.g 'All Englishmen are brave', 'Englishmen are brave when they break their crowns', and so on.

To generalize from the Jill example, suppose X reasons from A to B where the move from A to B is formally valid only if A is supplemented by a set of additional premises $A_1, \ldots, A_n$, then:

(1) X may not have explicitly entertained or accepted the propositions in an appropriate set $A_1, \ldots, A_n$; moreover, X may not have implicitly entertained or accepted *any* such set of propositions;

(2) In such cases, in which X does not even implicitly entertain or accept any appropriate set $A_1, \ldots, A_n$, there may be more than one set of propositions that X can legitimately advance when filling out his reasoning;

(3) If X is to be correctly described as reasoning from A to B then X must at least *intend* that there be some sequence of propositions $A_1, \ldots, A_n$ which together with A constitute a formally valid argument for B.

We should mention in passing that Grice devotes a good deal of attention to the question of what to add to the necessary condition in (3) in order to obtain a sufficient condition. He suggests that the intention specified in (3) should play an appropriate causal role in X's coming to think B.

We take (1)-(3) for granted. What concerns us is: what are the consequences of these points for the claim that utterers and audiences are 'implicitly guided' by procedures?

The claim that utterer's and audiences are so guided is motivated by the treatment of *unstructured* utterance-type meaning. Consider the H-W (handwave) example again. An utterer has in his repertoire the procedure of uttering H-W if he wants his audience to think that the utterer knows the route. Both the audience and the utterer *reason* from this premiss. The audience reasons to the conclusion that the utterer means that he knows the route. The utterer reasons to the conclusion that uttering H-W is an effective way of getting his audience to believe he knows the route. The possibility of such reasoning makes H-W a particularly efficacious way of meaning that one knows the route, and it is this sort of efficaciousness that makes it plausible to say that H-W means that one knows the route.

The rationale behind the treatment of *structured* utterance-type meaning is the same. The fact that utterers have resultant procedures creates the possibility of the same sort of reasoning with respect to sentences as occurs in the case of the unstructured utterance-type H-W. For example, suppose U utters 'I know the route', meaning thereby that he knows the route. U has the *resultant* procedure of uttering 'I know the route' if he wants his audience to think he knows the route. This resultant procedure is to play the role in reasoning that the 'plain, unresultant' H-W procedure plays in the unstructured utterance-type example.

We are to think of utterers as reasoning as follows: 'I want A to believe I know the route; therefore, I should utter, "I know the route"'. Audiences typically reason as follows: 'U uttered "I know the route"; therefore, U means U knows the route.' In each case, the 'therefore' is justified in part by the shared knowledge (and *perhaps* the knowledge that it is shared knowledge) that utterers have the resultant procedure of uttering 'I know the route' if he wants his audience to think he knows the route.

But why accept this view of communication? Surely it is *obvious* that utterers and audiences do not reason in this way. In answering this objection we will, for convenience, focus on the audience case. The first point to note is that an audience A need not *explicitly* think, 'U uttered, "I know the route"; therefore, U means U knows the route.' A may— and typically will—only implicitly think it. Moreover, there is no need to suppose that A thinks—*even implicitly*—any of the suppressed premisses needed to make his inference formally valid.

Compare Jill's reasoning: 'But he is an Englishman; therefore, he will be brave.' As we noted earlier, this thought may occur to Jill in a way that carries conviction with it. She thinks the thought while taking and intending the inference signalled by 'therefore' to be valid. But she does not think—even implicitly—any appropriate suppressed premiss. The suggestion is that we regard A in the same way. A (implicitly) thinks: 'U uttered "I know the route"; therefore, U means U knows the route'. A takes and intends the inference signalled by 'therefore' to be valid, but he does not—even implicitly—think any appropriate suppressed premisses.

But there is a problem here. Consider Jill. She could *explicitly* produce a formally valid argument which was an expansion of her thought, 'He is an Englishman; therefore, he will be brave.' So Jill could back up her use of 'therefore' by producing the necessary connecting links. Against the background of this ability, it seems reasonable to describe her as reasoning in an abbreviated way when she 'suppresses premisses'—i.e., when she *merely* thinks, 'He is an Englishman; therefore, he will be brave.' The 'therefore' is a promissory note that she can make good.

But do similar remarks hold of A? When A thinks, 'U uttered "I know the route"; therefore, U means that U knows the route', is the 'therefore' a promissory note that A can make good? Yes because A does know that U has the (resultant) procedure of uttering 'I know the route' if U wants A to believe that U knows the route. We saw earlier how the fact that U has this procedure can serve as a premiss in a formally valid argument that leads to the conclusion that U means that U knows the route (and from there to the conclusion that U does in fact know the route).

Of course, A may not discover this argument by himself. He may require instruction, coaxing, and careful reflection before he will accept and explicitly produce the argument. But this is no objection to regarding A as reasoning. After all, Jill may require instruction, coaxing, and careful reflection to fill in the complete reasoning, 'He is an Englishman, therefore he will be brave'. Of course, here is an obvious candidate suppressed premiss—'All Englishmen are brave'. But Jill may insist that she only thinks that certain Englishmen are brave. Her suppressed premiss is different, and it may not be obvious to her what it is. Is it 'Englishmen of Jack's description are brave'? And if so, what is the relevant description? She may seek the advice and opinion of others here.

Similarly, we may have to point out to A that he does know that U has the resultant procedure of uttering 'I know the route' if he wants his audience to think he knows the route. And it may require more instruction and reflection to get A to see that he knows the same sort of thing for each of an infinite number of sentences: that he knows that U has the resultant procedure of uttering 'Snow is white' if U wants A to think that U thinks that snow is white; that he knows that U has the resultant procedure of uttering 'Grass is green' if U wants A to think that grass is green; and so on. We consider the nature of such knowledge in the next section; the point to emphasize now is that the reasoning we have attributed to A is sufficient to allow us to see meaning as a reason-governed activity. Moreover, that *this sort* of reasoning is involved in meaning is made plausible by philosophical methods—by careful description, reflection, and delineation of the ways we talk and think.

But what about *basic* procedures? So far we have focused exclusively on resultant procedures. Do basic procedures play any role in utterer-audience reasoning? Grice emphasized in a recent conversation that he regarded this as an open question, although he sees serious difficulties standing in the way of a *yes* answer.

The idea behind the *yes* answer would be that utterer's basic procedures are 'suppressed premisses' in utterer–audience reasoning. To focus on the audience's reasoning, the idea is that when U utters 'I know the route' A reasons from the premiss that U has such-and-such basic procedures to the conclusion that U has the resultant procedure of uttering 'I know the route' if U wants his audience to believe he knows the route. A then reasons from that conclusion to the further conclusion that U knows the route. Of course, A does not *explicitly* think that U has such-and-such basic procedures. He *implicitly* thinks this.

The difficulty here is that it seems implausible to suggest that A implicitly thinks that U has such-and-such basic procedures. Consider Jill again. She reasons: 'But he is an Englishman; therefore, he will be brave'. Imagine that Jill implicitly thinks that all Englishmen are brave —where this proposition functions as a 'supressed premiss'. There are two points to note here. First, suppose we point out to Jill that her reasoning is incomplete—i.e., in need of supplementation if it is to be formally valid. Jill might reply: 'Yes, but I was taking it for granted —implicitly thinking—that all Englishmen are brave'. She supplies the missing premiss, and, in general, a reasoner who implicitly thinks a premiss can supply it on demand. But not always. Jill might have replied: 'I wonder what I was thinking. Probably something like, "All Englishmen are brave", or maybe just "Englishmen like Jack are brave", or something similar.' But even in this case Jill can produce a range of candidate 'suppressed premisses'.

To see the second point, consider a completion of Jill's incomplete reasoning: 'But he is an Englishman; all Englishmen are brave; therefore he will be brave.' This is a piece of reasoning that Jill could have explicitly produced completely and explicitly.

Reasoning involving basic procedures would not, it seems, exhibit either of the two features just noted. If asked to produce specifications of the basic procedures one was implicitly employing as premisses, one may be quite at a loss, and one certainly never explicitly produces a complete piece of reasoning in which specifications of basic procedures serve as premisses. And it does not help here to suggest that one turn to others for instruction, for how is one to evaluate the claim that *these*

were the basic procedures one was following? If we never produce complete pieces of reasoning in which specifications of basic procedures
function as premisses, it is difficult to see how we could have reason to
respond to such a claim by saying, 'Yes, I see; I could have been thinking
that way.' The problem is that one has virtually no ground to suppose
that one ever does reason in such a way.

We might try introducing a special or 'strong' sense of 'implicit'
here and argue that, in that sense, one implicitly thinks utterers have
such-and-such basic procedures. One might find this proposal attractive
if one thought—as, for example Fodor does—that the way to explain
psychological phenomena is to postulate 'internal representations'
manipulated in thinking and speaking. On this view the typical speaker
need not realize that he is manipulating such representations for it to
be legitimate to explain his thoughts and speech by attributing such
representations to him.

This view grants that—according to our common-sense notion of
reasoning, at least—we do not use specifications of basic procedures in
reasoning. But—so this suggestion goes—what does that matter?
All that matters is (1) that utterers and audiences have an internal
representation of procedures, and (2) that this representation plays a
role in speaking and understanding—a role that is, perhaps, very much
like the role premisses play in reasoning. A theory of meaning identifies the relevant internal representations and delineates their role in
speaking and understanding.

Whatever its merits, this is not Grice's view. As we said, Grice regards
the role of basic procedures in utterer/audience reasoning as an open
question. Other questions about basic procedures also remain open. In
particular, do all natural languages have the same basic procedures? Of
course the precise *content* of basic procedures will vary from language to
language in so far as the formulation of such procedures involves reference
to the vocabulary and surface syntax of a language. But perhaps the *form*
of such procedures is universal. We will not pursue these issues.

Instead we turn to two more general questions. Should we accept
this theory of meaning? Second, there is the question of the assumption of propositions. Does this cast doubt on the whole enterprise?

3. PSYCHOLOGICAL EXPLANATION AND MEANING

We want first to show how Grice's views about meaning are embedded
in, and gain support from, his views about psychological explanation.

Grice's concern is with *everyday* psychological explanation—explanation which employs everday psychological principles. By such principles we mean a relatively stable body of generally-accepted principles, of which the following are examples:

> If a person desires p, and believes if p then q, then—other things being equal—the person will desire q.
>
> If a person desires p and desires q, then—other things being equal—the person will act on the stronger of the two desires if the person acts on either.
>
> If a person stares at a coloured surface and subsequently stares at a white surface, then—other things being equal—the person will have an after-image.

We do not intend to suggest that all everyday principles are as simple and easy to formulate as these examples. As Grice repeatedly emphasizes, the principles we explicitly or implicitly employ are many, varied, rich, and subtle. Take desire. In everyday explanation we exploit 'an immense richness in the family of expressions that might be thought of as the "wanting family"; this family includes expressions like "want", "desire", "would like to ", "is eager to", "is anxious to", "would mind not . . .", "the idea of . . . appeals to me", "is thinking of", etc.' [Davidson.] Grice remarks that 'the likeness and differences within this family demand careful attention'. The systematic exposition of these likenesses and differences is itself an important (and not unpleasant) philosophical task.

But we are concerned with Grice's overall view of psychological explanation, and, to see what Grice thinks, it will be useful first to consider at some length how we would explain the behaviour of a certain sort of robot.

Suppose we are presented with a rather peculiar robot, and a diagram that we can use to predict and explain its behaviour. The robot is peculiar in that it has a panel of lights on its forehead—say sixty-four small lights in an eight-by-eight pattern, as described by the diagram.

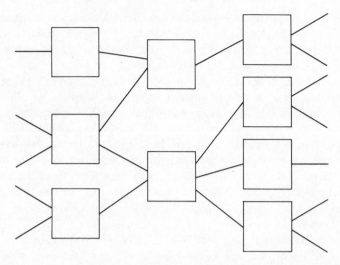

Each square represents a possible configuration of lights, and the diagram correlates possible configurations with each other. Some squares are correlated with more than one other square. For example,

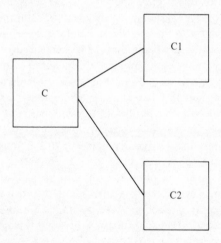

means that configuration C is followed by C1 *or* C2. (The diagram describes a finite, non-deterministic automaton; no transition probabilities are given.)

We can use the diagram to predict and explain the configurations that appear on the robot's forehead because the robot is so constructed that the configurations succeed one another in the ways represented in the diagram. So, if we observe configuration C, we can predict that C1 or C2 will follow. If we observe C1, we can explain its occurrence by pointing out that C must have preceded it.

All we can explain so far are configurations of lights. Can we explain *behaviour*—e.g., the robot's raising its left arm? Suppose we are provided with a table which has entries like: if configuraton C occurs at t, the robot will raise its arm at $t + 1$.

We succeed in predicting and explaining the robot's behaviour, except that occasionally our predictions are falsified; the robot does not always work according to the diagram. Temporary electronic defects and vagaries account for the falsified predications. The diagram and table represent the way the robot is *designed* to work, not the way it always does work.

Apart from the infrequent electronically-explained lapses, explanation and prediction proceed untroubled until one day a large number of our predictions are falsified. Suspecting a massive electronic disorder, we return the robot. The manufacturer explains that the robot was programmed to be self-regulating. The robot has an internal representation of the diagram and table we were given, and it was also programmed to use evaluative principles to determine whether to operate in accord with the diagram and table. For example, suppose the robot is in configuration C and that the immediate successor of C is C1. The robot determines by its evaluative principles not to move into C1, but to arrive at C2 instead. The robot was engineered so that it will in certain situations employ its evaluative principles, and so its states will change, in accord with the results of its evaluations.

When we ask for the evaluative principles, they are given to us, but they do not improve our predictive power as much as we may have hoped. First the robot has the power to formulate *new* subsidiary evaluative principles; it formulates these principles using its original evaluative principles plus information about the environment and the consequences of its past actions. We may simply not know, at any given time, exactly what subsidiary principles the robot is employing.

Second, the robot may—to some extent—revise or replace its original evaluative principles; that is, it may, in the light of some of its principles—original or subsidiary—plus information about its environment and past actions, revise or replace some of its original principles. So we may not know exactly what *original* principles the robot is using.

When we complain that we have lost our ability to predict and explain the robot's behaviour, we are told that the situation is not so bad. First, in programming the robot, certain evaluative principles were made immune to revision and replacement, so we can always count on the robot's operating with these principles. Second, we are not at a total loss to determine what evaluative principles—subsidiary or otherwise—the robot employs. We possess the diagram and table as well as knowledge of the original evaluative principles. The robot uses the diagram, table, and principles to arrive at new principles, and we can replicate this process. Third, we can replicate the processes that lead the robot to deviate from the diagram and table. To the extent that we have identified the robot's evaluative procedures, we can use them just as the robot does to determine whether it will act in accord with the diagram and table. Of course, there is the problem of determining when the robot will employ its evaluative principles, but we might be provided with a new table with entries like: if C occurs at t, the robot will employ its evaluative principles at $t + 1$. Fourth, we can often predict and explain the robot's behaviour just as we did before the evaluative principles complicated the picture, for the robot does not always employ its evaluative principles to diverge from the diagram and table. On the contrary, it was designed to minimize the use of these principles since their use requires significant time and energy.

An important part of Grice's view of everyday psychological explanation can be put this way: such explanation is similar to the explanation and prediction of the robot's behaviour. There are four points to note here.

First, everyday psychological principles play a role in explanation and prediction that is similar to the role of the diagram and table. Think of the robot's lights as representing psychological states. Then the diagram and table express relations among complexes consisting of psychological states and behaviour. Everyday psychological principles clearly express such relations (although, as we will see, this is not all they do).

Second, people use 'evaluative principles' in ways analogous to the use the robot makes of his. This point is an essential part of Grice's view of rationality. Grice holds

that the picture of rationality, given us by Plato and Aristotle and others, as something which essentially functions to regulate, direct, and control pre-rational impulses, inclinations, and dispositions, is the right picture. [Davidson.]

One of the things everyday psychological principles give us is a specification of how these 'pre-rational, impulses, inclinations, and dispositions' operate, just as the diagram and table represent how the robot operates apart from employing its evaluative principles. People can, through deliberation, rationally regulate, direct, and control pre-rational patterns of thought and action just as the robot can regulate, direct, and control its operation in accord with the diagram and table.

So what are the 'evaluative principles' people employ? Some of them are included among what we have been calling everyday psychological principles, for these principles do not *merely* specify how our pre-rational part operates. Consider for example:

If a person believes p and that p entails q, and the person believes not-q, then the person should stop believing p or stop believing q.

Conformity to this principle is a criterion of rationality (although this is not to say that the principle may not have exceptions in quite special circumstances).

Another important 'evaluative principle' is the conception of happiness. In 'Some Reflections about Ends and Happiness', Grice suggests that happiness consists in having a set of ends meeting certain conditions—where an important necessary condition is that the set of ends be 'suitable for the direction of life', and much of 'Some Reflections' is devoted to explaining this condition [Kant]. Grice suggests that if an individual asks what it is *for him* to be happy, the answer consists in identifying a system of ends which is a 'specific and personalized derivative, determined by that individual's character, abilities, and situation in the world, of the system constitutive of happiness in general'. This specific and personalized derivative figures prominently in deliberation, for a person may use it to regulate, direct, and control his pre-rational inclinations.

Third, recall that we imagined that the robot could replace and revise some of its evaluative principles. Analogously, a person may change his conception of what it is *for him* to be happy. But we also imagined that the robot had some evaluative principles it could not change. On Grice's view, a *person* has 'evaluative principles' that cannot change. Not because they are programmed in; rather, they are principles a person cannot abandon *if he is to count as rational*. For example, it is plausible to suggest that a person must, to count as rational, have and employ in deliberation at least some minimal conception what it is *for him* to be happy. Also it is plausible to suggest that this conception counts as a conception of *happiness* only if it is a 'specific and personalized derivative' of a conception of happiness in general. So to count as happy, a person would *have* to have and employ such a conception. (These examples do not, of course, exhaust the range of things one might hope to show necessary to counting as rational.) We should note here that our use of the word 'rational' is a looser use than Grice himself would indulge in; he regards 'rational' as a label for a cluster of notions he would distinguish. Our looseness is an expositional convenience.

Fourth, everday psychological predictions and explanations are sometimes falsified—like the prediction and explanations of the robot's behaviour. And, just as in the case of the robot, this reveals no defect in everyday psychological explanation. How can this be? In the robot example, the diagram and table specify how the robot is *designed* to function; obviously, minor deviations from the design do not justify regarding the information in the diagram and table as either false or useless. Can anything similar be true of people?

Something *somewhat* similar is true, according to Grice, and this because everyday psychology has special status. Grice argues:

The psychological theory which I envisage would be deficient as a theory to explain behaviour if it did not contain provision for interests in the ascription of psychological states otherwise than as tools for explaining and predicting behaviour, interests (for example) on the part of one creature to be able to ascribe these rather than those psychological states to another creature. Within such a theory it should be possible to derive strong motivations on the part of the creatures subject to the theory against the abandonment of the central concepts of the theory (and so of the theory itself), motivations which the creatures would (or should) regard as justified. Indeed, only from within the framework of such a theory, I think, can matters of evaluation, and so, of the evaluation of modes of explanation, be raised at all. If I conjecture aright, then, the entrenched system contains the materials needed to justify its own entrenchment; whereas no rival system contains a basis for the justification of anything at all. [1975b, p. 52.]

Suppose 'the entrenched system contains the materials needed to justify its own entrenchment; whereas no rival system contains a basis for the justification of anything at all'. Then while everyday psychology (or some preferred part of it) may not specify how we are designed to think and act, it does specify how we *ought* to think and act; for there can be no justification for failure to conform to (the preferred part) of everyday psychology.

There is another point which it is worth noting here in passing. If everyday psychology is uniquely self-justifying in the way Grice suggests, then we must reject the suggestion that everyday psychology is just a rough and ready theory that we will (or could) eventually abandon without loss in favour of a more accurate and complete scientific theory of behavior. Grice remarks:

We must be ever watchful against the Devil of scientism, who would lead us into myopic overconcentration on the nature and importance of knowledge, and of scientific knowledge in particular; the Devil who is even so audacious as to tempt us to call in question the very system of ideas required to make intelligible the idea of calling in question anything at all; and who would even prompt us, in effect, to suggest that since we do not really think but only think that we think, we had better change our minds without undue delay. [1975b, p. 53.]

Now let us turn to meaning. In 'Meaning Revisited', Grice sets out to

put one or two of the thoughts I have had at various times into some kind of focus, so that there might emerge some sort of sense about not merely what kind of views about the nature of meaning I am, or was, inclined to endorse, but also why it should be antecedently plausible to accept this kind of view. When I say 'antecedently plausible', I mean plausible for some reasons other than that the view in question offers some prospects of dealing with the intuitive data: the facts about how we use the word 'mean', and so on. So I will be digging just a little bit into the background of the study of meaning and its roots in such things as philosophical psychology. [1982, p. 224.]

It is worth emphasizing the point that the study has its roots in philosophical psychology, for one trend in contemporary philosophy has been to regard the study of meaning as 'first philosophy', as providing the framework and the tools for any other philosophical investigation.[13] This is clearly not Grice's view.

How can the roots of the study of meaning be in philosophical psychology? Consider the utterer's meaning. Grice employs his conception of everyday psychological explanation to provide a certain kind of rationale for his account of utterer's meaning. The rationale consists essentially of three claims: first, given our general psychological make-up (specified by everyday psychology) and given our environment, it is frequently highly conducive to realizing our ends that we be able to produce beliefs in each other. For example, suppose I need your help

[13] Michael Dummett.

to escape the riptide that is carrying me out to sea. You will help me if you believe I am caught in the riptide. How can I ensure that you will believe that?

Second, an especially effective way to produce this belief is to do something M-intending thereby that I am caught in the riptide. Consider what might happen if I do *not* have such an M-intention. Suppose I just thrash about in the water. I intended you to see that my swimming is ineffective, and to infer therefrom that I am caught. But you might think that I was simply having a good time splashing about, or that I was just pretending to be in trouble. If I can get you to realize that I intend by what I am doing to produce in you the belief that I am caught, that realization will give you a decisive reason to believe that I need help. So I do have a good and decisive reason to *M-intend* that I am caught.

And—and this is the third claim—I *have* the ability to M-intend that I am caught. It is an everday psychological fact that we can perform actions with the intention (1) that the audience believe p; (2) that the audience recognize the intention (1); (3) that this recognition be part of the audience's reason for believing p. This is a fact about our 'pre-rational part', analogous to the facts about the robot's behaviour which we can read off solely from the diagram and table without any appeal to its evaluative procedures. We are just so 'designed' that we M-intend things at various times. For example, in the riptide case, I would utter 'I am caught in the riptide' M-intending you to think that I am caught.

These three points show that it is rational for us to be so 'designed'. That is, it is rational for us to be pre-rationally structured so as to employ M-intentions. To see why, consider what we are doing in working through the three claims in question. We note that we have a certain pre-rational structure involving M-intentions, and we ask what can be said in favour of it. Given our ends and our environment, there is a good decisive *reason* to have such a pre-rational structure. So we discover that the M-intending structure passes rational muster; it does not have to be inhibited; rather it should be reinforced and guided.

The air of paradox in a pre-rational structure's being rational is easily dispelled. To label a structure pre-rational is merely to see it as present and operative independently of any attempt to evaluate whether and how it should be regulated, directed, and controlled. To call such a structure rational is to say that on evaluation one finds a good decisive reason to allow the structure to remain operative instead of trying to inhibit or eliminate it.

Grice sometimes expresses the fact that a pre-rational structure is rational by saying that it has a genitorial justification. [1975b, p. 36 f.] Suppose we are demi-gods—*genitors*, as Grice says—designing creatures. We are constructing them out of animal stuff, so we are making creatures that will perceive, desire, hope, fear, think, feel, and so on. The question before us is: exactly what psychological principles should our creatures obey? We want, so to speak, to decide on a specific diagram and table for them.

As we work on this problem, we discover that we have a good and decisive reason to make them such that they employ M-intentions, for we have built into them a desire for happiness, and as we survey their environment and their physical powers, it is clear that they have little chance for happiness (or even survival) unless they employ M-intentions. And, as benevolent genitors, we want them to have every chance of happiness. (In appealing to happiness in this way we have departed somewhat from Grice's treatment of creature construction. This deviation, which is expositionally convenient here, is corrected in the section on ethics.)

So as genitors we have a good and decisive reason to make our creatures M-intend. Grice infers from this genitorial *myth* that it *really* is rational—or, if one likes, that *we* really have a good reason—to be so pre-rationally structured that we M-intend. And the inference is a good one, for the technique of genitorial creature construction is a more picturesque way of establishing that M-intending passes rational muster. Grice sometimes uses this creature construction technique to *discover* what aspects of our pre-rational structure are rational. The idea is that the question 'What should we as genitors build into creatures with human psychological capacities living in a human environment?' is easier to answer than the question 'What aspects of our pre-rational structure are rational?'

As we have seen, M-intending is, for example, one structure that we can cite in answer to both questions. Consider how surprising it would be if language had no word that stood for M-intending. Our considerations reveal it not only as a rational, but as a very important, pre-rational structure. Of course, Grice does think that English has a word here: namely, 'mean'. This linguistic thesis combined with the identification of M-intending as a rational pre-rational structure provides a justification of Grice's account of utterer's meaning.

The concluding section of Grice's recent 'Meaning Revisited' is relevant here, as it further illuminates the rational aspect of M-intending (or speaker meaning as Grice calls it in 'Meaning Revisited'). Grice begins by saying that,

The general idea that I want to explore, and which seems to me to have some plausibility, is that something has been left out, by me and perhaps by others too, in the analyses, definitions, expansions and so on, of semantic notions, and particularly various notions of meaning. What has been left out has in fact been left out because it is something which everyone regards with horror, at least when in a scientific or theoretical frame of mind: the notion of value.

Though I think that in general we want to keep value notions out of our philosophical and scientific enquiries—and some would say out of everything else—we might consider what would happen if we relaxed this prohibition to some extent. If we did, there is a whole range of different kinds of value predicates or expressions which might be admitted in different types of case. To avoid having to choose between them, I am just going to use as a predicate the word 'optimal' the meaning of which could of course be more precisely characterized later. [1982, p. 237.]

Applying this idea to speaker-meaning (utterer's meaning, as we have been saying), Grice makes two suggestions: first that,

as a first approximation, what we mean by saying that a speaker, by something he says, on a particular occasion, means that p, is that he is in the optimal state with respect to communicating, or if you like, to communicating that p. Second, that the optimal state—the state in which he has an infinite set of intentions—is in principle unrealisable, so that he does not *strictly speaking* mean that p. However, he is in a situation which is such that it is legitimate, or perhaps even mandatory, for us to deem him to satisfy the unfulfillable condition. [1982, p. 242.]

The optimal state is what the analysis of speaker meaning specifies. Counter-examples advanced by Schiffer in *Meaning* suggest that this state is one in which a speaker has an infinite number of intentions. We will not discuss the counter-examples; we want to consider why it is reasonable to respond to them by granting that the analysis of speaker meaning specifies an unrealizable—but none the less *ideal* or *optimal*—state involving having an infinite number of intentions.

Consider an analogy. There is in sailing an optimal setting for the sails—a setting that maximizes forward thrust. Any reasonably complete text on sailing will explain at least some of the relevant aerodynamic theory. Now this optimal setting is difficult if not impossible to achieve while actually sailing—given continual shifts in wind direction, the sudden changes of direction caused by waves, and the difficulty in determining airflow patterns by sight. To deal with these practical difficulties, the text supplies numerous rules of thumb which are relatively easy to apply while sailing. Why not just drop the aerodynamic theory altogether and just provide the reader/sailor with the rules of thumb? Because they are *rules of thumb*. They hold (at best) *other things being equal*. To spot exceptions and resolve conflicts as well as to handle situations not covered by the rules, one needs to know what the aerodynamic optimum is. This optimum plays a crucial role in guiding the use of the rules of thumb.

Why should common sense psychology not avail itself of various optima in this way? It is plausible to think that it does given Grice's view of rationality as something that plays an evaluative and guiding role with respect to pre-rational inclinations and dispositions. Various optima would be especially suited to such a role. And why should speaker-meaning not be such an optimum? Indeed, there is some reason to think it is.

Resultant procedures: What can we say about sentence meaning? Is it possible to provide a rationale for the treatment of sentence meaning in the context of Grice's philosophical psychology?

The account of sentence meaning has an explanatory role. Consider that a speaker of a natural language can M-intend an extremely wide range of things, and typically his audience will know what he M-intends as soon as the audience hears what is uttered. Attributing resultant procedures to language-users explains these facts. There are two points to note:

First, suppose U has the procedure of uttering 'I know the route' if U wants A to think U thinks U knows the route. What does it mean to suppose this? *We can understand it as an everday psychological principle.* More precisely, the proposed principle is: if a competent English speaker wants an audience to think the speaker knows the route, then—other things being equal—the speaker may utter 'I know the route'. This qualifies as an everyday psychological principle and—perhaps most important—like (at least some) other everyday psychological principles this principle has a normative aspect. Both knowledge of and conformity to this principle are *required* if one is to count as a competent English speaker.

Turning from utterers to audiences, it is, for similar reasons, plausible to suggest that it is an everyday psychological fact that if a competent English speaker hears 'I know the route', then he will—other things being equal—think the utterer thinks he knows the route. (This principle could be derived from the first plus the assumption that speakers are, about certain things, trustworthy.)

There is nothing mysterious about such everyday psychological principles. They specify part of our psychological make-up, the way we are 'designed'—part of our pre-rational structure, and the fact that we are so 'designed', certainly explains the range of things we can M-intend and the ease with which we employ such M-intentions.

But—and this is the second point—we might have hoped for much more by way of explanation, for there are mysteries here. In particular, *what is it* for a person to have a resultant procedure? To see what the question asks, imagine having an answer of the form:

S has a resultant procedure P if and only if

. . . ,

where the dots are filled out by specification of certain psychological and behavioural features. This would provide us with an informative characterization of the psychological and behavioural capacities under-lying language use.

Since there are infinitely many resultant procedures, a reasonable way to provide answers would be (given any natural language) to specify a finite set of basic procedures (for that language), from which the infinitely many resultant procedures could be derived (in some suitable sense of 'derived'). Then we would provide a finite set of conditions of the form:

S has basic procedure P if and only if

. . . ,

where the dots are replaced by a suitable condition. But what counts as a 'suitable condition'? What psychological, behavioural, or other properties does one have to have to count as possessing a certain basic procedure P? As we said, Grice regards this as an open question. Of course, this is not to say that the question is unimportant; on the contrary, it is of fundamental importance if we want to know what capacities underlie language use.

One problem about Grice's account of meaning still remains: does the appeal to propositions not vitiate the whole project?

4. METAPHYSICS

Grice's ontological views are—at least—liberal. As Grice says when commenting on the mind–body problem in 'Method in Philosophical Psychology',

I am not greatly enamoured of some of the motivations which prompt the advocacy of psychophysical identifications; I have in mind a concern to exclude such 'queer' or 'mysterious' entities as souls, purely mental events, purely mental properties and so forth. My taste is for keeping open house for all sorts of conditions of entities, just so long as when they come in they help with the housework. Provided that I can see them work, and provided that they are not detected in illicit logical behaviour (within which I do not include a certain degree of indeterminacy, not even of numerical indeterminacy), I do not find them queer or mysterious at all. To fangle a new ontological Marxism, *they work therefore they exist*, even though only some, perhaps those who come on the recommendation of some form of transcendental argument, may qualify for the specially favoured status of *entia realissima*. To exclude honest working entities seems to me like metaphysical snobbery, a reluctance to be seen in the company of any but the best objects. [1975, pp. 30–31.]

One way entities can work is by playing a role in the explanation of what a proposition is. What would such an explanation look like? And, what sorts of entities would it put to work? Answering these questions will illustrate Grice's 'ontological Marxism' while clarifying the notion of a proposition.

What work do the entities in a theory of propositions do? They are to produce a theory meeting three constraints. First, there are systematic relations between sentences and propositions. For example, the sentence 'Socrates runs' is correlated with the proposition that Socrates runs; the sentence 'snow is white' with the proposition that snow is white, and so on. There are two determinants of the proposition (or propositions) to which a sentence is related. One is the syntactic form of the sentence. The sentences 'Clearly, John spoke' and 'John spoke clearly' are related to different propositions by virtue of the different syntactic relations among their respective parts. The other determinant is the meaning of the parts of the sentence. The sentence 'snow is white' is correlated with the propositions that snow is white in part because 'snow' means what it does. On Grice's theory this correlation between sentences and propositions is effected by language-users resultant procedures. An adequate theory of propositions should explicitly characterize this systematic relation between sentences and propositions. Since there are infinitely many sentences, one would presumably give such a characterization recursively.

The second constraint is that an account of what a proposition is should yield an adequate account of the relation of logical consequence that we exploit in everyday psychological explanation. For example, if you, by uttering an appropriate sentence, mean that you know the route and that Jones does as well, your audience may conclude that Jones knows the route. The conclusion, the proposition that Jones knows the route, is a logical consequence of the conjunctive proposition that you know the route and that Jones does as well. Given the assumption that you are trustworthy, your audience is entitled to the conclusion precisely because it is a logical consequence of the proposition you mean.

We frequently exploit such relations of logical consequence in everyday psychological explanation, and an adequate theory of propositions should provide us with an adequate characterization of this relation. One may think (as we do) that this task is not really distinct from exhibiting the systematic relations between sentences and propositions, but it is worth stating the second constraint separately to emphasize the role of logical consequence in psychological explanation, and hence the relation of a theory of propositions to such explanation.

The third constraint is that a theory of propositions should provide the basis, at least, for an adequate account of the relation between thought, action, and language on the one hand, and reality on the other. For example, one perceives the desk, walks over to sit at it, and utters sentences to mean things about it.

Since propositions are the items we specify in specifying the content of a thought, perception, intention, act of meaning, and so on, an account of propositions should at least provide the basis for an account of the relation between mind and reality.

Since Quine is the philosopher most generally associated with the rejection of propositions, it may be helpful briefly to compare his views with Grice's. Quine has two main arguments against propositions. The first is based on his arguments that synonymy is not a well-defined equivalence relation, the identity conditions for propositions are unclear and there is 'no entity without identity'.[14] On this issue, Grice

[14] See, for example, W. V. Quine, *Philosophy of Logic*, Prentice-Hall, 1970, pp. 2–10.

is not committed to an equivalence relation of synonomy (thus his remark about indeterminacy) but he parts company with Quine over whether clear identity conditions are required for a kind of entity. If they work they exist, whether we can always tell them apart or count them or not. There are many respectable entities for which we do not have criteria or identity. Suppose my favourite restaurant moves. Is it a new restaurant with the same name? Or suppose it changes owners and names but nothing else? Or that it changes menu entirely? Or that it changes chefs? It would be foolish to look for a single criterion to answer these questions—the answers go different ways in different contexts. But surely the concept of a restaurant is a useful one and restaurants do exist.

Quine's second objection is that propositions do no work. Grice denies this allegation. The main reason for disagreement is perhaps due to Quine's attitude that concepts such as belief and desire are of, at most, secondary importance in the unified canonical science that is his standard for ontology. Grice does not believe that everyday psychological discourse is a temporary pre-scientific expedient to be done away with as soon as possible. On the contrary, he believes that at least some psychological concepts and explanations play a fundamental role in both semantics and ethics. To quote the relevant passage a second time:

The psychological theory which I envisage would be deficient as a theory to explain behaviour if it did not contain provision for interests in the ascription of psychological states otherwise than as tools for explaining and predicting behaviour, interests (for example) on the part of one creature to be able to ascribe these rather than those psychological states to another creature because of a concern for the other creature. Within such a theory it should be possible to derive strong motivations on the part of the creatures subject to the theory against the abandonment of the central concepts of the theory (and so of the theory itself), motivations which the creatures would (or should) regard as justified. Indeed, only from within the framework of such a theory, I think, can matters of evaluation, and so, of the evaluation of modes of explanation, be raised at all. If I conjecture aright, then, the entrenched system contains the materials needed to justify its own entrenchment; whereas no rival system contains a basis for the justification of anything at all. [1975b, p. 52.]

Now suppose—as Grice thinks—certain ways of thinking, certain *categories*, are part of what is entrenched: there are certain concepts or categories that we *cannot avoid* applying to reality. The entities in these categories are *entia realissima*. We discover these categories by discovering what parts of everyday psychology are entrenched.

The idea that there are necessary categories of thought plays a role in Grice's views about ethics; in discussing these views we will see why certain principles of everyday psychology are self-justifying, principles concerned with the evaluation of ends. If *these same* principles played a role in determining what we count as *entia realissima*, metaphysics would be grounded in part in considerations about value (a not unpleasant prospect).

5. ETHICS

To understand Grice's view on ethics, we should return to the idea of creature construction in more detail. Suppose we are genitors—demigods—designing living creatures, creatures Grice calls *pirots*. To design a type of pirot is to specify a diagram and table for that type (plus evaluative procedures, if any). The design is implemented in animal stuff—flesh and bones (typically).

Let us focus on one type of pirot—a very sophisticated type that Grice (borrowing from Locke) calls 'very intelligent rational pirots'. (Think of them very roughly as creatures with the capacities for thought and action characteristic of persons.) Being benevolent genitors, we want to design these pirots so as to maximize their chances for survival. As Grice recently pointed out in conversation—by talk of survival, he does not, in the case of very intelligent rational pirots, mean simply *staying alive*. A full explanation of what Grice has in mind here would require an account of his views on teleology; however, for our purposes a full explanation is unnecessary. We need note only the following points.

First, in constructing pirots we build in certain ends, and for our purposes we may imagine ourselves as having a fairly free hand in deciding what ends to select. To build in an end is to construct the diagram and table so that the pirots have that end as a standing, constant end—an end where they strive to realize in all appropriate circumstances. The restriction to *appropriate* circumstances is necessary for two reasons. First, we will want to endow the pirots with a variety of ends, and we will not want a pirot to try to realize each end at each moment of time. We want them to schedule their pursuit of ends in a way that maximizes the realization of the whole array in the long run.

Second, we will, in the case of very intelligent rational pirots, want to give them the (limited) ability to eliminate (or inhibit for a long time the pursuit of) built-in ends should circumstances prove especially inappropriate. Now we can explain what, for present purposes, we mean by 'survival': to maximize chances for survival is to maximize chances for the realization of built-in ends.

How are we to design the pirots so as to maximize their chances for realizing the built-in ends? The answer would be easy if we could take as given a very detailed specification of the environment in which the pirots live. Then we could tailor the diagram and table to that specific environment by building in exactly the responses that the environment demands. But we cannot assume such a specific description of the environment; on the contrary, we know that the pirots will face a variety of changing environments. So we need to design the pirots to function effectively in the widest possible range of environments. We could, of course, avoid this if we were willing to descend periodically from Olympus in order to redesign the pirots in response to each significant change in the environment. But there is a more efficient way to achieve the same result: we give the pirots the ability to redesign themselves. There are two aspects to this ability.

First among the ends we build in is the end of being an *end-setter*. To be an end-setter requires that one have the (limited) ability to adopt new ends and to eliminate ends one already has. To have the end of being an end-setter is to have the end of employing this ability to adopt and eliminate ends. *This is not, as we will see, a complete specification of what it is to be an end-setter*, but it will suffice for the moment. By making the pirots end-setters we will enable them to redesign themselves by altering what they aim at.

Second, to enable pirots to determine when to use their end-setting ability, we given them an appropriate set of evaluative principles. These principles incorporate in the pirots some of our wisdom as genitors. We do not need to descend periodically to redesign them because in a sense we are always present—having endowed them with some of our divine knowledge.

What does this have to do with ethics? Grice answers this question in 'Method in Philosophical Psychology'. To interpret the reference to 'rational capacities and dispositions' in the following passage, recall that, given the connection between evaluative principles and rationality spelled out in section 4, we have, in giving the pirots evaluative principles, given them a capacity for rational evaluation.

Let me be a little more explicit, and a great deal more speculative, about the possible relation to ethics of my programme for philosophical psychology. I shall suppose that the genitorial programme has been realized to the point at which we have designed a class of pirots which, nearly following Locke, I might call 'very intelligent rational pirots'. These pirots will be capable of putting themselves in the genitorial position, of asking how, if they were constructing themselves with a view to their own survival, they would execute this task; and, if we have done our work aright, their answer will be the same as ours . . . . We might, indeed, envisage the contents of a highly general practical manual, which these pirots would be in a position to compile . . . . The contents of the initial manual would have various kinds of generality which are connected with familiar discussions of universalizability. The pirots have, so far, been endowed only with the characteristics which belong to the genitorial justified psychological theory; so the manual will have to be formulated in terms of that theory, together with the concepts involved in the very general description of living-conditions which have been used to set up that theory; the manual will therefore have *conceptual generality*. There will be no way of singling out a special subclass of addressees, so the injunctions of the manual will have to be addressed, indifferently, to any very intelligent rational pirot, and will thus have *generality of form*. And since the manual can be thought of as being composed by each of the so far indistinguishable pirots, no pirot would include in the manual injunctions prescribing a certain line of conduct in circumstances to which he was not likely to be subject; nor indeed *could* he do so even if he would. So the circumstances for which conduct is prescribed could be presumed to be such as to be satisfied, from time to time, by any addressee; the manual, then, will have *generality of application*.

Such a manual might, perhaps, without ineptitude be called an IMMANUEL; and the very intelligent rational pirots, each of whom both composes it and from time to time heeds it, might indeed be ourselves (in our better moments, of course). [1975b, pp. 40–1.]

We can both explain and motivate this approach to ethics by considering three objections. First, one may complain that the above remarks are extremely vague. In particular, what are the evaluative principles—the rational capacities and dispositions—with which we endow the pirots? These principles play a central role in compiling the manual (Immanuel). How can we evaluate the suggested approach to ethics until we are told what these evaluative principles are?

This complaint is somewhat unjust—in the context of 'Method in Philosophical Psychology' at least, for there Grice labels his remarks as speculative. But, more importantly, Grice has done a considerable amount of work directed toward providing this objection with the information it demands; this work includes investigations of happiness, freedom, reasoning, and teleology. While the examination of these projects is unfortunately beyond the scope of our introduction, we should comment briefly on Grice's work on happiness. In 'Some Reflections about Ends and Happiness', Grice develops an account of happiness, and on this account it is clear that *the conception of happiness could certainly function as a central 'evaluative principle' in endsetting.* It is also worth remarking here that Grice's views on happiness are very Aristotelian; Grice emphasizes the Kantian aspect of his view in the passage quoted, but when the views are worked out, one finds a blend of Kantian and Aristotelian themes.

The second objection is that Grice's approach makes it too easy to escape the demands of morality. What can Grice say to a person— or pirot—who rejects the manual, rejects moral demands and constraints? Suppose, for example, that a person reasons as follows:

If I continue to heed the voice of morality, I will continue on occasion to sacrifice my welfare and interests in favor of another's welfare and interests. Why should I be such a fool? After all, what am I after except getting as much as I can of what I want. Thorough-going egoism is the path to take; I'll have to resist these impulses to help others, in the way I resist sweets when I am dieting. Perhaps I will be able to condition such impulses out of myself in time.

Does Grice's approach have a reply to the consistent thorough-going egoist? It does—as Grice pointed out in a recent conversation; the considerations which follow are based on that conversation.

First we need to provide a more detailed account of end-setting. When we give our pirots the end of end-setting we have a *good reason* for giving them each of the evaluative principles in order to build in the capacity to redesign themselves, and we build in that capacity in order to maximize their chances of realizing their ends over the widest possible range of environments. So we have a good reason for giving them each of the end-setting evaluative principles: namely, each one contributes to the capacity for redisigning in a way that maximizes the chances of realizing ends. The pirots themselves are capable of recognizing that the evaluative principles make such a contribution, so *each pirot* has (or can have) a reason for having the evaluative principles. (We are assuming that contributing to the maximization of the realization of ends constitutes a good reason; a defence of this assumption would require an examination of Grice's view on teleology.)

A second essential point is that we design the pirots so that they do not simply adopt or eliminate ends at wll; rather, they do so *only when they have good reasons to do so—good reasons derived from the evaluative principles that govern end-setting.* We design them this way in order to maximize their chances for the realization of their ends. We want them to use their ability for end-setting only when the evaluative principles we have built in determine that a change of ends is called for in order to maximize the overall realization of ends. (In the typical case at least, an end-setter will only alter *some* of his ends as to maximize the realization of *all* his (remaining and newly adopted) ends.)

An end-setter then has the end of adopting or eliminating ends when he has good reasons to do so—where these reasons are provided by evaluative principles; and these evaluative principles are such that he has a good reason for having each of those principles. Let us call such an end-setter a *Gricean* end-setter.

Returning now to egoism, we can distinguish three different situations in which one might try to reject the 'demands of morality'. Before going on, one may insist on knowing what we mean by the 'demands of morality', but it is enough for present purposes that we agree that morality demands at least that one does not always treat others purely as means to one's own ends. It is this demand that the egoist described earlier rejects.

First, if the egoist is a Gricean end-setter who wishes to remain a Gricean end-setter, then he cannot abandon the non-egotistical principles since they are self-justifying and do not depend on other premises. Second, if the egoist envisioned is one who would cease to be a Gricean end-setter, this too is impossible for a rational agent. Being a Gricean end-setter is itself one of the self-justifying ends, and thus it can be abandoned only if one abandons reasoning. Finally, there is the question of whether an agent who is not a Gricean end-setter can be an egoist. Again the answer appears to be 'no', if the agent is rational and considers the question. For being a Gricean end-setter can be seen on reflection to be a self-justifying end, and thus must be adopted by any reflective rational agent.

Let this suffice as a brief indication of Grice's approach to the second objection, and let us turn to the third and last objection. This objection concerns what we have been calling 'the demands of morality'; the objection is that the notion of *demand* is vague. What do we mean by 'demand' when we talk of the 'demands of morality'? What kind of demand is this? What sort of claim is it that morality has on us? Grice has done a considerable amount of work relevant to this question— including 'Probability, Desirability, and Mood Operators', the John Locke Lectures, and recent work on Kant.

In explaining the claim morality has on us, Grice employs distinctions and notation provided by his theory of meaning.

We can begin with the sentence 'Pay Jones the money!' Grice assigns this sentence the following structure:

> ! + I pay Jones the money

where '!' is the imperative mood operator and 'I pay Jones the money' is a moodless sentence radical. This structure is embeddable in other sentences. In particular, it occurs in both 'I should pay Jones the money' and 'I should not pay Jones the money'. Grice assigns these the following structures:

> Acc + ! + I pay Jones the money;
>
> Not + Acc + ! + I pay Jones the money,

where 'Acc' may be read as 'it is acceptable that'. So if we read '!' as 'let it be the case that', the whole string, 'Acc + ! I pay Jones the money' may be read as: 'It is acceptable that (let) it be the case that I pay Jones the money' (whole 'Not + Acc + ! + I pay Jones the money' may be read as 'It is not the case that it is acceptable that (let) it be the case that I pay Jones the money').

In 'Probability, Desirability, and Mood Operators' Grice motivates this assignment of structures by arguing (in effect) that the sentence 'I should pay Jones the money' means—on the central and important reading—that it is acceptable that (let) it be the case that I pay Jones the money. The argument rests on an analysis of practical reasoning and on the analysis of sentence meaning.

Actually, Grice does not say that 'I should pay Jones the money' means what we just said it means. In 'Probability, Desirability, and Mood Operators' he is much more circumspect. After discussing probability inferences, he writes,

Bearing in mind the variety of interpretations to which sentences containing 'ought' and 'should' are susceptible, I find it natural to take, as practical analogues to sentences like 'an invalid is likely to be in retirement', sentences like 'it is desirable for an invalid to keep in touch with his doctor'. [Operators.]

For expositional purposes, we use 'should-sentences' since the interpretation we want these sentences to bear is clear, and the use of
'should-sentences' highlights the connections with ordinary moral
reasoning.

Suppose morality demands that I pay Jones the money; that is,
I act morally only if I pay Jones the money. Grice holds that this is
true only if an appropriate sentence (or thought) is derivable from my
evaluative principles—a sentence (or thought) whose underlying
structure is 'Acc + ! + I pay Jones the money'. I can, that is, derive
that it is acceptable that (let) it be the case that I pay Jones the money;
in other words, that I *should* pay Jones the money. Grice holds that
since I derive this from evaluative principles, it is *necessary*; that is, it is
necessary that I should pay Jones the money. There are two points to
note in order to explain the claim morality has on us.

First, Grice holds that the self-justifying evaluative principles are
necessarily true, and he holds that I can show, e.g. that it is necessarily
true that I should pay Jones the money, by constructing a suitable
derivation of 'I should pay Jones the money' from my self-justifying
evaluative principles. (These claims follow from a general view Grice
has of the nature of necessity, a view that we will not consider here.)
To be more precise, what I derive from my evaluative principles is a
sentence with the underlying structure:

Acc + ! I pay Jones the money,

which we read as 'It is acceptable that (let) it be the case that I pay
Jones the money'. Since it is possible to construct an appropriate
derivation it is *necessary* that it is acceptable that (let) it be the case
that I pay Jones the money. This is how we should understand attaching 'necessary' to a 'should-statement'. The sentence 'Necessarily, I
should pay Jones the money' expresses the *necessary acceptability of
the imperative* 'Pay Jones the money!' (Since my derivation will involve
contingent information about the circumstances C, we should represent
what I derive as 'I should *in these circumstances* C pay Jones the
money'; this will be what is necessary. We ignore this detail.)

Second, it does *not* follow from the fact that it is necessary that I
should pay Jones the money that I *will* pay him the money. Even if it is
necessary that it is acceptable that (let) it be the case that I pay Jones
the money, and even if I derive this, I may not act on it. It is true that
I cannot have a good reason *not* to act on it; after all, I have derived the
necessity of accepting the imperative, 'Pay Jones the money!'; and as

a Gricean end-setter I am committed to acting on such reasons; but this does not mean I will. A person is capable of irrationality—even in the face of acknowledged necessity.

Now we are in a position to explain what we mean by talk of the *demands* of morality. The demands of morality are expressed by necessary 'should-statements'. Or perhaps we may want to say that they are expressed by a special subset of such statements. We need not investigate this possibility since it would not alter the point we are making here—which is that the demands of morality express the necessity of rational agents accepting and acting on certain imperatives (in so far as they act rationally).

Consider the role elements of Grice's theory of meaning play in the above discussion of ethics, we have in a way returned to the starting-point of our exposition of Grice's views. And it is certainly high time we let the discoverer of M-intentions formulate some in response to what we have written. High time but not quite time. For one thing, we should note that the discussion of ethics resolves an issue we suppressed when discussing psychological explanation. At one point in that section, we wrote, with respect to M-intending, 'Given our ends and our environment, there is good and decisive reason to have such a pre-rational structure.' We did not raise the question of what makes those considerations into a reason; we tacitly assumed that relations to happiness and survival secured that the considerations counted as reasons. The ethics discussion points the way to detailed and informative treatment of this issue. Not that the discussion suggests that we were wrong to appeal tacitly to happiness and survival; on the contrary, it indicates that we should explain the reason-giving force of such considerations by examining the role they play for a Gricean-end-setter.

6. THE CONTRIBUTIONS

Patrick Suppes, 'The Primacy of Utterer's Meaning'. Suppes takes up a topic we did not treat in our discussion of meaning: the objections to Grice's taking the notion of utterer's meaning—not sentence meaning—as basic. As Suppes says, 'This feature of his theory has been severely criticized because of its deviation from the conception of semantics as an autonomous discipline independent of such general psychological considerations as speaker's intentions and listeners' recognition of intentions'. And he adds, 'I believe Grice is right and his critics wrong.' Suppes considers the criticisms of Ziff, Chomsky, and Yu, and in answering these criticisms he argues (among other things) that 'it is absurd to charge Grice with implicitly using a concept of sentence meaning'.

Andreas Kemmerling, 'Utterer's Meaning Revisited'. What Kemmerling revisists is the debate over the exact form of the analysis of utterer's meaning. Kemmerling's concern is to answer the charge (envisaged as a possible difficulty by Strawson and forcefully made actual by Stephen Schiffer) that, on Grice's analysis, an utterer can mean something only if he has an infinite number of intentions. Kemmerling's strategy involves appealing to notions of *value*. As we noted, Grice explores this idea himself in his own 'Meaning Revisited'; Grice considers simply granting that the correct analysis of utterer's meaning involves attributing an infinite number of intentions to the utter. Kemmerling proposes to cut the regress off before it begins.

Donald Davidson, 'A Nice Derangement of Epitaphs'. Davidson concludes his paper with the claim that '*if* conventions are somehow essential to speaker-hearer transactions imagined to take place with no further background. But conventions aren't essential to such speaker-hearer transactions. I leave it as an exercise to complete the inference'. Davidson reaches this conclusion through a critique of 'The assumption that communication by speech requires that a speaker and interpreter have learned or somehow acquired a common theory of interpretation —this may be otherwise described as being able to operate on the basis of shared conventions, or a mastery of grammar or other rules'. Davidson, as he points out, once made this assumption himself; his rejection of it and the reasons he advances to support this rejection lead him to a position that has affinities with Grice's position, with its insistence on the primacy of utterer's meaning. (There are interesting parallels in this regard between Davidson and Suppes.)

Stephen Schiffer, 'Compositional Semantics and Language Understanding'. Schiffer offers a counter-example to the thesis that every natural language must have correct compositional semantics. He draws consequences for physicalism and for Gricean treatment of meaning; as regards the latter, Schiffer argues that 'The Gricean account of sentence meaning can be correct only if natural languages have compositional semantics . . .; but natural languages neither have nor need compositional semantics'.

John Searle, 'Meaning, Communication, and Representations'. Searle begins by tracing out similarities and differences between his earlier views and Grice's views. He then turns to developing a new view which employs a notion of *representation*. There is a parallel between Schiffer and Searle here, but Searle's explanation of his notion of representation is quite different to Schiffer's treatment of his notion of mental representation. The key notion for Searle in (partially) characterizing representation is the notion of *conditions on the success of the utterance*. Searle's investigation of representation leads him to reject the primacy of utterer's meaning. As Searle says, 'Once we are prepared to distinguish meaning from communication instead of identifying them as most intention theorists have done, then the meaning intentions of the speaker which intentionalists insist are the "essence" of meaning are easily specified in terms of correspondence conditions on the success of the utterance, as specified by the correspondence theorists'.

P. F. Strawson, ' "If" and "⊃" '. Strawson considers two views of 'if . . . then . . .' The truth-functionalist view, and the consequentialist view. He explains and evaluates Grice's defence of the truth-functionalist view. The difficulty he raises for this defence is that arguments in its favour seem 'a little *too* powerful'. As he says, 'It seems to follow that it is actually *impossible* that there should exist in any language a conjunction of which the meaning can be characterized by saying that it carries the same general ground-consequent implications as "so" does without joining asserted propositions as "so" does'. And this, Strawson remarks, is 'excessively implausible'. The point is quite important, for Grice's defence of the truth-functionalist account of 'If . . . then' exploits the distinction between what is meant and what is only implicated. One wonders whether versions of Strawson's difficulty could be raised for other philosophical positions that rest on exploiting that distinction (for example, Grice's defence of the causal theory of perception).

Deidre Wilson and Dan Sperber, 'On defining "Relevance"'. In his William James Lectures, Grice introduces the maxim of relevance as one of several conversational maxims he employs to explain conversional implicature. Wilson and Sperber observe that, 'In the years since the William James lectures . . . no explicit account of relevance suitable for use in pragmatic theory has . . . emerged.' They outline an account of relevance which they think meets the demands of pragmatic theory. They explain relevance by appeal to inferential processes in the speaker involved in his comprehension of language. Their 'main claim is that, contrary to what has often been claimed, relevance is definable in logical terms'.

Jaakko Hintikka, 'Logic of Conversation as a Logic of Dialogue'. Hintikka is also concerned with Grice's conversational maxims— but with them all, not just the maxim of relevance. Hintikka begins by noting that 'Grice has emphasized . . . the importance of taking into account the nature of the whole discourse in which a speaker is engaged, and not just the particular proposition he or she is making. Yet when the time comes to conceptualize the results of such discourse theoretical observations Grice often seems to retreat back to formulations that pertain to utterances taken one by one . . .' Hintikka's own approach to the logic of conversation is game-theoretic. This approach allows him to develop a systematic and unified treatment of the logic of conversation that 'takes into account the whole nature of the discourse in which the speaker is engaged'.

Gordon Baker, 'Alternative Mind-Styles'. Baker takes exception to the approach to language illustrated by the last three papers. Baker notes that many philosophers and linguists 'are agreed that systems of rules lie behind the "working of language" and that an enterprise of immense importance is bringing this invisible structure to light'. Baker contends there is nothing invisible here to make visible: this conception of language is a misconception and he finds the antedote to this conception in the work of later Wittgenstein. Baker's critique of this conception raises an interesting question about Grice: to what extent is the structure Grice finds in language an 'invisible' structure? It is not clear to us that Grice does think of language in this way; resultant procedures, for example, are certainly 'visible'.

Richard Grandy, 'Some Misconceptions about Belief'. Grandy argues that—except in a trivial sense—belief is not a relation between a believer and a sentence or sentence-like item (i.e., a proposition). And what goes for belief goes for the other 'propositonal attitudes' as well. The considerations Grandy advances lend additional support to one important aspect of Grice's view on reasoning—the point that there are often a variety of equally good but different 'suppressed premisses' that we may legitimately attribute to a reasoner. This is just what one would expect given Grandy's view of belief. But Grandy's paper may also seem to count *against* Grice. After all, does Grice not treat meaning, intention, belief, and desire as relations in his theory of meaning? But there is no real inconsistency here. There *appears* to be since, for ease of exposition, *we* treated belief as a relation when describing resultant procedures. Grice does not do so (as one can see from 'Utterer's Meaning, Sentence Meaning, and Word Meaning'). He does not treat belief as a relation in those parts of his theory that one would use to explain linguistic behaviour.

John Perry, 'Perception, Action, and the Structure of Believing'. Perry outlines and motivates a semantics for belief sentences that treats belief as a relation. The conflict with Grandy is only apparent, however; in the kind of psychological theorizing with which Perry is concerned, belief is usefully treated as relation. This does not mean that a psychophysiological or even an information-processing model of thought and action should employ such a relation. Grandy's point is that *such scientific theories* should not do so. Perry's semantics—with its three-tiered approach—is in fact designed to avoid many of the pitfalls Grandy identifies. Perry's semantics, with its emphasis on perception and action, and with its anti-Fregean, anti-possible worlds motivation, is akin to proposals Grice makes in 'Method in Philosophical Psychology'.

Gilbert Harman, 'Willing and Intending'. Harman is concerned with the tripartite thesis Grice defends in his British Academy lecture, 'Intention and Uncertainty': the thesis that intentional action results from a special attitude of willing which is (a) distinct from belief and desire; (b) can occur in the absence of intention; (c) is a component of intention where intention is present. Grice opts for this thesis in preference to a proposal that would treat intention as a special kind of belief. Harman considers both proposals and finds merit in each.

We can see why Grice would favour a not purely 'cognitive' treatment of intention if we recall his views on rationality: what is essential to rationality is that it regulates pre-rational inclinations and dispositions. In this context, it is natural, although by no means inevitable, to think of intention as essentially involving a non-cognitive desiderative element.

We would like to add to Harman's detailed and sympathetic discussion Grice's description of his own wilful soul. In commenting on Davidson's treatment of wanting in 'Intending', Grice says:

It seems to me that the picture of the soul suggested by Davidson's treatment of wanting is remarkably tranquil and, one might almost say, computerized. It is the picture of an ideally decorous board meeting, at which the various heads of sections advance, from the standpoint of their particular provinces, the case for or against some proposed course of action. In the end the chairman passes judgement, effective for action; normally judiciously, though sometimes he is for one reason or another over-impressed with the presentation made by some particular member. My soul doesn't seem to me, a lot of the time, to be like that at all. It is more like a particularly unpleasant department meeting, in which some members shout, won't listen, and suborn other members to lie on their behalf; while the chairman, who is often himself under suspicion of cheating, endeavours to impose some kind of order; frequently to no effect, since sometimes the meeting breaks up in disorder, sometimes, though it appears to end comfortably, in reality all sorts of enduring lesions are set up, and sometimes, whatever the outcome of the meeting, individual members go off and do things unilaterally. [Davidson]

George Myro, 'Identity and Time'. Myro develops 'one of those ideas of Paul's': namely, that identity is time-relative. Objects may be identifical at one time and not at another. This proposal is aimed at resolving some (not all) of the perplexities about identity raised by Geach, Wiggins, and others. Myro's development of this idea bears in an interesting and illumunating way on traditional disputes about the nature of substance. Another important feature of his contribution is his careful discussion of the role of model theory in the treatment of metaphysical issues.

Alan Code, 'Aristotle: Essence and Accident'. Code begins by developing and expanding some ideas that "my dear friend and colleague H. P. Grice has advanced in connection with Aristotle's *Categories.*" Grice's idea is that the *Categories* employs two basic predication relations which Grice calls 'Izzing' and 'Hazzing'—which can be explicated by offering a set of axioms in which these notions figure. Code extends this approach to Plato and the later Aristotle. He is especially concerned with Aristotle's hylomorphic analysis of substance (an analysis that addresses some of the same issues that occupy Myro).

Nancy Cartwright, 'Fitting Facts to Equations'. Cartwright argues that 'fundamental equations (of physics) do not govern objects in reality; they govern only objects in models'. Cartwright traces the origin of the first part of this thesis to a seminar Grice conducted on metaphysics; she traces the second part of the thesis to another Grice seminar on metaphysics in which 'we talked about pretences, fictions, surrogates, and the like' and in particular about the 'as if' operator (as in 'The radiating molecules in an ammonia laser behave *as if* they are classical electron oscillators'). Cartwright concludes with a view of 'physics as theatre'. These concerns reflect Grice's long standing interest in the theory of theories.

Judith Baker, 'Do One's Motives Have to be Pure?' Kant thinks they do. Baker maintains that 'Kant demands both that we have a special moral motive and that it operates alone if our action is to have moral worth'. She suggests a reconstruction of the Kantian notion of acting from duty that avoids the usual objections to Kant's insistence on purity of motive. The key is to distinguish levels of motivation. Baker does not relate her discussion of Kant to Grice's recent work on ethics and Kant (some of which is, in fact, work done jointly with Baker), but there are important connections between Baker's treatment of moral motivation and the account Grice gives of the claim that morality has on us.

Richard Warner, 'Grice on Happiness'. Warner is concerned to bring out the Aristotelian aspects of Grice's account of happiness; he argues that the central notion of Grice's account—suitability for the direction of life—plays a role that closely parallels the role Aristotle assigns to the notion of activity of the soul in conformity with virtue. The point is an important one since, as we noted earlier, happiness is a likely candidate to serve as an evaluative principle, a principle that both regulates our pre-rational inclination and dispositions and also plays a role in end-setting. On Grice's account, happiness is well-suited to such a role. Warner formulates a condition of adequacy on accounts of happiness and assesses Grice's account in light of this condition.

2

REPLY TO RICHARDS

PAUL GRICE

PREAMBLE

I am greatly honoured and much moved by the fact that such a distinguished company of philosophers should have contributed to this volume work of such quality as a compliment to me. I am especially pleased that the authors of this work are not just a haphazard band of professional colleagues; every one of them is a personal friend of mine, though I have to confess that some of them I see, these days, less frequently than I used to, and much less frequently than I should like to. So this collection provides me with a vivid reminder that philosophy is, at its best, a friendly subject. I wish that I could respond individually to each contribution; but I do not regard that as feasible, and any selective procedure would be invidious. Fortunately an alternative is open to me. The editors of this volume, Richard Grandy and Richard Warner, have contributed an editorial which provides a synoptic view of my work; in view of the fact that I have so far published no book, that the number of my publications is greatly exceeded by the number of my unpublications, and that even my publications include some papers which are not easily accessible, their undertaking fulfills a crying need. But it does more than that; it presents a most perceptive and sympathetic picture of the spirit which lies behind the parts of my work which it discusses; and it is my feeling that few have been as fortunate in their contemporary commentators as I have been in mine. So I make my contribution a response to theirs, though before replying directly to them I allow myself to indulge in a modicum of philosophical autobiography, which in its own turn leads into a display of philosophical prejudices and predilections. For convenience I fuse the editors into a multiple personality called 'Richards', whose multiplicity is marked by the use of plural pronouns and verb-forms.

A. LIFE AND OPINIONS OF PAUL GRICE

A1. *Life*

As I look back upon my former self, it seems to me that when, fifty years ago, I began the serious study of philosophy, the temperament with which I approached this enterprise was one of what I might call *dissenting rationalism*.[1] The rationalism was probably just the interest in looking for reasons which would be found in any intelligent juvenile who wanted to study philosophy; the tendency towards dissent may, however, have been derived from, or have been intensified by, my father. My father, who was a gentle person, a fine musician, and a dreadful business man, exercised little personal influence over me but quite a good deal of cultural influence; he was an obdurate nineteenth-century liberal nonconformist, and I witnessed almost daily, without involvement, the spectacle of his religious nonconformism coming under attack from the women in the household—my mother, who was heading for High Anglicanism and (especially) a resident aunt who was a Catholic convert. But whatever their origins in my case, I do not regard either of the elements in this dissenting rationalism as at all remarkable in people at my stage of intellectual development. I mention them more because of their *continued* presence than because of their initial appearance; it seems to me that they have persisted, and indeed have significantly expanded, over my philosophical life, and this I am inclined to regard as a much less usual phenomenon.

I count myself wonderfully fortunate to have begun my philosophical studies as a pupil of W. F. R. Hardie, later President of my then college, Corpus Christi, the author of a work on Plato which both is and is recognized as a masterpiece, whose book on the Nicomachean Ethics, in one of its earlier incarnations as a set of lecture-notes, saw me through years of teaching Aristotle's moral theory. It seems to me that I learnt from him just about all the things which one can be taught by someone else, as distinct from the things which one has to teach oneself. More specifically, my initial rationalism was developed under his guidance into a belief that philosophical questions are to be settled by reason, that is to say by *argument*; I learnt also from him *how* to argue, and in learning how to argue I came to learn that the ability to argue is a skill involving many aspects, and is much more than

---

[1] As I read what I find myself to have written in this *Reply*, I also find myself ready to expand this description to read 'irreverent, conservative, dissenting rationalism'.

an ability to see logical connections (though this ability is by no means to be despised). I came also to see that though philosophical progress is very difficult to achieve, and is often achieved only after agonizing labours, it is worth achieving; and that the difficulties involved in achieving it offer no kind of an excuse for a lowering of standards, or for substituting for the goals of philosophical truth some more easily achievable or accessible goal, like rabble-rousing. His methods were too austere for some; in particular the long silences in tutorials were found distressing by some pupils (though as the years went by I believe the tempo speeded up). There is a story, which I am not sure that I believe, that at one point in one tutorial a very long silence developed when it was Hardie's turn to speak, which was at long last broken by Hardie saying, 'And what did you mean by "of"?' There is another story, which I think I do believe, according to which Isaiah Berlin, who was a pupil of Hardie's two or three years before me, decided that the next time a silence developed in one of his tutorials he was not going to be the one to break it. In the next tutorial, after Berlin had finished reading his essay to Hardie, there followed a silence which lasted twenty-five minutes, at which point Berlin could stand it no longer, and said something.

These tutorial rigours never bothered me. If philosophizing is a difficult operation (as it plainly is) then sometimes time, even quite a lot of time, will be needed in order to make a move (as chess-players are only too well aware). The idea that a professional philosopher should either have already solved all questions, or should be equipped to solve any problem immediately, is no less ridiculous than would be the idea that Karpov ought to be able successfully to defend his title if he, though not his opponent, were bound by the rules of lightning chess. I liked the slow pace of discussion with Hardie; I liked the breath-laden 'Ooohhh!' which he would sometimes emit when he had caught you in, or even pushed you into, a patently untenable position (though I preferred it when this ejaculation was directed at someone other than myself); and I liked his resourcefulness in the defence of difficult positions, a characteristic illustrated by the following incident which he once told me about himself. He had, not long since, parked his car and gone to a cinema. Unfortunately he had parked his car on top of one of the strips on the street by means of which traffic-lights were at that time controlled by the passing traffic; as a result, the lights were jammed and it required four policemen to lift his car off the strip. The police decided to prosecute. I indicated to him that this didn't surprise me at all and asked him how he fared. 'Oh', he said, 'I got off.' I asked him how on earth he managed that. 'Quite simply,' he answered, 'I just invoked Mill's Method of Difference. They charged me with causing an obstruction at 4.00 p.m.; and I answered that since my car had been parked at 2.00 p.m., it couldn't have been my car which caused the obstruction.'

Hardie never disclosed his own views to students, no doubt wishing them to think their own thoughts (however flawed and immature) rather than his. When one did succeed, usually with considerable difficulty, in eliciting from him an expression of his own position, what one got was liable to be, though carefully worked out and ingeniously argued, distinctly conservative in tone; not surprisingly, it would not contain much in the way of battle-cries or campaign-material. Aspiring knights-errant require more than a sword, a shield, and a horse of superior quality impregnated with a suitable admixture of magic; they require a supply, or at least a procedure which can be relied on to maximize the likelihood of access to a supply, of Damsels in Distress. In the later 1930s Oxford was rudely aroused from its semi-peaceful semi-slumbers by the barrage of Viennese bombshells hurled at it by A. J. Ayer, at that time the *enfant terrible* of Oxford philosophy. Many people, including myself, were greatly interested by the methods, theses, and problems which were on display, and some were, at least momentarily, inspired by what they saw and heard. For my part, my reservations were never laid to rest; the crudities and dogmatisms seemed too pervasive. And then everything was more or less brought to a halt by the war.

After the war the picture was quite different, as a result of the dramatic rise in the influence of Austin, the rapid growth of Oxford as a world-centre of philosophy (due largely to the efforts of Ryle), and of the extraordinarily high quality of the many young philosophers who at that time first appeared on the Oxford scene. My own professional life in this period involved two especially important aspects. The first was my prolonged collaboration with my former pupil, Peter Strawson. Our efforts were partly directed towards the giving of joint seminars; we staged a number of these on topics related to the notions of meaning, of categories, and of logical form. But our association was much more than an alliance for the purposes of teaching. We consumed vast quantities of time in systematic and unsystematic philosophical explorations, and from these discussions sprang our joint published paper *In Defense of a Dogma*, and also a long uncompleted work on predication and Aristotelian categories, one or two reflections of which are visible in Strawson's book *Individuals*. Our method of composition was laborious in the extreme; work was constructed together sentence by sentence, nothing being written down until agreement had been reached, which often took quite a time. The rigours of this procedure eventually led to its demise. During this period of collaboration we of course developed a considerable corpus of common opinions; but to my mind a more important aspect of it was the extraordinary closeness of the intellectual *rapport* which we developed; other people sometimes complained that our mutual exchanges were liable to become so abbreviated in expression as to be unintelligible to a third party. The potentialities of such joint endeavours continued to lure me; the collaboration with Strawson was followed by other collaborations of varying degrees of intensity, with (for example) Austin on Aristotle's *Categories* and *De Interpretatione*, with Warnock on perception, with David Pears and with James Thomson on philosophy of action, with Fritz Staal on philosophical-linguistic questions, and most recently with George Myro on metaphysics, and with Judith Baker on Ethics. I shall return shortly to the importance which I attribute to this mode of philosophical activity.

The other prominent feature of this period in my philosophical life was participation in the discussions which took place on Saturday mornings in term-time and which were conducted by a number of the younger Oxford philosophers under the leadership of Austin. This group which continued to meet up to, and indeed for some years after, Austin's death was christened by me 'The Play Group', and was often so referred to, though so far as I know never by, or in the presence of, Austin himself. I have little doubt that this group was often thought of outside Oxford, and occasionally, perhaps even inside Oxford, as constituting the core, or the hot-bed, of what became known as 'Ordinary Language Philosophy', or even 'The Oxford School of Ordinary Language Philosophy'. As such it no doubt absorbed its fair share of the hatred and derision lavished upon this 'School' by so many people, like for example Gellner, and like Gustav Bergmann who (it was said), when asked whether he was going to hear a paper delivered on a visit by an eminent British philosopher, replied with characteristic charm that he did not propose to waste his time on any English Futilitarian.

Yet, as I look back on our activities, I find it difficult to discern any feature of them which merited this kind of opprobrium. To begin with, there was more than one group or ill-defined association of Oxford philosophers who were concerned, in one way or another, with 'ordinary' linguistic usage; besides those who, initially at least, gravitated towards Austin, there were those who drew special illumination from Ryle, and others (better disciplined perhaps) who looked to Wittgenstein; and the philosophical gait of people belonging to one of these groups would, characteristically, be markedly different from that of people belonging to another. But even within the Play Group, great diversity was visible, as one would expect of an association containing people with the ability and independence of mind of Austin, Strawson, Hampshire, Paul, Pears, Warnock, and Hare (to name a few). There was no 'School'; there were no dogmas which united us, in the way, for example, that an unflinching (or *almost* unflinching) opposition to abstract entities unified and inspired what I might call the American School of Latter-day Nominalists, or that an unrelenting (or *almost* unrelenting) determination to allow significance only to what is verifiable united the School of Logical Positivism. It has, I think, sometimes been supposed that one dogma which united us was that of the need to restrict philosophical attention to '*ordinary*' language, in a sense which would disqualify the introduction into, or employment in, philosophical discourse of technical terminology or jargon, a restriction which would seem to put a stranglehold on any philosophical theory-construction. It is true that many, even all, of us would have objected (and rightly objected) to the introduction of technical apparatus before the ground had been properly laid; the sorry story of deontic logic shows what may happen when technologists rush in where a well-conducted elephant would fear to tread. We would also (as some of us did from time to time) have objected to the *covert* introduction of jargon, the use of seemingly innocent expressions whose bite comes from a concealed technical overlay (as perhaps has occurred with words like 'sensation' or 'volition'). But one glance at 'How to talk: Some Simple Ways', or at 'How to Do Things with Words' should be enough to dispel the idea that there was a general renunciation of the use of technical terminology, even if certain individuals at some moments may have strayed in that direction.

Another dogma to which some may have supposed us to be committed is that of the sanctity, or sacrosanctity, of whatever metaphysical judgements or world-pictures may be identified as underlying ordinary discourse. Such a dogma would, I imagine, be some kind of counterpart of Moore's 'Defence of Common Sense'. It is true that

Austin had a high respect for Moore. 'Some like Witters, but Moore's *my* man', I once heard him say; and it is also true that Austin, and perhaps some other members of the group, thought that some sort of metaphysic is embedded in ordinary language. But to regard such a 'natural metaphysic' as present and as being worthy of examination stops a long way short of supposing such a metaphysic to be guaranteed as true or acceptable. Any such further step would need justification by argument.

In fact, the only position which to my mind would have commanded universal assent was that a careful examination of the detailed features of ordinary discourse is required as a foundation for philosophical thinking; and even here the enthusiasm of the assent would have varied from person to person, as would the precise view taken (if any was taken) about the relationship between linguistic phenomena and philosophical theses. It is indeed worth remarking that the exhaustive examination of linguistic phenomena was not, as a matter of fact, originally brought in as part of a *direct* approach to philosophy. Austin's expressed view (the formulation of which no doubt involved some irony) was that we 'philosophical hacks' spent the week making, for the benefit of our pupils, direct attacks on philosophical issues, and that we needed to be refreshed, at the week-end, by some suitably chosen 'para-philosophy' in which certain non-philosophical conceptions were to be examined with the full rigour of the Austinian Code, with a view to an ultimate analogical pay-off (liable never to be reached) in philosophical currency. It was in this spirit that in early days we investigated rules of games (with an eye towards questions about meaning). Only later did we turn our microscopic eyes more directly upon philosophical questions.

It is possible that some of the animosity directed against so-called 'ordinary language philosophy' may have come from people who saw this 'movement' as a sinister attempt on the part of a decaying intellectual establishment, an establishment whose home lay within the ancient walls of Oxford and Cambridge (walls of stone, not of red brick) and whose upbringing was founded on a classical education, to preserve control of philosophy by gearing philosophical practice to the deployment of a proficiency specially accessible to the establishment, namely a highly developed sensitivity to the richness of linguistic usage. It is, I think, certain that among the enemies of the new philosophical style were to be found defenders of a traditional view of philosophy as a discipline concerned with the nature of reality, not with the character of language and its operations, not indeed with any mode of *representation* of reality. Such persons do, to my mind, raise an objection which needs a fully developed reply. *Either* the conclusions which 'ordinary language philosophers' draw from linguistic data are also linguistic in character, in which case the contents of philosophy are trivialized, *or* the philosopher's conclusions are *not* linguistic in character, in which case the nature of the step from linguistic premises to non-linguistic conclusions is mysterious. The traditionalists, however, seem to have no stronger reason for objecting to 'ordinary language philosophy' than to forms of linguistic philosophy having no special connection with ordinary language, such as that espoused by logical positivists.

But, to my mind, much the most significant opposition came from those who felt that 'ordinary language philosophy' was an affront to science and to intellectual progress, and who regarded its exponents as wantonly dedicating themselves to what Russell, in talking about common sense or some allied idea, once called 'stone-age metaphysics'. That would be the best that could be dredged up from a 'philosophical' study of ordinary language. Among such assailants were to be found those who, in effect, were ready to go along with the old description of philosophy as 'the queen of the sciences', but only under a re-interpretation of this phrase. 'Queen' must be understood to mean not 'sovereign queen', like Queen Victoria or Queen Elizabeth II, but 'queen consort', like Queen Alexandra or Queen Elizabeth the Queen Mother; and the sovereign of which philosophy is the queen-consort might turn out to be either science in general or just *physical* science. The primary service which would be expected of philosophy as a consort would be to provide the scientist with a pure or purified language for him to use on formal occasions (should there be such occasions). Some, I suspect, would have been ready to throw in, for good measure, the charge that the enterprise of 'ordinary language philosophy' is in any case doomed, since it presupposes the admissibility of an analytic/synthetic distinction which in fact cannot be sustained.

The issues raised in this attack are both important and obscure, and deserve a much fuller treatment than I can here provide, but I will do my best in a short space. I have three comments.

(1) The use made of the Russellian phrase 'stone-age metaphysics' may have more rhetorical appeal than argumentative force. Certainly 'stone-age' *physics*, if by that we mean a primitive set of hypotheses about how the world goes which might

(conceivably) be embedded somehow or other in ordinary language, would not be a proper object for first-order devotion. But this fact would not prevent something derivable or extractable from stone-age physics, perhaps some very general characterization of the nature of reality, from being a proper target for serious research; for this extractable characterization might be the *same* as that which is extractable from, or that which underlies, twentieth-century physics. Moreover, a metaphysic embedded in ordinary language (should there be such a thing) might not have to be derived from any belief about how the world goes which such language reflects; it might, for example, be derived somehow from the categorial structure of the language. Furthermore, the discovery and presentation of such a metaphysic might turn out to be a properly *scientific* enterprise, though not, of course, an enterprise in *physical* science. A rationally organized and systematized study of reality might perhaps be such an enterprise; so might some highly general theory in formal semantics, though it might of course be a serious question whether these two candidates are identical.

To repel such counter-attacks, an opponent of 'ordinary language philosophy' might have to press into service the argument which I represented him as throwing in for good measure as an adjunct. He might, that is, be forced to rebut the possibility of there being a scientifically respectable, highly general semantic theory based squarely on data provided by ordinary discourse by arguing, or asserting, that a theory of the sort suggested would have to presuppose the admissibility of an analytic/synthetic distinction.

(2) With respect to the suggested allocation to philosophy of a supporting role *vis-à-vis* science or some particular favoured science, I should first wish to make sure that the metaphysical position of the assigner was such as to leave room for this kind of assessment of roles or functions; and I should start with a lively expectation that this would not be the case. But even if this negative expectation was disappointed, I should next enquire by what standards of purity a language is to be adjudged suitable for use by a scientist. If those standards are supposed to be independent of the needs of science, and so not dictated by scientists, then there seems to be as yet no obstacle to the possibility that the function of philosophy might be to discover

or devise a language of that sort, which might even turn out to be some kind of 'ordinary' language. And even if the requisite kind of purity were to consist in what I might term such logico-methodological virtues as consistency and systematicity, which are also those looked for in scientific theories, what prevents us, in advance, from attributing these virtues to ordinary language? In which case, the ordinary-language philosopher would be back in business. So far as I can see, once again the enemy of ordinary-language philosophy might be forced to fall back on the allegations that such an attempt to vindicate ordinary language would have to presuppose the viability of the analytic/synthetic distinction.

(3) With regard to the analytic/synthetic distinction itself, let me first remark that it is my present view that neither party, in the actual historical debate, has exactly covered itself with glory. For example, Quine's original argument that attempts to define 'analytic' end up in a hopelessly circular tour of a group of intensional concepts disposes, at best, of only one such definitional attempt, and leaves out of consideration the (to my mind) promising possibility that this type of definition may not be the right procedure to follow—an idea which I shall expand in a moment. And, on the reverse side of the coin, the attempt by Strawson and myself to defend the distinction by a (one hopes) sophisticated form of Paradigm Case argument fails to meet, or even to lay eyes on, the characteristic rebuttal of such types of argument, namely that the fact that a certain concept or distinction is frequently deployed by a population of speakers and thinkers offers no guarantee that the concept or distinction in question can survive rigorous theoretical scrutiny. To my mind, the mistake made by both parties has been to try to support, or to discredit, the analytic/synthetic distinction as something which is detectably present in the use of natural language; it would have been better to take the hint offered by the appearance of the 'family circle' of concepts pointed to by Quine, and to regard an analytic/synthetic distinction not as a (supposedly) detectable element in natural language, but rather as a theoretical device which it might, or again might not, be feasible and desirable to incorporate into some systematic treatment of natural language. The viability of the distinction, then, would be a *theoretical* question which,

so far as I can see, remains to be decided; and the decision is not likely to be easy, since it is by no means apparent what kind of theoretical structure would prove to be the home of such a distinction, should it find a home.

Two further comments seem to me relevant and important. A common though perhaps not universally adopted practice among 'ordinary language philosophers' is (or was) to treat as acceptable the forms of ordinary discourse and to seek to lay bare the system, or metaphysic, which underlies it. A common alternative proposed by enemies of 'ordinary language philosophy' has been that of a *rational reconstruction* of ordinary language; in the words of Bishop Berkeley, it is proposed that we should speak with the vulgar but think with the learned. But why should our vulgar speech be retained? Why should we not be told merely not to think but also to speak with the learned? After all, if my house is pronounced uninhabitable to the extent that I need a new one, it is not essential that I construct the new one within the outer shell of the old one, though this procedure might sometimes be cheaper or aesthetically preferable. An attachment to the forms of ordinary discourse even when the substance is discarded suggests, but of course does not demonstrate, an adherence to some unstated principle of respect for ordinary discourse even on the part of its avowed enemies.

Second, whether or not a viable analytic/synthetic distinction exists, I am not happy with the claim that 'ordinary language philosophy' *presupposes* the existence of such a distinction. It might be that a systematic theoretical treatment of the facts of ordinary usage would incorporate, as part of its theoretical apparatus, material which could be used to exhibit such a distinction as intelligible and acceptable; but in that case, on the assumption that the theoretical treatment satisfied the standards which theories are supposed to satisfy, it would appear that the analytic/synthetic distinction would be *vindicated* not *presupposed*. For the distinction to be entailed by the execution of a programme is plainly not the same as it to be *presupposed* by that programme. For if it is to be presupposed by the programme of 'ordinary language philosophy', it would, I imagine, have to be the case that the supposition that anything at all would count as a successful execution of the programme would require a prior assumption of the viability of an analytic/synthetic distinction; and how *this* allegation could be made out I cannot for the life of me discover.

I turn now to the more agreeable task of trying to indicate the features of the philosophical operations of the Play Group which at the time, or (in some instances) subsequently, seemed to me to be particularly appealing. First, the entire idea that we should pay detailed attention to the way we talk seems to me to have a certain quality which is characteristic of philosophical revolutions (at least minor ones). I was once dining with Strawson at his college when one of the guests present, an Air Marshal, revealed himself as having, when he was an undergraduate, sat at the feet of Cook Wilson, whom he revered. We asked him what he regarded as specially significant about Cook Wilson as a philosopher; and after a good deal of fumbling, he answered that it was Cook Wilson's delivery of the message that 'what we know, we *know*'. This provoked in me some genteel silent mirth; but a long time later I realized that mirth was quite inappropriate. Indeed the message was a platitude, but so are many of the best philosophical messages: for they exhort us to *take seriously* something to which, previously, we have given at best lip service. Austin's message was another platitude; it in effect said that if in accordance with prevailing fashion one wants to say that all or some philosophical propositions are really about linguistic usage, one had better see to it that one has a proper knowledge of what linguistic usage is and of what lies behind it. This sophisticated but remorseless literalism was typical of Austin. When seeking a way of organizing a discussion group to entertain a visiting American logician, he said, 'They say that logic is a game; well then, let's play it as a game'; with the result that we spent a fascinating term, meeting each week to play that week's improved version of a game called by Austin 'Symbolo', a sequence (I suspect) of less thrilling ancestors of the game many years later profitably marketed under the name of 'Wff'n'Proof'.

Another appealing element was the fact that Austin had, and at times communicated, a prevalent vision of ordinary language as a wonderfully intricate instrument. By this I do not mean merely that he saw, or hoped one day to be able to see, our language conforming to a Leibnizian ideal of exhibiting an immense variety of linguistic pheno-mena which are capable of being elegantly and economically organized under a relatively small body of principles or rules. He may have had such a picture of language, and may indeed have hoped that some extension or analogue of Chomsky's work on syntax, which he greatly admired, might fill in the detail for us, thus providing new access to the Austinian science of grammar, which seemed to reside in an intellectual

Holy of Holies, to be approached only after an intensive discipline of preliminary linguistic studies. What I am imputing to him is a belief in our everyday language as an *instrument*, as manifesting the further Leibnizian feature of *purpose*; a belief in it as something whose intricacies and distinctions are not idle, but rather marvellously and subtly fitted to serve the multiplicity of our needs and desires in communication. It is not surprising, therefore, that our discussions not infrequently involved enquiries into the *purpose* or *point* of some feature of ordinary discourse.

When put to work, this conception of ordinary language seemed to offer fresh and manageable approaches to philosophical ideas and problems, the appeal of which approaches, in my eyes at least, is in no way diminished by the discernible affinity between them on the one hand and, on the other, the professions and practice of Aristotle in relation to τὰ λεγόμενα ('what is said'). When properly regulated and directed, 'linguistic botanizing' seems to me to provide a valuable initiation to the philosophical treatment of a concept, particularly if what is under examination (and it is arguable that this should always be the case) is a family of different but related concepts. Indeed, I will go further, and proclaim it as my belief that linguistic botanizing is indispensable, at a certain stage, in a philosophical enquiry, and that it is lamentable that this lesson has been forgotten, or has never been learned. That is not to say that I have ever subscribed to the full Austinian prescription for linguistic botanizing, namely (as one might put it) to go through the dictionary and to believe everything it tells you. Indeed, I once remarked to him in a discussion (with I fear, provocative intent) that I personally didn't care *what* the dictionary said, and drew the rebuke, 'And that's where you make your big mistake.' Of course, not all these explorations were successful; we once spent five weeks in an effort to explain why sometimes the word 'very' allows, with little or no change of meaning, the substitution of the word 'highly' (as in 'very unusual') and sometimes does not (as in 'very depressed' or 'very wicked'); and we reached no conclusion. This episode was ridiculed by some as an ultimate embodiment of fruitless frivolity; but that response was as out of place as a similar response to the medieval question, 'How many angels can sit on the point of a pin?' For much as this medieval question was raised in order to display, in a vivid way, a difficulty in the conception of an immaterial substance, so our discussion was directed, in response to a worry from me, towards an examination, in the first instance, of a conceptual question which was generally agreed among us to be a strong candidate for being a question which had no philosophical importance, with a view to using the results of this examination in finding a distinction between philosophically important and philosophically unimportant enquiries. Unfortunately the desired results were not forthcoming.

Austin himself, with his mastery in seeking out, and his sensitivity in responding to, the finer points of linguistic usage, provided a splendid and instructive example to those who were concerned to include linguistic botanizing in their professional armoury. I shall recount three authentic anecdotes in support of this claim. Geoffrey Warnock was being dined at Austin's college with a view to election to a Fellowship, and was much disconcerted, even though he was already acquainted with Austin, when Austin's first remark to him was, 'What would be the difference between my saying to you that someone is not playing golf *correctly* and my saying to you that he is not playing golf *properly*?' On a certain occasion we were discussing the notion of a principle, and (in this connection) the conditions for appropriate use of the phrase 'on principle'. Nowell Smith recalled that a pupil of Patrick Gardiner, who was Greek, wanting permission for an overnight visit to London, had come to Gardiner and offered him some money, saying 'I hope that you will not be offended by this somewhat Balkan approach'. At this point, Nowell Smith suggested, Gardiner might well have replied, 'I do not take bribes on principle.' Austin responded by saying 'I should not say that; I should just say "No, thanks".' On another occasion, Nowell Smith (again cast in the role of straight man) offered as an example of non-understandable English an extract from a sonnet of Donne:

> From the round earth's imagined corners,
> Angels, your trumpets blow.

Austin said, 'It is perfectly clear what that means; it means "angels, blow your trumpets from what persons less cautious than I would call the four corners of the earth".'

These affectionate remembrances no doubt prompt the question why I should have turned away from this style of philosophy. Well, as I have already indicated, in a certain sense I never have turned away, in that I continue to believe that a more or less detailed study of the way we talk, in this or that region of discourse, is an indispensable foundation for much of the most fundamental kind of philosophizing; for just how much seems to me to be a serious question in need of an answer. That linguistic information should not be just a quantity of collector's items, but should on occasion at least, provide linguistic Nature's answers to questions which we put to her, and that such questioning is impossible without hypotheses set in an at least embryonic theory, is a proposition which would, I suspect, have met general, though perhaps not universal, assent; the trouble began when one asked, if one actually ever did ask, what sort of a theory this underlying theory should be. The urgency of the need for such an enquiry is underlined by one or two problems which I have already mentioned; by, for example, the problem of distinguishing conceptual investigations of ordinary discourse which are philosophical in character from those which are not. It seems plausible to suppose that an answer to this problem would be couched in terms of a special *generality* which attaches to philosophical but not to non-philosophical questions; but whether this generality would be simply a matter of degree, or whether it would have to be specified by reference to some further item or items, such as (for example) the idea of *categories*, remains to be determined. At this point we make contact with a further issue already alluded to by me; if it is necessary to invoke the notion of categories, are we to suppose these to be linguistic categories (categories of expression) or *metaphysical* categories (categories of things), a question which is plainly close to the previously-mentioned burning issue of whether the theory behind ordinary discourse is to be thought of as a highly general, language-indifferent, semantic theory, or a metaphysical theory about the ultimate nature of things, if indeed these possibilities are distinct. Until such issues as these are settled, the prospects for a determination of the more detailed structure of the theory or theories behind ordinary discourse do not seem too bright. In my own case, a further impetus towards a demand for the provision of a visible theory underlying ordinary discourse came from my work on the idea of Conversational Implicature, which emphasized the radical importance of distinguishing (to speak loosely) what *our words* say or imply from what *we* in uttering them imply; a distinction seemingly denied by Wittgenstein, and all too frequently ignored by Austin.

My own efforts to arrive at a more theoretical treatment of linguistic phenomena of the kind with which in Oxford we had long been concerned derived much guidance from the work of Quine and of Chomsky on syntax. Quine helped to throw light on the problem of deciding what kind of thing a suitable theory would be, and also by his example exhibited the virtues of a strong methodology; Chomsky showed vividly the kind of way in which a region for long found theoretically intractable by scholars (like Jesperson) of the highest intelligence could, by discovery and application of the right kind of apparatus, be brought under control. I should add that Quine's influence on me was that of a model: I was never drawn towards the acceptance either of his actual methodology or of his specific philosophical positions. I have to confess that I found it a little sad that my two chief theoretical mentors could never agree, or even make visible contact, on the question of the theoretical treatment of natural language; it seemed a pity that two men who are about as far removed from dumbness as any that I have ever encountered should not be equally far removed from deafness. During this time my philosophizing revealed a distinct tendency to appear in formal dress; indeed the need for greater contact with experts in logic and in linguistics than was then available in Oxford was one of my main professional reasons for moving to the United States. Work in this style was directed to a number of topics, but principally to an attempt to show, in a constructive way, that grammar (the grammar of ordinary discourse) could be regarded as, in Russell's words, a pretty good guide to logical form, or to a suitable representation of logical form. This undertaking involved the construction, for a language which was a close relative of a central portion of English (including quantification), of a hand-in-hand syntax-cum-semantics which made minimal use of transformations. This project was not fully finished and has not so far been published, though its material was presented in lectures and seminars both inside and outside Berkeley, including a memorable summer colloquium at Irvine in 1971. An interest in formalistic philosophizing seems to me to have more than one source. It may arise from a desire to ensure that the philosophical ideas which one deploys are capable of full and coherent development; not unnaturally, the pursuit of this end may make use of a favoured canonical system. I have never been greatly attached to canonicals, not even those of first-order predicate logic together with set theory, and in any case this kind of formal enterprise would overtax my meagre technical equipment. It may, on the other hand, consist in the suggestion of notational devices together with sketchy indications of the laws or principles to be looked for in a system incorporating these devices; the object of the exercise being to seek out hitherto unrecognized analogies and to attain new levels of generality. This latter kind of interest is the one which engages me, and will, I think, continue to do so, no matter what shifts occur in my philosophical positions.

It is nevertheless true that in recent years my disposition to resort to formalism has markedly diminished. This retreat may well have been accelerated when, of all people, Hilary Putnam remarked to me that I was too formal; but its main source lay in the fact that I began to devote the bulk of my attentions to areas of philosophy other than philosophy of language: to philosophical psychology, seen as an off-shoot of philosophical biology and as concerned with specially advanced apparatus for the handling of life; to metaphysics; and to ethics, in which my pre-existing interest which was much enlivened by Judith Baker's capacity for presenting vivid and realistic examples. Such areas of philosophy seem, at least at present, much less amenable to formalistic treatment. I have little doubt that a contribution towards a gradual shift of style was also made by a growing apprehension that philosophy is all too often being squeezed out of operation by technology; to borrow words from Ramsey, that apparatus which began life as a system of devices to combat *woolliness* has now become an instrument of *scholasticism*. But the development of this theme will best be deferred until the next sub-section.

A2. *Opinions*

The opinions which I shall voice in this sub-section will all be general in character: they will relate to such things as what I might call, for want of a better term, *style* in philosophizing and to general aspects of methodology. I shall reserve for the next section anything I might have to say about my views on specific philosophical topics, or about special aspects of methodology which come into play within some particular department of philosophy.

(I) I shall first proclaim it as my belief that doing philosophy ought to be *fun*. I would indeed be prepared to go further, and to suggest that it is no bad thing if the products of doing philosophy turn out, every now and then, to be *funny*. One should of course be serious about philosophy; but being serious does not require one to be solemn. Laughter *in* philosophy is not to be confused with laughter *at* philosophy; there have been too many people who have made this confusion, and so too many people who have thought of merriment in philosophical discussion as being like laughter in church. The prime source of this belief is no doubt the wanton disposition which nature gave me; but it has been reinforced, at least so far as philosophy is concerned, by the course of every serious and prolonged philosophical association to which I have been a party; each one has manifested its own special quality which at one and the same time has delighted the spirit and stimulated the intellect. To my mind, getting together with others to do philosophy should be very much like getting together with others to make music: lively yet sensitive interaction is directed towards a common end, in the case of philosophy a better grasp of some fragment of philosophical truth; and if, as sometimes happens, harmony is sufficiently great to allow collaboration as authors, then so much the better.

But as some will be quick to point out, such disgusting sentimentality is by no means universal in the philosophical world. It was said of the late H. W. B. Joseph that he was dedicated to the Socratic art of midwifery; he sought to bring forth error and to strangle it at birth. Though this comment referred to his proper severity in teaching, he was in fact, in concert with the much more formidable H. A. Prichard, no less successful in dealing with colleagues than he was with students; philosophical productivity among his junior contemporaries in Oxford was low, and one philosopher of considerable ability even managed to complete a lifetime without publishing a single word. (Perhaps it is not entirely surprising that the undergraduates of his college once crucified him bloodlessly with croquet hoops on the college lawn.) The tradition did not die with Joseph; to take just one example, I have never been very happy about Austin's *Sense and Sensibilia*, partly because the philosophy which it contains does not seem to me to be, for the most part, of the highest quality, but more because its tone is frequently rather unpleasant. And similar incidents have been reported not so long ago from the USA. So far as I know, no one has ever been the better for receiving a good thumping, and I do not see that philosophy is enhanced by such episodes. There are other ways of clearing the air besides nailing to the wall everything in sight.

Though it is no doubt plain that I am not enthusiastic about *odium theologicum*, I have to confess that I am not very much more enthusiastic about *amor theologicus*. The sounds of fawning are perhaps softer but hardly sweeter than the sounds of rending; indeed it sometimes happens that the degree of adulation, which for a time is lavished upon a philosopher, is in direct proportion to the degree of savagery which he metes out to his victims. To my stomach it does not make all that much difference whether the recipient of excessive attachment is a person or a philosophical creed; zealotry and bandwagoning seem to me no more appealing than discipleship. Rational and dispassionate commendation and criticism are of course essential to the prosecution of the discipline, provided that they are exercised in the pursuit of philosophical truth; but passion directed towards either philosophers or philosophies is out of place, no matter whether its object is favoured or disfavoured. What is in place is respect, when it is deserved.

I have little doubt that it is the general beastliness of human nature which is in the main responsible for the fact that philosophy, despite its supposedly exalted nature, has exhibited some tendency to become yet another of the jungles in which human beings seem so much at home, with the result that beneath the cloak of enlightenment is hidden the dagger of diminution by disparagement. But there are perhaps one or two special factors, the elimination of which, if possible, might lower the level of pollution. One of these factors is, I suspect, a certain view of the proper procedure for establishing a philosophical thesis. It is, I am inclined to think, believed by many philosophers that, in philosophical thinking, we start with certain material (the nature of which need not here concern us) which poses a certain problem or raises a certain question. At first sight, perhaps, more than one distinct philosophical thesis would appear to account for the material and settle the question raised by it; and the way (generally the only way) in which a particular thesis is established is thought to be by the elimination of its rivals, characteristically by the detection of counter-examples. Philosophical theses are supported by elimination of alternative theses.

It is, however, my hope that in many cases, including the most important cases, theses can be established by direct evidence in their favour, not just by elimination of their rivals. I shall refer to this issue again later when I come to say something about the character of metaphysical argument and its connection with so-called transcendental argument. The kind of metaphysical argument which I have in mind might be said, perhaps, to exemplify a 'diagogic' as opposed to 'epagogic' or inductive approach to philosophical argumentation. Now, the more emphasis is placed on justification by elimination of rivals, the greater is the impetus given to refutation, whether of theses or of people; and perhaps a greater emphasis on 'diagogic' procedure, if it could be shown to be justifiable, would have an eirenic effect.

A second possible source of atmospheric amelioration might be a shift in what is to be regarded as the prime index of success, or merit, in philosophical enquiry. An obvious candidate as an answer to this question would be being right, or being right for the right reasons (however difficult the realization of this index might be to determine). Of course one must try to be right, but even so I doubt whether this is the best answer, unless a great deal is packed into the meaning of 'for the right reasons'. An eminent topologist whom I knew was regarded with something approaching veneration by his colleagues, even though usually when he gave an important lecture either his proofs were incomplete, or if complete they contained at least one mistake. Though he was often wrong, what he said was exciting, stimulating, and fruitful. The situation in philosophy seems to me to be similar. Now if it were generally *explicitly* recognized that being interesting and fruitful is more important than being right, and may indeed co-exist with being wrong, polemical refutation might lose some of its appeal.

(II) The cause which I have just been espousing might be called, perhaps, *the unity of conviviality* in philosophy. There are, however, one or two other kinds of unity in which I also believe. These relate to the unity of the subject or discipline: the first I shall call the *latitudinal unity* of philosophy, and the second, its *longitudinal unity*. With regard to the first, it is my firm conviction that despite its real or apparent division into departments, philosophy is one subject, a single discipline. By this I do not merely mean that between different areas of philosophy there are cross-references, as when, for example, one encounters in ethics the problem whether such and such principles fall within the epistemological classification of *a priori* knowledge. I mean (or hope I mean) something a good deal stronger than this, something more like the thesis that it is not possible to reach full understanding of, or high level proficiency in, any one department without a corresponding understanding and proficiency in the others; to the extent that when I visit an unfamiliar university and occasionally happens) I am introduced to, 'Mr Puddle, our man in Political Philosophy' (or in 'Nineteenth-century Continental Philosophy' or 'Aesthetics', as the case may be), I am immediately confident that either Mr Puddle is being under-described and in consequence maligned, or else Mr Puddle is not really good at his stuff. Philosophy, like virtue, is *entire*. Or, one might even dare to say, there is only one problem in philosophy, namely all of them. At this point, however, I must admit a double embarassment; I do not know *exactly* what the thesis is which I want to maintain, and I do not know how to prove it, though I am fairly sure that my thesis, whatever it is, would only be interesting if it were provable, or at least strongly arguable; indeed the embarassments may not be independent of one another. So the best I can now do will be to list some possibilities with regard to the form which supporting argument might take.

(i) It might be suggested that the sub-disciplines within philosophy are ordered in such a way that the character and special problems of each sub-discipline are generated by the character and subject-matter of of a prior sub-discipline; that the nature of the prior sub-discipline guarantees or calls for a successor of a certain sort of dealing with such-and-such a set of questions; and it might be added that the nature of the first or primary sub-discipline is dictated by the general nature of theorizing or of rational enquiry. On this suggestion each posterior sub-discipline S would call for the existence of *some* prior sub-discipline which would, when specified, dictate the character of S.

(ii) There might be some very general characterization which applies to all sub-disciplines, knowledge of which is required for the successful study of any sub-discipline, but which is itself so abstract that the requisite knowledge of it can be arrived at only by attention to its various embodiments, that is to the full range of sub-disciplines.

(iii) Perhaps on occasion every sub-discipline, or some element or aspect of every sub-discipline, falls within the scope of every other sub-discipline. For example, some part of metaphysics might consist in a metaphysical treatment of ethics or some element in ethics; some part of epistemology might consist in epistemological consideration of metaphysics or of the practice of metaphysical thinking; some part of ethics or of value theory might consist in a value-theoretical treatment of epistemology; and so on. All sub-disciplines would thus be intertwined.

(iv) It might be held that the *ultimate* subject of all philosophy is ourselves, or at least our rational nature, and that the various subdivisions of philosophy are concerned with different aspects of this rational nature. But the characterization of this rational nature is not divisible into water-tight compartments; each aspect is intelligible only in relation to the others.

(v) There is a common methodology which, in different ways, dictates to each sub-discipline. There is no ready-made manual of methodology, and even if there were, knowing the manual would not be the same as knowing how to *use* the manual. This methodology is sufficiently abstract for it to be the case that proficient application of it can be learned only in relation to the totality of sub-disciplines within its domain. (Suggestion (v) may well be close to suggestion (ii).)

(III) In speaking of the 'Longitudinal Unity of Philosophy', I am referring to the unity of Philosophy through time. Any Oxford philosophy tutor who is accustomed to setting essay topics for his pupils, for which he prescribes reading which includes both passages from Plato or Aristotle and articles from current philosophical journals, is only too well aware that there are many topics which span the centuries; and it is only a little less obvious that often substantially similar positions are propounded at vastly differing dates. Those who are in a position to know assure me that similar correspondences are to some degree detectable across the barriers which separate one philosophical culture from another, for example between Western European and Indian philosophy. If we add to this banality the further banality that it is on the whole likely that those who achieve enduring philosophical fame do so as a result of outstanding philosophical merit, we reach the conclusion that in our attempts to solve our own philosophical problems we should give proper consideration to whatever contributions may have been provided by the illustrious dead. And when I say 'proper consideration' I am not referring to some suitably reverential act of kow-towing which is to be performed as we pass the niche assigned to the departed philosopher in the Philosopher's Hall of Fame; I mean rather that we should treat those who are great but dead as if they were great and living, as persons who have something to say to us *now*; and, further, that in order to do this we should do our best to 'introject' ourselves into their shoes, into their ways of thinking; indeed to rethink their offerings as if it were ourselves who were the offerers; and then, perhaps, it may turn out that it *is* ourselves. I might add at this point that it seems to me that one of the prime benefits which may accrue to us from such introspection lies in the region of methodology. By and large the greatest philosophers have been the greatest, and the most self-conscious, methodologists; indeed, I am tempted to regard this fact as primarily accounting for their greatness as philosophers. So whether we are occupied in thinking on behalf of some philosopher other than ourselves, or in thinking on our own behalf, we should maintain a constant sensitivity to the nature of the enterprise in which we are engaged and to the character of the procedures which are demanded in order to carry it through.

Of course, if we are looking at the work of some relatively minor philosophical figure, such as for example Wollaston or Bosanquet or Wittgenstein, such 'introjection' may be neither possible nor worthwhile; but with Aristotle and Kant, and again with Plato, Descartes, Leibniz, Hume, and others, it is both feasible and rewarding. But such an introjection is not easy, because for one reason or another, idioms of speech and thought change radically from time to time and from person to person; and in this enterprise of introjection transference from one idiom to another is invariably involved, a fact that should not be bemoaned but should rather be hailed with thanksgiving, since it is primarily this fact which keeps philosophy alive.

This reflection leads me to one of my favourite fantasies. Those who wish to decry philosophy often point to the alleged fact that though the great problems of philosophy have been occupying our minds for $2\frac{1}{2}$ millennia or more, not one of them has ever been solved. As soon as someone claims to have solved one, it is immediately unsolved by someone else. My fantasy is that the charge against us is utterly wide of the mark; in fact many philosophical problems have been (more or less) solved many times; that it appears otherwise is attributable to the great difficulty involved in moving from one idiom to another, which obscures the identities of problems. The solutions are inscribed in the records of our subject; but what needs to be done, and what is so difficult, is to read the records aright. Now this fantasy may lack foundation in fact; but to believe it and to be wrong may well lead to good philosophy, and, seemingly, can do no harm; whereas to reject it and to be wrong in rejecting it might involve one in philosophical disaster.

(IV) As I thread my way unsteadily along the tortuous mountain path which is supposed to lead, in the long distance, to the City of Eternal Truth, I find myself beset by a multitude of demons and perilous places, bearing names like Extensionalism, Nominalism, Positivism, Naturalism, Mechanism, Phenomenalism, Reductionism, Physicalism, Materialism, Empiricism, Scepticism, and Functionalism; menaces which are, indeed, almost as numerous as those encountered by a traveller called Christian on another well-publicized journey. The items named in this catalogue are obviously, in many cases, not to be identified with one another; and it is perfectly possible to maintain a friendly attitude towards some of them while viewing others with hostility. There are many persons, for example, who view naturalism with favour while firmly rejecting nominalism; and it is not easy to see how any one could couple support for phenomenalism with support for physicalism. After a more tolerant (permissive) middle age, I have come to entertain strong opposition to all of them, perhaps partly as a result of the strong connection between a number of them and the philosophical technologies which used to appeal to me a good deal more than they do now. But how would I *justify* the hardening of my heart?

The first question is, perhaps, what gives the list of items a unity, so that I can think of myself as entertaining *one* twelvefold antipathy, rather than twelve discrete antipathies. To this question my answer is that all the items are forms of what I shall call Minimalism, a propensity which seeks to keep to a minimum (which may in some cases be zero) the scope allocated to some advertized philosophical commodity, such as abstract entities, knowledge, absolute value, and so forth. In weighing the case for and the case against a trend of so high a degree of generality as Minimalism, kinds of consideration may legitimately enter which would be out of place were the issue more specific in character; in particular, appeal may be made to aesthetic considerations. In favour of Minimalism, for example, we might hear an appeal, echoing Quine, to the beauty of 'desert landscapes'. But such an appeal I would regard as inappropriate; we are not being asked by a Minimalist to give our vote to a special, and no doubt very fine, type of landscape; we are being asked to express our preference for an ordinary sort of landscape at a recognizably lean time; to rosebushes and cherry-trees in mid-winter, rather than in spring or summer. To change the image somewhat, what bothers me about what I am being offered is not that it is bare, but that it has been systematically and relentlessly *undressed*.

I am also adversely influenced by a different kind of unattractive feature which some, or perhaps even all of these *bêtes noires* seem to possess. Many of them are guilty of restrictive practices which, perhaps, ought to invite the attention of a Philosophical Trade Commission; they limit in advance the range and resources of philosophical explanation. They limit its range by limiting the kinds of phenomena whose presence calls for explanation; some *prima facie* candidates are watered down, others are washed away; and they limit its resources by forbidding the use of initially tempting apparatus, such as the concepts expressed by psychological, or more generally intensional, verbs. My own instincts operate in a reverse direction from this. I am inclined to look first at how useful such and such explanatory ideas might prove to be if admitted, and to waive or postpone enquiry into their certificates of legitimacy.

I am conscious that all I have so far said against Minimalsim has been very general in character, and also perhaps a little tinged with rhetoric. This is not surprising in view of the generality of the topic; but all the same I should like to try to make some provision for those in search of harder tack. I can hardly, in the present context, attempt to provide fully elaborated arguments against all, or even against any one, of the diverse items which fall under my label 'Minimalism'; the best I can do is to try to give a preliminary sketch of what I would regard as the case against just one of the possible forms of minimalism, choosing one which I should regard it as particularly important to be in a position to reject. My selection is Extensionalism, a position imbued with the spirit of Nominalism, and dear both to those who feel that 'Because it is red' is no more informative as an answer to the question 'Why is an English mail-box called "red"?' than would be 'Because he is Paul Grice' as an answer to the question 'Why is that distinguished-looking person called "Paul Grice"?', *and* also to those who are particularly impressed by the power of Set-theory. The picture which, I suspect, is liable to go along with Extensionalism is that of the world of particulars as a domain stocked with innumerable tiny pellets, internally indistinguishable from one another, but distinguished by the groups within which they fall, by the 'clubs' to which they belong; and since the clubs are distinguished only by their memberships, there can only be one club to which nothing belongs. As one might have predicted from the outset, this leads to trouble when it comes to the accommodation of *explanation* within such a system. Explanation of the actual presence of a particular feature in a particular subject depends crucially on the possibility of saying what *would* be the consequence of the presence of such and such features in that subject, regardless of whether the features in question even do appear in that subject, or indeed in *any* subject. On the face of it, if one adopts an extensionalist viewpoint, the presence of a feature in some particular will have to be re-expressed in terms of that particular's membership of a certain set; but if we proceed along those lines, since there is only one empty set, the potential consequences of the possession of in fact unexemplified features would be invariably the same, no matter how different in meaning the expressions used to specify such features would ordinarily be judged to be. This is certainly not a conclusion which one would care to accept.

I can think of two ways of trying to avoid its acceptance, both of which seem to me to suffer from serious drawbacks. The first shows some degree of analogy with a move which, as a matter of history, was made by empiricists in connection with simple and complex ideas. In that region an idea could be redeemed from a charge of failure to conform to empiricist principles through not being derived from experience of its instantiating particulars (there being no such particulars) if it could be exhibited as a complex idea whose component simple ideas were so derived; somewhat similarly, the first proposal seeks to relieve certain vacuous predicates or general terms from the embarrassing consequences of denoting the empty set by exploiting the non-vacuousness of other predicates or general terms which are constituents in a *definition* of the original vacuous terms. (α) Start with two vacuous predicates, say (α_1) 'is married to a daughter of an English queen and a pope' and (α_2) 'is a climber on hands and knees of a

29,000 foot mountain'. (β) If α_1 and α_2 are vacuous, then the following predicates are satisfied by the empty set ϕ: (β_1) 'is a set composed of daughters of an English queen and a pope', and (β_2) 'is a set composed of climbers on hands and knees of a 29,000 foot mountain'. (γ) Provided 'R_1' and 'R_2' are suitably interpreted, the predicates β_1 and β_2 may be treated as coextensive respectively with the following revised predicates (γ_1) 'Stands in R_1' to a sequence composed of the sets *married to, daughters, English queens* and *popes*; and (γ_2) 'stands in R_2 to a sequence composed of the sets *climbers, 29,000 foot mountains*, and *things done on hands and knees*'. (δ) We may finally correlate with the two initial predicates α_1 and α_2, respectively, the following sequences derived from γ_1 and γ_2: (δ_1) the sequence composed of the relation R_1 (taken in extension), the set *married to*, the set *daughters*, the set *English queens*, and the set *popes*; and (δ_2) the sequence composed of the relation R_2, the set *climbers*, the set *29,000 foot mountains*, and the set *things done on hands and knees*. These sequences are certainly distinct, and the proposal is that they, rather than the empty set, should be used for determining, in some way yet to be specified, the explanatory potentialities of the vacuous predicates α_1 and α_2.

My chief complaint against this proposal is that it involves yet another commission of what I regard as one of the main minimalist sins, that of imposing in advance a limitation on the character of explanations. For it implicitly recognizes it as a condition on the propriety of using vacuous predicates in explanation that the terms in question should be representable as being correlated with a sequence of non-empty sets. This is a condition which, I suspect, might not be met by every vacuous predicate. But the possibility of representing an explanatory term as being, in this way or that, reducible to some favoured item or types of items should be a bonus which some theories achieve, thereby demonstrating their elegance, not a condition of eligibility for a particular class of would-be explanatory terms.

The second suggested way of avoiding the unwanted consequence is perhaps more intuitive than the first; it certainly seems simpler. The admissibility of vacuous predicates in explanations of possible but non-actual phenomena (why they would happen if they did happen), depends, it is suggested, on the availability of acceptable non-trivial generalizations wherein which the predicate in question specifies the antecedent condition. And, we may add, a generalization whose acceptability would be unaffected by any variation on the specification of its antecedent condition, provided the substitute were vacuous, would certainly be trivial. Non-trivial generalizations of this sort are certainly available, if (1) they are derivable as special cases from other generalizations involving less specific antecedent conditions, and (2) these other generalizations are adequately supported by further specifics whose antecedent conditions are expressed by means of non-vacuous predicates. The explanatory opportunities for vacuous predicates depend on their embodiment in a *system*.

My doubts about this second suggestion relate to the steps which would be needed in order to secure an adequately powerful system. I conjecture, but cannot demonstrate, that the only way to secure such a system would be to confer special ontological privilege upon the entities of physical science together with the system which that science provides. But now a problem arises: the preferred entities seem not to be observable, or in so far as they are observable, their observability seems to be more a matter of conventional decision to *count* such and-such occurrences as observations than it is a matter of *fact*. It looks as if states of affairs in the preferred scientific world need, for credibility, support from the vulgar world of ordinary observation reported in the language of common sense. But to give that support, the judgements and the linguistic usage of the vulgar needs to be endowed with a certain authority, which as a matter of history the kind of minimalists whom I know or know of have not seemed anxious to confer. But even if they were anxious to confer it, what would validate the conferring, since *ex hypothesi* it is not the vulgar world but the specialist scientific world which enjoys ontological privilege? (If this objection is sound, the second suggestion, like the first, takes something which when present is an asset, bonus, or embellishment, namely systematicity, and under philosophical pressure converts it into a necessity.)

I have, of course, not been attempting to formulate an argument by which minimalism, or indeed any particular version of minimalism, could be refuted; I have been trying only to suggest a sketch of a way in which, perhaps, such an argument might be developed. I should be less than honest if I pretended to any great confidence that even this relatively unambitious objective has been attained. I should, however, also be less than honest if I concealed the fact that, should I be left without an argument, it is very likely that I should not be very greatly disturbed. For my antipathy to minimalism depends much more on a concern to have a philosophical approach which would have prospects of doing justice to the exuberant wealth and variety of human experience in a manner seemingly beyond the reach of minimalists, than on the availability of any argument which would show the theses of minimalists to be mistaken.

(VI) But at this point some people, I think, would wish to protest that I am treating minimalism in much too monolithic a way. For, it might be said, while many reasonable persons might be willing to align themselves with me, for whatever reasons, in opposition to extensionalism and physicalism, when such persons noticed that I have also declared my opposition to mechanism and to naturalism, they might be prompted to enquire whether I wished to declare support for the ideas of the objectivity of value and of the presence of finality in nature, and to add that should I reply affirmatively, they would part company with me. Now I certainly do wish to affirm, under some interpretation, 'the objectivity of value'; and I also wish to maintain, again under some interpretation, 'the presence of finality in nature'. But perhaps I had better formulate in a somewhat more orderly way, one or two of the things which I do believe or at least would *like* to believe.

(1) I believe (or would like to believe) that it is a necessary feature of rational beings, either as part of or as a consequence of part of, their essential nature, that they have a capacity for the attribution of value. I also believe that it follows from this fact, together perhaps with one or more additional assumptions, that there is objective value.

(2) I believe that value, besides being objective, has at the same time intrinsic motivational force, and that this combination is rendered possible only by a constructivist approach rather than a realist approach to value. Only if value is in a suitable sense 'instituted by us' can it exhibit the aforesaid combination.

(3) The objectivity of value is possible only given the presence of finality or purpose in nature (the admissibility of final causes).

(4) The fact that reason is operative both in the cognitive and in the practical spheres strongly suggests, if it does not prove, that a constructivist approach is in order in at least some part of the cognitive sphere as well as in the practical sphere.

(5) The adoption of a constructivist approach makes possible, perhaps even demands, the adoption of a stronger rather than merely a weaker version of rationalism. That is to say, we can regard ourselves, *qua* rational beings, as called upon not merely to have reasons for our beliefs (*rationes cognoscendi*) and also for other attitudes like desires and intentions, but to allow and to search for, reasons for things to be

the case (at least in that area of reality which is constructed). Such reasons will be *rationes essendi*.

It is obvious that much of the terminology in which this programme is formulated is extremely obscure. Any elucidation of it, and any defence of the claims involved which I shall offer on this occasion, will have to wait until the second main section of this *Reply*; for I shall need to invoke specific theses within particular departments of philosophy. I hope to engage, on other occasions, in a fuller examination of these and kindred ideas.

B. COMMENTARY ON RICHARDS

Richards devote most of their ingenious and perceptive attention to three or four topics which they feel to be specially prominent in my work; to questions about meaning, to questions in and about philosophical psychology, rationality, and metaphysics, and finally to questions about value, including ethical questions. I shall first comment on what they have to say about meaning, and then in my concluding section I turn to the remaining topics.

B1. *Meaning*

In the course of a penetrating treatment of the development of my views on this topic, they list, in connection with what they see as the third stage of this development three problems or objections to which my work might be thought to give rise. I shall say something about each of these, though in an altered order; I shall also add a fourth problem which I know some people have regarded as acute, and I shall briefly re-emphasize some of the points about the most recent developments in my thinking, which Richards have presented and which may not be generally familiar.

As a preliminary to enumerating the question for discussion, I may remark that the treatment of the topic by Richards seems to offer strong support to my thesis about the unity (latitudinal unity) of philosophy; for the problems which emerge about meaning are plainly problems in psychology and metaphysics, and I hope that as we proceed it will become increasingly clear that these problems in turn are inextricably bound up with the notion of value.

(1) The first difficulty relates to the allegedly dubious admissibility of *propositions* as entities: 'In the explication of utterance-type meaning, what does the variable "p" take as values? The values of "p" are the

objects of meaning, intention, and belief—propositions, to call them
by their traditional name. But isn't one of the most central tasks of
a theory of meaning to give an account of what propositions are? . . .
Much of the recent history of philosophy of language consists of attacks
on or defences of various conceptions of what a proposition is, for the
fundamental issue involved here is the relation of thought and language
to reality . . . How can Grice offer an explication of utterance-type
meaning that simply takes the notion of a proposition more or less for
granted?'

A perfectly sound, though perhaps somewhat superficial, reply to
the objection as it is presented would be that in any definition of meaning which I would be willing to countenance, the letters '*p*', '*q*', etc.
operate simply as 'gap signs'; if they appear in a definiendum they will
reappear in the corresponding definiens. If someone were to advance
the not wholly plausible thesis that to feel F is just to have a Rylean
agitation which is caused by the thought that one is or might be F, it
would surely be ridiculous to criticize him on the grounds that he had
saddled himself with an ontological commitment to *feelings*, or to
modes of feeling. If quantifiers are covertly involved at all, they will
only be universal quantifiers which could in such a case as this be
adequately handled by a substitutional account of quantification. My
situation *vis-à-vis* propositions is in no way different.

Moreover, if this last part of the cited objection is to be understood
as suggesting that philosophers have been most concerned with the
characterization of the nature of propositions with a view to using
them, in this or that way, as a key to the relationships between language,
thought, and reality, I rather doubt whether this claim is true; and if it
is true, I would regard any attempt to use propositions in such a
manner as a mistake to which I have never subscribed. Propositions
should not, I think, be viewed as tools, gimmicks, or bits of apparatus
designed to pull off the metaphysical conjuring-trick of relating language,
thought, and reality. The furthest I would be prepared to go in this
direction would be to allow it as a possibility that one or more substantive treatments of the relations between language, thought, and reality
might involve this notion of a proposition, and so might rely on it to
the extent that an inability to provide an adequate theoretical treatment of propositions would undermine the enterprise within which
they made an appearance.

It is, however, not apparent to me that any threat of this kind of
disaster hangs over my head. In my most recently published work on

meaning (*Meaning Revisited*, 1981), I do in fact discuss the topic of the correspondences to be looked for between language, thought, and reality, and offer three suggestions about the ways in which, in effect, rational enterprises could be defeated or radically hampered should there fail to be correspondences between the members of any pair selected from this trio. I suggest that without correspondences between thought and reality, individual members of such fundamental important kinds of psychological states as desires and beliefs would be unable to fulfil their *theoretical* role, purpose, or function of explaining behaviour, and indeed would no longer be identifiable or distinguishable from one another; that, without correspondences between language and thought, communication, and so the rational conduct of life,would be eliminated; and that without direct correspondence between language and reality over and above any indirect correspondence provided for by the first two suggestions, no *generalized* specification, as distinct from case-by-case specification, of the conditions required for beliefs to correspond with reality, that is to be *true*, would be available to us. So far as I can see, the foregoing justification of this acceptance of the correspondences in question does not in any obvious way involve a commitment to the reality of propositions; and should it turn out to do so in some *unobvious* way—perhaps as a consequence of some unnoticed assumption—then the very surreptitiousness of the commitment would indicate to me the likelihood that the same commitment would be involved in *any* rational account of the relevant subject matter, in which case, of course, the commitment would be *ipso facto* justified.

Indeed, the idea of an inescapable commitment to propositions in no way frightens me or repels me; and if such a commitment would carry with it an obligation to give an account of what propositions are, I think this obligation could be discharged. It might, indeed, be possible to discharge it in more than one way. One way would involve, as its central idea, focusing on a primitive range of 'simple' statements, the formulation of which would involve no connectives or quantifiers, and treating each of these as 'expressing' a propositional complex, which in such cases would consist of a sequence whose elements would be *first* a general item (a set, or an attribute, according to preference) and *second* a sequence of objects which might, or might not, instantiate or belong to the first item. Thus the propositional complex associated with the sentence, 'John is wise', might be thought of consisting of a sequence whose *first* ('general') member would be the set of wise persons, or (alternatively) the attribute wisdom, and whose *second* ('instantial' or 'particular') member would be John or the singleton of John; and the sentence, 'Martha detests Mary', could be represented as expressing a propositional complex which is a sequence whose first element is *detestation* (considered either extensionally as a set or non-extensionally as an attribute) and whose second element is a sequence composed of Martha and Mary, in that order. We can define a property of *factivity* which will be closely allied to the notion of truth: a (simple) propositional complex will be factive just in case its two elements (the general and instantial elements) are related by the appopriate predication relation, just in case (for example) the second element is a member of the set (possesses the attribute) in which the first element consists. Propositions may now be represented as each consisting of a family of propositional complexes, and the conditions for family unity may be thought of either as fixed or as variable in accordance with the context. This idea will in a moment be expanded.

The notorious difficulties to which this kind of treatment gives rise will begin with the problems of handling connectives and of handling quantification. In the present truncated context I shall leave the first problem on one side, and shall confine myself to a few sketchy remarks concerning quantification. A simple proposal for the treatment of quantifiers would call for the assignment to each predicate, besides its normal or standard extension, two *special* objects associated with quantifiers, an 'altogether' object and a 'one-at-a-time' object; to the epithets 'grasshopper', ['boy', 'girl'], for example, will be assigned not only ordinary individual objects like grasshoppers [boys, girls] but also such *special* objects as *the altogether grasshopper* [boy, girl] and *the one-at-a-time grasshopper* [boy, girl]. We shall now stipulate that an 'altogether' special object satisfies a given predicate just in case *every* normal or standard object associated with that special object satisfies the predicate in question, and that a 'one-at-a-time' special object satisfies a predicate just in case *at least one* of the associated standard objects satisfies that predicate. So the altogether grasshopper will be green just in case *every* individual grasshopper is green, and the one-at-a-time grasshopper will be green just in case *at least one* individual grasshopper is green, and we can take this pair of statements about *special* grasshoppers as providing us with representations of (respectively) the statement that all grasshoppers are green and the statement that some grasshopper is green.

The apparatus which I have just sketched is plainly not, as it stands, adequate to provide a comprehensive treatment of quantification. It will not, for example, cope with well-known problems arising from features of multiple quantification; it will not deliver for us distinct representations of the two notorious (alleged) readings of the statement 'Every girl detests some boy', in one of which (supposedly) the universal quantifier is dominant with respect to scope, and in the other of which the existential quantifier is dominant. To cope with this problem it might be sufficient to explore, for semantic purposes, the device of exportation, and to distinguish between, (i) 'There is some boy such that every girl detests him', which attributes a certain property to the one-at-a-time boy, and (ii) 'Every girl is such that she detests some boy', which attributes a certain (and different) property to the altogether girl; and to note, as one makes this move, that though exportation, when applied to statements about individual objects, seems not to affect truth-value, whatever else may be its semantic function, when it is applied to sentences about special objects it may, and sometimes will, affect truth-value. But however effective this particular shift may be, it is by no means clear that there are not further demands to be met which would overtax the strength of the envisaged apparatus; it is not, for example, clear whether it could be made adequate to deal with indefinitely long strings of 'mixed' quantifiers. The proposal might also run into objections of a more philosophical character from those who would regard the special objects which it invokes as metaphysically disreputable.

Should an alternative proposal be reached or desired, I think that one (or, indeed, more than one) is available. The one which I have immediately in mind could be regarded as a replacement for, an extension of, or a reinterpretation of the scheme just outlined, in accordance with whatever view is finally taken of the potency and respectability of the ideas embodied in that scheme. The new proposal, like its predecessor, will treat propositional complexes as sequences, indeed as ordered pairs containing a subject-item and a predicate-item, and will, therefore, also like its predecessor, offer a subject-predicate account of quantification. Unlike its predecessor, however, it will not allow individual objects, like grasshoppers, girls, and boys, to appear as elements in propositional complexes; such elements will always be sets or attributes. Though less restrictive versions of this proposal are, I think, available, I shall, for convenience, consider here only a set-theoretic version.

According to this version, we associate with the subject-expression of a canonically formulated sentence a set of at least second order. If the

subject expression is a singular name, its ontological correlate will be
the singleton of the singleton of the entity which bears that name. The
treatment of singular terms which are not names will be parallel, but is
here omitted. If the subject-expression is an *indefinite* quantificational
phrase, like 'some grasshopper', its ontological correlate will be the set
of all singletons whose sole element is an item belonging to the extension of the predicate to which the indefinite modifier is attached; so
the ontological correlate of the phrase 'some grasshopper' will be the
set of all singletons whose sole element is an individual grasshopper. If
the subject expression is a *universal* quantificational phrase, like 'every
grasshopper', its ontological correlate will be the singleton whose sole
element is the set which forms the extension of the predicate to which
the universal modifier is attached; thus the correlate of the phrase
'every grasshopper' will be the singleton of the set of grasshoppers.
Predicates of canonically formulated sentences are correlated with
the sets which form their extensions. It now remains to specify the
predication-relation, that is to say, to specify the relation which has to
obtain between subject-element and predicate-element in a propositional
complex for that complex to be *factive*. A propositional complex will
be factive just in case its subject-element contains as a member at least
one item which is a subset of the predicate-element; so if the ontological
correlate of the phrase 'some grasshopper' (or, again, of the phrase
'every grasshopper') contains as a member at least one subset of the
ontological correlate of the predicate 'x is green' (viz. the set of green
things), then the propositional complex directly associated with the
sentence 'some grasshopper is green' (or again with the sentence 'every
grasshopper is green') will be factive.

   A dozen years or so ago, I devoted a good deal of time to this second
proposal, and I convinced myself that it offered a powerful instrument
which, with or without adjustment, was capable of handling not only
indefinitely long sequences of 'mixed' quantificational phrases, but also
some other less obviously tractable problems which I shall not here
discuss. Before moving on, however, I might perhaps draw attention to
three features of the proposal. *First*, employing a strategy which
might be thought of as Leibnizian, it treats subject-elements as being of
an order higher than, rather than an order lower than, predicate
elements. *Second*, individual names are in effect treated like universal
quantificational phrases, thus recalling the practice of old-style traditional logic. *Third*, and most importantly, the account which is offered
is, initially, an account of *propositional complexes*, not of *propositions*;

as I envisage them, propositions will be regarded as *families* of propositional complexes. Now the propositional complex directly associated with the sentence 'Some grasshoppers are witty', will be both logically equivalent to and numerically distinct from the propositional complex directly associated with the sentence 'Not every grasshopper is not witty'; indeed for any given propositional complex there will be indefinitely many propositional complexes which are both logically equivalent to and also numerically distinct from the original complex. The question of how tight or how relaxed are to be the family ties which determine propositional identity remains to be decided, and it might even be decided that the conditions for such identity would vary according to context or purpose.

It seems that there might be an approach to the treatment of propositions which would, initially at least, be radically different from the two proposals which I have just sketched. We might begin by recalling that one of the stock arguments for the reality of propositions used to be that propositions are needed to give us something for logic to be about; sentences and thoughts were regarded as insufficient, since the laws of logic do not depend on the existence of minds or of language. Now one might be rendered specially well-disposed towards propositions if one espoused, in general, a sort of Aristotelian view of theories, and believed that for any particular theory to exist there has to be a class of entities, central to that theory, the essential nature of which is revealed in, and indeed accounts for, the laws of the theory in question. If our thought proceeds along these lines, propositions might be needed not just as pegs (so to speak) for logical laws to hang from, but as things whose nature determines the content of the logical system. It might even be possible (as George Myro has suggested to me) to maintain that more than one system proceeds from and partially exhibits the nature of propositions; perhaps, for example, one system is needed to display propositions as the bearers of logical properties and another to display them in their role as contents, or objects of propositional attitudes. How such an idea could be worked out in detail is far from clear; but whatever might be the difficulties of implementation, it is evident that this kind of approach would seek to answer the question, 'What are propositions?', not by identificatory dissection but rather by pointing to the *work* that propositions of their very nature *do*.

I have little doubt that a proper assessment of the merits of the various proposals now before us would require decisions on some fundamental issues in metaphysical methodology. What, for example, determines whether a class of entities achieves metaphysical respectability? What conditions govern the admission to reality of the products of ontological romancing? What is the relation, in metaphysical practice, between two possible forms of identification and characterization, that which proceeds by dissection and that which proceeds by specification of output? Are these forms of procedure, in a given case, rivals or are they compatible and even, perhaps, both mandatory?

Two further objections cited by Richards may be presented together (in reverse order), since they both relate to my treatment of the idea of linguistic 'procedures'. One of these objections disputes my right, as a philosopher, to trespass on the province of linguists by attempting to deliver judgement, either in specific cases or even generally, on the existence of basic procedures underlying other semantic procedures which are, supposedly, derivative from them. The other objection starts from the observation that my account of linguistic communication involves the attribution to communicators of more or less elaborate inferential steps concerning the procedures possessed and utilized by their conversational partners, notes that these steps and the knowledge which, allegedly, they provide are certainly not as a rule explicitly present to consciousness, and then questions whether any satisfactory interpretation can be given of the idea that the knowledge involved is implicit rather than explicit. Richards suggest that answers to these objections can be found in my published and unpublished work.

Baldly stated, the reply which they attribute to me with respect to the first of these objections is that the idea that a certain sort of reasoning, which Richards illustrate by drawing on as yet unpublished work, 'is involved in meaning, is something which can be made plausible by philosophical methods—by careful description, reflection, and delineation of the ways we talk and think' (p. 13 of this book). Now I certainly hope that philosophical methods can be effective in the suggested direction, which case, of course, the objections would be at least partially answered. But I think that I would also aim at a sharper and more ambitious response along the following lines. Certainly the specification of some particular set of procedures as the set which governs the use of some particular langauge, or even as a set which participates in the governance of some group of languages, is a matter for linguists except in so far as it may rely upon some ulterior and highly general principles. But there may be general principles of this sort, principles perhaps which specify forms of procedure which do, and indeed must, operate in the use of any language whatsoever. Now one might argue for the existence of such a body of principles on the basis of the relatively unexciting, and not unfamiliar, idea that, so far as can be seen, our infinite variety of actual and possible linguistic performances is feasible only if such performances can be organized in a certain way, namely as issuing from some initial finite base of primitive procedures in accordance with the general principles in question. One might, however, set one's sights higher, and try to maintain that the presence in a language, or at least in a language which is actually used, of a certain kind of structure, which will be reflected in these general principles, is guaranteed by metaphysical considerations, perhaps by some rational demand for a correspondence between linguistic categories on the one hand and metaphysical, or real categories on the other. I will confess to an inclination to go for the more ambitious of these enterprises.

As regards the second objection, I must admit to being by no means entirely clear what reply Richards envisage me as wishing to make, but I will formulate what seems to me to be the most likely representation of their view. They first very properly refer to my discussion of 'incomplete' reasoning in my *John Locke Lectures*, and discover there some suggestions which, whether or not they supply *necessary* conditions for the presence of formally incomplete or implicit reasoning, cannot plausibly be considered as jointly providing a *sufficient* condition; the suggested conditions are that the implicit reasoner intends that there should be some valid supplementation of the explicitly present material which would justify the 'conclusion' of the incomplete reasoning, together perhaps with a further desire or intention that the first intention should be causally efficacious in the generation of the reasoner's belief in the aforementioned conclusion. Richards are plainly right in their view that so far no sufficient condition for implicit reasoning has been provided; indeed, I never supposed that I had succeeded in providing one, though I hope to be able to remedy this deficiency by the (one hopes) not too distant time when a revised version of my *John Locke Lectures* is published. Richards then bring to bear some further material from my writings, and sketch, on my behalf, an argument which seems to exhibit the following pattern: (1) That we should be equipped to form, and to recognize in others, M-intentions is something which could be given a genitorial justification; if the Genitor were constructing human beings with an eye to their own good, the institution in us of a capacity to deploy

M-intentions would be regarded by him with favour. (2) We do in fact possess the capacity to form, and to recognize in others, M-intentions. (3) The attribution of M-intentions to others will at least sometimes have explanatory value with regard to their behaviour, and so could properly be thought of as helping to fulfil a rational desideratum. (4) The exercise of rationality takes place primarily or predominantly in the confirmation or revision of previously established beliefs or practices; so it is reasonable to expect the comparison of the actual with what is ideal or optimal to be standard procedure in rational beings. (5) We have, in our repertoire of procedures available to us in the conduct of our lives, the procedure of *counting* something which approximates sufficiently closely to the fulfillment of a certain ideal or optimum as *actually* fulfilling that ideal or optimum, the procedure (that is to say) of *deeming* it to fulfil the ideal or optimum in question. So (6) it is reasonable to attribute to human beings a readiness to *deem* people, who approximate sufficiently closely in their behaviour to persons who have ratiocinated about the M-intentions of others, to have *actually* ratiocinated in that way. We do indeed deem such people to have so ratiocinated, though we do also, when called upon, mark the difference between their *deemed* ratiocinations and the 'primitive' step-by-step variety of ratiocination, which provides us with our ideal in this region, by characterizing the reasoning of the 'approximators' as *implicit* rather than *explicit*.

Now whether or not it was something of this sort which Richards had it in mind to attribute to me, the argument as I have sketched it seems to me to be worthy of serious consideration; it brings into play, in a relevant way, some pet ideas of mine, and exerts upon me at least, some degree of seductive appeal. But whether I would be willing to pass beyond sympathy to endorsement, I am not sure. There are too many issues involved which are both crucially important and hideously under-explored, such as the philosophical utility of the concept of *deeming*, the relations between rational and pre-rational psychological states, and the general nature of implicit thought. Perhaps the best thing for me to do at this point will be to set out a line of argument which I would be inclined to endorse and leave it to the reader to judge how closely what I say when speaking for myself approximates to the suggested interpretation which I offer when speaking on behalf of Richards. I would be prepared to argue that something like the following sequence of propositions is true.

(1) There is a range of cases in which, so far from its being the case

that, typically, one first learns what it is to be a ϕ and then, at the next stage, learns what criteria distinguish a *good* ϕ from a ϕ which is less good, or not good at all, one needs first to learn what it is to be a good ϕ, and then subsequently to learn what degree of approximation to being a good ϕ will qualify an item as a ϕ; if the gap between some item x and good ϕs is suffciently horrendous, then x is debarred from counting as a ϕ at all, even as a *bad* ϕ. I have elsewhere called concepts which exhibit this feature *value-oriented concepts*. One example of a value-oriented concept is the concept of *reasoning*; another, I now suggest, is that of *sentence*.

(2) It may well be that the existence of value-oriented concepts ($\phi_1, \phi_2 \ldots \phi_n$) depends on the prior existence of pre-rational concepts ($\phi_1', \phi_2' \ldots \phi_n'$), such that an item x qualifies for the application of the concept ϕ_2 if and only if x satisfies a *rationally-approved* form or version of the corresponding pre-rational concept ϕ'. We have a (primary) example of a step in reasoning only if we have a transition of a certain rationally approved kind from one thought or utterance to another.

(3) If ϕ is value-oriented concept then a potentiality for making or producing ϕs is *ipso facto* a potentiality for making or producing *good* ϕs, and is therefore dignified with the title of a *capacity*; it may of course be a capacity which only persons with special ends or objectives, like pick-pockets, would be concerned to possess.

(4) I am strongly inclined to assent to a principle which might be called a Principle of Economy of Rational Effort. Such a principle would state that where there is a ratiocinative procedure for arriving rationally at certain outcomes, a procedure which, because it is ratiocinative, will involve an expenditure of time and energy, then if there is a non-ratiocinative, and so more economical procedure which is likely, for the most part, to reach the same outcomes as the ratiocinative procedure, then provided the stakes are not too high it will be rational to employ the cheaper though somewhat less reliable non-ratiocinative procedure as a substitute for ratiocination. I think this principle would meet with Genitorial approval, in which case the Genitor would install it for use should opportunity arise.

(5) On the assumption that it is characteristic of reason to operate on pre-rational states which reason confirms, revises, or even (sometimes) eradicates, such opportunities will arise, provided the rational creatures can, as we can, be trained to modify the relevant pre-rational states or their exercise, so that without actual ratiocination the creatures

can be more or less reliably led by those pre-rational states to the thoughts or actions which reason would endorse were it invoked; with the result that the creatures can do, for the most part, what reason requires without, in the particular case, the voice of reason being heard. Indeed in such creatures as ourselves the ability to dispense in this way with actual ratiocination is taken to be an *excellence*: The more mathematical things I can do correctly without engaging in overt mathematical reasoning, the more highly I shall be regarded as a mathematician. Similar considerations apply to the ability to produce syntactico-semantically satisfactory utterances without the aid of a derivation in some syntactico-semantic theory. In both cases the excellence which I exhibit is a form of *judgement*; I am a good judge of mathematical consequences or of satisfactory utterances.

(6) That ability to produce, without the aid of overt ratiocination, transitions which accord with approved standards of inference does not demand that such ratiocination be present in an unconscious or covert form; it requires at most that our propensity to produce such transitions be dependent in some way upon our acquisition or possession of a capacity to reason explicitly. Similarly, our ability to produce satisfactory utterances does not require a subterranean ratiocination to acccount for their satisfactory character; it needs only to be dependent on our learning of, or use of, a rule-governed language. There are two kinds of magic travel. In one of these we are provided with a magic carpet which transports us with supernatural celerity over a route which may be traversed in more orthodox vehicles; in the other, we are given a magic lamp from which, when we desire it, a genie emerges who transports us routelessly from where we are to where we want to go. The exercise of judgement may perhaps be route-travelling like the first; but may also be routeless like the second.

(7) But problems still remain. Deductive systems concocted by professional logicians vary a good deal as regards their intuitiveness; but with respect to some of them (for example, some suitably chosen system of natural deduction) a pretty good case could be made that they not only generate for us logically valid inferences, but do so in a way which mirrors the procedures which we use in argument in the simplest or most fundamental cases. But in the case of linguistic theories even the more intuitive among them may not be in a position to make a corresponding claim about the production of admissible utterances. They might be able to claim to generate (more or less) the infinite class of admissible sentences, together with acceptable interpretations of

each (though even this much would be a formidable claim); but such an achievement would tell us nothing about how *we* arrive at the production of sentences, and so might be thought to lack explanatory force. That deficiency might be thought to be remediable only if the theory reflects, more or less closely, the way or ways in which we learn, select, and criticize linguistic performances; and here it is clear neither what should be reflected nor what would count as reflecting it.

There is one further objection, not mentioned by Richards, which seems to me to be one to which I must respond. It may be stated thus: One of the leading ideas in my treatment of meaning was that meaning is not to be regarded exclusively, or even primarily, as a feature of language or of linguistic utterances; there are many instances of non-linguistic vehicles of communication, mostly unstructured but sometimes exhibiting at least rudimentary structure; and my account of meaning was designed to allow for the possibility that non-linguistic and indeed non-conventional 'utterances', perhaps even manifesting some degree of structure, might be within the powers of creatures who lack any linguistic or otherwise conventional apparatus for communication, but who are not thereby deprived of the capacity to *mean* this or that by things they do. To provide for this possibility, it is plainly necessary that the key ingredient in any representation of meaning, namely *intending*, should be a state the capacity for which does not require the possession of a language. Now some might be unwilling to allow the possibility of such pre-linguistic intending. Against them, I think I would have good prospects of winning the day; but unfortunately a victory on this front would not be enough. For, in a succession of increasingly elaborate moves designed to thwart a sequence of Schifferian counter-examples, I have been led to restrict the intentions which are to constitute utterer's meaning to *M-intentions*; and, whatever might be the case in general with regard to intending, M-intending is plainly too sophisticated a state to be found in a language-destitute creature. So the unavoidable rearguard actions seem to have undermined the *raison-d'être* of the campaign.

A brief reply will have to suffice; a full treatment would require delving deep into crucial problems concerning the boundaries between vicious and innocuous circularity, to which I shall refer again a little later. According to my most recent speculations about meaning, one should distinguish between what I might call the *factual* character of an utterance (meaning-relevant features which are actually present in the utterance), and what I might call its *titular* character (the nested

M-intention which is *deemed* to be present). The titular character is infinitely complex, and so *cannot* be actually present *in toto*; in which case to point out that its inconceivable actual presence would be possible, or would be detectable, only *via* the use of language would seem to serve little purpose. At its most meagre, the factual character will consist merely in the pre-rational counterpart of meaning, which might amount to no more than making a certain sort of utterance in order thereby to get some creature to think or want some particular thing, and this condition seems to contain no reference to linguistic expertise. Maybe in some less straightforward instances of meaning there will be actually present intentions whose feasibility as intentions will demand a capacity for the use of language. But there can be no advance guarantee when this will be so, and it is in any case arguable that the use of language would here be a practically indispensable aid to thinking about relatively complex intentions, rather than an element in what is thought about.

B2. *Metaphysics, Philosophical Psychology, and Value*

In this final section of my *Reply to Richards*, I shall take up, or take off from, a few of the things which they have to say about a number of fascinating and extremely important issues belonging to the chain of disciplines listed in the title of this section. I shall be concerned less with the details of their account of the various positions which they see me as maintaining than with the kind of structure and order which, albeit in an as yet confused and incomplete way I think I can discern in the disciplines themselves and, especially, in the connection between them. Any proper discussion of the details of the issues in question would demand far more time than I have at my disposal; in any case it is my intention, if I am spared, to discuss a number of them, at length, in future writings. I shall be concerned rather to provide some sort of picture of the nature of metaphysics, as I see it, and of the way or ways in which it seems to me to underlie the other mentioned disciplines. I might add that something has already been said in the previous section of this *Reply* about philosophical psychology and rationality, and that general questions about value, including metaphysical questions, were the topic of my 1983 Carus lectures. So perhaps I shall be pardoned if here I concentrate primarily on metaphysics. I fear that, even when I am allowed the advantage of operating within these limitations, what I have to say will be programmatic and speculative rather than well-ordered and well-argued.

At the outset of their comments on my views concerning meta-physics, Richards say, 'Grice's ontological views are at least liberal'; and they document this assertion by a quotation from my *Method In Philosophical Psychology*, in which I admit to a 'taste for keeping open house for all sorts and conditions of entities, just so long as when they come in they help with the housework.' I have no wish to challenge their representation of my expressed position, particularly as the cited passage includes a reference to the possibility that certain sorts of entities might, because of backing from some transcendental argument, qualify as *entia realissima*. The question I would like to raise is rather what grounds are there for accepting the current conception of the relationship between metaphysics and ontology. Why should it be assumed that metaphysics consists in, or even includes in its domain, the programme of arriving at an acceptable ontology? Is the answer merely that that enterprise is the one, or a part of the one, to which the term 'metaphysics' is conventionally applied and so that a justification of this application cannot be a philosophical issue?

If this demand for a *justified* characterization of metaphysics is to be met, I can think of only one likely strategy for meeting it. That will be to show that success within a certain sort of philosophical under-taking, which I will with striking originality call First Philosophy, is needed if any form of philosophy, or perhaps indeed any form of rational enquiry, is to be regarded as feasible or legitimate; and that the contents of First Philosophy are identical with, or at least include, what are standardly regarded as the contents of metaphysics.[1] I can think of two routes by which this result might be achieved, which might well turn out not to be distinct from one another. One route would perhaps involve taking seriously the idea that if any region of enquiry is to be successful as a rational enterprise, its deliverance must be expressable in the shape of one or another of the possibly different types of theory; that characterizations of the nature and range of possible kinds of theory will be needed; and that such a body of characterization must itself be the outcome of rational enquiry, and so must itself exemplify whatever requirements it lays down for theories in general; it must itself be expressible as a theory, to be called (if you like) Theory-theory. The specification and justification of the ideas and material presupposed by any theory, whether such account falls within or outside the bounds of Theory-theory, would be properly called First Philosophy, and might

[1] In these reflections I have derived much benefit from discussions with Alan Code.

turn out to relate to what is generally accepted as belonging to the subject matter of metaphysics. It might, for example, turn out to be establishable that every theory has to relate to a certain range of subject items, has to attribute to them certain predicates or attributes, which in turn have to fall within one or another of the range of types or categories. In this way, the enquiry might lead to recognized metaphysical topics, such as the nature of being, its range of application, the nature of predication and a systematic account of categories.

A second approach would focus not on the idea of the expressibility of the outcomes of rational enquiry in theories but rather on the question of what it is, in such enquiries, that we are looking for, why they are of concern to us. We start (so Aristotle has told us) as laymen with the awareness of a body of facts; what as theorists we strive for is not (primarily) further facts, but *rational knowledge*, or *understanding*, of the facts we have, together with whatever further facts our investigations may provide for us. Metaphysics will have as its concern the nature and realizability of those items which are involved in any successful pursuit of understanding; its range would include the nature and varieties of explanation (as offered in some modification of the Doctrine of Four Causes), the acceptability of principles of logic, the proper standards of proof, and so on.

I have at this point three comments to make. *First*, should it be the case that, (1) the foregoing approach to the conception of metaphysics is found acceptable, (2) the nature of explanation and (understood broadly) of causes is a metaphysical topic, and (3) that Aristotle is right (as I suspect he is) that the unity of the notion of *cause* is analogical in character, *then* the *general* idea of cause will rest on its standard particularizations, and the particular ideas cannot be reached as *specifications* of an antecedent genus, for there is no such genus. In that case, *final* causes will be (so to speak) foundation members of the *cause* family, and it will be dubious whether their title as causes can be disputed.

Second, it seems very likely that the two approaches are in fact *not* distinct; for it seems plausible to suppose that explanations, if fully rational, must be systematic and so must be expressible in theories. Conversely, it seems plausible to suppose that the function of theories is to explain, and so that whatever is susceptible to theoretical treatment is thereby *explained*.

Third, the most conspicuous difficulty about the approach which I have been tentatively espousing seems to me to be that we may be in danger of being given more than we want to receive; we are not, for example, ready to regard methods of proof or the acceptability of logical principles as metaphysical matters and it is not clear how such things are to be excluded. But perhaps we are in danger of falling victims to a confusion. Morality, as such, belongs to the province of ethics and does not belong to the province of metaphysics. But, as Kant saw (and I agree with him), that does not preclude there being metaphysical questions which arise about morality. In general, there may be a metaphysics of X without it being the case that X is a concept or item which belongs to metaphysics. Equally, there may be metaphysical questions relating to proof or logical principles without it being the case that as such proof or logical principles *belong* to metaphysics. It will be fair to add, however, that no distinction has yet been provided, within the class of items about which there are metaphysical questions, between those which do and those which do not belong to metaphysics.

The next element in my attitude towards metaphysics to which I would like to draw attention is my strong sympathy for a *constructivist* approach. The appeal of such an approach seems to be to lie essentially in the idea that if we operate with the aim of expanding some set of starting points, by means of regulated and fairly well-defined procedures, into a constructed edifice of considerable complexity, we have better prospects of obtaining the explanatory richness which we need than if, for example, we endeavour to represent the seeming wealth of the world of being as reducible to some favoured range of elements. That is, of course, a rhetorical plea. but perhaps such pleas have their place.

But a constructivist methodology, if its title is taken seriously, plainly has its own difficulties. Construction, as normally understood, requires one or more constructors; so far as a metaphysical construction is concerned, who does the constructing? 'We'? But who are we and do we operate separately or conjointly, or in some other way? And when and where are the acts of construction performed, and how often? These troublesome queries are reminiscent of differences which arose, I believe, among Kantian commentators, about whether Kant's threefold synthesis (perhaps a close relative of construction) is (or was) a datable operation or not. I am not aware that they arrived at a satisfactory solution. The problem becomes even more acute when we remember that some of the best candidates for the title of constructed entities, for example numbers, are supposed to be eternal, or at least timeless. How could such entities have construction dates?

Some relief may perhaps be provided if we turn our eyes towards the authors of fiction. My next novel will have as its hero one Caspar Winebibber, a notorious English highwayman born (or so I shall say) in 1764 and hanged in 1798, thereby ceasing to exist long before sometime next year, when I create (or construct) him. This mind-boggling situation will be dissolved if we distinguish between two different occurrences; *first*, Caspar's birth (or death) which is dated to 1764 (or 1798), and *second*, my creation of Caspar, that is to say my making it in 1985 fictionally true that Caspar was born in 1764 and died in 1798. Applying this strategem to metaphysics, we may perhaps find it tolerable to suppose that a particular great mathematician should in 1968 make it true that (let us say) ultralunary numbers should exist timelessly or from and to eternity. We might even, should we so wish, introduce a 'depersonalized' (and 'detemporalized') notion of construction; in which case we can say that in 1968 the great mathematician, by authenticated construction, not only constructed the timeless existence of ultralunary numbers but also thereby depersonalized and detemporalized construction of the timeless existence of ultralunary numbers, and also the depersonalized construction of the depersonalized construction of . . . ultralunary numbers. In this way, we might be able, in one fell swoop, to safeguard the copyrights both of the mathematician and eternity.

Another extremely important aspect of my conception of metaphysical construction (creative metaphysical thinking) is that it is of its nature revisionary or gradualist in character. It is not just that, since metaphysics is a very difficult subject, the best way to proceed is to observe the success and failures of others and to try to build further advance upon their achievements. It is rather that there is no other way of proceeding but the way of gradualism. A particular bit of metaphysical construction is possible only on the basis of some prior material; which must itself either be the outcome of prior constructions, or perhaps be something original and unconstructed. As I see it, gradualism enters in in more than one place. One point of entry relates to the degree of expertise on the theorist or investigator. In my view, it is incumbent upon those whom Aristotle would have called 'the wise' in metaphysics, as often elsewhere, to treat with respect and build upon the opinions and the practices of 'the many'; and any intellectualist indignation at the idea of professionals being hamstrung by amateurs will perhaps be seen as inappropriate when it is reflected that the amateurs are really (since personal identities may be regarded as irrelevant) only ourselves (the professionals) at an earlier stage; there are not two parties, like Whigs and Tories, or nobles and the common people, but rather one family of speakers pursuing the life of reason at different stages of development; and the later stages of development depend upon the ealier ones.

Gradualism also comes into play with respect to theory development. A characteristic aspect of what I think of as a constructivist approach towards theory development involves the appearance of what I call 'overlaps'. It may be that a theory or theory-stage B, which is to be an extension of theory or theory-stage A, includes as part of itself linguistic or conceptual apparatus which provides us with a restatement of all or part of theory A, as one segment of the arithmetic of positive and negative integers provides us with a restatement of the arithmetic of natural numbers. But while such an overlap may be needed to secure intelligibility for theory B, theory B would be pointless unless its expressive power transcended that of theory A, unless (that is to say) a further segment of theory B lay beyond the overlap. Gradualism sometimes appears on the scene in relation to stages exhibited by some feature attaching to the theory as a whole, but more often perhaps in relation to stages exemplified in some department of, or some category within, the theory. We can think of metaphysics as involving a developing sequence of metaphysical schemes; we can also locate developmental features within and between particular metaphysical categories. Again, I regard such developmental features not as accidental but as essential to the prosecution of metaphysics. One can only reach a proper understanding of metaphysical concepts like *law* or *cause* if one sees, for example, the functional analogy, and so the developmental connection, between *natural* laws and *non-natural* laws (like those of legality or morality). 'How is such and such a range of uses of the word (the concept) x to be rationally generated?' is to my mind a type of question which we should continually be asking.

I may now revert to a question which appeared briefly on the scene a page or so ago. Are we, if we lend a sympathetic ear to constructivism, to think of the metaphysical world as divided into a constructed section and a primitive, original, unconstructed section? I will confess at once that I do not know the answer to this question. The forthright contention that if there is a realm of constructs there has to be also a realm of non-constructs to provide the material upon which the earliest ventures in construction are to operate, has its appeal, and I have little doubt that I have been influenced by it. But I am by no means sure that it is correct. I am led to this uncertainty initially by the fact that when I ask myself what classes of entities I would be happy to regard as original and unconstructed, I do not very readily come up with an answer. Certainly not common objects like tables and chairs; but would I feel better about stuffs like rock or hydrogen, or bits thereof? I do not know, but I am not moved towards any emphatic 'yes!' Part of my trouble is that there does not seem to me to be any good logical reason calling for a class of ultimate non-constructs. It seems to me quite on the cards that metaphysical theory, at least when it is formally set out, might consist in a package of what I will call ontological schemes in which categories of entities are constructively ordered, that all or most of the same categories may appear within two different schemes with different ordering, what is primitive in one scheme being non-primitive in the other, and that this might occur whether the ordering relations employed in the construction of the two schemes were the same or different. We would then have no role for a notion of *absolute* primitiveness. All we would use would be the relative notion of primitiveness-with-respect-to-a-scheme. There might indeed be room for a concept of authentic or maximal reality; but the application of this concept would be divorced from any concept of primitiveness, relative or absolute, and would be governed by the availability of an argument, no doubt transcendental in character, showing that a given category is mandatory, that a place must be found for it in *any* admissible ontological scheme. I know of no grounds for rejecting ideas along these lines.

The complexities introduced by the possibility that there is no original, unconstructed, area of reality, together with a memory of the delicacy of treatment called for by the last of the objections to my view on the philosophy of language, suggest that debates about the foundations of metaphysics are likely to be peppered with allegations of circularity; and I suspect that this would be the view of any thoughtful student of metaphysics who gave serious attention to the methodology of his discipline. Where are the first principles of First Philosophy to come from, if not from the operation, practised by the emblematic pelican, of lacerating its own breast. In the light of these considerations it seems to me to be of the utmost importance to get clear about the nature and forms of real or apparent circularity, and to distinguish those forms, if any, which are innocuous from those which are deadly. To this end I would look for a list, which might not be all that different from the list provided by Aristotle, of different kinds, or interpretations, of the idea of *priority* with a view to deciding when the supposition that A is prior to B allow or disallows the possibility that B may also be prior to A, either in the same, or in some other, dimension of priority. Relevant kinds of priority would perhaps include logical priority, definitional or conceptual priority, epistemic priority, and priority in respect of value. I will select two examples, both possibly of philosophical interest, where for differing m and n, it might be legitimate to suppose that the priority$_m$ of A to B would not be a barrier to the priority$_n$ of B to A. It seems to me not implausible to hold that, in respect of one or another version of *conceptual* priority, the legal concept of *right* is prior to the moral concept of *right*: the moral concept is only understandable by reference to, and perhaps is even explicitly definable in terms of, the legal concept. But if that is so, we are perhaps not debarred from regarding the moral concept as valuationally prior to the legal concept; the range of application of the legal concept *ought to be* always determined by criteria which are couched in terms of the moral concept. Again, it might be important to distinguish two kinds of *conceptual* priority, which might both apply to one and the same pair of items, though in different directions. It might be, perhaps, that the properties of sense-data, like colours (and so sense-data themselves), are posterior in one sense to corresponding properties of material things, (and so to material things themselves); properties of material things, perhaps, render the properties of sense-data intelligible by providing a paradigm for them. But when it comes to the provision of a suitably motivated *theory* of material things and their properties, the idea of making these *definitionally* explicable in terms of sense-data and their properties may not be ruled out by the holding of the aforementioned conceptual priority in the reverse direction. It is perhaps reasonable to regard such fine distinction as indispensable if we are to succeed in the business of pulling ourselves up by our own bootstraps. In this connection it will be relevant for me to reveal that I once invented (though I did not establish its validity) a principle which I labelled as *Bootstrap*. The principle laid down that when one is introducing the primitive concepts of a theory formulated in an object language, one has freedom to use any battery of concepts expressible in the meta-language, subject to the condition that counterparts of such concepts are subsequently definable or otherwise derivable in the object-language. So the more economically one introduces the primitive object-language concepts, the less of a task one leaves oneself for the morrow.

I must now turn to a more direct consideration of the question of how metaphysical principles are ultimately to be established. A prime candidate is forthcoming, namely a special metaphysical type of argument, one that has been called by Kant and by various other philosophers since Kant a *transcendental argument*. Unfortunately it is by no means clear to me precisely what Kant, and still less what some other philosophers, regard as the essential character of such an argument. Some, I suspect, have thought of a transcendental argument in favour of some thesis or category of items as being one which claims that if we reject the thesis or category in question, we shall have to give up something which we very much want to keep; and the practice of some philosophers, including Kant, of hooking transcendental argument to the possibility of some very central notion, such as experience or knowledge, or (the existence of) *language*, perhaps lends some colour to this approach. My view (and my view of Kant) takes a different tack. One thing which seems to be left out in the treatments of transcendental argument just mentioned is the idea that Transcendental Argument involves the suggestion that something is being *undermined* by one who is sceptical about the conclusion which such an argument aims at establishing. Another thing which is left out is any investigation of the notion of *rationality*, or the notion of a rational being. Precisely what remedy I should propose for these omissions is far from clear to me; I have to confess that my ideas in this region of the subject are still in a very rudimentary state. But I will do the best I can.

I suspect that there is no single characterization of Transcendental Arguments which will accommodate all of the traditionally recognized specimens of the kind; indeed, there seem to me to be at least three sorts of argument-pattern with good claims to be dignified with the title of Transcendental.

(1) One pattern fits Descartes's *cogito* argument, which Kant himself seems to have regarded as paradigmatic. This argument may be represented as pointing to a thesis, namely his own existence, to which a real or pretended sceptic is thought of as expressing enmity, in the form of doubt; and it seeks to show that the sceptic's procedure is self-destructive in that there is an irresoluble conflict between, on the one hand, *what* the sceptic is suggesting (that he does not exist), and on the other hand the possession by his act of suggesting, of the illocutionary character (being the expression of a doubt) which it not only has but must, on the account, be supposed by the sceptic to have. It might, in this case, be legitimate to go on to say that the expression of doubt cannot be denied application, since without the capacity for the expression of

doubt the exercise of rationality will be impossible; but while this addition might link this pattern with the two following patterns, it does not seem to add anything to the cogency of the argument.

(2) Another pattern of argument would be designed for use against applications of what I might call 'epistemological nominalism'; that is against someone who proposes to admit *y*s but not *x*s on the grounds that epistemic justification is available for *y*s but not for anything like *x*s, which supposedly go beyond *y*s; we can, for example, allow sense-data but not material objects, if they are thought of as 'over and above' sense-data; we can allow particular events but not, except on some minimal interpretation, causal connections between events. The pattern of argument under consideration would attempt to show that the sceptic's at first sight attractive caution is a false economy; that the rejection of the 'over-and-above' entities is epistemically destructive of the entities with which the sceptic deems himself secure; if material objects or causes go, sense-data and datable events go too. In some cases it might be possible to claim, on the basis of the lines of the third pattern of argument, that not just the minimal categories, but, in general, the possibility of the exercise of rationality will have to go.

(3) A third pattern of argument might contend from the outset that if such-and-such a target of the sceptic were allowed to fall, then something else would have to fall which is a pre-condition of the exercise of rationality; it might be argued, for example, that some sceptical thesis would undermine freedom, which in turn is a pre-condition of any exercise of rationality whatsoever.

It is plain that arguments of this third type might differ from one another in respect of the particular pre-condition of rationality which they brandished in the face of a possible sceptic. But it is possible that they might differ in a more subtle respect. Some less ambitious arguments might threaten a *local* breakdown of rationality, a breakdown in some particular area. It might hold, for instance, that certain sceptical positions would preclude the possibility of the exercise of rationality in the practical domain. While such arguments may be expected to carry weight with some philosophers, a really doughty sceptic is liable to accept the threatened curtailment of rationality; he may, as Hume and those who follow him have done, accept the virtual exclusion of reason from the area of action. The threat, however, may be of a *total* breakdown of the possibility of the exercise of rationality; and here even the doughty sceptic might quail, on pain of losing his audience if he refuses to quail.

A very important feature of these varieties of 'transcendental' argument (though I would prefer to abandon the term 'transcendental' and just call them *'metaphysical arguments'*) may be their connection with practical argument. In a broadened sense of 'practical', which would relate not just to action but also to the adoption of any attitude or stance which is within our rational control, we might think of all argument, even alethic argument, as practical perhaps with the practical tail-piece omitted; alethic or evidential argument may be thought of as directing us to accept or believe some proposition on the grounds that it is certain or likely to be true. But sometimes we are led to *rational* acceptance of a proposition (though perhaps not to *belief* in it) by considerations other than the likelihood of its truth. Things that are matters of *faith* of one sort of another, like fidelity of one's wife or the justice of one's country's cause, are typically not accepted on evidential grounds but as demands imposed by loyalty or patriotism; and the arguments produced by those who wish us to have such faith may well not be silent about this fact. Metaphysical argument and acceptance may exhibit a partial analogy with these examples of the acceptance of something as a matter of faith. In the metaphysical region, too, the practical aspect may come first; we must accept such and such thesis or else face an intolerable breakdown of rationality. But in the case of metaphysical argument the threatened calamity is such that the acceptance of the thesis which avoids it is invested with the alethic trappings of truth and evidential respectability. Proof of the pudding comes from the need to eat it, not vice versa. These thoughts will perhaps allay a discomfort which some people, including myself, have felt with respect to transcendental arguments. It has seemed to me, in at least some cases, that the most that such arguments could hope to show is that rationality demands the *acceptance*, not the *truth*, of this or that thesis. This feature would not be a defect if one can go on to say that *this* kind of demand for acceptance is sufficient to confer truth on what is to be accepted.

It is now time for me to turn to a consideration of the ways in which metaphysical construction is effected, and I shall attempt to sketch three of these. But before I do so, I should like to make one or two general remarks about such construction routines. It is pretty obvious that metaphysical construction needs to be disciplined, but this is not because without discipline it will be badly done, but because without discipline it will not be done at all. The list of available routines determines what metaphysical construction *is*; so it is no accident that it employs these routines. This reflection may help us to solve what has appeared to me, and to others, as a difficult problem in the methodology of metaphysics, namely, how are we to distinguish metaphysical construction from scientific construction of such entities as electrons or quarks? What is the difference between hypostasis and hypothesis? Tha answer may lie in the idea that in metaphysical construction, including hypostasis, we reach new entities (or in some cases, perhaps, suppose them to be reachable) by application of the routines which are essential to metaphysical construction; when we are scientists and hypothesize, we do not rely on these routines at least in the first instance; if at a later stage we shift our ground, that is a major theoretical change.

I shall first introduce two of these construction routines; before I introduce the third I shall need to bring in some further material, which will also be relevant to my task in other ways. The first routine is one which I have discussed elsewhere, and which I call *Humean Projection*. Something very like it is indeed described by Hume, when he talks about 'the mind's propensity to spread itself on objects'; but he seems to regard it as a source, or a product, of confusion and illusion which, perhaps, our nature renders unavoidable, rather than as an achievement of reason. In my version of the routine, one can distinguish four real or apparent stages, the first of which, perhaps, is not always present. At this first stage we have some initial concept, like that expressed by the word 'or' or 'not', or (to take a concept relevant to my present undertakings) the concept of value. We can think of these initial items as, at this stage, intuitive and unclarified elements in our conceptual vocabulary. At the second stage we reach a specific mental state, in the specification of which it is possible though maybe not necessary to use the name of the initial concept as an adverbial modifier, we come to 'or-thinking' (or disjoining), 'not-thinking' (or rejecting, or denying), and 'value-thinking' (or valuing, or approving). These specific states may be thought of bound up with, and indeed as generating, some set of responses to the appearance on the scene of instantiation of the initial concepts. At the third stage, reference to these specific states is replaced by a general (or more general) psychologial verb together with an operator corresponding to the particular specific stage which appears within the scope of the general verb, but is still allowed only maximal scope within the complement of the verb and cannot appear in subclauses. So we find reference to 'thinking p or q' or 'thinking it valuable to learn Greek'. At the fourth and last stage, the restriction imposed by the demand that the operators at stage three should be scope-dominant within the complement of the accompanying verb is removed; there is no limitation on the appearance of the operation in subordinate clauses.

With regard to this routine I would make five observations:

(1) The employment of this routine may be expected to deliver for us, as its end-result, *concepts* (in something like a Fregean sense of the word) rather than *objects*. To generate objects we must look to other routines.

(2) The provision, at the fourth stage, of full syntactico-semantical freedom for the operators which correspond to the initial concepts is possible only *via* the provision of truth-conditions, or of some different but analogous valuations, for statements within which the operators appear. Only thus can the permissible complexities be made intelligible.

(3) Because of (2), the difference between the second and third stages is apparent rather than real. The third stage provides only a notational variant of the second stage, at least unless stage four is also reached.

(4) It is important to recognize that the development, in a given case, of the routine must not be merely formal or arbitrary. The invocation of a subsequent stage must be exhibited as having some point or purpose, as (for example) enabling us to account for something which needs to be accounted for.

(5) Subject to these provisos, application of this routine to our initial concept ('putting it through the mangle') does furnish one with a metaphysical reconstruction of that concept; or, if the first stage is missing, we are given a metaphysical construction of a new concept.

The second construction routine harks back to Aristotle's treatment of predication and categories, and I will present my version of it as briefly as I can. Perhaps its most proper title would be *Category Shift*; but since I think of it as primarily useful for introducing new objects, new subjects of discourse, by a procedure reminiscent of the linguists' operation of nominalization, I might also refer to it as *subjectification* (or, for that matter, *objectification*). Given a class of primary subjects of discourse, namely substances, there are a number of 'slots' (categories) into which predicates of these primary subjects may fit; one is substance itself (secondary substance), in which case the predication is intra-categorial and *essential*; and there are others into which the predicates assigned in non-essential or accidental predication may fall; the list of these would resemble Aristotle's list of quality, quantity, and so forth. It might be, however, that the members of my list, perhaps unlike that of Aristotle, would not be fully co-ordinate; the development of the list might require not one blow but a succession of blows; we might for example have to develop first the category of arbitrary. It has to be properly motivated; if it is not, perhaps it fails to (quantity) and non-quantitative attribute (quality), or again the category of event before the subordinate category of action.

Now though substances are to be the *primary* subjects of predication, they will not be the only subjects. Derivatives of, or conversions of, items which start life (so to speak) as predicable, in one non-substantial slot or another, of substances, may themselves come to occupy the first slot; they will be qualities of, or quantities of, a particular type or token of substantials: not being qualities or quantities of substances, they will not be qualities or quantities *simpliciter*. (It is my suspicion that only for substances, as subjects, are *all* the slots filled by predicable items.) Some of these substantials which are not substances may derive from a plurality of items from different original categories; events, for example, might be complex substantials deriving from a substance, an attribute, and a time.

My position with regard to the second routine runs parallel to my position with regard to the first, in that here too I hold strongly to the opinion that the introduction of a new category of entities must not be arbitrary. It has to be properly motivated; if it is not, perhaps it fails to be a case of entity-construction altogether, and becomes merely a *way of speaking*. What sort of motivation is called for is not immediately clear; one strong candidate would be the possibility of opening up new applications for existing modes of explanation; it may be, for example, that the substantial introduction of abstract entities, like properties, makes possible the application to what Kneale called 'secondary induction' (*Probability and Induction*, p. 104 for example), the principles at work in *primary* induction. But it is not only the *sort* but the *degree* of motivation which is in question. When I discussed metaphysical argument, it seemed that to achieve reality the acceptance of a category of entities had to be *mandatory*; whereas the recent discussion has suggested that apart from conformity to construction-routines, all that is required is that the acceptance be *well-motivated*? Which view would be correct? Or is it that we can tolerate a division of constructed reality into two segments, with admission requirements of differing degrees of stringency? Or is there just one sort of admission requirement, which in some cases is over-fulfilled?

Before characterizing my third construction-routine I must say a brief word about *essential properties* and about *finality*, two Aristotelian ideas which at least until recently have been pretty unpopular, but for which I want to find metaphysical room. In their logical dress, essential properties would appear either as properties which are constitutive or definitive of a given, usually substantial, kind; or as individuating properties of individual members of a kind, properties such that if an individual were to lose them, it would lose its identity, its existence, and indeed itself. It is clear that if a property is one of the properties which define a kind, it is also an individuating property of individual members of a kind, properties such that if an individual were to lose them, it would cease to belong to the kind and so cease to exist. (A more cautious formulation would be required if, as the third construction routine might require, we subscribed to the Grice–Myro view of identity.) Whether the converse holds seems to depend on whether we regard spatio-temporal continuity as a definitive property for substantial kinds, indeed for *all* substantial kinds.

But there is another more metaphysical dress which essential properties may wear. They may appear as Keynesian generator-properties, 'core' properties of a substantive kind which co-operate to explain the phenomenal and dispositional features of members of that kind. On the face of it this is a quite different approach; but on reflection I find myself wondering whether the difference is as large as it might at first appear. Perhaps at least at the level of a type of theorizing which is not too sophisticated and mathematicized, as maybe these days the physical sciences are, the logically essential properties and the fundamentally explanatory properties of a substantial kind come together; substances are essentially (in the 'logical' sense) things such that in circumstances C they manifest feature F, where the gap-signs are replaced in such a way as to display the most basic laws of the theory. So perhaps, at this level of theory, substances require theories to give expression to their nature, and theories require substances to govern them.

Finality, particularly *detached* finality (functions or purposes which do not require sanction from purposers or users), is an even more despised notion than that of an essential property, especially if it is supposed to be explanatory, to provide us with *final causes*. I am somewhat puzzled by this contempt for detached finality, as if it were an unwanted residue of an officially obsolete complex of superstitions and priestcraft. That, in my view, it is certainly not; the concepts and vocabulary of finality, operating as if they were detached, are part and parcel of our standard procedures for recognizing and describing what goes on around us. This point is forcibly illustrated by William Golding in *The Inheritors*. There he describes, as seen through the eyes of a stone-age couple who do not understand at all what they are seeing, a scene in which (I am told) their child is cooked and eaten by iron-age people. In the description functional terms are eschewed, with the result that the incomprehension of the stone-age couple is vividly shared by the reader. Now finality is sometimes active rather than passive; the finality of a thing then consists in what it is supposed to *do* rather than in what it is supposed to suffer, have done to it, or have done with it. Sometimes the finality of a thing is not dependent on some ulterior end which the thing is envisaged as realizing. Sometimes the finality of a thing is not imposed or dictated by a will or interest extraneous to the thing. And sometimes the finality of a thing is not subordinate to the finality of some whole of which the thing is a component, as the finality of an eye or a foot *may* be subordinate to the finality of the organism to which it belongs. When the finality of a thing satisfies all of these overlapping conditions and exclusions, I shall call it a case of *autonomous* finality; and I shall also on occasion call it a *métier*. I will here remark that we should be careful to distinguish this kind of autonomous finality, which may attach to substances, from another kind of finality which seemingly will not be autonomous, and which will attach to the *conception* of kinds of substance or of other constructed entities. The latter sort of finality will represent the point or purpose, from the point of view of the metaphysical theorist, of bringing into play, in a particular case, a certain sort of metaphysical manœuvre. It is this latter kind of finality which I have been supposing to be a requirement for the legitimate deployment of construction-routines.

Now it is my position that what I might call finality-features, at least if they consist in the possession of *autonomous* finality, may find a place within the essential properties of at least some kinds of substances (for example, persons). Some substances may be essentially 'for doing such and such'. Indeed I suspect we might go further than this, and suppose that autonomous finality not merely *can* fall within a substances essential nature, but, indeed, if it attaches to a substance at all *must* belong to its essential nature. If a substance has a certain métier, it does not have to seek the fulfilment of that métier, but it does have to be equipped with the motivation to fulfil the métier should it choose to follow that motivation. And since autonomous finality is independent of any ulterior end, that motivation must consist in respect for the idea that to fulfil the métier would be in line with its own essential nature. But however that may be, once we have finality features enrolled among the essential properties of a kind of substance, we have a starting point for the generation of a theory or system of conduct for that kind of substance, which would be analogous to the descriptive theory which can be developed on the basis of a substance's essential descriptive properties.

I can now give a brief characterization of my third construction-routine, which is called *Metaphysical Transubstantiation*. Let us suppose that the Genitor has sanctioned the appearance of a biological type called Humans, into which, considerate as always, he has built an attribute, or complex of attributes, called Rationality, perhaps on the grounds that this would greatly assist its possessors in coping speedily and resourcefully with survival problems posed by a wide range of environments, which they would thus be in a position to enter and to maintain themselves in. But, perhaps unwittingly, he will thereby have created a breed of potential metaphysicians; and what they do is (so to speak) to reconstitute themselves. They do not alter the totality of attributes which each of them as humans possess, but they redistribute them; properties which they possess essentially as humans become properties which as substances of a new psychological type called *persons* they possess accidentally; and the property or properties called rationality, which attaches only accidentally to humans, attaches essentially to persons. While each human is standardly coincident with a particular person (and is indeed, perhaps, identical with that person over a time), logic is insufficient to guarantee that there will not come a time when that human and that person are no longer identical, when *one* of them, perhaps, but not the other, has ceased to exist. But though logic is insufficient, it may be that other theories will remedy the deficiency. Why, otherwise than from a taste for mischief, the humans (or persons) should have wanted to bring off this feat of transubstantiation will have to be left open until my final section, which I have now reached.

My final undertaking will be an attempt to sketch a way of providing metaphysical backing, drawn from the material which I have been presenting, for a reasonably unimpoverished theory of value; I shall endeavour to produce an account which is fairly well-ordered, even though it may at the same time be one which bristles with unsolved problems and unformulated supporting arguments. What I have to offer will be close to and I hope compatible with, though certainly not precisely the same as the content of my third Carus Lecture (original version, 1983). Though it lends an ear to several other voices from our philosophical heritage, it may be thought of as being, in the main, a representation of the position of that unjustly neglected philosopher Kantotle. It involves six stages.

(1) The details of the logic of value-concepts and of their possible relativizations are unfortunately visible only through thick intellectual smog; so I shall have to help myself to what, at the moment at least, I regard as two distinct dichotomies. *First*, there is a dichotomy between value-concepts which are *relativized* to some focus of relativization and those which are not so relativized, which are *absolute*. If we address ourselves to the concept *being of value* there are perhaps two possible primary foci of relativization; that of *end* or potential end, that *for* which something may be of value, as bicarbonate of soda may be of value for health (or my taking it of value for my health), or dumbbells may be of value (useful) for bulging the biceps; and that of *beneficiary* or potential beneficiary, the person (or other sort of item) *to* whom (or to which) something may be of value, as the possession of a typewriter is of value to some philosophers but not to me, since I do not type. With regard to this dichotomy I am inclined to accept the following principles. *First*, the presence in me of a concern for the focus of relativization is what is needed to give the value-concept a 'bite' on me, that is to say, to ensure that the application of the value-concept to me does, or should, carry weight for me; only if I care for my aunt can I be expected to care about what is of value to her, such as her house and garden. *Second*, the fact that a relativized value-concept, through a *de facto* or *de jure* concern on my part for the focus of relativization, engages me does not imply that the original relativization has been cancelled, or rendered absolute. If my concern for your health stimulates in me a vivid awareness of the value to you of your medication, or the incumbency upon you to take your daily doses, that value and that incumbency are still relativized *to your health*; without a concern on *your* part for your health, such claims will leave you cold.

The second dichotomy, which should be carefully distinguished from the first, lies between those cases in which a value-concept, which may be either relativized or absolute, attaches *originally*, or *directly*, to a given bearer, and those in which the attachment is *indirect* and is the outcome of the presence of a *transmitting* relation which links the current bearer with an original bearer, with or without the aid of an intervening sequence of 'descendants'. In the case of the transmission of relativized value-concepts, the transmitting relation may be the same as, or may be different from, the relation which is embodied in the relativization. The foregoing characterization would allow absolute value to attach originally or directly to promise-keeping or to my keeping a promise, and to attach indirectly or by transmission to my digging your garden for you, should that be something which I have promised to do; it would also allow the relativized value-concept of *value for health* to attach directly to medical care and indirectly or by transmission to the payment of doctor's bills, an example in which the transmitting relation and the relativizing relation are one and the same.

(2) The second stage of this metaphysical defence of the authenticity of the conception of value will involve a concession and a contention. It will be conceded that if the only conception of value available to us were that of *relativized* value then the notion of finality would be in a certain sense dispensable; and further, that if the notion of finality is denied authenticity, so must the notion of value be denied authenticity. A certain region of ostensible finality, which is sufficient to provide for the admissibility of attributions of relativized value, is 'mechanistically substitutable'; that is to say, by means of reliance on the resources of cybernetics and on the fact that the non-pursuit of certain goals such as survival and reproduction is apt to bring to an end the supply of potential pursuers, some ostensibly final explanations are replaceable by, or reinterpretable as, explanations of a sort congenial to mechanists. But if the concept of value is to be authentic and not merely 'Pickwickian' in character, then it is required that it be supported by a kind of finality which extends beyond the 'overlap' with mechanistically substitutable finality; autonomous finality will be demanded and a mechanist cannot accommodate and must deny this kind of finality; and so, as will shortly be indicated, he is committed to a denial of absolute value.

(3) That metaphysical house-room be found for the notion of absolute value is a *rational demand*. To say this is not directly to offer reason to believe in the acceptability of the notion, though it makes a move in that direction. It is rather to say that there is good reason for *wanting* it to be true that the notion is acceptable. There might be more than one kind of rational ground for this desire. It might be that we feel a need to appeal to absolute value in order to justify some of our beliefs and attributes with regard to relativized value, to maintain (for

example) that it is of absolute value that everyone should pursue, within certain limits, what he regards as being of value to himself. Or again, it might be that, by Leibnizian standards for evaluating possible worlds, a world which contains absolute value, on the assumption that its regulation requires relatively simple principles, is richer and so better than one which does not.

But granted that there is a rational demand for absolute value, one can then perhaps argue that within whatever limits are imposed by metaphysical constructions already made, we are free to rig our metaphysics in such a way as to legitimize the conception of absolute value; what it is proper to believe to be true may depend in part on what one would like to be true. Perhaps part of the Kantian notion of positive freedom, a dignity which as rational beings we enjoy, is the freedom not merely to play the metaphysical game but, within the limits of rationality, to fix its rules as well. In any case a trouble-free metaphysical story which will safeguard the credentials of absolute value is to be accepted should it be possible to devise one. I have some hopes that the methodology at work here might link up with my earlier ideas about the quasi-practical character of metaphysical argument.

(4) On the assumption that the operation of Metaphysical Transubstantiation has been appropriately carried through, a class of biological creatures has been 'invented' into a class of psychological substances, namely persons, who possess as part of their essential nature a certain métier or autonomous finality consisting in the exercise, or a certain sort of exercise, of rationality, and who have only to recognize and respect a certain law of their nature, in order to display in favourable circumstances the capacity to realize their métier. The degree to which they fulfil that métier will constitute them *good persons* ('good *qua*' persons); and while the reference to the substantial kind *persons* undoubtedly introduces a restriction or qualification, it is not clear (if it matters) that this restriction is a mode of relativization.

(5) Once the concept of *value-qua-member-of-a-kind* has been set up for a class of substances, the way is opened for the appearance of transmitting relationships which will extend the application of value-in-a-kind to suitably qualified non-substantial aspects if members of a kind, such as actions and characteristics. While it cannot be assumed that persons will be the only original instances of value-in-a-kind, it seems plausible to suggest that whatever other original instances there may be will be far less fruitful sources of such extension, particularly if a prime mode of extension will be by the operation of Humean

Projection. It seems plausible to suppose that a specially fruitful way of extending the range of absolute value might be an application or adaptation of the routine of Humean Projection, whereby such value is accorded, in Aristotelian style, to whatever would seem to possess such value in the eyes of a duly accredited judge; and a duly accredited judge might be identifiable as a good person operating in conditions of freedom. Cats, adorable as they may be, will be less productive sources of such extension than *persons*.

(6) In the light of these reflections, and on the assumption that to reach the goal of securing the admissibility of the concept of absolute value we need a class of primary examples of an unqualified version of that concept, it would appear to be a rational procedure to allot to persons as a substantial type not just absolute value *qua members of their kind*, but absolute value *tout court*, that is to say *unqualified* absolute value. Such value could be attributed to the kind, in virtue of its potentialities, and to selected individual members of the kind, in virtue of their achievements.

Such a defence of absolute value is of course, bristling with unsolved or incompletely solved problems. I do not find this thought daunting. If philosophy generated no new problems it would be dead, because it would be finished; and if it recurrently regenerated the same old problems it would not be alive because it could never begin. So those who still look to philosophy for their bread-and-butter should pray that the supply of new problems never dries up.

MEANING

3

THE PRIMACY OF
UTTERER'S MEANING[1]

PATRICK SUPPES

A central aspect of Grice's theory of meaning is the basic character of utterer's meaning. This feature of his theory has been criticized severely because of its deviation from the conception of semantics as an autonomous discipline independent of such general psychological concepts as speakers' intentions and listeners' recognition of intentions. I believe that Grice is right and his critics are wrong. The purpose of this essay is to offer my reasons for holding this view.

Before getting down to business, there are some preliminary matters to get out of the way. First, concerning the statement of Grice's views I primarily depend upon his three important articles (1957, 1968, 1969). The critics I shall explicitly consider are Chomsky (1975), Yu (1979), and Biro (1979).

I also want to make clear at the beginning that it is not my purpose here to give a detailed analysis of Grice's fundamental concept of utterer's occasion-meaning. As readers of Grice will remember, his programme is to use this basic notion to explicate at the next level of abstraction the concept of utterance-type occasion-meaning. At the next higher level is the analysis of the concept of the applied timeless meaning of an utterance-type (complete or incomplete) on a particular occasion of utterance. Finally, we reach the timeless meaning of an utterance-type. Because the criticisms of Grice have focused almost entirely on the nature of his programme rather than on the details, my intention is also to focus on the programme and try to explain why I think it is in principle sound.

Grice's own formulation and reformulatons of basic concepts are

---

[1] It is a pleasure to dedicate this paper to Paul Grice, who over the years has patiently instructed me on more philosophical points than I can hope to remember. I am indebted to Dagfinn Follesdal and Howard Wettstein for a number of useful criticisms of an earlier draft of this paper.

technical and intricate. It is a surprising feature of the critics I mentioned above that they do not enter into real details of these analyses. In order to make my discussion more or less consonant with those of the critics, I select one rather informal version from Grice (1969). Let p be a proposition and let $*\psi$ be a mood marker. As Grice puts it ψ is 'an auxiliary correlated with a propositional attitude ψ from a given range of propositional attitudes'. Grice's basic concept of meaning is then defined by him along the following lines.

U means by uttering x that $*\psi p =$ U utters x intending
  (1) that A should actively ψ that p
  (2) that A should recognize that U intends (1) and . . .
  (3) that the fulfilment of (1) should be based on the fulfilment of (2). [p. 171.]

I. CHOMSKY'S CRITICISM

Chomsky (1975, pp. 54–77) discusses Grice's theory of meaning along with a rather detailed discussion of related views of Searle and Strawson. I shall concentrate on what Chomsky says about Grice, but a number of his comments are of a general nature—in fact, most of them are general rather than specific and technical, and consequently are not necessarily aimed at Grice in particular. Also, I shall not go into some of the details of Chomsky's remarks, for a good many of them are specific replies to Searle's criticisms of Chomsky.

There are three central issues I have abstracted from the pages in Chomsky's book cited above. The first is the most important, but the other two bear on Chomsky's discussion of Grice. I do not expect Grice to agree entirely with me in my disagreements with Chomsky. On all three of the conceptual issues I mention I think that Chomsky is wrong. The three are these. First, is the concept of literal meaning required in the definition of utterer's meaning? Second, can we meaningfully talk about *the* rules of language? Third, is Grice a behaviourist?

1. *Literal meaning*

Chomsky's position is summarized in the following passage.

The notion 'literal meaning,' or some equivalent, again intrudes, and no way has been offered to escape the 'orbit of conceptual space' that includes the suspect abstract notions 'linguistic meaning' and the like, even if the utterer happens to have the postulated intentions with regard to a hypothetical audience, as is by no means necessary in the normal use of language.

One can imagine modifications of the proposed definition that would not involve incorrect claims about intentions, but not, so far as I can see, without introducing some notion like 'linguistic meaning.' [p. 68.]

Another pertinent passage a few pages later is the following:

We must distinguish between the literal meaning of the linguistic expression produced by S and what S meant by producing this expression (or by saying that so-and-so, whatever expressions he used). The first notion is the one to be explained in the theory of language; I can just as well ask, in the same sense of 'meaning,' what S meant by slamming the door. Within the theory of successful communication, we can, perhaps, draw a connection between these notions. The theory of meaning, however, seems quite unilluminated by this effort. [p. 76.]

These two passages state conclusions that are argued for in several different ways by Chomsky. I want to examine what appear to me to be the more important arguments he offers. One claim he returns to on several occasions is that speakers sometimes fail to have appropriate Gricean intentions, especially when there appears to be no intended audience. Chomsky cites various cases where the speaker has 'no intention of getting the hearer to know anything or to recognize anything, but what I say has its strict meaning, and I mean what I say' (pp. 63-4). Now, it seems to me there are two separate points to be made about what Chomsky repeats in several ways. First, there is a problem to be dealt with concerning the possible absence of an audience. It seems to me this is not a very serious problem and should be set aside at this point—I return to it in the next section on Yu. What is more important is to dig deeper into the concept of intention. Chomsky's counterexamples seem to be riding very much on a superficial and surface notion of intention, in fact, a notion that seems very behaviouristic. If I write in my diary or if I write some research notes to myself, it does not do, it seems to me, to say that I write something that has a strict meaning but that it does not make sense to talk about my 'intention to communicate'. It would certainly seem odd if someone asked me what I was doing, to say that I was writing something with strict meaning but of course it is not supposed to communicate anything. Another way of putting the matter is that communication is the primary act and meaning is an aspect of that primary act.

I can certainly agree that we do not have in Grice's writings or in Chomsky's criticisms of Grice or Searle, or in Searle's writings either, a really detailed theory of intention that we can bring to bear in this discussion in a precise way. But it seems to me that the kind of view of intention that Grice has is certainly outlined in general terms rather clearly, and it is not the rather simple view that Chomsky attributes to him. It should be mentioned, by the way, that the competing primary notion of the literal or linguistic meaning that Chomsky uses is similarly lacking in detailed specification.

A second objection of Chomsky's is that communication theorists, as he calls Grice, Searle, and Strawson, are not really concerned to build up the theory of meaning of an utterance from its component parts, and thus to have a principled account either of utterer's or linguistic meaning. All sides are guilty of this. Chomsky too does not provide a theory for building up meaning from an analysis of parts or in any way from a knowledge, let us say, of syntax. There is an attempted sketch for a much too simple formal language in Schiffer (1972), but it is clear from various things that Grice says that his attention to utterer's word meanings is meant to sketch how these matters are to be approached.

It seems to me, however, that there is a genuine issue here that we can discuss without requiring from either side a detailed theory of how we can determine the meaning of complex utterances or sentences. The communication theorists such as Grice argue that the framework of communication influences greatly the meaning of an utterance. Chomsky and others on his side take the opposite view. Some recent good examples of how even literal utterances are undetermined in terms of their strict meaning or literal meaning are to be found in Searle (1980). What I think we could grant Chomsky is that there are lots of sentences in scientific treatises and articles that have the kind of pleasing attributes he would like to see, but that these sentences are, from the standpoint of the primary use of language, highly non-standard. Even to this claim I will not grant very much. It is true perhaps of the theoretical parts of science but, as I have argued in Suppes (1982), matters are very different when one looks at the language of experimental science. The language is esoteric, context-dependent, and impenetrable from those outside the particular discipline. The real place that is context-dependent and, if you will, communication-dependent, is in the kind of casual give and take so characteristic of our daily conversations. The detailed analysis of most conversations will not get very far with consideration only of the literal meaning of words used. We must, over and over again, involve the speakers and listeners and their intentions in the conversation being analyzed after the fact.

One of Chomsky's central arguments about the primacy of literal meaning is that revisions of Grice's original characterization of utterer's meanings have moved more and more toward implicit use of 'rules' and 'conventions', which are ways of dragging in, illicit or otherwise, a concept of literal meaning. I do not buy this argument at all.

In another article, Grice (1982) has, in general terms, sketched the sense in which his approach to meaning provides a kind of proto-theory of how language came about and came to be used. It seems to me that an argument that this is not the correct order of develop-ment can scarcely be taken seriously. An account of the genesis of language that supposed that first came literal meaning and then, as a derivative from that, utterer's meaning, seems hard to conceptualize even in the barest and thinnest sort of outline. Surely, language must have begun from attempts at communication between a few individuals. At first these efforts at communication did not have very much stability of literal meaning. Only slowly and after much time did a stable com-munity of users lead to the abstract concept of literal meaning. In fact, 'abstract' is exactly the right term, taken in its primitive sense. There is no hard and fast platonic literal meaning that utterer's meanings attach themselves to and play upon in their need for dependence and shelter. The story surely is exactly the other way around. Utterers develop similar meanings, but not identical meanings. The commonality of experience of utterers is responsible for the possibility of abstract meaning, not the converse, but more on this in Section III.

2. *Some rules versus the rules of language*

Chomsky repeatedly refers to *the* rules of language, reflecting in such passages once again his commitment to what is essentially a platonic and abstract theory of language. I shall not argue about platonic meta-physics or ontology. My point is rather that Chomsky's conception of language as being embodied in a fixed set of rules used by speakers of that language seems to me an essentially mistaken notion. His argu-ments, stated in many different places, for the autonomy of syntax, affirm his beliefs on such matters, and are repeatedly given emphasis by his use of the phrase *the rules of language*. It seems to me impor-tant to challenge this notion as fundamentally incorrect. Certainly there are some rules of language that speakers and listeners share. We can begin with agreed-upon lists of words, some rules of grammar, some acoustical properties, etc. These matters are unexceptionable and easily stipulated by all parties. What is mistaken is to make the much stronger assumption that there is a fixed and complete set of rules that speakers and listeners share. A more defensible weaker thesis is that individual speakers and listeners have individually different rules. The rules they use are similar enough for them to understand each other and communicate with each other, but they are not using the same rules. It is only abstractions of their actually full-blown rules that lead to a concept of sameness. But this concept of sameness is a weak one, as weak as the concept of congruence in affine geometry that makes any two triangles congruent, a point that I expand on in Section III.

Let us start with the hypothesis that individual speakers and listeners can be characterized by a set of rules. What we notice at once when we begin to study these individual speakers in detail is that the same rules do not apply to them. Perhaps the easiest way to see this is in any attempt to characterize the prosody or rhythm of their speech, and surely anyone not committed to the written word as the final real embodiment of language will want to argue that rhythm and prosody of speech affect the meaning of speech and, therefore, utterer's meaning. There is another way to put the matter dramatically: the ease with which we all recognize individual speakers' voices. The differentiation we establish so readily between speakers is proof enough that if they are using rules to generate their spoken speech the rules are certainly different. I do not begrudge Chomsky his desire for a very generalized abstract theory of meaning, but he needs to recognize it for what it is—an abstraction that gets identity of rules across speakers only because of the coarseness of the abstraction. As in the case of triangles in affine geometry, Chomsky seems to have a kind of affine theory of meaning: we take a theory sufficiently weak and general to make the rules being used the same in a given linguistic community. But in real life we have a much more vivid and concrete geometry of meaning that we use continually, from the recognition of different speakers' voices to the recognition of an individual speaker's intention, rhythm, and prosody.

More radical argument

Let me in this same context turn to a more radical argument, which Grice himself might not accept. It is this. It is a mistake to suppose we can characterize the speech of even a single speaker by a complete set of rules. If we follow the discrete line of the Alexandrian grammarians, passing through Dionysius Thrax to Donatus and on to Chomsky, it might seem that we could talk about language being wholly rule-governed. I do not deny that of course there are partial rules, just as there are partial rules of walking or chewing. But when we look at the acoustical complexity of real speech, when we think about the features we all recognize intuitively without being able to identify acoustically or by rule, varying features of prosody, rhythm, individual quirks of grammar, etc., it seems hopeless to think that this marvellous complexity can be caught in any set of rules. Moreover, the attempts that we now have are so pitiful in character, so totally unsatisfactory, and so crude in approximation, that scepticism at the very idea of being able to capture language in rules is easily supported. Even so natural and obvious a property of a particular speaker's speech as the cadence of his individual rhythms is not discussed in the long treatise on the sounds of English by Chomsky and Halle (1968), and is certainly not discussed with any sophistication that is both mathematically and empirically satisfactory in any place that I know of. Chomsky likes to emphasize the creative use of language —his emphasis here I certainly agree with—but he speaks of this creative use as being generated by finite means and consequently by a finite set of rules. My point is that, once we leave the discreteness of syntax and deal with the continuous properties that we recognize in actual speech, it is a bold thesis that these can be parameterized in a finite way and do not contain complex elements distinctive of a given individual which can in no principled way be reduced to a fixed set of rules.

Many persons might agree with this negative argument about the possibility of having a complete set of rules for actual speech, but still maintain that such completeness is possible for syntax. This, too, I deny. Even at the regimented level of written language there is nothing like an adequate grammar of any natural language. Let me mention a personal example. Two students of mine have written dissertations on the grammar and semantics of the written language of elementary mathematics used in teaching children of about ten years of age. The grammars were far from complete even for this highly restricted topic, but when we examined the written language of mathematical textbooks for children of thirteen years it was not simply a matter of incompleteness, but a deeper sense of hopelessness at ever being able to approach grammatical completeness. Compared to the rhetoric of a Saintsbury or a Churchill these texts in term seem simple.

My own current conjecture, which is not essential to the rest of my argument, is this. Chomsky has told us only half the story. We are not only able to use a fixed set of rules to generate a potential infinity of utterances, but we are also as speakers and listeners continually creating new grammatical rules (not to speak of other aspects of language). These new rules, so I think, are ordinarily harmonious extensions of ones we are already using, but the constraints on their creation I cannot begin to characterize. I should emphasize here that I have in mind the creation of rules within the framework of what we would regard as a more or less homogeneous style, not new rules generated in the trail of an obvious stylistic metamorphosis. Here is a concrete example of what I mean. Let us write a grammar that gives a detailed analysis of every other sentence in the novels of Dickens, contains other general rules we might justify, but not by examining the omitted sentences, and does not permit any sentences we judge ungrammatical. My claim is that this grammar will not adequately parse the half of Dickens's sentences not considered, and still additional rules would be needed. Moreover, I think that speakers engage in such rule creation all the time. Both as speakers and listeners we are continually creating and learning new rules, engaging, if you will, in new practices.

But even with the newly created set of rules it is unlikely that we have grammatical rule-completeness. *Ad hoc* rules for single sentences scarcely count. Let me give a much simpler example to illustrate the point. For a variety of reasons there is and has been a strong interest in giving spelling rules for English, but in even such a relatively simple subject there is no complete set of rules, but sets of rules together with lists of exceptional individual words that account for varying percentages of whatever large population of English words are chosen. So, I claim, it is with sentences. We can and do speak and understand sentences that do not conform to any rules we have in our heads. The grammatical rules of our speech are not at all like the rules of chess. They are like the rules of a children's game that is not codified and is continually changing.

3. *Is Grice a behaviourist?*

Chomsky claims that Grice is a behaviourist and that consequently his programme suffers all the defects that Chomsky has alleged on numerous occasions are characteristic of empiricist theories about language. Here is what Chomsky says:

As for the reversion to behaviourism, it seems true of the most careful work within the theory. In what is, to my knowledge, the most careful and comprehensive effort to explain the meaning of linguistic expressions within this framework, Grice presents a system of definitions that rest not only on intentions but also on the speaker's 'policy', 'practice', and 'habit', on the idea of a 'repertoire of procedures'. To have a procedure in one's repertoire is to have 'a standing readiness (willingness, preparedness), in some degree to . . . ,' where 'a readiness (etc.) to do something [is] a member of the same family . . . as an intention to do that thing'. Grice recognizes the inadequacy of this analysis, but gives only some 'informal remarks' as to how a proper definition might be constructed. [p. 73.]

He continues a few lines later:

Grice's final case is intended to deal with the problem that a speaker may be 'equipped' to use expressions properly but have no readiness to do so. He suggests that a person may have a 'procedure for X' in the required sense if 'to utter X in such-and-such circumstances is part of the practice of many members of' the group to which the person belongs. That is, other members of the group '*do* have a readiness to utter X in such-and-such circumstances'. But for familiar reasons, this analysis is useless. There are no practices, customs, or habits, no readiness, willingness, or preparedness, that carry us very far in accounting for the normal creative use of language, whether we consider the practices of a person or of a group. [p. 74.]

It seems to me that Chomsky is badly off the mark in the passages I have quoted, and I want to try to explain why in some detail. Grice has used words like 'practice' and 'habit' and even the more technical word 'procedure' in their ordinary senses as they are used in ordinary discussion. He has not made technical concepts out of them as one might expect of some behavioural psychologists. There is nothing in any strong sense that is behaviourist about such talk—it is just ordinary talk about behaviour. There is also nothing exceptional in talking about practice, customs, or habits of language use. Grice certainly does not intend that these notions, as he has used them, give anything like a detailed account of the creative use of language. What Chomsky has to say is essentially a diatribe against empiricism, secondarily against behaviourism, and in the third place against Grice. In terms of more reasoned and dispassionate analyses of the matter, it seems to me that one would ordinarily think of Grice not as a behaviourist but as an intentionalist.

II. YU'S CRITICISMS

A rather recent comprehensive review of the literature on Grice's theory of meaning, along with a claim to give an analysis that brings out the nature of the Gricean mistakes 'in a perspicuous way' has been given by Yu (1979). In formulating his criticisms, Yu acknowledges that his greatest debt is to Chomsky's analysis and thus there is some overlap in what they have to say.

Minor points aside, Yu makes three criticisms of Grice. In my view, all three criticisms are mistaken. The first concerns the nature of explication or explanation and in particular whether Grice's theory of meaning is reportive or stipulative. The second concerns the case of intention in communcation when there is no audience present. The third criticism makes the claim that sentence meaning is prior to utterer's meaning.

Before making these criticisms, Yu introduces a preliminary distinction with which I agree. He points out that there are two kinds of general theses about language that we can be concerned with. One is to give an account of the genesis of language in the sense of how it developed in the course of human history. The second is to give an account of what it means for an organism or, more particularly, a person to have knowledge or possession of a language. Yu believes that Grice's programme is mainly concerned with the latter thesis, and with this I agree, although his sketch of how language came about in Grice (1982) has already been mentioned.

1. *Nature of explanation*

Within this framework the first criticism is that Grice or, as Yu puts it—to make the reference more general, the Griceans claim the following: (i) they can give necessary and sufficient conditions for sentence-meaning in terms of speaker-meaning and also necessary and sufficient conditions for speaker-meaning in terms of intention; (ii) the concept of intention is logically prior to the concept of speaker-meaning, and correspondingly, the concept of speaker-meaning is prior to that of sentence-meaning.[2] Yu introduces objections at this point on the basis of very general and rather bad arguments from the philosophy of science. One is that we do not know what *logically prior* means. Another closely related one is that we do not have any very precise notion of explication or explanation. In the case of explication, he wants to distinguish between explanations that are 'entirely stipulative, introducing

[2] To follow Yu's terminology I use here the phrase *speaker's meaning* by which I mean the same thing as Grice does by *utterer's meaning*. In the same way I do not intend to distinguish in any definite way here between the concept of literal meaning, as used by Chomsky, and the concept of sentence meaning, as used by Yu.

thereby a novel and technical notion', and reportive stipulations where 'the explicans has to characterize . . . correctly a pre-existing notion.' In my judgement this artificial dichotomy is as useful in the theory of explanation as is Aristotle's distinction between violent and natural motion in classical mechanics.

Any attempt to have a simple dichotomous characterization of explanations in this fashion is bad philosophy and bound to fail. Even relatively superficial reflection on any one of a number of conceptual examples in the history of mathematics, philosophy, or science bring out the artificial character of the distinction. Let me just mention a few. With the clarification of the difference between kinetic energy and momentum, a classic controversy in the early history of modern mechanics, a new distinction that did not exist before was created, but at the same time it was important to deal with a number of familiar complex phenomena. Any new distinction that did not would not be acceptable. So was this a reportive or stipulative case? Is the extension of the concept of addition from real numbers to complex numbers a reportive or stipulative explication? Is Russell's theory of descriptions reportive of stipulative? It seems evident that in important and interesting cases some aspects of a new concept are required to meet conditions of adequacy, to use Yu's phrase, as set by past experience and theory, while other aspects of a new concept are stipulative. Almost every important concept cuts across the two. It seems to me this is what we would expect of Grice's concept of utterer's meaning. We certainly have some intuitive ideas about utterer's meaning but we also do not have a very well-worked-out theory of the relevant phenomena. It is Grice's virtue to offer a theory that is far from explicit in our ordinary ideas, that may at certain points disturb or go beyond these intuitive ideas, but that in many respects satisfies our intuitions. Like other good proposals, Grice's explication of utterer's meaning is both reportive and stipulative.

2. *Problem of soliloquy*

Yu's second criticism picks up on a problem that is discussed by Grice himself, by Schiffer, Searle, and Chomsky. This is the question of how to apply Grice's characterization of utterer's meaning when an utterance is made with no audience present. Here it seems to me that Griceans have been more concerned than they should be with this problem, and have conceded more to their critics than they should have.

The problem is that when uttering something the utterer normally intends that an audience should actively respond to the utterance. It seems to me that Grice's idea is essential and correct. The primary use of language is for such communication, and it is hard to imagine language having been developed for any other major purpose. It is thus appropriate that utterer's meaning have its primary account in terms of intentions to influence an audience, but it by no means requires that such a complicated and extended skill should always be used only in its primary sense. Most complicated skills that we have can be used in ways other than the ways for which they were primarily developed. It is easy to think of some simple examples from among the repertoires of physical skills. Suppose that Jones is very interested in basketball and becomes very good at 'shooting baskets'. He develops his skill so as to do well in playing the game, but he also practices a great deal by himself and develops a true taste for shooting baskets alone. He develops a method of scoring and has a daily score based on the percentage of baskets shot out of those attempted in his backyard. The primary meaning of the skill makes sense only in the context of the game of basketball, but his additional use of that skill for pleasure and further training is derivative from that and is easily understood even though it is not exercised in the context of an actual game.

Smith is an excellent football-kicker. When held in an enemy prison camp he gets an important message out by kicking it in a can over the wall of the prison. His fellow prisoners tell him afterwards, 'Thank God you can kick like hell.'

And so it goes with a good talker. He has a complicated, useful, and powerful skill. He naturally uses it in supplementary ways to help himself remember things, to express his feelings even when alone, or to summarize his thoughts. The normal cases of speaking are addressed to an audience and have intentions with respect to the audience. It seems simple enough to extend the characterization to include those cases without an audience. I would expect a complicated skill like talking to be no more rigidly circumscribed in its meaningful use than any other such skill. Moreover, I would expect the noncentral uses to have no single, simple characterizations.

3. *Primacy of sentence meaning*

Yu's third argument, one that recurs in various forms in earlier criticisms of Grice, is that Grice's characterization of utterer's meaning is essentially circular in so far as it claims to be the basis of giving an account of the meaning of sentences, because the notion of the meaning of sentences is required in order to characterize that the intentions of the speakers are of the right kind. Yu's criticism seems to be based on the following two points. Sentence meaning is prior to utterer's meaning. Secondly, language can be used for many purposes, one of which is communication. Grice's proposal is one aimed at an account of communication, not of language. Such an account of communication must presume already and as logically prior an account of language and therefore of sentence meaning. The next section is devoted to this issue.

III. CONGRUENCE OF MEANING

Running through the criticisms of Chomsky and Yu, often explicitly, is an appeal to the idea of sentence meaning, but nothing very definite is said about this complicated and subtle notion. Given the many analyses of the concept of synonymy in work of several decades ago by Carnap, Church, Mates, Quine, and others, it is a little surprising to have the concept of sentence meaning referred to so casually by these critics of Grice's theory. (A good review of this earlier work is given in Quine, 1960.) Similar difficulties arise for saying when two proofs are 'the same', or even more recently, when two computer programmes are 'identical'.

I have argued earlier (1973) that the search for synonymy of sentences or, as often put, identity of propositions is mistaken, and that what we should have is what I have termed a geometrical theory of meaning. By this I mean that we replace the search for any fixed concept of synonymy by a hierarchy of concepts of congruence as is familiar in modern geometry. Thus, for example, we do not have in geometry one single notion of congruence, but one notion for Euclidean geometry, another for affine geometry, and another, say, for topology. In the same way, we have natural weaker and stronger senses of congruence of two sentences, and it is this notion of congruence of meaning that should be introduced and used in talking about sentence meaning. The rather casual paraphrases of meaning that are often used by Chomsky do not constitute a proper concept of sentence meaning, but only the rather coarse kind characteristic of paraphrase congruence.

It is not my purpose here to go into the technical details of my earlier ideas about congruence of meaning, but I want to use these ideas to develop some further remarks about the primacy of utterer's meaning. To do this it will be sufficient simply to give some examples of the different senses of congruence. The basic idea is that the syntactic structure enters into congruence as well as the referential character of a sentence. Thus, the following two sentences are congruent in a strong sense because their trees are syntactically isomorphic and denotationally identical. (By denotation I literally mean denotation, and not some peculiar sense of denotation one might find in generative semantics.)

> *All men are mortal.*
> *Every man is mortal.*

A second sense of congruence is that two sentences are permutationally congruent in meaning and form, but are not congruent in the sense of a strong congruence because the trees are not syntactically and denotationally isomorphic. Here are a pair of simple sentences illustrating permutational congruence:

> *John and Mary are here.*
> *Mary and John are here.*

The permutation of the order of proper names from one sentence to the other breaks apart the strong sense of congruence and leaves us with something weaker. A still weaker sense of congruence is that of paraphrase, mentioned earlier. In this case, only the denotation of the root of the tree for the entire sentence need be the same as its paraphrase.

To the extent that the kind of apparatus of congruence I have introduced for sentences is at all natural, it should be apparent that it has a direct extension to utterances. We now widen the concept of congruence to include features of the speech-act of utterance, and as we bring in an increasing number of factors we get absolute uniqueness, just as we do in geometry, namely, in the strongest sense of identity each utterance is only congruent with itself; that is, it is only identical with itself.

When we think about this natural progression of senses of congruence it seems to me absurd that Yu explicitly, and Chomsky perhaps less so, claim that sentence meaning is implicit in Grice's concept of utterer's meaning. I find this as ridiculous as saying that in any interesting sense affine congruence of triangles, for example, is somehow prior to Euclidean congruence. Certainly, affine congruence is weaker. After all, there is just one triangle in the affine plane up to congruence, but it is certainly not in any interesting way assumed as part of the concept of Euclidean congruence. What does seem to me obvious is that the richer and more concrete notion of utterer's meaning, when looked at from the standpoint of congruence, in no realistic sense whatsoever assumes a notion of sentence meaning. Let me make clear how the argument goes. There is no definite concept of sentence meaning. As in the case of geometry, the only systematic sense of sentence meaning is some particular sense of congruence of sentence meaning, but congruence of sentence meaning is clearly a weaker and more general concept than that of congruence of utterer's meaning. The particular facts and the particular acts of utterance form the basis of a stronger, more concrete, and more definite sense of meaning. It is confusion about sentence meaning that has misled Chomsky and Yu into thinking that there is a serious argument for the priority of sentence meaning over utterer's meaning.

In fact, to pursue this point a bit further it might be desirable to draw still another geometrical analogy. It might be said in response to what I have just said that I have put the shoe on the wrong geometry. It is Euclidean geometry that corresponds to what Chomsky and Yu have in mind in talking about sentence meaning, namely, the kind of geometry that has been around for a long time, just as talk about sentence meaning has been around for a long time. But it is easy for us to introduce a geometry stronger than Euclidean geometry, for example, a geometry that is sensitive not only to Euclidean geometry but also to orientation in space. Such a geometry in no way depends upon, and must assume as logically prior, the classical and traditional concept of Euclidean geometry. Let us call this concept that of oriented congruence. This is the kind of geometry that goes with much ordinary talk about the location of objects and events in daily experience.

It might still be objected that the fundamental feature of Euclidean geometry that is also characteristic of the idea of sentence meaning is present in oriented geometry but not correspondingly in utterer's meaning. This is the independence of context. In Euclidean geometry, oriented geometry, or affine geometry, a triangle is a triangle no matter what the context of the other points or figures. In fact, the very idea of other points or figures being present or absent is not a coherent concept in classical geometry. The same is implicitly the case for classical ideas of sentence meaning. The context of utterance should not affect the meaning. But all we need to do is to move from geometry to physics to pick a new analogy that is closer still to that of utterer's meaning. Physics is nothing but context. The motion of a particle is entirely different once a new particle comes close by. And so it is with utterer's meaning. The context as determined by the audience, the anxieties of the speaker, and so forth can have a significant and critical effect on utterer's meaning. I mean by this that the congruence of the utterance in the deepest and most detailed sense will depend upon these features as well as the features so characteristic of sentence meaning in the traditional sense.

In this sense my talk about a geometrical theory of meaning is mistaken. It is only in terms of the concept of congruence that I have talked about geometry. At the level of meaning itself, the analogy I would want to insist on as we move from sentence meaning to utterer's meaning is closer to physics than to geometry. It is a virtue of Grice's approach to bring out the importance of context and the importance of the concreteness reflected in utterer's meaning.

Because these matters have been so controversial, let me repeat once more my straightforward line on these matters. It is absurd to charge Grice with using implicitly a concept of sentence meaning once any systematic concept of sentence meaning is set forth. The reason is simple. Sentence meaning is going to entail a rather weak sense of congruence between utterances. The virtue of Grice's ideas is to require a strong sense of congruence. Perhaps the meek and the weak shall inherit the earth, but the strong shall not depend on them. Strong congruence of utterances does not depend on weak congruence in the sense of logical or conceptual dependence. Obviously, strong congruence implies weak congruence, and thus congruence of utterances implies congruence in the sense of sentence congruence, not conversely, but this we would expect and is completely unexceptionable.

IV. BIRO'S CRITICISM OF INTENTIONALISM

Grice's reduction, or partial reduction anyway, of meaning to intention places a heavy load on the theory of intentions. But in the articles he has written about these matters he has not been very explicit about the structure of intentions. As I understand his position on these matters, it is his view that the defence of the primacy of utterer's meaning does not depend on having worked out any detailed theory of intention. It is enough to show how the reduction should be thought of in a schematic fashion in order to make a convincing argument.

I do think there is a fairly straightforward extension of Grice's ideas that provides the right way of developing a theory of intentions appropriate for his theory of utterer's meaning. Slightly changing around some of the words in Grice (1968), we have the following example. U utters '"Phido is shaggy", if "U wants A to think that U thinks that Jones's dog is hairy-coated."' Put another way, U's intention is to want A to think U thinks that Jones's dog is hairy-coated. Such intentions clearly have a generative structure similar but different from the generated syntactic structure we think of verbal utterances' having. But we can even say that the deep structures talked about by grammarians of Chomsky's ilk could best be thought of as intentions. This is not a suggestion I intend to pursue seriously. The important point is that it is a mistake to think about classifications of intentions; rather, we should think in terms of mechanisms for generating intentions. Moreover, it seems to me that such mechanisms in the case of animals are evident enough as expressed in purposeful pursuit of prey or other kinds of food, and yet are not expressed in language. In that sense once again there is an argument in defence of Grice's theory. The primacy of utterer's meaning has primacy because of the primacy of intention. We can have intentions without words, but we cannot have words of any interest without intentions.

In this general context, I now turn to Biro's (1979) interesting criticisms of intentionalism in the theory of meaning. Biro deals from his own standpoint with some of the issues I have raised already, but his central thesis about intention I have not previously discussed. It goes to the heart of controversies about the use of the concept of intention to explain the meaning of utterances. Biro puts his point in a general way by insisting that utterance meaning must be separate from and independent of speaker's meaning or, in the terminology used here, utterer's meaning. The central part of his argument is his objection to the possibility of explaining meaning in terms of intentions.

Biro's argument goes like this:

1. A central purpose of speech is to enable others to learn about the speaker's intentions.
2. It will be impossible to discover or understand the intentions of the speaker unless there are independent means for understanding what he says, since what he says will be primary evidence about his intentions.
3. Thus the meaning of an utterance must be conceptually independent of the intentions of the speaker.

This is an appealing positivistic line. The data relevant to a theory or hypothesis must be known independently of the hypothesis. Biro is quick to state that he is not against theoretical entities, but the way in which he separates theoretical entities and observable facts makes clear the limited role he wants them to play, in this case the theoretical entities being intentions. The central idea is to be found in the following passage:

The point I am insisting on here is merely that the ascription of an intention to an agent has the character of an *hypothesis*, something invoked to explain phenomena which may be *described* independently of that explanation (though not necessarily independently of the fact that they fall into a class for which the hypothesis in question generally or normally provides an explanation). (pp. 250–1.) [The italics are Biro's.]

Biro's aim is clear from this quotation. The central point is that the data about intentions, namely, the utterance, must be describable independently of hypotheses about the intentions. He says a little later to reinforce this: 'The central point is this: it is the intention-hypothesis that is revisable, not the act-description' (p. 251). Biro's central mistake, and a large one too, is to think that data can be described independently of hypotheses and that somehow there is a clean and simple version of data that makes such description a natural and inevitable thing to have. It would be easy enough to wander off into a description of such problems in physics, where experiments provide a veritable wonderland of seemingly arbitrary choices about what to include and what to exclude from the experimental experience as 'relevant data', and where the arbitrariness can only be even partly understood on the basis of understanding the theories being tested. Real data do not come in simple linear strips like letters on the page. Real experiments are blooming confusions that never get sorted out completely but only partially and schematically, as appropriate to the theory or theories being tested, and in accordance with the traditions and conventions of past similar experiments. (Biro makes a point about the importance of convention that I agree with, but it is irrelevant to my central point of controversy with him.)

What I say about experiments is even more true of undisciplined and unregulated human interaction. Experiments, especially in physics, are presumably among the best examples of disciplined and structured action. Most conversations, in contrast, are really examples of situations of confusion that are only straightened out under strong hypotheses of intentions on the part of speakers and listeners as well.

There is more than one level at which the straightening-out takes place through the beneficent use of hypotheses about intentions. I shall not try to deal with all of them here but only mention some salient aspects. At an earlier point, Biro says:

The main reason for introducing intentions into some of these analyses is precisely that the public (broadly speaking) features of utterances —the sounds made, the circumstances in which they are made and the syntactic and semantic properties of these noises considered as linguistic items—are thought to be insufficient for the specification of that aspect of the utterance which we call its meaning. [p. 244.]

If we were to take this line of thought seriously and literally, we would begin with the sound pressure waves that reach our ears and that are given the subtle and intricate interpretation required to accept them as speech. There is a great variety of evidence that purely acoustical concepts are inadequate for the analysis of speech. To determine the speech content of a sound pressure wave we need extensive hypotheses about the intentions that speakers have in order to convert the public physical features of utterances into intentional linguistic items. Biro might object at where I am drawing the line between public and intentional, namely, at the difference between physical and linguistic, but it would be part of my thesis that it is just because of perceived and hypothesized intentions that we are mentally able to convert sound pressure waves into meaningful speech. In fact, I can envisage a kind of transcendental argument for the existence of intentions based on the impossibility from the standpoint of physics alone of interpreting sound pressure waves as speech.

Biro seems to have in mind the nice printed sentences of science and philosophy that can be found on the printed pages of treatises around the world. But this is not the right place to begin to think about meaning, only the end point. Grice, and everybody else who holds an intentional thesis about meaning, recognizes the requirement to reach an account of such timeless sentence meaning or linguistic meaning. In fact, Grice is perhaps more ready than I am to concede that such a theory can be developed in a relatively straightforward manner. One purpose of my detailed discussion of congruence of meaning in the previous section is to point out some of the difficulties of having an adequate detailed theory of these matters, certainly an adequate detailed theory of *the* linguistic meaning or *the* sentence meaning. Even if I were willing to grant the feasibility of such a theory, I would not grant the use of it that Biro has made. For the purposes of this discussion printed text may be accepted as well-defined, theory-independent data. (There are even issues to be raised about the printed page, but ones that I will set aside in the present context. I have in mind the psychological difference between perception of printed letters, words, phrases, or sentences, and that of related but different non-linguistic marks on paper.) But no such data assumptions can be made about spoken speech.

Still another point of attack on Biro's positivistic line about data concerns the data of stress and prosody and their role in fixing the meaning of an utterance. Stress and prosody are critical to the interpretation of the intentions of speakers, but the data on stress and prosody are fleeting and hard to catch on the fly. Hypotheses about speakers' intentions are needed even in the most humdrum interpretatins of what a given prosodic contour or a given point of stress has contributed to the meaning of the utterance spoken. The prosodic contour and the points of stress of an utterance are linguistic data, but they do not have the independent physical description Biro vainly hopes for.

Let me put my point still another way. I do not deny for a second that conventions and traditions of speech play a role in fixing the meaning of a particular utterance on a particular occasion. It is not a matter of interpreting afresh, as if the universe had just begun, a particular utterance in terms of particular intentions at that time and place without dependence upon past prior intentions and the traditions of spoken speech that have evolved in the community of which the speaker and listener are a part. It is rather that hypotheses about intentions are operating continually and centrally in the interpretation of what is said. Loose, live speech depends upon such active 'on-line' interpretation of intention to make sense of what has been said. If there were some absolutely agreed-upon concept of firm and definite linguistic meaning that Biro and others could appeal to, then it might be harder to make the case I am arguing for. But I have already argued in the discussion of congruence of meaning that this is precisely what is not the case. The absence of any definite and satisfactory theory of unique linguistic meaning argues also for moving back to the more concrete and psychologically richer concept of utterer's meaning. This is the place to begin the theory of meaning, and this theory itself rests to a very large extent on the concept of intention.

REFERENCES

Biro, J., 'Intentionalism in the Theory of Meaning', *The Monist*, 62 (1979), pp. 238–58.

Chomsky, N., *Reflections on Language*, New York, Pantheon Books, 1975.

Chomsky, N., and Halle, M., *Sound pattern of English*, New York, Harper and Row, 1968.

Grice, H. P., 'Meaning', *The Philosophical Review*, 66 (1957), pp. 377–88.

——, 'Utterer's Meaning, Sentence-Meaning, and Word-Meaning', *Foundations of Language*, 4 (1968), pp. 225–42.

——, 'Utterer's Meaning and Intentions', *The Philosophical Review*, 78 (1969), pp. 147–77.

——, 'Meaning Revisited', *Mutual Knowledge*, N. V. Smith (ed.), New York, 1982.

Quine, W. V., *Word and object*, Cambridge, Massachusetts Institute of Technology Press, 1960.

Schiffer, S. R., *Meaning*, London, Oxford University Press, 1972.

Searle, J. R., 'The Background of Meaning', in J. R. Searle, F. Kiefer, M. Bierwisch (eds), *Speech Act Theory and Pragmatics*, Dordrecht, Reidel, 1980, pp. 221–32.

Suppes, P., 'Congruence of Meaning', *Proceedings and Addresses of the American Philosophical Association*, 46 (1973), pp. 21–38.

Suppes, P., 'The Plurality of Science', in P. Asquith and I. Hacking (eds), *PSA 1978* (Vol. 2), East Lansing, Mich., Philosophy of Science Association, 1982.

Yu, P., 'On the Gricean Program about Meaning', *Linguistics and Philosophy*, 3 (1979), pp. 273–88.

4

UTTERER'S MEANING REVISITED

ANDREAS KEMMERLING

Grice's ideas of what it is to mean something by doing something, conceptually condensed in various analyses of 'utterer's (or speaker's) meaning', are today mostly disputed in the context of the question of how much—if any—semantics can be based on that concept. In this paper, I shall say nothing about this topic, but rather discuss some aspects of the analysis of 'utterer's meaning' itself. Since Schiffer's book *Meaning*, its details seem to be regarded as more or less settled, further scrutiny being disdained as sheer fussing over trifles and philosophically boring to boot.

So for a revisitor it seems wise to avoid niceties and to be brief, which is not always easy in discussing Gricean meaning. But I'll try my best. For the sake of brevity and perspicuity I introduce some informal abbreviations which render the analysans of Grice's (1957) original account of 'By uttering x, (some speaker) S meant something' in the following way:

[1] There is an audience A, and a reaction r such that[1]

    (1) $I_S(r_A)$

    (2) $I_S(B_A(I_S(r_A)))$

    (3) $I_S(B_A(I_S(r_A)) \backsim r_A)$

The abbreviations are to be read as follows: '$I_S(\text{---})$' is short for 'S uttered x intending (to bring it about) that ---'; '$B_A(\text{---})$' is short for 'A believes (or comes to believe) that ---'; 'r_A' is short for 'A does r'; '$\ldots \backsim r_A$' is short for 'The fact that $\ldots$ is at least part of a reason for A to do r', and this is to be taken to entail, together with an assumption of A's rationality, that if $\ldots$ then r_A.[2] More generally, '$\ldots \backsim \phi_Y(\text{---})$'

---

[1] This existential prelude already deserves qualifications, but I shall refrain from going into details since they do not have a bearing on the main points of the following. For a thorough discussion see Meggle (1981).

[2] This 'if $\ldots$ then ---' is not to be taken in the mere truth-functional sense, but as expressing a certain substantial connection between $\ldots$ and ---.

is short for 'The fact that . . . is at least part of a reason for Y to ϕ that —'.

In the following, I basically want to defend Grice's original analysis against several of its revisions which increase the number of intentions in the analysans. The fundamental characteristics of the sort of communication which the analysis is designed to elucidate are, I shall argue, not concerned at all by those revisions. Their point is a peripheral if not a negligible one which can be better accounted for anyway without ascribing further intentions to the speaker. This is what the first part of the paper is about. In the last part, I give a sketch of a reconstruction of the original analysis in which the concept of intention (or, more accurately, the concept of an action done with the intention to bring about a certain state of affairs) is eliminated in favour of the concepts of belief and desire. This somewhat more articulate account reveals —more clearly than does [1], I think—what I take to be the basic features of Gricean meaning, namely rationality and non-naturalness. In non-bizarre cases of meaning, an atmosphere of (if only restricted) trust and co-operation will (be assumed to) prevail; these aspects could be easily incorporated if one thought of them as further characteristics. Furthermore, the reconstruction uncovers hidden architectural details of the original analysis, e.g. how (2) derives from (1) together with part of what is meant by (3). The introduction of further intentions into the analysis will be seen to be something that cannot be done all too lightly; it takes more to justify such a step than merely presenting a 'counter-example' which would be removed by the ascription of an additional intention. Alleged counterexamples might be pointless, but intentions ascribed to rational agents might not be.

Before I turn to these things, just one step of progression by digression. How does the concept of utterer's meaning connect with a theory of linguistic meaning? Among other things, a theory of meaning is concerned with *what* we can do by uttering sentences and *how* we can do these things. Many things we can do with utterances are utterly irrelevant to the theory's subject: for example, ending a nap or frightening an absent-minded person. In order to achieve this, we just have to produce some noise, and this can be done by uttering any sentence. Austin's concept of illocutionary force can be thought of as being meant to pick out of the things that can be done by uttering sentences just those things that can be done by uttering *sentences* (as meaningful items). I take this to be the main characteristic of the category of illocution: to keep out anything that can be achieved by uttering a sentence which is not due to its being a meaningful item.

Austin ended up with a clearly narrower conception of illocutionary acts because of the specific examples he took into closer consideration, like christening, bequeathing, and marrying. Those things can be done only if they are done properly; they don't allow for dispensing with the formalities. Moreover, going through the motions of the formalities pertaining to these acts is often sufficient for doing them. So, in order to perform such acts, you just have to utter a certain sentence under certain circumstances, no matter what effects you want to bring about or actually bring about. Taking those acts to be typical of what can be done by uttering sentences smooths the way to a quite legalistic conception of illocutionary acts. According to such a conception, what illocutionary acts are is determined by a web of consequences conventionally associated with the performance of these acts; these consequences are thought of as speaker's and addressee's rights and duties emerging from the utterance (without being, in any interesting sense, caused by it). So what illocutionary acts are is basically determined by certain rules which distribute the respective consequential rights and duties. How illocutionary acts are performed is again a matter of rules, namely rules determining for any possible situation which utterance (if any) would constitute the performance of a given illocutionary act in this situation. These rules render certain words 'illocutionarily effective' for certain situations; performing an illocutionary act is simply happening to come up with such words in a relevant situation. This Prussian outlook on speaking a language fits in nicely with what the Red Queen says to Alice: 'When you've once said a thing, that fixes it, and you must take the consequences.'

Any such legalistic account is, I think, mistaken and misleading. It leaves out the essential point: why we talk, and how this connects with how we do it. This is mirrored in many of the taxonomies of illocutionary acts which speech act-theory abounds with. One finds acts ordered horizontally, according to several aspects of how they are performed and which kinds of consequences are triggered by their being performed. This is fine. But a vertical ordering—one which is sensitive to varying degrees of communicational importance and basic-ness—is not easily to be found along those lines. And even if the rule-oriented approach were phenomenologically acceptable, it certainly leaves out those unifying facts about linguistic communication which could contribute to getting a systematic theory of force going.

Grice's thought on communication has the desired quality of giving an account of this subject as a unified whole: it connects what is basically done by uttering meaningful items with why and how it's done. And it is thereby explained what renders an item meaningful, namely being used in this particular 'Gricean' way. This is, to me, part of what makes Grice's concept of utterer's meaning so fascinating: putting the fundamental *What, Why,* and *How* of linguistic communication into one smooth perspective.

Let me end this digression by hinting at (what I take to be) a more promising reference to the basic ingredients of a theory of force. On the surface of it, it's nothing but an exchange of slogans: swap 'No act without regulation' for 'Patefaction yields the action'. It's a good trade anyway. So, why not accept something like

(C) For any speaker *S*, addressee *A*, and utterance *x*: By *S*'s making it clear to *A* that, in uttering *x*, *S* wants to —, *S*, in uttering *x*, succeeds in —ing.

as a criterion of those acts the concept of illocutionary force was designed to capture? It fails to pick out many classical members of the original class. Naming a ship, bequeathing a watch, etc. are ruled out because the respective verb-phrases, if put in the slots, don't render (C) a true sentence. Let's have a look at what substitutions (C) admits: e.g. 'express', 'inquire', 'request', 'order', 'assert', 'agree', 'dissent', 'suggest', 'urge', 'congratulate', and 'accept'. That's not too bad. Of course, some inveterate legalists might come up with some misgivings about including some of these items on the list. But their objections, as far as I am familiar with them, are pretty prissy, mixing up what they take to be the proper way of doing these things with just doing them. The point of the Gricean twist of (C) is exactly to take us back to the essentials of communication, to lay bare *the way* those things get done —any way you do them. That's why I think that an elaborated version of (C) points to a basic layer of things that can be done by uttering sentences: things which can be done, in principle, by uttering anything whatever.

There are lots of internal problems with the envisaged criterion of illocutionary acts, for example those which are due to an inappropriate content of the act in question. Can I assert that the prime between 8 and 10 is divisible by 2? Assuming that every assertion is the performance of an illocutionary act if any assertion is, an important question, according to (C), is: Can I make it clear, by what I do, that I want to assert this somewhat off-beat content? (Making clear that I want to do this might turn out to be not as easy as simply uttering a semantically appropriate sentence; I might, additionally, have to present myself as an outstandingly stupid or ingenious fellow.) An answer to these questions requires at least two things: (a) getting clear about what an assertion is, and (b) getting clear about what makes one's desires clear consists in. Problem (b) is deeply entrenched in the concept of utterer's meaning and will be a leitmotif in the rest of the paper, the riff stemming from Grice, Strawson, Schiffer, Lewis, and Bennett. As regards (a), it has to be noted that (C) is supposed only to give a hint at which work should be done primarily but that it is not supposed to do this work or contribute to getting it done. (C) is to indicate nothing more than those acts which might be useful to get clear about first. The fact that an act is picked out by (C) doesn't tell us anything interesting about what kind of language-game it is. (C) only points to its being a basic game—basic in so far as the value of its being played is ranked sufficiently high not to have been overgrown by arbitrary restrictions on how to get the game in motion.

There are linguistic acts, of course, which have to be performed in a certain conventionally prescribed manner in order to be done at all. Their performance assumes the fulfilment of so-called 'happiness'-conditions over and above the fulfilment of the requirement to make one's relevant desires clear. Indeed, the fulfilment of additional happiness conditions can sometimes even eclipse the fact that this requirement is not fulfilled. This is undoubtedly an amazing fact about the organization of some forms of interaction (a judge can sentence somebody and yet, by the same token, make it quite clear that he does not want to). But those excesses and deformities of bourgeois convention do not make up the core of human communicaton. Conventions come and go. An account of linguistic communication has to try to capture primarily, what stays unaltered if it is to contribute something substantial to the theory of meaning.

Descriptions of linguistic acts have become entangled with the parochial paraphernalia of our elaborately sophisticated practices. Some criterion like (C) might help to get back to those acts which reveal quite purely a basic pattern of linguistic communication. And this pattern is, of course, what Grice's work on utterer's meaning is about.

REVISIONS

I am only concerned here with those revisions that were meant to protect the analysans against its being insufficient, and I omit details that would necessitate the introduction of new concepts (for example, 'mode of correlation', etc.). The first revision stems from Strawson (1964) and consists in the addition of

(4) $I_S(B_A(I_S(B_A(I_S(r_A)))))$

to the original analysans. Grice (1969) accepted this—if only provisionally—as well as the addition of

(5) $I_S(B_A(I_S(B_A(I_S(r_A))\sim r_A)))$

to (1)-(4), which arose from an objection presented by Schiffer, who —if only provisionally—even demanded a further step: namely the addition of

(6) $I_S(B_A(I_S(B_A(I_S(B_A(I_S(r_A))\sim r_A)))))$

to (1)-(5). Grice (1969) refused to follow, but Schiffer (1972), insatiably, suggested adding something to the original analysans which in effect is roughly equivalent to the following clause:

(S) For any condition c that we obtain from the original analysans, or from the application of S, add $I_S(B_A(c))$ to the conditions obtained so far.

This proposal requires someone who means anything at all by doing what he does to have infinitely many different and logically independent intentions with an indefinitely increasing degree of irreducible complexity. This makes any such proposal objectionable. As long as Gricean meaning is regarded as a fairly common phenomenon among human beings, such a position cannot in all consistency be held. At least, that is what I want to argue in the next few paragraphs.

Schiffer (in conversation) insists that on his actual proposal there is only one intention attributed to the speaker, although a complex one (consisting of infinitely many different and logically independent conjuncts with an indefinitely increasing degree of irreducible complexity). This intention is, very roughly, of the following type: $I_S[B_A(p)\&B_A(B_S(p))\&B_A(B_S(B_A(p)))\&\ . \ . \ .]$. Schiffer's point in favour of the 'only one intention'-claim is that a statement of the type 'S utters x with the intention to bring it about that p and q' does not entail a statement of the type '*S* utters *x* with the intention to bring it about that *p*'. I think that he is wrong to deny that the entailment-relation in question does obtain. But be that as it may, the fundamental question still remains: can we ever (correctly and with good reason) attribute such an infinitely complex intention to anyone, or at least to a common communicator?

We cannot do this, I contend, because of the indefinitely increasing degree of irreducible complexity of the conjuncts that make up the content of what would have to be intended. Plainly, what is intended (if only as an inseparable part of a complex intention) has to be intelligible to the person who is said to have the intention. Intentions of the kind under consideration are attributed to someone in order to explain why he does what he does; they are supposed to lead him to a certain action (or utterance, for that matter). But it is hard to see how an intention whose content is not intelligible to the intender (if there were such a thing) could lead him to a certain action instead of leading him to any other action or to none at all. What leads one nowhere or everywhere is not part of what one intends, so what is unintelligible to us is not part of what we intend.

Irreducible iterations of propositional attitude-operators, if sufficiently long, are not intelligible to us. Although we know that a sequence of, say, fifty billion 'You believe that I believe that'-items (followed, in the end, by something that couldn't be more obvious to us, as for example, 'we are in *Barney's Beanery*') represents a certain definite state of affairs, most of us are bound to fail to see which state of affairs that is. It is in this sense that the fifty-billion-item series is unintelligible to us. So most of us fail to be in a position to intend to bring about this state of affairs, even if it were only a somehow inseparable part of a very complex state of affairs. (Let's forget about the ones among us who can—or believe they can—do better in this respect; but if they are going to engage in developing a theory about our common ways of communicating, they should not forget about us who cannot.)

Weakening the concepts involved in the iteration is of no help; for example, substituting 'to have reason to believe' for 'to believe'.[3] The resulting sequence would still be of *irreducible* complexity, in contrast

[3] This is, in effect, to weaken Schiffer's (1972, p. 30 ff.) account of what he calls 'mutual belief' to Lewis's (1969, p. 52 ff.) account of what he, misleadingly, calls 'common knowledge'—a manœuvre of a kind recently recommended by Loar (1981, p. 250).

to, for example, an 'It is true that it is true that . . .'-sequence where, in order to find out what it says, we can simply wait for its last item; or an 'It is false that it is false that . . .'-series where we only would have to do a little counting while waiting for its last item. Complexity *qua* complexity does not yield unintelligibility, but irreducibility of high or very high complexity does—where the complex state of affairs described by a certain sequence, say *s*, is neither identical nor 'follows from' a less complex state of affairs whose description is embedded in *s* (or any composition of less complex states of affairs whose description is embedded in *s*). A 'You have reason to believe that I have reason to believe that . . .'-sequence might be thought to be less easily false than a corresponding 'You believe that I believe that . . .'-sequence, but as regards irreducibility of complexity, and hence intelligibility and 'intendability', they are on a par. So the objection to Schiffer's proposal would not be avoided.[4]

A quite analogous objection holds if the (outmost) intention-operator is changed into a belief operator, thereby yielding something of the following type: $B_S[B_A(p) \& B_A(B_S(p)) \& B_A(B_S(B_A(p))) \& \ldots]$. Although this is a better shot in several respects, it suffers from the same defect as the other one: nobody believes (or has reason to believe) what is unintelligible to him. The appeal to the unconscious, tacit, or implicit character of the belief in question doesn't save this epistemic monster. For, first, unintelligible content marks a limit not lightly to be dismissed even to tacit belief, and, second, the appeal to tacit belief itself is appropriate only if weaker means fail to explain satisfactorily what we want to explain. But, as will become apparent later, the explanatory goal can be reached equally well by weaker means, for example by a requirement like $\neg B_S \neg [B_A(p) \& B_A(B_S(p)) \& B_A(B_S(B_A(p))) \& \ldots]$ which does not face the problem of psychological reality but rather has a high prima-facie-plausibility. Anyway, it is not yet clear what this explanatory goal is supposed to consist in and whether it is worth being pursued at all. So let us turn to this.

---

[4] There is, in the last event, the possibility of its being claimed that, as a matter of fact, every speaker has acquired an infinitely iterated concept of the Lewisian or Schifferian kind—e.g. by having spontaneously developed an appropriate recursive definition—which he applies in forming his communicative intentions. Since nobody seems to want to go so far as to make such a wildly implausible claim, I prefer to discard it as deservedly undiscussed. A more elaborate version of this line of criticism is to be found in Kemmerling (1979).

DIAGNOSES

Its being afflicted by Multiple Intentionitis not only makes the analysis lose some of its innocent charm and attractiveness, it may make one even wonder what after all it is meant to be an analysis of. For a native speaker of the German language at least, it is clear right from the outset that the crucial point of the analysis is *not* to explicate the common concept of meaning something by doing, especially saying, something. For to mean something by an utterance, 'mit einer Äußerung etwas meinen', in the completely ordinary sense of that phrase, can, in German, be achieved without all intentions being, as Strawson put it, 'out in the open'. On the contrary, you can very well say that, for example, Apollo meant that the King would destroy his own kingdom, by saying 'If you cross that river, you'll destroy a mighty kingdom' to the poor consulting King (through the mouth of the Delphic Oracle). You can say that Apollo meant exactly this, even if he did not intend the King to arrive at that interpretation—in fact, even if he intended him to come to the false conclusion at which he (is said to have) actually arrived.

So, a German-speaking student of the Gricean analysis has to do without the aid of those conceptual intuitions that apparently underlie the Anglo-Saxon consensus that the famous so-called counterexamples (against the sufficiency of the analysans) given by Strawson and Schiffer earn their title. Unable to grasp it by virtue of his linguistic intuitions, he has to look for an explanation.[5] In doing this, one can rely on the assumption that the sort of (attempted) communication the Gricean analysis is about is hallmarked by (at least) two features: rationality of the process of communication and non-naturalness of the means used. Do the revisions account better for these features than the original analysis?

In the following consideration of this question I restrict myself to cases where the desired reaction of the audience consists in believing a certain state of affairs to obtain, i.e. I shall often talk of the conditions listed below as if they were the conditions of the original Gricean analysans.

[5] I have learnt that the above remarks tend to be understood as if I took the Gricean analysis to be a semantical analysis of the English word 'meaning'. But, of course, I do not, as will become apparent later on. The assumption—by now, I have reason to think, the mistaken assumption—underlying these remarks was that the English word 'meaning' may point somewhat more naturally to the phenomenon of human interaction which Grice's analysis is about than its German counterpart does.

[2] (1) $I_S(B_A(p))$
     (2) $I_S(B_A(I_S(B_A(p))))$
     (3) $I_S(B_A(I_S(B_A(p)))\backsim B_A(p))$

To take the non-naturalness factor first: The Gricean analysis is designed
to reveal what it is for arbitrary actions or action-products to stand
(on a certain occasion) in a non-natural meaning relation to any state of
affairs. Put in a dangerously different way, one might be tempted to say
that the analysis is designed to tell us what non-natural meaning is. Now
some stupid fellow might reason as follows: 'According to Grice, (S's
uttering) x had a non-natural meaning iff x was uttered with the three
intentions of the original analysans. But given these intentions, (S's
uttering) x still has a natural meaning, namely that S intends A to
believe that p. Since it is non-natural meaning we are after, let us see
what we can do about that. Well, we could repeat the trick and treat
the complete first clause of [2] just the way we treated "p" in [2]'.
Then he would get [3].

[3] (2) $I_S(B_A(I_S(B_A(p))))$
     (4) $I_S(B_A(I_S(B_A(I_S(B_A(p))))))$
     (7) $I_S(B_A(I_S(B_A(I_S(B_A(p))))))\backsim B_A(I_S(B_A(p))))$

The problem of non-naturalness would then have reached clause
(2), and he could proceed in the same way to overcome it. And so on,
for ever and ever. This could be called *Trying-to-Get-Rid-of-Naturalness-
by-Shifting-It*. But all this is obviously nonsense: first, the alleged
problem is not solved but only displaced (even if infinitely many
times) and, second, the whole 'problem' rests upon a misconception,
since things have neither natural nor non-natural meanings *simpliciter*,
rather one and the same thing can (on the same occasion) have
something as a non-natural meaning and some other things as natural
meanings.[6] [2] is designed to reveal the conditions which must be
satisfied for x (as uttered by S) to stand in a non-natural meaning
relation to p; but this is of course fully compatible with x being used
on that occasion as a natural sign for the fact that one or the other of
these conditions is satisfied.

Nobody commits howlers like these, so Trying-to-Get-Rid-of-
Naturalness-by-Shifting-It could not be the name of the game played
by the intention-increasers.

---

[6] Actually, one deep philosophical point of Grice's account is just that non-
natural meaning is, after all, nothing but a certain kind of natural meaning.

As regards the rationality factor, it is a remarkable trait of the analysis that the route by which the audience is supposed to be led to the desired reaction is intended to be rational, if only in the weak sense of being produced or supported by reasons (which may or may not be good reasons). Clause (3) brings in the aspect of rationality; the belief that S intends him to believe that p is intended to give A (the missing) part of a *reason* to believe that p. If everything works out nicely, A comes to believe that p for a reason. Now someone might, stupidly, reason as follows: 'By now, the analysans secures that A comes to believe that p rationally. But furthermore he is intended to come to believe that S intends him to believe that p. It is not yet secured that he comes to believe *that* rationally too. What can one do? Well, I could easily secure that along the same lines. The original analysis suggests that the scheme given in [4]—sometimes referred to as the Gricean Mechanism (GM)—is supposed by S to be satisfied by A.

[4] $B_A(I_S(B_A(p))) \top B_A(I_S(B_A(p))) \leadsto B_A(p)$

  $B_A(p)$

A's belief that p has been 'rationalized' by supposing that A believes that S intends him to believe that p, and by supposing furthermore that this second, complex belief provides for him a rational basis for the transition to the belief that p. I could rationalize A's belief that S intends him to believe that p by doing with that complex belief exactly what I just did with the belief that p'.—Repeating the trick yields [5].

[5] $\vdots$ $\vdots$

$B_A(I_S(B_A(I_S(B_A(p))))) \top B_A(I_S(B_A(I_S(B_A(p))))) \leadsto B_A(I_S(B_A(p)))$

  $B_A(I_S(B_A(p))) \top B_A(I_S(B_A(p))) \leadsto B_A(p)$

    $B_A(p)$

The problem of rationalizing would then have reached the belief which is represented at the topmost left in [5]. Boringly enough, he could go on repeating that trick for ever and ever. (That is what the dots are intended to indicate.) And if he were somehow to ascribe to S the intention to let A make all those transitions, he would *ipso facto* ascribe to S the intention to give A all the reasons for finally coming to believe that p. This could be called *Trying-to-Secure-Rationality-by-Endless-Complication*.

What is wrong with that? Before giving the obvious answer to this question, let me mention a certain harmless feature of this procedure.

On the right hand side of the [5] scheme there will appear more and more premisses that are not rationally founded. Hence, one could think that the problem of rationalizing is, so to say, only shifted from the left to the right and is therefore not solved at all. But this difficulty can easily be overcome just by S's crediting A wih the relevant *trust* in S. Just let S ascribe to A something like the following belief: 'Whatever S intends me (now, of certain things, for example his intentions, etc.) to believe, is the case.'[7] There seems nothing wrong *in principle* with letting S ascribe to A such a belief or open set of beliefs. (But then, of course, not everyone who communicates is like this speaker; and not every audience is like A is thought to be by S.)

The problems with the scheme obviously lie on its left-hand side. It is simply impossible to rationalize *all* of A's left-hand side beliefs in the suggested way—since a *regressus ad infinitum* fails to rationalize anything. At least one right-hand side belief must be rationalized in some other way; why not take one of a low level of intricacy, i.e. one with some degree of intelligibility and credibility? Having resort to higher-order beliefs, therefore, is only of apparent help since it does not solve the problem of rationalization but only displaces it—even if infinitely far away.

Moreover, an infinitely large part of the superstructure over the GM indicated in [5] must be completely superfluous. For one of these higher-order beliefs on the left-hand side of [5] must be rationalized by being connected with (S's doing) x without there being beliefs of still-higher order that, together with the relevant trust, render this connection rational along the considered regressive lines. That means, the truth of at least one of the statements listed in [6] must not (even partially) be due to the truth of a following one. ('x_S' is short for 'S does (or utters) x'.)

[7] Trust is not the only thing that could support the right-hand side of [5]. A's appropriate conditional beliefs—'If $I_S(B_A(p))$, then p', 'If $I_S(B_A(I_S(B_A(p))))$, then $I_S(B_A(p))$', etc.—could be backed up in some other way. Accordingly, in cases where the desired reaction is the performance of a certain action, the rational back up for A's wanting to perform this action conditionally upon his believing that S wants him to do this need not necessarily contain even a remote component of co-operation. It may even be that both want to harm each other. But cases of communication where the speaker relies on the GM but not on A's trust or A's (belief in S's) co-operativeness obviously run counter to the spirit of Grice's ideas. By adding some fussy supplementary conditions to the analysans we could eliminate such unintended cases of meaning. But this, in my opinion, would be to do them too much honour. I would prefer to accept them as cases of meaning, although as admittedly weird ones. I do not think it to be the task of the analysis to cover only those cases which *epitomize* Gricean meaning. (A little more about this below.)

[6] $x_S \leadsto B_A(I_S(B_A(p)))$

$x_S \leadsto B_A(I_S(B_A(I_S(B_A(p)))))$

$x_S \leadsto B_A(I_S(B_A(I_S(B_A(I_S(B_A(p)))))))$

$\vdots$

Together with the statement that S utters x, each of these statements would get the scheme of [5] going; of course, different statements would get it going at different points, with different degrees of nestedness, intricacy and, therefore, intelligibility and credibility. But at some point the utterance must get in touch with the left-hand side of [5] and then, with the assistance of the right-hand-side statements it goes all down the line to the desired belief that p.

Well, at least one of the connections represented by the statements listed in [6] must be provided—but which one? One answer says: all of them. This is as bold as it is bad since it eliminates the difference between (*a*) what A comes to believe by reasoning (and thereby relying on the conditional beliefs backing up the right-hand side of the scheme), and (*b*) what he obtains in a different way. In fact, this answer makes the whole right-hand side (except the bottom point) completely superfluous. We would obtain every belief on the left-hand side (except the one that p) without the assistance of the right-hand side in a purely rational way. But if S is able to produce the desired belief that $I_S(B_A(p))$ in A directly and still rationally, there is no point in his intending to produce other—and more complicated—beliefs which, after all, were only introduced to secure rationality of that desired belief.

Let me try to illustrate that point.

[7] names of routes   names of islands

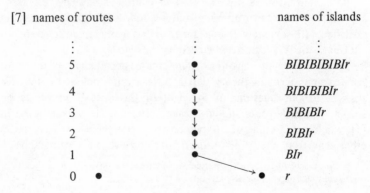

What is found in [7] is part of a map of the Sea of Communication. S is on the island with no name (bottom left) and he wants to go to the island r. The direct way to r is over troubled water, and as we all know: When the water is rough, the sailing is tough. But S wants to do it nice and easy. The island called '*Blr*' has a bridge connecting it with r. The bridges there are called 'rational connections', and one can walk over them only in the direction indicated by the arrow. The water between S's island and any island except r is so calm that S could use his small boat, called 'x'; but if he wanted to go to r directly he would have to use a heavy ship (called 'Natural Evidence'), and this would cause a lot of inconvenience which S prefers to avoid.

Let me mention some alien terminology to be found in theories about travelling in the Sea of Communication. Moving is called 'intending' over there, and the several routes one can take from S's island to r have specific names. Taking route 0 is called 'providing Natural Evidence for p' (p, of course, being the capital of r). Taking route 1—i.e. going to *Blr* and using the bridge to r—is called 'gricing'. Taking any other way (except route 0, of course) is called 'disgricing'. Various forms of disgricing are to be distinguished. In particular, to make one's way on route 2 is called 'to strawson'; but, to be careful, by saying of someone that he strawsons, one leaves it undetermined how he comes from *BlBlr* to *Blr*. To take route 2 and thereby going down on the bridges —i.e. to strawson in a special way—is called 'to schiffer in the first degree'; taking route 3 and using all three bridges downwards is accordingly called 'to schiffer in the second degree', and so on. One schiffers in the last degree if one moves up to an indefinitely, in fact, to an infinitely remote island, and if on one's long way down to r one crosses all the bridges.

To be sure, no one was ever seen to schiffer in any degree. Taking any other route than route 1 would mean a lot of trouble one could easily avoid;[8] somehow it appears to be altogether pointless, and to schiffer in the last degree is obviously impossible.

Before I close this chapter of tendentious geography and return to less frivolous meaning-theory, let us have a brief look at the possible answers to our queston. In the light of this analogy our question becomes, 'Which route should S take?' The infinite scheme given in [5] would require one of the two answers: 'He should take all routes other than 0 at once', and—apparently somewhat less demanding—

---

[8] 'Don't schiffer, if you can grice', and 'No kicks on route 66', these two sayings among foreign sailors come as no surprise.

'He should take the outermost route'; or, in the foreign tongue, 'He should grice and he should schiffer in all degrees', and 'He should schiffer in the last degree' respectively.

It is clear enough that these answers are not acceptable, and since nobody commits humbug like this, Trying-to-Secure-Rationality-by-Indefinite-Complication could not be the name of the game played by the intention-multipliers. But it is not yet clear at all how this problem, namely, at which point the utterance should get in touch with A's beliefs, is to be solved. We shall return to that question in a moment, when we have considered a third hypothesis about the causes of Multiple Intentionitis. Let me briefly sum up what we had before our side trip to the Sea of Communication.

As I take it, the Gricean analysis of the concept of utterer's or speaker's meaning is designed to be part of an analysis of one characteristic sort of human communication—that of rational communication by means of something that stands in a non-natural-meaning relation to what is communicated. The two crucial aspects of this enterprise —i.e. non-naturalness and rationality—do not seem to fare any better in the revisions that are overburdened with intentions than in the original analysis itself. Therefore, by now we have no rational, much less a natural (but that does not mean we have a non-natural) support for the introduction of further intentions.

The third diagnosis says that the *only* point of adding further intentions is to remove certain nice stories that are called 'counter-examples against the analysis'. But what is the point of those counter-examples? In the counter-exemplary stories, S invariably intends his audience to make at least one false assumption of an easily specifiable kind. So, for at least one true proposition of that kind, S invariably intends his audience not to come to believe it. Let us call those intentions *D-intentions* (from 'deceive') and *C-intentions* (from 'conceal') respectively. And let us say that both sorts of intentions are *bad*, whereas all intentions so far ascribed to S are *good*. In Strawson's counter-exemplary story, S satisfies the conditions of the original analysans; (4_1)–(4_5) represent what in addition is relevantly true in this story.

$$
\begin{aligned}
&(4_0)\ I_S(B_A(I_S(B_A(I_S(\neg r_A))))) \\
&(4_1)\ I_S(B_A(I_S(B_A(\neg I_S(r_A))))) \\
&(4_2)\ I_S(B_A(I_S(\neg B_A(I_S(r_A))))) \\
&(4_3)\ I_S(B_A(\neg I_S(B_A(I_S(r_A)))))
\end{aligned}
\quad\Bigg\}\quad D\text{-intentions}
$$

(4_4) $I_S(\neg B_A(I_S(B_A(I_S(r_A)))))$ *C*-intention
(4_5) $\neg I_S(B_A(I_S(B_A(I_S(r_A)))))$ no intention at all
    [(4_0) entails (4_1); (4_1) entails (4_2); etc.]

(Forget about (4_0); for our purposes it does not matter whether or not it is true in the story.) S having bad intentions is obviously nothing that detracts from the non-natural aspect of his trying to communicate. But how about the aspect of rationality? Firstly, the rationality of S's uttering x (in order to get A via the GM to do r) is clearly not impaired. Secondly, S's having such bad intentions need in no way affect the rationality of the process by which A is (supposed to be) led to do r; i.e. the original GM may—and, I suppose, usually will—work without A's relying on $I_S(B_A(I_S(r_A)))$. For, (a) it may well be that A, in the face of S's doing x, has reason to believe that $I_S(r_A)$, quite independently of his having the belief that $I_S(B_A(I_S(r_A)))$. And, (b) it is obvious that A's potential belief that $I_S(B_A(I_S(r_A)))$ has nothing to do with the rationality of A doing r conditionally on his believing that $I_S(r_A)$. So, S having bad intentions is fully compatible with its being the case that

(a) $x_S \smallsmile B_A(I_S(r_A))$,
(b) $B_A(I_S(r_A)) \smallsmile r_A$,   and
(c) S, in uttering x, relies on (a) and (b) being true.

So it is sufficient for the *success* of the communicative attempt that A is rational and fulfils the GM-conditions. The success does not depend on S's intentions being 'out in the open'.[9] The reason is simply this: if A comes to believe that $I_S(r_A)$ and this belief—given the background of his desires and other beliefs—is all he needs to come to do r, then any further speaker's intentions—good or bad, open or hidden—will be idle; success would be neither supported nor hampered by them or their being recognized. Hence in this sense, bad intentions do not (necessarily) detract from rationality (and success) in communication as envisaged by Grice.

At least on my interpretation, non-naturalness and rationality are by far the most important features of the sort of communication Grice's analysis is designed to account for. Therefore, at least on my interpretation, the point of those counterexamples cannot be very important. In fact, their point seems to be a 'moral' one:

[9] Cf. Schiffer (1982, p. 121) for an explicit claim to the contrary.

in communicating, one should have only good intentions. Strawson, Schiffer, and Grice—if only provisionally in his first revision of the original analysis —concluded that one should add the negation of (4_5) to the original analysans in order to get rid of this counterexample. That is, they required S to have the further intention (4). This way of dealing with counterexamples can be called *Getting-Rid-of-Bad-Intentions-by-Demanding-Good-Ones*; and I believe that this, at last, is the real name of the one and only game played by the intention-increasers.

But fortunately one does not need to join that game, since one can easily remove all those counterexamples by just forbidding S to have any bad intention instead. In fact, Grice, in his second revision of the original analysis, and Bennett in his book *Linguistic Behaviour*, proceeded along this much more intelligible and credible line, but there are still some difficulties about how they did it exactly. For the sake of brevity I will omit details, but just say that Grice did it a little too weakly—i.e. his method still allows for some bad intentions—and Bennett did it a little (but only *a very* little) too strongly—he in effect excludes some intentions that are not bad at all.[10] I prefer to do it by ruling out all and only C-intentions and thereby, *a fortiori*, all D-intentions as well. This can be achieved in the following way. The notion of a *Gricean p-sentence* is first defined ('*' stands for any number of negation-symbols):

> '*p' is a Gricean p-sentence;
> if s is a Gricean p-sentence, then '*I_S(*$B_A(s)$)' is
> one as well; and
> nothing else is a Gricean p-sentence.

Now let us say that S, in uttering x, is *in no way deceitful or secretive* towards A with respect to p iff it is not the case that S wants (and, *a fortiori*, it is not the case that he intends) A not to believe any proposition expressed by a true Gricean p-sentence. Then all counterexamples of the sort considered can be removed by adding the following to the original analysans:

(4*) In uttering x, S was in no way deceitful or secretive
      towards A with respect to (1)–(3).

The Gricean analysis of utterer's meaning is guided by three imperatives: Denaturalize! Rationalize! Moralize! To increase intentions

---

[10] For the details omitted, see Kemmerling (1980).

beyond the frame of the original analysis supports neither denaturalization nor rationalization, and it is a much too strong—and therefore a bad—way of moralizing. So, I conclude that we can remove all those horribly intricate intentions without losing anything essential to the Gricean analysis. In fact, I propose we just drop them; if you feel like moralizing, add clause (4*).

RECONSTRUCTION

So the revisions do not seem to be necessary, but a reconstruction may be helpful. In the last part of this paper I want to present a reconstruction of the original Gricean analysis in which the notion of doing something with a certain intention (or intending something by doing something) does not appear as a primitive concept. This reconstruction is mainly inspired by two things: first, in the discussion of the Gricean ideas the word 'intention' is used somewhat excessively and indistinctly, sometimes referring to beliefs and desires rather than to intentions properly so called. It should be possible to do a bit better. Second, from a more articulate account of the original analysans one could expect support for a substantial justification of the complex intentions. When he introduced them, Grice (1957) justified (the ascription of) these intentions by way of counterexamples, but there was no explanation of why S had these intentions when all he wanted was, after all, to produce a certain reaction in his audience. A 'substantial' justification would, at least, have to specify the further conditions which make S's complex intentions plausible in the light of his basic desire to get A to do r. The following reconstruction is designed to suggest what such a justification might look like.

The lines along which it proceeds are given by the following six conditions which I take to be (non-trivially) sufficient for 'S does x with the intention (or thereby intending) to bring it about that p'.[11]

(a) S does x.
(b) S wants that p.
(c) S believes that: p given that he does x.
(d) S does not believe that: p given that he does not x.
(e) There is no state of affairs q such that S wants that not-q and S believes that: q given that he does x.
(f) If (b)–(e) were not fulfilled, (a) would not be either.

[11] This is to be taken with a pinch of salt, since any niceties are avoided once again—even important ones such as deviant causal chains.

The fourth condition may appear unnecessarily strong, but '*S* believes that: . . . given that —' is taken to contain an 'other-things-being-equal' component: *S*'s beliefs are viewed as they are at a certain time *t* (which is not mentioned explicitly), and that he believes that: . . . given that —, says that if the belief that — were added (let's say at *t'*) to his *otherwise unaltered* body of beliefs, then the belief that . . . would also be one of his beliefs at *t'*.

Let me now introduce those conditions (again, informally abbreviated) that in my opinion, form the essentials of the Gricean analysis. I call them the *core* of the analysis.

(i) $W_S(r_A)$
(ii) $B_S(r_A//B_A(W_S(r_A)))$
(iii) $B_S(B_A(W_S(r_A))//x_S)$
(iv) $\neg B_S(r_A/\neg B_A(W_S(r_A)) \ \& \ x_S)$
(v) $\neg B_S(r_A/\neg x_S)$

'$W_S(-)$' is short for '*S* wants that —'; '$B_S(. . ./-)$' is short for '*S* believes that: . . . given that —'; '$B_S(\phi_Y(-)//. . .)$' is short for '$B_S(\phi_Y(-)/. . .)$ and *S* believes that . . . is at least part of a reason for *Y* to ϕ that —. And accordingly for '$B_S(r_A//. . .)$'.

Some brief comments on (ii), (iii), and (iv): In a case of Gricean meaning, *S* believes that *r* is under *A*'s rational control; i.e. he believes that *A* does *r* iff he has reason to do so. Maybe the most ingenious aspect of the Gricean analysis is that *S* thinks that *A*'s recognition of *S*'s want gives *A* (the missing part of) a reason to do *r*. This is what (ii) says, namely that *S* believes that: *A* does *r* given that *A* believes that *S* wants him to do *r*, and that *S* believes that *A*—via some unspecified background assumptions and/or wants—is provided with a reason to do *r* by his belief that this is what *S* wants him to do. Let us say that a little more briefly: *S* believes that *A* does *r on the rational condition* that *A* believes that *S* wants him to do it. Furthermore, *S* believes that *A* will come to that belief on the rational condition that *S* does or utters *x*. This is what condition (iii) tells us. Once again, *S* relies on some unspecified background assumptions on *A*'s part. And I think it an advantage of the analysis to leave them unspecified, since it depends on various and variable factors *which* specific assumptions of this sort *S* can expect *A* to have. Among other things, that will depend on such factors as: whether *x* is a conventional means for producing the desired reaction, or whether it is not; whether A knows (or, at least, is supposed by S to know) S's habits of doing things like x, or whether he does not; whether A is (assumed by S to be) fairly clever in detecting the intentions underlying actions, or whether he is not; and so on. I regard it as a desirable feature of the Gricean analysis that it covers lots of different cases of that kind and is not restricted to cases where certain specified background assumptions (and maybe even wants) on A's part are given. So this is the answer to the queston where the connection between the utterance and A's beliefs should be located. One should demand only that x is rationally linked with A's belief that S wants him to do r—and that means linked by any old appropriate background assumptions on A's part that do this job. And one should not demand that these assumptions contain higher-order beliefs or beliefs about higher-order intentions since that would unnecessarily restrict the applicability of the concept in question.

Condition (iv) states that S does not believe that his doing x has a natural meaning for A that leads him to do r without regard for the fact that S wants him to. This condition is strong enough to deal with all the undesired cases considered in Grice's original work, for instance it excludes the Herod-example but allows for the example where a picture is drawn of Mr Y displaying undue familiarity with Mrs X. But it is exactly weak enough not to make the concept of meaning too narrow to be interesting for an account of common linguistic communication.[12]

Under the label '*accessories* of the Gricean analysis' I list the following three conditions:

> (vi) S prefers his doing x to all other means he believes to be at his disposal to get A to do r.

[12] The stronger requirement '$B_S(\neg r_A / \neg B_A(W_S(r_A)))$ & x_S)' would exclude, for example, the possibility of S's meaning anything if he believed that A acted on the strict and literal meaning of x even if that were inconsistent with what A recognized S as wanting A to do. In cases where the desired reaction is the adoption of a belief it would be irrational in normal circumstances for A to act like this, wilfully ignoring the intention. Hence such cases are excluded by the fact that rationality is required by (ii) and (iii). But no irrationality is necessarily involved in cases where the desired reaction is an action on A's part, although such behaviour would be very unhelpful. If an attitude of mutual co-operation is taken to be a further characteristic of Grice's account of meaning (and it would be not unreasonable to do so) then (iv) should be replaced by the stronger version above. But since there are cases of communication where co-operation is (assumed by S to be) conspicuous by its absence, I prefer to retain (iv), cleaving, in case of doubt, to the more austere reconstruction of the Gricean concept.

(vii) $\neg \exists q(W_S(\neg q) \& B_S(q/x_S))$
(viii) If any of the statements (i), (iii), (v)-(vii) were not true,
      S would not do x.

From the core and the accessories we can derive the following consequences:

(C1) $B_S(r_A/x_S)$ from (ii) and (iii)[13]
(C2) $W_S(B_A(W_S(r_A)))$ from (i), (ii), (iv), (vi) and (C1)
(C3) $\neg B_S(B_A(W_S(r_A))/\neg x_S)$ from (ii), (iii), and (v)

Along the lines of (b)-(f) it follows that if S does x, then he does so thereby intending that A do r and that A come to believe that S wants him to do r:

(i)	(C2)
(C1)	(iii)
(v)	(C3)
(vii)	(vii)
(viii)	(viii)
$x_S \rightarrow I_S(r_A)$	$x_S \rightarrow I_S(B_A(W_S(r_A)))$

From the core and the accessories it follows that S, if he is rational and there are no overriding wants, does x. So, core and accessories provide the premises of a practical argument that leads S to do x. These conditions entail that S, when he does x, does so with the intention that A do r and that A come to believe that S wants him to do r. This second, complex intention is a consequence of S's desire to get A to do r, together with his beliefs and preferences about how to achieve this. These conditions secure that S believes that A has all he needs for a fully rational transition from S's uttering x to his own doing r. Furthermore, they secure that S does not take (his uttering) x to have a natural meaning for A which could lead A to do r regardless of what S wants him to do. Therefore, in that sense, rationality and non-naturalness are secured. If you are fond of the moral aspect as well, I recommend you to include an appropriately modified version of clause (4*) among the conditions of the reconstructed analysans.

---

[13] Assuming that '$\neg B_S(\neg x_S/B_A(W_S(r_A)))$' is trivially true, if meaningful at all.

The reconstruction yields a modest concept of Gricean meaning.[14] Anything which was clearly less than this could not, I suppose, be called Gricean. But besides what is mentioned in note 12, there is at least one point where it might seem plausible to demand a little more, namely condition (ii). Let us briefly consider the case where the desired reaction is A's adoption of a certain belief. In this case S could be required to think that it is trust that accounts for A's satisfying the GM—trust in the sense that A relies on two things: (a) that S himself believes what he wants A to believe, and (b) that confidence can be put in the correctness of S's belief. An invitingly simple way of incorporating trust would be to let S rely on A's satisfying the following scheme:

$$[8] \quad x_S \sim B_A(W_S(B_A(p))) \sim B_A(B_S(p)) \sim B_A(p),$$

thereby assuming that S supposes the two intermediate beliefs to be obligatory way-stations on any route leading from x_S to $B_A(p)$: the first being obligatory on any route from x_S to the second, the second being obligatory on any route from the first to $B_A(p)$, and there being no route from x_S to $B_A(p)$ except via the second. From this, together with S's preference for x_S to anything else he could do to get A to believe that p, it would follow (in addition to the reconstruction above) that S wants A to have the second intermediate belief—i.e. it would follow that $W_S(B_A(B_S(p)))$. From this new derivative desire a further speaker's intention, namely $I_S(B_A(B_S(p)))$, would result.

The new core and the new accessories would clearly be more complex than the old ones. And the additional complexity of the new conditions could not be justified merely by the fact that they exclude certain unintended cases which would otherwise have to be accepted as cases of meaning under the old conditions. I know only one sort of such cases. In these S supposes the GM to work because of A's reliance on two things: (a) that S disbelieves what he wants A to believe, and, strangely enough, (b) that confidence can be put in S's being mistaken in his disbelief.[15] But the mere exclusion of such cases is clearly not

[14] Core and accessories are even an irrelevantly little bit weaker than the original analysans: the reconstructed complex intention is weaker than (2). But the absence of a third intention is not to be taken as an indication of a further difference in strength, since the original condition (3) is not to be construed as ascribing to S an intention of the sort that is characterized by (b)–(f). I think that (ii) together with (vi) express approximately what Grice meant by (3).

[15] In elaborating stories along these lines it must not be forgotten, firstly, that $B_A(W_S(B_A(p)))$ does not, in S's opinion, cease to be (an indispensable part of) A's reason for believing that p, and, secondly, that S has no bad intentions. These two points make it a little hard to invent credible stories of the relevant kind.

enough to justify the introduction of all the conditions necessary for deriving the third intention just mentioned, because the exclusion could be achieved by much weaker means, for example by just adding '$\neg B_S(\neg B_A(B_S(p))/x_S)$' to the old accessories. What is needed for justification is that in all intended cases one can plausibly ascribe to S the view indicated by [8]. It is not sufficient for this purpose, as Bennett has reminded us, that the view indicated by [8] is correct, but rather it must not be the case that S simply has no beliefs about the details of A's transition from $B_A(W_S(B_A(p))$ to $B_A(p)$—except, of course, that it is rational. Whether A's not lacking such specific beliefs can plausibly be assumed (by S) for all cases one might like to regard as cases of meaning, I will not try to decide here.

Much the same can be said about an additional requirement of co-operativeness in the case where the desired reaction is the performance of an action. In this case, the basic route (assumed by the speaker) might be thought to be roughly of the following kind: (a) the utterance leads A to believe that S wants him to perform action a, (b) this belief leads A to want to do a, and (c) this leads him to do a. A less sparse account should be expected to tell us something about S's reason to assume a transition of the kind referred to in (b). Analogous to the bizarre possibility just considered for the indicative case, there is a bundle of strange ways for (b) to be satisfied which might be thought of as desirable to exclude. In particular, there are the cases where S and A have conflicting underlying interests (they might even want to harm each other wherever possible) which—because of appropriately differing beliefs about the results of A's doing a—lead to a coincidentally common desire that A do a. So S might assume A to reason as follows: 'S wants me to do a; but as regards things like a, he doesn't know what is good for him (in fact, he has a reliable tendency to desire things that turn out to be bad for him); so, probably, it will be bad for him if I do a; that's why I want to do a'. S then has good reason to utter x in order to (a) let A know that he wants him to do a, (b) make A thereby want to do a, and, in consequence, (c) bring it about that A does a. And all of this might be 'out in the open' (and it might even be intended to be so); common or mutual knowledge of Lewis's of Schiffer's sort would not make any difference.

To block far-fetched eccentricities of this and similar kinds, (b) might be dropped in favour of something that requires an attitude of genuine co-operativeness between S and A. (This requirement should not be too strong. It should not be so narrow as to exclude various acceptably mild forms of *S*'s egoism or dominance and *A*'s altruism and obedience. Common interest might be the purest basis of co-operation, but it is hardly the only one.)

But once again, the possibly desirable exclusion of queer cases does not, by itself, compel us to introduce another speaker's intention into the analysis. It might well be enough to just not allow the speaker to rely on certain odd beliefs.

So the moral of this is that not every 'counterexample' points to an additional speaker's intention, since any such intention arises only from the speaker's belief that a certain state of affairs must be brought about in order to satisfy his basic communicative desire by his preferred means. And obviously not everybody who means something by what he does, can be admired for having all, or even most of, the insights into the workings of rational communication which we owe to Paul Grice.[16]

REFERENCES

Bennett, Jonathan, *Linguistic Behaviour*, Cambridge University Press, Cambridge, 1976.

Grice, Paul, 'Meaning', *Philosophical Review*, 66 (1957), pp. 377–88.

——, 'Utterer's Meaning and Intentions', *Philosophical Review*, 78, (1969), pp. 147–77.

——, 'Meaning Revisited' (unpublished).

Kemmerling, Andreas, 'Was Grice mit "Meinen" meint' in G. Grewendorf (ed.), *Sprechakttheorie und Semantik*, Frankfurt a. M., 1979, pp. 67–118.

——, 'How Many Things Must a Speaker Intend/ (Before He is Said to Have Meant)?' *Erkenntnis*, 15 (1980), pp. 333–41.

Lewis, David, *Convention*, Cambridge, Mass., 1969.

Loar, Brian, *Mind and Meaning*, Cambridge, 1981.

[16] A somewhat different version of this paper was read at the conference on *The Theory of Language Use*, Bielefeld, in June 1979. I have benefited from discussions with Jonathan Bennett, Uli Blau, Brian Loar, Georg Meggle, Eike von Savigny, Stephen Schiffer, Tim Tillmann and, especially, Wolfgang Spohn. Thanks to all of them, as well as to Jay Rosenberg and Mark Helme for linguistic help and in particular for curbing my Rock'n Roll prose.

Two papers containing more recent reflections of Grice and Schiffer on the topic—Grice (unpublished) and Schiffer (1982)—came to my attention too late to take them into account here. Let me just mention that Schiffer seems sensitive to two points of criticism I put forward here: first, that the attribution of infinitely complex attitudes to a speaker is at least problematic, and, second, that some of the speaker's attitudes usually referred to as ('secondary') intentions might more properly be called beliefs. Cf. Schiffer (1982, pp. 121 and 125). However, there still remains considerable disagreement on other points.

Meggle, Georg, *Grundbegriffe der Kommunikation*, Berlin/New York 1981.

Schiffer, Stephen R., *Meaning*, Oxford University Press, Oxford, 1972.

——, 'Intention-Based Semantics', *Notre Dame Journal of Formal Logic*, 23 (1982), pp. 119–56.

Strawson, P. F., 'Intention and Convention in Speech Acts', *Philosophical Review*, 73 (1964), pp. 439–60.

5

A NICE DERANGEMENT OF EPITAPHS

DONALD DAVIDSON

Goodman Ace wrote radio sitcoms. According to Mark Singer, Ace often talked the way he wrote:

Rather than take for granite that Ace talks straight, a listener must be on guard for an occasional entre nous and me . . . or a long face no see. In a roustabout way, he will maneuver until he selects the ideal phrase for the situation, hitting the nail right on the thumb. The careful conversationalist might try to mix it up with him in a baffle of wits. In quest of this pinochle of success, I have often wrecked my brain for a clowning achievement, but Ace's chickens always come home to roast. From time to time, Ace will, in a jerksome way, monotonize the conversation with witticisms too humorous to mention. It's high noon someone beat him at his own game, but I have never done it; cross my eyes and hope to die, he always wins thumbs down.[1]

I quote at length because philosophers have tended to neglect or play down the sort of language-use this passage illustrates. For example, Jonathan Bennett writes,

I doubt if I have ever been present when a speaker did something like shouting 'Water!' as a warning of fire, knowing what 'Water!' means and knowing that his hearers also knew, but thinking that they would expect him to give to 'Water!' the normal meaning of 'Fire!'[2]

Bennett adds that, 'Although such things could happen, they seldom do.' I think such things happen all the time; in fact, if the conditions are generalized in a natural way, the phenomenon is ubiquitous.

Singer's examples are special in several ways. A malapropism does not have to be amusing or surprising. It does not have to be based on a cliché, and of course it does not have to be intentional. There need be no play on words, no hint of deliberate pun. We may smile at someone

---

[1] *The New Yorker*, 4 April 1977, p. 56. Reprinted by permission, © 1977, The New Yorker Magazine, Inc.

[2] Jonathan Bennett, *Linguistic Behavior*, Cambridge, 1976, p. 186.

who says 'Lead the way and we'll precede', or, with Archie Bunker, 'We need a few laughs to break up the monogamy', because he has said something that, given the usual meanings of the words, is ridiculous or fun. But the humour is adventitious.

Ace's malaprops generally make some sort of sense when the words are taken in the standard way, as in 'Familiarity breeds attempt', or 'We're all cremated equal', but this is not essential ('the pinochle of success'). What is interesting is the fact that in all these cases the hearer has no trouble understanding the speaker in the way the speaker intends.

It is easy enough to explain this feat on the hearer's part: the hearer realizes that the 'standard' interpretation cannot be the intended interpretation; through ignorance, inadvertence, or design the speaker has used a word similar in sound to the word that would have 'correctly' expressed his meaning. The absurdity or inappropriateness of what the speaker would have meant had his words been taken in the 'standard' way alerts the hearer to trickery or error; the similarity in sound tips him off to the right interpretation. Of course there are many other ways the hearer might catch on; similarity of sound is not essential to the malaprop. Nor for that matter does the general case require that the speaker use a real word: most of 'The Jabberwock' is intelligible on first hearing.

It seems unimportant, so far as understanding is concerned, who makes a mistake, or whether there is one. When I first read Singer's piece on Goodman Ace, I thought that the word 'malaprop', though the name of Sheridan's character, was not a common noun that could be used in place of 'malapropism'. It turned out to be my mistake. Not that it mattered: I knew what Singer meant, even though I was in error about the word; I would have taken his meaning in the same way if he had been in error instead of me. We could both have been wrong and things would have gone as smoothly.

This talk of error or mistake is not mysterious nor open to philosophical suspicions. I was wrong about what a good dictionary would say, or what would be found by polling a pod of experts whose taste or training I trust. But error or mistake of this kind, with its associated notion of correct usage, is not philosophically interesting. We want a deeper notion of what words, when spoken in context, mean; and like the shallow notion of correct usage, we want the deep concept to distinguish between what a speaker, on a given occasion, means, and what his words mean. The widespread existence of malapropisms and their kin threatens the distinction, since here the intended meaning seems to take over from the standard meaning.

I take for granted, however, that nothing should be allowed to obliterate or even blur the distinction between speaker's meaning and literal meaning. In order to preserve the distinction we must, I shall argue, modify certain commonly accepted views about what it is to 'know a language', or about what a natural language is. In particular, we must pry apart what is literal in language from what is conventional or established.

Here is a preliminary stab at characterizing what I have been calling literal meaning. The term is too incrusted with philosophical and other extras to do much work, so let me call what I am interested in *first meaning*. The concept applies to words and sentences as uttered by a particular speaker on a particular occasion. But if the occasion, the speaker, and the audience are 'normal' or 'standard' (in a sense not to be further explained here), then the first meaning of an utterance will be what should be found by consulting a dictionary based on actual usage (such as Webster's Third). Roughly speaking, first meaning comes first in the order of interpretation. We have no chance of explaining the image in the following lines, for example, unless we know what 'foison' meant in Shakespeare's day:

> Speak of the spring and foison of the year,
> The one doth shadow of your beauty show,
> The other as your bounty doth appear . . .[3]

Little here is to be taken literally, but unless we know the literal, or first, meaning of the words we do not grasp and cannot explain the image.

But 'the order of interpretation' is not at all clear. For there are cases where we may first guess at the image and so puzzle out the first meaning. This might happen with the word 'tires' in the same sonnet:

> On Helen's cheek all art of beauty set,
> And you in Grecian tires are painted new.

And of course it often happens that we can descry the literal meaning of a word or phrase by first appreciating what the speaker was getting at.

A better way to distinguish first meaning is through the intentions of the speaker. The intentions with which an act is performed are usually

[3] Shakespeare, Sonnet 53.

unambiguously ordered by the relation of means to ends (where this relation may or may not be causal). Thus the poet wants (let us say) to praise the beauty and generosity of his patron. He does this by using images that say the person addressed takes on every good aspect to be found in nature or in man or woman. This he does in turn by using the word 'tire' to mean 'attire' and the word 'foison' to mean 'harvest'. The order established here by 'by' can be reversed by using the phrase 'in order to'. In the 'in order to' sequence, first meaning is the first meaning referred to. ('With the intention of' with 'ing' added to the verb does as well.)

Suppose Diogenes utters the words 'I would have you stand from between me and the sun' (or their Greek equivalent) with the intention of uttering words that will be interpreted by Alexander as true if and only if Diogenes would have him stand from between Diogenes and the sun, and this with the intention of asking Alexander to move from between him and the sun, and this with the intention of getting Alexander to move from between him and the sun, and this with the intention of leaving a good anecdote to posterity. Of course these are not the only intentions involved; there will also be the Gricean intentions to achieve certain of these ends through Alexander's recognition of some of the intentions involved. Diogenes' intention to be interpreted in a certain way requires such a self-referring intention, as does his intention to ask Alexander to move. In general, the first intention in the sequence to require this feature specifies the first meaning.

Because a speaker necessarily intends first meaning to be grasped by his audience, and it is grasped if communication succeeds, we lose nothing in the investigation of first meaning if we concentrate on the knowledge or ability a hearer must have if he is to interpret a speaker. What the speaker knows must correspond to something the interpreter knows if the speaker is to be understood, since if the speaker is understood he has been interpreted as he intended to be interpreted. The abilities of the speaker that go beyond what is required of an interpreter —invention and motor control—do not concern me here.

Nothing said so far limits first meaning to language; what has been characterized is (roughly) Grice's non-natural meaning, which applies to any sign or signal with an intended interpretation. What should be added if we want to restrict first meaning to linguistic meaning? The usual answer would, I think, be that in the case of language the hearer shares a complex system or theory with the speaker, a system which makes possible the articulation of logical relations between utterances, and explains the ability to interpret novel utterances in an organized way.

This answer has been suggested, in one form or another, by many philosophers and linguists, and I assume it must in some sense be right. The difficulty lies in getting clear about what this sense is. The particular difficulty with which I am concerned in this paper (for there are plenty of others) can be brought out by stating three plausible principles concerning first meaning in language: we may label them by saying they require that first meaning be systematic, shared, and prepared.

(1) First meaning is systematic. A competent speaker or interpreter is able to interpret utterances, his own or those of others, on the basis of the semantic properties of the parts, or words, in the utterance, and the structure of the utterance. For this to be possible, there must be systematic relations between the meanings of utterances.

(2) First meanings are shared. For speaker and interpreter to communicate successfully and regularly, they must share a method of interpretation of the sort described in (1).

(3) First meanings are governed by learned conventions or regularities. The systematic knowledge or competence of the speaker or interpreter is learned in advance of occasions of interpretation and is conventional in character.

Probably no one doubts that there are difficulties with these conditions. Ambiguity is an example: often the 'same' word has more than one semantic role, and so the interpretation of utterances in which it occurs is not uniquely fixed by the features of the interpreter's competence so far mentioned. Yet, though the verbal and other features of the context of utterance often determine a correct interpretation, it is not easy or perhaps even possible to specify clear rules for disambiguation. There are many more questions about what is required of the competent interpreter. It does not seem plausible that there is a strict rule fixing the occasions on which we should attach significance to the order in which conjoined sentences appear in a conjunction: the difference between 'They got married and had a child' and 'They had a child and got married'. Interpreters certainly can make these distinctions. But part of the burden of this paper is that much that they can do ought not to count as part of their basic *linguistic* competence. The contrast in what is meant or implied by the use of 'but' instead of 'and' seems to me another matter, since no amount of common sense unaccompanied by linguistic lore would enable an interpreter to figure it out.

Paul Grice has done more than anyone else to bring these problems to our attention and to help sort them out. In particular, he has shown why it is essential to distinguish between the literal meaning (perhaps what I am calling first meaning) of words and what is often implied (or implicated) by someone who uses those words. He has explored the general principles behind our ability to figure out such implicatures, and these principles must, of course, be known to speakers who expect to be taken up on them. Whether knowledge of these principles ought to be included in the description of linguistic competence may not have to be settled: on the one hand they are things a clever person could often figure out without previous training or exposure and they are things we could get along without. On the other hand they represent a kind of skill we expect of an interpreter and without which communication would be greatly impoverished.

I dip into these matters only to distinguish them from the problem raised by malapropisms and the like. The problems touched on in the last two paragraphs all concern the ability to interpret words and constructions of the kind covered by our conditions (1)-(3); the questions have been what is required for such interpretation, and to what extent various competencies should be considered linguistic. Malapropisms introduce expressions not covered by prior learning, or familiar expressions which cannot be interpreted by any of the abilities so far discussed. Malapropisms fall into a different category, one that may include such things as our ability to perceive a well-formed sentence when the actual utterance was incomplete or grammatically garbled, our ability to interpret words we have never heard before, to correct slips of the tongue, or to cope with new idiolects. These phenomena threaten standard descriptions of linguistic competence (including descriptions for which I am responsible).

How should we understand or modify (1)-(3) to accommodate malapropisms? Principle (1) requires a competent interpreter to be prepared to interpret utterances of sentences he or she has never hear uttered before. This is possible because the interpreter can learn the semantic role of each of a finite number of words or phrases and can learn the semantic consequences of a finite number of modes of composition. This is enough to account for the ability to interpret utterances of novel sentences. And since the modes of composition can be iterated, there is no clear upper limit to the number of sentences utterances of which can be interpreted. The interpreter thus has a system for interpreting what he hears or says. You might think of this system as a machine which, when fed an arbitrary utterance (and certain parameters provided by the circumstances of the utterance), produces an interpretation. One model for such a machine is a theory of truth, more or less along the lines of a Tarski truth definition. It provides a recursive characterization of the truth conditions of all possible utterances of the speaker, and it does this through an analysis of utterances in terms of sentences made up from the finite vocabulary and the finite stock of modes of composition. I have frequently argued that command of such a theory would suffice for interpretation.[4] Here however there is no reason to be concerned with the details of the theory that can adequately model the ability of an interpreter. All that matters in the present discussion is that the theory has a finite base and is recursive, and these are features on which most philosophers and linguists agree.

To say that an explicit theory for interpreting a speaker is a model of the interpreter's linguistic competence is not to suggest that the interpreter knows any such theory. It is possible, of course, that most interpreters could be brought to acknowledge that they know some of the axioms of a theory of truth; for example, that a conjunction is true if and only if each of the conjuncts is true. And perhaps they also know theorems of the form 'An utterance of the sentence "There is life on Mars" is true if and only if there is life on Mars at the time of the utterance.' On the other hand, no one now has explicit knowledge of a fully satisfactory theory for interpreting the speakers of any natural language.

In any case, claims about what would constitute a satisfactory theory are not, as I said, claims about the propositional knowledge of an interpreter, nor are they claims about the details of the inner workings of some part of the brain. They are rather claims about what must be said to give a satisfactory description of the competence of the interpreter. *We* cannot describe what an interpreter can do except by appeal to a recursive theory of a certain sort. It does not add anything to this thesis to say that if the theory does correctly describe the competence of an interpreter, some mechanism in the interpreter must correspond to the theory.

Principle (2) says that for communication to succeed, a systematic method of interpretation must be shared. (I shall henceforth assume there is no harm in calling such a method a theory, as if the interpreter were using the theory we use to describe his competence.) The sharing comes to this: the interpreter uses his theory to understand the speaker;

[4] See the essays on radical interpretation in my *Inquiries into Truth and Interpretation*, Oxford, 1984.

the speaker uses the same (or an equivalent) theory to guide his speech. For the speaker, it is a theory about how the interpreter will interpret him. Obviously this principle does not demand that speaker and interpreter speak the same language. It is an enormous convenience that many people speak in similar ways, and therefore can be interpreted in more or less the same way. But in principle communication does not demand that any two people speak the same language. What must be shared is the interpreter's and the speaker's understanding of the speaker's words.

For reasons that will emerge, I do not think that principles (1) and (2) are incompatible with the existence of malapropisms; it is only when they are combined with principle (3) that there is trouble. Before dicussing principle (3) directly, however, I want to introduce an apparent diversion.

The perplexing issue that I want to discuss can be separated off from some related matters by considering a distinction made by Keith Donnellan, and something he said in its defence. Donnellan famously distinguished between two uses of definite descriptions. The *referential* use is illustrated as follows: Jones says 'Smith's murderer is insane', meaning that a certain man, whom he (Jones) takes to have murdered Smith, is insane. Donnellan says that even if the man that Jones believes to have murdered Smith did not murder Smith, Jones has referred to the man he had in mind; and if that man is insane, Jones has said something true. The same sentence may be used *attributively* by someone who wants to assert that the murderer of Smith, whoever he may be, is insane. In this case, the speaker does not say something true if no one murdered Smith, nor has the speaker referred to anyone.

In reply, Alfred MacKay objected that Donnellan shared Humpty Dumpty's theory of meaning: ' "When *I* use a word", Humpty Dumpty said, . . . "it means just what I choose it to mean." ' In the conversation that went before, he had used the word 'glory' to mean 'a nice knockdown argument'. Donnellan, in answer, explains that intentions are connected with expectations and that you cannot intend to accomplish something by a certain means unless you believe or expect that the means will, or at least could, lead to the desired outcome. A speaker cannot, therefore, intend to mean something by what he says unless he believes his audience will interpret his words as he intends (the Gricean circle). Donnellan says,

If I were to end this reply to MacKay with the sentence 'There's glory for you' I would be guilty of arrogance and, no doubt, of overestimating the strength of what I have said, but given the background I do not think I could be accused of saying something unintelligible. I would be understood, and would I not have meant by 'glory' 'a nice knockdown argument'?[5]

I like this reply, and I accept Donnellan's original distinction between two uses of descriptions (there are many more than two). But apparently I disagree with *some* view of Donnellan's, because unlike him I see almost no connection between the answer to MacKay's objection and the remarks on reference. The reason is this. MacKay says you cannot change what words mean (and so their reference if that is relevant) merely by intending to; the answer is that this is true, but you can change the meaning provided you believe (and perhaps are justified in believing) that the interpreter has adequate clues for the new interpretation. You may deliberately provide those clues, as Donnellan did for his final 'There's glory for you'.

The trouble is that Donnellan's original distinction had nothing to do with words changing their meaning or reference. If, in the referential use, Jones refers to someone who did not murder Smith by using the description 'Smith's murderer', the reference is none the less achieved by way of the normal meanings of the words. The words therefore must have their usual reference. All that is needed, if we are to accept this way of describing the situation, is a firm sense of the difference between what *words* mean or refer to and what *speakers* mean or refer to. Jones may have referred to someone else by using words that referred to Smith's murderer; this is something he may have done in ignorance or deliberately. Similarly for Donnellan's claim that Jones has said something true when he says 'Smith's murderer is insane', provided the man he believes (erroneously) to have murdered Smith is insane. Jones has said something true by using a sentence that is false. This is done intentionally all the time, for example in irony or metaphor. A coherent theory could not allow that under the circumstances Jones' sentence was true; nor would Jones think so if he knew the facts. Jones' belief about who murdered Smith cannot change the truth of the sentence he uses (and for the same reason cannot change the reference of the words in the sentence).

---

[5] Keith Donnellan, 'Putting Humpty Dumpty Together Again', *The Philosophical Review*, 77 (1968), p. 213. Alfred MacKay's article, 'Mr Donnellan and Humpty Dumpty on Referring' appeared in the same issue of *The Philosophical Review*, pp. 197–202.

Humpty Dumpty is out of it. He cannot mean what he says he means because he knows that 'There's glory for you' cannot be interpreted by Alice as meaning 'There's a nice knockdown argument for you'. We know he knows this because Alice says 'I don't know what you mean by "glory"', and Humpty Dumpty retorts, 'Of course you don't—til I tell you'. It is Mrs Malaprop and Donnellan who interest me; Mrs Malaprop because she gets away with it without even trying or knowing, and Donnellan because he gets away with it on purpose.

Here is what I mean by 'getting away with it': the interpreter comes to the occasion of utterance armed with a theory that tells him (or so he believes) what an arbitrary utterance of the speaker means. The speaker then says something with the intention that it will be interpreted in a certain way, and the expectation that it will be so interpreted. In fact this way is not provided for by the interpreter's theory. But the speaker is nevertheless understood; the interpreter adjusts his theory so that it yields the speaker's intended interpretation. The speaker has 'gotten away with it'. The speaker may or may not (Donnellan, Mrs Malaprop) know that he has got away with anything; the interpreter may or may not know that the speaker intended to get away with anything. What is common to the cases is that the speaker expects to be, and is, interpreted as the speaker intended although the interpreter did not have a correct theory in advance.

We do not need bizarre anecdotes or wonderlands to make the point. We all get away with it all the time; understanding the speech of others depends on it. Take proper names. In small, isolated groups everyone may know the names everyone else knows, and so have ready in advance of a speech encounter a theory that will, without correction, cope with the names to be employed. But even this semantic paradise will be destroyed by each new nickname, visitor, or birth. If a taboo bans a name, a speaker's theory is wrong until he learns of this fact; similarly if an outrigger canoe is christened.

There is not, so far as I can see, any theory of names that gets around the problem. If some definite description gives the meaning of a name, an interpreter still must somehow add to his theory the fact that the name new to him is to be matched with the appropriate description. If understanding a name is to give some weight to an adequate number of descriptions true of the object named, it is even more evident that adding a name to one's way of interpreting a speaker depends on no rule clearly stated in advance. The various theories that discover an essential demonstrative element in names do provide at least a partial rule for adding new names. But the addition is still an addition to the method of interpretation—what we may think of as the interpreter's view of the current language of the speaker. Finding a demonstrative element in names, or for that matter in mass nouns or words for natural kinds, does not reduce these words to pure demonstratives; that is why a new word in any of these categories requires a change in the interpreter's theory, and therefore a change in our description of his understanding of the speaker.

Mrs Malaprop and Donnellan make the case general. There is no word or construction that cannot be converted to a new use by an ingenious or ignorant speaker. And such conversion, while easier to explain because it involves mere substitution, is not the only kind. Sheer invention is equally possible, and we can be as good at interpreting it (say in Joyce or Lewis Carroll) as we are at interpreting the errors or twists of substitution. From the point of view of an ultimate explanation of how new concepts are acquired, learning to interpret a word that expresses a concept we do not already have is a far deeper and more interesting phenomenon than explaining the ability to use a word new to us for an old concept. But both require a change in one's way of interpreting the speech of another, or in speaking to someone who has the use of the word.

The contrast between acquiring a new concept or meaning along with a new word and merely acquiring a new word for an old concept would be salient if I were concerned with the infinitely difficult problem of how a first language is learned. By comparison, my problem is simple. I want to know how people who already have a language (whatever exactly that means) manage to apply their skill or knowledge to actual cases of interpretation. All the things I assume an interpreter knows or can do depend on his having a mature set of concepts, and being at home with the business of linguistic communication. My problem is to describe what is involved in the idea of 'having a language' or of being at home with the business of linguistic communication.

Here is a highly simplified and idealized proposal about what goes on. An interpreter has, at any moment of a speech transaction, what I persist in calling a theory. (I call it a theory, as remarked before, only because a description of the interpreter's competence requires a recursive account.) I assume that the interpreter's theory has been adjusted to the evidence so far available to him: knowledge of the character, dress, role, sex, of the speaker, and whatever else has been gained by observing the speaker's behaviour, linguistic or otherwise. As the

speaker speaks his piece the interpreter alters his theory, entering hypotheses about new names, altering the interpretation of familiar predicates, and revising past interpretations of particular utterances in the
light of new evidence.

Some of what goes on may be described as improving the method of
interpretation as the evidential base enlarges. But much is not like that.
When Donnellan ends his reply to MacKay by saying 'There's glory for
you' not only he, but his words, are correctly interpreted as meaning
'There's a nice knockdown argument for you'. That's how he intends us
to interpret his words, and we know this, since we have, and he knows
we have, and we know he knows we have (etc.), the background needed
to provide the interpretation. But up to a certain point (before MacKay
came on the scene) this interpretation of an earlier utterance by
Donnellan of the same words would have been wrong. To put this
differently: the theory we actually use to interpret an utterance is
geared to the occasion. We may decide later we could have done better
by the occasion, but this does not mean (necessarily) that we now have
a better theory for the next occasion. The reason for this is, as we have
seen, perfectly obvious: a speaker may provide us with information
relevant to interpreting an utterance in the course of making the
utterance.

Let us look at the process from the speaker's side. The speaker wants
to be understood, so he intends to speak in such a way that he will be
interpreted in a certain way. In order to judge how he will be interpreted, he forms, or uses, a picture of the interpreter's readiness to
interpret along certain lines. Central to this picture is what the speaker
believes is the starting theory of interpretation the interpreter has for
him. The speaker does not necessarily speak in such a way as to prompt
the interpreter to apply this prior theory; he may deliberately dispose
the interpreter to modify his prior theory. But the speaker's view of the
interpreter's prior theory is not irrelevant to what he says, nor to what
he means by his words; it is an important part of what he has to go on
if he wants to be understood.

I have distinguished what I have been calling the *prior theory* from
what I shall henceforth call the *passing theory*. For the hearer, the prior
theory expresses how he is prepared in advance to interpret an utterance of the speaker, while the passing theory is how he *does* interpret
the utterance. For the speaker, the prior theory is what he *believes* the
interpreter's prior theory to be, while his passing theory is the theory
he *intends* the interpreter to use.

I am now in a position to state a problem that arises if we accept the distinction between the prior and the passing theory and also accept the account of linguistic competence given by principles (1)–(2). According to that account, each interpreter (and this includes speakers, since speakers must be interpreters) comes to a successful linguistic exchange prepared with a 'theory' which constitutes his basic linguistic competence, and which he shares with those with whom he communicates. Because each party has such a shared theory and knows that others share his theory, and knows that others know he knows (etc.), some would say that the knowledge or abilities that constitute the theory may be called conventions.

I think that the distinction between the prior and the passing theory, if taken seriously, undermines this commonly accepted account of linguistic competence and communication. Here is why. What must be shared for communication to succeed is the passing theory. For the passing theory is the one the interpreter actually uses to interpret an utterance, and it is the theory the speaker intends the interpreter to use. Only if these coincide is understanding complete. (Of course, there are degrees of success in communication; much may be right although something is wrong. This matter of degree is irrelevant to my argument.)

The passing theory is where, accident aside, agreement is greatest. As speaker and interpreter talk, their prior theories become more alike; so do their passing theories. The asymptote of agreement and understanding is when passing theories coincide. But the passing theory cannot in general correspond to an interpreter's linguistic competence. Not only does it have its changing list of proper names and gerrymandered vocabulary, but it includes every successful—i.e. correctly interpreted—use of any other word or phrase, no matter how far out of the ordinary. Every deviation from ordinary usage, as long as it is agreed on for the moment (knowingly deviant, or not, on one, or both, sides), is in the passing theory as a feature of what the words mean on that occasion. Such meanings, transient though they may be, are literal; they are what I have called first meanings. A passing theory is not a theory of what anyone (except perhaps a philosopher) would call an actual natural language. 'Mastery' of such a language would be useless, since knowing a passing theory is only knowing how to interpret a particular utterance on a particular occasion. Nor could such a language, if we want to call it that, be said to have been learned, or to be governed by conventions. Of course things previously learned were essential to arriving at the passing theory, but what was learned could not have been the passing theory.

Why should a passing theory be called a theory at all? For the sort of theory we have in mind is, in its formal structure, suited to be the theory for an entire language, even though its expected field of application is vanishingly small. The answer is that when a word or phrase temporarily or locally takes over the role of some other word or phrase (as treated in a prior theory, perhaps), the entire burden of that role, with all its implications for logical relations to other words, phrases, and sentences, must be carried along by the passing theory. Someone who grasps the fact that Mrs Malaprop means 'epithet' when she says 'epitaph' must give 'epithet' all the powers of 'epitaph' has for many other people. Only a full recursive theory can do justice to these powers. These remarks do not depend on supposing Mrs Malaprop will always make this 'mistake'; once is enough to summon up a passing theory assigning a new role to 'epitaph'.

An interpreter's prior theory has a better chance of describing what we might think of as a natural language, particularly a prior theory brought to a first conversation. The less we know about the speaker, assuming we know he belongs to our language community, the more nearly our prior theory will simply be the theory we expect someone who hears our unguarded speech to use. If we ask for a cup of coffee, direct a taxi driver, or order a crate of lemons, we may know so little about our intended interpreter that we can do no better than to assume that he will interpret our speech along what we take to be standard lines. But all this is relative. In fact we always have the interpreter in mind; there is no such thing as how we expect, in the abstract, to be interpreted. We inhibit our higher vocabulary, or encourage it, depending on the most general considerations, and we cannot fail to have premonitions as to which of the proper names we know are apt to be correctly understood.

In any case, my point is this: most of the time prior theories will not be shared, and there is no reason why they should be. Certainly it is not a condition of successful communication that prior theories be shared: consider the malaprop from ignorance. Mrs Malaprop's theory, prior and passing, is that 'A nice derangement of epitaphs' means a nice arrangement of epithets. An interpreter who, as we say, knows English, but does not know the verbal habits of Mrs Malaprop, has a prior theory according to which 'A nice derangement of epitaphs' means a nice derangement of epitaphs; but his passing theory agrees with that of Mrs Malaprop if he understands her words.

It is quite clear that in general the prior theory is neither shared by speaker and interpreter nor is it what we would normally call a language. For the prior theory has in it all the features special to the idiolect of the speaker that the interpreter is in a position to take into account before the utterance begins. One way to appreciate the difference between the prior theory and our ordinary idea of a person's language is to reflect on the fact that an interpreter must be expected to have quite different prior theories for different speakers—not as different, usually, as his passing theories; but these are matters that depend on how well the interpreter knows his speaker.

Neither the prior theory nor the passing theory describes what we would call the language a person knows, and neither theory characterizes a speaker's or interpreter's linguistic competence. Is there any theory that would do better?

Perhaps it will be said that what is essential to the mastery of a language is not knowledge of any particular vocabulary, or even detailed grammar, much less knowledge of what any speaker is apt to succeed in making his words and sentences mean. What is essential is a basic framework of categories and rules, a sense of the way English (or any) grammars may be constructed, plus a skeleton list of interpreted words for fitting into the basic framework. If I put all this vaguely, it is only because I want to consider a large number of actual or possible proposals in one fell swoop; for I think they all fail to resolve our problem. They fail for the same reasons the more complete and specific prior theories fail: none of them satisfies the demand for a description of an ability that speaker and interpreter share and that is adequate to interpretation.

First, any general framework, whether conceived as a grammar for English, or a rule for accepting grammars, or a basic grammar plus rules for modifying or extending it—any such general framework, by virtue of the features that make it general, will by itself be insufficient for interpreting particular utterances. The general framework or theory, whatever it is, may be a key ingredient in what is needed for interpretation, but it can't be all that is needed since it fails to provide the interpretation of particular words and sentences as uttered by a particular speaker. In this respect it is like a prior theory, only worse because it is less complete.

Second, the framework theory must be expected to be different for different speakers. The more general and abstract it is, the more difference there can be without it mattering to communication. The theoretical possibility of such divergence is obvious; but once one tries to imagine a framework rich enough to serve its purpose, it is clear that such differences must also be actual. It is impossible to give examples, of course, until it is decided what to count in the framework: a sufficiently explicit framework could be discredited by a single malapropism. There is some evidence of a more impressive sort that internal grammars do differ among speakers of 'the same language'. James McCawley reports that recent work by Haber shows

. . . that there is appreciable variation as to what rules of plural formation different speakers have, the variation being manifested in such things as the handling of novel words that an investigator has presented his subjects with, in the context of a task that will force them to use the word in the plural . . . Haber suggests that her subjects, rather than having a uniformly applicable process of plural formation, each have a 'core' system, which covers a wide range of cases, but not necessarily everything, plus strategies . . . for handling cases that are not covered by the 'core' system . . . Haber's data suggest that speakers of what are to the minutest details 'the same dialect' often have acquired grammars that differ in far more respects than their speech differs in.[6]

I have been trying to throw doubt on how clear the idea of 'speaking the same dialect' is, but here we may assume that it at least implies the frequent sharing of passing theories.

Bringing in grammars, theories, or frameworks more general than, and prior to, prior theories just emphasizes the problem I originally presented in terms of the contrast between prior theories and passing theories. Stated more broadly now, the problem is this: what interpreter and speaker share, to the extent that communication succeeds, is not learned and so is not a language governed by rules or conventions known to speaker and interpreter in advance; but what the speaker and interpreter know in advance is not (necessarily) shared, and so is not a language governed by shared rules or conventions. What is shared is, as before, the passing theory; what is given in advance is the prior theory, or anything on which it may in turn be based.

What I have been leaving out of account up to now is what Haber calls a 'strategy', which is a nice word for the mysterious process by which a speaker or hearer uses what he knows in advance plus present data to produce a passing theory. What two people need, if they are to understand one another through speech, is the ability to converge

[6] James McCawley, 'Some Ideas Not to Live By', *Die Neuern Sprachen*, 75 (1976), p. 157. These results are disputed by those who believe the relevant underlying rules and structures are prewired. My point obviously does not depend on the example, or the level at which deviations are empirically possible.

on passing theories from utterance to utterance. Their starting points, however far back we want to take them, will usually be very different —as different as the ways in which they acquired their linguistic skills. So also, then, will the strategies and stratagems that bring about convergence differ.

Perhaps we can give content to the idea of two people 'having the same language' by saying that they tend to converge on passing theories; degree or relative frequency of convergence would then be a measure of similarity of language. What use can we find, however, for the concept of a language? We could hold that any theory on which a speaker and interpreter converge is a language; but then there would be a new language for every unexpected turn in the conversation, and languages could not be learned and no one would want to master most of them.

We just made a sort of sense of the idea of two people 'having the same language', though we could not explain what a language is. It is easy to see that the idea of 'knowing' a language will be in the same trouble, as will the project of characterizing the abilities or capacities a person must have if he commands a language. But we might try to say in what a person's ability to interpret or speak to another person consists: it is the ability that permits him to construct a correct, that is, convergent, passing theory for speech transactions with that person. Again, the concept allows of degrees of application.

This characterization of linguistic ability is so nearly circular that it cannot be wrong: it comes to saying that the ability to communicate by speech consists in the ability to make oneself understood, and to understand. It is only when we look at the structure of this ability that we realize how far we have drifted from standard ideas of language mastery. For we have discovered no learnable common core of consistent behaviour, no shared grammar or rules, no portable interpreting machine set to grind out the meaning of an arbitrary utterance. We may say that linguistic ability is the ability to converge on a passing theory from time to time—this is what I have suggested, and I have no better proposal. Buf if we do say this, then we should realize that we have abandoned not only the ordinary notion of a language, but we have erased the boundary between knowing a language and knowing our way around in the world generally. For there are no rules for arriving at passing theories, no rules in any strict sense, as opposed to rough maxims and methodological generalities. A passing theory really is like a theory at least in this, that it is derived by wit, luck, and wisdom from a private vocabulary and grammar, knowledge of the ways people get their point across, and rules of thumb for figuring out what deviations from the dictionary are most likely. There is no more chance of regularizing, or teaching, this process than there is of regularizing or teaching the process of creating new theories to cope with new data in any field—for that is what this process involves.

The problem we have been grappling with depends on the assumption that communication by speech requires that speaker and interpreter have learned or somehow acquired a common method or theory of interpretation—as being able to operate on the basis of shared conventions, rules, or regularities. The problem arose when we realized that no method or theory fills this bill. The solution to the problem is clear. In linguistic communication nothing corresponds to a linguistic competence as often described: that is, as summarized by principles (1)-(3). The solution is to give up the principles. Principles (1) and (2) survive when understood in rather unusual ways, but principle (3) cannot stand, and it is unclear what can take its place. I conclude that there is no such thing as a language, not if a language is anything like what many philosophers and linguists have supposed. There is therefore no such thing to be learned, mastered, or born with. We must give up the idea of a clearly defined shared structure which language-users acquire and then apply to cases. And we should try again to say how convention in any important sense is involved in language; or, as I think, we should give up the attempt to illuminate how we communicate by appeal to conventions.

6

COMPOSITIONAL SEMANTICS AND LANGUAGE UNDERSTANDING

STEPHEN SCHIFFER

I

It is conceded by most philosophers of language,

Professor Donald Davidson wrote in 1967, and I think the same is true today,

. . . that a satisfactory theory of meaning must give an account of how the meanings of sentences depend upon the meanings of words. Unless such an account could be supplied for a particular language . . . there would be no explaining the fact that we can learn the language: no explaining the fact that, on mastering a finite vocabulary and a finitely stated set of rules, we are prepared to produce and to understand any of a potential infinitude of sentences.[1]

That is to say (nearly enough), it is widely believed that every natural language has what I shall presently call a *compositional semantics*, and the reason for this belief is the belief that:

> [U] It would not be possible to account for a human's ability to understand utterances of indefinitely many novel sentences of a language without the assumption that the language had a compositional semantics.

None the less, as I shall make plain, I am inclined to believe that (a) no natural language has a compositional semantics, and that, therefore, (b) [U] is false.

The most elementary point about the semantics of sentences about propositional attitudes,

Professor Tyler Burge has recently proclaimed,

is that such sentences have the form of a *relational* propositional attitude predicate with singular argument places for at least a subject

---

[1] Davidson (1967), p. 304.

(e.g. a person) and something believed (thought, desired, intended, said). This latter . . . is, with some qualifications, the semantical value of the grammatical object of the propositional attitude verb.[2]

In other words, *the relational theory of propositional attitudes*, Burge claims, is correct: believing is a relation to things believed, to values of the quantifiable variable 'y' in the schema 'x believes y' (or 'x believes that y'), to things having truth-valuational properties which determine the truth-valuational properties of beliefs. My present belief that snow is white is true, this theory has it, just in case what I believe—the referent of the singular term 'that snow is white'—is true.[3]

I believe that there is this important connection between the CS theory alluded to by Professor Davidson—the theory that each natural language has a correct compositional semantics—and the relational theory of propositional attitude verbs endorsed by Professor Burge: that, if the CS theory is correct, then so is the relational theory. For the relational construal of propositional attitude verbs is the only feasible construal of them *relative to the assumption that natural languages have compositional semantics.* Consequently, there can be no cogent denial of the relational theory that does not carry with it the claim that English (and every other natural language) does not have a compositional semantics.

For if σ is any well-formed indicative sentence of English, then ⌜believes that σ⌝ is a well-formed predicate phrase. Since there are infinitely many such predicate phrases, no finitely statable compositional semantics (and, we shall see, a compositional semantics is by definition finitely statable) can treat them as semantically primitive. A compositional semantics must therefore treat 'believes' (or 'believes that') as semantically primitive. And, for reasons that cannot now be considered, it happens, I dare say, that the only tenable way this can be done is to treat 'believes' (or 'believes that') as a relational predicate; i.e. as a predicate with argument places for singular terms.

At the same time, I am inclined to believe that the relational theory of propositonal attitudes is false. For, if believing is a relation to things believed, then there must be some true account of what those things

<hr/>

[2] Burge (1980). The qualifications, ignored in my restatement, pertain to *de re* constructions.
[3] If Davidson's version of the relational theory (1969) is correct, the demonstrative 'that' is the singular term which refers to what I believe, and its referent is the occurrence, following its occurrence, of 'snow is white'.

are—propositions (of one kind or another), mental representations, sentences or utterances of a natural language, or whatever. But I find compelling reasons for rejecting each of the possible candidate answers. Since I also believe that the relational theory of propositional attitudes has got to be right if natural languages have compositional semantics, I have a compelling reason for believing that natural languages do not have compositional semantics.

But that is not directly the topic of this paper.[4] If no natural language has a compositional semantics, then [U], the commonly accepted rationale for the CS theory, must also be false. My primary purpose in this paper is to make a case for the falsity of [U], to give some reason for supposing that our ability to comprehend utterances in a public language does not presuppose a compositional semantics for that language.

In the next section I elaborate on the CS theory and the reason for believing it. In section III, to clear the air for better reasons, I dismiss two bad reasons for thinking that the theory of language understanding will not need recourse to a compositional semantics. The correct reason is given in secton IV, and section V discusses the bearing of these matters on two other issues, physicalism and the Gricean programme in semantics.

II

The thesis in question is that every natural language has a correct compositional semantics, and I shall say that:

[CS] A *compositional semantics* for a language L is a finitely statable theory which ascribes properties to, and defines recursive conditions on, the finitely many vocabulary items in L in such a way that, for each of the infinitely many sentences of L that can (in principle) be used to make truth evaluable utterances, there is some condition (or set of conditions) such that the theory entails that an utterance of that sentence is true iff that condition (or a certain member of the set) obtains.

The notion of a compositional semantics for a language L is closely related to that of what has come to be called a *meaning theory for L.*

---

[4] It is, however, among the topics of my book in progress, *Remnants of Meaning*, to be published by Bradford Books/MIT Press.

This latter is a theory that specifies the meanings of all the expressions of L, and specifies recursions which show how these meanings determine the meanings of complex expressions in L. [CS] does not entail that a compositional semantics for L will be a meaning theory for L, but a meaning theory for L may well be at least a compositional semantics for L (and more), and those for whom 'semantics with no treatment of truth conditions is not semantics'[5] will maintain that it must be.

For much, perhaps all, of what I shall eventually say against the need for compositional semantics in the theory of public language understanding, 'meaning theory' may be substituted for 'compositional semantics'; this will even apply if one's favourite construal of a componential meaning theory does not require it to be a *truth-conditional* componential semantics. Still, I am unwilling to take the broader notion of a meaning theory, as lately defined, as my avowed target. First, the notion of 'meaning' as it there occurs has virtually no content, but is at best a place-holder for some theoretically serviceable notion. Second, as we shall presently see, the intuitive considerations which motivate the need for a finitely statable meaning theory do indeed motivate the need for a compositional semantics in the sense of [CS]. Third, I do not want to sever the link, already remarked on, with the relational theory of propositional attitudes, and I doubt that one can so much as make sense of the claim that propositional attitude predicates are relational other than in terms of their playing a certain role in the determination of the truth conditions of the sentences in which they occur.

Finally, I trust that it is obvious—if only from the fact that a meaning theory may be a compositional semantics—that a compositional semantics for L may, but need not, take the form of an extensional, finitely axiomatized theory of truth for L in the style of Tarski, somehow relativized to utterances of sentences. Indeed, a compositional semantics might even directly take the form of a recursive axiomatization of the Gricean facts about the sentences of the language used by a given population.[6]

Why does the CS theorist suppose that for each natural language there is a correct compositional semantics? His reason is the familiar one, already stated in [U], that he cannot see how to account for the ability of users of a natural language to understand utterances in it

---

[5] Lewis (1972), p. 169.   [6] See Davies (1984).

without supposing that there is a correct compositional semantics for that language. After all, he reasons, one who has mastery of a natural language L has somehow acquired, after a relatively brief period of exposure to utterances of a finite number of sentences in L, the ability to understand indefinitely many sentences of L that are wholly novel to him, never before encountered. Now, in encountering a novel but understood sentence, one is not being confronted with novel words, but with familiar words put together, via familiar constructions, in a novel way. This strongly suggests that there can be no explaining one's mastery of a natural language independently of the specification of compositional mechanisms which generate the meanings of complex expressions out of the meanings of simpler ones.

From the fact that a meaning theory for a language must state compositional mechanisms which reveal the ways in which the meanings of sentences are determined by the meanings of the words composing them, it does not yet follow that the meaning theory must be a truth-condition entailing componential semantics of the sort characterized in [CS]. That further hypothesis is, however, motivated by the further observation that:

(a) to understand an utterance is to know what propositional speech acts were performed in it,

and that:

(b) one cannot know what speech acts in the assertive mode were performed without knowing their truth conditions: if in uttering 'Someone was burned' a speaker said that someone was swindled, then to understand that utterance one must know that the speaker said that, and that requires knowing that what was said, and hence the utterance as well, was true just in case someone was swindled.

In other words: to understand a public language is to have the ability to understand utterances in it; and to understand an utterance in the assertive mode is to know that it is true provided that such and such is the case, where what the speaker said in the utterance was precisely that such and such was the case. All this, the theorist feels, does strongly motivate the assumption that natural languages have compositional semantics in the sense defined.

III

We will understand better what is to come later if we appreciate now that, in subscribing to the CS theory, the astute CS theorist is *quite correctly* undeterred by (a) a certain potentially misleading way of using the phrase 'theory of language understanding', and (b) a certain fallacious argument to show that understanding a natural language does not presuppose a compositional semantics for that language.

Both (a) and (b) have as their point of departure the topical thesis —with which a CS theorist may be altogether sympathetic—that we think in a 'language of thought', perhaps even, suitably interpreted, the very same language we speak. (How could the CS theorist be anti-pathetic? The empirical hypothesis that we are information-processors and thus think (i.e. process) in a neural machine-language is consistent with any philosophical position that is itself consistent with our thoughts having physical realizations.)

Current dogma, which I will not immediately scrutinize, has it that the correct theory of content, or meaning, for the inner system of mental representation will have two components: (1) a *conceptual role* component, and (2) a truth-theoretic, *referential semantic* component.[7] The referential semantics, which is just one of your standard, finitely axiomatized truth theories, will not be at issue in this section.

The conceptual role component assigns conceptual roles to expressions of the inner system. The conceptual role of a subsentential expression is the contribution it makes to the conceptual roles of the infinitely many sentences in which it occurs. The conceptual role of an inner sentence is a counterfactual property of that sentence, which property is specifiable independently of any semantic properties the sentence might have, and in a way which details the causal or transitional role of that sentence in the formation of perceptual beliefs, and in theoretical and practical reasoning. Not only is the conceptual role of a formula specifiable without reference to the formula's truth condition, it also fails to determine it: the neural sentence whose tokening realizes my belief that water [$= H_2O$] is potable may be exactly the same neural sentence, with exactly the same conceptual role, as the one that realizes my Twin Earth *Doppelgänger's* belief that twater [$=XYZ$] is potable.[8]

It is natural to equate a conceptual role theory for the language of

---

[7] See Field (1977 and 1978); Loar (1981 and 1982); McGinn (1982); and Schiffer (1981a and 1981b).

[8] Putnam (1975); see also Burge (1982).

thought with a theory of language of thought understanding. For, to understand a language is to know how to use it, but to 'use' a system of mental representation is just for its formulae to have conceptual roles. Thus, two computers from the same assembly line may use, and so understand, the same inner code, even though, as one has been placed on Earth, the other on Twin Earth, sentences that are understood the same way have different truth conditions. Since the conceptual role theory for Mentalese is independent of any referential semantical theory of Mentalese, the theory of understanding for Mentalese, construed as a conceptual role theory, does not presuppose a compositional semantics for Mentalese.

To understand a *public* language, on the other hand, is to have the ability to understand utterances in it. And to understand an utterance is to know what propositional speech acts, with what truth conditions, were performed in it. So it ought to be obvious that, from the fact that

(1) the theory of understanding for the inner system of mental representation does not presuppose a compositional semantics for that system,

it clearly does *not* follow that

(2) the theory of understanding for one's public language does not presuppose a compositional semantics for that language.

Suppose, to emphasize the point, that we wanted to programme a very sophisticated information-processor, Louise, so that she could understand spoken utterances in English; so that, for example, upon hearing an utterance of 'She was green' Louise could come to know that the utterer said that a certain woman was inexperienced, and thus that the utterance was true just in case that woman was inexperienced. Relative to this supposition, the question as regards the need for a compositional semantics in the theory of *public* language understanding may be posed thus:

> Would we have to programme Louise so that she represented, or somehow realized, a compositional semantics for English?

It is the (correct) opinion of the astute CS theorist that no answer whatever to this question is forthcoming from the assumption that the theory of understanding for Louise's *lingua mentis*, her neural (or electronic) code, is a conceptual role, 'use' theory that does not presuppose a compositional semantics.

It is sometimes held that a person's language of thought is his natural language; that English speakers think in English, French ones in French, etc. Of course, all that this can plausibly mean is that there is some salient, but unspecified, relation between one's public language and one's system of mental representation which makes that a useful way to talk. But what would make that a useful way to talk? For the inner code to be one's spoken language it is not enough that there be a meaning-preserving mapping from inner formulae onto outer ones that assigns the same syntactic analysis to all correlated pairs of formulae; for such a mapping could obtain between distinct natural languages. But perhaps the 'thinking in English' metaphor would be warranted if, in addition to the foregoing requirement, it were also the case that one's acquisition of one's outer, spoken language *causally* accounted for one's acquisition of one's isomorphic internal language.

If one's language of thought is English, in the foregoing sense, then the theory of understanding English *qua language of thought* will be a conceptual role theory that presupposes no compositional semantics for English. But from this nothing whatever follows about the need for a compositional semantics in the account of one's understanding of spoken English—that is, in the account of one's ability to know what propositional speech acts are performed in spoken utterances. The use of language in *thought* is one thing, its use in *speech* another. These are different phenomena, to be explained by different theories.

Now we are in a position to appreciate why the astute CS theorist is deterred neither by (a) a certain potentially misleading way of using the phrase 'theory of language understanding', nor by (b) a certain questionable argument.

As regards (a), the CS theorist is well aware of a recent tendency to promote 'use' theories of language understanding which do not presuppose truth-conditional semantics. He knows, for example, that Hilary Putnam has written that

the theory of language understanding and the theory of reference and truth have much less to do with one another than many philosophers have assumed,

following this with the sketch of a conceptual role account of 'language use' from which it is clear that 'nothing in this account of "use" says *anything* about a correspondence between words and things, or sentences and states of affairs'.[9] But a theorist can see the wisdom in this without renouncing his belief in [U]: the correctness of a non-truth-conditional, 'use' theory of 'understanding' *for the role of language in thought* would imply nothing about the need for a compositional semantics in the theory of a person's ability to understand spoken utterances. Perhaps, the CS theorist may concede, it is true that, in acquiring English as a first language one is acquiring two capacities —the ability to understand English utterances and the ability to think in English—and perhaps it is true that an account of the latter capacity would make no appeal to a compositional semantics; none the less, the question remains open as to whether a compositional semantics will be needed to explain the former capacity, namely, the ability to know what propositional speech acts speakers perform in their utterances.

The argument alluded to in (b) is Gilbert Harman's.[10] He has not been confused by any pun on 'language use', but has been forcefully explicit in denying that a compositional semantics is needed to explain even the public, communicative use of language, *given that one thinks in one's natural language*. His argument evidently has these two premisses:

(1) We would need a compositional semantics for English only if understanding spoken utterances were a matter of *decoding* a message expressed in one language, English, into a distinct language, Mentalese.

(2) But, since we think in English, no such decoding takes place: 'words are used to communicate thoughts that would ordinarily be thought in those or similar words'.[11]

The CS theorist ought to deny (1), protesting that what should be at issue is not how we represent thoughts, but how we manage to ascribe truth-valuational properties to utterances, however we represent those utterances as having those properties.

Thus, we may imagine, Ralph utters the sounds 'She beat him'; you have an auditory perception of them and form the correct belief that Ralph said that a certain female completed a certain running race ahead of a certain male, and that, therefore, Ralph's utterance is true just in case that female did finish ahead of that male. Let it be granted that you think in English, and thus do not decode messages spoken in English into a distinct Mentalese: How does that show that no compositional semantics is needed to explain the processing that took you from

[9] Putnam (1978).   [10] Harman (1975).   [11] Ibid., p. 271.

the auditory stimulation to the knowledge that Ralph's utterance was true just in case a certain state of affairs obtained?

IV

A person S utters a sentence σ. Another person, A, hears S's utterance of σ and, even though he has never before encountered σ, instantaneously forms the correct belief that S, in uttering σ, said that such and such, and that, therefore, what S said, and thus his utterance of σ, is true provided that such and such is the case. In the event, A understands, or knows the meaning of, σ, understands S's utterance of σ, and manifests his understanding of the language to which σ belongs.

It is the claim of the CS theorist that, in order correctly to account for the language understanding capacity manifested by A in his processing of S's utterance, we shall at some point need to postulate a compositional semantics for the language in question. More generally, it may be said, and I think with only a little exaggeration, that, among those who hold the CS theory for a considered reason, that considered reason is [U], the conviction that, without the assumption of a compositional semantics, there could be no explaining a person's ability to comprehend indefinitely many utterances of indefinitely many novel sentences.[12]

If I am right to doubt that any natural language has a compositional semantics, then I must find fault with [U], and that is the burden of this section. My goal, however, will not be to explain our language understanding capacity in a way that does not imply that the languages we understand have compositional semantics. The explanation of our capacity to understand natural language utterances would be an empirical, scientific undertaking, the business, surely, of cognitive psychology and psycholinguistics. My present purpose is merely to provide a *counterexample* to [U], and thus to show that it is possible that we should be so constituted that our language comprehension abilities proceed without access to a compositional semantics for the language we comprehend. My counterexample to [U] takes the

[12] "Only a little exaggeration" because, as I shall later acknowledge, the "two-factor" theory of mental representation described on p. 180 does imply a way of arguing that one's public language has a compositional semantics, even if that assumption is not needed to explain one's *understanding* of that language. It may, however, be fair to say that, with the possible exception of Katz [16], Ch. 1, [U] has been the only reason explicitly offered in the literature for supposing natural languages to have compositional semantics.

form of a description of a possible world in which it is the case that (1) a certain person, Harvey, has the ability to understand utterances of indefinitely many novel sentences of a certain language E_1, itself containing infinitely many sentences, and that (2) the explanation of Harvey's ability does not invoke a compositional semantics for E_1.

Although the example of Harvey's comprehension of E_1 is plausibly a counterexample to [U], E_1 falls short of being a full-blown natural language, and this might suggest that it is owing to features of natural languages not shared by E_1 that a compositional semantics will have to be invoked in explaining our ability to understand utterances in natural languages such as French or English. So, as my objective is to undermine the standard motivation for supposing that our natural languages have compositional semantics, I shall incrementally complicate the Harvey example to the point where he represents a possible model of us. In the end I shall also suggest how certain other special features of Harvey, perhaps not shared by us, may be removed without detriment to the main point.

Harvey, in the possible world now to be characterized, is an information-processor, and so thinks (i.e., processes) in an inner neural machine language—his *lingua mentis*, so to say—which I shall call 'M'. It is a contingent but nomological fact about Harvey that he has a belief just in case he stands in a certain computational relation to a tokened sentence of M. To make this vivid we may pretend that there is in Harvey's head a large box marked 'B', and that a sentence of M is tokened as a belief just in case a token of that sentence occurs in B.[13] Further, for every belief which Harvey can have, there is a unique sentence of M whose occurrence in B would realize that belief. Consequently, there is just one formula μ such that Harvey believes that snow is white if and only if μ occurs in B. Since sentences of M realize beliefs, they have semantic, or representational, features: it is fair to say, for example, that μ, the formula whose occurrence in B realizes the belief that snow is white, 'means' that snow is white. However, I shall make no further stipulation about the semantics of the neural code M; I even leave it open as to whether or not M, in accordance with the two-factor theory described on p. 180, requires a compositional semantics (which I would deny): for, it will soon be evident, our present issue is whether we can account for Harvey's processing of spoken

[13] For simplicity I suppose that Harvey is limited to finitely many beliefs.

utterances without supposing that the processing proceeds in accordance with a compositional semantics for his public language, and it will be clear that we can so account for Harvey's understanding of his public language, even if it were the case (which it is not) that the inner code M required a compositional semantics to account for its representational features. Nevertheless, it will have to be acknowledged that, if M has a compositional semantics, then so does Harvey's public language, even if that compositional semantics need not be adverted to in explaining Harvey's ability to understand public language utterances. This means that [U] is not the *only* possible rationale for supposing natural languages to have compositional semantics; that, even if Harvey is a counterexample to [U], there would remain the possibility of establishing that his public language required a compositional semantics, even though that compositional semantics played no role in the full story of the processing which realizes Harvey's understanding of spoken utterances. But this concession, which has more bark than bite, is best looked at again after Harvey has been shown to be a counterexample to [U].

Anyway, Harvey, *qua* computer, is endowed with certain *belief-forming mechanisms*. These mechanisms determine the conditions under which a given sentence of M will occur in Harvey's B-box. If we suppose that, roughly speaking, the appearance of a given sentence in B at a time t is determined by sensory stimulations and the contents of B at times immediately preceding t, then the belief-forming mechanisms determine *how* the occurrence of a sentence in B is a function of sensory stimulations and other sentences occurring (or not occurring) in B. Thus, for every sentence of M, the belief-forming mechanisms will determine a very complex counterfactual property that details the way in which the occurrence of that sentence in B is determined by sensory stimulations and other sentences in B. I shall call this complex, counterfactual property of an inner sentence, with some trepidation, its *conceptual role* (as before, the conceptual role of a subsentential expression is its contribution to the conceptual roles of the sentences in which it occurs). I call it that because I need a label and others in the literature have such a property in mind by their use of 'conceptual role'; my trepidation is due to my not wanting to be party to various theoretical claims which others make about the counterfactual properties which I am calling 'conceptual roles'. In particular, I am not proposing conceptual roles as part of a theory of mental content (I am not here proposing any theory of mental content).

Harvey's spoken language, and that of the linguistic community to which he belongs, happens to be nonindexical, unambiguous English, which language I call 'E$_1$'. My task now is precisely this: to make further stipulations that will show that Harvey's ability to understand utterances in E$_1$ does not presuppose a compositional semantics for E$_1$. If I can do this, then we shall have a counterexample to [U], the hypothesis in question.

Now Carmen utters the sequence of sounds, 'Some snow is purple'. Harvey has an auditory perception of Carmen's utterance and immediately knows, notwithstanding the novelty of the sound sequence uttered, that Carmen said that some snow was purple, and, consequently, that her utterance is true just in case some snow is purple. As this transition manifests Harvey's ability to understand utterances of novel sentences of E$_1$, my task amounts to this: to state general principles, applicable to any utterance in E$_1$, that (a) will take Harvey from

[1] his belief that Carmen uttered the sounds 'Some snow is purple'

to

[2] his belief that Carmen said that some snow was purple, and thus what she said, and so her utterance, is true just in case some snow is purple,

but that (b) will not require Harvey's processing to realize, or be in accordance with, a compositional semantics for E$_1$.

I think it may be useful, before turning to my stipulations about Harvey, to see what the CS theorist would have to say about him. That theorist, subscribing to [U], must claim that, in order correctly to account for the transition from [1] to [2], we must suppose that Harvey's internal processing somehow realizes, or represents, a compositional semantics for E$_1$. Now the language comprehension process that begins with Harvey's auditory perception and terminates with his belief about what Carmen said is realized by a sequence of tokened occurrences of inner formulae. The CS theorist is constrained to say that some of these formulae represent segments of Carmen's utterance as having certain semantic values, and that, on the basis of this, and in accordance with a certain compositional semantics for E$_1$, some formula later in the comprehension sequence represents Carmen's entire sound sequence as having a certain semantic value. This representation, the CS theorist will doubtless want to say, interacts with other formulae representing general psychological, or psychosemantical, principles applicable to speakers of any language, and this interaction in turn results in there being in Harvey's B-box a formula which represents Carmen as having said that some snow was purple. The CS theorist may regard it as an empirical question, to be resolved by scientific research, whether the compositional semantics (or grammar, as it used to be called in Cambridge, Mass.) is itself internally represented, or whether Harvey is simply 'hard-wired' so as to process in conformity with a certain compositional semantics, not itself internally represented.

But what are these 'semantic values', and what form will the compositional semantics which ascribes them take? I am aware of no answer that will help us to understand Harvey's comprehension process. This makes it difficult (for me) to assess the claim that, in order for Harvey to have the language comprehension ability he is stipulated to have, his internal processing must somehow have some sort of access to some sort of compositional semantics for E_1. In proposing, as I shall now do, that Harvey's understanding of E_1 might proceed without access to a compositional semantics for E_1, I am hardly flying in the face of an already available explanatory theory of that understanding.

Here, at any rate, is how, without appeal to a compositional semantics, we can account for Harvey's ability to understand utterances in E_1: we can stipulate that certain expressions in the inner code M have conceptual roles that do explain the transition from [1] to [2], and all others like it, but do not presuppose a compositional semantics for E_1. I shall explain.

Let

[3] Nemrac derettu 'sŭm' 'snō' 'ĭz' 'pûr'pəl',

[4] Nemrac dias taht emos wons si elprup,

and

[5] Nemrac's ecnarettu si eurt ffi emos wons si elprup

be (graphemic representations of) the sentences of the inner code M that realize, respectively, Harvey's beliefs that Carmen uttered the sequence of sounds 'some snow is purple', that Carmen said that some snow was purple, and that Carmen's utterance is true iff some snow is purple.[14]

My intention is to show that Harvey is a counterexample to [U] by

---

[14] I owe the idea of backwards English to its occurrence in Lycan (1984), where it is used to a different end.

showing how 'dias taht' and 'eurt' can have conceptual roles that (a) do not presuppose a compositional semantics for E_1, but (b) do explain the transition from the occurrence of [3] in Harvey's B-box to the occurrence there of [4] and [5] (and, of course, all of Harvey's other utterance comprehension transitions).

To do this I do not need to specify the entire conceptual roles of 'dias taht' and 'eurt'. I assume that [4] and [5] have whatever conceptual roles are necessitated by virtue of their being formulae whose occurrence in Harvey's B-box would realize the beliefs that Carmen said that some snow was purple and that Carmen's utterance is true iff some snow is purple. But it is clear that there is nothing in the conceptual roles thus necessitated that presupposes a compositional semantics for E_1; for someone who did not understand E_1—say, a monolingual speaker of Serbo-Croation—could, without knowing the meaning of 'some snow is purple', correctly believe, perhaps by being told, that Carmen, in uttering that sentence, said that some snow was purple, and that, therefore, what she said, and her utterance as well, is true if and only if some snow is purple. Consequently, my question is this: Given that [4] and [5] realize the foregoing beliefs, what stipulations can be made about the conceptual roles of 'dias taht' and 'eurt' that would explain the transition in Harvey from [1] to [2], and all other utterance comprehension processes, but would not presuppose a compositional semantics for E_1?

In order to state these conceptual roles I need first to assume the existence of a certain function. Let 'δ' be a variable over those structural descriptions in M that, like the description "sǔm'⌢'snō'⌢'ĭz'⌢'pûr'pəl", refer to sound sequences that are well-formed formulae of E_1, and let 'μ' range over sentences in M, Harvey's internal system of mental representation. Then, I stipulate, there is a recursive function f, issuing in statements of the form

$$f(\delta) = \mu,$$

from structural descriptions in M of the kind described to sentences of M, such that:

(i) f is definable in terms of formal features of the expressions in its domain and range, without reference to any semantic features of any expressions in either M or E_1; and

(ii) if the referent of δ can be used to say that p, then $f(\delta)$ would token the belief that p.

(In making this stipulation I am tacitly assuming that each sentence in E_1 is relevantly correlated with just one sentence in M; otherwise the description of the mapping would be slightly more complex. The existence of f, relative to this assumption, would seem to be unproblematic, in the same way that it is unproblematic that there should be a recursive mapping of French sentences onto English sentences that is statable without reference to any semantic features of those sentences, but yet maps each French sentence onto its English translation.)

The conceptual role of 'dias taht' is now stipulated to be such that:

If the sentence

$\ulcorner \alpha$ derettu $\delta \urcorner$

is in Harvey's B-box and $f(\delta) = \mu$, then, *ceteris paribus*, so is the sentence

$\ulcorner \alpha$ dias taht $\mu \urcorner$

(where 'α' is a variable over singular terms in M). Thus, if

'Nemrac derettu 'sŭm'⌢'snō'⌢'ĭz'⌢'pûr′pəl''

is in B and, as happens to be the case, f ("sŭm'⌢'snō'⌢'ĭz'⌢'pûr′pəl''") = 'emos wons si elprup', then *ceteris paribus*, so is

'Nemrac dias taht emos wons si elprup'.

So, in this way, the conceptual role of 'dias taht' automatically guarantees that, if Harvey believes that Carmen uttered 'Some snow is purple', and certain further conditions obtain, then he will believe that she said that some snow was purple.

Readers of this volume need hardly to have it pointed out that it would derogate from the plausibility of the hypothesis that Harvey even remotely approximated to being a model of us if we supposed him to be so 'programmed' that, upon hearing a sentence which in fact meant p, he automatically believed that the utterer said, or meant, that p. Hence the *ceteris paribus* clause, which, of course, is just a stand-in for a fuller specification of the conceptual role.

There is more than one psychologically feasible way of cashing out the *ceteris paribus* clause consistently with my other stipulations, and without smuggling in a compositional semantics for E_1. However, I will stipulate Harvey to satisfy a style of completion to which I am particularly drawn, as I think that it, or a variant of it, is one that may well have application to us.

I have in mind an analogy between utterance comprehension processes and a possible view of perceptual processes. Given a glimpse of a typical collie, I will believe off the bat that the creature is a dog. At the same time, I do not regard the creature's doggy appearance as being a sufficient condition for its being a dog, as I would disbelieve it to be a dog were I to become convinced that the creature was the bizarre mutant offspring of two turtles. In view of this, one *might* suppose that the transition from the initial visual stimulus, the sight of the creature, to the belief that it was a dog involved an inference to the best explanation, one that invoked a belief that possession of a doggy appearance was some high degree of evidence that its possessor was conspecific with some sample of creatures that was somehow determinative of the species *dog*.

However, for reasons that cannot now be broached, I believe that this 'inference to the best explanation' view is implausible. I think that a closer approximation to the truth would eschew inference and see me 'programmed' so as to believe straightaway, upon seeing the creature with a doggy appearance, that it is a dog, *unless* I already possess some *defeating* belief, such as the belief that the creature's parents are turtles.

With this in mind, I suggest that we think of the further specification of the conceptual role of 'dias taht', left open by the *ceteris paribus* clause, as being such that, upon hearing Carmen utter 'Some snow is purple', Harvey will straightaway come to believe that she said that some snow was purple, unless Harvey's B-box already contains some defeating sentence, such as one that realizes the belief that it is mutually obvious to him and Carmen that she does not believe that some snow is purple. But I will make no (foolish) attempt to delimit the class of potential defeaters, and so must leave the characterization of the *ceteris paribus* clause in the present sketchy state.

Faced now with the prospect of having to write out the conceptual role of 'eurt' in backwards English, I realize that it is time to depart from this tiresome convention, and to suppose, merely for intelligibility of exposition, that E_1 is written English, the 'same language' in which Harvey thinks.[15] The conceptual role of 'says that' in M (= E_1), now to replace that of 'dias taht', may be stated thus (where 'σ' ranges over

[15] We may suppose that Harvey's B-box contains a very large blackboard, and that a sentence of E_1 occurs in B just in case a token of it is written on that blackboard. Those who are fastidious about grammar may notice that I have taken minor liberties with tense constructions in E_1.

sentences of inner and outer E_1, and '$\bar{\sigma}$' is a structural description of the sentence σ):

If the sentence

⌜α uttered $\bar{\sigma}$⌝

is in Harvey's B-box, then, *ceteris paribus*, so is

⌜α said that σ⌝.

Then the example already used comes out as follows.

If

'Carmen uttered "Some snow is purple"'

is in B, then, *ceteris paribus*, so is

'Carmen said that some snow is purple'.

(I was reluctant to begin with this simplification, for fear that the reader might worry that, in the stipulation that Harvey thought and communicated in E_1, semantic assumptions were being entailed that might imply the existence of a compositional semantics for E_1. But there should not be any anxiety on this score now, given that we know how to translate into the tiresome but more explicit convention. Notice that the earlier function f has implicitly been replaced by a purely disquotational function, which maps the quotation description of each sentence of E_1 onto its referent, that very sentence of which it is a quotation description.)

This brings me to *the conceptual role of 'true' in M*, which I stipulate to be such that:

If

⌜α said that σ⌝

is in B, then so is

⌜What α said (viz., that σ), and so α's utterance, is true iff σ⌝.

Consequently, having arrived at the belief that Carmen said that some snow was purple, Harvey automatically believes as well that what she said and her utterance are true just in case some snow is purple.

So much for Harvey's mastery of his public language E_1. Harvey, I submit, is plausibly a counterexample to [U], the evident motivation for supposing that natural languages have compositional semantics. We have provided enough of a description of the possible world in which Harvey resides to make plausible the claim that (a), by virtue of the conceptual roles of certain semantic expressions in his inner code, Harvey has the ability to understand utterances of indefinitely many novel sentences of E_1, and that (b) the account of Harvey's processing of spoken utterances does not require E_1 to have a compositional semantics. And if Harvey constitutes a counterexample to [U], then, if there is a good reason to think that natural languages have compositional semantics, it cannot be that the assumption of a compositional semantics for a public language is needed to explain a person's finitely based ability to know the meanings of—that is, to understand utterances of—the sentences of that language. Despite the artificial simplicity of E_1, the issue with the CS theorist is squarely joined over it.

Yet one might now wonder if the need for a compositional semantics does not arise in the need to accommodate one or another of those features that separate E_1 from English: indexicality and ambiguity. It might especially be thought that a need for a compositional semantics will enter with indexicals, in the need to explain how, from a speaker's utterance of 'He's retired', one can know that what was said was that Nixon was retired. Let us turn, then, to E_2, which is E_1 supplemented with indexicals, that is, singular terms whose reference is context dependent. My strategy, as before, is to stipulate conceptual roles for expressions in M (now, for convenience, taken to be written, unambiguous English) that account for Harvey's ability to understand utterances in E_2, but do not presuppose a compositional semantics for E_2.

I first stipulate that M contains the predicate

$$\xi_1\text{'s utterance of } \xi_2 \text{ refers to } \xi_3 \ [= \text{Ref}\,(\xi_1, \xi_2, \xi_3)]\,.$$

No doubt this predicate has a complex conceptual role in M, one which links it with predicates ascribing communicative intentions to the utterer; but that is not anything that needs now to be specified; we may take it for granted that the conceptual role of 'Ref' permits its application in comprehension processes involving utterances containing indexicals. It remains to be shown that the role of this predicate can cohere with a noncompositional account of understanding.

The revised conceptual role for 'says that' is as follows (where each t_i is an indexical of E_2, α and each β_i is an internal singular term, and '$\Sigma\,(t_1, \ldots, t_n)$' is a structural description of the sentence Σ in which occur the indexicals $t_1, \ldots, t_n$):

If the sentences

$\ulcorner\alpha$ uttered $\overline{\Sigma (t_1, \ldots, t_n)}\urcorner$

and

$\ulcorner$Ref $(\alpha, \bar{t}_1, \beta_1)$ and $\ldots$ and Ref $(\alpha, \bar{t}_n, \beta_n)\urcorner$

are in Harvey's B-box, then, *ceteris paribus,* so is

$\ulcorner\alpha$ said that $\Sigma (\beta_1, \ldots, \beta_n)\urcorner$.

The conceptual role for 'true' remains the same. Thus, if

'Ralph uttered "He is retired" '

and

'Ralph's utterance of "he" refers to Nixon'

are in B, then, *ceteris paribus*, so are

'Ralph said that Nixon is retired'

and

'What Ralph said, as well as his utterance, is true iff Nixon is retired.'

Likewise, if

'Ralph uttered "She believes that he gave it to her" '

and

'Ref (Ralph, "she", Sally) and Ref (Ralph, "he", George) and Ref (Ralph, "it", the Hope diamond) and Ref (Ralph, "her", Liz)'

are in B, then, *ceteris paribus*, so are

'Ralph said that Sally believes that George gave the Hope diamond to Liz'

and, of course,

'What Ralph said [etc.] is true iff Sally believes [etc.] '.

There is a weak sort of compositionality now implicated in the conceptual role of 'says that' in M, since we are taking account of some aspects of an utterances's internal structure. But, of course, no compositional semantics is being relied on, because each n-ary predicate of E_2, however complex, is being treated noncompositionally, *as if* it were primitive. The upshot is that, by making stipulations about the conceptual roles of 'says that' and 'true' in M, we can explain, without recourse to a compositional semantics for E_2, Harvey's ability to understand indefinitely many utterances of indefinitely many novel sentences in his public, indexical language. Indexicality, then, does not carry with it the need for a compositional semantics.[16]

I turn now to E_3, which is full-blown English, and to Harvey's ability to comprehend utterances of ambiguous sentences. However, to keep the discussion simple, I shall ignore indexicality, thus in effect showing how ambiguity can be added, without incorporation of a compositional semantics, to E_1.

Let us suppose that M—English *qua* language of thought—has the predicate 'means the same as', the conceptual role of which permits Harvey to have in his B-box sentences such as

[6] 'Cape' means the same as 'short sleeveless cloak' and 'promontory of land'

and

[7] 'Henry bought a cape' means the same as 'Henry bought a short sleeveless cloak' and 'Henry bought a promontory of land'.

The occurrence of [7] in B is of course dependent on the occurrence of [6] in B, but to explain this we need only to stipulate that the conceptual role of 'means the same as' requires Harvey to have in B the sentence:

If e means the same as é, then $\ulcorner$. . . e . . .$\urcorner$ means the same as $\ulcorner$. . . e′ . . .$\urcorner$.

There is nothing in the conceptual role of 'means the same as', as it occurs in Harvey's head, that requires a compositional semantics for E_3. To accommodate Harvey's ability to understand utterances of ambiguous sentences we may revise the conceptual role of 'says that' thus (where 'σ' ranges over sentences of the outer E_3, and 'μ' over

---

[16] In a similar vein we can allow for a degree of compositionality induced by truth-affecting recursion clauses for connectives and quantifiers, while also insisting that, as there is no finite way of specifying semantic values for the basic predicates of the language, it enjoys no compositional semantics.

sentences of M, inner E_2: it may be assumed that the language of thought is ambiguity-free):

If the sentences

⌜α uttered σ̄⌝

and

⌜σ̄ means the same as $\bar{\mu}_1$ and $\bar{\mu}_2$⌝

and

?

are in Harvey's B-box, then, *ceteris paribus*, so is

⌜α said that μ_1⌝.

The task of filling in the missing mentalese sentence is analogous to the task of specifying the *ceteris paribus* clause: suggestions here are perforce speculations on empirical issues, ideally to be resolved by some future cognitive psychology. Still, as a first approximation, or gesture, towards the *sort* of filling we might expect, we may stipulate that, in Harvey's head at least, the lacuna is to be filled by this sentence of M:

⌜It is more probable that α believes that μ_1 than that α believes that μ_2⌝.[17]

Then we know that, if Harvey has in B the sentences

'Ralph uttered "Henry bought a cape"', '"Henry bought a cape" means the same as ". . . short sleeveless cloak" and ". . . promontory of land"',

and

'It is more probable that Ralph believes that Henry bought a short sleeveless cloak than that he believes that Henry bought a promontory of land',

then, *ceteris paribus*, so, too, is

'Ralph said that Henry bought a short sleeveless cloak'.

Harvey is now plausibly a counterexample to the claim that there

---

[17] Of course, in a more adequate rendering there would be trade-offs with other factors such as conversational appropriateness.

could be no correct account of a person's ability to understand *natural language* utterances that did not imply that natural languages have compositional semantics. But there is still something that we can do that Harvey has not yet been equipped to do, and which has bearing on the nature of radical interpretation.

Not enough has been stipulated about M to show that Harvey, upon hearing Pierre utter 'La neige est blanche', can figure out that Pierre said that snow was white, or that Mrs Malaprop, in uttering 'Regular exercise is enervating' said that regular exercise was energizing. Let me then simply stipulate that M contains the predicate

$$\xi_1 \text{ means for } \xi_2 \text{ what } \xi_3 \text{ means for } \xi_4,$$

the conceptual role of which is such that (where 'σ' is a variable over all sound or mark sequences):

If

$\ulcorner \alpha \text{ uttered } \bar{\sigma} \urcorner$

and

$\ulcorner \bar{\sigma} \text{ means for } \alpha \text{ what } \bar{\sigma}' \text{ means for me} \urcorner$

are in B, then, *ceteris paribus*, so is

$\ulcorner \alpha \text{ said that } \sigma'. \urcorner$

The implicit point about radical interpretation is as follows. In radical interpretation we seek explicit propositional knowledge that will enable us to understand utterances in the native's language J. Since J contains infinitely many sentences, the knowledge sought must be expressible in a finitely statable theory of J. It might be thought that this theory could be a correct *translation manual* from J into the interpreter's public language. Surely, one can understand utterances in J if one can translate J sentences into one's own. But Davidsonians have been scornful of translational theories of radical interpretation. For one could know a procedure for translating one language into another without knowing what the sentences of either language meant. When one translates into one's own language, it is clear, one relies on one's *prior knowledge* of what the sentences of the translating language mean; 'but this is knowledge of precisely the kind that was to be accounted for in the first place'.[18] Consequently, it is felt, the translational approach to interpretation

[18] Evans and McDowell (1976).

serves only to enable us to conceal from ourselves our utter incapacity to do what we ought to be doing. What we ought to be doing is stating [not a translation manual, which can be known without knowing what the sentences of either the translated or the translating language mean, but] something such that, if someone knew it, he would be able to speak and understand the language.[19]

Thus, for the Davidsonian, the explicit knowledge needed in radical interpretation is knowledge of a 'meaning theory', a finitely statable theory that 'explicitly states something knowledge of which would suffice for interpreting utterances of speakers' of J.[20] Obviously, if this is correct, then every natural language has a compositional semantics.

The mistake in this line of reasoning is in the presupposition that a meaning theory is needed to account for one's understanding of one's own language. It is true that in radical interpretation one seeks a finitely statable theory explicit knowledge of which will enable one to interpret utterances in J. But for Harvey the only finitely statable theory needed is a *translation manual* from J into Harvey's public language; as no compositional semantics is needed to explain Harvey's understanding of his own public language, no compositional semantics, no 'meaning theory', is needed for J.

I have tried to describe a possible world in which a person's ability to understand utterances in a natural language does not presuppose a compositional semantics for that language. While I recognize that my sketch has been too incomplete to prove the point, I hope that it has not been too incomplete to make it plausible.

Now the person in my possible world is a human computer; he thinks in a neural machine-language, a language of thought, and I accounted for his ability to comprehend utterances in his public language by stipulating conceptual roles for expressions in his inner code. Yet the language of thought assumption, which I do not dismiss as having application to us, has been merely heuristic, and the story need not have been told in terms of conceptual roles of inner formulae, but could have been couched, with only minor adjustments, in terms of the functional, or causal, properties of the neural states which realize our beliefs. Actually, I think that even that much cranial penetration may already be more than is required to explain our capacity to comprehend natural languages; but I recognize that these are topics for another occasion.

[19] Ibid., p. ix.   [20] Davidson (1976), p. 33.

There is, however, a remaining question, one already alluded to, that is still for this occasion.

I have construed [U], in its application to Harvey, as being the processing explanation imputed to the [U]-theorist on p. 187–8. This, I take it, is a fair reading of the rationale suggested by Davidson, certainly the dominant, if not the only, sort of rationale discernible in the literature. At all events, it is a basis for subscribing to the CS theory that must be taken seriously, and my concern in constructing Harvey has been merely to refute that motivation for the CS theory, by showing how Harvey could understand spoken English, even though his processing of spoken utterances was not in accordance with any compositional semantics for English.

At the same time I left open the question of whether a compositional semantics would be needed to account for the semantic, or representational, features of Harvey's inner code M; to account, that is to say, for what makes an occurrence of 'emos wons si elprup' in Harvey's B-box an instance of his believing that some snow is purple. But if M has a compositional semantics, and there exists the function f described on p. 189, then E, Harvey's public language, will also have a compositional semantics. This would by no means show that Harvey was not, in the way detailed, a counterexample to [U], but it would mean that there remains a basis for thinking that natural languages have compositional semantics that has not yet been disarmed. This may seem strange, given that I began this essay by motivating my attack on [U] by my wanting to deny that natural languages have compositional semantics. One may wonder why I have chosen to reply to one argument for the CS theory (the one suggested by [U]), but not another (the one implicit in the two-factor theory of mental representation).

There is a reason. I had been led to deny the CS theory by my views on propositional attitude content—that is, on mental representation. These views not only reject the relational theory of belief (see p. 176), but also the two-factor theory of mental representation: beliefs are indeed true or false, and do indeed have "content" (one of my beliefs is that the Pope is Polish), but, I want (in my forthcoming book) to say, there is neither a need nor the possibility of explicating the semantic or representational features of beliefs in terms of truth-theoretic notions that would require a compositional semantics for the believer's inner system of mental representation.[21] Thus, I wanted to deny a

[21] I am thus taking back the line advanced in [27], that a truth-theoretic semantics would be needed in the construction of a "reliability theory" for an

certain claim about natural languages—namely, that they have compositional semantics—because of views that I held on propositional attitude content. From this perspective, the special importance to me of [U], the Davidsonian motivation for the CS theory, is precisely that it does not proceed from assumptions about propositional attitude content; it purports to establish that natural languages have compositional semantics without relying on any special assumptions about the truth-theoretic content of beliefs.

V

I have not tried to show that natural languages do not have compositional semantics, but only that the assumption that they do is not *required* to explain one's ability to understand natural language utterances. At the same time, my dominating interest in showing this is to pave the way for arguing, on some other occasion, that no natural language has a compositional semantics. In this final section I want briefly to discuss the ramifications of denying the CS theory for two other issues: physicalism and Gricean semantics.

Sillier philosophers can be imagined than the one who began his theorizing about language and thought with a degree of expectation of achieving a theory that would accommodate the following suppositions.

A. *Some marks and sounds have interlinguistically ascribable semantic properties.* For example, each of the six sentences resulting from

‘Snow is white’   }   { means that snow is white

‘La neige est blanche’ }   { can be used to say that snow is white

                           { is true iff snow is white

is true, and the semantic predicate phrases contained in them ascribe the same properties to both subject sentences.

B. *We have beliefs (and other propositional attitudes) with determinate content.* For example, the sentence

Paul and I believe that at least some snow is white

is, quite literally, true, and, it may be added, the sentence ascribes

agent—that is, a theory which exploits an agent's beliefs as reliable indicators of external-world states of affairs. On these matters I am much in sympathy with an unpublished *MS* of Hartry Field's, "Thought Without Content."

precisely the same property—the one expressed by the predicate 'believes that at least some snow is white'—to both of us.

C. *These semantic and psychological facts are not irreducibly semantic or psychological, but can be revealed to be facts statable by sentences devoid of semantic or psychological terms; and if these facts, like functional facts, are not themselves physical facts, then they, like functional facts again, are at least realized by physical facts.* This assumption need reflect no confidence in the enterprise known as conceptual analysis, but merely the inability to accept that semantic and psychological properties, being irreducible, are primitive and inexplicable. The sentiment here is that, surely, somewhere down the line such facts must cash out into a bedrock of physical facts which determine all of the semantic and psychological facts there are. Clearly, the feeling is, the fact that, say, 'Fido' refers to Fido cannot be accepted as a brute, primitive, irreducible fact; surely that thought violates those physicalistic scruples which ought to guide any rational inquiry into our nature and that of the world we inhabit. This conviction is held so strongly by some that they are willing to urge that one should not be prepared to maintain that there *are* semantic or psychological facts unless one is prepared to maintain that such facts are reducible to physical facts.

D. *The Gricean programme in semantics is essentially correct, and the semantic reduces to the psychological in the style of that programme.* That is, a certain notion of communication, or speaker's meaning, is to be taken as foundational in the theory of meaning by defining it, without reference to anything overtly semantic, in terms of acting with the intention of producing belief or action in another, all other public language semantic notions then to be defined in terms of the reduced notion of speaker's meaning.[22]

Our imagined philosopher would doubtless have many reasons for subscribing to this attractive programme, paramount among them perhaps being that: (a) the only feasible reduction of the semantic and the psychological to the physical is via the reduction of the semantic to the psychological, and (b) the Gricean programme is the only feasible programme for reducing the semantic to the psychological. (I have argued for (a) elsewhere;[23] (b) I take to be obvious (on reflection).)

---

[22] See especially Bennett (1976); Grice (1957, 1968, 1969, and 1982); Loar (1976 and 1981); Schiffer (1972, 1981a, 1981b, and 1982); and Strawson (1964 and 1971).

[23] Schiffer (1982).

Yet the philosopher who was not silly to begin in this way may come to realize that, alas, it would be silly to continue in it.

He will certainly encounter trouble over his physicalistic assumption (C), and we may imagine him becoming convinced that no such reduction is to be had. If, he comes to realize, it is a fact that be believes that Los Angeles is smoggy, then that fact is not physicalistically reducible; it is not a fact statable in a non-mentalistic idiom. But what is our theorist now to do? Is he to bite the eliminativist bullet and deny that we have beliefs with content and words with meaning, or, even worse, to recant, to renounce the scruples of the natural scientist and 'just surface listlessly to the Sargasso Sea of mentalism'?[24]

Not, push having come to shove, quite, the theorist is likely to respond. And to prepare the way for the resolution of his dilemma he will insist that we need to be clearer than we have so far been about *reduction* and *physicalism*. As I myself have been drawn to his solution, I shall state it for him in *propria persona*.

It will help to begin by distinguishing between:

(a) the reduction of *extralinguistic* psychological *entities*— substances (believers), states or events (beliefs), or properties (believing that such and such, being a belief that such and such)

and

(b) the reduction of psychological *sentences*.

When, as regards (a), our concern is with objective, language independent things, of whatever ontological category, then to say that As reduce to Bs is just to say that As *are* Bs. Reduction here is identity. If, for example, belief properties reduce to functional properties, then every belief property is identical to some functional property.

Sometimes talk of reduction has as its topic predicates or the sentences containing them. To say in the context of the mind/body problem that A-sentences reduce to B-sentences will mean that every A-sentence enjoys some suitably strong equivalence relation, typically necessary equivalence, to some B-sentence.

The distinction between entity-reduction and sentence-reduction is easily elided if one supposes that there are objective, language-independent belief properties, properties such as being a belief that Fido is a dog. For their reduction would induce the corresponding reduction for belief sentences, and a reduction of belief sentences

_____
[24] Quine (1975), p. 91.

would virtually assure the identification of belief properties with properties specifiable in a non-mentalistic idiom.

The distinction between entity-reduction and sentence-reduction becomes of interest when one entertains the possibility that (a) there are no belief properties, but (b) there are true belief-ascribing sentences. Taking this possibility seriously, one cannot glibly identify physicalism with the doctrine that there are no irreducibly-mental entities—either substances, events, or properties. For that would leave open the possibility of a position whose physicalistic credentials are not immediately evident: namely, the position which affirms:

   (i) that nothing extralinguistic is irreducibly psychological;
  (ii) that there are no belief properties;
 (iii) that there are true, but irreducible, belief-ascribing sentences.

It will be useful, then, to follow the distinction between entity-reduction and sentence-reduction with a corresponding distinction between what—if we can divest the term of its emotive connotations—may be called two kinds of physicalism:

  (a) *Ontological Physicalism*: there are no extralinguistic irreducibly psychological entities of any ontological category.
  (b) *Sentential Physicalism*: there are no irreducibly psychological sentences.

The two kinds of physicalism will roughly coincide if there are belief properties; but they become interestingly different when, for whatever reason, one contemplates denying that such properties exist. Consequently, one cannot argue merely from the truth of Ontological Physicalism to the truth of Sentential Physicalism.

The favoured resolution of the theorist's dilemma is now simply this: to accept Ontological Physicalism, but reject Sentential Physicalism. I am inclined to take the failure to reduce belief predicates to show that there are no belief properties, construed as objective entities whose existence is genuinely independent of the predicates which are thought to express them; for, if there were such belief properties, they would not, for compelling reasons here left unsaid, be irreducible.[25] Ontological

[25] I hope that it goes without saying that, while I deny the existence of genuinely language-independent belief properties and facts, I can certainly accept the pleonastic use of these terms that is without theoretical import, such as the use of 'fact' in 'It is a fact that Ralph believes that Fido is a dog'. In denying the existence of language-independent belief properties I am denying (*inter alia*) the Fregean view that there exists a certain abstract entity, the property of

Dualism is indeed insupportable. But Sentential Dualism, for reasons that also remain to be revealed, is not.

There is, however, a problem with this solution to the theorist's dilemma: this piecemeal nominalism is liable to seem *ad hoc*, a facile solution to a local problem.

It is precisely at this point that the case against the CS theory becomes relevant to the issue of physicalism. For if the CS theory is wrong for the reason I have suggested, then *the denial of the existence of belief properties is mandatory*. For suppose that what I earlier suggested (but did not attempt to prove) is right, and that we should reject the CS theory because (i) the only feasible construal of belief predicates consonant with that theory is the relational theory of those predicates, but (ii) the relational theory is false. Then it can be shown that there *cannot* be belief properties.

For assume that (a) belief predicates such as 'believes that flounders rarely snore' do express genuinely objective, language-independent belief properties, and that (b) as the relational theory is false, there is no correct treatment of 'believes' as being semantically primitive. Then there would be an *infinity* of *semantically primitive* belief predicates, the semantic values of which were the primitive, *noncomposite* belief-properties they expressed, and English would certainly be unlearnable. But English is eminently learnable. Therefore, it is not the case that (a) and (b), that is, there are no belief properties if the relational theory of propositional attitude verbs is false. As an Ontological Physicalist who is convinced that there are true belief sentences, I welcome this result.

The Gricean programme of defining semantic predicates in terms of psychological ones is, for me at least, drained of most of its appeal and much of its motivation by the failure of Sentential Physicalism. But that is not the connection between Gricean semantics and compositional semantics on which I wish to conclude.

Griceans have had quite a lot to say about the correct analysis of speaker's meaning, but surprisingly little to say about the meaning of linguistic expressions, and even less to say about those vehicles of meaning which might well be thought the primary interest of philo-

---

believing that snow is white, such that the predicate 'believes that snow is white' means what it does by virtue of its standing in a certain contingent relation to that property.

sophers of language—sentences of natural languages. This is not without an explanation.

It is definitive of the Gricean programme that I have called 'intention-based semantics'[26] that, for every sentence σ of every natural language L, there is some property ϕ, constitutive of the meaning of σ in L, such that:

(1) ϕ has a specification in wholly psychological terms, which include, in particular, those propositional attitudes deemed by the Gricean theorist to be constitutive of speakers' meaning;

(2) by virtue of having ϕ, σ is a *conventional means* among speakers of L for performing acts of speaker's meaning of a certain type;

(3) σ's being ϕ entails that σ has whatever meaning σ happens to have in L.

The picture we then get in regard to language understanding is this: a speaker utters a (perhaps novel) sentence σ; an audience hears the utterance and somehow forms the belief that σ is ϕ, for some ϕ satisfying (1)–(3); from his belief that σ is ϕ, together with certain other beliefs, the audience concludes that the speaker, in uttering σ, meant, and said, that such and such.

Now what are these psychological ϕs, and how is the theorist to account for a finite creature's ability to correlate a potential infinity of sentences with a potential infinity of such psychological properties? I am personally aware of nothing in the literature that even comes close to being a plausible answer to this question. The reason, I suggest, is this: (a) the Gricean account of sentence meaning can be correct only if natural languages have compositional semantics, finitely statable theories that, for the Gricean, assign to each of the infinitely many sentences of a language that complex, composite psychological property constitutive of its meaning; but (b) natural languages neither have nor need compositional semantics. I leave it to the reader to draw the rude inference, and I trust Paul to be forebearing of my apostasy.[27]

---

[26] See Schiffer (1981b and 1982).

[27] This paper has benefited from my discussions with Hartry Field, Mike Harnish, Brian Loar, Christopher Peacocke, John Pollock, Keith Quillen, Michele Schiffer, and Richard Warner.

REFERENCES

Bennett, J., *Linguistic Behaviour*, Cambridge University Press, Cambridge, 1976.

Burge, T., 'The Content of Propositional Attitudes', delivered at the 1980 APA Western Division Meetings; abstract published in *Noûs*, 14 (1980), pp. 53–8.

——, 'Other Bodies', in *Thought and Object*, ed. A. Woodfield, Oxford University Press, Oxford, 1982.

Davidson, D., 'Truth and Meaning', *Synthese*, 17 (1967), pp. 304–28.

——, 'On Saying That', in *Words and Objections*, eds D. Davidson and J. Hintikka, D. Reidel, Dordrecht, 1969.

——, 'Reply to Foster', in *Truth and Meaning: Essays in Semantics*, eds G. Evans and J. McDowell, Oxford University Press, Oxford, 1976.

Davies, M., 'Taylor on Meaning-Theories and Theories of Meaning', *Mind*, 93 (1984), pp. 85–90.

Evans, G., and McDowell, J., 'Introduction', in *Truth and Meaning: Essays in Semantics*, eds G. Evans and J. McDowell, Oxford University Press, Oxford, 1976.

Field, H., 'Logic, Meaning, and Conceptual Role', *Journal of Philosophy*, 74 (1977), pp. 379–409.

——, 'Mental Representation', *Erkenntnis*, 13 (1978), pp. 9–61.

Grice, H. P., 'Meaning', *Philosophical Review*, 66 (1957), pp. 377–88.

——, 'Utterer's Meaning, Sentence-Meaning, and Word-Meaning', *Foundations of Language*, 4 (1968), pp. 225–42.

——, 'Utterer's Meaning and Intentions', *Philosophical Review*, 78 (1969), pp. 147–77.

——, 'Meaning Revisited', in *Mutual Knowledge*, ed. N. V. Smith, Academic Press, London, 1982.

Harman, G., 'Language, Thought, and Communication', in *Language, Mind and Knowledge* (Minnesota Studies in the Philosophy of Science, vol. VII), ed. K. Gunderson, University of Minnesota Press, Minneapolis, 1975.

Katz, J., *Semantic Theory*, Harper & Row, New York, 1972.

Lewis, D., 'General Semantics', in *Semantics of Natural Languages*, eds D. Davidson and G. Harman, Reidel, Dordrecht, 1972.

Loar, B., 'Two Theories of Meaning', in *Truth and Meaning: Essays in Semantics*, eds. G. Evans and J. McDowell, Oxford University Press, Oxford, 1976.

——, *Mind and Meaning*, Cambridge University Press, Cambridge, 1981.

——, 'Conceptual Role and Truth Conditions', *Notre Dame Journal of Formal Logic*, 23 (1982), pp. 272–83.

Lycan, W., *Logical Form in Natural Language*, MIT/Bradford Press, Cambridge, 1984.

McGinn, C., 'The Structure of Content', in *Thought and Object*, ed. A. Woodfield, Oxford University Press, Oxford, 1982.

Putnam, H., 'The Meaning of "Meaning"', in *Philosophical Papers Vol. II: Mind, Language and Reality*, Cambridge University Press, Cambridge, 1975.

———, *Meaning and the Moral Sciences*, Routledge and Kegan Paul, London, 1978.

Quine, W., 'Mind and Verbal Dispositions', in *Mind and Language: Wolfson College Lectures 1974*, Oxford University Press, Oxford, 1975.

Schiffer, S., *Meaning*, Oxford University Press, Oxford, 1972.

———, 'Truth and the Theory of Content', in *Meaning and Understanding*, eds. H. Parrot and J. Bouveresse, de Gruyter, Berlin, 1981a.

———, 'Indexicals and the Theory of Reference', *Synthese*, 49 (1981b), pp. 43–100.

———, 'Intention-Based Semantics', *Notre Dame Journal of Formal Logic*, 23 (1982), pp. 119–56.

Strawson, P. F., 'Intention and Convention in Speech Acts', *Philosophical Review*, 73 (1964), pp. 439–60.

———, 'Meaning and Truth', in *Logico-Linguistic Papers*, Methuen, London, 1971.

7

MEANING, COMMUNICATION,
AND REPRESENTATION

JOHN SEARLE

I

The purpose of this paper is to explore some, though by no means all, of the relationships between the concepts of meaning, communication, and representation. More precisely, its aim is to explore the relations between the notion of speaker meaning—what it is for a person to mean something when he issues an utterance or performs some other action by which he means something—and the notions of representation and communication. Its aim is not, however, to explore the ordinary usage of the three English verbs 'mean', 'communicate', and 'represent'. The verb 'mean' and the corresponding noun 'meaning' in particular are notorious sources of confusion; and I do not believe they adequately express the notion that I am trying to analyse. Notice, incidentally, that 'mean' does not translate comfortably into either French or German. It has no exact equivalent among the group that includes 'meinen', 'bedeuten', 'vouloir dire', and 'signifier'. The problem I am discussing can be posed without using any of these words. It is this. People perform illocutionary acts: they make statements, give orders, ask questions, etc. In doing so they make noises, or marks on paper; they draw pictures, or wave their arms about, etc. Now my problem is: what must be added to these noises, marks, etc., in order that they should be statements, orders, etc.? What, so to speak, must be added to the physics to get the semantics? In short, that question can be posed as, 'What is it for a speaker to mean something by an utterance?', but it should not be thought that the question is solely or even primarily about the meaning of 'meaning' in English.

In the past, following Grice, I have argued that the concept of intention was the crucial element in the analysis of meaning. I still

¹ Versions of this paper were delivered at the University of Hamburg (1974) and at the APA Western Division (1976).

believe that to be the case, but I believe that the precise role of intention in the analysis of meaning has been at least partly misdescribed by
Grice, myself, and other authors. I will begin this discussion by sum-
marizing my previous views in order to place my present views in the
context of past discussions of this subject: when a speaker utters a
sentence and means it literally, that is, when he means literally what he
says, he performs an illocutionary act and the performance of that
illocutionary act (assuming the context is appropriate) consists in
uttering the sentence with a certain set of intentions directed at a
possible hearer. One can summarize these intentions by saying that
they are:

(a) the intention to produce a certain illocutionary effect in the
    hearer,
(b) the intention to produce this effect by getting the hearer to
    recognize the intention to produce the effect,
(c) the intention to produce the recognition by means of the
    hearer's knowledge of the rules governing the sentence.[2]

This analysis was inspired by Grice's work on meaning, but there are
some crucial differences between my analysis and his.[3] One of them
is this: Grice argued that the intended effects of meaning were what
Austin called perlocutionary effects. Thus, for example, if I say, 'It's
raining', and mean it, for Grice, I intend to produce in some audience
the *belief* that it is raining; or if I say, 'Leave the room', and mean it,
I intend to produce in the audience the response of leaving the room.[4]
I have argued against Grice that the intended effects of meaning are not
perlocutionary but rather illocutionary; that is, I have argued that when
I say, for example, 'It's raining', I may say it and mean it without any
intention of *convincing* or *persuading* my audience or otherwise getting
them to believe it or even getting them to believe that I believe it. I may
be quite indifferent as to whether the audience believes what I say, or
whether or not any perlocutionary effects are produced at all. I argued
against Grice that the intended effect of meaning was *understanding*

---

[2] J. R. Searle, *Speech Acts*, Cambridge University Press, 1969, pp. 49–50.

[3] Most obviously, Grice was concerned with a general account of meaning
and I was concerned with applying that account to the special case of literal
utterance for the purpose of developing a theory of speech acts.

[4] 'Meaning', *Philosophical Review*, 1957. The analysis is modified in later
articles, but the modifications all rely on perlocutionary effects. 'Utterers Meaning
and Intentions', *Philosophical Review*, 1969, pp. 147 ff., and 'Utterers Meaning,
Sentence Meaning, and Word Meaning', *Foundations of Language*, 1968.

and that a non-circular account of understanding could be given in terms of the commitments of the speaker in making the utterance. In brief, Grice argued that meaning-intentions were intentions to produce a *response* in a hearer. I argued that meaning-intentions were intentions to produce *understanding* in the hearer, and that understanding consists in the knowledge of the conditions on the speech act being performed by the speaker. It is the knowledge of these conditions that I have called the 'illocutionary effect'.

So much by way of past claims. But now the question forces itself on us: if my objections to Grice are really valid why can't I extend them to my own account? I argued against Grice that one can say something and mean it and still not intend to produce any response or action by the hearer. But why can there not be cases where one says something, means it, and does not intend to produce understanding in the hearer? In a case, for example, where I know that my hearer is not paying any attention to me I might feel it my duty to make a statement even though I know he will not understand me. In such cases the speech act is indeed defective, because the speaker fails to secure illocutionary up-take; but even in such cases it seems clear that the speaker means *something* by what he says even though he knows his speech act is defective. Furthermore, what shall we say about cases of soliloquy where the speaker talks to himself or writes in a diary or a journal? In the past I have dealt with such objections as follows: the soliloquy case is simply the limiting case of communication, where the speaker (S) is identical with the hearer (H). Soliloquy on this account is in principle not different from any other form of discourse. It differs only in the fact that S and H are identical. The written journal or diary that one keeps is a form of communiction to one's self, though perhaps to one's *future* self, and hence is an attempt to produce an illocutionary effect on one's self or on one's future self.[5] And the case where one makes a statement in the full knowledge that one's hearer will not understand it again seemed to me not a serious counterexample, because that it is a defective or infelicitous speech act is already determined by the concept of the speech act in question. The failure to secure illocutionary uptake is one in which a speech act can be defective. But even in such cases one acts *as if* one were communicating, and thus it seemed to me that the communication case remained the primary case.

Perhaps such answers are really satisfactory as ways of dealing with

[5] See Grice, 1969, pp. 174 ff., for a similar response to this objection.

these alleged counterexamples. But in any case I believe the counter-examples are now paving the way for a more radical objection. Like most speech act theorists I have analysed meaning in terms of com-munication. The intentions that are the essence of meaning are inten-tions to produce effects on hearers, that is, they are intentions to communicate. But it now seems to me, for reasons I want to explain in this article, that in at least one sense of 'meaning', communication is derived from meaning rather than constitutive of meaning. Communica-tion, one might say, is a consequence of meaning, but meaning exists independently of the intention to communicate that meaning.

As a preliminary formulation, I shall argue that a speaker's uttering something and meaning something by it consists in the speaker's utter-ing something with the intention that his utterance should represent the world in one or more of the possible illocutionary modes, and that the intention to communicate is the intention that these meaning intentions should be recognized by the hearer. In order to make these claims clear I want to begin the analysis afresh.

II

Suppose you wanted to communicate something to someone with whom you had no common language. Suppose furthermore that it mattered very seriously that you succeed, that it was a question of some urgency. Just to have a concrete example to work with, let us suppose that while you are driving through Calabria your car suffers a broken crankshaft. Let us suppose that you locate a mechanic but he speaks no English and you speak no Italian. How would you go about communicating to him that your crankshaft was broken? Since the crankshaft is inside the engine block, there is no way you can show him the crankshaft. But if you knew what a crankshaft looks like and you had a pencil and paper handy a perfectly natural way to go about communicating that your crankshaft was broken would be to draw a picture of an engine block with a broken crankshaft inside it. Perhaps you might also direct his attention to your engine block so that he would know which crankshaft and which engine block was in question. With reasonable luck and reasonable skill at drawing you might succeed in communicating to him the fact that your crankshaft was broken.

Let us now attempt to describe the salient features of this very primitive communication situation.

(1) In drawing the picture the 'speaker' (S) *represents* the state of affairs of his crankshaft—being broken. Once drawn, the picture then can be said to *represent* that state of affairs.

(2) If his efforts are successful S will succeed in *communicating* to the 'hearer' (H) that his crankshaft is broken. If S succeeds, the picture can be said to *communicate* to H the fact that the crankshaft is broken.

But now notice that what is represented is not quite the same as what is communicated. What is represented is a state of affairs, but what is communicated is not a state of affairs, but one might say, the representation of that state of affairs. In English this is concealed by an ambiguity of 'that' clauses. One can, without too much awkwardness, say either that the picture represents (the fact) that your crankshaft is broken, or that it communicates (the fact) that your crankshaft is broken. But the corresponding noun phrases reveal the fundamental difference: the picture represents your broken crankshaft and it represents your crankshaft as broken, but it does not make any sense to say that it communicates your broken crankshaft or that it communicates your crankshaft as broken. Rather one must say: it communicates that your crankshaft is broken. The picture as a material object is used both to represent and to communicate; however, it is not used to communicate the object represented, but rather the representation of it. One might say in the terminology of speech-act theory that the representation consists of a propositional content in an illocutionary mode, and that this propositional content represents the state of affairs, but it is the propositional content in that mode and not the state of affairs that is communicated.

Furthermore, in the example, the representation of the broken crankshaft is clearly separable from the communication of the fact that the crankshaft is broken. This is brought out by the fact that one can represent without communicating, or without any intention to communicate. For example, I might just draw the picture to have a picture of my broken crankshaft without any desire or intention to communicate the fact that the crankshaft is broken to anyone. Nor does it seem correct to say in such cases that I am communicating with my future self, or acting as if I were communicating with someone else. For I might, for example, deliberately draw the picture with the intention that there be no communication at all. I might intend to destroy the picture or draw it in disappearing ink, for example. In this example, at least, it seems to me that representation is both prior to, and independent of, communication. It is *independent* in the sense that one may represent without any intention to communicate, and it is *prior* to in the sense that what one communicates is dependent on there being a representation which is communicated. In such cases, at least, one communicates one's representations; and one can represent without communicating, but one cannot communicate without representing.

The question about this example now divides into two parts. How does the picture represent and how does it communicate? What makes the picture into a representation is not a physical property of the picture, nor is the representing relation solely a matter of the resemblance between the picture and the broken crankshaft. Resemblance, though it is clearly a help in pictorial communication, is not a sufficient condition of representation, whether pictorial or otherwise. My left boot resembles my right boot. It may even have been made with the intention that it should resemble my right boot, but that is neither a sufficient nor a necessary condition of its being used to represent my right boot. My left boot does not represent anything at all, however much it may resemble other objects.

What then, so to speak, has to be added to the picture to make it into a representation? The obvious answer is that in order for the picture to be a representation of a state of affairs the speaker must produce it with the intention that it represent that state of affairs. (The element of production here is not crucial: the speaker might *use* an antecedently existing picture to represent his broken crankshaft.) The intention that the object should represent seems to be a crucial element in the representing relation. Our first tentative hypothesis then is this: in order that an entity X represent some state of affairs A, it must be the case that there is some person S such that S intends that X represent A. In colloquial speech we might say that S must use X to represent A, or S must produce X with the intention that it represent A, where these formulations either state explicitly or imply the intention to represent on the part of S.

Though I think this point is true, and though it does specify a necessary condition for the application of the concept of representation, it is obviously no more than a preliminary to the analysis of the concept because it employs the notion of representation itself. One cannot analyse representation in terms of the intention to represent without circularity or infinite regress. In order that we get a non-circular analysis of representation we must ask the next question: what is it that one intends when one intends that X represent A? what exactly do

I intend, for example, when I intend that the picture represent my broken crankshaft? The answer to that question, if it is to have any real explanatory power, should be given in terms that employ no such semantic notions as reference, truth, meaning, propositions, etc. Perhaps, in the end, it will prove impossible to give an answer that does not employ such notions. However, at least a start on such an answer can be made by showing how representing relates to intentional behaviour generally.

It is a general feature of intentional behaviour that it can succeed or fail, and that the intentions determine the conditions of success and hence the conditions of failure. My intention that the picture represent will be successful under certain conditions and not under others. My intention to represent can at least in part be analysed as the intention that certain conditions be satisfied, and these conditions are conditions of success of the utterance. How exactly can we specify these conditions? The most obvious way to get at these conditions would be to ask what counts as a failure. When would we say the speaker had made a 'mistake'? In the case of the broken crankshaft an obvious mistake would be made if S's crankshaft were not broken. If S's crankshaft is not broken then he has made a mistake in representing it as broken. In this case, the intention to represent the state of affairs that the crankshaft is broken consists at least in part in the intention that a condition of success of the utterance should be that the crankshaft is broken (and that this state of affairs should exist independently of the utterance). And in general we may say that whenever S produces X with the intention that it represent a state of affairs A then it must be the case that S produces X with the intention that a criterion of success of his action should be that A obtains, independently of the utterance.

Notice that so far the intentions to represent can be specified quite independently of the intentions to communicate. However, the converse does not seem to be the case. The intention to communicate (at least in the sort of example we have been considering) requires a representation which is to be communicated, and the representation itself requires the intentions of the sort that we have just discussed. What, then, exactly is the intention to communicate? Let us continue with our example of the Calabrian crankshaft.

In that example S will have succeeded in communicating to H that his crankshaft is broken as soon as H recognizes that the picture is a representation of that state of affairs. S's intention to communicate, therefore, is the intention that H should recognize the picture as a representation of that state of affairs. But as we have already seen, that the picture is a representation consists (at least in part) in the fact that S intends that it be a representation. But if that is the case, then it seems natural to conclude that the intention to communicate is the intention to produce in H the knowledge that the picture represents a certain state of affairs, by means of H's recognition of S's intention that it should represent that state of affairs.

On this account, something rather like the Gricean analysis is a natural development of my account of representation: for if I intend that the hearer should know that I intend the utterance to represent a certain state of affairs, then as soon as he recognizes that I intend him to know it he will know it. It is a general feature of intentions that if I intend the hearer to know my intentions, then as soon as he recognizes my intention that he should know, he will know. The mistake was to suppose that the speaker's communication intentions and speaker meaning were identical. We might say that Grice and I (in different ways) analysed communication or communicative meaning but that we did not yet see the prior role of representations in meaning. On my present account the primary meaning intentions are intentions to represent and they are independent of and prior to the intention to communicate those representations. A primary-meaning intention is an intention to represent; a communication intention is an intention that the hearer should know the representing intention.

I believe that the distinction between representation and communication was disguised by the concentration on speech acts rather than pictures, for in the standard speech situation the utterance both represents and communicates, and it is tempting (and, in general, correct) to construe a failure to communicate as a failure of the speech act; but with pictures the fact that the picture can represent a certain state of affairs is clearly independent of the question of whether it is ever used to communicate anything to anybody.

Schematically the argument of this section, as applied to this example and others like it can be stated as follows:

1. *In U (utterance) of X, S means that A,*

in one sense of 'meaning' is equivalent to;

2. *In U of X, S intends that X represent the state of affairs that A,*

which entails;

3. *In U of X, S intends that a criterion of success of U of X will be
   that the state of affairs that A obtains independently of U;*
4. *In U of X, S communicates (intentionally) that A to H*

entails 1., which is equivalent to 2. 4, then, is equivalent to:

5. *In U of X, S intends$_1$ that S represent the state of affairs that A,
   and S intends$_2$ that H recognizes intention$_1$. H recognizes inten-
   tion$_2$ and thereby recognizes intention$_1$.*

III

I now turn to cases involving the use of language. The case of drawing
a crankshaft did not involve any explicitly linguistic elements (though
I am for present purposes ignoring the vexed question as to how much
of our habits of pictorial representation rest on conventions of a
linguistic kind). Confining our attention to simple indicative sentences,
let us begin this part of the analysis by asking a Wittgensteinian sort
of question: What is the difference between saying, for example, 'It's
raining', and meaning it and saying it without meaning it? Wittgenstein
asks us these questions at least partly in order to point out that 'meaning' is not the name of an introspective process, like having a memory
image or feeling a pain. And he is no doubt right in calling attention to
the difference between meaning something and having interior mental
processes. But none the less there is a difference between saying something and meaning it and saying it without meaning it. What exactly is
the difference? The difference between saying it is raining and meaning
it, and saying it without meaning it can be got at by again examining
the question, what counts as a mistake? What counts as a relevant
objection? If I say, 'It's raining' and mean it, then if I look out of the
window and see that the sun is shining and the sky is blue, I am committed to recognizing these states of affairs as relevant to my utterance
in a way that I am not so committed if I originally said, 'It's raining'
without meaning it. What this suggests is that saying something and
meaning it is a matter of intending that one's utterance represent a
certain state of affairs, which state of affairs (assuming the utterance
is literal) is determined by the rules governing the elements of the
sentence one utters.

The pattern of analysis that is suggested here is parallel to that
of the non-linguistic case. Stated informally, it goes as follows:

(1) For simple indicative sentences of the sort used to make

statements saying something and meaning it, it is a matter of uttering a sentence with the intention that it represent a certain state of affairs, which state of affairs will be determined by the rules governing the elements of the sentence uttered, as uttered in that particular context.

(2) The intention that it represent a certain state of affairs is at least partly the intention that certain conditions are conditions of success of the utterance.

(3) At least one of the conditions of success is that there must exist the relevant state of affairs, independently of the making of the utterance.

On this account, as on the earlier account it is possible to mean something without any communication intentions. What, then, is introduced into the situation if we assume that the speaker is attempting to communicate something? What is involved if the speaker says something and means it and intends to communicate what he means? As in our early example it is, I believe, primarily a matter of S intending to produce in H the knowledge that his utterance is intended as a representation of a certain state of affairs. On this account the primary meaning intentions are intentions that one's utterance represent, and communication intentions are intentions to produce in hearers the knowledge that one is intending to represent. What once seemed such a puzzling and mysterious feature of communication, namely that one suceeds in one's intentions by getting the hearer to recognize those intentions, now seems an automatic consequence of the analysis of meaning in terms of representation, for it is a general feature of intentions that as soon as you recognize my intention A that you should know my intention B, you will know my intention B; and this is a general feature of intentions with no special relevance to language or meaning.

Notice, furthermore, that this account of meaning and communication is in no way inconsistent with the view that the fundamental purpose of language is communication. Language provides us with public systems of representation, and thereby allows representations to be readily communicated from one speaker-hearer to another in virtue of their common knowledge of the rules of language.

IV

I now turn to the question of how these conclusions can be generalized to apply to the theory of speech acts and to sentences used to perform speech acts other than statements. So far we have considered only the nature of meaning and representation as they apply to utterances of the statement class, but of course not all illocutionary acts are statements and we must now consider the question, how does the concept of representation apply to other kinds of illocutionary acts? The hypothesis suggested by the argument so far is that different kinds of illocutionary acts, in so far as they have propositional contents, can be regarded as different modes in which utterances represent reality: an assertive mode, a directive mode, a commissive mode, and so on. If we see the basic form of the illocutionary act as $F(p)$, then the different illocutionary points will be indicated by the Fs and the illocutionary points will determine the different ways in which the ps are related to the world. And these modes of representation will, in turn, be analysable as conditions on the success of utterances. For reasons that are independent of the argument of this paper I believe that illocutionary acts divide into five different basic types.[6] These are:

(1) *Assertives*. The defining point or purpose of the members of the assertive class is to commit the speaker (in varying degrees) to something being the case, to the truth of the expressed proposition. All of the members of this class are assessable on the dimension of assessment which includes 'true' and 'false'. This class includes *inter alia* statements, assertions, explanations, descriptions, and characterizations. All the members of this class have the word-to-world direction of fit.

(2) *Directives*. The defining illocutionary point of these consists in the fact that they are attempts (in varying degrees) by the speaker to get the hearer to do something. Examples of this class are orders, commands, requests, prayers, entreaties, invitations, pleadings, and implorings.

(3) *Commissives*. The defining illocutionary point of a commissive is to commit the speaker (again in varying degrees) to some future course of action. Examples of commissives are promises, vows, threats, pledges, contracts, bets, and guarantees. Both directives and commissives have the world-to-word direction of fit.

(4) *Expressives*. The defining illocutionary point of this class is to express the psychological state specified in the sincerity condition about a state of affairs specified in the propositional content. The paradigm expressives are thanks, congratulations, apologies, condolences, welcomes, greetings, and applause. In general, they have no direction of fit.

[6] See J. R. Searle, 'A Classification of Illocutionary Acts', in *Expression and Meaning*, Cambridge University Press, 1979, pp. 1–29.

(5) *Declarations.* It is the defining characteristic of this class that the sucessful performance of one of its members brings about the correspondence between the propositional content and reality. Successful performance guarantees that the propositional content corresponds to the world. Examples are declaring war, pronouncing someone man and wife, adjourning a meeting, excommunicating, christening, appointing, resigning, and nominating. It is a general feature of declarations that they require an extralinguistic institution for their performance.[7] They have both directions of fit.

If we extend the analysis of the preceding sections to these different kinds of speech acts, our hypothesis would be that each basic type of speech act, that is, each illocutionary point, marks a different mode of relating utterances to the world: and that amounts to saying that the different basic illocutionary points are determined by the different intentions that speakers have regarding the ways that their utterances should represent reality. Since, as we have seen, the concept of intending to represent reality can be analysed at least partly in terms of intending that certain conditions of success be met, then the different illocutionary points can be defined at least partly in terms of the different conditions of success that the speaker intends in making the utterance. In each case the essential condition on the speech act will be specified as a necessary condition of the success of the utterance as intended, when the utterance is intended as a member of the relevant class. The basic idea here is the old one that the meaning of a statement is somehow given by its truth conditions, the meaning of a command is given by its obedience conditions, the meaning of a promise is given by its fulfilment conditions, and so on. But the problem is to spell out those conditions in terms of the intentions of the speaker in making the utterance. And it is necessary to do that in order to explain how the utterance *represents* anything, since the matching of utterances and conditions does not by itself give any sense to the notion that the utterance represents the conditions, or even has anything to do with them. And it is only in virtue of the *representing* relation that the utterance can be said to have a meaning at all.

For the first three classes—assertives, directives, and commissives —the specification of the relevant necessary conditions is fairly easy, and can be stated as follows:

---

[7] Examples where a declaration can be performed outside an extralinguistic institution are either declarations about language itself, e.g. 'I abbreviate "Free on Board" as FOB', or supernatural, e.g. 'Let there be light!'

1. S uttered X and meant the U of X as an assertive that p has as a necessary condition that:

> In the U of X, S intended that a criterion of success of U of X will be that there exist a state of affairs such that p, which is causally independent of the U of X.[8]

2. S uttered X and meant it as a directive to H to do A has as a necessary condition that:

> In U of X, S intended that a criterion of success of the U of X will be that H does A, at least partly because of the recognition by H that S intends the U of X as a reason for doing A.

3. S uttered X and meant it as a commissive to do act A has as a necessary condition that:

> In U of X, S intended that a criterion of success of the utterance will be that S does A, at least partly because S intends that the U of X function as a reason for doing A.

When we come to the topic of expressives it is necessary to introduce two new concepts, both of which are related to, but neither of which is analysable in terms of the concepts of representation and communication. These two new concepts are expression and presupposition. I shall not attempt to analyse these concepts, but only to illustrate their relation to our main topic of discussion. Consider a paradigm case of an expressive illocutionary act. In an example such as, 'I apologize for stepping on your toe', the truth of the propositional content that I stepped on your toe is not asserted but is rather presupposed, and the essential condition, the illocutionary point of the total speech act, is to express sorrow or regret for the state of affairs that is presupposed in the propositional content condition. In general, the notion of a presupposition of a speech act is the notion of a condition on the felicitous performance of that speech act, and in this case, a condition on the performance of the speech act is that the proposition should be true; however, it is not the point of the speech act to commit the speaker to that proposition being true. The point of the speech act of, for example, apologizing, is simply to express sorrow or regret about the state of affairs specified in the proposition. But the truth of the proposition is taken for granted, it is presupposed. It is

---

[8] This requires a slight modification for self-reference cases, where the 'state of affairs' is not independent of U.

generally the case with presuppositions whether in expressive or other sorts of speech acts, that the illocutionary point of the utterance can only succeed if the presuppositions are satisfied, but the presuppositions are not themselves intended as specifying the point of the speech act.

With the concept of expression, however, unlike the concept of representation, there is no condition for success other than the intention that the utterance should be an expression of the relevant psychological state. If I intend my utterance as an expression of such and such a state, then it will be an expression of that state. Of course, I may not succeed in communicating that expression, that is my hearer may or may not recognize my intentions. But there is no condition of success on expressions other than simply the intention that the utterance should be an expression. Therefore the following tautological statement of a necessary condition for expressives emerges.

4. S uttered X and meant it as an expressive of a state E about the state of affairs that p has as a necessary condition that:

> In the U of X, S intended that the U of X be an expression of E, presupposing that p.

We have already seen that declarations have two special features not common to the other types of illocutionary acts. First, since the illocutionary point of the declaration is to bring about some new state of affairs solely in virtue of the utterance, declarations have both directions of fit; and second, in order that this be achieved it is a general feature of declarations that they require some extralinguistic institution within which the utterance is made. Therefore, the conditions that form the necessary meaning conditions of a declaration can be stated as follows:

5. S uttered X and meant it as a declaration that p has as necessary conditions:

> In the U of X, S intended that some new state of affairs p be brought about solely in virtue of the U of X. In the U of X, S intended to employ the constitutive rules of some institution within which he is acting.

This completes our account of the general modes of meaning. In accordance with the discussion of communication in our previous sections it is easy to see how to extend this analysis of meaning to cover communication: the intention to communicate in each of these cases will consist in the intention that H should know S's meaning intention, that is at least partly that H should know each of the intentions specified in the above analyses. But as soon as H recognizes a communication intention (that is, the intention that he should know a meaning intention) he will know the meaning intention, hence communication is derivative from meaning and not conversely.

It might seem from this analysis that there is an asymmetry between the analysis of directives and other types of speech acts. The meaning of directives seems to be specified in terms of intended perlocutionary effects, since directives involve the intention that the hearer should do something in virtue of the utterance, and the others do not seem to involve any reference to perlocutionary effects on the hearer. This distinction, however, does not show that directives have a different kind of meaning: because the propositional content condition on directives requires that there be a reference to the hearer and the predication of some future course of action by the hearer, and because the direction of fit is world-to-word, any specification of the speaker's meaning will involve a specification of an action by the hearer. But in this case, as in the other cases, the illocutionary point is a matter of relating the propositional content to the world in a certain way. The difference between directives and other kinds of speech acts derives not from some difference in the way the utterances have meaning, perlocutionary in the one case and illocutionary in the others, but rather from the different propositional contents in the different cases. Furthermore, many names of speech acts contain the notion of communication between speaker and hearer. Thanking, congratulating, apologizing, warning, promising, and many others all involve the notion of communication between speaker and hearer. It is not surprising that the names of many speech acts should make essential reference to communication since that is what these various kinds of speech acts are for and indeed what language in general is for. None the less, within each of these cases it is possible to distinguish the meaning intentions from the communicating intentions.

V

By way of concluding this paper, I want to make a few brief remarks about how the analysis it contains might be further developed and how these issues relate to certain other issues in the philosophy of language.

A. *Falsehood and rules*

There is a persistent mistake in contemporary philosophy of language which the present analysis avoids; it is to suppose that falsehood is a violation of linguistic rules. It is quite amazing how often this mistake is made, but a moment's reflection will show that it is a mistake. For example, the weatherman who predicts rain only to be confronted by a sunny day violates no rule of language. He is simply mistaken. The rules of language must, indeed, determine what counts as success and failure; and for the assertive class this means that they must determine what counts as truth and falsehood. In the same way the rules of a game must determine what counts as winning and losing. That truth is a condition of success must be internal to the notion of a statement. But just as the man who loses the game does not thereby break the rules, so the man who makes a false statement does not thereby violate the rules of language. Lying and cheating are indeed rule violations, but that is quite a different matter. The rules of language must also determine what counts as fulfiling or breaking a promise, obeying or disobeying an order, but the man who breaks a promise or disobeys an order does not thereby violate any linguistic rules. Neither does the man who makes a false statement. The idea that there is an extra truth convention has the effect of separating the notion of representation from its conditions of success, but the conditions of success are internal to the notion of representation.

B. *Constitutive rules*

I have tried to construct the analyses of section IV without using any constitutive rules, or any rule-impregnated notions such as obligation or authority (with the exception of the analysis of the class of declarations, which require extralinguistic institutions anyway). If, in the end, these analyses are successful they will enable us to achieve some of the objectives of my earlier analyses of speech acts with a much weaker apparatus. Aside from the methodological advantages of this approach —it enables us to account for the data with a simpler set of hypotheses —a further advantage is that it suggests certain possibilities of how our present rather elaborate and articulated linguistic institutions might have evolved from simpler prelinguistic forms. Just as our present elaborate systems of constitutive rules in such institutions as marriage or private property may have evolved from such pre-institutional practices as the cohabitation of men and women or the sheer physical possession of material objects, so such institutions as promising or stating may have evolved from such prelinguistic practices as representing reality in various modes. It is an empirical question whether language did evolve from prelinguistic practices, but it would be presumptuous to exclude the possibility a priori. For some theories of language, for example Chomsky's, it is hard to see how, according to the theory, it would even be possible for language to evolve from simpler prelinguistic forms.

Once I have the apparatus of constitutive rules it becomes relatively easy to state both necessary and sufficient conditions on different types of illocutionary acts in the manner of Chapter 3 of *Speech Acts*. In that work I was concerned to analyse illocutionary acts performed in the literal utterances of sentences in a language. The apparatus necessary to get from 'the physics to the semantics' involved sentences (specified purely syntactically), rules (attaching to those sentences), conditions (specified by the rules), and intentions (by the speaker to invoke those rules). In this paper the account does not begin with literal utterances of sentences, but outside language altogether. Here the apparatus includes only intentions and conditions. If my present account is on the right track, and if the distinction between representation and communication is really valid, then the theory of *Speech Acts* can be seen as a special case of a more general theory of meaning and communication.

C. *The 'Homeric struggle'*

Of the various attempts to analyze meaning in contemporary philosophy, two seem to me particularly fruitful, and one way to see the theory advanced in this article is to see it as an attempt to combine the best features of the two approaches. The first approach, which has its near ancestry in Frege and Wittgenstein's *Tractatus* and receives its most influential recent exposition in Davidson's writings[9] derives from the insight that to know the meaning of a statement is to know under what conditions it is true or false. This approach associates meaning with truth conditions.

The second approach, which has its recent ancestry in the work of the later Wittgenstein and Austin, and receives a recent influential version in Grice's writings, sees meaning as essentially tied to such notions as use and intention. Just to have labels we might call these theories 'correspondence theories' and 'intentionalist theories' respectively. Strawson[10] has described the conflict between them as

[9] 'Truth and Meaning', *Sythese* 17 (1967), pp. 304–23.
[10] 'Meaning and Truth', in P. F. Strawson, *Logico-Linguistic Papers*, Methuen, 1971.

a 'Homeric struggle'. But the fundamental insight of each theory seems to me correct; the mistake is to suppose that the two theories are necessarily in conflict. To know the meaning of a statement is indeed partly to know under what conditions it is true or false, and similarly to know the meaning of a command is at least partly to know under what conditions it is obeyed or disobeyed; to know the meaning of a promise is at least partly to know under what conditions it is kept or broken. But none of this is inconsistent with the intentionalist view that to mean something is to have a certain set of intentions. Once we are prepared to distinguish meaning from communication, instead of identifying them as most intentionalist theorists have done, then the meaning intentions of the speaker, which the intentionalists insist are the 'essence' of meaning, are easily specified in terms of the correspondence conditions on the success of the utterance, as specified by the correspondence theorists.

THE LOGIC OF CONVERSATION

8

'IF' AND '⊃'

P. F. STRAWSON

The object of this paper is to bring about a confrontation, at a fairly general level, of two views about the meaning, or conventional force, or sense, of 'if . . . then . . .'. I do not suggest that these two views exhaust the possibilities.

One of these views may be called the truth-functionalist view. On this view, 'if . . . then . . .' really has precisely the same meaning or conventional force as '⊃'. If we are prone to think otherwise, it is, according to this view, because we are tempted to count as part of the *meaning* of 'if' certain features which do not belong to its meaning, though they are characteristic of central cases of its *use*. (Let me remark how the wider bearings of this particular conflict are indicated here.) A view of this kind is succinctly expressed by Quine as follows:

Only those conditionals are worth affirming which follow from some manner of relevance between antecedent and consequent—some law, perhaps, connecting the matters which these two component state-ments describe. But such connection underlies the useful application of the conditional without needing to participate in its meaning. Such con-nection underlies the useful application of the conditional even though the meaning of the conditional be understood precisely as '~(p. ~q)'. [*Methods of Logic*, London, 1974, p. 16.]

The most powerful arguments I have heard employed in this cause are due to Paul Grice. I shall refer to them in what follows.

The view that 'if . . . then . . .' is identical in conventional force with '. . . ⊃ . . .' is sometimes accompanied by reservations about counter-factual conditionals.[1] But if it is to be attractive, I think it will have to be forced through for counterfactuals as well. For if (*if*) the right way of tackling the whole question of conditionals is, among other things, to try to settle the question of the meaning, or meanings, of the expres-sion 'if . . . then . . .', then we are faced with the alternative of saying

[1] Quine op. cit., p. 14: 'Whatever the proper analysis of the contrafactual conditional may be, we may be sure in advance that it cannot be truth-functional.

either that 'if . . . then . . .' has the same meaning, or that it has different meanings, in such cases as the following—I go back a little in recent history for my example:

(1) Remark made in the summer of 1964:

'If Goldwater is elected, then the liberals will be dismayed.'

(2) Remark made in the winter of 1964:

'If Goldwater had been elected, then the liberals would have been dismayed.'

It seems obvious that about the least attractive thing that one could say about the *difference* between these two remarks is that it shows that, or even that it is partly accounted for by the fact that, the expression 'if . . . then . . .' has a different meaning in one remark from the meaning which it has in the other. So I shall assume that the truth-functionalist view must somehow be extended to cover the counterfactual cases, and shall suggest a way in which this might be done.

The other of the two views to be brought into confrontation with each other might be called the consequentialist view. It is the view that 'if . . . then . . .' is first cousin in conventional force to 'so'. To make sure we do not take too narrow a view of what this involves, it is best to begin by looking at some examples of remarks of the form 'p, so q'.

(1) Today is Monday, so tomorrow will be Tuesday.
(2) There is a red sky tonight, so we shall have a fine day tomorrow.
(3) He has been travelling all day, so he will be tired when he arrives.
(4) He saw she was in difficulties, so he went to her assistance.
(5) The petrol ran out, so the car just stopped.
(6) He has disobeyed, so they will punish him.
(7) You have disobeyed, so I shall punish you.
(8) Melbourne is in Australia, so the sea is salt.

Anyone who asserts any of these sentences asserts, of course, both of the constituent propositions conjoined by 'so'. He asserts that p and he asserts that q. But he does more than this. He implies that there exists what I shall refer to vaguely as some ground-consequent relation between the matter affirmed in the antecedent proposition and the matter affirmed in the consequent proposition. I put it in this rather vague way because the ground-consequent relation involved need not always be of the same kind. Often what is implied (or a part of what is implied) is that the truth of the proposition that p is a sufficient reason, either absolutely or in the circumstances of the case, for taking the proposition that q to be true also. We can find this feature present in examples (1), (2), (3), and (6)—also, as I shall show later, in example (8). The word 'so' in all these cases is, we might say, an inference-marker. Where 'so' thus marks an inference, the kinds of consideration which underlie the inference may be different. Thus in (1) we have a deductive implication. In (2), the state of affairs affirmed in the antecedent proposition is a reliable *sign* of, but not a *cause* of, what is predicted in the consequent proposition. In (3) what is affirmed in the antecedent is a *cause* of what is affirmed in the consequent. In (6) what is reported in the antecedent constitues a *reason* which, it is implied, the agents will find sufficient *for acting* in the way predicted in the consequent.

In examples (4), (5), and (7), 'so' will not normally be operating as an inference-marker. Nevertheless its use in each case implies that there exists, between the matter affirmed in the antecedent and the matter affirmed in the consequent, a relation belonging to one or another of those types which generally underlie the use of 'so' as an inference-marker. Thus what is implied in case (4) is that what is affirmed in the antecedent constituted the agent's reason for acting as he is reported as acting in the consequent. What is implied in case (5) is that what is reported in the antecedent was the cause of what is reported in the consequent; in case (7) that what is affirmed in the antecedent is the speaker's reason for acting as he announces that he is going to act.

Now let us look at case (8). Case (8) at first looks a little odd. And the reason why it looks a little odd is that it does not seem that there could exist, between what is affirmed in the antecedent and what is affirmed in the consequent, any such relation—whether deductive, natural, or 'rational'—as normally underlies the use of 'so' as an inference-marker. Indeed, of course, there is no such relation in this case. And it is a matter of some importance to notice that 'so' can perfectly well function as an inference-marker even in the absence of any such relation; that two propositions can perfectly well be related by a ground-consequent relation of the inferential kind even when this does not rest directly on any of those natural or deductive or 'rational' types of ground-consequent relation which normally underlie an inferential ground-consequent relation. To see how this can happen, we need to do no more than imagine a situation in which someone is informed, by an informant whose knowledgeability and veracity he has reason to accept, that at least one of a certain pair of propositions is false. We can imagine such a thing happening, perhaps, as part of a test of some kind, or in the context of some sort of general knowledge game. There need be no other kind of connection between the two propositions than what is conferred upon them by this context. Thus one proposition could be the proposition that Melbourne is in Australia, the other the proposition that the sea is not salt. For the recipient of our information, whom we may suppose to be antecedently ignorant of the location of Melbourne and the composition of the sea, the question of whether Melbourne is in Austrialia and the question of whether the sea is not salt now come to be mutually dependent questions to the extent that he can infer from the truth of either of these propositions the falsity of the other. Let him find out, by consulting an atlas, that Melbourne is in Australia. Then he can properly link the two propositions by the use of the inference-marker 'so'. He can properly say:

Melbourne *is* in Australia, so the sea *is* salt.

We can imagine other cases in which propositions not connected by any of the kinds of connection which normally underlie a ground-consequent relation of the inferential kind may nevertheless acquire such a relation. Thus we may imagine a somewhat neurotic character who never makes positive or unqualified assertions accept on matters on which he is well informed, but is subject to bursts or phases of compulsive lying. All his assertions come, we may suppose, in clearly demarcated groups; so that we know antecedently—for such is the nature of his disorder—that the remarks falling within any given group are either all true or all false. Then if p and q are remarks belonging to the same group and we want to know whether q is true, we can satisfy ourselves by finding out that p is true and arguing 'p, so q', even though the subject-matters of the two remarks are quite unconnected.

To sum up as far as we have gone. When something of the form 'p, so q' is said, i.e. when two assertive clauses are linked by 'so', then it is asserted that p and it is asserted that q—and also it is implied that there exists between the matter affirmed at p and the matter affirmed at q either a ground-consequent relation of the inferential kind or a ground-consequent relation of one of the types which normally underlie a ground-consequent relation of the inferential kind or both.

Two things seem obvious: (1) what particular kind of ground-consequent relation is implied in any case is not (solely) a matter of the meaning or conventional force of 'so'; (2) the meaning or conventional foce of 'so' is sufficient (though not necessary) to ensure an implication that there is some kind of ground-consequent relation between the two propositions. In other words, (1) it would be wrong to say 'In each case there is some kind of ground-consequent relation which is conventionally implied by "so"'; but (2) it would be right to say 'In each case it is conventionally implied by "so" that there is some kind of ground-consequent relation'. (Comparison may usefully be made with 'hence', 'consequently', 'therefore'.)

The above seems uncontroversial. It also seems uncontroversial to remark that for every statement containing 'so' and carrying a ground-consequent implication, one or more corresponding statements could be framed containing 'if' instead of 'so' which carried, somehow or other, a *corresponding* ground-consequent implication. I say 'corresponding' and not 'the same', since the clauses of an 'if . . . then . . .' statement, unlike the clauses of a 'so' statement, are not asserted. Thus, while it might be implied in a 'so' statement that one actual state of affairs *was*, say, the cause of another, or *was* an agent's effective reason for acting in a certain way, the corresponding implication in the corresponding 'if . . . then . . .' statement would be rather that a hypothetical state of affairs *would be* or *would have been*, in given circumstances, sufficient to cause another, or that a hypothetical state of affairs *would be* or *would have been* an agent's effective reason for acting in a certain way.

Now to set out the consequentalist view of 'if . . . then . . .'. Summarily it is the view that just as 'so' *conventionally* implies the existence of some ground-consequent relation between the propositions it conjoins without conventionally implying the relation to be of one kind rather than another, so 'if . . . then . . .' *conventionally* implies the existence of some ground-consequent relation between the propositions it conjoins without conventionally implying the relation to be of one kind rather than another—the difference being that 'so' is coventionally restricted in its employment to conjoining propositions which are *asserted* in the use of the sentence containing the conjunction, while 'if . . . then . . .' is conventionally restricted in its employment to conjoining propositions which are unasserted in the use of the sentence containing the conjunction. *Prima facie* there is nothing incoherent or otherwise objectionable in the idea of a linguistic device possessing just the conventional force assigned, on this view, to 'if . . . then . . .'. And if there is such a device, there will be plenty of occasions for employing it. We have plenty of occasion for drawing, or setting out, the consequences of suppositions, indicating that this is what we are doing, just as we have plenty of occasion for drawing, or setting out, the consequences of known truths or accepted propositions, indicating that this is what we are doing.

On this view, then, as I have already remarked, 'if' and 'so' are first cousins in conventional force or meaning. On the truth-functionalist view, on the other hand, there is no such kinship between 'if' and 'so' as regards their conventional force or meaning. For on this view 'if' carries no *conventional* implication of a ground-consequent relation of any kind between propositions. 'If' is, rather, a near relation of 'and' and 'not', which are similarly free from any such conventional implications.

Though two views are opposed on this important point, there are two other important points on which the partisans of both can consistently agree. In the first place, they can both agree that one who asserts a conditional statement is committed, in virtue of the conventional force of 'if', to the rejection, as false, of the proposition that results from conjoining the affirmation of the first constituent proposition of his conditional with the negation of its second constituent proposition. More briefly, one who affirms 'if p, then q' is committed to the denial of 'p.~q'. and is so committed in virtue of the meaning of 'if'. Obviously this is a very direct consequence of the truth-functionalist view; for on that view, the affirmation of the conditional 'if p, then q' has exactly the same conventional force as the denial of the conjunction 'p.~q'. But it is also a consequence, though not quite such a direct one, of the consequentialist view. For on that view the use of the form conventionally commits the speaker to the implication that the truth of p either would be (in the case in which its truth is understood to be an open question) or would have been (in the case in which it is understood to be false) either absolutely, or in the circumstances obtaining, sufficient to guarantee that q also was true. But one cannot consistently combine this view with the admission that p is in fact true and q in fact false. So it follows from the consequentialist thesis regarding 'if' that one who asserts a conditional statement is committed, in virtue of the conventional force of 'if', to rejecting as false the corresponding conjunction of the form 'p.~q'.

The second important point on which both parties can consistently agree is that typical or central case of the use of 'if . . . then . . .' are cases in which it is somehow *implied* that there is a ground-consequent relation of some kind between the coupled propositions. This, of course, is a direct consequence of the consequentialist view, whereas it does not appear to be a direct consequence of the truth-functionalist view. But equally it does not appear to be inconsistent with the truth-functionalist view. For something may be implied by what a man says, or by his saying it, without this implication being part of the conventional force or meaning of the words he uses. But though the defender of the truth-functionalist view can (it seems) consistently admit that the implication is regularly present while denying that it is conventional, he is (it seems) faced with a challenge and a task: the task, namely, of explaining why, given that 'if' has a merely truth-functional meaning, it nevertheless regularly carries the ground-consequent implication.

This is the challenge which has been so effectively taken up by Grice in a paper unfortunately unpublished. Although, relying on memory, I cannot do justice to the subtlety and complexity of the argument, I can, I think, recall some of its main features; and where memory fails, or in areas which Grice did not enter (such as the topic of counterfactual conditionals), I shall invent similar arguments. Although I think these arguments are powerful, I do not think they are conclusive. I think, in fact, that the consequentialist thesis is more realistic than the truth-functionalist thesis, even if it is less beautiful. So I will try to present the issue as an open one, while not disguising the fact that the weight of argument seems to me to fall, on balance, on the consequentialist side.

The governing aim of the argument we have to consider is to show that, on the assumption that the conventional meaning of 'if . . . then . . .' is entirely exhausted by the meaning-rules for '. . . ⊃ . . .', the ground-consequent implications which an 'if-then' statement may carry can be explained as the result of the operation of certain general principles of assertive discourse. These principles exert their influence impartially over the whole field of such discourse, though the way in which they operate to generate implications in different kinds of case depends, of course, on the meanings of the expressions peculiar to each kind of case. Moreover, according to this view, it is possible to show not only that the normal 'if-then' implications *can* be explained on these lines, given the assumption of a purely truth-functional conventional force for 'if . . . then . . .'; it is possible also to show, by reference to the general nature of meaning and implication, that they *should* be so explained; that this assumption and this explanation are not only *consistent* with the generally admitted facts, but also *correct*.

Of the general principles of assertive discourse just referred to, two in particular are relevant to the argument. They are:

(1) That one should not make an unqualified assertion unless one has good reason to think it true;

(2) That, subject to the previous principle being observed, one should not (unless one has some special justification for doing so) deliberately make a *less* informative statement on the topic of conversational exchange when one has just as good grounds for making, and could, with equal or greater economy of linguistic means, make, a *more* informative statement. (This could perhaps be seen as a corollary of a more general point about not deliberately withholding relevant information.)

Such principles are consequences of the more general assumption still that the purpose of assertive discourse is to be helpful, rather than the reverse, to one's partners in a conversational exchange. Evidently, this assumption does not always hold good, for example when you are being interrogated by an enemy. Nor does it hold good in a straightforward form when you are playing certain kinds of game. But apart from such special situations as these the assumption is one that we in fact generally make. Indeed it has a much more fundamental status than this way of putting it suggests. It might be said to be a precondition of the possibility of the social institution of language.

Now let us take the first of our two principles in conjunction with the truth-functional hypothesis about the meaning of 'if . . . then . . .'. On that hypothesis it seems to follow that there are three types of independently admissible grounds on which one could assert a conditional statement without violating the first principle: the case in which one knows (or has good reason for thinking) merely that the antecedent is false; the case in which one knows (or etc.) that the consequent is true; and the case in which, though lacking sufficient reason for thinking the antecedent false or for thinking the consequent true, one has sufficient reason for thinking that the conjunction of the antecedent with the negation of the consequent is false.

However, if we now add the requirement that we should not violate the second principle (the principle of maximum informativeness), then the number of cases of minimal conditions for asserting the conditional drops from three to one. The statement that it is false that p or the statement that it is true that q are each of them more informative than the statement that it is not the case that it is true that p and false that q.

Each of the first two statements is more informative than the third in the straightforward sense that it entails the third and is not entailed by it. So, by the principle of maximum informativeness, one should not make the third statement when one is in a position to make either of the other two.

But if one has good reason, other than knowledge of the falsity of p or the truth of q, for denying the conjunction of the truth of p with the falsity of q, then *eo ipso* one has good reason for holding that a ground-consequent relation holds between the proposition that p and the proposition that q (in that order). It does not matter whether the basis of one's rejection of the conjunction is knowledge of causal laws or of what agents would count as reasons for acting or of deductive implications, or, again, whether it is simply a case of two propositions between which there is no direct connection of any of these kinds but in respect of which one comes to know without knowing the falsity of p or the truth of q, that the combination of truth-values, p.~q, does not in fact obtain. This last is the case I illustrated in discussing the ground-consequent relation implied in the sentence, 'Melbourne is in Australia, so the sea is salt'; and one has exactly the same ground for holding the two propositions to be so related when, knowing in this way that the conjunction is false, but not having found out the antecedent to be true, one says instead: '*If* Melbourne is in Australia, *then* the sea is salt'. (Knowledge merely of the falsity of the conjunction confer on the question whether q a *dependence* on the question whether p which is quite lacking if knowledge of the falsity of the conjunction is itself based on knowledge of the falsity of p or of the truth of q (or both).)

So then every case in which one has good reason, other than knowledge of the falsity of p or of the truth of q, for denying the conjunction of the truth of p with the falsity of q is a case in which one has good reason for holding that a ground-consequent relation relates the proposition that p and the proposition that q in that order.

Now any audience of any piece of assertive discourse is entitled to assume, in the absence of any special reason to suppose the contrary, that its author (the speaker) is observing the general principles of all assertive discourse. Hence any audience of a *conditional* statement (it being still assumed that the conventional force of 'if p, then q' is the same as that of 'p ⊃ q') is entitled to assume, in the absence of special reason, that the author of the conditional statement has good reason for thinking that a ground-consequent relation holds between the proposition that p and the proposition that q. It might be said that in

general one who embarks on the enterprise of assertive discourse
tacitly implies that he is observing the general principles of that activity;
and hence that in general what he says implies the truth of any proposition (over and above the one he explicitly asserts) which he must have
good reason for holding true if, in saying what he says, he is observing
those general principles. Thus the fact that a conditional assertion of
ordinary speech normally carries a ground-consequent implication is
shown to be consistent with the assumption that there is no more to
the conventional force of 'if . . . then . . .' than there is to the meaning
of '. . . ⊃ . . .'.

I have given this part of the argument in the barest schematic outline. There is room for much qualification and addition. Here is one
addition, for which Grice cannot be held responsible, by means of
which an upholder of the truth-functionalist view might attempt to deal
with the case of counter-factual conditionals. Suppose there is a proposition, p, the falsity of which is known to a speaker and his audience
and is known by both to be known to both. Yet the speaker may issue
a conditional statement of which the antecedent corresponds to the
proposition that p, and the statement may, in the regular way, imply
a ground-consequent relation between antecedent and consequent. How
is this to be explained on the assumption that the conventional force of
his assertion is merely that of the negation of a conjunction? It might
be said that this assumption is in any case untenable in most instances
of this kind, for the speaker's choice of tense and mood will normally
conventionally indicate or imply his having knowledge of, or grounds
for belief in, the falsity of the antecedent. This in itself a debatable
contention—so we will consider the case under two heads: first,
on the assumption that the debatable contention is false, and second,
on the assumption that it is true.

On the assumption that the debatable contention is false and that
the whole relevant conventional force of the assertion is truth-functional,
it looks as if the principle of greater informativeness must have been
blatantly violated. But because it has been *blatantly* violated, there is
no risk of misleading the audience in the way in which the audience
would be misled if the principle were violated, but not blatantly. That
is to say, the speaker runs no risk of misleading the audience into the
belief that he has no sufficient ground for thinking that it is false that
p. So the speaker is at any rate not violating the more fundamental
principle that one should not mislead one's audience or deliberately
conceal relevant beliefs or information.

Here it is possible to appeal to another principle, which might be called the principle of informative *point*: which is that a man seriously engaged in the enterprise of informative discourse must take it that what he says has or may have some informative value for his audience. The only or the most obvious way of saving this principle, in the case of a speaker who denies a conjunction when it is common ground to himself and his audience that he knows one of the conjuncts to be false, is that he has some ground for the denial which is independent of knowledge of the falsity of the conjunct in question. A straightforward application of the principle of greater informativeness rules out the possibility of this other ground being simply knowledge of the falsity of the other conjunct (i.e. of the truth of consequent of the conditional). So we are left with the remaining alternative, namely with its being knowledge of the existence of some causal or other type of basis for that implication of a ground-consequent relation which set us our original problem. Thus the existence of the ground-consequent implication is explained consistently with the hypothesis that the implication is no part of the conventional force of the words used.

The argument is similar in principle for the assumption that the falsity of p is conventionally implied by the form of words chosen for the counterfactual. The appeal lies once more to the principle of informative point. Why conventionally commit yourself *both* to the denial of one of the conjuncts *and* to the weaker or less informative denial of the conjunction unless you have a ground for the latter which is additional to and independent of your ground for the former? Someone might object to the form of the explanation in this case on the ground that the very existence of a distinctive grammatical structure which explicitly carried a *conventional* commitment to the denial of one of the conjuncts, would seem inexplicable unless it also carried a *conventional* commitment to an independent ground for the denial of the conjunction. But it would be open to the truth-functionalist simply to admit this and then maintain that this last conventional commitment was simply a product of the other two, and hence no part of the meaning of 'if . . . then . . .', taken by itself.

So far the aim of the argument has been simply to show that the fact that 'if . . . then . . .' statements normally carry a ground-consequent implication can be explained in a way consistent with the assumption that such an implication is no part of their meaning or conventional force; that (if we set aside the debatable issue about the negative implications of forms appropriate to counterfactual conditionals) we can represent the agreed facts as consistent with the hypothesis that 'if . . . then . . .' statements have the same meaning as the corresponding material implication statements, that in fact, they *are* such statements. The next step is to try to strengthen the hypothesis by discrediting its rival. Here the following powerful argument may be used. If the ground-consequent implication were part of the conventional meaning or force of 'if . . . then . . .', it should be possible to find an alternative construction such that by using this construction instead of 'if . . . then . . .' we could eliminate the ground-consequent implication from any statement while still committing ourselves to the lesser thing which is expressed by the truth-functional connective of logic. (For remember that everyone agrees that, whatever 'if . . . then . . .' means, it at least carries, in virtue of its conventional force, a commitment to the denial of 'p.~q'.) The general point can be illustrated with the help of another conjunction, namely the conjunction 'but'. Everyone agrees that part of the meaning of the conjunction is that of the truth-functional conjunction sign, expressed in ordinary language by the word 'and'. The conjunction 'but' also carries, we will assume without debate, a *conventional* implication of some sort of adversative relation obtaining, in the circumstances, between the propositions expressed by the clauses it conjoins. This implication is part of its meaning. But just in so far as this implication of opposition is correctly attributed, in the case of any statement, to the meaning of 'but', we can always frame another corresponding statement from which this implication is eliminated but which retains the merely conjunctive force of the original, simply by replacing 'but' by 'and'.

But by the arguments already developed, no such manœuvre is possible in the case of 'if . . . then . . .'. It would be no good replacing 'if p, then q, by 'p ⊃ q'. or 'not both p and not-q' or by 'the combination of truth-values, first true, second false, is unrealized in the case of the ordered pair of propositions, p and q'. For in every case in which an 'if p, then q' statement in fact carries the implication which, on the consequentialist hypothesis, conventionally attaches to the 'if . . . then . . .' form, the operation of the principles previously referred to would ensure that the substitute statement carries exactly the same implications, though not, of course, as a part of the conventional force of the expressions used. Summarily: if an implication is conventional, it is eliminable; the implications in question are not eliminable, therefore they are not conventional.

The trouble with this argument is that it is really a little *too* powerful.

For if it is cogent, it seems to follow that it is actually *impossible* that there should exist in any language a conjunction of which the meaning can be characterized by saying that it carries the same general ground-consequent implications as 'so' does without joining asserted propositions as 'so' does. But it seems excessively implausible to maintain that it is actually impossible that there should exist an expression with such a meaning, when the meaning in question can be perfectly coherently explained. If the proposition that the existence of such an expression is possible is incompatible with some theoretical principle about meaning, it would seem more rational to modify the principle than to declare the proposition to be false. But if we do agree to modify the relevant principle, then the argument takes on a new look. From looking very fierce, it suddenly turns to looking very mild. For it now amounts to no more than a challenge to the holder of the consequentialist view to explain why the conventional implication he holds out for cannot be eliminated, as it can in other cases. But if seen as a challenge, it must be seen as a self-answering challenge. For the demonstration that the relevant implications cannot be eliminated by the substitution-method already contains the explanation of the reason *why* they cannot be eliminated. So that argument can be dismissed.

Indeed the upholder of the consequentialist view might be tempted by the successful repulse of this argument into a counter-attack. Let us express his thesis as follows: just as 'p, so q' might be called for (or a) conventional argument-form, so 'if p, then q' might be called the conventional quasi-argument-form. Quasi-argument differs from argument in that the premisses are, in the expression of a quasi-argument, entertained rather than asserted. Quasi-argument is something we have many occasions for just as argument is something we have many occasions for. It is entirely reasonable, therefore, to expect that language should contain a particle of which the conventional force is parallel to that of 'so' in the respects in which quasi-argument is parallel to argument and differs from that of 'so' in the respects in which quasi-argument differs from argument. But if there is a strong presumption that there exists in such a particle in language, there is an equally strong presumption that 'if' is such a particle. For it is a good candidate, and there is no better.

The counter-attack could be further developed. It could be contended, for example, that the meaning conventionally assigned to 'p ⊃ q' is inherently unstable, and could not preserve itself unmodified in the natural conditions of language-use. What the truth-functionalist account presents as reasons why 'if' normally carries implications denied to be part of its conventional meaning, the consequentialist theory can present as reasons why '⊃', if put to use in practice instead of 'if', would inevitably acquire the conventional implications which, on this view, are part of the meaning of 'if'. Only in the specially protected environment of a treatise on logic can '⊃' keep its meaning pure.

I do not think it could be claimed that these counter-attacking arguments are *decisive*. We still have two conflicting theses, each, perhaps, with difficulties of its own to face. We should remember that though each denies something which the other asserts, they are not necessarily exhaustive of the possibilities. If we are to adjudicate between them or—perhaps—to reject them both, we must do so in the light of (1) the degree of success with which each copes with its particular difficulties, and (2) any general considerations about meaning which bear on their acceptability.

9

ON DEFINING RELEVANCE

DEIRDRE WILSON AND DAN SPERBER

1. *Introduction*

Under the category of RELATION, I place a single maxim, namely 'Be relevant'. Though the maxim itself is terse, its formulation conceals a number of problems that exercise me a good deal . . . I find the treatment of such questions exceedingly difficult, and I hope to revert to them in a later work. [Grice, 1975, p. 46.]

In these cautious terms Grice, in his William James Lectures, introduced a maxim of relevance which, together with maxims of truthfulness, informativeness, and perspicuity was to form the basis for his exciting and influential approach to pragmatics. In the years since then, in spite of the considerable amount of research done in and on the Gricean pragmatic framework, no explicit account of relevance suitable for use in pragmatic theory has emerged.[2] Indeed, there has been considerable scepticism over whether any such account is in principle possible.[3]

[1] We would like to thank the participants in the 1980 Pragmatics Workshop at Asilomar, California, and in particular Herb Clark, Paul Grice, Larry Horn, Jerry Morgan, Ellen Prince, Ivan Sag, and Bonnie Webber, for stimulating comments on an earlier version of this paper. We are also grateful to Diane Brockway, Robyn Carston, Jerry Katz, Ruth Kempson, and Yuji Nishiyama for their help.

[2] The following is a representative sample of comments:

'. . . no attempt to apply formal semantic theory to this notion [relevance] has been successful enough to provide a model that would be usable in pragmatics' [Thomason, 1973, p. 12].

'That relevance is relevant to linguistic description is painfully apparent . . . Equally apparent is the almost complete absence of any kind of formal linguistic treatment of the notion' [Gazdar, 1979, p. 45].

'. . . current accounts of conversational interaction depend crucially upon the undefined notion of "relevance"' [Werth, 1981, p. 130].

[3] See, for example, the following comments:

'Relevance is not a precise logical category . . . the word is used to convey an essentially vague idea' [Berlin, 1938-9, p. 21].

'Conventionally, considerations of relevance are apt to be relegated to the rhetorical rather than the logical dimension of assessment of arguments' [Haack, 1978, pp. 16-17].

Where definitions have been attempted, they have been approached in rhetorical, emotional, or aesthetic rather than logical terms.[4] Yet since utterance comprehension involves a substantial inferential element, it is not unreasonable to expect the drawing of inferences to contribute in some way to judgements of relevance. In this paper we want to argue that there is an intimate connection between inference and relevance, and that an approach to relevance in inferential terms can yield fruitful results for pragmatic theory.

2. The nature of relevance

It is usual to treat relevance as a property of utterances or a relation between an utterance and a text or discourse. However, relevant information may be derived not only from utterances and other communicative acts, but also from memory, observation, and inference. We shall treat relevance in the first instance as a property of propositions (information units, combinations of sense and reference); subsidiary definitions of relevance for utterances or discourses are relatively easy to construct. Similarly, we shall treat a proposition as relevant in the first instance, not to a text or discourse but to a context, where a context is a stock of information derived not only from preceding discourse, but also from memory, observation, and inference. From the formal point of view, a context is simply a set of propositions of arbitrary size and content. From the psychological point of view, both size and content are subject to considerable constraints; these will be ignored for the moment and discussed in a later section.

The interpretation of an utterance involves, on the one hand, identification of the proposition the speaker has expressed, and on the other hand, the processing of this proposition in a context provided by the hearer and consisting, as we have seen, of information derived from a variety of sources. To process a proposition is simply to extract

'. . . the notion of connection or dependence being appealed to here is too vague to be a formal concept of logic' [Suppes, 1957, p. 8].

'The difficulty of treating relevance with the same degree of mathematical sophistication and exactness characteristic of treatments of extensional logic led many influential philosopher–logicians to believe that it was *impossible* to find a satisfactory treatment of the topic' [Anderson and Belnap, 1975, p. xxi].

[4] For some recent attempts, see van Dijk, 1979, Dascal, 1977, and Werth, 1981. Van Dijk equates relevance with degree of importance in discourse, Dascal relates it to satisfaction of a conversational demand, and Werth equates it with appropriateness to the meaning of the previous utterance, together with the context.

information from it; to process it in a context is to supply additional background information which contributes in some way to its processing. The processing of a proposition may be treated in largely inferential terms. For example, the processing of (1) might involve the use of (1) as a premiss, together with the background information in (2), to deduce the conclusion in (3):

(1) Jackson has just bought a Rolls Royce, but his wife refuses to drive in expensive cars.
(2) The Rolls Royce is an expensive car.
(3) Jackson's wife refuses to drive in his Rolls Royce.

In this case, the processing of (1) involves going through the steps needed to draw a certain set of inferences, and the context will be, or at least include, the set of background assumptions, such as (2), used as supplementary premisses in the inferential process.

When a proposition P is added to a context $C_1 \ldots C_n$, two distinct types of inference process involving P as a premiss may take place. On the one hand, P may be taken as the sole premiss, and its logical implications obtained. These are, of course, invariant from context to context, but we can say that P is *informative* in the context $C_1 \ldots C_n$ iff P has at least one logical implication not implied by $C_1 \ldots C_n$.

The processing of P in a context $C_1 \ldots C_n$ may also yield a further set of implications, this time context-dependent: the set of propositions which are logically implied not by P alone, nor by $C_1 \ldots C_n$ alone, but by the union of P and $C_1 \ldots C_n$. Call these the *contextual implications* of P in the context $C_1 \ldots C_n$. For example, consider a context consisting of the two propositions (4a) and (4b):

(4) a. If the Chairman resigns, Jackson will take over his duties.
   b. If Jackson takes over the Chairman's duties, the company will go bankrupt.

If proposition (5) is added to this context, conclusions (6) and (7) may be obtained as contextual implications of (5) in the context (4a)-(4b):

(5) The Chairman has resigned.
(6) Jackson will take over the Chairman's duties.
(7) The company will go bankrupt.

Propositions (6) and (7) are contextual implications of (5) in this context: they are logically implied by the union of (4) and (5), but by neither (4) alone nor (5) alone.

As informativeness in a context is definable in terms of logical implication, relevance in a context might be approached in terms of contextual implication. We shall say that a proposition is relevant in a context $C_1 \ldots C_n$ iff it has at least one contextual implication in $C_1 \ldots C_n$. Intuitively, being relevant in a context is a matter of connecting up with the context in some way. According to this proposal, relevance in a context is a matter of connecting up with the context in a highly specific way: so as to have contextual implications in that context. By this definition, because (5) has contextual implications in the context (4), it would be relevant in that context as well.[5]

This inferential approach to relevance would fit naturally into an inferential theory of comprehension. In processing a proposition in a context, the hearer would automatically derive its contextual implications, on the basis of which the relevance of the proposition would be established. In fact, one might go further and claim that the purpose of processing a proposition is precisely to establish its relevance, making relevance the foundation stone of pragmatic theory. Whatever its initial plausibility, however, this proposal can not be seriously entertained without answers to a number of questions being provided. Here we shall briefly consider the three that seem to us most urgent. It is perhaps worth mentioning that none is exclusive to our particular approach. The first, which has to do with the nature of the inference rules used, arises in any inferential pragmatic theory. The second, which has to do with the fact that relevance is a matter of degree, arises in any theory in which relevance plays a role. The third, which has to do with the nature and identification of contexts, arises in any pragmatic theory in which context plays a role. The answers we shall give, unlike the questions themselves, are often possible only within the sort of framework that we propose.

3. *The deductive system*

Suppose the logic used in deriving contextual implications is a standard one, say a standard natural deduction system. Then for any context Q and any proposition P, the conjunction of P and Q will be a contextual implication of P in the context Q: *P and Q* is logically implied by the union of P and Q, but by neither P alone nor Q alone. Every proposition will have at least one contextual implication in every context and hence, according to our definition of relevance, will be relevant in

[5] Goodman 1961 defines a notion of 'relative aboutness' along somewhat similar lines, although with rather different purposes.

every context; which is absurd. Therefore, either the logic used in deriving contextual implications is not a standard one, or our approach to relevance is incorrect.

In fact, quite independently of this approach to relevance, there is good reason to think that the logic used in utterance comprehension is not a standard one. On the one hand, it must be much more extensive, providing rules for every concept that can play a role in the inferential processing of propositions, including many that are of no particular interest to logicians. On the other hand, it must be more restrictive in certain ways. For example, the standard logical implications of a single proposition P include many propositions which would never in fact be derived during comprehension of an utterance expressing P:

(8) a. P & P
    b. P ∨ P
    c. − −P
    d. P ∨ Q
    e. −P → Q
    f. Q → P.

It is in general simply false that a hearer, given an utterance expressing P, might think that any of the implications in (8) was part of the speaker's intended message, and any inferential account of comprehension must provide some method of excluding them.

The need for some restriction is compounded by the fact that the rules which give rise to (8) may reapply to their own output, yielding infinite sets of logical implications along the lines in (9):

(9) a. (P & P) & P . . .
    b. (P ∨ P) ∨ P . . .
    c. . . . − − − − P
    d. (P ∨ Q) ∨ R . . .
    e. . . . −(−P → Q) → R . . .
    f. . . . R → (Q → P).

The full set of logical implications of a proposition could thus not in principle be drawn in any step-by-step way during the finite amount of time it takes to process a proposition.

The inferences in (8) and (9) are in some sense trivial. The rules which give rise to them are fairly easy to characterize: they are rules which may apply to any proposition at all, regardless of its form or content, and which may thus reapply indefinitely to their own output.

There are two possible reactions to the problem of trivial inferences and the rules which give rise to them. Most theories of comprehension which consider the problem at all retain something equivalent to a standard logic, but attempt to restrict its functioning in some way. It is felt that in certain circumstances a trivial rule might be needed, and it would be too drastic a move to eliminate all trivial rules entirely.[6] We feel, on the contrary, that the more drastic approach is correct.

Our hypothesis is that the deductive system used in spontaneous information processing is a purely interpretive one, in the sense that each of its rules requires, for its application, the presence of a particular concept in the proposition or propositions being processed. In other words, each rule is essentially an elimination rule. Such a system could contain something like the standard rule of *and*-elimination, which applies only to propositions in which *and* is present, but could have no equivalent of the standard rule of *and*-introduction, which imposes no conditions on the form or content of the propositions to which it applies. Such a system, though it could contain elimination rules for a wide range of concepts not treated at all in standard logics, could contain no rule which permits the derivation of any of the propositions in (8) or (9) from the single premiss P.

In a system of this type, the problem of trivial inferences would not arise. In particular, since there would be no rule of *and*-introduction, it would not be possible, given a proposition P and an arbitrary context Q, to derive the trivial implication $P \& Q$ as a contextual implication of P in the context Q. The elimination of the problem of trivial inference thus automatically provides a solution to the first of the problems raised by the proposed account of relevance.[7]

The inferential processing of a proposition could now be conceived of as carried out by an automaton which, given a proposition, a finite

---

[6] See, for example, Johnson-Laird, 1975.

[7] This is the only one of our three problems to be treated by relevance logicians. The system we envisage has some similarity to Parry's system of 'analytical implications' as outlined in Anderson and Belnap, 1975. It is sometimes suggested that a rule of *and*-introduction would be needed to derive R in the following circumstances: the context contains P and $(P \& Q) \to R$, and the new information to be processed is Q. However, we are not claiming that the most empirically adequate system of elimination rules contains only those envisaged in standard logics. There is good reason to think that in the above circumstances, the hearer would automatically convert $(P \& Q) \to R$, in a single step, to $P \to (Q \to R)$, which would combine with P to yield $Q \to R$ before Q was ever presented. On presentation of Q, the hearer could thus proceed directly to the conclusion R. For further discussion, see 'Reply to Gazdar and Good', in Sperber and Wilson, 1982.

context, and a set of non-trivial inference rules as input, would derive the full, finite set of non-trivial logical implications of the union of the proposition with the context as output. These would include the contextual implications of the proposition in the context. One could then compare the contextual implications that a given proposition would have in different contexts, or that different propositions would have in the same context. One could also compare the *amount* of processing that different propositions would require in a given context, or that a given proposition would require in different contexts, where the amount of processing is the number of steps that some automaton would have to go through in order to be sure of deriving all the contextual implications of a proposition in a context. Leaving special cases and technicalities aside, amount of processing is determined by, on the one hand, the number of non-trivial logical implications of the proposition being processed, and on the other hand, the number of non-trivial logical implications of the context. The simplest effective automaton would merely examine each of the members of the cartesian product of these two sets to check whether any inference rule applied. Roughly speaking, the greater the semantic complexity of the proposition being processed, and the larger the context, the greater the amount of processing that will be required.[8] We shall argue that degrees or comparisons of relevance are based on assessments of numbers of contextual implications on the one hand and amount of processing on the other.

4. *Degrees of relevance*

Grice's maxim simply says 'Be relevant'. If, as we have suggested, being relevant is merely a matter of expressing a proposition which has at least one contextual implication in a context accessible to the hearer, such a maxim would constrain the speaker, and hence guide the hearer, hardly at all. However, if degrees of relevance could be defined, or some basis for comparisons of relevance could be given, then some much more constraining maxim such as 'Try to be as relevant as is possible in the circumstances' might be proposed, and interpretation would take place under correspondingly severer constraints. In this section, we shall provide a basis for comparing the relevance of different propositions in

[8] There is, of course, a third factor affecting the amount of processing that a certain proposition requires in a given context, namely the number of contextual implications itself: each contextual implication adds one derivational step. However, we can ignore this factor, since it does not contribute to an assessment of amount of processing independent of the assessment of number of contextual implications, which is what we are after.

a fixed context, going on in the next section to deal with context selection and assessment in variable contexts. The examples considered will be highly unrealistic, partly because utterance comprehension does not take place in fixed contexts, and partly because actual contexts are unlikely to be as small as those used here. We shall also make the simplifying assumption that speakers not only aim at maximal relevance, but succeed in their aim, so that the hearer's task is merely to choose the interpretation that is maximally relevant. In a fuller account this simplifying assumption would be dropped. Examples and discussion should thus be taken only as an illustration of the criteria around which a fuller account could be constructed.

If relevance is linked to contextual implications, it seems reasonable that the more contextual implications a proposition has in a given context, the more relevant it is. We shall say that, other things being equal, the more relevant of two propositions in a given context will be the one with more contextual implications. However, a further factor must be taken into account. Two propositions may have the same number of contextual implications in a certain context, but one may be more semantically complex than the other, and contain whole stretches of information that do not connect up with the context and make no contribution to relevance. Intuitively, the existence of this extraneous information detracts from the relevance of the proposition. Because it also increases the amount of processing required, we shall say, for reasons that will become clearer in the next section, that, other things being equal, the more relevant of two propositions in a given context is the one which requires least processing. In assessments of relevance, there are thus two factors to take into account: on the one hand, numbers of contextual implications, and on the other hand, the amount of processing needed to obtain them.

To illustrate this, take the context in (10):

(10) a. The tickets cost £1 each.
   b. People may buy more than one ticket.
   c. The person who bought the green ticket wins the prize.
   d. The prize is £100,000.
   e. Anyone who wins £100,000 can fulfil the dreams of a lifetime.

If a hearer had only the information in (10), and a speaker knew that all of (11)–(13) were true, which of these propositions should the speaker, aiming at maximal relevance, choose to express?

(11)   James bought the green ticket.
(12)   Charles bought the blue ticket.
(13)   James bought the green ticket, and today is Tuesday.

(11) and (12) require roughly the same amount of processing,[9] since they have parallel logical structures and are being processed in the same context. Of these two propositions, it is therefore the one with the most contextual implications that will be the more relevant. While (12) has only the single contextual implication (14), (11) has the set of contextual implications (15)–(18):

(14)   The blue ticket cost Charles £1.
(15)   The green ticket cost James £1.
(16)   James wins the prize.
(17)   James wins £100,000.
(18)   James can fulfil the dreams of a lifetime.

Hence (11) is more relevant than (12) in this context.

In comparing (11) and (13), the same two factors—number of contextual implications and amount of processing—must be taken into account. In this case, (11) and (13) have exactly the same contextual implications, but require different amounts of processing. Because (13) entails (11), (13) requires every step of processing that (11) requires, and more besides. By the proposed criteria, it is the proposition which requires the smallest amount of processing—that is, (11)—that is the more relevant in the context. Of the three propositions (11)–(13), it is thus (11) that is selected as most relevant by the proposed criteria, and this accords with intuitive judgements of relevance.

These criteria do not, and need not, always yield such clear-cut results. For example, they do not say what the result would be of comparing (12) and (13), which differ both in the amount of processing required and in their numbers of contextual implications. They are designed to yield clear-cut results in just those cases where human beings can make clear-cut judgements of relative relevance. The sort of comparisons among different propositions that a hearer is called on to make during utterance comprehension are generally more like those in (11) and (12), and (11) and (13), than (12) and (13). For example, a hearer may have to choose among various candidate disambiguations and reference assignments for a given utterance. In most cases of

---

[9] With the unimportant qualification suggested in footnote 8.

reference assignment, and many of disambiguation, the candidate propositions to be compared will share much of their logical structure, as do (11) and (12), and may enter into entailment relations, as do (11) and (13). Moreover, in the normal case the alternative candidates differ so grossly in numbers of contextual implications that comparisons are quite straightforward, and only a single proposition will be worth considering. When no single candidate clearly emerges, we predict that the hearer will be unable to decide which interpretation is intended.[10]

So far we have assumed that contexts are arbitrary sets of propositions, fixed in advance. In looking at examples (11)–(13) above, the reader may have been tempted to expand context (10) in one way or another to increase the relevance of the proposition being processed: introducing, for instance, assumptions which would combine with the extraneous information in (13) to permit further contextual implications to be derived. In real life, contexts are not fixed in advance, but are chosen at least partly in function of the proposition being processed. It is to the question of context selection, or context construction, that we now turn.

5. *Context selection*

The problem of context selection is not unique to our framework. Any adequate theory of comprehension must describe the role of background assumptions in utterance interpretation, and the principles by which they are selected to play this role. In our framework, the role of background assumptions is to provide premises which will combine with the proposition being processed to yield contextual implications. The goal of processing is in general to maximize, as far as possible, the relevance of the proposition being processed: that is, to obtain the maximum of contextual implications in return for any given amount of processing. We want to show that because variations in context may increase or decrease the relevance of the proposition being processed, the goal of maximizing relevance may simultaneously guide the choice of context.

The hearer of an utterance has available a set of potential contexts from which an actual context must be chosen. We assume that there is

[10] In a fuller account, it could be shown that a speaker who did not believe that one clear candidate would emerge, or who caused the hearer to hesitate between alternative interpretations, would not have been observing the principle of maximal relevance. See Sperber and Wilson, 1986, for further discussion.

a small, immediately accessible context, fixed in advance, and consisting of the proposition which has most recently been processed, together with its contextual implications. When new information is received, say from an utterance, it will be processed in this most immediate context. If the initial context is (19) and the proposition expressed by the utterance is (20), some degree of relevance is immediately achieved:

(19) If the interest rate has risen, the company will go bankrupt.
(20) The interest rate has risen.

It may happen, however, that unless the initial context is extended in some way, no degree of relevance can be achieved. This would be so if, with the same initial context, the proposition expressed were not (20) but one of (21)–(23):

(21) The interest rate has done what you said it would do.
(22) The interest rate has done what the sun does every morning.
(23) The interest rate has done this. [speaker demonstrates]

If the goal of processing is to maximize the relevance of the information being processed, the hearer will be forced to add to the initial context (19) further information, which may be remembered from earlier discourse (in the case of (21)), recovered from encyclopaedic memory (in the case of (22)), or derived from sense perception (in the case of (23)). The goal will be to find, from the most immediately accessible source, premises which will combine with the proposition beng processed, to yield the maximum of contextual implications in return for the available amount of processing.

As these examples show, the accessibility of potential contexts may be altered by the content of the proposition being processed, which may direct the hearer's attention in one case to the physical environment, in another to the preceding discourse, in another to encyclopaedic memory. More complex examples require simultaneous or sequential extensions of the context in a variety of different directions, and there is no principled limit on the number of extensions that may be needed to establish the relevance of a given proposition. Each extension provides a new potential context in which the proposition could be processed, up to a maximal context consisting of the entire contents of the hearer's accessible memory.

If there were only one direction of extension, the set of potential contexts for processing a given proposition would be strictly ordered, ranging from a smallest, most easily accessible initial context, through ever larger, less accessible extensions, up to a most inclusive, least accessible context containing everything the hearer knows. Because of the variety of possible directions of extension, the actual situation is rather more complex; however, there is a partial ordering of potential contexts, with a series of ever more inclusive contexts extending out from the initial context in various directions.

If the set of potential contexts is structured in this way, every extension of the initial context will incur a double cost in processing terms. First, each extension increases the size of the context, and the larger the context, the greater the amount of processing. Second, later extensions are harder to access, and accessing itself is presumably a step-by-step procedure with associated costs in processing. Hence, every extension of the context increases the cost of processing, and must be expected, other things being equal, to decrease the relevance of the proposition being processed.

We shall say that a proposition is relevant in a set of contexts $K_1 \ldots K_n$ iff it is relevant in at least one context which is a member of that set, and that it is more relevant in K_1 than K_2 if, other things being equal, it has more contextual implications in K_1 than in K_2, or, other things being equal, the amount of processing required to obtain the implications it has in K_1 is smaller than the amount required to obtain the implications it has in K_2. Maximizing the relevance of a given proposition is therefore a matter of choosing a context which maximizes its contextual implications and minimizes the amount of processing; in other words, it is a matter of maximally efficient processing.

This approach to the assessment of relevance in variable context can be illustrated with the following highly simplified example. Assume that there is an initial context (24C1), to which (24C2), (24C3) and (24C4) may be added, in that order:

(24) C1: Jackson has chosen the date of the meeting.

   C2: If the date of the meeting is February 1st, the Chairman will be unable to attend.

   C3: If the Chairman is unable to attend, Jackson's proposals will be accepted.

   C4: If Jackson's proposals are accepted, the company will go bankrupt.

A hearer aiming to maximize the relevance of (25) or (26) in this set of contexts should only be willing to incur the extra costs of extending the context in return for a compensating increase in the number of contextual implications:

(25) The date of the meeting is February 1st.
(26) The date of the meeting is February 5th.

In the initial context C1, (25) has the single contextual implication (27), and (26) the single contextual implication (28):

(27) Jackson has chosen February 1st as the date of the meeting.
(28) Jackson has chosen February 5th as the date of the meeting.

In this context, both propositions are relevant, and indeed, because of their similarities in logical structure, context, and contextual implications, both will be equally relevant.

If the initial context is extended to include C2, (25) gains the further contextual implication (29):

(29) The Chairman will be unable to attend.

The extension would be worthwhile if the cost of accessing C2 was not so great as to outweigh the gain in contextual implications. If the context is further extended to include C3, and then C4, the additional contextual implications (30) and (31) are in turn obtained:

(30) Jackson's proposals will be accepted.
(31) The company will go bankrupt.

Again, if the accessing costs are not too high, these extensions would both be worthwhile. Thus, someone processing (25) in the set of contexts C1–C4 might have good reason to continue expanding the context up to its maximum size, because every expansion would increase the relevance of (25).

In the case of (26), the results of any extension beyond the initial context C1 would be quite different. Each extension incurs an extra cost in processing, but without any compensating increase in contextual implications. Whichever context is chosen, only the single contextual implication (28) is obtained. Thus, someone processing (26) in the set of contexts C1–C4 would have no reason to extend the context beyond the initial stage C1, because every expansion would decrease the relevance of (26).

Within this inferential framework, it is thus possible to see in principle how context selection might take place, and more specifically, how a proposition might help to determine its own context, subject to constraints of accessibility and relevance. In a more realistic account, more serious attention would have to be given to the choice of particular directions for extension of the context. For example, the hearer of (26) would probably not give up at context C1, but would look for relevance in another direction. Similarly, more attention would have to be paid to the question of how processing costs are balanced against numbers of contextual implications in real-life situations. For example, at what point would the hearer of (25) decide that the cost of new extensions to the context had become too high? These are empirical questions, which we have not tried to solve directly, and to which, moreover, we believe that there will be different answers for different people in different circumstances.

The relation of our work to these and other such empirical questions in the theory of comprehension is indirect. For example, we do not believe that a hearer, in disambiguating an utterance, will actually compare all its possible interpretations and rank them for relevance before deciding what has been said. What we have tried to describe is not the procedures used in disambiguation but the goal these procedures are designed to achieve, the property they are designed to diagnose. Our claim is that the interpretation the speaker should have intended, and the one the hearer should choose, is the one that satisfies a principle of maximal relevance. Knowing the goal, it should become easier to describe the procedures, and it is in this way that our work may contribute to descriptive work on comprehension.

The assumptions crucial to our framework are, first, that comprehension is a largely inferential process, the role of context being essentially to provide premises for the calculation of contextual implications, and second, that the contextual implications of a proposition in a finite context are themselves finite. With these assumptions it is possible to see how context selection might in principle take place; without them the framework would collapse. What is in some ways less important is our choice of terminology. For us, 'relevance' is a technical term, designed to play a role in an overall pragmatic theory rather than to approximate everyday usage. We do believe that a quite substantial range of everyday intuitions about relevance are captured within this theory, and hence that this choice of terminology is quite appropriate. However, the terminology could be questioned without the overall framework being affected at all.

6. Conclusion

Grice regards the practice of observing the maxims of conversation as not merely 'something that all or most do IN FACT follow but as something that it is REASONABLE for us to follow, that we SHOULD NOT abandon' [Grice 1975, p. 48]. He is uncertain why this should be so, and suggests that an answer must await a clarification of 'the nature of relevance and the circumstances in which it is required' [p. 49]. The answer suggested by our attempted clarification is as follows.

In cognitive terms, what human beings are looking for in the information they process is relevance. Processing involves effort, and will only be undertaken in expectation of some reward in terms of contextual implications; the greater the expected reward, the more effort one will be prepared to undertake. Expectations of relevance are not constant across all individuals and circumstances, and a speaker or writer who consistently disappoints the expectations of an audience will cause a downward readjustment in their subsequent expectations, and may lose their attention entirely. If we want you to read our work, it is thus in our interest to aim at as high a level of relevance as we possibly can, creating expectations which will induce you to continue reading our work with the attention we think it deserves. Given the brute facts of cognitive psychology, this is rational, or at least reasonable, behaviour, although not particularly altruistic or virtuous.

It follows that information that has been deliberately communicated, unlike information from other sources, comes with a guarantee that a certain level of relevance has been attempted, if not achieved. It is this guarantee that makes the difference between merely uttering sentences in front of someone and saying something to someone, that justifies the disambiguation of meaning and the calculation of implicatures, that defines a separate field of pragmatics. Pragmatics so conceived is about the way in which the universal search for relevance is both served and exploited in verbal communication, and the study of relevance is its foundation stone.[11]

REFERENCES

Anderson, A. R. and N. D. Belnap, *Entailment*, Princeton University Press, 1975.

[11] For discussion of Grice's contribution to pragmatics, see Wilson and Sperber, 1981; for further discussion of the framework described in this paper, see Sperber and Wilson, 1982; for an attempted outline of a pragmatic theory, see Sperber and Wilson, 1986.

Deirdre Wilson and Dan Sperber

Berlin, I., 'Verification', in *Proceedings of the Aristotelian Society*, 1938–9.

Dascal, M., 'Conversational Relevance', in A. Margalit (ed.), *Meaning and Use*, D. Reidel, 1979.

van Dijk, T., 'Relevance Assignment in Discourse Comprehension', in *Discourse Processes*, 2 (1979), pp. 113–126.

Gazdar, G., *Pragmatics: Implicature, Presupposition and Logical Form*, Academic Press, 1979.

Goodman, N., 'About', in *Mind*, LXX, 277 (1961), pp. 1–24.

Grice, H. P., 'Logic and Conversation', in P. Cole and J. Morgan (eds), *Syntax and Semantics 3: Speech Acts*, Academic Press, 1975, pp. 41–58.

Haack, S., *Philosophy of Logics*, Cambridge University Press, 1979.

Johnson-Laird, P. N., 'Models of Deduction', in R. J. Falmagne (ed.), *Reasoning: Representation and Process*, Lawrence Erlbaum, Hillsdale, NJ, 1975.

Sperber, D. and D. Wilson, 'Mutual Knowledge and Relevance in Theories of Comprehension', in N. V. Smith (ed.), *Mutual Knowledge*, Academic Press, 1982, pp. 61–131.

―― and ――, *Relevance: Communication and Cognition*, Blackwell, 1986.

Suppes, P., *Introduction to Logic*, D. van Nostrand, 1957.

Thomason, R., 'Semantics, Pragmatics, Conversation and Presupposition', unpublished mimeo, Philosophy Dept. University of Pittsburgh, 1973.

Werth, P. N., 'The Concept of Relevance in Conversational Analysis', in P. N. Werth (ed.), *Conversation and Discourse*, Croom Helm, 1981, pp. 129–54.

Wilson, D. and D. Sperber, 'On Grice's Theory of Conversation', in P. N. Werth (ed.), *Conversation and Discourse*, Croom Helm, 1981, pp. 155–78.

10

LOGIC OF CONVERSATION AS
A LOGIC OF DIALOGUE

JAAKKO HINTIKKA

Though a longtime keen admirer of Paul Grice's work, I frequently find myself ambivalent *vis-à-vis* the way he codifies and systematizes his insights.[1] These perceptive insights have often pertained to the 'logic' (in the widest sense of the word) of *discourse* phenomena. Grice has emphasized more forcefully than any other recent philosopher —and also longer than any of his colleagues—the importance of taking into account the nature of the whole discourse in which a speaker is engaged and not just the particular proposition he or she is making. Yet when the time comes to conceptualize the results of such discourse-theoretical observations, Grice often seems to retreat back to formulations that pertain to utterances taken one by one rather than to the interplay of different utterances in discourse. This does not diminish the value of Grice's observations, but it prompts the question as to whether they—or at least some of them—could perhaps be accommodated, with profit, within a different, more flexible framework in which the dynamics of discourse are spelt out more explicitly.

Another way of making a closely related point is to suggest that the contrast Grice draws between formal logic and the 'logic' of conversation is misplaced. What is wrong, or insufficient, about current formal logic is not that it is formal, but that it is developed only on the sentence level, that is to say, so as not to take into account the interrelations of different sentences in discourse. What is important is to take these intersentential relations into account, and whether one does it formally or informally is of a lesser consequence.

It is for this reason that I have dared to flaunt the term 'logic' in the title of this paper without any quotation marks.

[1] The classical—and unfortunately the only printed—statement of Grice's ideas is 'Logic and Conversation' in Peter Cole and Jerry L. Morgan, editors, *Syntax and Semantics*, vol. 3: *Speech Acts*, Academic Press, New York, 1975. pp. 41–58. (All references not otherwise specified are to this paper.)

These points apply even more obviously to the work of Paul Grice's former student and sometime associate, Peter Strawson. If we open, almost at random, his paper 'Identifying Reference and Truth-Values',[2] we find an abundance of such locutions as 'purpose of assertive discourse' (p. 237), 'presumption (on the part of the speaker) of ignorance (on the part of the audience) of some point to be imparted in the utterance' (p. 237), 'the scope of the audience's identifying knowledge' (p. 239), 'the speaker's intention' (p. 241), 'antecedently introduced class' (p. 251), etc.

An especially striking feature in such locutions is the frequency of references to what the speaker and the hearer *know*. Yet the main applications of Strawson's observations are to such things as the contrast between asserting and presupposing or to the relation of this contrast to failures of reference, where both subject matters are dealt with in terms of one utterance at a time and not in terms of interrelations of successive utterances. A typical question raised in this department is: if an expression in an assertion fails to refer, is the assertion false, or should we speak instead of a failure as a presupposition? Whatever one wants to say about such matters, they are likely to be the least interesting and least distinctive part of the 'logic' of discourse. The futility of formulations which turn on considering only one utterance at a time is illustrated by the fact that few interesting and true generalizations can be set up in such a way. For instance, if it is said (as Strawson tried to maintain at one time) that a failure of reference in an assertively uttered sentence causes a failure of presuppositions and makes truth-values inapplicable, it remains to be explained why a sentence like

(1) The present King of France does not exist

(or, more idiomatically, 'There's no such person as the present king of France') is true even though it contains the vacuous term 'the present king of France'. The same goes for statements like

(2) If there were such a person as the present King of Romania, he would have to be a shrewd politician to have been able to survive on his throne.

Admittedly, Strawson writes that 'it no longer seems to me important

---

[2] *Theoria*, vol. 30 (1964), pp. 96–118; reprinted in E. D. Klemke, editor, *Essays on Bertrand Russell*, University of Illinois Press Urbana, Illinois, 1970, pp. 236–55. (Page references here are to the reprint.)

to come down on one side or the other in this dispute' as to whether failures of reference cause truth-value gaps. But instead of dealing with the queston in terms of the relation of the utterance in question to other ones, Strawson merely says that both competing 'conceptions are tailored . . . to emphasize different kinds of interest in statement', in other words, he merely refers to the general interests that someone might have in the proposition uttered or perhaps in the whole discourse in question, instead of focusing on the specific mechanism through which the utterance of a proposition serves these ends. Likewise, Strawson uses the notion of presupposition in a way that shows that it is an attribute of a particular assertive utterance. (For example, ' . . . is not something asserted, but something presupposed, by the speaker's utterance', op. cit., p. 244.)

A constructive example of the kinds of conceptualizations I am missing in Strawson's work is my own analysis of the relation of a question to its (conclusive) answers.[3] Not only does this analysis deal with the relation of two different utterances. The resulting criterion of (conclusive) answerhood is in terms of what the questioner knows. Furthermore, it turns out to have most interesting consequences for the role of the questions and answers in discourse. I shall be relying on this theory later in the present essay. How natural this use of a suitable theory of questions and answers is is shown by the fact that Strawson himself occasionally brings in the notion of question in order to make his point. ('But suppose the statement occurring in the context of the question . . .', p. 251.) He nevertheless considers this as a mere 'hypothesis' which serves to bring out his ideas better (p. 252). What I am suggesting here, and illustrating later in this paper, is that the concepts of question and answer can be used as an explicit ingredient of one's theory for the purpose of developing further the very ideas of Strawson and Grice.

Grice is, commendably, much more explicit about the discourse character of the phenomena he is interested in that Strawson. This is reflected by his emphasis on the conversational character of the phenomena he studies in 'Logic and Conversation'. But even there I miss explicit discussions of the interplay of different kinds of utterances.

[3] Cf. Jaakko Hintikka, *The Semantics of Questions and the Questions of Semantics* (Acta Philosophica Fennica, vol. 28, no. 4), North-Holland, Amsterdam, 1976 (distributed by the Academic Bookstore, Helsinki); 'What Is the Answer to This Question? And Other Questions in the Theory of Questions and Answers' in Morscher, Neumaier, and Zecha, editors, *Philosophie als Wissenschaft/Essays in Scientific Philosophy*, Comes Verlag, Bad Reichenhall, 1981, pp. 261–77.

For instance, Grice's justly famous conversational maxims concern what can legitimately be expected of *one particular utterance* in a conversation where the purpose is 'exchange of information'.

Grice says that one of his 'avowed aims is to see talking as a special case or variety of purposive, indeed rational, behavior' (p. 47). If so, the bag of conceptual tools one can profitably use in studying conversational logic should be a special case, or a variety, of the conceptual tools one uses in studying the rationality of human behaviour in general. One such tool is game theory, which is especially promising in the direction in which I wish Grice had ventured deeper, namely, in the direction of conversational strategies and strategy selection. For what this theory is all about is basically just the problem of strategy selection, whether or not the strategies in question are competitive or co-operative ones. (Philosophers have perhaps been put off by the unfortunate name of the theory, which in the light of hindsight ought to have been dubbed *strategy theory* rather than *game theory*, for the latter term is easily but mistakenly taken to exclude the study of co-operative strategies.) In order to illustrate the promise of this approach, I shall sketch a simple model of purposive dialogues of a certain kind, and then show how some Grice-type ideas can perhaps be accommodated in this simple model.[4]

The model is simplicity itsef. Two speakers make 'moves' alternately. There are four different kinds of moves:

(*a*) Assertoric moves.
(*b*) Interrogative moves.
(*c*) Deductive moves.
(*d*) Definitory moves.

The first move by each player must be an assertoric one; otherwise the players are free to choose the type of move they make when their turn comes.

(*a*) In an assertoric move, the player making it puts forward a new proposition (a new 'thesis').

(*b*) In an interrogative move, the player making it addresses a question to the opponent, who answers it if it can be answered. The answer is then added to the list of the answerer's theses.

---

[4] For an account of these question-answer games, see Jaakko Hintikka, 'Rules, Utilities, and Strategies in Dialogical Games' in Lucia Vaina and Jaakko Hintikka, editors, *Cognitive Constraints in Communication*, D. Reidel, Dordrecht, 1984, pp. 277–294.

(c) In a deductive move, the player making it draws a logical conclusion from the totality of his/her opponent's theses and the conclusions he/she has drawn from them earlier.

In practice, deductive steps can best be thought of as being codified in a Beth-type semantical *tableau* that each player uses as his/her 'scorecard'.[5] Deductive steps will then be steps of *tableau* construction according to the usual rules.

An application of a rule of *tableau* construction can split the *tableau* into two *subtableaux*. All the rules (a)-(d) are applied relative to some pair of *subtableaux* of the two opponents.

(d) In a definitory move, the player making it introduces a new non-logical symbol by an appropriate explicit definition.

The goal of each player is to prove the totality of his/her theses using his/her opponent's theses as the sole initial premisses, including of course one's opponent's answers to one's questions. This goal can be varied, however. For instance, instead of trying to prove a collection of theses, each player might want to prove an answer to a given question by using one's opponent's answers as the only available premisses. Then the resulting modified dialogical game can be characterized as an attempt to answer a 'big' principal question by means of a number of answers to the 'small' questions a player poses to his or her opponent.

The importance of the ends or aims in a discourse, so aptly stressed by Grice, is built into my model dialogues through their definition as games in the sense of game theory. For, as every serious student of game theory knows, it is the array of possible outcomes ('pay-offs') that essentially determines the strategy structure in a game. And it is these pay-offs that define the ends of the dialogue.

It is hence important to realize precisely how these 'pay-offs' are thought of as being determined. One thing that counts is the concrete outcome of the dialogue. Since we are trying to model information-seeking dialogues, one main consideration will be the information-content of the theses that a player has managed to prove.[6] The higher this information-content, the greater the pay-off. This motivates the players to make assertoric moves, which otherwise would appear

---

[5] The *tableau* method was introduced by E. W. Beth in 'Semantical Entailment and Formal Derivability', in *Mededelingen der Koninklijke Nederlandse Akademie van Wetenschappen*, Afd. Letterkunde, NR, vol. 18, No. 13, Amsterdam, 1955, pp. 309–42; reprinted in Jaakko Hintikka, editor, *The Philosophy of Mathematics*, Oxford University Press, 1969, pp. 9–41.

[6] For the notion of information that is presupposed here, see my own contributions to Jaakko Hintikka and Patrick Suppes, editors, *Information and Inference*, D. Reidel, Dordrecht, 1970.

inexplicable. (They make my task more difficult, for they add to the list of what I have to prove, and they make my opponent's task easier by providing him or her with additional premisses.)

It is nevertheless important to realize that pay-offs do not depend only on the end product of a game, but on the entire course which the game took in order to reach the end position. In my dialogical games, one particularly important possibility is that by making certain types of moves a player incurs a 'cost' or 'payment' to be charged against that player's eventual pay-off. One aspect of strategy selection thus assumes the form of asking how much it is worth for a player to 'pay' for the right of making a certain move.

Yet it is not the case, either, that the pay-off of a player is merely the sum total of costs (positive or negative ones) of the successive individual moves plus the value of the outcome. In principle, it may depend also on the 'holistic' features of the entire succession of moves, for example, on the number of moves it has taken a player to prove his or her theses, or on whether one's opponent has accomplished his/her task before one does it oneself.

Different ways of determining the pay-offs (i.e., different ways of defining my dialogical games) result in different optimal strategies. In spite of their apparent simplicity, my question–answer games are thus capable of considerable subtlety.

We have not exhausted, either, the subtleties of the ways in which the end or aims of my dialogical games influence what happens in the course of a game. The 'aim' of a dialogue of the kind just explained can mean two different things. They are not always easy to distinguish from each other in the applications of our model, but they are none the less important to keep apart in the interest of conceptual clarity. First, the aim of setting up the dialogue in the first place is to model certain possible or actual information-seeking procedures. This imposes certain further restrictions on the rules of the 'game' to be defined. Violations of the resulting rules are instances of pointless or irrational behaviour in one sense of these words.

Second, once the game has been set up, we can speak of a player's end or aim in the game, defined by his or her pay-offs. Admissible moves which do not further these ends are strange, and perhaps even irrational.

An example of the former is the fact that the presuppositions of questions (in a sense which I have spelt out elsewhere) have to be taken into account in the game rules. For instance, we may require that the presupposition of a question asked by one of the players must occur in the left column of that player's *tableau* before he or she is allowed to put that question to the opponent. Alternatively, we may allow a question to be asked even when its presupposition does not occur in the left column of that player's *tableau*, provided we also allow the addressee of the question to respond, not by giving an answer, but by denying the presupposition. Without some such restriction, there obviously is no point in setting up our dialogical game as a serious model of information-seeking by questioning.

There is nevertheless more trade possible between the two kinds of 'aims' than might first appear. For instance, it might seem that we need a hard-and-fast prohibition against some kinds of questions in order not to trivialize our games completely. In the variant game described above where each player's end is to answer a big initial question by putting a number of 'small' questions to one's opponent, an absolute line between 'big' and 'small' must apparently be drawn. For otherwise a player could instantly trivialize the game by putting the initial big question on his or her opponent.

In ruling out such askings of the principal (initial) question, we are following the sagacious precedent of Aristotle, who forebade the so-called fallacy of *petitio principi*. Literally, this means the asking of the principal question, and Richard Robinson has in effect shown that Aristotle's maxim in fact coincided with mine.[7] Thus Aristotle was not ruling out a fallacious inference, but an illicit move in the questioning games practised in the Academy.

It can be argued that one partial way of ruling out unlimited *petitio principii* is to allow in one's questions only a limited number (e.g. one) of layers of quantifiers. This limitation turns out to be connected with a large number of fascinating concepts and problems in the philosophy of logic and mathematics.[8] However, other limitations are also needed.

Interestingly, it can be argued that these restraints need not be absolute after all. It turns out useful for my purposes to replace an absolute prohibition against certain types of attempted moves by a principle of pay-off determination which assigns a stiff 'fee' or 'penalty' to such moves. If such a fee is stiff enough, its effect is the same as that of an absolute prohibition. But making the restraint a matter of degree makes it possible, for example, to compare the value

---

[7] Richard Robinson, 'Begging the Question 1971', *Analysis*, 31 (1971), pp. 113-17.

[8] For some of them, cf. my book *Logic, Language-Games, and Information*, Clarendon Press, Oxford, 1973.

of several different kinds of violations of prima facie restraints to the player committing them. The underlying reason for this is of course the one Grice in effect emphasizes: both the absolute rules of my games and the pay-off structure are different ways of codifying what the overall purpose of these games is.

After these simplified model dialogues have been set up, what can we say about the role of conversational expectations and conversational implications and other similar phenomena in them? Perhaps the easiest concept is that of a presupposition, in spite of the fact that this concept is in many respects exceptionally unclear. One thing that is immediately obvious is that the presuppositions of different kinds of moves are entirely different, in whatever reasonable way you may want to interpret the notion of presupposition.

(i) The only way of construing the presupposition of the output sentence of an interrogative move (that is, the sentence which is entered into the game *tableau*) is to identify it with the presupposition of the question to which it is an answer.

(ii) In contrast, the presuppositions of a definitory move are the usual presuppositions of explicit definitions. For instance, if I want to put forward the definition

(3) $(x)(y) \quad (f(x) = y \equiv D[x, y])$

for a new function f, I must have established, that is, I must have occurring in the left column of my game *tableau*, the following sentences:

(4) $(x)(\exists y) D[x, y]$

(5) $(x)(y)(u) \quad (D[x, y] \,\&\, D[x. u] \supset y = u)$

(iii) The 'presuppositions' of a deductive move are simply the conditions on which a step of *tableau* construction can be carried out.

(iv) As far as the presuppositions of an assertive move are concerned, there is no obvious sense that we can make the notion. Such moves can be more or less advantageous to the player who makes the move, but there is no obvious absolute condition that has to be satisfied.

These observations throw some interesting light on the concept of preuppositions such as Strawson and others have used it.[9] First of all,

---

[9] Over note 2 above, cf., for example, *Mind*, 59 (1950), pp. 320–44, reprinted in Klemke, op. cit. (note 2 above), pp. 147–72. (Page references here are to the reprint.)

we can see it cannot be the monolithic notion it is all too often taken to be. Different kinds of utterances (different kinds of 'moves') have entirely different kinds of presuppositions in my sample dialogues, let alone in real-life ones.

A second point is that Strawson's notion of presupposition as applied to a factual statement is clearly best construed as a presupposition in the sense (i), that is, as the presupposition of the (tacit) question to which the utterance under consideration is thought of as being an answer to. Strawson occasionally reveals how very close his own way of thinking is to this idea; witness, for example, the following passage:

A literal-minded and childless man asked whether all his children are asleep will certainly not answer 'Yes' on the ground that he has none; but nor will he answer 'No' on this ground. Since he has no children, the question does not arise. To say this is not to say that I may not use the sentence 'All my children are asleep', with the intention of letting someone know that I have children, or of deceiving him into thinking that I have. Nor is it any weakening of my thesis to concede that singular phrases of the form 'the so-and-so' may sometimes be used with a similar purpose.[10]

Here Strawson is to all intents and purposes assimilating to each other the presuppositions of questions and the presuppositions of the use of definite descriptions.

Of course it is not determined by an utterance alone what question it should be thought of as an answer to in my games, or even whether it should be construed as an answer (part of an interrogative move) or as an assertion (assertive move). But this underdeterminacy is merely a corollary to the discourse character of the notion of presupposition. It is also matched by the vagaries of the notion in its earlier use in the literature. Strawson and others will have to explain somehow why the existence of a unique present King of France is not presupposed in (2) whereas it is presumably presupposed by many other assertions in which the definite description occurs, including the famous Russellian example,

(6) The present King of France is bald.

I am not saying that Strawson cannot give, or has not given, such an account. It is nevertheless relevant to note that in my model explanation is virtually immediate. The sentence (6) is most naturally thought of as an answer to the question

[10] Op. cit. (note 9), p. 172.

(7) Is the present King of France bald?

whereas (2) is equally readily construed as an answer to following one:

(8) Is there such a person as the present King of France?

Now the presupposition of (7) in the precise sense defined in my theory of questions is equivalent to

(9) There exists such a person as the present King of France

whereas (8) has in my theory a vacuous presupposition.

A further point of partial agreement between Strawson and my model lies in the nature of the appropriate response to the situation in which a presupposition is violated. On my construal, this means that the question to which the sentence S in point is thought of as an answer has a false supposition. In such circumstances, the appropriate move is not to negate S. This is not a correct answer any more than S was. The right response by the speaker (the addressee of a question) is to deny the presupposition.

This discourse-theoretical phenomenon—the failure of a yes-or-no *question* to have an answer when its presupposition is violated—seems to me the true counterpart to Strawson's earlier doctrine that an *assertion* fails to have a truth-value if its 'presupposition' is not satisfied. The two ideas are easily confused, but nevertheless are in reality quite different. The discourse-theoretical idea is obviously correct, while Strawson's sometime view is extremely dubious.

Strawson himself argues for his (later) view of assertions in terms of the corresponding questions in 'Identifying Reference and Truth-Values' (note 2 above), pp. 251-252. There Strawson acknowledges the dependence of what we have to say of an assertive utterance on the question on which the speaker's interest is centred. But he conceptualizes this interest as an unanalysed background feature of the context instead of considering explicitly the relation of an assertive utterance to the question it is taken to be an answer to.

On my principles, it is also understood at once why the so-called presuppositions of assertive utterances are nevertheless closely related to the presuppositions of questions, in a natural sense of 'presupposition'. My quote from Strawson above illustrates this point, and so does an abundance of other examples. For instance, the stealthy presupposition of the question,

(1) Has Harry stopped seeing other women?

is obviously closely related to the presupposition of the statement

(11) Harry has not stopped seeing other women

even though someone might argue that (11) is literally true whenever Harry has not even begun doing so.

In general, other things being equal, the denial of a presupposition of a question, particularly of a wh-question, is a less informative proposition than an answer to it. Hence, *ceteris paribus*, it is not rational of a speaker to violate presuppositions in my dialogical games. Yet, as all aggressive prosecutors (and some precocious children) know, asking a question without having established its presupposition may be a way of making one's opponent admit the presupposition. Witness, for example, Inspector van der Valk making use of such a ploy in trying to find out who has sent poison-pen letters to several good citizens of Drente. For the purpose, he is questioning a man whom he suspects of also having received some letters but who is denying it. (I am changing the quote a little for my purpose.)

'Never?' . . . Van der Valk picked rough, direct phrases; street words. 'These nice bits you have here in the white overalls—never kissed one of them? Never craftily sort of slid your hand up a skirt when no one was looking? . . .'
Outrage, looking like a dying cod.
'How dare you—how can you—I would never dream—I swear to you —never, never, never . . . .' . . .
'But didn't the letters accuse you of these things?' Van der Valk asked cheerfully. The poor wretch stopped dead.
'But I destroyed all the letters.'
'Now we are getting somewhere.'

(Nicholas Freeling, *Double Barrel*, Vintage Books, 1981, p. 76.)

Likewise, Grice's conversational maxims can be accommodated in my model, which throws some interesting light on them. By and large, they turn out much less monolithic than Grice's presentation perhaps suggests. They are typically complex resultants of several different factors, often compromises between forces that are pulling in different directions.

In order to illustrate these points, consider Grice's first maxim, which he calls the maxim under the category of quantity (p. 45):

(12) 'Make your contribution as informative as is required (for the current purposes of the exchange.'

Grice adds, hesitatingly, the complementary maxim:

(13) 'Do not make your contribution more informative than is required.'

It seems to me that Grice underestimates the force of (13). He relates it to danger of confusing the hearer, and to the possible failure of relevance because of the extra information. There is nevertheless operative, both in my sample dialogues and in ordinary discourse, a different pressure against extra information. Everything a player of my dialogical games says can be used against him (or her) by the opponent. The more one says, the more one has to prove oneself, and the more premisses one concedes to one's opponent. Hence, the prima facie maxim of rationality is in this case something like

(14) 'Make your contribution as uninformative (weak) as is compatible with the purpose of the discourse.'

The reality and force of (14) should not be underestimated. The maxim (14) is an important ingredient in what is sometimes known as the *principle of charity*. It tells one to interpret a speaker's utterances in such a way as to make them likeliest to be true, which in practice amounts to making them as weak (*un*informative) as possible. As has been emphasized among others by Donald Davidson, the principle of charity plays an extremely important role in all interpretation and understanding of what people actually say.

A modest example is offered by sentences containing more than one quantifier. One of the principles governing the scopes of such quantifiers, when they occur in the same clause, is the left-to-right order. Yet this is often overruled by the principle of charity. Cases in point are the following:

(15) This is a dangerous street. Someone is hit here by a car every month.

(16) Someone is occupying every telephone booth.

Purely logically speaking, 'Someone' ought to have the wider scope in these sentences, a fact that is brought home to us by responding to (15) by saying: 'How can the poor chap survive?' or to (16) by saying, 'How can one man do that?' Yet in actual discourse, 'every' is in fact given the wider scope.[11]

---

[11] The principle of charity is also the reason why it is so difficult to come up with clear-cut examples of irreducible branching (standard) quantifiers in natural

Yet (14) does not tell the whole story. In my model dialogues, a participant will in the end be better off the more informative his or her established conclusions are. This makes it rational in some cases to stick one's neck out and put forward more information than the rules of the game require. However, that is a rational thing to do only if the player in question thinks that he or she can eventually prove the proffered thesis. Here the consequences of the first Gricean maxim converge with those of the second one (p. 46), the maxim under the category of quality which consists of one 'supermaxim', namely,

(17) 'Try to make your contribution one that is true'

and two more specific maxims:

(18) 'Do not say what you believe to be false'

and

(19) 'Do not say that for which you lack adequate evidence.'

It is the consequence of (19) that we are approaching here, even though (19) itself needs a minor generalization, suggested by my regimented dialogues. Instead of (19), we should really say,

(20) 'Do not say things for which you cannot reasonably expect eventually to acquire conclusive evidence.'

We shall return to the second maxim soon. Meanwhile, we may register the fact that Grice's first maxim (12) in any case has to be applied differently to different kinds of moves in my simplified model discourse. (How much more differently must it apply to different utterances in real life!) In the case of assertive moves, there is no clear norm as to what the degree of informativeness is that is required by the current purposes in the dialogue. As we saw, what it is rational for a speaker to utter does not depend on the informativeness of his or her statement alone, but also—and especially—the ease at which the player in question is justified in thinking that the thesis can be proved.

Grice's first maxim sits most happily on the utterances which are answers to a question asked in an interrogative move. For in such cases, there is a clear requirement present on the informativeness of the languages. Because of the great logical force of sentences containing irreducible branching quantifier structures, the principle leads a hearer to linearize the quantifiers tacitly. Cf. here my paper, 'Quantifiers in Natural Languages: Some Logical Problems' in Esa Saarinen, editor, *Game-Theoretical Semantics*, D. Reidel, Dordrecth, 1979, pp. 81–117, especially pp. 90–1.

utterance. It is implied by the requirement that the utterance must be a (full) answer to the question, assuming that one is possible in the circumstances. I have analysed the conditions of full (or 'conclusive') answerhood in detail elsewhere.[13] They are the cornerstone of any satisfactory theory of questions and answers.

The contrast between what can be said of different kinds of moves *vis-à-vis* Grice's first maxim illustrates vividly the need of taking into account the interrelations between utterances in trying to capture the logic of conversation. At the same time, the fact that Grice's own formulation applies primarily to answers to questions shows how in many discussions in the literature declarative utterances are tacitly assumed to be answers to questions. This tendency was noted above in Strawson, and it seems to me that it is operative also in Grice's conversational maxims.

Like Grice's first maxim, his second one turns out to be a many-splendoured thing to a larger extent than first meets the eye. In my simplified dialogues, the requirements (17) and (18) apply perhaps most naturally and most directly to answers to questions. There is little point in trying to model information-seeking discourse by means of my question–answer games unless it is required that the answers a player receives from other parties in the dialogue are true.

But what about assertions? In constructing my model dialogue, I have provided the players only with the Popperian motivation, which rewards informative and therefore bold and improbable theses, in so far as assertive moves are concerned. Does this not directly violate Grice's maxim (19)? Am I going to land in the same predicament as Popper who, after having first renounced all probabilistic measures of evidential support, nevertheless had to embark on a desperate and on the whole unsuccessful quest of a measure of 'truthlikeness'? Or is Grice committing the mistake against which Popper has been preaching and mistakenly preferring safety to information?

Grice can be vindicated in the main here, however. It can be shown —I have sketched an argument to that effect elsewhere[13]—that if my opponent gives true answers to my questions, if the opponent is fairly well-informed, and if the effects of my own answers can be discounted, then it is *ceteris paribus* in my own best interests to put forward true theses. Honesty, in brief, is the best policy in my information-seeking games even without any irreducible assumptions that the dialogue partners are truthful in their theses. Or, to put the point in somewhat

---

[12] See the references in note 3 above.   [13] See note 4 above

different terms, if my opponent is truthful and well-informed in answering my questions, then I had better be truthful in my assertions.

If these observations show anything, they show how extremely complex in nature Grice's maxims are in spite of their apparent simplicity. They are not, and cannot be, the rock bottom of a satisfactory analysis of the logic of conversation.

The same complexity attaches even more blatantly to Grice's third maxim, the maxim of relation. It says simply, 'Be relevant'. However, a survey of the different cases quickly shows that the only reasonable explication the notion of relevance that is relevant here is the following: an utterance in my dialogical games is relevant if it is in conformity with the rules and is believed by the speaker to further his or her interests in the game, that is, to tend to increase the speaker's pay-offs. This observation, although apparently not very helpful, has a certain interest in discourse theory in general. For instead of the relevance of the several utterances in a dialogue I could collectively speak of the *coherence* of the dialogue. My claim implies in effect that the only reasonable explication of coherence in a dialogue is in terms of the rationality of the strategies the different speakers are following.

I can argue for this conclusion by examining the different kinds of moves one by one. (i) There is no hard-and-fast criterion as to when an assertoric move coheres with the rest of a question–answer dialogue. Coherence is in this case completely a matter of how much the speaker is in a position to establish by means of questions and deductions. (ii) In the case of interrogative moves, the minimal condition they have to satisfy in order to be coherent is that the questioner has established the presupposition of the question. (Moreover, the response has to be a conclusive answer to the question.) However, over and above these basic requirements, an interrogative move is the more coherent the more obviously it serves the questioner's purposes. (iii) The only absolute condition on the coherence of a deductive move is its conformity with the usual rules of inference, in our case, with the rules of *tableau* construction. (iv) Likewise, the sole black-and-white condition of the coherence of a definitory move is that its presuppositions are satisfied. In the case of both (iii) and (iv) we also have to consider how well the move serves the player's ends.

These indices of coherence pertain prima facie to entirely different things. The only way of bringing them under the same roof is to consider the move in question in relation to the goals of the speaker. We have already seen that this cannot be done directly, by reference to a single move, but only by the mediation of the overall strategies the move can instantiate.

This formulation may seem to be incomplete in that it does not cover the conformity to explicit game rules as a prerequisite of coherence. It was seen above, however, that there is no sharp distinction beween the ends of a player as codified by the strict rules of the game and as codified by the pay-off structure. Hence this objection is not conclusive.

The fourth Gricean maxim, falling under the category of manner, is different in kind from the first three maxims, and does not interest us here.

The most important point still remains to be made. In a way, it is a generalization of the point anticipated in the very beginning of this paper. Grice wants to consider utterances from the vantage point of how they further the ends of fact-stating (possibly also fact-finding) discourse. Now the conceptualization of those purposes in terms of game theory immediately leads to a most important general point. It is implicit in the central concept of all game theory, namely the concept of strategy. What it amounts to is that normally it is impossible to tell whether a single move (for example, one particular utterance) serves to further a player's ends. This question can only be raised if we know how this player's choice concerning the one move under consideration is correlated in his/her planning with the other moves the same player makes. All such choices are summed up in the game-theoretical concept of *strategy*. (Informally speaking, a player's strategy is a rule which determines his/her moves in all the conceivable circumstances that can come up during the game, including all the possible stores of information that player might have available at the time of a move.) The question of rationality cannot in general be raised in relation to individual moves, for their effect on the course of a game depends on the other moves the players make, but it can be raised—and must be raised—in relation to strategies.

It follows that if one follows Grice and assimilates the question of conversational expectations and conversational implications to the general questions of rationality in pursuing one's ends, the resulting maxims should pertain to conversational strategies and not to individual utterances. Hence Grice's maxims, which are in effect formulated in terms of the latter, can only be approximations. There will inevitably be exceptions to them, even in the normal circumstances in which they are thought of as being applicable in the first place.

Moreover, it is in such prima facie exceptions that we can sometimes find the most brilliant instances of a strategy choice, at least in an information-seeking dialogue. Take, for instance, the requirement of relevance, that is, Grice's third maxim. What can possibly be prima facie more irrelevant than some of Sherlock Holmes's most famous lines? In interviewing witnesses about the mysterious nocturnal disappearance of the famous racing horse *Silver Blaze* and the death of its trainer, who was discovered the same morning killed out on the heath, Sherlock asks a nearby shepherd whether his flock has been all right recently, and receives the weird answer that a couple of sheep have gone lame.

What can be more irrelevant, more in violation of all reasonable conversational expectations than Holmes's question? And the reason for this appearance of irrelevance is precisely the one emphasized by Grice: Sherlock's question does not seem to further the ends of his discourse in the slightest. And there is indeed a sense which it does not do so—*alone*. That his question and the answer he received actually further the aims of Holmes's fact-finding discourse cannot be seen from them alone. For the purpose, we have to see how they fit into a place in the famous sleuth's overall chain of reasoning. (They turn out to be a splendid confirmation of what Sherlock had 'deduced' concerning the events of the fateful night.)

Hence the conversational maxims which serve to characterize conversational relevance cannot refer to an utterance alone, independently of its context in a discourse. In the last analysis they can only pertain to entire strategies.

One useful index of this fact is the occasional need to *explain* an utterance. However much there is to be said for the good old British maxim, 'Never apologize, never explain', as a social rule, an analyst must sometimes break the etiquette and restore conversational coherence by means of explanations. The explanations relevant here are typically indications of how an utterance serves as a step in an entire strategy. One can, for instance, explain Sherlock Holmes's apparently pointless query by pointing out the conclusion for which Sherlock was trying to find further confirmation. (The trainer had stolen *Silver Blaze* himself for the purpose of laming it with a surgical knife. In order to learn how to do so, he had surreptitiously tried the technique on a couple of nearby sheep.) This phenomenon of conversational explanations is an indication that the status of an utterance *vis-à-vis* conversational goals is not an attribute of our isolated utterances, not even if the purpose of the whole discourse is known and fixed, but can be changed by spelling out the speaker's overall strategy. Perhaps what is needed in the theoretical discussion of this matter is a plea for explanations to match Austin's plea for excuses.

The urgency of such a plea is enhanced by the following observation. There are excellent theoretical reasons, approximating a strict proof, to think that the need of explanations cannot ever be eliminated completely. By this I mean the following: it can be argued that the question of whether a given utterance in my dialogical games serves the purposes of the speaker optimally, or the question of to what comparative degree it serves these purposes, admits no decision method. In other (simplified) words, it cannot always be seen from an utterance alone, even in its context in discourse, whether or not it serves the speaker's purposes in that discourse. If conversational expectations are defined by reference to these purposes, as Grice aptly suggests, then it cannot be decided on the basis of an utterance alone whether it satisfies the conversational expectations (conforms to the ultimate 'conversational maxims'). Even when it does, this cannot always be seen without explanations, which hence are an indispensable tool in making the rationality of rational discourse patent.

This observation throws further light on the nature of Grice's conversational maxims. Even if one takes into account the discourse character of realistic conversational principles, a defender of Grice's maxims faces a dilemma. If one wants to make them actually and universally applicable in conversation, and hence effective, one will always find exceptions to them. The other horn of the dilemma is to give up effectivity. Then one can indeed have strict (exceptionless) conversational principles. But then one loses the direct applicability of one's maxims. In some cases, their applicability can only be established by means of explanations. Then it is not an immediately observable fact of conversation whether or not a given utterance satisfies them, even if the speaker's ends in the discourse are known.

Even though I have frequently departed from the letter of Grice's own formulations in this essay, it is unmistakable that the decisive inspiration for it comes from Grice. I have always thought that the best tribute one can pay to an important philosopher is to develop his (or her) ideas further. That is what I have tried to do here.

11

ALTERNATIVE MIND-STYLES

GORDON BAKER

Paul Grice is one of the few of the previous generation of philosophers from whom I have learned something of profound importance about how philosophy ought to be conducted. No doubt I have learned far less than he taught, and hence I have profited less from his work than he might reasonably hope. What I found admirable from the first was his skilful advocacy of heresies, not so much the particular heresies which he advocated (now transformed by his success into orthodoxies). He revealed the virtues of a healthy scepticism about what most philosophers took for granted, and he opened up topics that many had assumed to be worked out.

This essay is an expression of gratitude for this goodly inheritance. It may seem a somewhat doubled-edged present, if not a veritable Trojan horse. For my intention is to raise philosophical questions about the very framework in which he constructs ingenious answers to what he considers to be basic philosophical questions. Only another philosopher could possibly recognize this as an intention to honour anybody! More soberly, this essay might be viewed as a recipe for a much-needed antidote to the intellectual intoxication brought on by deep draughts of 'Method in Philosophical Psychology', 'Utterer's Meaning and Intentions', 'Some Aspects of Reason', or 'The Logic of Conversation'.

1. FREGE'S VISION

It seems to us now that very occasionally somebody has brought about a transformation in the climate of thought in philosophy. Frege is one of these outstanding figures. He inaugurated the modern period in the philosophy of mathematics. He swept away the logic of the syllogism with its supporting doctrine of analysing propositions into subjects and predicates; he replaced it with a system of logic incomparably more powerful and elegant, and his new creation has survived intact to the present day.

We also credit Frege with a host of spectacular achievements in philosophical logic. He allegedly developed the idea that predicates should be analysed as function-names in the semantic analysis of declarative sentences. He is reputed to have given the first correct semantic definitions of the logical constants: truth-table definitions of the constants of the propositional calculus, and the standard semantics for quantifiers. With the distinctions of objects from concepts and of second-level concepts from first-level ones, he adumbrated the simple theory of types and thus anticipated the viable part of Russell's account of type-differences. The concept of sense was employed to solve the paradox of identity and to give the first analysis of sentence-meaning as truth-conditions. He introduced the distinction between sense and force which is indispensable for generalizing truth-conditional semantics to the whole of any natural language. He first perceived the important truth that the meaning of a sentence is compounded out of the meanings of its parts according to its structure, and so he handed us the key to answering the fundamental question of how it is possible to understand a sentence never before encountered. And he furnished the correct account of the application of numbers in counting. This formidable list is merely a minimal opening bid for a compilation of his achievements. Some commentators would argue vehemently for other claims: that he anticipated the picture theory of meaning in the *Tractatus*, that he fore-shadowed Wittgenstein's later refutation of psychologism about meaning, etc. But to certify Frege's indisputable genius, there is no need to adjudicate on any claims not unanimously acknowledged even if this strategy might seem to some to understate his merits.

On closer inspection, however, some of the lustre appears thin and chipped. The attribution to him of several of his putative central achievements is questionable. He did not believe that the business of logic centres on the semantic analysis of sentences, and he lacked the notion of truth-conditions familiar from the *Tractatus*; hence he was at two removes from the idea that the concept of sense grows out of the conception of sentence-meaning as truth-conditions. Similarly, he never formulated truth-table definitions of his primitive logical constants; these symbols have tabular explanations in *Begriffsschrift*, though they cannot coherently be construed as names of *truth*-functions, while the demand for completeness of definition in the *Basic Laws* excludes the legitimacy of truth-table explanations and undermines any rationale for distinguishing the logical primitives from any other first-level concept-words. Whatever resists the solvent of this textual scrutiny suffers from further defects. First, important ingredients of his thinking are seriously mistaken. He built his logical system on the presupposition that any cogent inference must have true premisses, and the very idea of function/argument analysis, in his view, presupposes that sentences are proper names of objects (originally of judgeable-contents, later of truth-values). Second, major arguments are incredibly weak, and occasionally altogether wanting. No case is made for the notorious doctrine that the reference of a sentence in indirect speech is its customary sense. The crucial claim that predicates name functions ('concepts') stands merely on an analogy with the symbolism of function-theory, and no defence is indicated against obvious (and devastating) counter-arguments. The thesis that the reference of a sentence is a truth-value rests on a sequence of equivocations and question-begging steps of inference. Philosophical criticism dissolves away much of the body of this thought and leaves a heap of disconnected bones. Even this remnant may be less impressive than it seems. The present ignorance of nineteenth-century logic forestalls our noticing that many apparently original ideas are in fact inherited from his predecessors. The catalogue of Frege's unquestioned achievements contains numerous false entries. Compiling a revised edition is an important task for the history of philosophy in the present day.[1]

What seems initially surprising and then, on deeper reflection, most noteworthy is the almost universal absence of any recognition of the enormous gap between Frege's reputation and the contents of his writings. How can the myths survive when modern publications have made all of his work available to a wide audience and when an increasing interest in it attracts an increasing number of able philosophers to study it? The explanation must be that we are fascinated by certain general contours of his thought so that we are ready to dismiss detailed examinations of his work as focusing on trivia, perhaps even to castigate detailed criticism as malicious sniping at the memory of a genius. The crucial question then is what we find so entrancing.

One answer is that we are impressed by the elegance and technical sophistication exemplified in Frege's formal logic. We are inclined to agree with the judgement that he fashioned

---

[1] This is the main business of G. P. Baker and P. M. S. Hacker, *Frege: Logical Excavations*, Oxford University Press, New York, and Basil Blackwell, Oxford, 1984. Claims dogmatically stated here are explained and defended there in detail.

a new instrument, a logic, which in delicacy and range and power far surpassed anything that went by this name before, a subject revealing to this day new and unexpected depths.[2]

He invented and brought to maturity the first-order predicate calculus, and he opened the road to fruitful studies in metalogic. He is the very model of a virtuoso logician, and we interpret technical ingenuity of such a high order as a symptom of depth of understanding.[3]

A second answer is that he rejuvenated the traditional paradigm for developing theories of meaning, what Wittgenstein called 'the Augustinian picture of language'.[4] The notion that the meaning of a word is an object correlated with it had been transformed by classical empiricism into the notion that words stand for ideas, and this had come to seem problematic and confused. Syllogistic logic, incorporating the contention that every assertion expresses a relation between exactly two ideas, generated further strains and called for a sweeping application of the distinction between the grammatical form of a declarative sentence and the logical form of the proposition expressed. Frege cleared the ground of this clutter. He purified the Augistinian picture of the psychologism introduced by empiricism; mental entities (ideas) are replaced by Platonic ones (senses) which by themselves, that is independently of such empirical relations as resemblance, determine what entities (concepts or objects) are their references. He discovered entities having novel logical forms (concepts and relations of different levels), and he identified a galaxy of new logical forms of thoughts, thereby licensing the possibility of a general (though not strictly universal) correspondence of thought-structures with sentence-structures. An attractive paradigm threatened with asphyxiation by masses of qualifications was granted a new lease of life,[5] and it lives on with new vigour even now.

A third source of charm is a vision of a double isomorphism holding between language and thoughts and between thoughts and

[2] F. Waismann, *How I See Philosophy*, ed. R. Harré, Macmillan, London, 1968, p. 15.

[3] Cf. E. Husserl, *Logical Investigations* (trans. J. N. Findlay), Routledge & Kegan Paul, London, 1970, vol. 1, pp. 249 f.

[4] L. Wittgenstein, *Philosophical Investigations*, Blackwell, Oxford, 1953, §§ 1 ff. For detailed analysis and criticism see G. P. Baker and P. M. S. Hacker, *Wittgenstein: Understanding and Meaning*, Blackwell, Oxford, and Chicago University Press, 1980, pp. 33 ff.

[5] Partly through the direct influence of Frege's thinking, exploitation of this paradigm reached its zenith in the logical atomism of Russell and Wittgenstein.

the world. This is immediately perspicuous in a diagram that Frege devised;[6]

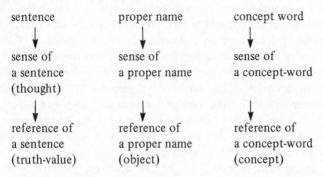

Both the sense and the reference of a proper name are completely unlike the sense and the reference of a concept-word; each of the first are 'saturated' entities, each of the second 'unsaturated'. In a logically perfect language, sentence-composition would exactly correspond to thought-composition, and hence only an unsaturated expression would count as a concept-word, only a saturated one as a proper name. Concept-script is meant to put the realization of this ideal within practical grasp. In principle isomorphism of language with thought can be attained, and in practice there is a great measure of correspondence. The isomorphism of thoughts with the world takes care of itself. Frege advanced the comforting idea that this is the best of all possible worlds from a logical point of view—or at least very nearly so for someone fortunate enough to be a native speaker of German.

The combination of these ideas amounts to a revitalization of the Pythagorean dream. His logic is built on a radical generalization of the mathematical concept of a function (the one current in his day!). His concept-script revamps statement-making discourse in the symbolism familiar from algebra and real analysis. The theses that ordinary predicates stand for concepts, that concepts are really functions, and that thoughts are isomorphic with the world, together imply that the categories of abstract function-theory are the ultimate metaphysical categories. For the very first time the vista opened of a sophisticated theoretical science of the objects of thought, even the prospect of an advanced science of language.[7] Although the world, thought, and

---

[6] Frege, *Philosophical and Mathematical Correspondence*, Blackwell, Oxford, 1980.

[7] Frege did not himself pioneer the application of function theory to the

language are not made of numbers, at each level philosophical analysis reveals that the ultimate building-blocks are objects and functions. Frege conquered new domains and subjected them to the sway of mathematics just as Newton had.[8] The visionary aspect of Frege's work rides on the back of an elaborate theory, the doctrines of a quasi-science. He emphasized this point. He compared the logical analysis of thoughts with the chemical decomposition of matter, and he declared that his discovery of the two logical objects the True and the False was as important as the discovery of a pair of new elements in chemistry. What may seem now to us to be bizarre redefinitions of familiar terms ('concept', 'object', 'function') undoubtedly struck him as revelations about the real natures of what these non-technical terms had always designated. The fruits of his scientific investigations were, in his view, an axiomatization of the general laws of logic and the rigorous demonstration that arithmetical truths are analytic, but he foresaw parallel theories dealing with other subject-matter.

The presuppositions of Frege's theory-building are important, though seldom remarked or discussed. First, it must be possible to make genuine *discoveries* in logic. In his view, no language-user had known the sense or the reference of numerals or of the predicate 'number' until he revealed it. Likewise, the incorporation of syllogistic reasoning within quantification theory shows that those who had produced or followed proofs in Euclidean geometry had unbeknownst to themselves really been making use of the basic laws of logic which Frege first discovered. He also claimed to have discovered the true nature of mathematical induction. Formal definitions of words may be hidden in their patterns of use, and the genuine principles of correct reasoning may be hidden in the canons actually applied in justifying and criticizing arguments. Secondly, it must make sense to *criticize* or *reform* established patterns of word-use or acknowledged forms of reasoning. Frege often engaged in such revisionism. Negatively, he ruled that the standard form for speaking about concepts is logically incoherent because it violates his type-restrictions, and he accused us

syntactical analysis of sentences (*pace* P. T. Geach, 'Frege', in G. E. M. Anscombe and P. T. Geach, *Three Philosophers*, Blackwell, Oxford, 1967, pp. 142 ff.)

[8] A similar concept informed Boole's earlier construction of a logical algebra. 'The laws of thought, in all of its processes of conception and of reasoning, in all those operations of which language is the expression or the instrument, are the same kind as are the acknowledged processes of Mathematics . . . . [H]uman thought, traced to its ultimate elements, reveals itself in mathematical forms.' G. Boole, *The Laws of Thought*, Dover, New York, 1958, pp. 422 f.

of error in conceiving of truth as a property of thoughts.[9] Positively, he argued that mere narrow-mindedness prevents our recognizing that category-restrictions among objects are logically unjustifiable, so that we should define numerical and even logical operators over all objects whatever. In his eyes, natural languages are not in good logical order, and their speakers have a duty imposed by the laws of logic to put matters right. Finally, Frege's theorizing manifests an unshakable *commitment* to the general applicability of abstract function-theory. He acted as if he knew in advance of detailed investigation that *somehow* logic could be built on the notions of function and argument. The original theory in *Begriffsschrift* grew out of the hypothesis that judgeable-contents were the values of the functions basic to logic. The *Basic Laws* elaborated a new theory, duplicating function/argument analysis at the level of sense and at the level of reference, and thenceforth both thoughts and truth-values were treated as basic values of functions. In practice Frege behaved like somebody who declared that the form of his theory was fixed, but who conceded that only the construction of a successful theory of this form would reveal what the subject-matter of the theory really was.

The immense attractions of Frege's general vision together with his deep commitment to the spirit of rigorous scientific inquiry call forth the reverence widely accorded to his work. Would it not be conclusive proof of philistinism to fail to join the general adulation? Before drawing this conclusion we might reflect on the fact that his repute has not always been so great, and his writings not always the object of respect. Indeed, *Begriffsschrift* was mocked by one of the most eminent logicians of that period and ignored by most of the rest. Does it have a single invariant philosophical value? Is deplorable ignorance in the nineteenth century and exemplary sagacity in the mid-twentieth the only explanation of its changing fortunes? Or a proper explanation at all? Might its elevation to greatness not reveal more about us than about it? If a book and a head brought into sudden contact give off a hollow thud, it need not be the book that is hollow. Conversely, even if such contact gives rise to a revelation, the book may not be the Gospels. A fundamental shift in the intellectual climate and in the interests of philosophers may have occasioned the striking reassessment of Frege's worth. This hypothesis is reinforced by noting that the object of our admiration often turns out not to be his idea at all, but something that we have projected

[9] 'On Sense and Reference', in P. Geach and M. Black (eds), *Translations from the Philosophical Writings of Gottlob Frege*, Blackwell, Oxford, 1960, p. 64.

onto his thought from another source (often, it seems, from the *Tractatus*) and then idolized. The writings of a philosopher are treacherous: they seem to be windows, but most readers perceive little but reflections of themselves.

2. SUPERSTITION AND DOGMATISM

Frege evidently conceived logic and the philosophy of mathematics to be an investigation of the realm of Platonic entities conducted in conformity with the canons of scientific rigour. His system, it seems, is to be assessed according to the criteria for the adequacy of a scientific theory: mathematical elegance, simplicity, and explanatory power. Our reluctance to dismiss any of his work as simply ridiculous stems in part from a deep commitment to the appropriateness of scientific methodology in philosophy. What seems to us truly absurd is patent departure from these norms.

This pervasive ideal can be reformulated more positively. Philosophers, like scientists, are urged to combine hard-headedness with open-mindedness. Hard-headedness demands wielding Occam's razor; speaking of theoretical or abstract entities requires justification, and it must be eschewed whenever satisfactory justification is not forthcoming. Similarly, there is the requirement of maximum explanatory power with minimum complexity of theories; a minimal set of primitive propositions should be sought to provide a theoretical unification of 'observed' regularities (in what is perceived, in language, in the stream of consciousness, etc.). Open-mindedness demands banishing all inviolable preconceptions about the phenomena to be explained. It should include a serious attempt to exorcize all dogmatism, to scrutinize the grounds for each belief, and to call in question whatever has no more secure basis than custom or traditional authority. Methodological or Cartesian doubt is the pure form of this generalized sprit of Protestantism. What could be more worthy of admiration than a combination of hard-headedness with open-mindedness? Would any deliberate deviation from this ideal be tolerable in principle, or more likely to lead to philosophical insight in practice?

Impeccable though its credentials seem, the scientific ideal is problematic in application to philosophy. There is superstition in avoiding superstition, and so too the attempt to avoid all forms of dogmatism produces fresh dogmatism all the more insidious for being nearly imperceptible. Suspicion of theoretical or abstract entities is perhaps the most obvious case. This has ramifying roots among which two pre-conceptions stand out. The first is the idea that a word has meaning in virtue of standing for some entity which is its meaning. The second is the general empiricist presumption that the basis of all language consists of words directly correlated with perceptible entities (objects and properties, whether mental or physical or both). Together these conten-tions cast doubt on whether terms purportedly standing for impercep-tible entities have any significance at all, and hence they demand some act of atonement for the sin of introducing the names of 'theoretical' or 'abstract' entities into discourse. Only if a particular 'ontological commitment' is unavoidable should it be granted absolution. The important and seldom noticed fact is that this whole conception rests on at least two dubious assumptions about the nature of meaningful language. The very idea of 'ontological commitment' depends on the legitimacy of the Augustinian picture, since otherwise the question of whether an expression had a proper place in a scientific theory could not be taken to raise any issue at all about ontology! The worship of hard-headedness in its current form is far from being presupposition-free; rather, it emanates from a muddle about meaning which itself stands in need of philosophical investigation.

The veneration of open-mindedness is equally dangerous in philo-sophy. It leads straight into a subtle dogmatism. To maintain an open mind on a particular matter is to suppose that the answers to relevant questions have yet to be discovered. However admirable in science, this idea is suspect in application to philosophy. The real risk of dogmatism here originates, as Wittgenstein noted, from 'the conception that there are questions the answers to which will be found at a later date. It is held that, although a result is not known, there is a way of finding it'.[10] Where does danger lurk here? What alternative strategy could conceiv-ably be an improvement? At first sight there seems no plausible answer to either question. But reflect: to suppose that the answers to philo-sophical questions await discovery is to presuppose that the questions themselves make sense and stand in need of answers (not already available). Why should this not be a fit subject for philosophical scrutiny? Questions cannot be posed *in vacuo*. The formulation of a question, certainly of any that is deep and penetrating, presupposes a framework of thought which may be complex and widely ramifying. Questions, just as much as assertions, carry presuppositions. To pose

[10] *Ludwig Wittgenstein and the Vienna Circle: Conversations recorded by Friedrich Waismann* Blackwell, Oxford, 1979, p. 182.

a particular question is to take some things for granted, to put some things beyond question or beyond doubt, to treat some things as matters of course. Once this is acknowledged, can a philosopher reasonably turn his back on investigating the questions posed in philosophy and simply join in a co-operative search for answers, as it were, to God-given questions? The ideal of open-mindedness is dangerous because it precipitates us into answering questions. We should, on the contrary, make serious efforts at raising questions about the questions commonly viewed as being genuinely philosophical. Perhaps the proper answers to such questions is often, even if not always, further *questions*![11]

The defects of simple-minded open-mindedness have been much emphasized even in respect of science itself. Philosophers of science have noted that the construction of any scientific theory occurs within a particular framework of concepts and assumptions. It takes place within the horizon of possibilities embodied in a particular paradigm. But any scientist who vaunts his own open-mindedness is in danger of mistaking a relative freedom from presuppositions with an absolute one, as if his scientific visions were bounded by no horizon at all. Philosophers run the same risk too. But in addition they may forget that it is at least as much their business to inspect paradigms (both scientific and philosophical) as to construct theories. Therefore, there is the added risk that adherence to the ideal of open-mindedness will divert their efforts from paradigm-scrutiny into paradigm-elaboration. (A powerful gravitational field here threatens to draw philosophy into the orbit of science.)

Philosophers who guide themselves by the ideals of science are no more perfect than scientists in adhering to them, and no less immune than scientists to correlative illusions. They are apt to conflate mathematical sophistication with explanatory power. As if expertise in symbolic techniques were inseparable from an understanding of what is (allegedly!) symbolized! Philosophers are also exposed to the danger of sliding down the slippery slope of success. Quantification theory is an exemplary case. Frege began with a modest, perhaps instrumental conception: the representation of general judgements in his concept-script would be of utility in checking the cogency of inferences in rigorous demonstrative sciences.[12] By the end of his life he had come to think that formulae in concept-script gave an accurate picture of

---

[11] L. Wittgenstein, *Remarks on the Foundations of Mathematics* (first edn) Blackwell, Oxford, 1964, Part II, §5.
[12] G. Frege, *Begriffsschrift*, Preface.

the structure of thought and the world.[13] He probably thought, as others do, that he had discovered *the* true logic of multiple generality.[14] His successors have made even more sweeping claims: quantification theory belongs to the depth structure of every natural language,[15] and the whole system of classical logic delineates the essence of language, thought, and the world.[16] Modesty seems but the febrile offspring of caution, instantly killed off by the least whiff of success. Finally, philosophers are prey to the opposite danger in the face of apparent failure. They are tempted to explain away difficulties by contrasting apparent with real refutations of their theories, and they are prone to patch things up by myriad *ad hoc* modifications, pursuing the mirage that the salvation of a beleaguered theory lies in some hitherto undreamt of feat of technical ingenuity.

Frege's thought illustrates these dangers clearly. He dogmatically denied that truth is a property of thoughts, asserting instead that the True is really the reference of what we misleadingly call true judgements. He invented the sense/reference distinction to salvage his function/argument analysis in the face of his need to link concepts logically with their extensions for the purpose of establishing his logicism.[17] And he brushed off the deep incompatibility between the multiple polyadicity of ordinary predicates and the thesis that predicates stand for functions (since functions are differentiated into types by the number of their arguments). Although everything can be classified as a merely apparent deviation from a simple uniform pattern, to follow this strategy renders vacuous, and hence pointless, the assertion of genuine conformity at an allegedly deeper level.

The risk of lapsing from the standards set is not the principal problem with the application of scientific ideals to the activity of philosophizing. The fundamental issue is whether these ideals are appropriate at all in philosophy. The elaboration and testing of detailed scientific theories makes sense only within the framework of ideas and assumptions that generally pass unquestioned. In the absence of

[13] Frege, *Correspondence*, p. 63, and *Posthumous Writings*, Blackwell, Oxford, 1979, p. 266.
[14] Cf. M. Dummett, *Frege: Philosophy of Language*, Duckworth, London, 1981, pp. 8 ff.
[15] Cf. J. Lyons, *Semantics*, Cambridge, 1977, vol. I, pp. 147 f. and vol. II, p. 458.
[16] L. Wittgenstein, *Tractatus Logico-philosophicus*, Routledge & Kegan Paul, London, 1961, 6.12, 6.1231 ff., and 6.13.
[17] For a vindication of this controversial thesis, see Baker and Hacker, *Frege: Logical Excavations*, part II.

consensus on a paradigm, theory-construction comes to a halt. The focus of interest is on the empirical adequacy of theories, not on passing judgements on paradigms that serve as norms of representation for theories and observations alike. Philosophy should reverse this order of priority. Otherwise it would put the most crucial matters beyond question. To accept a question as making good sense and embark on building a philosophical theory to answer it is already to make the decisive step in the whole investigation.

How does the philosophical problem about mental processes and states and about behaviourism arise?—The first step is the one that altogether escapes notice. We talk of processes and states and leave their nature undecided. Sometime perhaps we shall know more about them—we think. But that is just what commits us to a particular way of looking at the matter. For we have a definite concept of what it means to learn to know a process better. (The decisive movement in the conjuring trick has been made, and it was the very one that we thought quite innocent.)[18]

This insidious dogmatism is conspicuous in Frege's system. The construction of his concept-script began with the purpose of replacing the traditional logical analysis of judgements into subjects and predicates by a decomposition into function and argument. But, at the outset, he gave no clear explanation of what entities are the values of these functions; apparently 'judgeable-contents' were to reveal their nature through further investigation. Ultimately he decided (or discovered!) that a pair of distinct entities (a thought and a truth-value) correspond to each putative judgeable-content. In a parallel way he arrived at the thesis that simple proper names have senses. The logical significance of any expression he assumed is determined by its being correlated with some entity. A complex proper name he held to indicate a mode of presenting an object as the value of a function for an argument, and this (abstract) entity is its sense. This account is inapplicable to simple unanalysable names. None the less, persuaded that their logical significance was not exhausted by their correlation with objects, he concluded that they too *must* be correlated with some (abstract) entities, though he had no explanation to give of what their senses might be.

Similar preconceptions dominate contemporary philosophy of language. One of the most notable is preoccupation with forms of expression. Efforts to account for the various uses of sentences set out from the presumption that particular uses, or perhaps ranges of uses,

[18] Wittgenstein, *Philosophical Investigations*, §308.

are somehow determined by the forms of uttered sentences (together, of course, with their constituent terms). The search is launched for semantic mood-makers, for features that mark sentences off as metaphorical or ironic, etc. The obvious failure to find requisite characteristics merely diverts the hunt into the realm of depth structures. The underlying idea is unshakable: somehow difference in use must be encapsulated in difference in forms (or constituents), even if we have no inkling of how this is accomplished. The moral to be drawn from these examples of dogmatism is that no amount of open-mindedness about details in theory-construction can compensate for an *idée fixe* about the nature of the question to be answered. Negatively, this means that serious reflection, especially that of the clever, may be ruined by 'un noyeau d'erreur qui attire et assimile tout à lui-même'.[19] Positively, it means that one insight at the beginning is worth more than ever so many somewhere along the way. Wherever a philosopher states that something *must* be thus-and-so, however it may appear, and particularly when he describes things as being 'tacit', 'implicit', 'unconscious', 'below the surface', we should reach immediately for a large retort of cynical acid and apply it liberally to everything in the neighbourhood.

Fascination with scientific theorizing diverts philosophers' attention from their proper business. The unexamined question is not worth answering, the unexamined presupposition not worthy of adherence. Unless philosophical questions suddenly all dissipate like a mist, the task of philosophy must be literally endless. For, it should be to raise questions about every question, still more obviously to raise questions about every answer to a philosophical question. What most urgently needs questioning is the legitimacy of any general framework of thinking which gives rise to a co-ordinated set of philosophical questions and an elaborate theory giving detailed and unifying solutions to them. Far from encouraging this activity, the veneration of scientific open-mindedness in philosophy is a superstition engendering a myriad of further superstitions.

3. HIDDEN DEPTHS

Suppose it were conceded that there are serious doubts in principle about the application of scientific ideals to philosophical investigations. None the less, it might be objected, we lack any viable alternative

[19] J. Joubert, *Pensees Essais etc.,* Paris, 1850, vol. I, p. 170.

guides. The human condition condemns us to reasoning always in some framework of concepts and assumptions (a 'conceptual scheme'). Moreover, there is urgent work to be done. It must fall to philosophy to tackle such issues as the general connections between mental states and behaviour, between thought and language, and between fact and value. Clearly much here is not perfectly understood, perhaps not understood at all. There are mysteries to be fathomed, explanations and clarifications to be given. Instead of deploring the absence of any possibility of thought unbounded by some intellectual horizon, should we not press on with the business of explaining, and thus coming to understand, what is opaque because of its depth and profundity?

Such a call to action is very persuasive. It draws its strength from a pervasive and deep aspect of our contemporary culture: the myth of hidden systems. This idea ramifies through our *Weltanschauung* and sprouts forth in many different places. We are easily charmed by explanations resting on recursion formulae: since such a formula generates all the infinity of solutions to multiplying any pair of natural numbers, we are inclined to accept that a child who knows how to multiply must have really mastered the technique of deriving answers to multiplication problems from applying the underlying recursion formula. His ability might be claimed to consist in his (implicit) mastery of this recursive technique. We are readily captivated by determinism applied to the physical world: we accept with no difficulty the contention that all events belong to a single comprehensive network of causal relations, that none stand aloof, as it were, from the rest. The picture of the physical world as a vast clockwork strikes us as interesting and worth considering, not as ridiculous. Psycho-physical parallelism evokes the same response: undergraduates and journalists chatter indifferently about the mind and the brain, and even a regimen of Socratic questioning often fails to elicit the faintest glimmer of awareness of any reasons for insisting on a distinction. Few would dare to *mock* the comparison of the brain with computer hardware or of the mind with computer software. The idea that the whole of culture, or various aspects of it, are epiphenomena is widely treated as a credible and interesting suggestion. There is a widespread relish in reductionism of all forms. The contrast of appearance and reality appeals to us provided that dismissing what is familiar as merely apparent is compensated for by showing it to be the surface manifestations of some underlying system. Even crude and rebarbative features of the purported reality do not dampen enthusiasm for reductionism (e.g. psychological hedonism or Freudian psychology). Claims to have discovered new systems beneath apparent chaos (e.g. in history, art, or education) evoke respectful attention rather than instant rejection or contempt. We picture ourselves as afloat on a sea of limitless depth.

One focal point of this mythology is language. Thinking about language naturally starts from the assumption that language is a system, or even a system of interrelated systems: phonology, orthography, syntax, semantics, and pragmatics. These systems are thought to be described, defined, or characterized by sets of rules, just as a game such as chess is to be analysed. Since the set of sentences recognized to be grammatical is held to be infinite, and since so too is the set of sentences understood by a competent speaker, the rules of syntax and semantics are claimed to generate recursively the sets of grammatical and intelligible sentences (respectively). Consequently, each of these sets of rules itself constitutes a structured system.[20] A philosopher may take his task to be the delineation of a general strategy for constructing a detailed description of the system of semantic rules underlying a natural language.[21] A linguist, by contrast, will probably press on with detailed theory-construction, convinced that the general principles of semantic rules are known, though the exact content of these rules is still to be discovered.[22] But all are agreed that systems of rules lie behind the workings of language, and that bringing this invisible substructure to light is an enterprise of immense importance. According to this picture of language, we come to think 'that if anyone utters a sentence and *means* or *understands* it he is operating a calculus according to definite rules'.[23] Of course, the competent speaker is not conscious of these rules, perhaps of none of them. To suppose that he was would be manifestly absurd. Instead, he is alleged to have 'tacit' or 'implicit' knowledge of the relevant semantic rules and to have the practical ability to communicate without awareness of the theoretical principles underlying his activities.

Philosophers are particularly susceptible to the allure of the idea that language masks systems of rules. They are attracted to enlist in the ranks of those seeking a rigorous scientific theory of semantics, especially when they are allotted honourable posts in this co-operative

[20] Cf. Neil Smith and Deirdre Wilson, *Modern Linguistics: The Results of Chomsky's Revolution*, Penguin, Harmondsworth, 1979, pp. 13 f. and 31.

[21] For example, M. Dummett, *Truth and Other Enigmas*, Duckworth, London, 1978, pp. 440 f. and 454 f.

[22] N. Chomsky, *Rules and Representations*, Blackwell, Oxford, 1980, p. 90.

[23] Wittgenstein, *Philosophical Investigations*, §81.

enterprise. They march under the banner of 'constructing a theory of meaning for a natural language', and they dream of attaining to comprehensive explanations of the nature of language, mind, and the world by bringing order to the realm of semantic theories. All of this enthusiasm diverts them from scrutiny and criticism of the mythology that nurtures their vision.

What launches philosophers on the various quests of discovering hidden system beneath apparent chaos is the conviction that many important matters have not yet been understood. But what justifies that initial idea? Where does it originate from? An even more basic question is what it means to say of somebody that he lacks understanding of something. Does it makes sense for a philosopher to claim that he does not already understand the nature of language, the cause of his sense experience, the relation of mental states to behaviour, etc.? For if not, there is apparently no scope for explanation or clarification of these matters, *a fortiori* none for explanations revealing hidden systems!

Let us begin here. Failing to understand is correlative to understanding (and to misunderstanding). So what we evidently need is an understanding of what it is to understand something. There is obviously a vast range or family of cases displaying many points of resemblance and many crucial differences. Consider what it is to understand algebraic topology or a particular theorem; the principle of inertia or Newtonian mechanics; the duodecimal system; domestic electric circuits or practical electronics; the development section of the first movement of Mozart's G-minor quintet, the structure of the B-minor mass, or the classical symphony; the last couplet of Shakespeare's first sonnet, Joyce's *Ulysses*, or the Gothic novel; how to prune roses; etc. The criteria for understanding are very different in these different cases, and so too the criteria for not understanding or misunderstanding. A violinist may display his misunderstanding of the structure of a movement by misphrasing a bit of his part; a student may manifest his failing to understand a proof by his inability to produce parallel proofs of related theorems or by his incapacity to complete the proof if its structure is altered; and a gardener may demonstrate his understanding of pruning hybrid tea roses by wielding his secateurs in the proper way.

The point of reviewing these commonplaces is to raise the question of how *philosophical* understanding fits into this spectrum of cases, and how lack of *philosophical* understanding is supposed to be manifested.

What shows that there are deficiencies in our understanding that philosophy might remedy? Is it the occurrence of specific puzzles and antinomies, for example, Russell's paradox or Frege's antinomy about concepts? If so, why is the construction of a general theory the appropriate treatment? Perhaps detailed probing in the immediate vicinity of the problem would prove more efficacious. And is a theory needed at all? There are many sorts of puzzlement calling for quite different approaches, for example, bewilderment about how to fit a set of parallelograms and triangles together to form a rectangle. Much theory-building in philosophy seems motivated not by specific paradoxes, but by a general diffuse sense of wonder and bafflement. We contemplate a familiar form of inference involving adverbs (e.g. 'He departed quickly, so he departed'), and then, clutching our brows in anguish, we wonder how adverbs 'really work'. This bafflement itself is baffling, for the problem does not arise out of any serious uncertainty about whether any such specific arguments are valid. When addressed with this question, why should we not reply 'Don't you know?'? Very often, as in this case, the suspicion is that the puzzlement is the product of prior commitment to a philosophical theory. Our difficulty about adverbs is that they do not fit neatly into first-order quantification theory; we have faith that this system of logic must really be sufficient to account for all valid arguments. But why elevate this recalcitrance of adverbs to fit our preconceptions about logic into the allegation that we do not *understand* the role of adverbs in language? It is predetermined by the question what would count as understanding here. But would there be any advantage in achieving 'understanding' apart from the removal of misattributed lack of understanding? Fitting adverbs into quantification theory would further understanding only in the sense in which finding a cure for an iatrogenic disease would be a contribution to public health.

Where there is absence of understanding, there is scope for explanation, clarification, or elucidation. These concepts are correlative to understanding. If one person fails to understand something and a second person, who does understand it, explains it to him, then what is explained *is* what the first does not understand and what the second does. Explanations give understanding. (But the connection is internal, not causal.) Predictably, the variety of cases of understanding is matched by a range of interrelated cases of explanation. Consider explaining a word by giving a synonym, by translating it, by analyzing it in a definition *per genus et differentiam*, or by pointing to a sample;

explaining how to behave in church by giving a description of an appropriate demeanour or by setting an example; explaining how to cut dovetails by supplying a diagram or a model to follow; explaining how to construct proofs by mathematical induction; explaining why Napoleon marched on Moscow or the origins of the First World War; explaining why water expands when it freezes; etc. The criteria for giving correct explanations differ in these different cases, and so too do the criteria for completeness of explanations, where there is any such thing as completeness.

Once again the point of reviewing the variety of explanations and the variable criteria of correctness is to raise the question of how *philosophical* explanations fit into this spectrum of cases. Are they uniform in kind? Must all satisfactory ones have the structure and role of theories in the physical sciences? What are the criteria of correctness for philosophical explanations? Does it make sense to speak of their completeness, and if so, what are the criteria of completeness? Are they always clarifications of the meanings of problematic expressions? To the extent that they are, how do they relate to the practice of everyday explanation of words and phrases? If they overlap, then must their forms not be as diverse as the forms of ordinary explanations? How to fit ostensive definitions, samples, or explanations by examples into an axiomatic calculus of meaning-rules calls for considerable ingenuity and a blanket refusal to take these explanations at face value. If philosophical clarifications of meaning diverge from ordinary explanations, how are they endowed with the status and role of meaning-*rules*? Whence derives their authority to pass judgements on the correctness or incorrectness of disputed applications of language? Can anything lacking the normative powers of ordinary explanations of words be intelligibly characterized as a clarification of *meaning* at all?

Diversity in the forms and roles of philosophical explanations is to be expected from the diversity of kinds of misunderstanding and lack of understanding to be rectified, and divergence in form and function from scientific explanations is also to be expected because many conceptual perplexities arise precisely from questions by-passed or suppressed in the education of scientists and mathematicians.

Both understanding and explanations are subject to assessment along a scale running from depth or profundity to superficiality or triviality. A superficial understanding of something is a close cousin to lack of understanding, and a superficial or trivial explanation is something scarcely worth possessing. Not surprisingly, then, philosophers aim at deep understanding, and to this end they search for deep explanations. But what is their ideal of depth? What is their yardstick for measuring profundity? The terms 'deep' and 'profound' carry a considerable range of connotations. Prominent among them are being recondite, recherché, unfamiliar, difficult to comprehend. But it would be naïve to suppose that we move 'beyond superficiality' and achieve profundity in explanations simply

by a readiness to undertake perhaps far-reaching idealization and to construct abstract models that are accorded more significance than the ordinary world of sensation, and correspondingly, by readiness to tolerate unexplained phenomena or even as yet unexplained counter-evidence to theoretical constructions that have achieved a certain degree of explanatory depth in some limited domain.[24]

Descarte's *Meditations* are surely not to be condemned as superficial on the grounds that he avoided any explicit theory-construction and made no use of mathematics in expounding his arguments! Profundity must be a concept as many-facetted as the concepts of understanding and explanation.

What the appropriate criteria are for profundity in philosophy depends on a clarification of the nature of philosophical understanding and of philosophical explanation. From the outset, however, we should be on our guard against a tendency to pass the judgement that whatever does not meet the standards of depth for a scientific explana-tion is *ipso facto* defective in philosophy. A one-sided vision inclines us to apply a monolithic conception of profundity, to venerate techni-cal sophistication and the reduction of the familiar to what is mysterious, hidden, and even uncanny. As a corrective, we should bear in mind other ingredients of depth. Questions may be deep because they concern issues that move us. Perplexity about time and scepticism about the future interlock with human anxiety and insecurity. Puzzle-ment about the relation of mind and body links up with the importance of establishing others' beliefs, desires, emotions, etc., and with worry about one's own fate (death and immortality). Controversies about values concern matters of crucial importance to our own happiness and well-being. Perhaps much of the apparent depth of philosophy derives from its treatment of questions that are not purely intellectual. An explanation may also be deep because it is strikingly simple or because it makes something apparently complex utterly transparent.

[24] Chomsky, *Rules and Representations*, p. 96.

Notable scientific theories share in this aspect of depth, but the purest forms occur elsewhere, especially in mathematics and logic. Frege effected a simplification and ordering of reasoning involving generalizations; by viewing expressions of generality as second-level functions, he reduced an apparent welter of forms of reasoning to variations on a single theme. Similarly, by taking truth-tables to characterize the significance of logical constants and by treating tautology as the defining characteristic of logical truth, Wittgenstein revealed something already present (but hitherto unnoticed) in Frege's explanations. In such cases the profundity of an explanation turns on its working an alternation in how we view something known and familiar. The explanation involves a shift of aspect. Sometimes lack of understanding and the need for explanation arise from the fact that 'the aspects of things that are most important for us are hidden because of their simplicity and familiarity'.[25] Reflection on the obvious varieties of depth in explanations should convince us that profundity is not a matter of the form of the explanation (whether it contains mathematical symbols or theoretical terms, whether it is simple or difficult to survey, whether it states something familiar), but rather a matter of the context in which it occurs and the use to which it is put.

These observations about understanding, explanations, and depth are not intended to settle the question of the nature of philosophy. They are meant to demonstrate that the question is not yet settled. If the ideal of science reigns over philosophers, it does not occupy the throne by divine right. It does so by the acquiescence of its subjects. And the question whence derives their duty of obedience to this monarch is a legitimate and important philosophical question.

4. WITTEGENSTEIN'S TRANSFORMATION: RULES

The combative nature of philosophers has ensured that the imperialism of the scientific ideal over philosophy has met with some resistance. A few scattered voices have been raised in opposition. But the most sustained negative case is Wittgenstein's set of remarks on philosophy in the *Philosophical Investigations*.

One thread that ties the *Tractatus* to his later work is Wittgenstein's opposition to Russell's advocacy of 'scientific method in philosophy'. According to Russell, philosophy should aim at a theoretical understanding of the most general aspects of the world by pursuing the

[25] Wittgenstein, *Philosophical Investigations*, §129.

methodology of the advanced physical sciences. Covering-law explanations should be sought to unify apparently diverse data, and where
several are viable, theoretical economy and degree of inductive confirmation are the criteria for selecting the fittest. Wittgenstein retorted
that philosophy does not consist of statements or theses at all; that its
'propositions' are not theories or hypotheses, but purely descriptive
accounts of the logical syntax of language; that Occam's razor and
measures of inductive support are inapplicable to propositions plotting
the bounds of sense; and that the statements of everyday language
are in perfect logical order, immune to rectification or modification
in the light of philosophical theorizing. This persistent antipathy to
Russell's fundamental ideas is perhaps the most conspicuous point of
continuity between the *Tractatus* and the *Investigations*.

This continuity is an important candle to illuminate the later
enigmatic epigrams about philosophy. But it is no sooner lit than
extinguished. Wittgenstein's later remarks are widely construed as
laying down a blanket ban on any generalization, as denying that
language exhibits any systematic structure at all. According to this
influential interpretation, we should constantly remind ourselves that
words are extraordinarily vague and flexible in meaning, and that the
patterns for their correct use are always more or less indeterminate. The
only legitimate task for a philosopher is still destructive: 'whenever
someone else wanted to say something metaphysical, to demonstrate
to him that he had failed to give a meaning to certain signs in his sentences'.[26] Apart from exposing the nonsense of philosophical pro-
nouncements, one should be content to leave *everything* as it is. This
wholly negative conception seems short of intrinsic merits, and it
conflicts with other prominent aspects of Wittgenstein's thought. His
earlier views about the descriptive task and prophylactic nature of
philosophy did not prevent the production of the complex and sophisticated system presented in the *Tractatus* as an account of the essence of
language. His later writings are peppered with generalizations of
apparent importance, for example that inner states stand in need
of outward criteria, that the meaning of a word is its use in language, and
that confusions about mathematics parallel those about psychological
phenomena. Moreover, the crucial notion of an *Übersicht* (synopsis,
bird's-eye view) seems to presuppose a degree of system or interrelated-
ness capable of being surveyed. Foisting on Wittgenstein an exclusively
negative verdict on the value of generalization or systematization has

[26] Wittgenstein, *Tractatus*, 6.53; cf. *Philosophical Investigations*, § 116.

the corollary that either his practice manifests a misunderstanding of his own principles or his characterization of philosophy is disingenious. This unflattering conclusion could be circumvented by ascribing to him a more subtle and sophisticated positive conception of philosophy as the antithesis to Russell's scientific conception.

To explore this matter in detail and to establish the complete contour of Wittgenstein's later conception of philosophy would be a lengthy undertaking. My aim is at once more modest and more ambitious: simply to furnish the key to unlock the gate to this μακρότερος ὄδος. But that key itself is locked away. How can we gain access to it? Here two ideas suggest a strategy. The first is the thought that continuity in opposition to Russell between the *Tractatus* and the *Investigations* might mask a discontinuity in the rationale for the opposition. Russell's set of theses might have more than one contrary. The second idea is to question the provocative and plausible thesis that Wittgenstein's comments on philosophy in the *Investigations* have no organic connection with the contents of his substantive remarks.[27] Would we really be unable to reconstruct his views from careful study of a text from which the methodological declarations had been expurgated? Both these lines of thought indicate that we should cast around more widely to see whether his characterization of philosophy has any intimate liaisons with what are obviously the leading themes of the *Investigations*.

Pursuing this line of enquiry leads immediately to promising results. According to Wittgenstein's account, the primary task of philosophers is clarifying the meanings of problematic expressions, making perspicuous the rules for their correct use (their 'grammar') or their *de jure* role in speech. His interest in language is analogous to the study of the powers of chess pieces. Understanding a word consists in knowing how to use it correctly or in mastering the rules for its correct use, while misunderstanding it involves entanglement in these meaning-rules. The grammar of a word is the set of rules relevant to determining the correctness of its applications. This idea seems a platitude; it pervades almost all of the modern philosophy of language. But in the context of Wittgenstein's thought, this platitude has a cutting edge. He took seriously the implications of the assertion that the clarification of meaning centres on the formulation of *rules*. By doing this, he connected his extensive (and controversial) analysis of the nature of rules and of

[27] Cf. Crispin Wright, *Wittgenstein on the Foundations of Mathematics*, Duckworth, London, 1980, p. 262.

rule-following with the concepts of meaning and understanding, thus indirectly relating his remarks on philosophy to leading ideas in his elucidation of rules. This throws a flood of light on his conception of philosophy and integrates it into the mainstream of the *Investigations*.

Gathering in this harvest presupposes an understanding of the crucial points established in his clarification of what rules are and what it is to follow a rule.[28] A sentence formulates a rule only if it is used in a range of distinctive normative activities, for example, in giving instruction on how something is to be done, in justifying or criticizing particular performances, in guiding someone who aims to do something or who seeks to correct errors in his own performances. Its status as a rule does not depend on its grammatical form, but on its use or application. This is perhaps clearest when rules are concretized in charts, tables, samples, or signposts; nothing intrinsic to such objects fixes their role as rules, but only the extrinsic feature of how they relate to certain human practices. Following a rule is an intentional action. There are a range of familiar criteria for whether somebody is following a particular rule, for example that he actually cites a formulation of this rule to rebut criticism of his behaviour or that he appeals to the rule in deliberating about what to do. It is crucial to note that somebody may conform to a rule that he does not follow, because it is, for example, unknown to him. The truism that rule-following is an intentional action has the implication that there is no such thing as somebody's following a rule hidden from his awareness or unknown to him, *a fortiori* no such thing as his following a rule never discovered and formulated or his following a possible rule which is not an actual one. There is no possibility of penetrating the behaviour of an agent and discovering that he is, unbeknownst to himself, really following a hitherto unsuspected rule. At worst he may lose sight of what rule he is following and need to be reminded of it.

The purpose of these humdrum observations is to dispel the illusion that there are hidden depths to be plumbed in the matter of rule-governed practices and the activity of following rules. There is no such thing as an undiscovered or unacknowledged rule governing any practice; there is rather the possibility of adopting new rules in place of, or in addition to, established ones. Reflection on the role of rules

[28] For a more detailed account, see G. Baker, 'Following Wittgenstein: Some Signposts for Philosophical Investigations §§143–242' in S. Holtzman and C. Leich (eds), *Following a Rule*, Routledge & Kegan Paul, London, 1981, pp. 31 ff.

makes this point obvious. Rules have a distinctive 'direction of fit': if behaviour governed by a rule fails to conform with the rule, the behaviour is faulted, not the rule. Hypotheses and scientific explanations have the reverse 'direction of fit': if the phenomena fail to square with the hypothesis, it is faulted, not the descriptions of the phenomena. A hypothetical rule is therefore incoherent, as if each of two rods could on a single occasion each be used to measure the other. There is also no such thing as tacit or implicit rule-following; there is rather *conformity* to rules unknown to the agent. Measuring with rulers provides an illuminating analogy. To wield a rod in certain ways for various familiar purposes is to use the rod as a ruler to measure objects, while absence of these purposes or deviation from this practice disqualifies the activity for the description 'measuring something'. Where the agent lacks the appropriate purposes, the fact that another who had them might be properly said to measure an object in going through the same motions does not license the conclusion that the original agent was 'tacitly' or 'implicitly' measuring this object! In respect of the *rules* of a practice and the activity of *following* these rules, there is literally nothing to be discovered.

Wittgenstein brought these general considerations to bear on meaning-rules.[29] Explanations of meaning do serve in various ways as standards for the correct use of expressions. They have a role in the justification or criticism of applications of words; they are employed sometimes as guides as to what to say; and they have a major role in language-teaching. Consequently, they may be rightly called *rules*. And in speaking we may correctly be said to *follow* these rules. Indeed, in giving a correct explanation of a particular word to justify its application, a speaker satisfies a criterion for following the rule constituted by this explanation. Conversely, if he sincerely refuses to acknowledge a putative meaning-rule as a rule that he was following, then he satisfies a criterion for *not* having followed it. Nothing but acknowledged explanations of meaning satisfy the standards of rules for the correct use of words. If specification of meaning is exhausted by meaning-rules, and if the meaning of an expression is what is understood in understanding it, then understanding does not transcend the capacity to give explanations correct by the standards of the practice of explanation. What we understand is just what we explain. The slogan 'The meaning of

[29] For further elaboration of these issues, see Baker and Hacker, *Wittgenstein: Understanding and Meaning*, pp. 69 ff. and 664 ff.

a word is what is explained in explaining its meaning' has a bite much more vicious than its bark.

The idea of characterizing meaning exclusively in terms of rules has important implications that Wittgenstein subsumes under the label 'the autonomy of grammar'. Two are striking. First, grammar diverges radically from our picture of a system or calculus of rules. It might best be called a *motley* of rules. Its rules are not uniform in form or in application. Explanations are really as different as they seem. They comprise analysis *per genus et differentiam*, ostensive definition, explanations by charts or by authoritative example, contrastive paraphrase, etc. Some can be invoked as general principles to justify particular applications of words, while others cannot. Moreover, they cannot be unified into a deductive system either by filling in derived rules or by postulating primitive rules on the model of covering-law explanation. For, although a rule-formulation may be held to stand in entailment relations with other sentences, whether or not these sentences formulate *rules* depends on how they themselves are used, and that is independent of their logical relations. Grammar is no more systematic than it *seems*. The second aspect of the autonomy of grammar is that explanations of meaning cannot be justified (and hence cannot be faulted). They are free-floating creations like the planets. Nothing holds them in place. There is nothing behind the rules of grammar; there is, as it were, no logical machinery. What could conceivably justify setting up such a rule? One apparent possibility we have already dismissed: a rule cannot be justified by appeal to a putative primitive rule (or axiom) from which it can be derived. Can facts justify a rule? Is it validated by the nature of the world, thought, or language? Or potentially invalidated by any such facts? Only its *utility* depends on the facts. But we are free to frame rules with no significant application. This form of independence from matters of fact is what Wittgenstein emphasized in relating rules to decisions. Whether a sentence formulates a rule depends solely on how we treat it, and there is no logical compulsion to use it in the way that we actually do. All justifications for applications of words come to an end. In fact they come to an end in the citation of appropriate rules. Therefore we reach rock-bottom in the language-game in appealing to established explanations of meaning.

5. THE BATTLE AGAINST THE BEWITCHMENT OF PHILOSOPHY BY MEANS OF SCIENCE

As his general clarification of the nature of rules and of rule-following directly supports his conception of the autonomy of grammar, so the picture of grammar as a motley of free-floating rules directly informs Wittgenstein's conception of philosophy.

Rejection of the presuppositions of Frege's philosophizing follows immediately from the autonomy of grammar. There is no such thing as a discovery about the rules that we are following. 'One might even given the name "philosophy" to what is possible *before* all new discoveries and inventions.'[30] Empirical investigations are therefore irrelevant, but so too are logical deductions. 'The work of the philosopher consists in assembling reminders . . .',[31] especially of those aspects of our rule-governed activities which are 'hidden because of their simplicity and familiarity'.[32] There is equally no such thing as a cogent criticism or justification of any established rule of grammar.

> Philosophy may in no way interfere with the actual use of language; it can in the end only describe it.
>
> For it cannot give it any foundation either.
>
> It leaves everything as it is.[33]

The citation of an antinomy which appears to demonstrate that grammar is incoherent manifests a misunderstanding or confusion about the role of explanations of meaning which is not remedied by adopting some technical strategem to block the derivation of this antinomy.

It is the business of philosophy, not to resolve a contradiction by means of a mathematical or logico-mathematical discovery, but to make it possible for us to get a clear view (*Übersicht*) of . . . [what] troubles us: the state of affairs *before* the contradiction is resolved [i.e. entanglement in our own rules].[34]

Finally, prior commitment to a particular form of philosophical explanation actually generates philosophical problems and puzzles. The characteristics of grammar cannot be foreseen even in outline, and the uses (and usefulness) of an explanation cannot be predicted from its form. To avoid unjustifiable or empty moves in philosophy we must

---

[30] Wittgenstein, *Philosophical Investigations*, §126.
[31] Ibid., §126.   [32] Ibid., §129.   [33] Ibid., §124.   [34] Ibid., §125.

refuse, for example, to treat abstract function theory as a preconceived idea to which the world or language *must* correspond, and instead employ it simply as an *object of comparison*. Dogmatic prejudices are inimical to clarity about the geometry of concepts.

Russell's plea for scientific method in philosophy evidently rests on mistaken presuppositions akin to Frege's. It presumes that philosophy consists of statements—statements marked off from those in science and everyday life by their generality. But the philosopher should aim to give perspicuous formulations of meaning-rules. Moreover, an adversary's acknowledgement of each rule is essential if it is to count as a rule that he is following. There is therefore no scope for advancing theses: everything must be a matter of mutual agreement on rules. *A fortiori* there is no place for hypotheses or explanations in philosophy. Its status as an explanation or hypothesis debars a sentence (or what it expresses) from having the normative role essential to a rule. This makes the criteria for judging the worth of hypotheses in science irrelevant to elucidations of meaning in philosophy. Occam's razor and degree of inductive support are as inapposite in assessing clarifications of colour-words or number-words as they are for judging the performance of a pianist or the merits of a Canaletto.

The constrast with Russell and Frege contributes towards understanding Wittgenstein's conception of philosophy in the *Investigations*. So too does contrasting it with the conception presented in the *Tractatus*. Inspection of these details supports the initial hunch that the ground for opposition to Russell shifts markedly between the *Tractatus* and the *Investigations*.

First, the *Tractatus* is prefaced with the sweeping claim, 'I believe myself to have found, on all essential points, the final solution of the problems [of philosophy]'.[35] The central business of philosophy was finding a solution to the '*single* great problem':[36] 'My whole task consists in explaining the nature of the proposition'.[37] The correct delineation of the general form of a proposition completed this programme. It constituted a single vantage point from which everything could be seen aright. The *Investigations* repudiates not only the putative solution, but also the ambition to seek for any substitute. The aim is merely to clear away sundry misunderstandings about the use of words. The method is to assemble reminders about the rules of grammar

[35] Wittgenstein, *Tractatus*, Preface.
[36] L. Wittgenstein, *Notebooks 1914–1916*, Blackwell, Oxford, 1961, p. 23.
[37] Ibid., p. 39.

which are targeted on removing specific misunderstandings, like thera-
pies for particular diseases. In this way, 'Problems are solved (difficulties eliminated), not a single problem'.[38] The therapist establishes 'an
order in our knowledge of the use of language: an order with a particular
end in view; one out of many possible orders; not *the* order'.[39] Clarity
about this limited goal frees the philosopher from the paralysing
demand that any satisfactory eludication of the grammar of a word
such as 'language' or 'sentence' must give a single formula that once and
for all guarantees that all philosophical confusions about these notions
shall completely disappear.[40] Different clarifications of a single expression may be useful for eliminating different confusions, and possible
confusions are limitless and hence cannot be eliminated in advance.
Although for every philosophical problem there is *some* method for
removing it, Wittgenstein no longer thought that a single correct logical
point of view would simultaneously remove every confusion, actual or
possible.

Secondly, the *Tractatus* held that the philosopher needs to deploy
formal concepts to delineate the bounds of sense. These super-concepts
cannot be used to form meaningful sentences. The notorious conclusion
was that the correct logical point of view is ineffable. It is shown by
philosophical sentences that are literally nonsensical. As an alternative
to this paradox, some might prefer the idea that philosophizing is an
activity of clarifying what makes sense and thereby indicating what
does not;[41] but then this is a paradoxical activity since it has no intelligible product. The *Investigations* exposed these illusions. The so-called
formal concepts are expressed by words such as 'language', 'number',
'experience', 'sentence', and 'world', which have genuine uses in our

[38] Wittgenstein, *Philosophical Investigations*, § 133.

[39] Ibid., § 132.

[40] This provides the key to resolving two conundra in interpreting the
Investigations. It is implied that philosophers err in answering such questions as
'What is language?' or 'What is a proposition?' by supposing that 'the answer to
these questions is to be given once for all; and independently of any future
experience' (§ 92). Wittgenstein further states, 'The real discovery is the one that
makes me capable of stopping doing philosophy when I want to' (§ 133). Is the
point not that what may be perplexing or misunderstood cannot be foreseen, so
that what is needed to answer a request for clarification cannot be determined once
and for all? And conversely, that failure of a specific clarification to resolve some
future confusion does not detract from or call into question its satisfactoriness
in eliminating a present one? Grammar is independent of future experience, but
requirements for philosophical elucidations may differ from age to age.

[41] Schlick popularized this interpretation of the *Tractatus*. Cf. M. Schlick,
Gesammelte Aufsätze, Gerold, Vienna, 1938, pp. 130 ff.

language—uses as humdrum as those of such words as 'table', 'lamp', and 'door'. Philosophically puzzling words acquire an aura of mystery by being torn out of their natural environments and used in radically different contexts without any of the necessary clarification of their novel grammatical roles. 'As if [its] sense were an atmosphere accompanying a word, which it carried with it into every kind of application.'[42] The alleged nonsensicality of all applications of formal concepts rests on a further misconception. The distinctive feature of proper grammatical clarifications is that they are formulations of rules; the difference in role between rules and statements accounts for their peculiarity without recourse to the doctrine of ineffability. What needs to be clarified by philosophy can be said and should be said clearly.

Thirdly, according to the *Tractatus*, logic presented 'the *a priori* order of the world: i.e., the order of *possibilities*, which must be common to both world and thought'.[43] The rationale for this thesis was that 'logic is not a field in which *we* express what we wish with the help of signs, but rather one in which the nature of the natural and inevitable signs speak for itself.'[44] This rests on the idea that arbitrary assignments of meanings to signs have ineluctable consequences. 'Although there is something arbitrary in our notations, *this* much is not arbitrary—that *when* we have determined one thing arbitrarily, something else is necessarily the case. (This derives from the *essence* of notation.)'[45] The rules governing the logical syntax of language cannot be laid down by fiat or even intelligibly stated. Logical order is 'the *hardest* thing there is';[46] it is given by the logical structure of the world. It cannot be violated; it takes care of itself. This characterization of logic is the diametrical opposite of the conception in the *Investigations*. At every point it conflicts with a proper recognition of the autonomy of grammar. Principles of logic are *rules* for correct inference. They are part of the grammar of language, and hence independent from each other. It is a radical misconception to conceive of logical laws as *derived* rules whose justification rests on other rules of grammar ('semantic rules'). And the ineluctable character of logic is the expression of our demand that these rules be inexorably applied. Their crystalline purity is not a result of investigation, but a *requirement*. A correct view of the autonomy of grammar stands on its head the account of logic (and of formal concepts) presented in the *Tractatus*. As in

[42] Wittgenstein, *Philosophical Investigations*, §117.   [43] Ibid., §97.
[44] Wittgenstein, *Tractatus*, 6.124.   [45] Ibid., 3.342.
[46] Wittgenstein, *Philosophical Investigations*, §97.

revolving a kaleidoscope, we find also that everything else changes its aspect.

The picture of philosophy sketched in the *Investigations* is not by any means wholly negative. It offers an account of the sources of philosophical perplexity, and it outlines what is required for effective cure. These positive suggestions grow off the same root-stock as the criticisms of scientific conceptions of philosophy, namely the autonomy of grammar. The fact that meaning-rules are in perfect logical order, however heterogeneous and unsystematic they may seem, has the dramatic consequence that the doubts, paradoxes, perplexities, and accusations of incoherence marshalled against them by philosophers must rest on misconceptions and confusions. The kind of reflection which reaches its acme in the works of great philosophers is what generates the need for the clarificatory activity which is the proper labour of philosophers. The importance and pervasiveness of philosophical confusion gives this task its immense significance. In each case the aim is nothing less than a perfectly clear view of those parts of the network of meaning-rules in which our thinking is prone to become entangled.

One consequence of this idea is that philosophical clarification is strictly purpose-relative. Since grammar is in perfect order, whenever its application proceeds without any hitches the philosopher has no employment. Clarification here would be as idle as the attempt to repair a machine that is running smoothly and efficiently. Conversely, when hitches do arise in particular applications of meaning-rules, the philosopher's business is solely to remove them, to make these particular problems completely disappear. A procedure which works in one case is thereby vindicated in that case, even if it has no general utility. If, for example, somebody is plunged into perplexity because he views rules as Platonic entities, it may be helpful to encourage him to think of a sentence as an instrument and of its meaning as its use and then to consider a rule to be a sentence used in a distinctive range of normative activities. Or somebody puzzled about how an ostensive definition can be the formulation of a meaning-*rule* may find illumination in regarding a sample as a symbol and an ostensive definition as a rule licensing the substitution of one partly concrete symbol for another verbal one. Philosophers standardly object that clarifications such as these do not cover every case or that they raise as many problems as they solve; for example, viewing a rule as a sentence with a particular use fails to account for the intelligibility of the statement that two sentences may formulate the same rule, and treating a sample as a sign does not show the nonsensicality of the request to translate a particular sample (e.g. a metre-stick) into French! Such objections are inappropriate. The crucial matter is that each particular explanation does remove a particular problem, that it does serve a particular therapeutic purpose. Its failure to provide a panacea, or even the possibility that it may be used elsewhere to generate new confusions, does not detract from this concrete achievement. Conversely, the fact that an idea dissolves a wide range of problems generates no presumption that it will cure every confusion. To insist that quantification theory must provide a synopsis of all sound forms of reasoning, even those involving adverbs, modality, and tenses, is as silly as the accusation that penicillin is worthless unless it cures every disease. Relativity to specific purposes differentiates the criteria for satisfactoriness of philosophical clarification from those for the correctness of scientific explanations. It further generates a resemblance with attempts to expose new aspects of things, say of works of art. A percipient observer may, for example, reveal an elaborate geometrical symmetry in a painting by Ucello, thus adding a new dimension to appreciation of this particular work. The value of this insight is independent of whether a similar structure can be discerned in any other Renaissance painting. Philosophical elucidations share this autonomy of aspect-seeing. Fascination with the scientific canon of generality results in unwarranted contempt for valuable achievements.

Wittgenstein diagnosed the principal sources of philosophical misunderstanding as misleading analogies in language and simplistic pictures of the world. We are inclined to presume that expressions of the same syntactic form must have identical uses; for example that numerals name Platonic entities because they are employed as nouns, that equations are assertions because they are read as declarative sentences, or that all generalizations have the same logical role because they exemplify the same sentence structure. We also unreflectively apply a host of pictures; for example the inner/outer picture of the relation of mind and behaviour, the localization of thinking in the head, the conception of speech as the encoding of thoughts, and the notion of communication as the transfer of thoughts from one mind to another. Philosophers take these data and ruthlessly follow up their implications, undeterred by apparent absurdity. This is not simply the perpetration of blunders by the intellectually deranged. Rather, it manifests the extent to which philosophical confusion is the product of the will, not of the intellect, and hence it indicates the necessity for a kind of conversion to eliminate deep misunderstanding. Philosophical confusion often betrays desires and passions that we all share to some degree. There is a real *craving* for generality. We are dissatisfied with the motley appearance of meaning-rules, and we hanker after something more homogeneous, systematic, and elegant. We do not have respect for a procedure of clarifying a particular domain of grammar which has no wider applicability. Similarly, we are deeply *attached* to certain fundamental pictures. We struggle to preserve them when they are threatened by recalcitrant 'data', perhaps viewing them as our only bulwark against the discomforts of intellectual chaos. To many it must seem that surrendering the notion of hidden depth and unity in language would make any investigation of meaning-rules flat, stale, and unprofitable. Though we are frequently captive to pictures, this is generally in accord with our own volition. Prising somebody away from his own desires and passions is an enterprise of the utmost delicacy and one requiring infinite ingenuity and resourcefulness.

The methods for eliminating the confusions to which philosophers are prey cannot be circumscribed in advance.

Philosophy unties the knots in our thinking, which we have tangled up in an absurd way; but to do that, it must make movements which are just as complicated as the knots. Although the *result* of philosophy is simple, its methods for arriving there cannot be so.[47]

Occasionally something resembing theory-construction in science proves useful. The invention of the calculus of first-order predicate logic broke the tyranny of the traditional doctrines that all judgements had subject-predicate structure and that all genuine inferences were syllogistic; it simply presented an attractive and workable alternative. But even here such an invention threatens to foster a new set of confusions unless it is explicitly treated as a model of comparison, not as a theory portraying the ideal case to which everything really approximates.

Other methods are often efficacious. One is to expose as nonsensical the questions to which puzzle-generating theories are meant to provide the answers. An appropriate counterquestion may reveal an underlying confusion or a bizarre presupposition. It may successfully make fun of a supposedly deep problem. The question motivating semantic investigations in philosophy and linguistics alike is, 'How do we understand sentences that we have never encountered before?' The illusion that this question makes sense rests partly on a misassimilation of understanding

[47] L. Wittgenstein, *Philosophical Remarks*, Blackwell, Oxford, 1975, §2.

to the category of processes or acts. If understanding is seen to be an ability, then the question becomes as absurd as the question 'How do you own a house?' or 'How do you have the ability to break a twig?'. The puzzle about understanding novel sentences is often rephrased as the question 'How is it possible for a competent speaker of English to know the meanings of *infinitely many* sentences?' Should we deny that anybody does understand infinitely many sentences? Or should we clutch our heads in amazement and exclaim 'How wonderful—to learn to understand infinitely many sentences, and in so short a time! How clever we are'?[48] Such reflections manifest confusion about what it means to speak of the infinite. 'If you say "How terrific!", if your head reels—you can be sure [that you have] the wrong image.'[49] Philosophical questions are often in desperate need of clarification, and they tend to lose any aura of mystery upon careful inspection.

Pictures underlying theory-instruction in philosophy also require investigation. They often feed on one-sided diets of examples. To consider language as a system seems natural, but we readily slip from this harmless picture into the view that meaning-rules must be uniform in kind and unified within a single axiomatic structure. This conception of a system is exemplified by Euclidean geometry, but not by many structures to which we unhesitatingly apply the term 'system'[50] (e.g. the Imperial system of weights and measures, the British transport system, or the system of allocating children to neighbourhood high-schools!). We forget that systems may be more or less systematic and that there is no prima facie case at all for likening the grammar of English to an axiomatized calculus! One useful method for countering such distortions is to highlight differences among what is subsumed under a given concept, to stress that apparent differences are real (e.g. that explanations of meaning do exemplify a variety of patterns) and to issue reminders that in grammar all differences are big differences. Other methods include inventing indeterminate or deviant cases, imagining facts of nature to be altered, and pin-pointing absurd consequences of apparently straightforward applications of apparently clear pictures. The basic thrust of Wittgenstein's procedures is to show the disutility of forcing phenomena under Procrustean forms of representation and to demonstrate the baselessness of philosophical scruples arising from their resistance.

[48] Cf. L. Wittgenstein, *Wittgenstein's Lectures on the Foundations of Mathematics*, ed. C. Diamond, Harvester, Hassocks, 1976, p. 31.
[49] Ibid., p. 253.   [50] Cf. Wittgenstein, *Philosophical Investigations,* § 100.

Wittgenstein's conception of philosophy is in head-on collision with the pervasive scientific conception. Philosophy consists in purpose-relative clarifications of meaning-rules, and grammar is autonomous. Properly understood this excludes the legitimacy of any form of theory-construction. Attempts to render uniform and systematic any meaning-rules which are multiform and independent yield only illusory extensions of grammar, since the products lack the normative status of rules. There is no 'action at a distance' in grammar.[51] Attempts to support what cannot in principle be justified (or criticized) are as futile as erecting papier mâché columns to improve the stability of a sky-scraper.[52] Justifications of language-use come to an end within the rules of grammar. The scientific conception of philosophy leads to the proliferation of nonsense. It does not tackle the confusions giving the impetus to theory-construction, and it diverts attention away from the paradigms which its theories embroider. The impulse towards simpli-fication, schematization, generalization, and idealization is powerful. In Wittgenstein's view it is as it were the original sin of the intellect. It makes the construction of scientific theories possible—and philosophy necessary!

6. BIG BANGS AND PERPETUAL MOTION

The conception of philosophy elaborated by Wittgenstein stands in conflict with the scientific conception now dominant. Explanatory theories are wholly unlike synopses (*Übersichten*) of rules of 'grammar', and the methods appropriate for scientific investigations contrast with the methods productive of insight into conceptual connections. This incompatibility amounts to a clash of *Weltanschauungen*. The spirit informing his writing, Wittgenstein remarked,

is different from the one which informs the vast stream of European and American civilization in which all of us stand. *That* spirit expresses itself in an onwards movement, in building ever larger and more com-plicated structures; the other in striving after clarity and perspicuity in no matter what structure . . . .[T]he first adds one construction to another, moving on and up, as it were, from one stage to the next, while the other remains where it is and what it tries to grasp is always the same.[53]

[51] L. Wittgenstein, *The Blue and Brown Books*, Blackwell, Oxford, p. 14; and L. Wittgenstein, *Philosophical Grammar*, Blackwell, Oxford. 1974, p. 81.

[52] Cf. Wittgenstein, *Philosophical Investigations*, § 217.

[53] Wittgenstein, *Philosophical Remarks*, p. 7.

Philosophy so conceived sets itself the formidable task of standing firm against the flood tide of contemporary thought. It is at risk of being swept into the ocean of science. Hence in a deep sense it is opposed to science. Its proper business is not to contribute to physics or mathematics, nor even to redesign experiments or to interfere with procedures of proof. It should not meddle in the internal affairs of the sciences. Rather its task is to criticize the wider significance commonly claimed for scientific or mathematical findings (Cantor's diagonal proof, Russell's paradox, Godel's incompleteness theorem, Heisenberg's uncertainty principle, etc.) and also to question the presupposition or overt declaration that the way of science is alone appropriate to any serious intellectual enquiry. The aim is merely to curb the imperialist propensities of science. This provides ground enough for bitter conflict.

Philosophy according to this specification is difficult to locate on the intellectual map. It cannot be circumscribed in the ways standard for other disciplines. It has no distinctive subject-matter; there are no indispensible philosophical concepts and no body of philosophical truths. Everything falls within its purview. Similarly, there are no indispensible philosophical methods and none that are sacrosanct. Any procedure may be appropriate, even questions, jokes, metaphors, or imaginative invention. Philosophy cannot be ranked alongside the sciences, or above or below them. Being incomparable with them, it may seem anomalous and amorphous.

Still worse, this conception of philosophy may seem incomprehensible. How does the activity of philosophizing promote *understanding*? How is what is not already well understood *explained* or *clarified*? And wherein lies the *profundity* or *importance* of philosophy? Enslaved to the ideals of science, we may find these questions impossible to answer. Philosophy in this mould 'seems only to destroy everything interesting, i.e. all that is great and important . . .[a]s it were all the buildings, leaving behind only bits of stone and rubble'.[54] The refutation of this condemnation and the answers to the puzzles about Wittgenstein's conception of philosophy can be discovered only through a basic reorientation, a recognition of the limitations of the scientific ideal. The first step is to acknowledge the variety of forms of understanding, of explanation, and of profundity. The second is to question whether those forms fundamental in science are appropriate to philosophy. Does lack of a theory unifying apparently diverse phenomena show that there is something not understood? Perhaps it is the insistent urge to

[54] Wittgenstein, *Philosophical Investigations,* §118.

construct explanations of what is clear and unproblematic that betokens lack of understanding. Might a more suitable criterion of lack of understanding not be entanglement in applying meaning-rules? And a better criterion of understanding be the ability to find one's way about in the maze of actual meaning-rules without encountering any hitches? If so, the appropriate concept of explanation should be the capacity to give such understanding and to remove such misunderstanding. The focus would then not be on the form of statement made (e.g. whether it has the form of a covering law), but on its role or use in the course of philosophical therapy. A good explanation in philosophy might be comparable not to a scientific theory unifying phenomena and supporting predictions, but to the successful clarification of a style of painting or the cultivation of insight and understanding of classical music. And why measure the profundity of a philosophical explanation by the standards fitting for a law of physics? A more appropriate standard would refer to the importance of the misunderstanding promoted by the explanation. The thinking of the devotee of the scientific ideal for philosophy is surely bounded in a nutshell if he cannot even imagine the possibility of serious philosophical activity conducted along totally different lines.

It is tempting to assimilate this contrast in conceptions of philosophy to some familiar distinction. We might treat it as an instance of the opposition between optimism and pessimism: the optimists believe that they confront problems which can be solved by dint of rigorous and systematic thinking, whereas the pessimists contend that the important questions are mysteries which transcend our powers to arrive at solutions.[55] Or we might view the rift in philosophy as nothing deeper than a contrast in style of expository writing: some prefer their arguments dressed in Gothic letters, logical symbolism, and algebraic computations, whereas others insist on classic English prose fully intelligible to the interested layman. Such reinterpretations of the issue are radically mistaken, tending to trivialize a profound difference. There is a continental divide within the tradition of analytic philosophy —separate watersheds of thought resting on differing insights and different forms of reasoning. A bird's-eye view of the boundary is difficult to attain. Perhaps the contrast is most illuminatingly characterized by dividing philosophers into those who find satisfaction in thinking that the world, language, and the mind are full of mysteries,

[55] This contrast is prominent in the writings of Chomsky (e.g. *Rules and Representations*, Blackwell, Oxford, 1980).

perplexities, and deep antinomies, calling for magical solutions by reference to theories of unbelievable sophistication, and those who discern no value in questions and answers that are not crystal clear, intelligible to any thoughtful person, and beyond dispute. The first live for the gradual penetration of hidden depths and resent any demonstration that their problems grow out of confusion; they view the second as blind or philistine. The second abhor dubious assertions in reply to nonsensical questions and thirst for perfect clarity; they see the first as mystery-mongers who participate in worthless verbal rituals. As Wittgenstein noted, no intellectual difference could cut more deeply.

Although philosophers hive themselves off from each other, some of the products of their reflections manage to cross the boundary between them. Wittgenstein's writings are sometimes argued to embody an embryonic theory of the mind or a novel theory of meaning,[56] and hence his private language argument may be incorporated into the work of some theory-builders. Conversely, something intended to be part of a theory may be accorded a different value by a philosopher seeking for a puzzle-dissolving synopsis of grammar; it may be reinterpreted as a form of representation of rules of meaning, a model for comparison with familiar rules. The use of definite descriptions may be compared (and contrasted!) with that of proper names,[57] or formulae in quantification theory may be compared (and contrasted!) with ordinary forms of generalization.[58] What must be avoided is treating these paradigms as idealizations to which everything really conforms despite appearances to the contrary. A form of representation is legitimate and often helpful provided that its application takes care of itself. Forcing it upon phenomena produces distortion, symptoms of which are the use of such qualifiers as 'unconscious', 'imperceptible', 'tacit', 'implicit', etc. Desire for depth induces an insouciance about obvious differences. The sanction against this activity is a choice between falsity and vacuity. If, for example, a philosopher discovers that all words are 'really' names, then what he asserts is false if he uses 'name' correctly, and

---

[56] For example, Dummett, *Truth and Other Enigmas*, pp. 16 ff. His suggestion for interpreting Wittgenstein as an 'anti-realist' was taken up and differently developed by G. P. Baker, 'Criteria: a New Foundation for Semantics', *Ratio*, 16 (1974), pp. 156 ff; P. M. S. Hacker, *Insight and Illusion*, Oxford, 1972; and Wright, *Wittgenstein on the Foundations of Mathematics*.

[57] Cf. Wittgenstein, *Philosophical Investigations*, § 79.

[58] Wittgenstein, *Philosophical Remarks*, 87 ff., and *Philosophical Grammar*, pp. 165 ff.

otherwise it involves an apparently pointless determination to redefine 'name' as a synonym for 'word'. Provided forms of representation are not mistaken for revelations of essence or panaceas for all puzzles, they have a legitimate place in anybody's philosophy. Only the practice of total immersion is dangerous.

Most general remarks about philosophy are intended to effect a conversion to a new point of view. The reader is meant to be swept along on a wave of enthusiasm to adopt a novel outlook on a vast range of issues. Perhaps he is supposed to see that the philosophy of language holds the key to all philosophical problems, or that the principle of verifiability produces instant answers to every question. He is at least offered the prospect of immediate transport to the Promised Land, even if he is so benighted that he fails to take this up. My purpose is different: not to drive anybody out of the paradise of the scientific conception of philosophy, but rather to produce a travel brochure. There is a failure of imagination to be remedied. To somebody who has lived always in a jungle, it may be unintelligible how anybody might wish to live in a desert or even in the Garden of Eden. This essay is meant to depict the pleasures of perpetual motion in philosophizing, the unceasing examination of questions. It attempts to make comprehensible the philosophical merit in cultivating the sophisticated *naïveté* of the perceptive and intelligent alien who scrutinizes our pattern of life, thought, and speech. Possibly a certain clarity of vision, or even nobility of mind, may reward a philosopher for the discomforts of being a perpetual exile.[59]

---

[59] Many of the ideas developed in this essay arise out of work on Frege and Wittgenstein jointly carried out with Peter Hacker. I gladly acknowledge an immense debt to him. For this reason, however, I should also make clear that the overall interpretation of Wittgenstein's later conception of philosophy which I sketch here differs considerably in points of emphasis and nuance from the account that he would prefer.

PHILOSOPHICAL PSYCHOLOGY

12

SOME MISCONCEPTIONS ABOUT BELIEF[1]

RICHARD E. GRANDY

The concept of belief attracts attention from many philosophical quarters—philosophers of language debate the logical forms of belief sentences, metaphysicians ponder whether the objects of belief are sentences or propositions, and philosophers of mind wonder whether other animals have beliefs. My goal in this paper is to identify some fundamental assumptions common to almost all philosophers[2] who argue any side of these issues, and to show that these basic assumptions are unjustified.

I. BELIEF AND ATTITUDES

The first assumption is that true belief reports, at least those of the so-called *de dicto* type,[3] describe a relation between the believer and an object, either a sentence or proposition, and more specifically that they report an attitude that the believer has toward the sentence or proposition. In fact, 'believe', 'know' and related verbs are often referred to as sentential or propositional attitude verbs. I begin by considering why such a description has some plausibility.

In some cases belief is very closely bound to an attitude toward a sentence. Michael, having set his new computer a task and accepting its result, will assent to the sentence:

6,643,213 is a prime number.

Since he seems knowledgeable about numbers and forthcoming in his

---

[1] I am indebted to Paul Grice for an extremely helpful conversation that clarified the main ideas of this paper; several of the examples were suggested by S. Denbeigh Galoop; conversations with members of the Rice University Philosophy Department led to many improvements in an earlier draft. None of them are responsible for any errors or unclarities.

[2] At least two exceptions are Daniel Dennett and Steven Stich, as is evident from their recent papers in Woodfield (1982).

[3] I shall confine the discussion to *de dicto* beliefs until Section VI, where I will argue that *de re* and *de dicto* are not two kinds of belief.

responses we have no reason to doubt that Michael believes that 6,643,213 is a prime.[4]

In other cases, however, it seems indubitable that belief is not an attitude toward the content sentence.[5] Aristarchus believed that the earth was round, but he presumably never had any attitudes toward any English sentences. (The reason that I am confident that he had no attitudes toward English sentences is not just that they did not exist during his lifetime—one can have attitudes toward things that do not yet exist—but rather the fact that he had no concept of the English language.)

Two responses can be offered in defence of a sentential attitude approach. The first would be to claim that what is relevant is the attitude that Aristarchus would have had if he had known sufficient English. The second is that what is relevant is the attitude that Aristarchus had to various Greek sentences. Although the two views are distinct, it would appear that most of the evidence for the counter-factual claim would consist of the attitudes that Aristarchus actually had to Greek sentences.

In either case, it is not possible to construe the belief report as attributing to Aristarchus an attitude toward the content sentence of the report. The most plausible sentential analysis appears to be that for Aristarchus to believe that S there must be a sentence S' of a language spoken by Aristarchus such that Aristarchus stands in relation R_1 to that sentence S', and S' stands in relation R_2 to S. This form of analysis is not new, of course; its first explicit formulation is probably to be found in Carnap (1947).

The propositional account of belief is motivated partly by the difficulties of the sentential account, and partly by the thought that some organisms may have beliefs that are not expressible in a language that they speak, the thought that belief can outrun language. To put the idea into a form more readily comparable with the sentential account, we see that Aristarchus believes that S just in case:

> There is a proposition P such that Aristarchus stands in rela-
> tion R_3 to P and P stands in relation R_4 to S.

---

[4] It is an interesting and difficult question whether Michael currently believes 6,643,212 is not a prime, even though there is no doubt that he would believe it if asked. The attempt to answer the question by saying that he does not actually know it yet but that he potentially believes it because he believes all even numbers greater than 2 are non-prime fails, for I think it equally problematic whether he believes 6,643,212 is even.

[5] The 'context sentence' in a belief report is the one that appears after 'X believes that'.

Looking more closely at R_3, we can see that this must be an attitude of assent or belief. While I do not know how to formulate the following principle exactly, it seems plausible that to have such an attitude toward something one must either be in some causal relation to the object or have some representation of it. (The 'or' is not exclusive.) Thus we can rewrite the propositional analysis of belief as:

> There is a proposition P such that Aristarchus stands in relation R_5 to P*, P* represents P, and P stands in relation R_4 to S.

Notice that the function of the proposition in the analysis is to provide the intermediate term that connects the representation P* with the sentence S via the two relations of representing and R_4. Thus if we let R_6 abbreviate 'there is a proposition P that is represented by P* and that bears R_4 to S' we can rewrite the analysis once more as:

> There is a representation P* such that Aristarchus stands in R_3 to P* and P* bears R_6 to S.

Now this indicates that the proposition is irrelevant except in so far as appeal to propositions clarifies the relation R_6. (More precisely, the question is whether some equivalent relation can be provided that does not proceed via propositions.)

II. BELIEF AND RELATIONS

There is an obvious sense in which belief is a relation between individuals and either sentences or something that sentences stand for. This sense is the modern analytic one in which taking any English sentence and replacing two noun phrases by distinct variables produces a relation. Thus, for example, if we take the sentence

> Beth's father-in-law once lived near Milwaukee.

we can obtain the relation

> x's father-in-law once lived near y.

This is not likely, however, to be a very interesting relation since it is improbable that it will fit into any significant theory, either commonsensical or scientific, and also since it is composed from more important relations.

Given these remarks, it would be inconsistent to deny that belief is any kind of relation, but I want to suggest that it has at least some of the features of the example just cited. Belief does figure in common sense reports and, by some accounts, in common sense theories, but I want to question how satisfactory and significant these theories are, and also eventually to suggest that the belief 'relation' is a composite one built from more interesting ones.

III. THE CONTENT OF BELIEFS

(a) *Canine content*

Before considering the issue of how the content sentence in belief reports is related to behaviour of humans, I wish to digress to consider the analogous question, recently much disputed, about dogs. Suppose that Denbeigh is a small dog who enjoys chasing, catching, and retrieving tennis balls. Basketballs and footballs are too large, baseballs are too hard on the mouth, and squash balls have too little bounce to bother with.

At this instant a tennis ball is thrown across the yard and Denbeigh sprints toward the point where it will strike the ground. It is natural to explain this action by saying that:

(i) he believes that the tennis ball will strike the ground there;
(ii) he wants to catch the tennis ball before it strikes the ground.

This explanation is right surely in so far as it discriminates this bit of action from squirrel-chasing, cat-harassing, or general exhibitions of exuberance. But a number of philosophers have objected to the explanation on further reflection. Specifically, they[6] object to the attribution of the belief that 'the tennis ball' will strike the ground. Even though he has watched the odd game of tennis, he surely has no concept of the game of tennis, and *a fortiori,*[7] no concept of 'a ball used in a game of tennis'. Worse than that, it is unclear whether he has the unmodified concept of a ball:

1 (a) A spherical or almost spherical body.
2 (a) Any of various rounded movable objects used in sports and games.[8]

---

[6] 'They' include Dennett (1969) and Stich (1979).

[7] Actually, the whole question of 'having a concept' is far more complex than can be dealt with here. On further investigation, it may prove that one can have a concept of a tennis ball without having the concept of tennis; concepts may not be isomorphic in structure to their various linguistic representations.

[8] *American Heritage Dictionary.*

Recently, Armstrong (1973) has attempted to defend the attribution of canine beliefs. He grants that the attribution of contents such as 'That is a tennis ball' are misleading, but suggests that future investigation of canine cognition would lead us to a detailed description that could be used instead of the expression 'tennis ball', which is a crude approximation necessitated by our current state of ignorance. We might, for example, discover that the objects that produce the distinctive tennis ball behaviour are all and only those that are approximately spherical, between 2.25 and 3.25 inches in diameter, and rebound at least 40 per cent from a concrete floor. This leaves Armstrong in the rather embarassing position of suggesting that it is satisfactory to attribute beliefs to canines because eventually the unacceptable but temporary (i) will be replaced by:

(ia) Denbeigh believes that the approximately spherical object that is between 2.25" and 3.25" in diameter, compressible 20 per cent, and that rebounds from a concrete surface at least 40 per cent, will strike the ground there.

Surely any problems that Denbeigh has with 'tennis' and 'ball', both of which he has had some experience of instances of, pale beside his lack of understanding of sphericity, inches, diameters, and the like.

Armstrong was cognizant of this objection and tried to ward it off by claiming that the attribution in (ia) is to be understood as totally *de re*, that is, that the predicate expressions as well as the referential expressions are to be taken *de re*. Stich (1979) has more recently objected rightly that this totally *de re* belief concept is totally novel and unexplicated. Further, if one is going to avail oneself of this move for (ia) it may work just as well for (i).

To summarize this subsection—it appeared that (i) and (ii) were a plausible explanation of Denbeigh's action. But upon examination the content attributed in both of these sentences seems unjustifiable and thus the purported explanation fails. Since the main argument for attributing beliefs (and desires) to dogs is their explanatory force, it appears that we have no reason to make such attribution.

(b) *Human contents*

Backtracking to a fraction of a second before the ball was thrown, we find Andy, a human five-year-old, about to throw the tennis ball for Denbeigh. Andy is throwing the tennis ball because he enjoys playing fetch with Denbeigh and believes that Denbeigh will chase and retrieve the tennis ball. He would not throw the ball if he believed that the consequence would be that he would have to retrieve it himself. Does Andy believe that if he throws the tennis ball Denbeigh will retrieve it? Suppose that he can utter the sound 'tennis ball' more or less appropriately on this occasion, but that his conceptual connections are at best vague, for example, he does not know what tennis is. Moreover, we can assume that his ability to discriminate tennis balls from other similar objects is not much more precise than, or different from, Denbeigh's discriminations. And while he may be able to utter the phrase 'tennis ball' with some appropriateness, he is totally unfamiliar with such concepts as 'diameter' and 'inches'. This only shows that some of the same problems arise for human children as arise for animals, which will likely not surprise many.

But I want to argue that the same problem arises for adults. Consider Andrea, an adult tennis player about to hit an overhead. The tennis ball is approaching with a horizontal velocity of 65 ft./sec., a vertical velocity of 8 ft./sec., and a vertical acceleration due to gravity of 32 ft./sec.^{2}, and is 40 feet away 20 feet above the ground. Andrea swings and expertly dispatches the ball.

We can explain her swinging at exactly the time and place she did by attributing to her the belief that 0.5 seconds before the impact the ball had a horizontal velocity of 65ft./sec., etc. And since she is acquainted with the relevant portions of physics, there is no immediate absurdity in attributing those beliefs to her. In other circumstances, given the opportunity, the initial conditions, and time to calculate, she could perfectly well form an unquestionable belief about the velocity and acceleration of the tennis ball. But in the circumstances described there is a problem—she would deny having any belief about the velocity or height of the ball of the form we need to attribute to explain the action. Her timing of the stroke had no more to do with knowledge of physics than does Denbeigh's ability to catch a thrown ball.

We have a conflict then between two principles. The first is that the content sentence in belief reports is supposed to provide an explanation of behaviour, and unless we attribute a quite precise content to Andrea's belief, we cannot explain her success. But there also seems to be a principle that if the content sentence is in a language spoken by the believer then the believer should be disposed to assent to the sentence when being truthful.

IV. BELIEF AS REPRESENTATION

The widespread view of belief is that what is reported in a belief report is a relation between the believer and some sentence-like object.[9] The believer's overall state of belief is composed of the separate relations to many of these objects.

This seems to me to be fundamentally wrong. People have overall internal representations of the world, and for a given person at a specific time there is a single overall representation. Moreover, the representation is, so to speak, a multi-media one; some information will be represented in an image-like way, some information in language related ways, and others as well (Kosslyn, 1980).

A belief report is a partial description of translation of the internal representation. The fact that in belief reports the content sentences are linguistic reflects only the fact that reports are sentences, not on the structure of the representation being reported.[10] One can perfectly intelligibly and correctly report that a map says that Houston is further south than San Diego without implying that the map has sentences on it, or that it has attitudes towards anything.

Among the things that are represented internally are, of course, sentences—those that are heard, read, and spoken. But the portion of an internal representation that represents a sentence is not itself a sentence any more than the grooves in a phonograph record or a linguist's phonological representation of a sentence are themselves sentences. And the representation of a written sentence must be different from that of a spoken one if the reader/hearer can recall whether the sentence was written or heard.

To avert one possible misunderstanding, let me note that my remark above about a portion of an internal representation being of a sentence should not be taken as inconsistent with my earlier insistence that representations are global. A dot on a map may represent Chicago, but it does not do so by virtue of a special intrinsic relation between that

[9] By 'sentence-like' I mean to include propositions. The claim that belief is such a relation is more plausible when one restricts it to occurrent beliefs as in Lycan (1980). However this seems to me an unpromising restriction, for eventually we want to understand the relation between occurrent beliefs and the rest of the internal states that produce them. Even in the restricted sense the claim is not unproblematic (Grandy, 1980).

[10] On pain of regress. The phrase 'language of thought' is picturesque but misleading since the basic internal representations must be non-conventional and unlearned and there is good evidence they are non-linear, non-acoustic, and non-spatial.

dot and Chicago. Rather, it is the relation between that dot and all of the other elements of the map, and the correspondence between the total set of elements and some geographical area that is the basis of the representation. Dots represent cities because the map as a whole represents an area—you do not make a map by utilizing dots that have independent diverse representational relations of their own.[11]

The suggestion that internal states are like maps is not novel: it can be found, for example, in Armstrong (1973). My view differs from Armstrong's, however, in that I claim that the representation has a holistic character whereas Armstrong thinks of the belief state as consisting of many representations of propositions. Moreover, he has a complex and rather unsatisfying account of how the representations succeed in representing because they are composed from simple ideas which have intrinsic representing power. (Heil, 1980, discusses some of the problems.) I would contrast the conception I am advocating, which we might call the cartographic, with the alternative, which we might call congressional. Congress collectively represents the people because individual members each represent some group of people because of a relation that they bear to that group. The representativeness of the whole derives from the relations the members bear to the world. But in a map it is the overall structure of the map and its relations to a region of space that makes it a representation of the region.

The most basic mode of internal representation is fundamental and nonconventional. It is the form of representation that we share with creatures of lesser cognitive capacities.

But we are also capable of a second, less direct, learned, and partially conventional mode of representation *via* language. Persons who are knowledgeable speakers of English will have as part of their vocabulary 'armadillo' and even though they may have had no perceptual encounters with armadillos, they will have internal representations of the word. And since the word in English refers to the creatures, in this indirect sense the speaker's internal representation includes a portion that represents armadillos. It is because of this dual possibility of representation that we have the conflict discussed in the last section. Denbeigh can have the linguistically-unmediated, that is perceptual, representation of a moving tennis ball, but cannot have the linguistic representation. Andrea can have either but will not in general have

---

[11] To avert misunderstanding, within the general representational context causal relations may determine specific representational relations. But it is because of the context that the causal relation produces representation, not vice versa.

them at the same time. Since we tend to concentrate our explanations of behaviour on the grosser aspects of our behaviour, we lose sight of the divergence when we seek finer-grained explanations.[12]

V. KINDS OF REPRESENTATION

One respect in which representations can vary is the degree of specificity of portions thereof, both perceived and actual. Consider three would-be sloop buyers—Jack, Jim, and John. Each of them believes that he is going to buy a sloop. Jack has decided from his general preferences and his finances that it would be desirable and possible to have a sloop. Since he believes many sloops are for sale and that they are within his means, he believes he will buy one. Which one is a matter for further thought.

In contrast, Jim and John have made up their minds which sloop they each want. Both could give a description and recount the several visits they have made to contemplate the soon-to-be-possessed boats. There are, we assume for our purposes, no internal differences between Jim and John—each has the same images, descriptions, memories, and so on—but there are differences in external relations. Jim has indeed visited the same sloop three times, whereas John's three visits were to similar but distinct sloops without his realizing it.

Readers sympathetic to causal theories may suggest that the sloop relevant to John's state is the one causally responsible for his desire. But we can well imagine that the first sighting at a distance awakened his interest, the second strengthened it, and the third clinched matters. Without the third he might never have made up his mind; without the first two the third would not have sufficed. I am not unsympathetic to attributing causal interactions importance, but want to point out that causation comes in many kinds and can be relevant in many ways. The story for reference is undoubtedly much more complex than it is for perception for example, which is already a mess (*Vide* Ziff, 1972; and McLaughlin, 1981).

The point of this tri-partite example is to urge that Jim and John are in the same kind of belief state, one that is different from Jack's. This point seems to have been generally overlooked, perhaps because in Quine's (1956) original discussion and almost all the subsequent

---

[12] While rewriting an earlier draft I discovered that in 1912 G. E. Moore advocated, though for slightly different reasons, at least the negative portion of Section IV (Moore, 1953, p. 265).

literature the contrast has been specificity *and* existence as opposed to non-specificity *and* non-existence (e.g., unicorns). Another possible reason is the strong tendency engendered by literature on the subject to identify the specificity of belief with 'knowing who'. This is puzzling since the specificity of *belief* is transmuted into a question of *knowledge*. The ungrammatical 'believing who' is obviously not a likely candidate for a paraphrase of specificity, but 'believing one knows who' would seem serviceable. Jim and John believe they know which sloop they will each buy; Jack does not believe he knows which he will buy.

VI. KINDS OF REPORTS

What of *de re* beliefs? Thus far I have been focusing exclusively on so-called *de dicto* beliefs, but there is a strong suggestion in the earlier discussion that the usual line on *de re* belief is wrong. If *de dicto* beliefs do not have sentences or propositions or anything of that ilk as objects, then it would be at least odd, if not inconsistent, for *de re* beliefs to be attitudes toward ordered pairs of objects and open sentences or propositional functions.

There is an argument, usually tacit, that there must be two kinds of belief. (At least prima facie, though many authors after distinguishing two kinds attempt to show the reducibility of one to the other.)

(a) Belief is a relation between a believer and some object or objects.
(b) A correct belief report describes the relation and objects.
(c) There are two distinct kinds of correct belief report.
(d) Therefore, there are two distinct belief relations or objects.

Having denied (a) earlier, the denial of (b) is a natural sequel. Note that we need not, however, reject (c). There may be two different and correct ways of reporting a belief even if (a) is false—what we must do is make sense of what these ways are. If we succeed in this we can clarify matters by showing that *de re/de dicto* is not a matter of two kinds of belief but of two kinds of reports of belief.[13]

Consider first the usefulness of a *de re* report in the prediction of behaviour. In Quine's classic example, while at the beach Ralph has briefly glimpsed from a distance Ortcutt dressed in a trench coat with his hat pulled down over his face. It is reported that Ralph believes Ortcutt to be a spy. But as the story is told and the report usually

---

[13] Chisholm (1980) almost makes this point in noting what he takes to be an ambiguity in the notion of *de re* belief.

interpreted, this does not mean that if we confront Ralph with Ortcutt in plain view that he will accuse him, or recognize him. Nor that even if we took Ralph back to the beach he could pick out Ortcutt from other similarly dressed individuals under the same circumstances. Nor even whether Ralph would respond in the same situation by re-identifying Ortcutt when seen. In short, we know nothing about Ralph's future behaviour except that he will act as though he believes someone he saw at the beach is a spy.

The reporter's specification of Ortcutt in reporting Ralph's belief may have any of several different purposes. It may be amusing to the hearer who knows both Ortcutt and his peculiar habit of lurking at the beach, or it may be to indicate what caused poor Ralph's currently distressed state. While it may say something about the cause, or possibly even the remedy, of Ralph's state, it says nothing about the state itself.

The distinction between *de dicto* and *de re* reports can be likened to that between direct discourse and indirect discourse reports. They differ in their faithfulness to the exact words uttered, but they do not differ by reporting two distinct kinds of utterances. The cases are only analogous, of course, since internal representations are not themselves discourse or linguistic, nor can they be quoted. (You can put nonsense strings in quotes, but not neurophysiological states.) But it would be just as much a mistake to infer the existence of two ways of believing as it would be to infer the existence of two ways of speaking.

Some of the reasons for varying referring phrases in giving *de re* reports are the same as those for making the same substitution in indirect discourse. The hearer may be familiar with a referring expression not known to or used by the speaker/believer. Or the conventions of conversational English may require shifts. If I am reporting to Sam what George said, and George said 'Sam will lend you $5' I will report this to Sam by saying 'George said you would lend me $5'.

VII. THE LOGICAL FORM OF BELIEF REPORTS

My suggestion is that a better analysis of belief reports would be that 'Michael believes that 6,643,213 is a prime' be analysed as:

A. Some assertive portion of Michael's internal representation of the world can be rendered as '6,643,213 is a prime'.[14]

---

[14] The expression 'rendering' has been borrowed from Goodman to emphasize the intermedial aspects of the matter.

I grant that in the sense of 'relation' discussed in Section II this makes belief a relation between Michael and a sentence-like object. But the fundamental relations are between Michael and his internal representation of the world, and between the latter, the English sentence, and the world. (In saying that this is an analysis I do not intend to claim that (A) is what a speaker means in giving the belief report, but that (A) is a good way of explaining what is meant.)

The qualification 'assertive' is required to differentiate belief from desire and also to avoid problems that would arise if internal representations are sufficiently like linguistic ones that a conditional has 'parts' that are not themselves asserted. The adjective would have to be cashed in terms of the functional role the portion of the representation plays in behaviour, perception, and the like.

The expression 'rendering' may not be the optimal one for the relation, but it is better than either 'translation', which suggests that the internal representation is quasi-linguistic, or 'description', which underplays the representative qualities of what is being rendered. One feature that rendering shares with translating is that the optimal rendering or translation of something may depend not only on that thing but also on what others are to be rendered or translated. Translating 'kennen' or 'know' is unproblematic in a context where 'wissen' does not occur, and one may even be able to translate both into 'know' for some purposes, but clearly not for all.

Thus, returning to our example of Andrea from Section III, we can see that 'Andrea believes the tennis ball has a velocity of 65 ft./sec.' is a tempting rendering of her state on the tennis court, but we are given pause by the fact that we are also inclined to render her state in the physics laboratory in the same way. And the two states differ considerably.[15] She could not have been in the second (laboratory) state without considerable linguistic and cognitive training; she could have been in a state relevantly similar to the first without any training of that kind.

Such conflicts do not always arise though. Denbeigh could never be in a state resembling that of the trained physicist. The reason we feel

[15] Note that Kripke's puzzle about belief (Kripke, 1979) arises partly on the premiss that proper names are rigid designators, but also on the less-questioned premiss that propositions are the objects of belief. The puzzle is not puzzling given my suggestion, for an agent can have several distinct elements of a representation that an external observer can see all represent the same city. The only problem is how to render that in a language like English which has only one such term.

somewhat inclined to deny him any beliefs at all is, I suspect, that in Andrea's case we prefer to reserve the belief report for the second of the competing states. And thus we do not wish to use it to apply to Denbeigh when he is in the first sort of state. Some other belief states are unproblematic (in this respect)[16] for humans, for Michael could not be in any state plausibly rendered as '6,643,213 is a prime' without linguistic and arithmetic training.

Of the other crucial term in my analysis, 'representation', I have not a great deal to say, for I am not an expert and even the experts are only beginning their experiments. I should remind the reader that the mode of representation is mostly nonconventional. (Though I do not want to suggest that it is *unmodified* by linguistic and other training.) Usually, when R represents X for S, S must learn how the representation R is related to X, what the conventional or nonconventional relations are between R and X. But cognitive agents do not learn how their internal representation relates to the world. In this sense they have a special access to the information. But the information is not private in the Wittgensteinian sense, for it is conceivable that a sufficiently advanced cognoneurophysiology might eventually permit us to utilize the representations of others more directly than we now do. The person has special access to their representation in something like the way they have special access to their limbs—they can move them in ways we cannot.

To avert one possible misunderstanding, let me note that the agent's special access does not mean that the agent has a special knowledge of how the representation relates to the world. The representation may be, and always is to varying degrees, confused and inaccurate, and any higher level aspects of the representation concerning which portions are confused or inaccurate are themselves subject to the same potential flaws. The representation is used rather than interpreted; changing to a different type of representation or a different type of interpretation is not possible. What makes R the *agent's* representation and also makes it a *representation* is that it is continually modified by the agent's perceptions and guides action.[17]

[16] There remains the question of footnote 2, though we might resolve it if we think of the representation as not only a matter of information but also of processes for dealing with inputs. But this is stretching the ordinary concept of belief.

[17] Recent discussions (Perry, 1979, 1982; Lewis, 1979) suggesting that not *all* beliefs are attitudes toward propositons are based on perceptual aspects of representations and are, I would contend, partial recognition of my general point.

The reader will recall that given the modified formulations of sentential and propositional analyses at the end of Section I, the major differences between my proposal and those bear primarily on the nature of the representation. First, I do not find it plausible that all the required representations will be sentential in nature. The primary argument that has been given for the sentential claims is Lycan's:

Every belief I know is a belief *that* . . . ; the verb 'believe' can take as its grammatical object only a clause or some pronoun that stands in anaphorical for one . . . . Thus to each belief that is even hypothetically reportable there corresponds an actual or potential sentential structure. (1980, 24.)

This argument is unconvincing; we could argue in parallel that since every report of what a painting or picture shows contains a sentence that paintings and pictures consist of sentences.[18]

Secondly, in opposition to the propositional account I do not find it plausible that the internal representation is built up out of representations of propositions. Since no detailed theory of this kind has been produced it is difficult to argue against it. Instead I am offering (unsolicited) advice that research will progress faster by paying attention to the internal representation and its relation to sentences directly, and forgetting propositions.[19]

REFERENCES

Armstrong, David M., *Belief, Truth and Knowledge*, Cambridge University Press, 1973.

Chisholm, Roderick, 'The Logic of Believing', *PPQ*, 61 (1980), pp. 31–49.

Dennett, Daniel, *Content & Consciousness*, New York, Humanities Press, 1969.

——, 'Beyond belief' in A. Woodfield (ed.) *Thought & Object*, Oxford University Press, 1982.

Kripke, Saul, 'A puzzle about belief', in *Meaning and Use*, ed. Margalit, Reidel Publishing Company, Dordrecht, 1979.

[18] This is not strictly true, for a painting may show the President of the United States, but equally someone may believe the President of the United States. Thus just as Lycan must restrict attention to belief *that* the parallel argument restricts attention to paintings showing *that*.

[19] Between the writing of this paper and publication of the volume similar ideas have been presented by Dennett (1982), Stich (1983), and Peacocke (1984).

Lewis, David K., 'Attitudes *de dicto* and *de se*', *The Philosophical Review*, 87 (1979), pp. 513–43.

Lycan, William, 'Toward a humuncular theory of belief', typescript.

Moore, G. E., *Some Main Problems of Philosophy*, The Macmillan Company, New York, 1973.

Peacocke, C., *Sense & Content*, Oxford University Press, 1984.

Perry, John, 'The Problem of the essential indexical', *Noûs*, 13 (1979). pp. 3–22.

——, 'Perception, Action, and the Structure of Believing', this volume.

Quine, W. V., 'Quantifiers and propositional attitudes', reprinted in *Ways of Paradox*, Harvard University Press, Cambridge, Mass., 1976.

Stich, S., *From Folk Psychology to Cognitive Science*, MIT Press, Cambridge, Mass., 1983.

13

PERCEPTION, ACTION, AND
THE STRUCTURE OF BELIEVING

JOHN PERRY

Psychology has its beginning in ethological observation, Grice says. Systematic philosophical psychology, appropriately enough, has its beginning in ethological fiction, Grice's Toby and his fellow squarrels.[1] Toby and the other squarrels often gobble nuts in front of them, particularly after doing without nuts for some time. The theoretical apparatus we use to describe this in an explanatorily promising way allows us to say such things as *Toby prehends nuts as in front of him* and *Toby judges on nuts in front, for squarrel food*. Appeal to certain laws or near-laws then allows the explanation of Toby's gobbling. Prehending is a type of proto-perception, and judging a type of proto-belief. *Prehending nuts as in front of him* and *judging, on nuts in front, for squarrel food* are states instantiated at different times, in front of different nuts, by different squarrels; gobbling is a type of act, similarly instantiated by different squarrels at different times; when successful, different nuts are gobbled. Thus the laws relate (proto) perceptual states, (proto) belief states, and types of action.

This is all, I think, just as it should be, not only for squarrels, prehension, judging, and gobbling but also for humans, perception, belief, desire, and action. Psychological theory must deal with perceptual states, belief states, desire states, and types of action if it is to be general and systematic. The laws which relate these states and types of action and their combinations to one another as typical causes and effects must square with ethological observation and make ecological sense.

A widely held conception of the structure of belief makes this impossible. The conception is the progeny of an inadequate semantics

[1] H. P. Grice, 'Method in Philosophical Psychology (From the Banal to the Bizarre)', *Proceedings and Addresses of the American Philosophical Association*, 1974-5.

for attitude reports due to Frege but attractive to many. This in turn is the result of an inadequate semantics for the sentences embedded in canonical attitude reports. The inadequate theory has been and is being developed in great complexity and detail, with impact on disciplines from metaphysics to syntax. When Grice's programme of creature-construction reaches the point where it can give us a 'genitorial' justification for the psychological laws or near-laws that govern us, we should have a reasonably clear idea of what these laws are. This requires, I think, a new semantic perspective.

I explain the problem and show how a new semantical perspective, situation semantics, promises a solution. Situation semantics, developed by Jon Barwise and me,[2] brings back into semantics a notion banned by Frege in 'Sense and Reference', the idea that sentences stand for something like facts.[3,4] It incorporates many of the insights of David Kaplan's three-tiered semantics, with its formal recognition of the sort of meaning that demonstratives and indexicals have.[5] The importance of this type

[2] See Jon Barwise and John Perry, 'Semantic Innocence and Uncompromising Situations', *Midwest Studies in Philosophy*, 1981; 'Situations and Attitudes', *Journal of Philosophy*, November 1981; *Situations and Attitudes*, Bradford Books, MIT Press, 1983. The present paper was actually written in the autumn of 1980, before the last two items mentioned, while actively working out the ideas of situation semantics with Barwise. It was heavily revised in the spring of 1982, incorporating some developments made in the theory in the meantime. The following papers, although not very up to date as far as situation semantics goes, explain the basic ideas and motivations reasonably well: Jon Barwise, 'Scenes and Other Situations', *Journal of Philosophy*, September 1981; John Perry, 'Frege on Demonstratives', *Philosophical Review*, 86, no. 4, October 1977; 'The Problem of the Essential Indexical', *Nous*, 13 (1979); 'Belief and Acceptance', *Midwest Studies in Philosophy*, 5, 1980; 'A Problem About Continued Belief', *Pacific Philosophical Quarterly*, October 1980; Jon Barwise and John Perry, 'The Situation Underground', in Jon Barwise and Ivan Sag (eds), *Stanford Working Papers in Semantics*, Stanford, 1980.

[3] Gottlob Frege, 'On Sense and Reference', in *Translations from the Philosophical Writings of Gottlob Frege,* edited and translated by Peter Geach and Max Black, Oxford, 1960, pp. 64 ff.

[4] Many authors have seen the need for facts or at least events in philosophy generally and semantics in particular. Our real situations are in many ways similar to Davidson's events, or at least are motivated by many of the same considerations and in response to Davidson's many insights concerning the need for events. Davidson was convinced by an argument we call the 'slingshot' that events or situations could not serve as the semantic values of sentences, as they do in situation semantics; we discuss the argument in 'Semantic Innocence and Uncompromising Situations'. Our abstract situations are close to the Brandt–Goldman–Kim notion of event. See Alvin Goldman, *A Theory of Human Action*, Englewood Cliffs, 1970; and Jaegwon Kim, 'On the Psycho-Physical Identity Theory', *American Philosophical Quarterly*, 3 (1966).

[5] David Kaplan, 'Dthat' and 'On the Logic of Demonstratives', in *Contemporary*

of expression has long been championed by a distinguished minority of philosophers of language, including C. S. Peirce, Arthur Burks, and Hector-Neri Castenada.[6] It is not surprising that a philosophy of language and mind that wishes to take our relation to the environment seriously must also take seriously *this, that, I, now,* and *here.*

This paper began as a discussion of the role of *I* in memory, occasioned by certain theses advanced by Grice in 'Personal Identity'.[7] A bit like the *monstera gigantiea,* a vine mentioned later, the paper grew towards a near-by protuberance which cast a shadow on the original enterprise, leaving its roots behind. The protuberance was the semantics of indexicals and demonstratives. I end, however, with some remarks about *I* reminiscent of the themes that were once the core of the paper.

THE TWO FACES OF BELIEF

Reports of the form *X believes that S,* where *X* designates a person and *S* is a sentence, appear to be of subject-object form. The subject is a believer, the object an entity designated by the that-clause, and the transitive verb is *believes.* We can speak of *X* and *Y* believing the same thing, of there being something that *X* believes, and so forth. The identity of the object believed or *propositon* seems to have much to do with the embedded sentence *S.*

Traditionally, propositions have been expected to play two roles. On the one hand, they identify states of the world. *It is true that Caesar was a Roman* makes a claim about the world, a claim that is either right or wrong depending on what the world is or was like. But propositions are also thought to identify belief-states. Thus *Smith believes that Caesar was a Roman,* tells us something about the state of Smith's mind.

This dual role is connected with two uses we make of belief reports. We can use them as *evidence* about what the world is like: Turvey, a reliable authority on lunch, believes that lunch is served. So we believe it too, and go to lunch. We also use belief reports as parts of *explanations*

Perspectives in the Philosophy of Language, ed. Peter A. French, Theodore E. Uehling, Jr, and Howard K. Wettstein, Minneapolis, 1979, pp. 383–412, and *Demonstratives,* mimeo, UCLA Philosophy Department.

  [6] See A. W. Burks, 'Icon, Index, and Symbol', *Philosophy and Phenomenological Research,* Vol. IX, 1949, and references therein; and Hector-Neri Castenada, 'Indicators and Quasi-indicators', *American Philosophical Quarterly,* vol. 4, 1967.

  [7] H. P. Grice, 'Personal Identity', *Mind,* 50, 1941.

about how people act: Turvey believes lunch is served; that is why he is leaving his office and running towards the cafeteria.

Propositions are identified by sentences, and thus seem to reflect logical relations among sentences (or perhaps impose them). So, using propositions to characterize the world, we can infer the truth of *that ψ* from the truth of *that φ* and *that φ only if ψ*. But this logical structure is also useful in characterizing beliefs. I appeal to authority:

> Our attitudes fit into a causal network. In combination, they cause much of our behaviour; they are caused in part by the stimuli we receive from our surroundings and in part by one another. In attempting to systematize what we know about the causal roles of the attitudes, we find it necessary to refer to the logical relations among the objects of the attitudes.[8]

The phrases *objects of the attitudes* and *objects of belief* have three possible uses (at least). The ambiguity would be harmless, at least in the case of belief, if propositions really had the dual role envisaged. The phrase *object of belief* most naturally means those entities designated by the direct-object phrases in belief reports. So the object of Elwood's belief that Caesar was a Roman is whatever *that Caesar was a Roman* stands for. The phrase might mean those entities we are interested in when we use belief as evidence, the states the world either is or is not in. Or it might mean those entities that characterize our belief states in a way that allows us to systematize their causal roles, those entities in terms of which we should characterize states of the believer for purposes of explaining behaviour. If propositions are

---

[8] David Lewis, 'Attitudes *De Dicto* and *De Se*', *Philosophical Review*, 87, no. 4, October 1979, p. 514. In this typically subtle and elegant paper Lewis describes an alternative treatment of what I called 'self-locating belief' in 'Frege on Demonstratives'. Then, exploiting his modal realism, he treats all beliefs as self-locating. The modal realism does make a lot of streamlining possible. But I think our views on the structure of believing are very close. I suspect I do not agree with his remark in the footnote on page 541, that it is 'unfortunate that the study of the objects of belief has become entangled with the semantic analysis of attributions of belief.' This is supported by reference to the claims that 'belief is is in the head', and that 'the main purpose of assigning objects of attitudes is . . . to characterize states of the head . . .' (p. 526). Given the difference between belief as evidence about the world and belief as explanation of the believer's actions, these claims suggest an over-simple picture, which too easily leads us to think that our way of reporting beliefs is not 'straightforward'. Compare, 'Vision is in the head'. Surely, in some sense, true. The eyes and visual centres are all in the head. It does not follow that the point of saying what people see is mainly to describe their heads, or that, to the extent that we do report perception for that purpose, the expressions used will refer to what occurs in the head.

the designata of that-clauses, identify states of the world, and identify states of believers, then propositions are the objects of belief in all three senses.

Experience with perception should raise doubts about this comfortable convergence of theoretical roles. Like belief reports, canonical perception reports identify a perceiver, a relation, and an object. But the point of the traditional arguments from illusion and perceptual relativity (properly construed) is just that the objects of perception in the first two senses are not the objects of perception in the third.

Suppose Smith says 'Elwood sees Hoover Tower'. *Hoover Tower* stands for Hoover Tower. That Elwood sees it might tell us something important about the world, most obviously that wherever Elwood is, Hoover Tower is there to be seen. But the facts of the relativity of perception show that there are countless ways to see Hoover Tower. The states we are in when we see Hoover Tower depend on our perspective and other conditions of perception, not just what we see. The actions that are appropriate for us, given certain desires, also vary with our position, relative to the object seen. So we should expect the ways of seeing Hoover Tower, and not the mere fact of seeing it, to be linked systematically with action and desire. A person who wants to reach Hoover Tower will turn one way if he sees it the way one does when one stands on the north side of it, another way when he sees it as one does when one is to the south side of it.

Not only are there many perceptual states one could be in when seeing Hoover Tower, those same perceptual states could conceivably be involved in seeing something else. The perceptual state one is in when one sees Hoover Tower from one hundred yards on a foggy day in Palo Alto is quite a bit like that which one is in when one sees the Nebraska State Capitol Building from one hundred and fifty yards in Lincoln. We could use this fact to fool someone, were we so inclined and adequately funded.

Objects perceived, physical objects for the most part, do not serve well to classify perceivers for the purpose of explaining their behaviour. This is recognized in common sense psychology. We would never expect to explain what a person does just in terms of what they see, without, at least implicitly, considering the spot from which they see it. If I tell you that Smith wanted to get to Hoover Tower, and saw it from the Athletic Department, then I have given a reasonable explanation for his walking south. If he saw it from an aeroplane I have not given a reasonable explanation for his walking south. It is also recognized that what is seen and the place from which it is seen sometimes give the wrong suggestion. If conditions are abnormal, one may not see things the way one usually does from that spot. In that case, we expect behaviour appropriate to the spot from which things would ordinarily look that way.

In ordinary language, we have a variety of devices for describing our perpetual states independently of what we see when we are in them on a given occasion. For example, we explain mistakes by saying one thing looked like another; this can mean that we were in the state one is usually in when one perceives a thing of the latter sort. One can imagine a very systematic attempt to describe perceptual states, however. One might have a catalogue of photographs, taken of various objects from various angles, and have people pick out one that shows 'what things looked like'. Such a system of identifying perceptual states, though less than the last word scientifically, might have its uses. Then the system of photographs used to individuate the perceptual states would be the 'objects of perception' in the third sense indicated. This would be a very dangerous usage, however. For confusing the usages, but keeping the system of identifying perceptual states, one might begin to think of the photographs, or something akin to them, as what we *really* see. The third use of *objects of perception* seems best avoided altogether.

I think an approach similar to that described for perception (which is intended to be relatively non-controversial), is needed in the philosophy of belief. The reason is that nothing can play both of the roles that propositions are supposed to play in the traditional theory.

The states an object is in at a time are distinguished from the relations in which it stands to other things at that time. That grass is green is a true proposition. It is not true just for certain persons or from certain positions, it is simply true. Its being true, we might think of as a state of the world, rather than a relation that the world stands in to certain people, or certain positions within it. But if propositions correspond to such states of the world (and this is how I shall use the term), then there are no general and systematic links between belief in propositions, perception, and action.

To 'systematize what we know about the causal role of attitudes', we need states that are typically caused in normal perceivers by certain perceptual states and states that typically cause, in normal believers, certain kinds of actions. Belief in a proposition will not fill this theoretical need, so long as propositions identify states of the world. The proposition one comes to believe through perception will concern the objects in one's environment; someone in some other place, looking at other objects, will not acquire belief in the same proposition, even if his perceptual state is the same. And the proposition, belief in which leads me to run or to reach out for a morsel of food, will not lead someone else, in some other place at some other time, to act in the same way.

Consider the proposition that the door to Building 90 at Stanford is open. Belief in this proposition can have no systematic and general links with action. Even holding desires constant for the general population, what one should do depends not just on the fact that the door is open and one's desire (say) that it be shut, but where one is. Some with this desire and belief should walk downstairs and shut it. Others should phone and ask Julius to close it. A monk in Tibet, who has been apprised of the situation and desires that all doors be shut, really has no appropriate course of action open to him. Aristotle, who was awfully smart, may have foreseen that the door would be open, and have thought that philosophers should be kept warm. Apart from adding a footnote, 'Close the door!' to his *Ethics* (much studied in Building 90), it's hard to imagine what he could have done about it.

Standing in front of Building 90, one comes to believe that the door is open by seeing it open. But given the uniformity of Stanford's Inner Quad, one would be in the same perceptual state when looking at Building 30's open door (the numerals are obscured when the doors are open). But one would thereby be led to a different belief, that *that* door was open.

What we perceive—Building 90 or Building 30—is a matter not just of how we see things, but also of our position in the world. What we do —close the door of Building 90 or close the door of Building 30—is a matter not just of how we move but also of where we are and what we touch. If psychology, common-sense or otherwise, is to be systematic and general, it will be concerned with ways of perceiving and ways of acting, the same theory applying to the philosophy major in front of Building 90 and the English major in front of Building 30. A similarly two-faceted account of the structure of belief is needed.

ACCEPTANCE AND BELIEF

Consider this unlikely conversation:

> Sarah: It's Tuesday. So you should empty the dustbin.
> Joe: I agree, I should empty the dustbin.
> Jim: So you believe that Joe should empty the dustbin.

I shall say that Sarah *accepts* the sentence *You should empty the dustbin*. By *sentence*, I mean the meaningful English sentence. Joe accepts *I should empty the dustbin*. Sarah does not accept *I should empty the dustbin*, but she thinks that when Joe says it, he says something true. And Joe does not accept *You should empty the dustbin*, although he thinks that when Sarah says it, she says something true. The sentences one accepts at a given time are those one uses or would use to describe the world to oneself and others. But description is just one activity among many; the sentences one accepts are those which guide one's actions generally. Some sentences, like *Caesar was a Roman* one usually accepts for a long time if one accepts them at all. Others, like *I should empty the dustbin*, one usually does not accept for long.

I suggest that the sentences one accepts give us a pretty good way of identifying the belief states one is in. I take belief states to be dispositions to do various things, including use various sentences in various ways, and so this is a case of identifying a multiply-manifested disposition by one of its upshots. Thus belief states are identified by the behaviour they cause in articulate adults in suitable circumstances. But belief states and belief will be attributable to pre-linguistic children and animals in so far as we are motivated to identify the states they are in with those of articulate adults. This is conceivable because the disposition to accept a sentence may be the disposition to do much else that is more important. This approach not only does not preclude the attribution of belief states to organisms without language, it facilitates it. Individuation of belief state by sentence accepted, rather than propositions believed, makes it possible to link some of these states systematically with perceptual situations on the one hand and environmental threats and opportunities on the other. This is precisely the step that is needed to make sense of belief without language.

Acceptance must be distinguished from belief. Belief is an attitude we have towards propositions in virtue of accepting sentences, or being in the states that dispose us to accept them. Propositions I take to be abstract complexes of objects and properties; details are found in the next section. As Jim points out, Sarah and Joe believe the same thing; the proposition that Joe should empty the dustbin. The fact that they believe it in virtue of accepting different sentences manifesting different belief states, I shall put as they believe it *in different ways*. Of course, they both accept *Joe should empty the dustbin*, so there is a way they both believe it. But this is not necessary: one or the other might not know Joe's name. They might also accept the same sentence, and thereby believe different things. For example, if they both accepted *You should empty the dustbin*, there would be a sharp disagreement.

Acceptance is not belief that a sentence is true, although one will believe that one's own uses of the sentences one accepts will be true, if one reflects on it. The analogy with perspective may be helpful. I have a certain perspective on Hoover Tower from my office. I realize that other positions give other perspectives, and I can imagine having those perspectives, and might even produce some rough drawings. I believe that those are how Hoover Tower looks from various angles. Of the drawing from the angle I have, I believe that it shows how Hoover Tower looks from where I am. And I can focus on the way it looks to me now even without a drawing, and if I reflect upon it I will certainly agree that this is how Hoover Tower looks from here, now. But believing that about how it looks should not be identified with its looking that way to me, now. Similarly, my acceptance of *Hoover Tower is over there*, should not be confused with my belief that the sentence, as uttered by one in my position and looking in the direction that I am, is true. Accepting it is not thinking that it is true, but being in a certain kind of state identifiable by it.

When we describe beliefs, we usually identify the believer, the time at which the believing occurs, and the proposition believed. This is what Jim does in the example. A sincere first-person present-tense belief report—*I believe that such and such*—will embed in the that-clause a sentence accepted by the believer. But this is the exceptional case. Thus if Joe were to say 'Sarah believes that I should empty the dustbin', his belief report would be true, but he would not have embedded the sentence that Sarah accepts, which is not *I should empty the dustbin*, but *You should empty the dustbin*.

This may lead us to suppose that how a person believes a proposition is not very important. But often it is crucial. When we seek to explain a person's behaviour by their beliefs it is ultimately the way they believe, not what they believe, that is important.

In the example, we may confidently expect Joe to collect the dust-bin and head for the door, while Sarah continues her studies. Their behaviour thus differs dramatically. But their beliefs are the same. It is the difference in what they accept that appears to coincide with the difference in behaviour. All well-behaved children will behave as Joe does when they accept *I should empty the dustbin*, even though each will believe something different.

Consider the English major and the philosophy major of the last section. They are in the same perceptual state, the one a normal perceiver is in looking at a building of a certain type with an open door. But of course they see different things. One sees one open door, the other sees the other. Each is led to a belief state that is systematically and generally tied to such a perceptual state in a wide range of human beings, that state identified by acceptance of *That door is open*. They believe in the same way, though of course they believe different things. The one believes the door is open, the other believes the other door is open. The belief state, given certain desires (where a similar distinction will have to be made), is linked with a certain type of action: closing that door. They both perform actions of this type, but in so acting, close different doors.

The sentences whose acceptance will be systematically linked to perception and action typically contain demonstratives and indexicals: *That rock is coming at me, I'd better duck, This door is open*, etc. We need an account of meaning that comprehends such expressions.

SITUATION SEMANTICS

The framework I shall use is the situation semantics theory that Jon Barwise and I are developing. The basic idea of situation semantics is that the meaning of a sentence is a relation between situations. First we shall look at the notion of a situation, then at the relation theory of meaning.

Situations. The basic metaphysical idea is that reality consists of real situations, objects having properties and standing in relations at space-time locations. But we should not think of real situations as made up of separately existing objects, relations, and locations standing in some higher-order relation. Rather, objects, relations, and locations are abstractions from the flux of real situations, from what there ultimately is. They are at the most basic level of abstraction, but they are abstract. Such abstraction is the only way we have of dealing with the uniformities in reality, the recurring pattern of adjustment to which, whether through Divine Plan, evolution, or practical reasoning, is a precondition to effective action.

We assume that each situation s has a location l, ($l = loc(s)$) and a type s, ($s = type(s)$). The type is a relation between n-place relations, n individuals, and 1 and 0 (whose role in this scheme will be explained shortly). Where we have a real situation s with $loc(s) = l$ and $type(s)$ s, then if

$s(\text{runs, Albert}) = 1,$

Albert is running at *l*. Situation types, like objects and properties and locations, are abstract; they represent *uniformities* across real situations. The type *s* just mentioned represents what all situations in which Albert is running have in common, while s' represents what all situations in which Albert is not running have in common, where

$s(\text{runs, Albert}) = 0$

Now one can see the point of the 1s and 0s. They allow us to distinguish situation types which represent Albert as not running from those that are merely silent on the matter. Consider these two situation types:

$s(\text{barks, Mollie}) = 1$
$s(\text{barks, Fido}) = 0$
$s(\text{barks, Mollie}) = 1$

The first represents Mollie as barking and Fido as not barking; the second represents Mollie as barking but does not represent Fido as doing anything.

A pair $\langle l, s \rangle$ of a location and a situation type is an *abstract* situation. An *actual situation* is an abstract situation that corresponds to a real situation. That is,

$\langle l', s' \rangle$ *is actual if there is a real situation* s *such that* $loc(\text{s}) = l'$ *and* $type(\text{s}) = s'$ [9]

Other abstract situations are non-actual. Actual and non-actual situations are just set-theoretical objects, that do or do not correspond to real situations. In particular, non-actual situations fail to correspond to real ones, rather than corresponding to non-real ones.

There is, then, a gap between real situations, the stuff of the world, and abstract situations, actual and non-actual. The difference is obscured by calling them all *situations* and also by using, as I shall, the variable s to range over both. *Situations* will usually be used for abstract situations, with *real* added when needed.

Linguistic meaning. In situation semantics, the linguistic meaning of

---

[9] This way of putting things builds in a decision about the question of how many situations there are at a location. If we think there is only one, whose type includes everything that is going on at a location, then we should want to require that s' be part of *type*(s).

a sentence is a relation between situations, between an utterance on the one hand, and a described situation on the other. Suppose someone says, 'This table was built by you'. For this *utterance* to be true, a certain relation will have to hold between it and another situation. Let's call the utterance **u** and the situation it describes **s**. Then the relation in question is this one:

There are objects *a, b, c*, locations *l, l′* and types *u* and *s* such that:

(i) $\mathbf{u} = \langle l′, u \rangle$
(ii) $\mathbf{s} = \langle l, s \rangle$
(iii) l temporally precedes $l′$
(iv) $u(\text{speaks to, a, b}) = 1$
(v) $u(\text{demonstrates, a, c}) = 1$
(vi) $u(\text{table, c}) = 1$
(vii) $s(\text{builds, b, c}) = 1$

This is a complex relation that holds between abstract situations, involving many different individuals and locations. A true utterance occurs when there are there situations in this relation that each correspond to reality: an actual utterance of *This table was built by you*, and an actual, properly related, episode of table building.

A theory of linguistic meaning assigns to expressions of a language relations between utterances and elements of described situations, in such a way that the correct relations for sentences emerge.[10] We indicate the meaning of an expression α with $[\![\alpha]\!]$. This is a relation between utterances and situations if α is a sentence, otherwise, elements of situations. Thus

$$_\mathbf{u}[\![\alpha]\!]_\mathbf{s}$$

is an instance of the form

$$_aR_b$$

Here are some semantic rules of this form.

(a) $_\mathbf{u}[\![\textit{built by}]\!]_r$ iff r is the relation of being built by.

---

[10] I am simplifying here, by sticking to situations, rather than bringing in *courses of events*. A course of events is a set of situations, hence a set of pairs of locations and situation types, hence a relation in extension between locations and situation types. Such a relation can be thought of as a partial function from locations to situation types. So a course of events is a dynamic version of a situation, it represents what is going on at locations, or more precisely, part of what is going on at some locations.

(b) $_\mathbf{u}[\![\,you\,]\!]_\mathbf{b}$ iff   there is an individual a, a location l and a type u such that
- (i) $\mathbf{u} = \langle l, u \rangle$
- (ii) $u(\text{speaker}, a) = 1$
- (iii) $u(\text{addresses}, a, b) = 1$

Note that '$\mathbf{u}$' does not appear on the right hand side of (a). *Built by* stands for a certain relation, independently of the facts of the utterance.[11] But *you* works very differently, since who a use of *you* stands for depends on who the speaker is addressing.

Here are the rest of the rules we need to handle our simple sentence.[12]

(c) $_\mathbf{u}[\![\,table\,]\!]_p$ iff p is the property of being a table.

(d) Where α is a common noun, *this α* is a noun phrase; $_\mathbf{u}[\![\,this\ \alpha\,]\!]_c$ iff   there is a location l, a type u, a property p and and individual a such that
- (i) $\mathbf{u} = \langle l, u \rangle$
- (ii) $u(\text{speaker}, a) = 1$
- (iii) $u(\text{demonstrates}, a, c) = 1$
- (iv) $_\mathbf{u}[\![\,\alpha\,]\!]_p$
- (v) $u(p, a) = 1$

(e) Where α is a transitive verb and β is a noun phrase, $\alpha\beta$ is a verb phrase; $_\mathbf{u}[\![\,\alpha\beta\,]\!]_{a,\,s,\,l}$ iff   there is a relation r, an individual c and a type s such that
- (i) $_\mathbf{u}[\![\,\alpha\,]\!]_r, {}_\mathbf{u}[\![\,\beta\,]\!]_c$
- (ii) $\mathbf{s} = \langle s, l \rangle$
- (iii) $s(r, a, c) = 1$.

(f) Where β is a verb phrase, *was β* is a full verb phrase; $_\mathbf{u}[\![\,was\ \beta\,]\!]_{a.\,s'}$ iff   there are locations l, l', and a type u such that
- (i) $\mathbf{u} = \langle l, u \rangle$,
- (ii) l' temporally precedes l, and
- (iii) $_\mathbf{u}[\![\,\beta\,]\!]_{a.\,s',\,l'}$

[11] Although we could treat the language spoken as an additional parameter of the utterance, and for certain purposes this is useful.

[12] Of course, these rules are not intended to be the final word, just to give the flavour of what a theory of meaning looks like in situation semantics. Rule (f). for example, would not fare very well as the fragment got larger.

(g) Where α is a noun phrase   iff   there is an individual a
and β is a full verb phrase,   such that
$\alpha\beta$ is a sentence; $_u[\![\alpha]\!]_a$ and $_u[\![\beta]\!]_{a,s}$
$_u[\![\alpha\beta]\!]_s$

Meaning, interpretation, and information. Utterances are ways of conveying information, and although there are all sorts of information that an utterance can convey, the central case is that in which the utterance is true, and the information conveyed is that the conditions for the utterance's being true are met. On the relation theory of meaning, the truth conditions of an utterance pertain to two situations, the utterance and the subject matter situation. They must be related in a certain way, and both be actual, for the utterance to be true. And there are cases in which the information we gain is limited to this. Suppose I get a postcard in the mail, with no signature, no return address, no picture to indicate where it came from, and the postmark blurred. Written on it are the words *I am having a good time.* What constraints are placed on the world, if I assume that the writing of this card was a true utterance? Just this,

> There are actual situations **u** and **s**, a type u, location l and an individual a such that
> (i) $_u[\![\textit{I am having a good time}]\!]_s$
> (ii) $\mathbf{u} = \langle l, u \rangle$
> (iii) $u(\text{writes, this card, a}) = 1$
> (iv) l temporally precedes the present moment.

By knowing the conditions under which an utterance is true, and knowing something about the utterance, we learn about the subject matter, the described situation. Thus, if I know that you wrote the card last week, I learn that you were having a good time last week. This is clearly the normal pattern, knowing about the utterance, and learning about the subject matter. By fixing the facts of the utterance, and only allowing the situation to vary, we get the notion of interpretation:

> The interpretation of an utterance **u** of an expression α, is the set $\{s \mid _u[\![\alpha]\!]_s\}$

Consider my utterance to Jane, of *This table was built by you.* There are many situations in the interpretation of this utterance. The utterance is true if any of them are actual. They all have Jane building this table at some time previous to my utterance, but they vary in every other conceivable way. Some have World War II avoided by timely diplomacy, others have it happening as it did, others do not consider it.[13] Each of these situations has a type that is defined upon Jane and this table; these objects are the subject matter of the utterance. Nothing else makes it into the subject matter, not even me.

This last point is important. When we use natural language, we tend to focus on interpretation. The most common notion of saying the same thing, is just uttering something with the same interpretation. If you say, pointing at Jane, and picking up a reference to the table, *She built that table*, we would ordinarily say that you said just what I did, that Jane built the table. The meaning of the sentences we use is not the same. And if it were the same, we might not have said the same thing. If you were talking to Albert and used the sentence *That table was built by you*, you would not have said what I did, but something quite different. Even in reporting utterances, it is the interpretation we worry about, not the meaning. You could report what I said as *He said that Jane built that table,* or even *He said that Jane built the table in the living room by the fireplace.* You are not reporting the meaning of the sentence I used, but the interpretation of my utterance.[14] This point carries over into the other propositional attitudes, such as belief and knowledge. Given this focus on interpretation, it is natural to capture one thing that has been meant by *propositions* with the interpretation of the utterance of a declarative sentence, a set (or class) of situations. This is how I shall use the term in this essay. So used, it conforms to the first two uses of *object of belief*, propositions are the designata ($\approx$ interpretation) of that-clauses, and are the entities we are interested in when we use belief reports as evidence about the world. But the propositions in this construal do not give us the fine-grained way of classifying belief states that we would need to systematize their causal role. That job, as we shall see, is played by meanings.

This focus on interpretation in natural language leads one into thinking that all of the information we get from an utterance is information about the subject matter. But this is just not so. When we hear or read sentences that we take to be making true statements, we must simultaneously build up a picture of the utterance and of the subject matter. Often what we learn about the utterance, the general situation

---

[13] Here the lack of courses of events in this exposition makes accurate statement of the point impossible.

[14] This thesis is defended at length in 'Situations and Attitudes', and at greater length, with changes, in *Situations and Attitudes*.

of the speaker, is more important than what the speaker says. A hostess hears a child say 'This chair is funny looking'. She knows a little about the utterance situation from the fact that she can hear the voice. Taking the statement as true, she can fix the interpretation of *this*; there is only one funny looking chair in the house. This, together with the meaning of *the chair*, fixes the utterance situation in more detail, and she shouts, 'Don't sit on that chair, it is a valuable antique.' What she learned was not that a certain chair was funny looking, which she already knows, but that a child was near her favourite antique. Another example, Elwood's brother has made it to San Francisco, but is lost. He calls and says, 'This phone booth is next to a large tower that looks like a fire-hose nozzle.' Elwood learns where his brother is, though his brother has not *said* anything about himself at all.

If the normal focus on interpretation is not properly understood, the other ways of getting information can seem mysterious. Sentences like *I am Elwood Fritchey* and *This city is San Francisco* can seem rather odd. If Elwood says the first one, he has said something necessarily true. If anyone else says it, they have said something necessarily false. And when Elwood says the first, it seems to have the same interpretation as *Elwood Fritchey is Elwood Fritchey*, when anyone else says it. And yet when he says it, I learn something, for I learn who I am talking to.

Let us introduce the notion of the inverse interpretation:

The inverse interpretation of a use of α relative to s, is that set $\{u \mid {}_u[\![\alpha]\!]_s\}$

Relative to any actual situation s, the only utterances in the inverse interpretation of *I am Elwood Fritchey* are ones in which Elwood Fritchey is the speaker, and the only utterances in the inverse interpretation of *This city is San Francisco* are ones in which the speaker is demonstrating San Francisco. If you and I are at Powell and Geary, and you say 'This is San Francisco', not pointing to a place on a map, but just the area around you, I learn that we are in San Francisco.

If we equate meaning and interpretation, perhaps lumping them together under something called 'truth conditions', then information of the sort just noted will be hard to deal with. We may deny it any semantic status, but this is a mistake because the constraints placed on the identity of the speaker and other aspects of the utterance situation are as closely related to the meaning of the sentence used as the constraints its truthful use places on the described situation. We may shove all the information we can get into the interpretation, so that we think that what is said contains implicit reference to the speaker and so forth. These strategies are both instances of what we call the *fallacy of misplaced information*. Given a relational perspective on meaning, we do not need to misplace information. The truth of an utterance of a sentence with a given meaning puts a set of interrelated constraints on two situations, the utterance and the subject-matter situation. When we recognize a truthful utterance, or take one to be true that is not, we pick up information, or misinformation, about both situations. The usual case is to know a lot about the utterance and learn about the subject matter, but cases where the basic drift of information is in the other direction are quite common.

So far, we have taken one thing about the utterance, the expression, to be given. But this is not always so. Indeed, when you report my utterance of *This table was built by you* by saying, 'He said that Jane made that table', your auditor learns the interpretation of my utterance without learning which expression I used. But the expression is constrained to be one that would have that interpretation, as used by me, in the situation I was in. Given further knowledge about that situation, you may be able to figure out just what words I uttered. This sort of reasoning, and its analogues with reports about what a person believes or knows, is very important, as we shall see.

PERCEPTION, ACCEPTANCE, AND ACTION

This account allows us to see why the acceptance of certain sentences can be systematically linked with perception and action. By a *context* let us mean a situation like an utterance, except for the speaking or writing of a sentence. Given the way we have been using *utterance*, there are still a lot of facts left: who and where the potential speaker is, and how he or she is connected to the wider world.[15] A context belongs

[15] The facts about an utterance that are relevant to interpretation can be divided in various useful ways. We have generally divided them into facts about the discourse situation and connections. The former are publically observable facts such as the identity of the speaker and the time and place of the utterance. The latter are basically causal connections to objects in the wider world. The interpretation of a use of *I* requires only the first sort of facts, the discourse situation. The interpretation of a use of a proper name requires the latter sort of fact, a lesson to be learned from the theories of Donnellan and Kripke. Some kinds of expression require both sorts of facts for their interpretation, but they are still relevant in ways worth keeping separate. For example, the object demonstrated may be constrained by facts about the discourse situations, but further

to the inverse interpretation of an expression relative to a situation just in case the utterance got by adding the production of the expression would. Finally, let us say that a context that belongs to the inverse interpretation of an expression relative to some actual situation, belongs to the *actual inverse interpretation* of the expression.

The acceptance of a sentence φ will be systematically and generally linkable to one's perceptual situation, if one's situation can often be determined to belong to the actual inverse interpretation of φ perceptually. This does not require that all situations in the inverse interpretation of φ be perceptually similar, but that there be a subset of those that are. Thus *This is a fir tree* can be directly linked with perception, even though some situations in its actual inverse interpretation could not be perceived to be in it, because it is dark or the fir tree is disguised as an elm.

The beliefs that can be acquired directly through perception seem to be those which are about the perceptible properties of objects in one's environment. This can be so because there are sentences whose acceptance for each person guarantees a belief about just those objects in that person's environment, and whose acceptance therefore can be directly and systematically linked to the perceptual states one is in when one is in certain kinds of situations.

Let us distinguish between sentences with bland and rich inverse interpretations. Those with bland inverse interpretations are those that are or come close to being eternal sentences. Their utterance has the same interpretation, no matter who says them and where and what they are attending to. Their meanings are insensitive to the context. Such sentences cannot be linked with perception in a systematic way. This can only happen if the sentence has a rich inverse interpretation, if its meaning puts heavy restrictions on the kinds of situations in which it can be uttered truly.

Similarly, the acceptance of φ will be linkable with action if there is a type of action that is generally advisable for speakers in situations in its actual inverse interpretation. For example, every speaker in a situation in the actual inverse interpretation of *There is a rock coming at me* should duck. Again, we get at the truth of a simple idea, that beliefs about the threats posed and opportunities afforded by objects in one's environment lead directly to action.

causal facts are probably also relevant; which of the various chairs in a room a speaker refers to with *this chair* may turn on which one the speaker is attending to.

From this perspective, we can see the source of the tension created by the notion of the 'objects of the attitudes'. If they are to be true or false, corresponding to states the world might or might not be in, the common objects of belief of various people in various places and times, they correspond to interpretations of utterances. If they are to serve the purposes of psychological classification, they should correspond to meanings of sentences with rich inverse interpretations. The class of those who accept as I do is not the class of those who believe as I do. Many believe that I have a deadline; many of them are fishing, attending plays, and the like. But most of those who accept *I have a deadline* sit in front of their typewriters, thinking hard and feeling pressurized.

From this point of view, the importance of sentences with bland interpretations may seem a bit of a mystery. This is because to see how the acceptance of sentences can be linked to perception and action, we have had to ignore, in thinking about language, the very thing that makes language so important to us, the ability it gives us to communicate and hold information in ways that is not tied in any very immediate way to perception and action. An animal or a child will duck if a ball is thrown at them; there seems little point in attributing an intervening belief state. The perceptual states can lead to ducking through design of the organism without belief intervening. If the only sentences we had were those capable of being directly linked to perception and action, those sentences would be useless. Their having a use requires two things. There must be some natural dispositions to act in certain ways, given certain perceptual states;[16] the acceptance of sentences can be seen as taking over this causal role. Second, there must be some other way besides perception of the objects in one's environment to come to accept these sentences. The acceptance of sentences puts another node in the network of psychological states, one that can have the effect of perception without all of its risks. It is this second factor that makes sentences with constant meanings so important.

ON INTERPRETATION

Sentences, or tokens of them, travel. They travel quickly through the air as sounds, and slowly through the mail as marks. They are published,

[16] The term *state* suggests much too static a way of looking at things, particularly things having to do with perception; I use it in spite of that, because of another set of suggestions it has, where the states of a thing at a time are contrasted with a wider set of properties dependent on its relations to the wider world.

stored away in libraries, and sometimes read, at later times and far away places. The utterance is in general not the same as the situation of interpretation, the time and place when the utterance is understood, and information gained from it.

Let us say that to interpret a sentence heard or read or otherwise apprehended is to find a sentence with the same interpretation in one's own situation, as the apprehended sentence had in the utterance of origin.[17]

We can distinguish several kinds of interpreting.

Interpreting up. This is to find an interpreting sentence with a less sensitive meaning. My friend in San Francisco sends me a card on which he has written, 'This city has dilapidated cable cars.' I write in the draft of my travel-guide: 'San Francisco has dilapidated cable cars.' Note that the sentence I find is not insensitive. It has tense and a proper name. But it is in less sensitive than the sentence I read on the card; it has a constant or near-constant interpretation over a wider range of change in the context.

Interpreting down. This is to find a more sensitive sentence with the same interpretation. On a trip to San Francisco I read in my Mobil-Guide, 'San Francisco has dilapidated cable cars.' I write on my notepad, 'This city has dilapidated cable cars.' Or I think it. But I do not get on the cable cars I see.

Lateral interpreting. This is to find a sensitive sentence to interpret a sensitive sentence. My friend shouts, 'You are about to be hit by a rock.' I think, 'I am about to be hit by a rock.'

We can always interpret a sentence, if we know its meaning. I get the postcard described above with no signature, no postmark, and no picture. I interpret: *The author of the postcard was having a good time when he or she wrote it.* Such a sentence is pretty useless in forming expectations or guiding action. Theoretical semantics is the systematic development of a theory of such (practically) useless interpreting

---

[17] This is a dangerous usage. Sentence-*types* don't have interpretations, but meanings; they have interpretations relative to contexts. But we can think of sentence-*tokens* as having interpretations in an extended sense, the interpretations of the utterance which produced them. Xerox machines and other things complicate the latter notion, but I shall ignore such complications. This may be the point to indicate that I try to italicize mentioned sentence-types, but use quotation marks with verbs like the *says* of direct discourse. There is a theory of indirect discourse, which is that it is the mention of a sentence type, but I am not at all sure that theory is right. It must have something to it, however, or I wouldn't have so much trouble adhering to the convention I have described.

sentences, in some language previously explained, of an appropriately formidable appearance.

These three types of interpreting have different purposes, different advantages, different disadvantages, and different requirements, even within the general project of gathering information.

Upwards interpretation allows the retention of information through change of discourse situation. *San Francisco has dilapidated cable cars* will have the same interpretation as I move about the world and for others reading my guide book. *This city has dilapidated cable cars* does not have this virtue. Upwards interpreting requires relatively insensitive expressions for the subject matter and knowledge of the utterance.

Downwards interpreting is used to generate expectations and guide actions. It requires knowledge of one's own situation. I could go from accepting *San Francisco has dilapidated cable cars* to accepting *This city has dilapidated cable cars* because I accepted *This city is San Francisco*. Having done so, I expect to see such cable cars, and avoid getting into them.

Thus it is the very blandness of inverse interpretation which makes insensitive sentences unsuited for direct linkage to perception, that makes them eminently suited for storing information thus acquired.

These reflections lead to the following picture of the structure of accepted sentences, or *doxastic structure*, in a normal believer. It has three levels. At the top are the insensitive sentences. At the bottom are those suited for direct linkage with perception and action. Tying these two levels together are the *orienting* sentences like *This city is San Francisco* and *That person is Richard Sklar* and *I am Elwood Fritchey*. Such a structure may be said to be in *perfect equilibrium* when the structure is closed under strong logical consequence.[18] This happens only rarely one assumes, but I use *equilibrium* loosely, to mean approaching perfect equilibrium. For example, if *That person is Richard Sklar* is accepted and so is *Richard Sklar helps tourists in distress*, then *That person helps tourists in distress* is accepted. A structure is properly oriented when the orienting sentences are true in the context, and more or less fully oriented when there are a good number of them.

Given these rather vague notions, we can list some vague expectations we have about doxastic structures: programme stability and generality; relative fullness and stability of orientation; relative stability of belief.

Programme stability and generality. The programme of an individual

---

[18] φ is a *strong logical consequence* of ψ when the interpretation of ψ in any context is included in the interpretation of φ in the same context.

relates perceptual states to doxastic or belief states, doxastic states to each other, and doxastic and affective states to types of expectation and action. This is our loose version of Lewis's vision, a picture that the Gricean programme in philosophical psychology can help bring into focus.

A programme is reliable if it takes us from perceptual states to the acceptance of sentences that are true in the contexts in which the speakers are likely to be in those perceptual states, from sentences that are true in contexts to others that are, and from accepted sentences to appropriate actions. I think of the notion of a reliable programme as a generalization of David Kaplan's concept of something true in virtue of the logic of demonstratives. The latter is a sentence true in every context, even though it doesn't have the same true content ($\approx$ interpretation) in every context. *I am speaking* is such a sentence. It's true, whoever says it, although what they say varies from speaker to speaker and time to time. A reliable programme need not be so flawless, just something that works out in most contexts. And truth isn't always the relevant measure of success. Consider *Never do today what can be put off until tomorrow*. It gives us different advice every day, usually good.

A more sophisticated notion of a reliable programme would consider changes from state to state that are reliable as one's discourse situation changes in automatic ways, as time passes.

We expect such programmes to be stable within individual and across members of a species, and to make ecological sense. The first attribute makes the elucidation of such programmes a reasonable part of empirical psychology, the latter accounts in part for the illumination provided by Grice's programme.

Relative fullness and propriety of orientation. We expect people to recognize the objects in their environment and, by and large, to know who they are and approximately where they are, and the like. This requires changes in the doxastic structure as time passes, and they and other objects move about and change. If they are aware of the passage of time, and little else, there will be an orderly transition of the whole structure. If aware of their own movement, local changes occur at the top level where their own name occurs, and massive changes at the bottom two levels. If aware of changes in other objects (of a relatively non-catastrophic nature), local change occurs at all three levels.[19]

---

[19] Compare J. J. Gibson, 'The Optical Information for Self-Perception', chapter 7 in *The Ecological Approach to Visual Perception*, Boston, 1979.

Relative stability of beliefs. We expect beliefs by and large to remain the same, except as necessitated by changes in accord with the principles just adumbrated. Thus we expect the doxastic structure to change so as to preserve what is believed, the interpretation of the accepted sentences. But we do not expect generality of belief. We expect different individuals to have different beliefs, not mainly because of disagreements about what the world is like, but because different individuals interact with and are concerned about different parts of the world.

Common-sense psychology is a psychology of differences. It has locutions built to focus on the way in which individuals differ; this means it focuses on what is believed, and not just what is accepted, because by the first two principles it assumes that difference of belief gives rise to appropriately different action. Given the assumptions of normal programming and relative full and proper orientation, classification by what is believed, the interpretation of the accepted sentences, rather than the accepted sentences themselves, make sense. Relative to these assumptions, what is believed isolates a deeper dispositional property than what is accepted does; the latter changes to accommodate the former.[20] We also have a reasonably rich vocabulary for describing orientation or lack of it: *recognizes, knows who, where,* and the like. And we have ways of cancelling the presumption of orientation when disorientation occurs.

When we speak of orientation, we have in mind, first and foremost, orientation towards objects in the environment. This is the requirement for making effective use of beliefs held at the upper level of our doxastic structure. But it is a fact of human life that we have many ways of designating individuals, and the modes of designation are tied to actions directly and indirectly through different parts of our doxastic structure. We can speak of orientation here too.

Elwood is at a party and wants to look up a passage in *Word and Object*. He stands next to Marcia. I say, 'Elwood believes that Marcia has a copy of *Word and Object* in her backpack.' I know he believes this, because I said to him 'Marcia has a copy of the book you are looking for', just before the party. You expect him to ask her for it, and are puzzled when he does not. But Elwood is not fully oriented; he does not know who Marcia is. He cannot downward interpret in an effective manner, and so he cannot use his belief effectively.

Later Elwood is at home. He wants to call the person whom he was first told about, and later came to learn was standing next to him,

[20] See 'A Problem About Continued Belief' for more about this.

who knew so much about Quine. But he does not know who that woman is; that is, he cannot interpret upwards in the way necessary to use the information, stored in an insensitive way in the phone book, which has a lot of Marcias in it. It has often been noted that *knowing who* and like expressions seem to vary a lot in their applicability depending on context. But there is a system behind it. These expressions are used to describe an interpretive ability suitable for the task at hand.

Knowing who is being able to interpret information effectively for the task at hand. So knowing who is a species of knowing how. As used with reference to humans, it is usually a knowing how that is supported by acceptance of some sentence. But such interpretive ability is not always based on acceptance. We should add three more species of interpretation.

Interpreting in: interpreting information made available in ordinary perception (as opposed to perception of sentences) into accepted sentences.

Interpreting out: using information in accepted sentences to act effectively in ways directed towards objects in one's environment.

Interpreting through: acting on objects as a direct result of perceiving objects.

The concept of orientation is applicable here also. A shark that perceives a flounder by detecting a change of ionization in the water through which he swims turn towards the flounder, gives chase, and eats it. A tree casts a shadow on a *monstera gigantea*. The vine grows towards the tree, then climbs it, leaving its roots behind. In both cases it is natural to speak of orientation: information about environmental objects was converted by a reliable programme into action, or something like it, directed towards the same object. These programmes are very reliable, but by taking the shark or the vine out of its ecological niche we could produce something resembling disorientation; language is not necessary for identity problems, although it helps.

Neither the shark nor the vine need to interpret up. In each case, the constant presence of the object throughout the episode eliminates the need for anything like a constant expression. *Information that is always available in the environment need not be retained in the head.* Intentionality has its origins in the ecological description of organisms, the borrowing of terms for environmental objects to describe states of the organism. Such descriptions require systematic interaction with the environment, not internal representations of it.

If the tree towards which the vine grows is cut, it has to wait until a different tree casts a new shadow before it changes direction. The shark we can imagine to be more sophisticated. After chasing one flounder, it heads back towards another, through whose perimeter of ionization it passed during the chase. To make sense of this we have to attribute a little more to the shark, something a little like our doxastic structures, that enable it to continue to believe in a perceptually inaccessible flounder.

When the shark perceived the flounder, the information it picked up was as much about it as about the flounder; it is its direction and distance from the flounder that is crucial, not the absolute location of the prey. And in returning to the flounder of second choice, the shark had to keep track of where it had gone, not just where the flounder had stayed. Does this mean that the shark needs also be to credited with some primitive precursor of *I*?

SOME REMARKS ABOUT *I*

The shark needs no precursor of *I*, no self-referring perturbation of shark consciousness, no self-specifying blot in shark vision. It needs none because it has no access to information about itself except through perception, and no use for the information, except in action. The difficulty in grasping this point has less to do with the difficulty of imagining what it is like to be a shark, than with seeing clearly the connection between the meaning of *I* and its role in perception, cognition, and communication.

I stands for the person who uses it. This simple rule hardly seems to invest *I* with sufficient meaning to give it the very special place in self-knowledge that philosophers have accorded it. There seems to be an immediacy and salience to knowledge that we formulate with *I*. Most famously, Descartes begins his climb out of the pit of doubt with *I think*, not *Descartes thinks* or *The author of the **Meditations** thinks*. Hector-Neri Castañeda has enriched philosophy with many examples of this importance.[21] A version of one: Ivan Tovar, heir to a famous fortune, does not claim it, in spite of reading accounts in the papers of the search for Ivan Tovar, the riches that await him, and so forth. Why? Because he has amnesia, and does not accept *I am Ivan Tovar*.

---

[21] Hector-Neri Castañeda, ' "He": A Study in the Logic of Self-Consciousness', *Ratio*, 8 (1966); 'On the Logic of Attributions of Self Knowledge to Others', *The Journal of Philosophy*, 65 (1968).

He does accept *Ivan Tovar has many riches awaiting him* but not *I have many riches awaiting me*. So he does not act.

Some philosophers have thought such importance shows that the rule cited cannot be the whole truth about *I*, perhaps not even an important part of it. Frege thought that *I* must have a special sense for each of us, a sense that determines that person as reference when he uses *I*.[22] Anscombe suggests that *I* should not be thought of as a referring expression at all, for she feels that to suppose that it is leads us to take it not to refer to persons but to selves, a metaphysical nuiscance.[23]

The special importance of *I* is easily accounted for in terms of our framework. Those who accept *I have many riches awaiting me* do not believe the same thing, they may even disagree. But they all believe something that makes it reasonable for them to take steps to obtain their riches. Membership in this class of people projects onto behaviour, more or less. But membership in the class of people who believe that Ivan Tovar has many riches awaiting him does not project onto obtaining behaviour. So Ivan's membership in the second class leaves him just like a lot of other people, while his membership in the first would lead us to expect him to seek his riches.

We can get a lot of knowledge about ourselves through perception. And knowledge about ourselves is quite relevant to action. The meaning of the word *I* makes it peculiarly appropriate for identifying a certain causal role. Acceptance of *I*-sentences, although determining different beliefs for each of us, plays a very similar role for all of us. That is why the first person is indispensable for philosophers who want to isolate an important class of doxastic states.

But indispensable as *I* is for philosophers in identifying such states, it is not necessary for someone to have mastered *I* to be in them. Children learn to use their own names before they master the intricacies of *I* and *you*. Katie may respond to *Katie get in here* and insist *Katie wants a cookie* long before she masters the first person.

It is not surprising that use of one's own name precedes the use of *I*, or can. *Katie wants a cookie* is not in general an effective thing to say if one wants a cookie. But for Katie, it works well. If she gets in the habit of using it whenever she is cookie-deprived, it will work well. We can make the same point about an expression like *this city*. As long as

---

[22] Gottlob Frege, 'The Thought: A Logical Inquiry', trans. by A. M. and Marcelle Quinton, *Mind*, 65 (1956).

[23] G. E. M. Anscombe, 'The First Person', in Samuel Guttenplan, ed., *Mind and Language*, Oxford, 1975.

Katie does not travel, sentences like *It is raining in Palo Alto* can be linked to her perceptual state. When she begins to travel, she will have to break this link.

Katie will not ever cease to be a Katie. But she may meet other kids with the same name. She may meet adults who do not know her name, and whose names she does not know. In these situations, *I* and *you* must be mastered.

When a perceivable entity *a* is constantly in *X*'s environment, *X* can link a sentence with an insensitive expression for *a* to her perceptual states. The constant expression can play the role of a demonstrative or indexical. But the opposite is also the case. An indexical or demonstrative phrase can play the role of a constant expression in the retaining of information in just such a case. The distinction between a reliable sentence—one that makes a truth whenever uttered, but not always the same one—and an insensitive sentence becomes blurred. *This planet isn't a bad place to live, all things considered* has a very secure place in the doxastic structure of all but the choosiest non-astronauts. Does it belong at the top level of our doxastic structure or at the bottom?

I has a similarly blurred status, even for astronauts. Wherever I go, I am always there, standing right behind whatever is in front of me, the one with a head I cannot see, and a body that disappears under a moustache.

The fact that we can get by with our name and not *I* is based on the same fact as that we can get by with *I* and not our name. Both are needed for more complicated forms of life. I need my name to look up my own phone number. But I need *I* to engage in Cartesian doubt. Among the things I might doubt is whether my parents fooled me as to my name. They might have trained me to say *Thomas E. Dewey wants a cookie* when cookie-deprived, as a sort of misguided patriotic joke. It seems easier to worry about this than to worry about whether I got fooled or confused about the meaning of *I*, but if I wanted to worry about that, my name might come in handy. But suppose I wanted to worry about both at the same time. How could I think of myself?

Even a name is not necessary. The gannet folds its fragile wings gracefully to its side just before it hits the water, when it dives for a fish. It does not fold its wings when it sees other gannets about to hit the water. It knows the difference between *its* hitting the water and *that bird's* hitting the water. But it seems all wrong to think of the gannet receiving or using information that makes specific reference to itself at all. It has no use for *I*. Indeed, the gannet, a bird with a rather long protruding neck, usually does not even have a decent amount of itself in its own visual field. If we wanted to paint a picture of what the gannet sees, it would just be a picture of water, with the faint outline of a fish below the surface. And what seems true for the gannet really seems true for us. We often see parts of our body. But we do not need to see parts of our body to know where we are in relation to the objects we see in the environment.

In just those cases in which either a name or a constant expression will do, because what is designated is always there, neither is really needed. The entity can be built into the semantics of the informational medium, without any perturbation in the medium, any name or indexical or disruption in the sensory field to designate that entity.

Consider the language I use with my dog: *Come, Go, Food, Sit, Stop that*. The dog interprets these; her actions and expectations vary (somewhat) with what I shout. Quite apart from whether this or anything like it could qualify the dog as penetrating the essence of language, the dog surely gets information from my verbal activity. We could take the meaning of each of these expressions to be a relation between an utterance of mine and situations involving my dog. This would be reasonable, in that the dog takes these to be commands for her. It would be misleading in that she has no apparatus for taking them in any other way.

We might say that my commands are pre-interpreted for the dog. She does not need to interpret them up, down, or laterally. Perception is kind of like that. The information that we get at a certain spot in the world is information about objects in the neighbourhood of that spot in a form suitable for the person at that spot. As long as this is the only source of information we have about ourselves, we need no way of designating ourselves, indexical or insensitive. Our entire perceptual and doxastic structure provides us with a way of believing about ourselves, without any expression for ourselves. As soon as we begin to get information about ourselves in other modes that need to be laterally or downwards interpreted to be effectively used, we will need to take some expressions as standing for us; to do so will be to interpret the information in a certain way. If Katie comes when we call *Katie* she has it right. She still does not need *I*. She only really needs that to produce information about herself, not to interpret it. The first indexical she will take to designate her will probably be *you*, as said by her mother, standing before her, posing some threat or affording some opportunity.[24]

[24] Jon Barwise and Michael Turvey gave me a lot of help with this. Various parts of this paper were included at talks given at Stanford, Harvard, the University of Washington, and the University of British Columbia. I am grateful to the philosophers at those places for a number of probing questions and helpful comments. This paper was first completed while I was at the Center for Advanced Study in the Behavioural Sciences. I am grateful for financial support from the Center, the National Endowment for the Humanities, the Andrew Mellon Foundation, and Stanford University. Revisions have been influenced by comments from Michael Bratman, Hector-Neri Castañeda, Julius Moravcsik, Howard Wettstein, and others, including someone who returned a copy of an earlier version with very useful comments, but no name.

14

WILLING AND INTENDING

GILBERT HARMAN

Does intention involve the belief that one will do as one intends? Some who have thought carefully about this question have answered 'yes'; others have answered 'no'. I want to suggest that, whatever may be true of ordinary usage, it is useful to distinguish two notions here—for reasons I will explain. I will use the term 'intending' and related terms for the stronger notion, so that intending in this sense does involve believing one will do as one intends. I will use the term 'willing' for the weaker notion, so that willing does not involve believing one will do as one wills.

In particular I will be discussing the following thesis:

Intentional action results from a special attitude of willing which
(a) is distinct from belief and desire,
(b) can occur in the absence of intention, but
(c) is a component of intention where intention is present.

H. P. Grice argues for such a thesis in his important British Academy lecture, 'Intention and Uncertainty'.[1] The issues this lecture raises are interestingly complex. I am not satisfied that I fully understand them. Nevertheless, in this paper I hope to show (1) Grice's argument for the thesis is inconclusive, (2) the thesis is nevertheless probably true and there is such an attitude of willing that *can* occur in the absence of intention, (3) the notion of willing is conceptually more basic than the notion of intending, but (4) willing of the sort that can initiate action can occur only as a component of intending and only if one believes one will do as one wills.

I begin with a terminological point. I am going to use the term 'willing' as the name of a putative attitude, like belief, desire, or intention. Grice, like many other philosophers,[2] uses the term to name an

[1] H. P. Grice, *Intention and Uncertainty*, Oxford, Oxford University Press, 1971; page references below to *Proceedings of the British Academy*, 57 (1971), pp. 263–79.
[2] For example, H. A. Prichard, 'Acting, Willing, and Desiring', *Moral Obligations*,

occurrence, an 'act' of will, although Grice denies that willing is properly called an act or action. Conceivably Grice might wish to identify the putative attitude of willing as a disposition to will in the occurrent sense, just as some philosophers distinguish dispositional and occurrent senses of belief.[3] I prefer to talk directly about the attitudes of belief and willing without trying to analyse these attitudes in terms of occurrences. This means that the thesis I am attributing to Grice is somewhat different from the one he himself puts forward. But I believe that the thesis I am attributing to Grice is at least as plausible as the one he actually puts forward and is at least as well supported by Grice's argument.

Before stating that argument, however, I must take up a preliminary point. Grice's argument presupposes that if one intends to do something, one believes one will do it. As a claim about English, this is highly controversial because, although many who have written about intentions agree with that strong claim,[4] there are also many others who disagree and say that, if an intention requires a belief at all, the required belief is at most merely the belief that there is some chance one will do what one intends.[5] In the end, I do not think it is important whether Grice is right about English. But some discussion of this linguistic issue may be useful.

In thinking about this it is important to distinguish intending from trying or intending to try. To say that Isabel intends to beat Judy in their next chess game would seem to be to say something stronger than Isabel merely intends to try to beat Judy. It does not seem enough merely that her aim is to beat Judy. If she is to intend to beat Judy she must, it seems, have a certain confidence that she will win. Perhaps she must believe she will win. She might 'hype' herself up for the game by getting herself to believe she will win.

Similarly, suppose Herbert's boat sinks. The nearest land is five miles away and Herbert is a poor swimmer. Nevertheless, Herbert sets out with the aim of swimming ashore. Does he intend to swim ashore? He certainly intends to try—but it would seem that more is required

Oxford, Oxford University Press, 1949; Wilfrid Sellars, 'Fatalism and Determinism', in Keith Lehrer (ed.), *Freedom and Determinism*, New York, Random House, 1966; Bruce Aune, *Reason and Action*, Dordrecht, D. Reidel, 1977.

[3] For example, H. H. Price, *Thinking and Experience*, London, 1953; Sellars, op. cit.

[4] For example, Stuart Hampshire and H. L. A. Hart, 'Decision, Intention, and Certainty', *Mind*, 67 (1958), pp. 1–12; Monroe Beardsley, *Intending*, in A. I. Goldman and J. Kim, *Values and Intentions*, Dordrecht, D. Reidel, 1978.

[5] For example, Bruce Aune, op. cit.; Donald Davidson, 'Intending', in Yovel, *Philosophy of History and Action*, Dordrecht, D. Reidel, 1978.

if he is flatly to intend to swim ashore. What more? Here again perhaps belief is needed. If Herbert is to intend to make it, he must get himself to believe he will make it.

Cases of this sort provide some support for the strong claim that intending involves belief that one will succeed. There are also reasons for thinking that certain cases that seem to tell against the strong claim actually do not. This can be seen if two points are kept in mind. First, the notions of intending and belief can be used more or less strictly. In thinking about cases one must take care to use the same standards for belief as for intending. And, second, one must not simply assume that, if someone does something intentionally, it follows always that he or she intended to do it.

Let us consider these points in turn. Consider, first, the undoubted fact that George can now intend to go to New York tomorrow even though he realizes that something may always come up that will prevent him from getting there. For example, his car may break down half way there—or he may simply change his mind. This may appear to show that George does not flatly believe he will go to New York tomorrow even though he intends to go. It might be suggested that George believes merely that he will go if he can and does not change his mind. But in fact the example is quite inconclusive. For George can now *believe* he will go to New York tomorrow even though he realizes that something may come up and that he may change his mind. And clearly he cannot believe that he will go to New York tomorrow without believing he will go. So the fact that he can intend to go while realizing he may not does not show he can intend to go without believing he will go.

We use the worlds 'believe' and 'belief' loosely. We can say that George believes he will go to New York although he realizes he may not —or we can say he does not flatly believe he will go but believes only that he will go if he can and does not change his mind. Our use of the term 'intend' is equally loose and parallels our use of 'believe'. We can say either that George intends to go or that George intends to go if he can and does not change his mind. Perhaps it seems that George can intend to go to New York tomorrow without believing he will do it only if one fails to apply the same standards in ascribing intention and belief.

Failing to apply the same standards to belief and intending may be one reason why some people deny that if someone intends to do something he believes he will do it. Another is a possibly over-simple view about the relation between doing something intentionally and intending to do it. Clearly one can try to do something without positively believing one will succeed; if in such a case one does succeed, it is sometimes correct to say one acted intentionally. For example, Karen might try to kill Lyle by pushing him into the water—not knowing whether he will be able to swim ashore. If he drowns, she kills him intentionally. This may seem to show that someone can intend to do something without positively believing she will do it. But again the example is inconclusive. It is not obvious that someone can do something intentionally only if he or she intends to do it. That supposition is at least controversial. Perhaps, it is enough to intend to try. It can be argued that sometimes there is not even an intention to try, if what one does is a foreseen consequence of something else intended. Karen realizes that in pushing Lyle into the water she reveals to the others her true attitude towards Lyle. She does not want to do that but thinks it cannot be helped, this being her last chance to kill Lyle. She intentionally reveals to the others her true feelings about Lyle but it is not clear that she intends to do that; perhaps she merely realizes that she is doing that. If so, someone can do something intentionally without intending to do it.

But enough of 'perhaps' and 'maybe'. Is Grice's strong claim true or false as a claim about the ordinary use of 'intend'? I think it is hard to say. I find that when I consider cases, I am inclined to agree with Grice's strong claim that intention involves the belief that one will succeed. But I sometimes waver a bit about certain cases. And when I poll groups of people I find that opinion is often divided about cases and, indeed, that some people make confident judgements that conflict with Grice's strong claim.

Albert the basketball player makes a last desperate throw from half court as the clock runs out without really expecting the ball to go in but hoping that it will. Does he intend to throw a basket? Many people confidently say he does, although that seems wrong to me.

It seems marginally better to me to say he throws with the intention of making a basket. More generally, I find I am more inclined to see a difference between intending and intending to try than to see a difference between acting with an intention and acting with an intention to try. So, although I would not agree that poor Harold intends to swim to the shore unless he believes he will make it, I am not sure I object to saying he swims with the intention of swimming to the shore (although I feel some objection to this). Am I imagining things? And what does it mean? Perhaps there is some temptation to use the noun 'intention' for aim, and less temptation (for some of us anyway) to carry over that temptation to the verb 'intend'. But this is mere speculation on my part.

I think that this much can be said. Although many people's judgement of cases conflicts with Grice's strong claim that intending requires the belief one will succeed, there are also many other people whose judgements about cases seem in accordance with that claim. Perhaps there are two uses of the term 'intend'—some people using it in one way, others using it the other way. This suggests that there is a use of 'intend' (and perhaps also 'intention') for which Grice's strong claim is correct. Supposing there is such a use, from now on (unless otherwise indicated) I will use the terms 'intend' and 'intention' in that sense for which Grice's claim is true. If one intends in this sense to do something then one believes one will do it. I will argue later that it is useful to have this notion of intention, that intention in this sense represents a distinctive and unified phenomenon.

Now Grice observes that, if intending involves belief in this way, a puzzle arises as to how that belief could be justified. It seems that the belief could not be based on evidence, for if it was one could not intend to do the thing in question; one would merely predict one was going to do it. But then it seems the belief can never be justified. Grice's resolution of this puzzle is to suppose that there is an attitude towards doing something, call it the attitude of *willing*, which is, or is like, intending in the other sense (if there is one) not involving belief. Grice speaks of 'willing that one should do something', where the 'should' is the subjunctive of 'shall' and is not equivalent to 'ought to'. Grice assumes the attitude of willing satisfies three conditions.

(1) One can know immediately that one wills that one should do something in the same way one can know immediately that one believes something.

(2) What one knows, when one knows that one wills that one should do something, does not entail that one believes one will do it.

(3) One intends to do something if and only if
   (a) one wills that one should do it
   (b) one believes that one's present will that one should do that thing will result in one's doing it.

If there is an attitude of willing satisfying these conditions, then the belief one has when one intends to do something is after all based on evidence, where a crucial part of the evidence is that one wills that one should do the thing in question. For one can have immediate knowledge of one's will and one can know from past experience that under certain conditions one does what one wills one should do.

Grice presents this analysis after rejecting a different analysis of intention as a special kind of assurance about what one will do which is independent of evidence. He reports that in an unpublished paper he himself once put forward a version of the rejected analysis, which he traces back to G. F. Stout.[6] (Rumour has it that the publication of a similar idea by Hampshire and Hart[7] prompted Grice to develop his alternative analysis.) He argues that the rejected analysis must count as unjustified the belief that one will do as one intends.

I will begin with some points of detail concerning Grice's final account of intending in terms of willing. Then I will develop a version of the rejected account of intending as a special kind of belief— a version which is able to deal with Grice's sceptical puzzle. Finally, I will consider how we might decide between these two accounts.

First, a minor point. Consider clause (3b) of Grice's analysis of 'one intends to do something':

(b) one believes that one's present will that one should do that thing will result in one's doing it.

This clause is acceptable only for what I will call 'positive intentions', and therefore needs some modification to allow for conditional intentions and what I will call 'negative intentions'. A possible substitute might be this:

(b′) one believes that one's present will that one should do that thing results in its being guaranteed or at least settled that one does it.

One can have the conditional intention of going swimming tomorrow if it does not rain, without believing that one's will is definitely going to result in anything at all, since one is presumably aware that it may well rain tomorrow. No doubt, one believes that, if it does not rain, one's present 'will' will result in one's going swimming tomorrow. But that is not the same as believing that one's present 'will' will definitely result in something; namely, one's going swimming if it does not rain.

[6] G. F. Stout, 'Voluntary Action', *Mind*, n.s., 5 (1896), pp. 354–66, reprinted in Stout's *Studies in Philosophy and Psychology*, London, MacMillan, 1930.
[7] Stuart Hampshire and H. L. A. Hart, 'Decision, Intention, and Certainty', *Mind*, 67 (1958), pp. 1–12.

It is even clearer that one can have the negative intention of not going swimming without believing that one's not going swimming will result from one's present 'will' since one may well believe that one will go swimming only if one positively decides to go. In such a case, one may suppose perhaps that one's not deciding to go will result in one's not going; but one need not suppose that one's not deciding to go results from one's deciding not to go, since one does not have to suppose that, unless one decided not to, one would definitely decide to go. (Why then does one *decide not* to go swimming rather than merely *not decide* to go? Perhaps simply to settle this isssue so that one may turn one's attention to other matters.)

With that point out of the way, let us consider what sort of attitude willing might be and how it might be related to other attitudes. Grice claims that willing occurs not only when one intends to do something but also when one wishes whole-heartedly for something. It might be said against this that in many, even most, cases of intention, one's attitude is not at all like wishing whole-heartedly for something. One does various things, intending to do each, but with no very passionate commitment to doing them. On the other hand, all cases of intentions do share with wishing whole-heartedly a certain commitment of the will. The extra passion involved in wishing whole-heartedly for something may simply be due to the fact that there is no obvious or easy way to satisfy one's wish oneself.

Consider someone who must choose one of several possible routes to a destination. It might seem that Mabel can arbitrarily form the intention of taking one of these routes without her attitude being at all like wishing whole-heartedly that she should take the route. But we must be careful here. Before making her decision she has no attitude towards that route like wishing whole-heartedly she should take that route. But once she has decided, she will hope to succeed in taking that route to her destination.

Similarly, when John is offered an apple from the basket of apples, he may not have a prior attitude that is like wishing whole-heartedly to take a particular one of the apples. But when he decides on a particular apple, his will is committed to taking that apple even though the commitment in this case is not a passionate one and is easily deflected.

So much for the relation between willing and wishing whole-heartedly for something. Let us next consider the relation between willing and trying or intending to try. To begin with: might the willing that is involved in intending be identified with intending to try? No, because not all intentions involve intending to try. It may be that positive intentions do involve this. If one intends to carry the suitcase to the car but fails to get it all the way there, it is still true that one tried, and so perhaps true that one intended to try. This is so even when one has a positive intention to do something one believes one can do, as we say, 'without trying', an intention to raise one's hand at a given signal, for example. If the signal is given and one has not changed one's mind but one is for some reason unable to raise one's hand, still one tries and so perhaps intended to try.[8] But other cases are different. The conditional intention of going swimming tomorrow if it does not rain involves no unconditional intention to try something, namely going swimming if it does not rain; it involves only a conditional intention to try something if it does not rain. And the negative intention of not going swimming does not have to involve any sort of intention to try not to go swimming. So, since all intention is supposed to involve willing, willing cannot be identified with intending to try.

Does intending to try to do A always involve willing that one should do A? No, because there are cases of trying to do A in which actually succeeding is not one's goal. One might try to throw a ball over someone's head, expecting the ball to arrive waist high, having been told that otherwise one's throw will fall short. One might try to defeat an atomic power plant's security system as a way of testing it, hoping one will not be able to succeed. One might try to push over a wall in order to build up one's arm muscles.[9]

More specifically, one can try as a test to defeat the atomic power plant's security system and be unhappily sure that one will succeed without it being true that one intends to defeat the plant's security system. This shows that no attitude involved in trying to defeat the plant's security system can count as willing that one should defeat the plant's security system, since no such attitude satisfies condition (3) on willing.

(3) one intends to do something if and only if
    (a) one wills that one should do it
    (b′) one believes that one's present will that one should do that thing results in its being settled that one does it.

---

[8] This example and this method for discovering when someone tries are from Brian O'Shaughnessy, 'Trying As the Mental Pineal Gland', *Journal of Philosophy*, 70 (1973), pp. 365–86.

[9] I owe these examples to Grice's lectures on intention and trying at Brandeis University in the early sixties.

Nevertheless, it might plausibly be suggested that willing that one should do a given thing is involved in the more ordinary cases of intending to try to do something, when doing that thing is one's goal.[10] In these more ordinary cases it does seem that, if one not only intends to try to do *A* but also believes one will succeed in doing *A*, then one intends to do *A*. And this suggests that willing that one should do *A* might be identified with having as one's goal that one do *A*.

Distinguishing these two ways in which one can try to do *A* also helps to explain something about our use of the adverb *intentionally*. I have already observed that we sometimes may count a person as having done something intentionally even though he or she did not flatly intend to do that thing but, strictly speaking, merely intended to try to do it, not being at all sure of success. This is so, for example, if the agent acts in the face of what ought to be some reason against doing the act in question. If there is no such reason it often seems wrong to say that the agent acts intentionally. So it seems wrong to say that one intentionally rolls a seven with a pair of dice even though that was what was what one was trying to do. That seems wrong, anyway, unless the dice are loaded or one is so skilled that one can roll a seven at will. And it seems wrong in the same way to say one intentionally shoots a bulls-eye if it is merely a lucky shot, even though one was trying to shoot a bulls-eye. But the sniper is correctly said to kill the enemy officer intenionally even though it is a lucky shot, because here the sniper acts in the face of what ought to be at least a prima-facie reason not to shoot the officer. Furthermore—and this is what is particularly relevant to our present concerns—we count such an act as intentional only if the case involves the more usual sort of intending to try to do something where doing that thing is the agent's goal.[11]

For example, suppose that it would be a bad thing to defeat the power plant's security system, because news of this would inevitably emerge, leading others to attempt to defeat the security system in order to get inside to steal atomic fuel. Now consider two cases.

In *case 1*, Albert, a worker in the plant, has inadvertently left inside the plant a library book which is due today. Albert wants to retrieve the book so he will not have to pay a fine, but he is not supposed to be in the plant at this time. So Albert attempts to defeat the security

[10] Here and elsewhere I am indebted to Susan Wolf's comments on an earlier draft.

[11] I overlooked this in my discussion of *intentionally* in 'Practical Reasoning', *Review of Metaphysics*, 29 (1975-6), pp. 433-4, p. 445 fn. 7.

system in order to sneak in and get his book back. In such a case, if Albert succeeds in defeating the security system, he is properly described as having intentionally defeated the security system.

In *case 2*, Betty tests the security system by attempting to defeat it, hoping that she will not be able to succeed. She knows that there is a chance that she will succeed, which will have bad consequences, but she thinks that this risk is worth taking given the need to test the system. If she does succeed in defeating the security system, despite her hopes, it seems incorrect to describe her as having intentionally defeated the security system.

Given a theory of willing like Grice's, we can say that the relevant difference between these cases is that in case 1 Albert's intention to try to defeat the security system involves Albert's willing that he should succeed in defeating the security system, whereas in case 2, Betty's intention to try to defeat the security system does not involve willing that she should succeed. The general principle might be that one does something intentionally only if one wills that one should do it (or one's doing it is a foreseen consequence of something one wills that one should do).[12] It is a strong reason to think there is such an attitude of willing that the notion of willing can be used in this way to account for the conditions under which someone does something intentionally.

Let us now turn to a different issue. Grice aruges that we must resist the temptation to think of one's occurrent willing as itself something one does in order to bring about, or at least try to bring about, some desired result; otherwise, he argues, there will be an infinite regress, for then one must will that one wills, and one must will that one wills that one wills, and so forth.[13] But this is not a conclusive objection. The regress may be a harmless one, as is the case, for example, if the relevant willing refers to itself so that the relevant sort of willing that one should do *A* is willing that because of one's so willing it should be guaranteed, settled, or at least more likely that one will do *A*. If willing is self-referential in this way, then any instance of willing is also an instance of willing that one wills, so the regress is harmless.[14]

---

[12] Cf. 'Practical Reasoning'. Note that this principle says 'only if', not 'if and only if'.

[13] This regress is also noted in Wilfrid Sellars, 'Fatalism and Determinism', loc. cit., pp. 156–7; Gilbert Ryle, *The Concept of Mind*, London, Hutchinson, 1949, p. 67; and H. A. Prichard, 'Acting, Willing, Desiring', p. 192.

[14] I discuss advantages of and objections to such self-referential attitudes in 'Reasoning and Explanatory Coherence', *Midwest Studies in Philosophy*, 5 (1980), pp. 163–82; and in 'Practical Reasoning'.

Furthermore, willing is surely not something that merely *happens* to a person. Forming an attitude of willing is something one does, because of results one expects from the willing. This is obvious in the case of arbitrary decisions and negative intentions. One arbitrarily selects one out of the possible routes for one's trip. This is something one actively does, not something one finds oneself doing, as one might find that one prefers to go by one route rather than another. One arbitrarily chooses a route because a choice must be made if one is to get under way. That choice then leads to others. One makes the choice because it enables one to go on to the others and eventually make the trip. Similarly, one decides to stay at home and not go swimming because of the expected benefits of so deciding. These benefits need not include primarily the benefits of staying at home as compared with those of going swimming, but may be mainly the benefits of having decided that question so that one may think about other matters. It is true that there are intentions one has because of benefits one expects from doing as one intends. But then one expects the same benefits from willing as one does, since one believes one's will settles it that one does the thing in question.

Consider also how willing initiates action. Grice holds that, if one wills that A should happen, where it is immediately within one's power to bring about A and one realizes this, then one's willing will initiate an act of bringing about A. But that cannot be true.[15] Simply willing that A should happen is not enough. One can wish whole-heartedly for A and therefore will that A should happen, realizing it is immediately within one's power to bring about A, without having any inclination at all to bring about A oneself, if what one hopes for is that A should happen without being brought about by oneself. One might suppose, for example, that A's occurrence, if not brought about by oneself, would indicate that God loves one. If one's willing is to produce an inclination to bring about A, one must will not only that A should happen but also that A should be brought about by oneself, which is to will that one should will in such a way that one brings about A. Only such a willing can initiate an act of bringing about A. Normally, of course, when one wills that A should occur and realizes that bringing about A is immediately within one's power, one also wills that one should bring about A—but not always, as we have just seen. So, the sort of willing that initiates action must be a willing that one's willing should initiate a given action. In other words, the willing that initiates action is itself something one wills should occur.

[15] The following argument is from an unpublished paper by Claudia Mills.

But that is enough about Grice's theory of willing. Recall that he puts his theory forward as an alternative to the Hampshire–Hart sort of theory which treats an intention as a special kind of belief which involves a disposition to take steps required for making the belief true. It is now time to see whether we can make sense of that sort of theory. Grice argues that such a theory must be rejected because the relevant belief could never be justified. More specifically he says this:

For if my going to London is to depend causally on my acceptance that I shall go, the possession of satisfactory evidence that I shall go will involve possession of the information that I accept that I shall go. Obviously, then, I cannot (though others can) come to accept that I shall go on the basis of satisfactory evidence; for to have such evidence I should have *already* to have accepted that I shall go. I cannot decide whether or not to accept that I shall go. [p. 274]

Grice also puts his objection like this:

If we ask why (assuming the theory to be correct) I hold a belief such that I shall go abroad, the only possible answer is that I believe this because, for example, it is something I should particularly like to be the case, or something that I think ought to be the case . . . So, to put it crudely, the theory represents having an intention as being a case of licensed wishful thinking. [p. 262]

But this is surely oversimplified. If one is to be justified in forming what we might call the intention-belief that one shall go abroad, it is not enough that one would particularly like to do so or ought to do so. It is also required that one be justified in believing the conditional proposition that, if one does form that intention-belief, one will go abroad; and one can presumably be justified in believing *that* only on the basis of empirical evidence. Furthermore, if one is justified in believing this conditional proposition, then forming the intention-belief that one should go abroad is not mere wishful thinking. For wishful thinking is precisely thinking that something is so because one wants it to be so where one is not justified in believing the corresponding conditional proposition.

Moreover, if one has evidence for the relevant conditional proposition, then when one forms the intention-belief that one shall go abroad one is justified in believing that one is going to go abroad. For one will be justified in believing the proposition that one has that intention-belief, which together with the relevant conditional proposition logically implies that one will go abroad. So, even though it is true that one cannot in this case *come* to accept that one will go on the basis of satisfactory evidence, when one accepts the proposition that one will go one can then be justified on the basis of satisfactory evidence in doing so. Similarly, as Derek Parfit has observed, an insomniac might be justified on the basis of satisfactory evidence in believing he will stay awake because of that very belief, although he cannot base the belief on that evidence. On the other hand, one is justified in accepting a proposition as an intention-belief only if one is *simultaneously* justified both by the empirical evidence and by practical considerations concerning one's desires, what one ought to do, and so forth. Practical reasoning must reflect this double requirement.

Parfit's insomniac shows that an intention belief is not just a self-referential belief that the very belief will lead one to do something. Is the intention to do something then simply a self-referential belief of the relevant sort plus the disposition to take whatever steps are required? No. For let us suppose that Parfit's insomniac wishes to test a particular type of sleeping pill. His procedure is to take the pill and then to do everything he can to stay awake. He hopes to find that the pill will put him to sleep despite his best efforts to stay awake. After some time he begins to doubt that the pill will work. He begins to suspect that he is going to be successful in staying awake. He realizes that the belief that he will stay awake is all he needs to stay awake. He comes at last to have the self-referential belief that this very belief results in its being settled that he will not fall asleep.

The insomniac has a self-referential belief of the relevant form and is, moreover, disposed to take steps required in order to stay awake. So an intention is not simply a belief of the relevant sort plus a disposition of the relevant sort. If an intention is a belief, it must be a belief of a sort that can account for the disposition. How? Through practical reasoning. If one intends to do A, that intention gives one a reason to take the steps necessary for doing A. The intention therefore produces a disposition to take such steps. If one merely believes that one will do something—even if this is the self-referential belief that that very belief results in its being settled that one will do that thing—that belief does not give one the same sort of reason to take the steps required to do it and therefore does not in the same way account for one's dispositon (if any) to take such steps. The insomniac testing the sleeping pill is disposed to take the steps required for him to stay awake, but this disposition is not explained in the relevant way by his self-referential belief.

This belief is not what gives the insomniac reasons to take those steps —so the belief cannot be an intention to stay awake.

What features of an intention allow it to have this function that other beliefs do not have? It is not clear how on this approach we are to answer this question except to say that that is what an intention is. Certain psychological states have this dual function—they serve as representations of certain aspects of the future and are therefore like beliefs; but they also serve as reason providing ends, leading to other states of the same sort and ultimately to actions. These states we call intentions.[16]

So we now have two accounts of intention. The first analyses intention as a combination of an attitude of willing plus a belief. The second treats an intention as itself a special kind of belief. We have so far been given no reason for taking these accounts to be competing and it is possible that they are simply different ways of looking at the same thing. One says an intention is X plus a belief. The other says an intention is a belief plus Y. Maybe X=Y.

Nevertheless, two interesting issues arise when we contrast the two theories. One of these issues is more conceptual, the other more empirical or psychological. The more conceptual issue is whether willing is a conceptually more basic notion than intending. Given the notion of willing, Grice offers a definition of intending. Is it or is it not possible to go the other way and define willing in terms of intending in any interesting way? The more psychological or empirical issue concerns the extent to which willing can occur without believing one will do as one wills, that is, without intending.

Taking the conceptual issue first, let us consider how we might attempt to explain willing in terms of intending. Perhaps we could first explain trying, then willing. I suspect that the notion of trying is itself

---

[16] Grice endorses this rather indirect way of specifying psychological attitudes in 'Method in Philosophical Psychology', *Proceedings of the American Philosophical Association*, 48 (1974-5), pp. 23-53. See also Hilary Putnam, 'Minds and Machines', in Sidney Hook (ed.), *Dimensions of Mind*, New York, New York University Press, 1960; 'Psychological Predicates', in Capitain and Merrill (eds), *Art, Mind, and Religion*, Pittsburgh, University of Pittsburgh Press, 1967; both reprinted (the latter under the title 'The Nature of Mental States') in Hilary Putnam, *Mind, Language, and Reality: Philosophical Papers*, volume 2, Cambridge, Cambridge University Press, 1975. Also Jerry A. Fodor, *Psychological Explanation*, New York, Random House, 1968; David Lewis, 'An Argument for the Identity Theory', *Journal of Philosophy*, 63 (1966), pp. 17-25, and 'Psychological and Theoretical Identifications', *Australasian Journal of Philosophy*, 50 (1972), pp. 249-58; Gilbert Harman, *Thought*, Princeton, NJ, Princeton University Press, 1973, chapter 3.

a rather loose collection of ideas encompassing various ways of approximating actually doing A intentionally. One can intend to try to do A by intending any of the following things: to do A, to do A if one can, to do what is most likely to result in one's doing A, to do what will count as doing A if the world co-operates, to do what *would* count as doing A if the world *were* to co-operate, etc. Then the notion of willing might be explained in terms of the notion of trying in some such way as this: one wills that one should do something if and only if either (i) one wishes whole-heartedly that one will do it, or (ii) one intends to do it,[17] or (iii) one intends to try to do it where actually doing it is one of one's goal.

A serious problem remains, namely to explain what it is for actually doing something to be one of one's goals. This notion is needed not only to construct a notion of willing but also to explain what it is to do something intentionally in certain cases, as we have seen in our discussion of attempts to defeat an atomic power plant's security system. It might be plausibly suggested that the relevant notion of goal has to be explained in terms of willing: actually doing something is one of one's goals if and only if one wills that one should do that thing. If so, the analysis of willing offered in the second approach is circular and that approach must after all make appeal to a primitive notion of willing, so that it fails to offer an alternative to the first approach.

It might be thought we could explain the relevant notion of goal in a noncircular way in terms of practical reasons one has, along something like the following lines.[18] Actually doing something is one of one's goals if and only if one's reasons for intending to try to do that thing include a desire actually to do it. Whether that idea can be made to work depends of course on how the theory of practical reasoning is developed. I see a difficulty here. It would seem that the theory of practical reasoning must say that reasoning modifies desires by modifying what one desires all things considered, one's 'all-out desires', where all-out desires cannot be identified with or reduced to non-all-out desires and/or intentions. The theory must surely recognize the independent existence of such all-out desires if only because they are sometimes instanced as hopes (if one is not convinced the desired thing will happen). Willing can now be identified with all-out desiring. Willing effective in action can be identified with all-out desiring that that very

[17] We can't eliminate this clause because, as noted above, a negative intention, e.g. to stay home and not go swimming, need involve neither an intention to try to stay home nor the goal of staying home.

[18] Here and elsewhere I am indebted to Carolyn McMullen.

all-out desire should have a certain effect. But this amounts to accepting willing as a notion that is not to be explained in any interesting way in terms of intention. So willing does seem in this sense conceptually more primitive than intending.

Finally, let us consider the more empirical or psychological issue concerning the extent to which willing can occur in the absence of intending. Here I think we must distinguish the sort of willing that can initiate action from the other sort of willing involved say in hoping that something will happen without any help from oneself, the sort of willing perhaps also involved in simply wishing whole-heartedly for something. Clearly the second sort of willing can occur in the absence of intending. But I believe there are reasons to suppose the first sort of willing cannot so occur. I suggest that we are so constructed that any of us can thus will that he or she should do something only if he or she believes he or she will do that thing.

Let us restrict our attention to this sort of willing—the sort that can initiate action. Then I want to argue that such willing is probably constrained to occur only, as part of intending, when one believes one is going to do as one wills. My argument appeals to practicality and feasibility. I claim that it is much easier to decide what to will if willing is thus constrained than if it is not; indeed a system of practical reasoning in which willing was quite unconstrained by belief in this way would probably not be feasible at all. For how would a creature with such unconstrained willing decide what to will? It could not simply consider how much it wants various outcomes and then will that it should bring about the outcome it most wants. The creature must also consider the likelihood of success, because if obtaining the most favoured outcome is unlikely the creature might do better to aim at something that is not so desirable but is more likely to be attained. It must also consider the possible side effects of pursuing one or another goal. It might be suggested that the creature ought to calculate the expected utility of willing one thing rather than another, and then form that attitude of willing that maximizes expected utility. But that would involve extensive assignments of probability and utility of an unmanageable sort. There is abundant evidence that people do not handle probabilities very well.[19] I suspect the reason is that no finite

[19] See, for example, Amos Tversky and Daniel Kahneman, 'Judgment under Uncertainty: Heuristics and Biases', *Science*, 185 (1974), pp. 1124-31. Richard Nisbet and Lee Ross, *Human Inference: Strategies and Shortcomings of Social Judgment*, Englewood Cliffs, NJ, Prentice-Hall, 1980.

creature could make much use of probabilities without running into a combinatorial explosion of memory capacity needed to keep track of relevant probabilities. (For example, if probabilities are updated by R. C. Jeffrey's analogue of conditionalization,[20] then to keep track of the probabilities of n logically unrelated propositions one needs to record $2^n - 1$ independent probabilities. To use Jeffrey's method to calculate the new probability of a given proposition which results from changes in m other logically unrelated propositons requires at least 2^m multiplications.)

This difficulty does not arise if probabilities other than 1 or 0 can be ignored. Suppose for example that the creature knows that, if it wills one thing, a certain outcome is guaranteed; if it wills a second thing, a different outcome is guaranteed; and if it wills a third thing, a still different outcome is guaranteed. Suppose it knows that any other consequences of its willing can be disregarded. Then it needs only to decide which of these outcomes it prefers. It need not assign to any outcome a numerical utility of a sort that can be combined with a probability in a calculation of expected utility.

Now a creature might be so designed and so situated that it could make the most of its decisions in this second way. It might for example be designed so as to consider willing something only if it believed that so willing would result in an outcome it had previously determined it wanted. In the absence of reasons to suppose otherwise, it would normally suppose that the other possible effects of so willing could be disregarded. The creature might be so situated that in fact this procedure worked out well most of the time.

In other words, it may well be feasible for a creature to operate in the world with attitudes of constrained willing, where willing (of the sort that can initiate action) is always intending. It is quite likely that it is not possible for a creature to operate in the world with attitudes of unconstrained willing, because of the combinatorial explosion this may involve. So there are reasons to think that our willing is constrained, rather than unconstrained.

Of course, under certain conditions, even a creature like us whose actions arose from intentions rather than unconstrained willing could reach a decision on grounds of expected utility—if probabilities were well defined, for example, in terms of frequencies; if some sort of numerical measurement of utility made sense, for example, in monetary

[20] R. C. Jeffrey, 'Probability Kinematics', in *The Logic of Decision*, New York, McGraw-Hill, 1965.

terms; and if the creature had the specific goal of maximizing expected utility calculated in these terms. Presumably this would happen only rarely. More often—but still infrequently—such a creature will decide to *try* to do something without being sure of success. It forms the goal of trying to do something—perhaps because much will be lost if it does not try, as in trying to escape from its enemy, or because much is to be gained from success, or because something is to be gained from the trying itself, as in the enjoyment of playful competition.[21]

So I see some distinctive truth in both of the theories Grice discusses. His own theory is useful in bringing out the important conceptual role of the notion of willing. The Hampshire-Hart type of theory is useful in indicating that actions arise from intentions rather than from unconstrained willing.

[21] I discuss this further in "Rational Action and the Extent of Intention," *Social Theory and Practice* 9 (1973), pp. 123-42.

METAPHYSICS

15

IDENTITY AND TIME

GEORGE MYRO

I

It is not uncommon to encounter difficulties in trying to understand philosophically the relationship between the concept of time and the concept of identity. In this essay I should like to set out and recommend a proposal—which was, within my ken, first made by H. Paul Grice—concerning one group of such difficulties. The main idea of the proposal, as I see it, is that temporal qualifications—such as: today, a year ago, at noon on Saturday, 17 January 1981, and so on—should be regarded as applying systematically and uniformly (though, perhaps, in some cases, 'trivially') to all statements, including statements of identity.

What are the difficulties in question? I shall try to make them emerge from some examples (none of which is novel or exciting).

Suppose that on Monday morning I take a piece of wax and fashion it into a vase, which I then put on my mantelpiece to stand there in lonely splendour. It is no doubt admired by my friends and myself throughout Monday. But in the middle of the night I become dissatisfied. I get up, crush the vase, mould the piece of wax into a bust of Aristotle, and put it back on the mantelpiece to be admired by my friends and myself throughout Tuesday. Now, what is the relationship between the vase, the bust of Aristotle, and the piece of wax?

Suppose that a wooden ship which once sailed around the world is put into the centre of a market-place as a public monument to the world-circumnavigation. For one reason or another, various planks and pieces of wood are gradually removed from the ship and replaced by new ones—until one day not a single bit of the original wood remains in the old ship. Meanwhile, the original planks and pieces of wood have been transported to Texas and reassembled there into a ship very much like the one which stands in the centre of the market-place. Now, what is the relationship between the two ships and the wood which has been transported?

It is easy to come up with further examples of this sort. We ourselves are rather like the ship in the market-place. For we are told that in the course of time our own planks are replaced by others, and the ones which are removed from us no doubt go into other ships. Invite a group of people to a party, and in all probability at the end each will contain some atoms from each.

The second example—about the ship—raises a special problem which I am *not* going to discuss. And that is: which of the two ships —the one in the market-place or the one in Texas (if either)—is the 'original' ship—the one which sailed around the world? I shall suppose that it is the ship in the market-place which is the 'original' one. But I think that the points which I shall be making can be made *mutatis mutandis* if one opts for any other plausible alternative.

The example about the ship can be extended a bit to raise a question which appears to be another instance of the sort I want to discuss. Suppose the ship in the market-place (in spite of the replacement of wood) deteriorates beyond repair. So that the city may not lose a famous public monument and tourist attraction, the city fathers arrange to have the other ship transported back from Texas and set up in the market-place in place of the decayed one. Now, what is the relationship between the two ships and the tourist-attracting monument?

Well, what is difficult about these questions? Let us confine ourselves to the piece of wax. It would have been natural for me to say on Monday: this piece of wax is a vase (if for some reason this is not obvious to my friends). And also: this vase is a piece of wax (though of course cunningly shaped). For this and other reasons, it seems not unnatural to conclude that the vase is *identical* with the (cunningly shaped) piece of wax. And on Tuesday it would have been equally natural to say: this piece of wax is a bust of Aristotle—and also: this bust of Aristotle is a (in a different way cunningly shaped) piece of wax—and to conclude in a parallel fashion that the bust of Aristotle is *identical* with the (in a different way cunningly shaped) piece of wax. But it would be not at all natural to say that my vase is *identical* with my bust of Aristotle (unless by way of aesthetic judgement). Let us review: the vase is *identical* with the piece of wax, and the bust is *identical* with the piece of wax, but the vase is *not identical* with the bust. Do we have a break-down of the transitivity of identity? Again, the piece of wax is to be found on the mantelpiece on Tuesday, but the vase is not. Do we have a more general break-down of Leibniz's Law? Or is it that, contrary to appearances, we do not have cases of identity here? Or what?

I believe there is some tendency, when confronted with examples and questions such as these, to take refuge in one or another of several familiar philosophical positions, some extreme ones among which are:

(1) Change is an illusion. Nothing really changes.
(2) The world really consists of imperishable substances or sub-strata, which in the course of change acquire and lose characteristics.
(3) The world really consists of momentary entities (events?) none of which exists, or, perhaps, even *can* exist, over a period of time, and change consists in the succession of some of these by others.

Perhaps one a little less extreme is:

(4) The world really consists of space-time 'worms' which overlap here and then, share 'temporal slices'.

I am sure there are others. Indeed, there are two more which have a certain contemporary appeal. One of these is:

(5) There is no concept of identity *tout court*. Identity is always relativized to a concept.

When we think of things as being the same, we must always be going on to specify: the *same what*. Thus we should not either affirm or deny that the vase is just identical with the bust. Rather, we should affirm that the vase is the *same piece of wax* as the bust, and of course deny that the vase is the *same vase* or the *same bust* or the *same artifact* as the bust. Something like this position has been advocated by Peter Geach (who, incidentally, regards Frege as an ally in this). And the other of the two positions is:

(6) In spite of appearances, the relationships between the vase and the piece of wax, and the bust and the piece of wax, are not relationships of *identity*. Rather, they are relationships of '*constitution*'. The vase is only constituted, or made out of, the piece of wax, and so is the bust. There are other cases in which we might be misled into thinking that we have a relationship of identity. Thus in the extension of my example about the ship, one might be inclined to think that the tourist-attraction is *identical* with the first ship, and also with the second ship. And then be baffled by the fact that the two ships are not identical and have different characteristics. (And perhaps to

escape the bafflement be enticed into position (5), confining oneself to saying that the two ships are the *same tourist-attraction* but of course not the *same ship*.) But what we should realize is that each ship only functions as, or plays the role of, the tourist attraction. The various difficulties arise out of mistaking either of two special relations—that of *constitution* and that of *function*—for the relation of identity. Something like this position has been advocated by David Wiggins (who, incidentally, suggests that this view is an interpretation of Aristotle).

I shall not be able to discuss even these last two positions—Geach's and Wiggins's—systematically. I shall simply summarize some results of reflection on them and then go on to outline Grice's approach to the difficulties. I am not *fully* convinced that Grice's approach is completely correct or completely adequate, but I find it the most attractive of those familiar to me. And perhaps in the end it is not really incompatible with the others but only emphasizes something which they do not.

In his book *Identity and Spatio-Temporal Continuity*, Wiggins, in setting out his own position, criticizes Geach's. I am not convinced that Wiggins succeeds in showing Geach's theory to be untenable; but he does succeed, I think, in calling attention to difficulties within it. I think he makes three main points in connection with this.

1. The concept of identity is strongly linked with Leibniz's Law, and this connection cannot be seriously weakened without winding up with a concept of something other than identity.
2. Geach's notion of concept-relative identity is in various ways at odds with Leibniz's Law and so is a poor candidate for a notion of identity.
3. Cases of the sort which might be regarded as supporting Geach's position—my examples are of this sort—can be better accounted for by an alternative theory—Wiggins's—which is not at odds with Leibniz's Law.

It is common ground between the two theories that we do, and perhaps must, use constructions of the sort: A is the same F as B. But whereas Geach holds that such constructions express identity relative to the concept F between A and B (and that there is no relation of just plain identity), Wiggins maintains that such constructions express just plain identity—and also something else—(and that there is no relation of concept-relative identity). Let us take a brief look at how Wiggins proposes to interpret constructions of this sort. I think his proposal for my examples amounts to the following:

The vase is the same piece of wax as the bust

should be understood as tantamount to:

The piece of wax of which the vase is constituted is identical with the piece of wax of which the bust is constituted

and

The first ship is the same tourist-attraction as the second ship

should be interpreted somewhat as follows:

The tourist-attraction as which the first ship functions is identical with the tourist-attraction as which the second ship functions.

(Note that 'the tourist-attraction' must be regarded as picking out not a *type* of tourist-attraction—e.g. '(a ship which is the) centre-piece of a public place', but a particular *instance* of a tourist-attraction—e.g. 'the centre-piece of *that* market-place, *to wit*, the ship or replica of the ship which circumnavigated the world'. For the city in question might contain a further ship in the centre of a second market-place, commemorating whatever you please; and even come later to contain a still further ship in the centre of the first market-place commemorating, say, a naval victory.)

The point I want to stress is that on Wiggins's view, we have in each of the two cases three distinct objects, none of which is identical with either of the other two. In the first case: the vase, the bust, and the tourist-attraction; in the second case: the first ship, the second ship, and the tourist-attraction. It will also be seen that in parallel fashion we have two further distinct objects: the 'original' wood, and the 'new' wood.

It seems to me that Wiggins's proposal has four major objectionable features:

1. It multiplies senses. A statement of the form: A is B—has besides the predicative interpretation, five others, namely:

A is identical with B
A constitutes B
A is constituted of B
A functions as B
A is something which B functions as

But a statement of the form: A is the same F as B—has in principle (in addition to Wiggins's special sense (roughly): A is identical with B, and A is 'essentially' F) twenty-five different interpretations. For the general form of analysis of such a statement is (if I am right):

The F thing which stands in relation W to A is identical with the F thing which stands in relation W' to B

and we have a choice of five relations for W and for W', namely the five just enumerated as senses of: A is B. Such opportunity for ambiguity and equivocation is to be avoided if possible.

2. It multiplies entities. And this in two ways. First, there is a multiplicity of *types* of particulars:[1] there are familiar objects, such as vases and ships; and there are pieces of stuff which constitute these objects, such as pieces of wax and masses of wood; and then there are role- or function-particulars which familiar objects play or perform, such as landmarks, monuments, and tourist-attractions. And, second, there is a potentially indefinite multiplicity of *particulars* in any given place at a given time. In the centre of the market-place at a given time there is the tourist-attraction, and also the ship, and also the collection of planks. On my mantelpiece on Monday there is the vase, and also the piece of wax. But what if the piece of organic matter which is wax on Monday and Tuesday is transformed (through my switching from art to chemistry) into plastic by Wednesday? We should have to say that the piece of organic matter was on my mantelpiece on Monday —in company with the vase and the piece of wax. And what if (through advancing to nuclear physics) I transmute the piece of solid stuff from organic matter into metal by Thursday? Then the piece of solid stuff must have been there in company with the vase, the piece of wax, and the piece of organic matter. Is there here a stopping point beyond which one could not conceive of going? Such multiplicity seems undesirable.

3. Though Wiggins succeeds in preserving the link between identity and Leibniz's Law, he fails to account for a connection between

[1] This multiplicity seems to remain in Grice's proposal as well.

Leibniz's Law and the supposed relations of constitution and function. For they seem to behave with respect to Leibniz's Law very much like identity. If my vase weighs two pounds, has a tulip-shape, is pale yellow, smells nice, and is located in the centre of the mantelpiece, so, on Monday, does the piece of wax—and not, it seems, by a possibly surprising law of nature. On a given day, the wood, the ship, and the tourist-attraction cast the same shadow, skin the same knees, and feed the same termites. It would further complicate Wiggins's theory if we were to account for these facts along the following lines:

> 'weighs two thousand pounds' sometimes means: (literally) weighs two thousand pounds—sometimes means: is constituted out of something which (literally) weighs two thousand pounds —sometimes means: is something as which something which (literally) weighs two thousand pounds functions—etc.

More dubiously and with various restrictions, something analogous seem to hold for the relation of being the same F. If the vase is the same piece of wax as the bust, then if the vase weighs two pounds, so does the bust. But here we are perhaps prepared to see that this is so only given the law of nature to the effect that, normally, a piece of wax does not (appreciably) change in weight over an approximately short period of time. And certainly, it is not the case that if the vase has a tulip shape, so does the bust.

4. It fails to explain how the wood fails to be a ship—even though the wood is shaped like a ship, floats like a ship, conveys cargo like a ship, etc. The wood is *awfully* ship-like!

At this point I must say that both Geach's and Wiggins's theses appear to be designed to account also for various types of cases other than those of my examples. To take one instance, if Jones is both the mayor of the city and the dean of the college, we might be at first tempted into holding that the mayor is identical with the dean and then be baffled by our willingness to say that the mayor declared a city-wide curfew together with our reluctance to say that the dean did. Geach would propose to help us out by distinguishing between two identity relations: being the *same man* (which the mayor and dean are) and being the *same official* (which the mayor and dean are not). Wiggins would propose to help us out by holding that there are three *distinct* particulars here: Jones, the mayor, and the dean, of which the first *functions* as each of the other two. Both proposals are supposed to account for the apparent break-down of Leibniz's Law.

Now it seems that for cases such as this one, also, something very much like (a restricted) Leibniz's Law does hold for the relations between any two of: Jones, the mayor, and the dean. If any one of these is blond, plays tennis, and has three daughters, so does each of the other two—and not, it seems, as the result of any law of nature.

I mention cases of *this* sort mainly to point out that the proposal which I shall espouse is not designed to deal with them. Very roughly, there are various sorts of cases in which our inclination to attribute identity comes into conflict with our inclination to accept Leibniz's Law without qualification. In some of these cases, the difficulty can be traced to *time*; in others it cannot. The proposal I shall espouse is designed to deal only with the former.

With respect to *such* cases—let us return to my vase made out of wax—Wiggins's acceptance of Leibniz's Law in an unrestricted and, in particular, unqualified-with-respect-to-time form forces him to deny identity between the vase and the piece of wax. For they (and similarly for other cases involving time) have different life histories. The vase exists for only one day. The piece of wax, longer. But now special provision must be made so that the 'new' alleged relation between the vase and the piece of wax exemplifies some principle rather like Leibniz's Law. For the vase and the piece of wax *must* share a great many properties. Geach relativizes identity to concepts right from the start and, along with this, proposes a form of Leibniz's Law relativized to concepts. The relation between the vase and the piece of wax continues to appear to be something *like* identity.

The scope of this essay precludes further discussion of ways[2] of dealing with the difficulties different from the way proposed by Grice.

It was, if I recollect correctly, in the summer of 1971 that a group met weekly in Berkeley to discuss Wiggins's then new book and the issues it raised. We kept running into difficulties. Towards the end of one of the later meetings (perhaps the last), Paul Grice said he thought the solution (to the difficulties raised by cases involving *time*) was that A could be identical with B at one time and fail to be identical with B at another. My own (unspoken) reaction to this was that this was 'one of those ideas of Paul's', ingenious and boldly simple in initial conception and incapable of being coherently worked out in full detail. I set to reflecting just where the attempt at a full working out would break down. To my surprise, no such point came into view. So I continued,

---

[2] For a recent discussion and references, see Griffin, N., *Relative Identity*, Clarendon Press, Oxford, 1977.

now with the growing conviction that the proposal might be viable. As the shape of a fairly full coherent working-out became clear, insuperable paradoxes came into view. But further scrutiny showed not only that they were superable, merely apparent, but that they were clues to further insights. In all of this I was immeasurably helped by Paul Grice's generosity with his ideas and in other ways, as well as by suggestions of students, both here, at Berkeley, and at the University of Minnesota in Minneapolis. It now seems to me that this 'one of those ideas of Paul's' is correct and an idea of great philosophical fruitfulness. Since I have, over the years, had relevantly similar experiences with quite a number of ideas Paul Grice has put forth, I have formed a 'Grice Rule': If what he says strikes me initially as 'can't be right', then it is almost certainly right; if what he says strikes me initially as 'almost certainly right', then it can't be right. The correctness of this rule has been borne out over and over again. Obviously, it would not be in good taste for me to reveal whether Paul Grice has ever said anything that struck me initially as 'almost certainly right'.

Let us, then, try to deal with the difficulties which emerge from the examples with which I began by deploying Grice's idea that A can be identical with B at one time and fail to be identical with B at another. I think that we should not regard this as a 'new' notion of identity, relativized, identity-at-a-time—any more than we should, in dealing with an object changing from being red to being green, regard outselves as needing a 'new' notion of being red, relativized, being-red-at-a-time. The idea is simply that we should regard statements—*not excluding statements of identity*—as subject to temporal qualifications in a systematic and uniform way. Thus, we are to envisage having in a 'regimented' sort of way:

> at t, A is red
> at t′, A is green (not red)

and:

> at t, A = B
> at t′, A ≠ B

such that, in suitable circumstances, *both* members of each pair are true.

For my example of the vase and the bust of Aristotle made, at various times, from the same piece of wax, we should have as true:

> on Monday, the piece of wax = the vase
> on Monday, the piece of wax is on the mantelpiece

> on Monday, the vase is on the mantelpiece
> on Tuesday, the piece of wax is on the mantlepiece
> on Tuesday, the vase is not on the mantelpiece
> on Tuesday, the piece of wax ≠ the vase
> on Tuesday, the piece of wax = the bust of Aristotle
> at *all* times, the vase ≠ the bust of Aristotle

This raises at once questions about Leibniz's Law. Well, we are envisaging imposing temporal qualifications on statements in general, systematically and uniformly. We would, for example, say:

> at *all* times, if A is red, then A is not green.

Why should we not treat Leibniz's Law in the same way:

> at *all* times, if A = B, then A is F if and only if B is F

We might call this 'Leibniz's Law subject (like other statements) to temporal qualification'. We now see why, *on Monday*, the vase and the piece of wax *must* share properties, such as being on the mantelpiece, weighing two pounds, having a tulip-shape, being pale yellow, and smelling nice.

But we *do* encounter a complication. For it seems that, *on Monday*, the piece of wax has the property of going to be, on Tuesday, on the mantelpiece, whereas the vase lacks this property. But also we see what to do about this complication. For the property in question, representable by the open sentence:

> on Tuesday, x is on the mantelpiece

is one the possession of which *at any time* is *dependent* on the possession of another property—namely, being on the mantelpiece —at a certain time or times—namely, on Tuesday. And this is reflected in the open sentence representing the property in question by the actual occurrence of a temporal qualification—namely, 'on Tuesday'.

So the general way of dealing with the complication is to divide properties into those which are '*time-free*'—like being on the mantelpiece—which are represented by open sentences *not* containing temporal qualifications, and those which are '*time-bound*'—like being on the mantelpiece on Tuesday—which are represented by open sentences which do contain temporal qualifications. And what must be done is that 'Leibniz's Law subject (like other statements) to temporal qualification' is to be, in addition, *restricted* to properties which are '*time-free*'

—properly represented by open sentences (or 'predicates') which do not (relevantly) contain temporal qualifications.[3]

One may reasonably feel that this additional restriction is *no* addition within the spirit of the original idea but only an addition within the letter. For the original idea envisages that on Monday, the piece of wax is identical with the vase, while on Tuesday the piece of wax is, but the vase is not, on the mantelpiece. Should we, then, not, in all consistency, envisage that on Monday the piece of wax is, but the vase is not, *going to be on Tuesday* on the mantelpiece? The additional restriction on 'Leibniz's Law subject (like other statements) to temporal qualification' is merely a reflection of this point.

It now appears that it may very well be the case that at any given time A and B are identical even though their life-histories differ.

What can be done to make clear whether this is or is not the correct account of the matter? This itself is not clear. One thing that can be done is to set out a general theoretical account of the logical relationships among statements, with studied attention to temporal qualification. If no hitches develop, one can then attempt to survey how well the general theoretical account concords with what we seem to see with respect to particular cases and topics.

II

Nowadays, a favourite method of setting out a general theoretical account of logical relations among statements is to describe a 'formal' or 'formalized' 'system' and then give more or less detailed hints for correlating suitable elements of this system with statements expressed in the vernacular. A system of this sort—let us call it System G— which incorporates Grice's idea that statements of identity, along with other statements, are to be subject to temporal qualification, and, indeed, in such a way that in some cases at t, A = B, while at t', A ≠ B, can, indeed, be described. I shall here try to convey a general idea of the system and give a more precise characterization elsewhere.

[3] Obviously, quite a bit more could be said about this. One can easily get worried about the quasi-metaphysical notion of the possession of a property at all times being *dependent* on the possession of another property at a certain time or times. And one may have Goodmanesque (*à la 'grue'*) worries about corresponding open sentences or 'predicates'. The starting point would seem to be that being 'time-free' is intimately connected with being a property such that it is possible to have it at one time and fail to have it at another, independently of any purely temporal ordering of the times in question.

System G is really a rather minor modification of a standard Predicate Calculus with Identity (PCI) designed to fulfil three desiderata:

1. it permits us to express the idea that so-and-so is the case at one time but not at another, and, in particular,
2. permits us to express the idea that a particular thing exists at one time but not at another, and
3. permits us to express the idea that thing A and thing B are identical at one time but not at another.

No doubt, these desiderata can be attained in a number of alternative ways. Indeed, Grice himself has registered to me his strong dislike of various features of the way I have chosen. But I find it the most attractive and so steam ahead.[4]

1. Syntactically, that so-and-so is the case at time t will be represented by prefixing a symbol for time t to a formula which is, in the first instance, simply one of the familiar ones of PCI or augmented by Parsons' Operator discussed below, separating the two, for ease of reading with a bar. For example:

$$t \mid (Fa \,\&\, \exists x(Gx \,\&\, Hxa)), t \mid [b] \, Fb$$

Such expressions are, of course, to be subject to truth-functions. But it also proves convenient to allow quantifiers occurring outside of the scope of a time-symbol but binding variables within that scope, predication with respect to and quantification over time-symbols themselves, and subjecting such expressions, in turn, to temporal qualification. Thus, for example:

$$\exists t \, t \mid \exists x(\exists t' \exists t'' \, (t < t'' \,\&\, t' \mid Fx \,\&\, t'' \mid \sim Fx))$$

Such expressions are to be called 'proto-formulae' and are to be divided into two kinds: those in which any individual variables and constants have occurrences outside the scope of any time-symbol are to be *merely proto-formulae* and *proto-sentences*. and only those in which this feature is not found are to be *formulae* and *sentences*.

2. Syntactically, that a particular object *exists* at time t will be represented by a device which is a modification of an idea of Paul Grice's put forward in another connection.[5]

---

[4] It may be worth noting that a number of the other ways, including a 'tense-logic', may be obtained from the one I have chosen essentially as *notational variants*, 'by definition'. (At least, if enough 'rules' or 'axioms' characterizing the 'nature of time' are incorporated.)

[5] Grice, H. P., 'Vacuous Names' in Davidson, D. and Hintikka, J., *Words*

This idea drives a wedge between the notions of 'some' and 'all', represented by quantification, on the one hand, and the notion of existence, represented by an additional device, on the other. It allows (or can be easily adapted to allow) us to say truly that *something* (i.e. Pegasus) is a winged horse—even though Pegasus does not exist, and, indeed, there do not exist any winged horses—without 'onto-logical commitment' to Pegasus or winged horses. Similarly, we might want to say that *someone* (say Plato) is now admired, exerts influence, and excels every living philosopher—even though he no longer exists and there does not now and, indeed, could not now exist anyone excelling (in philosophy) every living philosopher.

The main idea of Grice's proposal can be explained briefly thus. He wishes to extend the notion of '*scope*' to individual-symbols and truth-functional connectives, and thereby distinguish, for example:

It is not the case that Pegasus is in the San Francisco Zoo.

from:

Pegasus is not in the San Francisco Zoo.

In the former, negation has the largest 'scope', the existence of Pegasus is not required for the truth of the whole, and the whole is in fact true. Whereas in the latter, the name 'Pegasus' has the largest scope, the existence of Pegasus is, consequently, required for the truth of the whole, and so the whole is false (or, some might want to say: has no truth-value).

The details of Grice's actual proposal are rather complicated. But the idea important for our purposes is that there should be a way to indicate 'scope' of individual-symbols. And this idea can be easily exploited by adopting a simplifying suggestion of Charles Parsons'. So let us introduce a device (call it *Parsons' Operator*) consisting of an individual-symbol within square brackets to be prefixable to formulae and proto-formulae, so that we may distinguish between, for example,

Fb

and

[b] Fb

and Objections, Dordrecht, D. Reidel, 1969. I am also attracted by the idea of simply representing existence by a predicate: $t \mid Ex$ — instead of: $t \mid [x]\ x = x$. This is a saving of one syntactical construction and two 'inference-rules'. For I have been so far unable to discern any distinctive logical features of an existence-predicate within a system of the present general sort.

The former does not require for its truth the existence of b, whereas the latter does. The 'inference rules' governing this device are essentially;

$$[\beta]\, \phi \vdash \phi$$

$$\phi,\, [\beta]\, \psi \vdash [\beta].\phi$$

It will be seen that one proto-formula which is true if and only if a exists is: [a] a = a—but there are infinitely many others.

3. Syntactically, that A is identical with B at t has already been provided for:

$$t \mid a = b$$

I trust that a good enough idea of the 'formation rules' of System G has been conveyed. The details are to be published elsewhere.

In matters of this kind, it is customary to turn one's attention to the 'semantics' of the system being described. About this I will keep mum at the present. I shall make some remarks which, I hope, will be helpful, and a fairly precise discussion of two different 'semantics' will be published elsewhere.

Instead, I shall here try to give a general idea of the 'inference-rules' of System G.

The 'inference-rules' are really a rather minor modification of standard 'natural deduction' rules for PCI. I shall briefly sketch the main differences. The details are in a discussion to be published elsewhere.

1. Only *sentences* (i.e. not expressions which are merely *proto-sentences*) are to form lines in a derivation.

2. All but one (the 'introduction of premisses (suppositions) rule') of the familiar 'rules' have both 'Internal' and 'External' versions —depending upon whether the 'inferential transformation' takes place *within* the scope of a time-symbol or *not*—but are with an exception to be noted, otherwise unchanged. I think the idea is best got across by illustration:

'Internal'	'External'
k | (Fa & Fb)	k | Fa & k | Fb
∴ k | Fa	k | Fa
k | ∀xFx	∀t t | Fa
∴ k | Fa	∴ k | Fa

'*Internal*'   '*External*'

   k | ∀t t | Fa
∴ k | k | Fa

   k′ | Fa   k | Fb
∴ k′ | ∀xFx   ∴ ∀t t | Fb

   k′ | k | Fb
∴ k′ | ∀t t | Fb

for the last three: *provided* 'the constant in question:—'a' or 'k',
as appropriate—does not occur in the 'inferred' line or any of the
'premisses (suppositions)' of the 'given' line.

3. The exception of a familiar 'rule' which undergoes a further
modification is—as may be expected from previous discussion—the
'Internal' version of Leibniz's Law. The idea is that given, for example,

   k | a = b

and any formula,

   k | . . . .

one may infer any formula

   k | – – – – – – – –

which results from replacing occurrences of 'a' by occurrences of 'b'
or *vice versa—provided no such replacement has taken place at an
occurrence which is within the scope of an occurrence of some time-
symbol other than 'k'*. This is the 'formal' upshot of our discussion of
'time-free' and 'time-bound' properties/predicates.

4. Some 'rules' are needed to govern the new devices. The two
needed for Parsons' Operator have already been discussed. Three are
needed for temporal qualification.

   k | ϕ ⊢ ϕ—*provided ϕ is a sentence*

    ϕ ⊢ k | ϕ—(ϕ is already required to be a *sentence*)
   ~k | ϕ ⊣ ⊢ k | ~ϕ

5. Presumably, 'rules' (or 'axioms') will be wanted to characterize
the 'nature of time', for example:

$$\wedge \vdash (k < k' \ \& \ k' < k'') \supset k < k''$$

$$\wedge \vdash k < k' \supset \exists \ t(k < t \ \& \ t < k')$$

and/or others, though these may be regarded as outside the 'formal' development of the system.

It may be helpful to give as an illustration a derivation correct both downwards and upwards (if taken to be not part of a larger derivation):

$$k \mid \forall x Fx$$
$$k \mid Fa$$
$$k' \mid k \mid Fa$$
$$k' \mid \forall x \ k \mid Fx$$

This completes the sketch of the 'syntax' of System G. We must now try to tackle matters 'semantical'.

III

There is a familiar way, or cluster of ways, of describing the 'semantics' of a system such as System G. It is said to be done in a 'meta-language', which is usually a more or less 'regimented' (sometimes *very much* 'regimented') version of English (or some other 'natural language'). But the problems with which we have started are, in part, problems about the nature of English (and similar languages). Are statements of identity subject to temporal qualification in such a way that A can be identical with B at one time but not at another? If so, then one might want, in describing in English the 'semantics' of System G, to bring into prominence those features of English which are relevantly related to this fact. This seems to amount to saying that in using English as the 'meta-language' for this purpose, one might want to 'regiment' it into, in effect, an interpreted version of System G. For, perhaps, only thus can one describe the 'semantics' of System G in a clear and coherent way. It seems to me, reasonably clearly, that at least one *can* do this by proceeding in this way.

Supposing it is so, one may still harbour worries about what it shows. One cannot help having some lingering feeling that one is pulling oneself up by one's boot-straps. Still, doing the job may be illuminating and thought-provoking.

Fortunately, however, it is possible to describe a sort of 'semantics' for System G in a version of English 'regimented' in such a way as to keep entirely out of prominence those features with which System G is designed to deal. This may convince one of the viability of System G (whatever exactly that may mean). But because of the way this job is done, it carries with it a pressure to think that the viability of System G thus demonstrated does not show that identity is variant with respect to time, but, rather, the opposite. For, in this way of describing the 'semantics' of System G, the objects 'semantically correlated' to the elements of the system are not—at least, explicitly regarded as—capable of being identical at one time and not at another. Some form of mildly recondite tinkering brings it about that expressions of System G which notationally suggest time-variant identity come out, or turn out to be capable of coming out, true.

Thus we are caught between two fires: either describing the 'semantics' in what might appear to be a question-begging way or describing it in a way which might make it appear that the system fails to represent time-variant identity.

My own opinion is that the first approach does give the 'correct', intended 'semantics' of System G in its application to the vicissitudes of things in the course of time. The second approach gives only a *simulated* 'semantics' by attending to an assemblage of objects *at one time*, or unchanging over time, which is in a way isomorphic to the vicissitudes in the course of time. But the second approach, being more familiar, is still capable of making clear important features of System G.

My procedure will be to discuss some issues, clarity concerning which seems to help with the first approach, and then to sketch its gist. A concise formulation of it and of the second approach is in a discussion to be published elsewhere.

I have suggested that regarding Leibniz's Law as subject to temporal qualification—including the restriction to 'time-free' conditions—clears the way for the thesis that identity—like all other 'time-free' properties and relations—is subject to time. But there is another obstacle, or cluster of obstacles, in the way. I believe that a discussion of this will throw light on a plethora of puzzles and discomforts.

The business with Leibniz's Law may be granted to make clear how it might be that, today, the ship is identical with the wood, even though, a year ago, the ship was (still) in the market-place, but the wood was not (was in the lumber-yard). But (it may be said) if, today, the ship is truly identical with the wood, then, today, there is just *one*—relevantly prominent—object in the centre of the market-place, and what about *this object*, a year ago—was it in the market-place or was it not (was it in the lumber-yard)? We seem to have a paradox.

I would like to make a general suggestion for dealing with this sort of difficulty. The suggestion summarily put, is that in order to consider (in a familiar way) with respect to an object whether it is at time t such-and-such, one must identify or single-out the object by means of a condition which the object satisfies *at t* uniquely. And for this purpose, a condition which an object satisfies *at some other time* uniquely may prove insufficient.

The application of the suggestion to the illustrative puzzle is as follows: if we wish to discuss the whereabouts *a year ago* of an object, it is not enough to identify the object as the *one* which is *today* in the centre of the market-place. We must identify the object as the *one* which was *a year ago* such-and-such. It does not matter *what* condition we use, *provided* it is one which the object satisfied *a year ago* uniquely. For example, all three conditions: being today in the centre of the market-place, being a ship which is today in the centre of the market-place, being (a mass of) wood which is today in the centre of the market-place—are candidates for identifying conditions. But, in our example, the first of these conditions was *not*, and only the other two *were*, uniquely satisfied a year ago. So the first condition *will not do* for discussion of the whereabouts a year ago of any object, while the other two *will*. And now we have a non-paradoxical answer to our question—or, rather, non-paradoxical answers to our answerable questions: the ship which is today in the market-place was in the market-place a year ago; the wood which is today in the market-place was not (was in the lumber-yard).

It is tempting to see the situation in a different light. Someone says to us: where was that (pointing?) object (which is now in the centre of the market-place) a year ago? We do not know how to answer, knowing that the ship was (still) in the market-place, but the wood was in the lumber-yard. We say: what do you mean—the ship in the market-place or the wood in the market-place? Only when he answers, can we, in turn, answer. It is tempting to interpret this as our asking *which of two different objects* in the centre of the market-place does he mean (or is he or might he be interested in).

But this is not the only way to see the situation. We can think of our asking him what he means not as asking which of two different objects he means, but, rather, as asking which of two different answerable questions he (is or might be interested in) posing:

A year ago: the object which was (*then*) uniquely a ship which is today uniquely in the market-place, where was it?

A year ago: the object which was (*then*) uniquely (a mass of) wood which is today uniquely in the market-place, where was it?

The suggestion is that we must try to find out which of these questions he (is or might be interested in) posing because his spoken question, taken *au pied de la lettre*, is:

A year ago: the object which was *then* uniquely an object which is today uniquely in the market-place, where was it?

and as such is unanswerable, since (*ex hypothesi*) there was *not* a year ago any uniquely such object. The condition of being in the centre of the market-place *is* uniquely satisfied *today*. But the condition of being today uniquely in the market-place was *not* uniquely satisfied a year ago.

The suggestion I am making is this. A statement which can be regarded as of the form:

The A thing is at t B

is to be further regarded as being of the form:

At t, the (then) uniquely A thing is B

allowing for suitable reworking of the phrase represented by 'A'. If we make the supposition that a Russellian treatment is to be accorded to such forms, and use '1xAx' to represent[6]: x is uniquely A—we shall have:

$$t \mid \exists x(1xAx \ \& \ Bx)$$

We may illustrate this with respect to our example in, one may hope, suggestive notation:

The ship in the market-place (today) was last year in the market-place.

$$1 \mid \exists x(1x(Sx \ \& \ t \mid 1xMx) \ \& \ Mx)$$

The wood in the market-place (today) was last year not in the market-place

$$1 \mid \exists x(1x(Wx \ \& \ t \mid 1xMx) \ \& \ \sim Mx)$$

[6] Notation of the form: $1x \ldots x \ldots$ may be regarded as abbreviating: $\forall y(\ldots y \ldots \equiv y = x)$—where the dotted lines represent any proto-formulae differing only in the replacement of the variables at all free occurences. An inductive procedure is needed to specify such abbreviations with full strictness and generality, if elimination of such abbreviation is to be unique. I suppress Parsons' Operator as inessential to the discussion.

These form a consistent[7] set with:

t | ∃x 1xMx

that is: today there is just *one* object in the market-place.

Notice that the two statements:

t | ∃x(1xMx & 1 | Mx)

t | ∃x(1xMx & 1 | ~Mx)

which generate an air of paradox are actually mutually consistent and, indeed, are (in our example) both true. Because of the proposed re-interpretation of Leibniz's Law, they do not generate the inconsistent:

t | ∃x(1x Mx & 1 | Mx & 1 | ~Mx)

and—it is being suggested—they are *not* to be read as:

The object (today) in the market-place was last year in the market-place.

The object (today) in the market-place was last year not in the market-place.

These would be represented by:

1 | ∃x(1x t | 1xMx & Mx)

1 | ∃x(1x t | 1xMx & ~Mx)

and these are (since we are adopting the Russellian treatment) both false, because

1 | ∃x 1x t | 1x Mx

is false.

I believe that if we reject the supposition that a Russellian treatment is to be accorded to statements of the sort under discussion, we shall be able to give a more elaborate account which will, nevertheless, dispel the air of paradox more or less along the same lines.[8]

---

[7] Though in the absence of 'semantics' for system G, consistency would be undefined—except 'syntactically', e.g. not generating both φ and ~φ *via* the 'rules of reference'.

[8] I venture to suggest that more or less the same approach is to be adopted with respect to statements involving (alethic) modality. Roughly, a statement of the form:

The A thing could have been B.

is to be construed along the lines:

I have said that for a discussion whether a certain object is at t such-and-such, the object must be identified or singled out by some condition which *at t* it satisfies uniquely. I have said that, in general, it does not matter what this condition is, *provided* the requirement is fulfilled. But one should expect that we would want to have available to us conditions which would allow us to discuss the state of an object at any and every time by being satisfied by that object uniquely at any and every time—and, indeed, '*a priori*'. Such conditions are available as conjunctions of conditions which (as an '*a priori*' matter) an object satisfies at *all* times with conditions which an object satisfies uniquely at some time. Thus, some object is at all times uniquely an object which (as an '*a priori*' matter) at all times[9] is a ship and today is uniquely in the market-place. And so we can discuss the vicissitudes in the course of time of *the ship which is today in the market-place* and of *the (mass of) wood which is today in the market-place* and make such remarks as that the ship in question is at some time identical with and at other times distinct from the (mass of) wood in question.

One may see here room for a notion of being 'essentially' a ship or being 'essentially' a (mass of) wood. And in a discussion to be published elsewhere I have set out a compressed account of an attempt to spell out such a notion.

IV

I believe that attention to matters of the sort discussed above will help to resolve similar puzzles which may arise when we move to more explicitly 'semantical' considerations. For example, one may wish to consider for what values of the variable 'x' the formula '1| Mx' (in the intended interpretation) comes out true (within the context of our example). And one may come to feel that the variable cannot be regarded as taking (*inter alia*) as value the alleged *single*—relevantly prominent—object which is today in the centre of the market-place. For would the formula come out true or false for that value of the

> In some possible world, the object which is ('there') uniquely A is B

again allowing for suitable reworking of the phrase represented by 'A'. For example:

> In some possible world, today, the object which is ('there', 'now') uniquely [a ship which is *in this world*, today, uniquely in the market-place] is (made of/identical with a mass of) steel.

[9] Or, at any rate, at all times at which it *exists*. There seem to be options as to how to construe remarks about the state of objects at times which they do not exist.

variable—in view of the fact that the ship was, while the wood was not, in the market-place last year? One is moved to hold that the formula comes out true for the ship as value of 'x' and comes out false for the wood as value of 'x'. And then one is further moved to hold that there are, therefore after all, *two* objects involved.[10]

The point to keep in mind is that, just as in the puzzle previously discussed to consider whether the formula '1 | Mx' comes out true for a particular value of 'x'—since it involves considering whether that value of 'x' was in the market-place a year ago—requires that the value of 'x' in question be identified or singled out in some way such that it is determinate which of the objects *a year ago* it is. And simply specifying that it is the object which is *today* in the centre of the market-place is insufficient, since, though there is only one such object today, *a year ago* there were *two* objects which satisfied this condition.

We must rethink the notion of value of variable with attention to temporal qualification. The following may be suggestive, if not quite philosophically rigorous. When a variable 'takes as value' an object, then *at each time* some one object is uniquely such that *at every time* that object is the unique value of the variable. So we may speak with respect to any time, of the object which the variable 'has as value' *at that time*. Now we may consider two such 'cases' of 'taking a value'. It may happen that at some times t, the object which the variable 'has as value' in the one 'case' at t is identical at t with the object which the variable 'has as value' in the other 'case' at t; while at other times t', the object which the variable 'has as value' in the one 'case' at t' is *not* identical at t' with the object the variable 'has as value' in the other 'case' at t'. Thus, for two 'cases' of 'taking a value', there may be times such that the values of the variable are at those times identical, and times such that at those times the values of the variable are distinct. But the differences between the two 'cases' of 'taking a value' should not be promoted into a temporally unqualified distinctness of the objects 'taken as value'. The object 'taken as value' in one 'case' is at some times identical with, at other times distinct from, the object 'taken as

---

[10] This feeling is reinforced by taking a glance at what I have labelled as *simulated* 'semantics' for System G. But that is just because such 'semantics' *is simulated*. It can be described within a framework within which temporal qualifications can be suppressed, identity does not vary with respect to time, and, consequently, variation of identity with respect to time has to be *mimicked* by a certain sort of non-identity. A discussion at Stanford of the general topic of this paper prompted the first six paragraphs of this section and a reordering of the exposition. Thanks, in particular, to John Etchemendy.

value' in the other 'case'. Or, at any rate, so we should think if we allow that the ship is at some times identical with and at other times distinct from the (mass of) wood.

Now, we can see through our puzzle. In one 'case' the variable 'x' 'takes as value' the ship, in another 'case' it 'takes as value' the wood. The object which 'x' 'has as value' *today* in the first 'case' is *today* identical with the object which 'x' 'has as value' today in the second 'case'—it is, indeed, the single thing in the centre of the market-place today. But the object which x 'had as value' *last year* in the first 'case' was *not last year* identical with the object 'x' 'had as value' *last year* in the second 'case'. And the formula '1|Mx' comes out true for that object as value of 'x' which 'x' 'had as value', last year in the *first* 'case' —namely the ship—and comes out false for that object as value of 'x' which 'x' 'had as value' last year in the second 'case'—namely the wood—even though the former and the latter are *today* identical.[11]

But, perhaps, it is more philosophically rigorous to regard a 'case' of a variable 'taking as value' an object as an *ordered couple* of that variable and that object. Now it is even easier to see that (if we hold on to the view that the ship and the wood are identical today) the ordered couple ⟨'x', the ship⟩ and the ordered couple ⟨'x', the wood⟩ have *the same* second term *today*, but had *distinct* second terms *last year*. If we hold on to a principle of extensionality, we should hold that the ordered couples themselves are identical *today*, but were distinct *last year*. (And, similarly, we should hold that the 'cases' in terms of which we were thinking before were two at some times but only one at others.)[12]

This brings to mind that we must re-think our notions of *set* with attention to temporal qualification before we can employ that notion in describing the intended 'semantics' of System G. First, the relation of set-membership is to be subjected to temporal qualification: $t \mid x \in y$. So which objects belong to a set may change over time. For example, one would expect that an object belongs to the set of things which are red at all and only those times at which the object is red. But if we want to allow such sets as, for example, the set of things which were red at *some specific time t*, we encounter a complication. Let us return to our ship s and our wood w and consider the set of things which were in the market-place last year, $\hat{x}1 \mid Mx$. What belongs

[11] The failure of substitutivity in accordance with our formulation of Leibniz's Law suggests that we are dealing with '*time-bound*' notions as our reflections and a scrutiny of the 'definition of truth' confirm.

[12] Rather analogous remarks, *mutatis mutandis*, can be made about the value of a variable being at t something which does not exist at t.

to this set *today*? It seems that the ship does, for it was in the market-place last year. But today the ship is identical with the wood, so the wood belongs to the set, even though the wood was *not* in the market-place a year ago. That is, if:

$$t \mid s \in \hat{x}1 \mid Mx$$

$$t \mid s = w$$

then,

$$t \mid w \in \hat{x}1 \mid Mx$$

but,

$$\sim t \mid 1 \mid Mw$$

Is this an insurmountable paradox? We, certainly, would get a contradiction if we maintained (even with some adaptation of the usual provisions to preclude the *familiar* set-theoretic paradoxes), for any time t:

$$t \mid (x \in \hat{y} \ldots y \ldots \equiv \ldots x \ldots)$$

unless we artificially exempted the set-membership relation from substitutivity in accordance with our formulation of Leibniz's Law —artificially, because the set-membership relation does not seem '*time-bound*' and, certainly, notationally is not. But a small modification suffices to preclude contradiction. We should maintain (with some adaptation of the usual provisions to preclude the familiar set-theoretic paradoxes), instead, for all times t:

$$t \mid (x \in \hat{y} \ldots y \ldots \equiv \exists z(x = z \& \ldots z \ldots))$$

The only unpleasant consequence of this is that sets $\hat{x} \ldots x \ldots$ and $\hat{x} \sim \ldots x \ldots$ are not in every case exclusive: they may fail to be when $\ldots x \ldots$ is '*time-bound*'. So the ship, that is, the wood, is today a member both of the set of things which were in the market-place a year ago and also of the set of things which were not in the market-place a year ago. But this seems not to cause any serious difficulties. As we have already seen, ordered couples and other entities, such as functions, construed as certain kind of sets in more or less the usual ways may be identical at some times and distinct at others. For example, if today but not at other times all and only philosophers are wise, then the set of philosophers and the set of the wise are identical today but not at other times.

Because the membership of sets changes over time, it will be useful to counter-act this feature, as we move to more explicit consideration of matters 'semantical'. For example, it will be useful to have a notion of a set of ordered *n*-tuples such that all their terms are *at one time or another* members of a certain set. For example, {⟨the ship, the wood⟩} was even last year a set of ordered couples all of whose terms are *at one time or another* (namely today) members of the set of things in the market-place, even though the wood was not last year a member of that set. Another notion that is useful is that of a '*temporally rigid*' function: one which, loosely speaking, has 'same' arguments and values at all times. But words fail me here. A '*temporally rigid*' function f is one that satisfies the condition:

$$\forall t \mid \forall x \forall y(f(x) = y \supset \exists z \exists u(x = z \,\&\, y = u \,\&\, \forall t't' \mid f(z) = u))$$

We are now ready to turn our attention to the intended 'semantics' of System G.

We could give one or another 'definition of truth' for sentences (and, as it turns out, *proto-sentences*) of System G, thereby *fixing* the interpretation of its non-logical constants. It is more customary and, in various ways, more useful to give a once-and-for-all 'definition of truth with respect to a model', which leaves the interpretation of the non-logical constants *unfixed*. The intended interpretation then can be given later simply by selecting a particular 'model' as the intended one. I shall sketch a 'definition with respect to a model'.[13]

A model of the intended sort is to be any ordered quintuple of a non-empty set of objects, a non-empty set of times, a temporally-rigid function from predicates of degree *i* to sets of ordered *i*tuples all of whose terms are at one time or another members of the domain of objects (and from sentential letter to 'T' or 'F'), a temporally rigid function from individual constants to objects which are at one time or another members of the domain of objects, and a temporally-rigid function from time-constants to objects which are at one time or

---

[13] It is not clear to me, but it *may* be that this way of proceeding will not turn out to be as useful as one might expect it to be. For it may, perhaps, turn out that some 'possible' models of the intended sort will not be 'actual'. For example, it is quite likely that no 'two' objects are repeatedly identical and distinct over exactly five billion times (intervals). So there will not *be* a model of the sort described with such objects 'in it'. And this will make the 'truth in a model' approach useless for definitions of such logical notions as consequence and consistency. Perhaps this can be mitigated by adding an artificial time-ordering which will 'rearrange the times'. But, in any case, we can have recourse to the *simulated* 'semantics' for the definition of the logical notions.

another members of the domain of times. A γ-variant of a model is, as usual, a model which differs from the first at most in the value which the appropriate function has for γ as argument.

If we pay attention to temporal qualification, we will expect that explicit definitions will be of the form:

$$\forall t \mid \forall x_1 \ldots \forall x_n (F x_1 \ldots x_n \equiv --- x_1 \ldots x_n ---)$$

and inductive definitions will be of the form: $\forall t \mid$, followed by the clauses of the inductive definition. The definition of 'truth with respect to a model' is not to be an exception. We would thus define in effect 'truth with respect to a model m *at time* t'—though the proper expression of this would be of the form: $t \mid T\phi m$. A consequence of this is that we define 'truth with respect to a model' also for *proto-sentences* such as 'Mw'. But these will, in general, be true with respect to a model *at some times but not at others*. This is, of course, just what we should expect. For 'the wood is in the market-place' (temporally unqualified) is true today but was false a year ago. *Sentences* of System G, on the other hand, will, as one should expect, retain the same truth-value at all times, just as (read tenselessly) 'In year k the wood is in the market-place' does not change its truth-value over time.

Well, what about the inductive clauses of the definition of 'truth with respect to a model'? They are *exactly* the usual ones—*including* the clause for identity-sentences of the form: a = b! Except, of course, that additional clauses are needed for the devices of temporal qualification and the device used to represent existence. Of these, the novel ones are, in effect:

if ϕ is $\kappa < \kappa'$, then $T\phi m$ iff the time assigned by m to κ is earlier than the time assigned by m to κ'

if ϕ is $\kappa \mid \psi$, then $T\phi m$ iff at the time assigned by m to κ, $T\psi m$

if ϕ is $[\beta]\psi$, then $T\phi m$ iff $T\psi m$ and the object assigned by m to β exists.

Of course, we are to remember that we are supposing that our meta-language deals with temporal qualification and existence in the ways being recommended and so itself has an overall structure like that of System G.

A further observation may be of interest. If we choose to interpret some time-constant, say 'n', as having the meaning of 'now', then we should regard as an interpretation of System G a set S of models m differing only in what time is assigned to 'n' and *correlated* with t if and only if m assigns t to 'n'. Then, at any time a proto-sentence is to be true with respect to this *correlation* of the set of models if and only if the proto-sentence is true at that time with respect to the model correlated to that time. This may help us to think about McTaggartian problems about time.

I see a last bit of support for Grice's proposal concerning time and identity in the systematic consideration that, whereas the atemporal, 'absolute', notion of identity can be introduced into System G *'by definition'* as: $\forall t \; t \,|\, x = y$, Grice's conception of identity as subject to temporal qualification cannot be thus recovered from 'absolute identity'.[14]

But, *perhaps*, on the other hand, . . .

[14] I venture to suggest that the same point, *mutatis mutandis*, can be made concerning identity *vis-à-vis* (alethic) modality. Indeed, System G can be easily reinterpreted as a 'modal logic without tears', and by repeating the moves whereby System G was obtained from PCI one can obtain a 'modal temporal logic with tiers without tears'. It is also not unlikely that the formal structure of system G can be useful for detailed investigation of propositional attitudes.

16

ARISTOTLE: ESSENCE AND ACCIDENT

ALAN CODE

1. GENERAL REMARKS ON THE PROJECT

In order to make sense of the development of Aristotle's thought on predication and his debt to Plato, it is necessary to see his metaphysical investigations against a shared background of problems, principles, and concepts. It is important to see both the *Categories* and the middle books of the *Metaphysics* as rejecting some of, but continuous with, Platonic metaphysics. The scope of *Metaph. Z* is determined by the question: 'What is substance?', and *Z*1 explains that this query is tantamount to the fundamental ontological question over which Aristotle and his predecessors have repeatedly puzzled: 'What is Being?'. The subsequent discussion in Book *Z*, seen by Aristotle as both building and improving upon previous thought, is to a very large extent concerned with the problem of explaining (starting with an account of the applicability of words to things) the connection between the correct use of language and an objective, language-independent reality. In virtue of *what* are things (correctly) called whatever they are called? It is from Plato that he inherits both this problem and the general ontological framework within which he investigates it. The framework assumes a basic distinction between what a thing *Is* as opposed to what it *Has*, and enables both Plato and Aristotle to approach the problem by distinguishing cases in which a word is applicable to an object in virtue of what that object Is from derivative cases in which a word may be applied to some entity Y in virtue of Y's Having something that Is X (for some X appropriately related to the word in question). In the former case, but not in the latter, the entity to which the word is applied is called whatever it is called (as a result of that application) in virtue of itself: It is καθ' αὐτὸ λεγόμενον. It is in virtue of its *essence* that a substance Is the very thing that it Is.

It is impossible to understand this facet of Aristotelian essentialism, and hence impossible to understand the early history of the essence/accident distinction, without taking into account the following principle, argued for in *Metaph.* Z6:

> Z6 THESIS: All things πρῶτα καὶ καθ᾽ αὑτὰ λεγόμενα (primary and called what they are called in virtue of themselves) are one and the same as their essence.[1]

This thesis is an alternative way of expressing Aristotle's requirement that the definiens and the definiendum must, in a correct definition of a substance, signify one and the same entity. Mediating this requirement on definition and the Z6 thesis is the idea that an essence is the ontological correlate, or signification, of the definiens of such a definition.[2] In the middle books of the *Metaph.*, primary substance is *substantial form*,[3] and the definition of a primary substance says what that substance Is. The essential nature of the form (as expressed in its definition) is identical with that single subject of which its nature is essentially predicable—that is, the form itself by itself.[4] Being identical with its own essence, the account saying what it Is (the definition signifying its essence) applies to it in virtue of Being exactly what it Is. It is individual in that it is essentially predicable of itself alone.[5]

---

[1] *Metaph.* Z6, 1032ª4-6; see also 1031ᵇ11-14, 18-20; Z11, 1037ª33-ᵇ4.

[2] This interpretation of the Z6 thesis was worked out in collaboration with H. P. Grice, though its subsequent development has been my own. It was originally presented in a paper ('The Relation Betwen Form, Matter and Composite in Aristotle's *Metaphysics* Z') at a conference held by the University of Victoria in January 1979 (sponsored by the Canada Council). I argued that 1031ᵇ28-1032ª4 contains an argument for the numerical sameness of each definable substance with its essence, and that this argument involves an argument for the numerical sameness of the signification of a definiendum and the signification of the associated definiens.

[3] I rely here upon J. L. Ackrill's distinction between species and form— a contrast reflected in two distinct Aristotelian uses of the word 'εἶδος'. See 'Aristotle's Definitions of *psuche*', reprinted in *Articles on Aristotle*, vol, 4, ed. by J. Barnes, M. Schofield and R. Sorabji, Duckworth, 1979, esp. pp. 67-8. He also points out that 'man' has both its usual use (to pick out the species) and a possible use in which it refers to the form of a composite. Discussion with Professor Ackrill helped me to understand the relation between this distinction and the Z6 thesis. I also refer the reader to John A. Driscoll's detailed discussion of this distinction in 'ΕΙΔΗ in Aristotle's Earlier and Later Theories of Substance', *Studies in Aristotle*, ed. by D. J. O'Meara, Catholic University Press, 1981, pp. 129-59. This study reached me only after the writing of the present paper.

[4] εἶδος αὐτὸ καθ᾽ αὑτό (Z11, 1037ª2).

[5] See D5 and D6 is Section 2 below. The claim that Aristotle held a doctrine of *individual* form is compatible with, but does not entail, that he associated a different form with each particular material substance. For a discussion of the latter idea, see Wilfrid Sellars, 'Substance and Form in Aristotle', *Journal of Philosophy*, 54 (1957), pp. 688-9, Rogers Albritton, 'Forms of Particular

This notion of substantial form must be understood in the context of hylomorphic analysis. The *form* is the formal component of a particular hylomorphic compound, and is universal in relation to the matter of which it is predicable. By way of contrast, the *Categories*, an early treatment of some of the issues discussed in *Metaph. Z*, makes use of neither matter nor individual form. The interpretation of the recalcitrant Z6 text involves establishing its place in the development of Aristotle's views by comparing it with this earlier treatise (as well as some other relevant portions of the corpus). Only in this way can we see how and why he has expanded and modified the earlier treatment of substance and predication in order to accommodate the hylomorphic analysis of particulars.

Since Aristotle's own development as well as his strong dissent from Plato as to the structure and detail of reality, and the way language attaches to it, takes place against a shared background, we should try to give a neutral characterization of this common framework. Once such a sketch has been provided, we may investigate fundamental shifts and disagreements by formulating for each metaphysical doctrine the smallest set of principles which, when added to that framework, generate its pertinent features. Rather than following the more usual practice of discussing essentialist claims in terms of a first-order predicate calculus with modal operators, I begin by developing and expanding some ideas that my dear friend and colleague, H. P. Grice, has advanced in connection with Aristotle's *Categories*.[6] He employs two basic predication relations, which he calls 'Izzing' and 'Hazzing', when stating the definitions and specifying the operations involved in the construction of a theory of substance and categories. In extending these ideas to the interpretation of Plato and the later Aristotle, I have changed only the names, leaving as a matter for joint investigation the inquiry into what they are.

Some of Aristotle's ontological vocabulary can be understood in terms of these two basic notions, and it is possible, by displaying a number of ontological theorems couched in this terminology, to give

Substances in Aristotle's *Metaphysics*', same issue, pp. 699–708, and (more recently) Edwin Hartman, *Substance, Body, and Soul: Aristotelian Investigations*, Princeton, 1977, and Michael Frede, 'Individuen bei Aristoteles', *Antike und Abendland*, 24 (1978), pp. 16–39.

[6] In Section III ('Semantic Multiplicity and Copulative Being') of 'Aristotle on Being and Good', read at the conference mentioned in n. 2. I am indebted to his paper as well as to our discussions on this topic. Some of the formal principles and definitions in Section 2 (below) are adapted from his work.

a semi-formal treatment of many of the most interesting features of this framework. I then further enlarge the area of discussion by attempting to connect the various ontological ideas to the problem of explaining the applicability of words to things.

The main task of this paper is to show that the logic of Being and Having is a promising tool for the articulation of some of the basic ideas that Aristotle employs in his efforts to construct a sophisticated and flexible semantics together with a metaphysics of substance. Consequently, in what follows I offer the results of my own attempts to reconstruct Aristotle's understanding of Plato and the subsequent development of his own ideas on essence and accident. When characterizing and contrasting a 'Platonic' position and two Aristotelian positions (roughly, the *Cat.* and *Metaph.*), I present textual evidence and argument in order to make the main outline of my interpretation plausible, but still more detailed analysis of individual passages and arguments is required to sustain it. Often my interpretation is simply stated without adequate discussion of the alternatives.

2. THE LOGIC OF BEING AND HAVING

(A) *Formal Principles*

FP1   X Is X

FP2   if (X Is Y and Y Is Z), then X Is Z

FP3   if X Has Y, then it is not the case that X Is Y

FP4   X Has Y iff X Has something that Is Y

(B) *Total Definitions*

D1   X is predicable (κατηγορεῖται) of Y iff either Y Is X *or* Y Has something that Is X

D2   X is I-predicable (predicable καθ' αὐτό, essentially predicable) of Y iff Y Is X

D3   X is H-predicable (predicable κατὰ συμβεβηκός, accidentally predicable) of Y iff Y Has something that Is X

D4   X=Y iff (X Is Y and Y Is X)

D5   X is individual (ἄτομον) iff (necessarily) for all Y it is the case that (if Y Is X, then X Is Y)

D6   X is particular (καθ' ἕκαστον) iff (necessarily) for all Y it is the the case that (if X is predicable of Y, then (X Is Y and Y Is X))

D7   X is universal ($\kappa\alpha\theta\delta\lambda o\upsilon$) iff (possibly) there is a Y such that (X is predicable of Y and it is not the case that (X Is Y and Y Is X))

(C) *Partial Definitions*

D8   if X is $\tau\delta\delta\epsilon$ $\tau\iota$ (a this some*what*), then X is individual

D9   if X is a (separable) Platonic Form, then (X is $\tau\delta\delta\epsilon$ $\tau\iota$ and X is universal)

(D) *Ontological Theorems*

T1   X is predicable of Y iff either Y Is X *or* Y Has something that Is X, but not both

T2   X is I-predicable of X

T3   if X is H-predicable of Y, then X≠Y

T4   X is not H-predicable of X

T5   if X is particular, then X is individual
(note: the converse of T5 is *not* a theorem)

T6   if X is particular, then nothing that is not identical with X Is X

T7   nothing is both particular and a (separable) Platonic Form

T8   if X is a (separable) Platonic Form, then nothing that is not identical with X Is X

T9   if X is particular, then there is no (separable) Platonic Form Y such that X Is Y

T10   if X is a (separable) Platonic Form, then ((if X is predicable of Y and X≠Y), then Y Has X)

T11   if (X is a (separable) Platonic Form and Y is particular), then (X is predicable of Y iff Y Has X)

(E) *Platonic Principle*

PP1   each universal is a (seperable) Platonic Form

(F) *Platonic Theorem*

PT1   each universal is $\tau\delta\delta\epsilon$ $\tau\iota$

PT2   if X is particular, then there is no Y such that (Y≠X and Y is I-predicable of X)

PT3   if (X is predicable of Y and X≠Y), then X is H-predicable of Y

(G) *Aristotelian Principle*

AP1   if (X Has Y and X is particular), then there is a Z such that (Z≠X) and X Is Z)

(H) *Aristotelian Theorems*

AT1   if (X is particular and Y is universal and predicable of X), then there is a Z such that (X≠Z and Z is I-predicable of X)

AT2   if there are particulars of which universals are predicable, then not every universal is τόδε τι

3. PRELIMINARY DISCUSSION OF THE LOGIC OF BEING AND HAVING

Before examining the ways in which these ideas are embodied in the Platonic and Aristotelian theories, I would like to discuss the notions of Being and Having in a *fairly* neutral manner and explain some of the terminology that will later be used when discussing their theories. An adequate elucidation would require a detailed discussion of actual texts, some of which occurs in subsequent sections. This section will do no more than to provide a preliminary understanding of the logic of Being and Having.

Not every occurrence of a form of the verb 'to be' (εἶναι) expresses Being. For instance, the word 'is' in the sentence 'Socrates is brave' expresses Having; likewise for 'Socrates is a grammarian'. Furthermore, not every occurrence of a form of the verb 'to have' (ἔχειν) expresses Having. Socrates has a father, but his father is not predicable of him, and so he does not Have his father. Having is the relation specified in *Metaphysics* Δ23, 1023^{a}11-13: an item is Had by a subject that receives that item in the way that some bronze Has the form of a statue, or a body Has a disease.[7] To avoid confusing Being and Having with other concepts which may also be expressed by the relevant verbs, the words are usually capitalized when used in the technical sense being investigated.

I do not know all of the principles governing these relations, nor do I know to what extent the English language actually expresses these

---

[7] This is not to be confused with a use of "ἔχειν" which is confined to one category (see *Topics* A9, 103 ^{b}20-23; cf. *Cat.* 4, 2^{a}3). This more general use of the word stands for the relation that obtains between a thing and a property or form (see also *Cat.* 15, 15^{b}17-19). (Notice that FP4 requires that a subject has present in it the species and genera of the individual qualities in it, *pace* J. L. Ackrill, *Aristotle's 'Categories' and 'De Interpretatione'*, 1963, p. 74.)

concepts by means of the verbs 'to be' and 'to have'. Plato and Aristotle both tried to give theoretical characterizations of the two notions. Although they both investigate the *same two relations*, Being and Having, they offer competing theories as to what those relations are. Plato identifies Being with τὸ εἰλικρινῶς ὄν ('pure' Being), and identifies Having with μέθεξις (participation).[8] In the *Categories*, the two predication relations 'καθ᾽ ὑποκειμένου λέγεται' ('said of a subject') and 'ἐν ὑποκειμένῳ ἐστίν' ('present in a subject') are treated as the converses of Being and Having, respectively.[9] Though Plato and Aristotle will sometimes ascribe very different principles to these relations, and use different terminology to discuss them, their accounts none the less have a large area of overlap. (In much the same way, one might say that a philosopher who identifies *personal identity* with continuity and connectedness of ideas is setting forth an account of a single concept that some other philosopher might identify with spatio-temporal continuity of the body. They would be offering rival accounts of the same concept, and when they disagree they are arguing and disagreeing about that concept.)

Aristotle thinks that 'man' and 'animal' are the *names* of the species man and the genus animal, respectively, just as 'Socrates' is the name of Socrates. He regards the following three statements as true, and wishes to understand the copula in each case in terms of the same basic and primitive sense of 'is':

(a) Animal Is animal.
(b) Socrates Is animal.
(c) Man Is animal.

In each, the item named by the term 'animal' is essentially predicated of the item named by the subject expression.

Due to the lack of an indefinite article in Greek it is difficult to translate or paraphrase a Greek author's statements about predication. Omission of the Article in English can leave one with a sentence of

---

[8] On τὸ εἰλικρινῶς ὄν see Gregory Vlastos, 'Degrees of Reality in Plato', *Platonic Studies*, Princeton, 1971, pp. 58-75. Aristotle does not seem to observe the Form/character distinction (found, for instance, at *Phaedo* 102 D-E) when reporting Platonist views. I here ignore the complications raised by the introduction of this distinction.

[9] The *Cat.* uses the vocabulary cited, and does not talk in terms of essential ot accidental predication. However, I believe that understanding *predication* in terms of Being and Having does fit the *Cat.* distinctions, as well as its use of 'predicable' (see, for instance, 3ª3-4; cf. *De Int.* 7, 17ª39-40), provided that a particular can be 'said of' itself—see n. 11.

dubious grammaticality (witness (a)-(c)), while supplying it can suggest unwanted readings. Sometimes we have a choice as to whether to supply the article with the predicate term only, or with both subject and predicate. The choice can make a difference to sense. Usually in what follows I place the article in parentheses or omit it altogether in an attempt to ward off unwanted implications.

I have often heard it said that it is a mistake to take 'man' and 'animal' (or their Greek counterparts) as names of universals, and a language which, like English, makes use of an indefinite article makes the mistake easier to detect. It is claimed that the correct English version of (a) is '*an* animal is *an* animal', whereas the correct English for (b) is 'Socrates is an animal' (not '*a* Socrates is *an* animal').[10] If the word 'animal' were functioning as a name it would be improper to place the indefinite article in front of it. If so, then Aristotle cannot be right in holding that the copulas in (a), (b), and (c) express a relation between the items named by the subject and predicate terms (let alone the same relation in each case). This line of reasoning is suspect, but rather than pursue the issue let us simply note that Aristotle is making assumptions that many philosophers reject.

A modern reader might be none the less willing to accept the idea that in some sense natural kind terms are names, but what they name are sets. Hence the copula cannot express the same relation in all three statements. Perhaps in (a) and (c) it expresses set inclusion, and in (b) set membership. One might then claim that the fact that a singular term functioning as such does not accept the indefinite article (or quantificational idioms) whereas kind terms do, does not indicate that the kind terms are not names. Instead it shows that the relation between Socrates and the item named by 'animal' is not the same as the relation between the item named by 'man' and that named by 'animal'. Thus English is indeed a better guide to 'logical form' than Greek. If a distinction is to be drawn between the essential and the accidental, we must be able to attach sense to the idea that some such memberships or inclusions hold necessarily, others contingently. If this cannot be done, we reject essentialism. (I have doubts about this line of thought too.)

It is by no means clear that one can recapture an Aristotelian essence/ accident distinction having started in this way from a set-theoretical base. In any case, the Greek philosophers did not have the notions of

[10] Note that Aristotle was aware that the proper name of a particular man does not accept quantificational idioms (*Metaph.* Δ9, 1018ᵃ1-4).

a set or a class, at least as they are exploited in modern theories, and Aristotle does not use such notions in his own analysis of predication. The universals named by 'man' and 'animal' are not sets or classes, and the *same* predication relation links the universal animal to the universal man, and both to the particular man Socrates.

On the other hand, an analysis of 'Socrates is brave' that takes 'brave' as naming the set of brave things will find the same predication relation at work in both that statement and (b) above. Aristotle, however, does not take the word 'brave' to name either the universal bravery or a set. It is a name applied to brave things in virtue of the fact that they Have the universal. Thus, where a set-theoretical analysis claims to find two relations, Aristotle finds only one; but where Aristotle claims to find two, the other is content with one. In order to evaluate the viability of Aristotle's approach we must try to develop a theory based upon his own primitives and see how successful it is. It will not do to say that Aristotle has fallen into the trap of searching for substances corresponding to substantives, or has confused set-membership with set-inclusion. He has done neither. He has tried to develop a theory of predication which makes use of universals that are not sets, and predication relations that are not relations between sets.

The question as to whether Plato or Aristotle are committed to some form of 'self-predication' is ambiguous, and the ambiguity is not resolved by carefully distinguishing various set-theoretical readings of the copula. There are two basic predication relations, and so there are two forms of *self*-predication. It is a fundamental truth that each item is I-predicable of itself. Since a predicable cannot belong essentially and accidentally to the same subject, it is also a basic truth that no item is H-predicable of itself. Everything Is essentially itself, and nothing accidentally Has itself.[11] Most discussions of self-predication seem to

[11] Since each universal is self-I-predicable, it follows that each universal is 'said of' itself, and hence an item can be a ὑποκείμενον for itself. (A universal is self-I-predicable because it is identical with its essence, and *that* is I-predicable of it.) However, in the *Cat.* a primary substance is not predicable of a subject, and consequently is not 'said of itself'. Since FP1 requires that each particular is I-predicable of itself, this is a minor departure from the *Cat.* (However, the Greek for 'subject', ὑποκείμενον means underlying thing, and it is a bit odd to describe an item as underlying itself.) *Metaph.* Δ18, 1022ᵃ25–27, suggests (provided we do not follow E and J in omitting καθ' αὐτὸν Καλλίας) that Callias is predicable of himself in the way that his essence is. (Allowing Callias to be I-predicable of himself gives us a simpler and more elegant theory, and causes no theoretical problems.)

Post. An. A4, 73ᵃ34–ᵇ5, makes it clear that nothing can belong both essentially and accidentally to the same thing (see D2 and D3 with FP3), and in the

be concerned with H-predicability,[12] but some writers have treated
I-predications like 'man is (a) man' as instances of self-predication.[13]
It is quite important to avoid confusing these two very different ways
in which an item might be said to be predicable of itself. Notice that
if Plato accepts self-H-predicability for even a single Form, he is saddled
with an inconsistency unless he rejects FP3.

The analysis of identity in terms of reciprocal Being in D4 is not
found in any Aristotelian text. This comes as no surprise, since Aristotle
does not clearly accept the idea that a particular is essentially self-
predicable. Quite briefly, Aristotle characterizes numerical sameness as
follows:[14]

> X is numerically the same as Y iff whatever is predicable of X is
> predicable of Y, and whatever is predicable of Y is predicable
> of X.

The identity conditions for definable terms are given by their definitions—that is, by their essential properties. Material particulars, however, may be co-specific and thus share all essential properties, and yet
still be numerically distinct 'on account of their matter'.[15] The definition of identity in D4 requires that each item, whether universal or
particular, Is itself, and it characterizes identity as two-way, or reciprocal, Being. The relationship between D4 and the discussions of numerical sameness in Aristotle is problematic, and the former is not intended

middle dialogues Plato seems to sharply distinguish each Form from its participants—i.e the things that Hve it (see *Rep.* 376D 1-3, 579C 7-9; *Phaedo* 103B
2-C 1, 104B 6-9; Cf. *Metaph.* 991ᵃ2-3). Alexander Nehamas has suggested to me
that FP3 is abandoned in the later dialogues (thus the One which Is One can Have
unity, and hence be one thing; the Different not only Is Different, but also Has
the Different.

[12] See, for instance, Gregory Vlastos, 'The Unity of the Virtues in the *Prota-
goras*', p. 258, n. 97, and 'Self-Predication and Self-Participation in Plato's Later
Period', both in *Platonic Studies*. Most scholars have followed the usage that
Vlastos introduced.

[13] See G. E. L. Owen, 'The Platonism of Aristotle', reprinted in *Articles on
Aristotle*, vol. 1, ed. by J. Barnes, M. Schofield and R. Sorabji, Duckworth,
1975, esp. pp. 21-2. Vlastos introduced the term in such a way as to apply *only*
to cases of self-H-predicability; thus his complaint (p. 258, n. 97) that Owen
applies the term to the very cases Vlastos originally wished to *exclude* by the
introduction of that label.

[14] See *Topics* H, 152ᵇ25-29. (*Metaph.* Δ9 gives a treatment of numerical
sameness that applies only to things having matter—see 1018ᵃ4-6 with Δ6,
1016ᵇ32-3).

[15] See *Metaph.* Z8, 1034ᵃ7.

as an adequate analysis of the latter. However, the use of '=' in this paper does conform to that definition.[16]

It is important not to confuse D5 with D6. An *individual* is an item that cannot be truly I-predicated of another item—whether or not it can be H-predicated of other things is not determined by the content of D5. Some individuals, such as the individual white (τὸ τὶ λευκόν) of *Categories* 2, 1ᵃ27, are H-predicable of other things; other individuals, like Socrates, cannot be truly H-predicated of anything at all. A *particular*, on the other hand, is an item that is of such a nature that it cannot be truly I-predicated *or* truly H-predicated of another item. Although all particulars are individuals, the converse implication does not hold.[17]

The principles, definitions, and theorems in Section 2, A–D, can be used to describe part of the ontological framework common to Plato and Aristotle. To examine some of the important *differences* we must consider principles that one accepts and the other rejects. The principle AP1 is accepted by Aristotle but not by Plato. The idea behind this principle is that a particular cannot receive accidental properties unless it Is something essentially. Aristotle holds, against Plato, that sensible particulars must Be something or other definable in order to Have any properties—each must be τόδε τι, a 'this some*what*', where the τι is the something definable that τόδε Is.[18] What Has properties must Be something knowable.

Plato rejects AP1, and with it rejects AT1 and AT2. However, he

---

[16] G. E. R. Lloyd has pointed out that since Socrates is not essentially a philosopher who died in 399 BC by drinking hemlock, D4 seems to require that Socrates is not identical with the philosopher who died in that year and in that way. D4 needs to be supplemented with an account of accidental sameness (for which see *Metaph.* Δ9).

[17] See T5. This use of 'ἄτομον seems to come from the practice of making 'divisions' on a genus/species chart, not from Democratean theories. (See *Cat.* 1ᵇ6, 3ᵇ12 and *Met.* Z8, 1034ᵃ8; D6 and D7 seem to fit *De Int.* 7, 17ᵃ39–ᵇ1.) Michael Frede ('Individuen bei Aristoteles', *Antike und Abendland*, 24 (1978), pp. 16–39) thinks that the *Cat.* uses the term for that which although a 'subjective part' of something, does not itself have such parts (p. 21), and argues that by the time he writes the *Metaph.*, Aristotle has abandoned this use of the term (p. 31). My D5 requires that individuals do not have subjective parts, but does not require that they must themselves be subjective parts of something. I suggest that D5 fits the use of the term in *Metaph.* Z8.

[18] See Owen, pp. 24–5. The expression 'τόδε τι' is sometimes used in such a way that the τι is the 'something' that the τόδε picks out. Sometimes, however, it seems to involve quantification over essential properties, one of which is the essence of the τόδε in question. (It is grammatically possible that the 'τόδε' picks out the essential nature, and the τι ranges over the items endowed with the essence. On the former reading, 'Socrates is τόδε τι' generalizes 'Socrates is this man'; on the latter, it generalizes 'Socrates is a certain man'.)

accepts a principle that Aristotle rejects, namely PP1. He also accepts
the theorems PT1, PT2, and PT3. The last two embody the idea that
particulars are not endowed with essential natures, but merely Have
accidental properties without Being anything definable. This is incompatible with AP1. Theorems PT2 and PT3 are consequences of Plato's
belief that the universal (the One Over Many) is τόδε τι.

4. LINGUISTIC PREDICABILITY

Plato and Aristotle use Being and Having (or, ontological predicability,
which comes to the same thing given our definitions) to explain linguistic predicability (L-predicability). A simple subject-predicate sentence
may be used to make a simple affirmative statement in which one item
is predicated of another (usually distinct) item. For example, one may
use the sentences 'Socrates is (a) man' and 'Socrates is (a) grammarian'
to assert the propositions that Socrates is (a) man and Socrates is (a)
grammarian, respectively. The above statements will be true and the
linguistic predicates 'man' and 'grammarian' applicable just in case man
and grammatical knowledge are ontologically predicable (in the appropriate way) of Socrates.

L-predicability is a relation between linguistic predicates (L-
predicates) and things. An L-predicate is a word or phrase (often an
adjectige, noun, or definiens) which serves as the grammatical predicate in a simple subject-predicate sentence, and which introduces a
non-linguistic universal.[19] If L is an L-predicate that is L-predicable
of X, this holds *either* in virtue of the fact that the associated universal
is I-predicable of X *or* in virtue of the fact that the associated universal
is H-predicable of X. If a universal Y is I-predicable of X, then both the
name of that universal and the definiens of its definition are L-predicable
of X. For example, if (as Aristotle thinks) man is I-predicable of
Socrates, and that Is what Socrates Is in his own right, it follows that
both the noun 'man' (which names the universal in question) and the
corresponding defining expression are L-predicable of him. If a universal Y is H-predicable of X, then that fact does not prevent a name of
Y from being L-predicable of X, but in no case can the definiens of the
definition of Y be truly L-predicated of X.[20] For instance, the adjective

[19] The term 'introduces' is not intended to be a translation of anything in the
text.
[20] See *Cat.* 2ª19–34 and 3ª15–20. Although these claims are taken from the
Cat., they seem to describe Platonic theses as well, though not in Platonic terminology (see *Phaedo* 103 E–104 B).

'brave' is L-predicable of Socrates if and only if the signification of the noun 'bravery' is H-predicable of him. (The words 'brave' and 'bravery' introduce the same universal.) Aristotle claims that the brave are so-called paronymously from the bravery that they Have.[21] He also thinks that though bravery is H-predicable of Socrates (assuming that he is brave), neither the name 'bravery' nor the definiens of the definition of bravery may be truly L-predicated of him, for Socrates is not brave in virtue of what he Is.

The above is a way of regarding Plato's and Aristotle's use of a theory of ontological predication in their explanations of the correct application of language to reality. An L-predicate truly applies to an object just in case the application of the L-predicate to the object results in a true statement. A true statement results when the object stands in the appropriate relation, Being or Having, to the universal associated with the L-predicate.[22]

5. ARISTOTLE'S UNDERSTANDING OF PLATO

It is important to stress that the Platonic position explored in this paper may differ in certain respects from what one finds in the Platonic dialogues. The 'Plato' of this paper is seen through Aristotle's eyes. It is a topic for further discussion whether and to what extent Aristotle is criticizing the ideas found in the dialogues.

Since Aristotle saw himself as breaking from Plato, an account of what he took Plato's views to mean is needed in order to fully appreciate the origin and content of his own thought. To devise such an account we should rely upon the remarks he makes about Platonism (both in the extant works and as recorded in Alexander's commentary on the *Metaph.*), and try to determine what he must have made of certain key passages in the dialogues. For example, since Aristotle thinks that the TMA poses a serious difficulty for the Platonist, he must have supposed that the latter was committed to the existence of a separable αὐτοάνθρωπος.[23] However, it is well-known that the *Phaedo*

[21] See *Cat.* 1ª12–15 and 10ª27 ff. The notion of paronymy is Aristotelian, not Platonic. Plato treats certain adjectives (e.g. 'large', 'equal') that apply to particulars as *names* of the corresponding universal, but Aristotle considers this to be a mistake.

[22] I do not mean to suggest that the notion of L-predicability is reduced to ontological notions. Furthermore, it is important to keep in mind that in cases of L-predication is a linguistic expression interpreted in a certain way that is applied to the object, not an uninterpreted expression.

[23] See M. Hayduck's text of Alexander of Aphrodisias' commentary on

shows no clear commitment to such Forms, and the *Parmenides* expresses doubt on this very point shortly before Parmenides initiates a
series of objections to the theory of separable Forms—and one of
those objections is usually thought to be the 'Third Man Argument'
(132 A 1-B 2). None the less, the Platonist with whom I am concerned
does believe in a separable Form of Man.

It is possible that in some cases Aristotle actually misunderstood
Plato. There are many other factors, however, that one should consider
when trying to explain apparent discrepancies between 'Plato' and
Plato. First, Plato's philosophy had a development, and so the position
considered in this paper at best represents a single stage of that development (and not necessarily a stage reproduced in full in any dialogue).
Indeed, if we may suppose that early Aristotle and late Plato are contemporaries, and that *both* reject the classical middle period theory of
Forms, Aristotle might be criticizing views that Plato had already
abandoned. Secondly, some of the tenets of 'Plato' may be dialectical accretions—details and refinements made when trying to put the
best face possible on the theory being investigated. (One might compare
this with the dialectical treatment of the 'man is the measure' doctrine
in the *Theaetetus*.) Thirdly, in an aporematic treatment one develops
certain strands of a predecessor's thought while ignoring or slighting
others. The resulting picture distorts the historical truth while pursuing philosophical truth.[24] Fourthly, Aristotle makes use of his own
technical vocabulary in describing and criticizing Plato. He gives a
presentation of the latter's views that is more systematic as well as more
formal than anything in the middle period dialogues.[25] Finally,
Aristotle believed that some of Plato's views were inconsistent.[26] We

Aristotle's *Metaphysics* in *Aristotelis Metaphysica Commentaria*, vol. 1, Berlin,
1891, 84.25. See PP1.

[24] Further, it may even lack elements crucial to a proper understanding of the
original whole. For instance, Aristotle was quite familiar with both the *Timaeus*
and the *Phaedo*. None the less, the *Cat.* seems oblivious to the important role
those works assign to *soul* in explaining life and movement (even though
Aristotle's view in the *De Anima* owes quite a bit to those dialogues), and as a
result 'Plato' is in some ways less sophisticated than Plato. Perhaps Aristotle
thought that immortal souls had no place in a metaphysics bent upon making
a firm and exhaustive dichotomy between a realm of Being and a realm of cease-
less Becoming. If so, he may have realized that Plato wanted both, but chose to
ignore Plato's views on souls in some contexts.

[25] This kind of systematization can put into a clear light issues that are initially
obscure or confused, and may make obvious certain options and entailments
that one might otherwise fail to notice.

[26] For instance, *Metaph.* M9, 1086ª32-34, with ᵇ6-7, tells us that those who

cannot simply assume that Plato was always consistent, and that it is Aristotle who is at fault if we discover that his various reports on Platonic theses add up to an inconsistent Platonic metaphysics. (Of course I do not mean to suggest that we should assume that Aristotle is always right.)

It is far beyond the scope of this paper to settle the many different issues involved in a full assessment of his understanding of Plato. I have merely mentioned some of the relevant factors. In the next section I sketch a Platonic position to which Aristotle responds. The portion of that position presented here is intended to be internally consistent, and something that could have been believed by the author of the *Phaedo*.[27]

6. PLATO ON BEING AND HAVING

The importance of the Socratic 'What Is X?' question cannot be over-emphasized in a discussion of Platonic Being. Socrates thought that his search for definitions of ethical universals was indispensable to virtue, and hence to happiness (or εὐδαιμονία), and, in general, to living well. Throughout his searches, he assumed the following:

SOCRATIC PRINCIPLE: If X Has Y, then the definition of Y is L-predicable of X.

The content of the definition of the F is a *standard* which may be used to settle ethical disputes (see *Euthyphro* 6E). Suppose that Euthyphro maintains that the prosecution of his father is holy (i.e Has the holy), but his relatives deny this. The dispute may be settled by one who is in possession of a correct definition of the holy. If the definition of what it is to be holy applies to his action, then (and only then) is his action indeed holy. Whatever is 'such as' this standard is holy, and whatever is not 'such as' the standard is not holy.

Plato rejects this Socratic principle, and instead endorses:

PLATONIC PRINCIPLE: If a particular X Has a Form Y, then the definition of Y is not L-predicable of X.

Whereas Socrates assumed that the definition of the F applies to all of

---

treat the Ideas as universals also at the same time treat them as separable particulars. Since a particular is not a universal (see D6 and D7), this position is logically incoherent. (See also *EN* 1096^{a}34–1096^{b}5; *Metaph.* I 1059^{a}10–14.)

[27] In the next section I do not attribute to Plato the view that both the name and the definition of man are L-predicable of particular men, although Aristotle does at times take the Platonist to be committed to it—see n. 26.

the F particulars, and that each of those particulars is 'such as' the
essence (οὐσία) of the F itself, Plato believed that the many F particulars are all *deficient* in being 'such as' the F itself, and that striving to be
such, they none the less fall short (see *Phaedo* 74). This is the famous
Platonic separation of the universal. The universal, X, is logically
separable from entities of type E only if the definition of the X cannot
apply to any entity of type E (and accounts of the sense in which they
are F do not apply to X, nor are they contained in the definition that
does apply to X). Aristotle reports that Socrates did not separate the
universal, but that the Platonists, having accepted the quest for universals and definitions, did separate the objects of universal definition (*Metaph.* M4, 9).

Plato's realm of separable Being is *not* the realm of existence, though
of course its inhabitants are supposed to exist. Rather, it is the domain
of definable entities—the objects about which one asks the Socratic
'What Is X?' question. This question is a request for a definition that
says what X really Is.[28] Being the sole bearer of its definition, each real
Being Is what it Is all by itself and in its own right—it alone really and
truly Is X. The realm of Being *includes* the single item that Is X in the
fullest sense: namely, the X itself. It is a realm of Being in that it consists solely of such entities. Thus, only X itself really and truly Is X,
and so X itself is a real Being. For instance, the Form, the beautiful
itself, is the only thing that really and truly Is beautiful. Hence it is a
real Being.

Just as the word 'Helen' names a certain sensible particular, so the
word 'beautiful' names (in this theory) something that exists in addition to all of the sensible particulars. It names the beautiful itself, and
this Plato takes to be an external and separable Form. In general, for
any definable entity X there will be many things besides X itself that
are quite correctly called 'X', even though X itself is the *only* thing to
which the *definition* of X properly applies (since it alone is, strictly
speaking, the bearer of the name 'X'). The realm of Being *excludes*
the many Xs (the many things that are merely called 'X') because none
of them really and truly Is X. Thus, since only one thing, the beautiful
itself, really Is beautiful, and 'beautiful' is the name of that very thing,
Plato must explain how it is that Helen can quite correctly be called

---

[28] The 'What is X?' (τὸ τί ἐστι) question is answered by a definition that says
what X Is (ὃ ἔστιν X). The word 'ἔστι' has exactly the same sense in the question
and the answer: it expresses Being. Further, the word 'X' functions as subject in
both, and the whole phrase 'ὃ ἔστιν X' stands for the content of the definition
of X.

'beautiful'. How is it that the name of the beautiful itself is applicable to Helen? Of course, if she were identical with the beautiful, there would be no problem here. But she is not. After all, no sensible particular is a proper subject for definition.

Plato accounts for and explains the application of language to items in the sensible realm in terms of what those items Have (at least in some key cases, in terms of the separable Forms in which they participate), not in terms of what they Are—for there is nothing definable or scientifically knowable that they Are. The forms, but not the sensible particulars, are endowed with essential natures—the very natures that the Forms Are.[29]

Aristotle would, I think, find in the *Phaedo* the doctrine that a word may be applicable to an object either in virtue of what that object *Has* or in virtue of what that object *Is*. The word 'large' is applicable to Simmias not in virtue of what he Is, but rather in virtue of the largeness that he Has.[30] Similarly, the number three is rightly called 'odd' in virtue of the fact that it Has the μορφή (shape, form, or character) of the Form of the odd.[31] By way of constrast, the word 'odd' is applicable to the Form itself (αὐτὸ τὸ εἶδος), to Oddness, not in virtue of its Having the character of the odd, but in virtue of its Being ὅπερ τὸ περιττόν (i.e. in virtue of what it Is).[32]

The *Phaedo* holds, at least in cases where there are Forms of opposites, that there is always a word (which *we* would classify as an adjective) that applies to a Form in virtue of what that Form Is, and applies to other things in a derivative way, in virtue of something that they Have.[33] Although I cannot find convincing evidence that the *Phaedo* treats all universals as separable Forms (PP1), this claim is a part of the position Aristotle attacks. If we add PP1 to the *Phaedo*, then the theory holds that the word 'man' applies truly to Socrates because of something he Has (to wit, the Form Man), and not because of anything he Is.

[29] In so far as the Having *de re* of necessary properties in grounded in essence, this is connected with the idea that all necessity is *de dicto*.

[30] This is one way of interpreting *Phaedo* 102 B 8–C 1 with C 10 ff. (cf. B 4–6).

[31] The example at 103 E 6–104 A 7 is meant to illustrate 103 E 2–5 (ὥστε μὴ μόνον αὐτὸ τὸ εἶδος ἀξιοῦσθαι τοῦ αὐτοῦ ὀνόματος εἰς τὸν ἀεὶ χρόνον, ἀλλὰ καὶ ἄλλο τι ὃ ἔστι μὲν οὐκ ἐκεῖνο, ἔχει δὲ τὴν ἐκείνου μορφὴν ἀεί, ὅτανπερ ᾖ).

[32] See 103 E 5–104 A 3; cf. *Parmenides* 130 E 5–131 A 2. Note that the number three is necessarily odd, but is not what the odd itself Is.

[33] Things which Are opposites (the opposites themselves) are carefully distinguished from the things that Have those opposites (103 B 2–C 1; see also 104 B 6–9). The name of an opposite (e.g. the large) also applies to the things that Have it.

It is not the case that Socrates Is (a) man. The Form, and only the Form, Is man, and it is simply not true that Socrates Is the Form (ie. Is what man Is). Socrates merely Has, or participates in, man, without Being man. In general, the inhabitants of the sensible realm Are not the natures in which they participate.

Since the Form Man is an individual, nothing but the Form Is (a) man. The word 'man' as well as the corresponding definition are both truly applied to the Form in virtue of what that Form Is. Underlying this semantical fact is the ontological fact that the Form is I-predicable of itself. Since particular men Have the Form, whereas the Form Is (a) man, it follows that the term 'man' does not apply to both man and particular men in the same way. Contrary to the Aristotelian position, a particular man participates in man, whereas only man really Is (a) man. Aristotle can attack this by arguing that since the definition of man is L-predicable of precisely that class of entities to which the word 'man' is applicable, man must be I-predicable of each of the many men.

The *Meno* contains a mistake that is of a piece with the mistake about Man. Here Plato seems to think that just as the various kinds of bee all Have the Form of Bee in common, so too the various virtues all Have a single Form because of which they are virtues.[34] Furthermore, strictly speaking roundness is not shape, but rather a certain shape (σχῆμά τι). This is because there are other shapes as well.[35] Furthermore, same point is made about *virtue*. Each of the particular kinds of virtue is a certain virtue, but strictly speaking none is virtue. This is because no matter which particular virtue one considers, there are others as well. The moral is that a generic kind term applies in a strict sense to the kind itself (for instance, ὃ δὴ ὀνομάζεις σχῆμα, 74 D 8), to that which Is the kind, even though the species of that genus may also be called by the generic kind term.[36] The latter merely Have the kind. Aristotle could criticize this for treating the species of a genus as Having that genus. The definition of the genus, he would argue, is L-predicable of the species, and hence the genus is I-predicable of the species.

The *Phaedo* mistakenly treats adjectives as though they were names for the entities introduced by the corresponding abstract nouns. The adjective 'large' is dealt with as though it were the proper name of largeness. Plato conflates the statement that largeness is largeness with the statement that largeness is large, and regards them as having the

---

[34] *Meno* 72 A-D (C 7-8: ἕν γέ τι εἶδος ταὐτὸν ἅπασαι ἔχουσιν δι' ὃ εἰσὶν ἀρεταί).

[35] 73 E 3-6, 74 B 5-7; cf. 74 C 7-8.

[36] τὰ πολλὰ ταῦτα ἐνί τινι προσαγορεύεις ὀνόματι (74 D 5-6).

same truth-value. As long as Plato conflates 'X is F' with 'X is F-ness', and fails to consider alternative interpretations of the copula, he will maintain that F-ness alone Is F.[37] However, once he hits upon the importance of the distinction between 'hot' and 'hotness' (or 'white' and 'whiteness'; and in general, between 'such' and 'suchness'),[38] and hence ceases to treat adjectives as names, he is in a position to see that the copula requires different interpreations in different sentences. The copula in 'X is large' does not express the same concept as the copula in 'X is largeness'. This realization paves the way for a search for new interpretations of the copula. Such a search is initiated in the *Sophist* (see 255 E 11–256 D 10), and is continued by Aristotle.[39]

7. ARISTOTLE ON BEING AND HAVING IN THE 'CATEGORIES' AND THE 'ORGANON'

The *Categories* carefully distinguishes between cases in which an adjective 'F' is L-predicable of an object and cases in which a corresponding noun 'F-ness' is applied to F-ness, and holds that if F-ness is H-predicable of some item, then (in general) there will be an expression 'F' that is (in virtue of this fact) L-predicable of that item. In such a case the item is called 'F' paronymously from F-ness. The adjective 'white', for instance, is L-predicable of Socrates because whiteness (the universal signified by the noun 'whiteness') is H-predicable of him. The noun 'whiteness', however, cannot be truly predicated of Socrates. Plato and Aristotle can both agree that the word 'white' is L-predicable of Socrates because he Has whiteness, and hence both should deny that largeness is predicable of him in the same way as it is predicable of itself.

Aristotle takes over from Plato a distinction between cases in which both a name and the definition of a predicable truly apply to some subject and cases in which although the subject Has the predicable, the definition does not apply to it. For Aristotle, the definition of X signifies the essence of X. Consequently, if the definition of man is

---

[37] Further, since Largeness Is not Smallness, indeed cannot Be, it follows that Largeness cannot Be small. In general, no opposite can Be its own opposite (*Phaedo* 102 D 5–103 A 2; B 4–5; C 1–2; C 7–8; 104 B 7–8). Likewise, it is not true that Socrates Is large, for Socrateness Is not Largeness. Part of the point at 102 B 8–C 2 is that it is not true that Socrates Is large—rather he Has the large.

[38] See *Theaetetus* 182A 7–B 2.

[39] I would like to thank Vanessa Whang for help in reformulating parts of this section and parts of Section 4. In writing the present section, I benefited from Alexander Nehamas's 'Self-Prediction and Plato's Theory of Forms', *American Philosophical Quarterly*, 16 (1979), pp. 93–103.

'biped animal', then *biped animal* is the essence of man. The essence is simply the signification of the account that says what X Is. Once we discover the correct definition of *man* we are in a position to L-predicate that definition of each thing that we classify as a man, thereby predicating the essence of man of those items. However, even prior to the discovery of the definition we may assert that each thing that Is (an) X Is the very F that X Is. We may use the phrase 'ὅπερ τὸ X' (elliptical for 'ὅπερ τὸ X ἐστιν'—the very F that X Is)[40] to predicate the content of the definition of X (i.e. the essence of X) of each thing that Is (an) X. The essence of X is ὅπερ X ἐστιν. For instance, since Socrates Is (a) man, we know even in advance of the discovery of the correct definition of man that Socrates Is the very F that man Is. Since man Is man, we also know that man Is the very thing that man Is (whatever that turns out to Be). I do not believe that this implies that Socrates = man. Rather, such statements are used to assert that the essence of man is predicable (*per se*) of Socrates, or man, or whatever the subject may be. The statement that Socrates Is the very thing that man Is should be construed as asserting that the essence of man is I-predicable of Socrates. This, of course, does not entail that Socrates is predicable of man. Thus it does not entail that Socrates = man (see D4).

The contrast between cases in which the definition of a predicable *does* apply to a subject and those in which it *does not* is equivalent to the distinction between Being and Having. However, the *Categories* (unlike the *Phaedo*) accounts for and explains the application of words to items in the sensible realm in terms of what the sensible particulars *Are* as well as what they *Have*. Aristotle holds, in opposition to Plato, that sensible particulars are endowed with essential natures. The word 'man', for example, applies to Socrates because of something he Is (to wit, (a) man), and not because of anything he Has. Socrates does not Have man, rather, he Is (a) man. Both the name 'man' and the corresponding definitions are L-predicable of him precisely because man is I-predicable of him.[41]

For Plato, the substances are all bearers of I-predicables, but in addition can be H-predicated of other things. The *Categories* is

---

[40] See *Cat.* 36ᵇ6, *Metaph.* Z4 1030ª3, *SE* 179ª5. (Also, consult *Cat.* 6ª38, 39; 11ª25, 26–27, ᵇ24, 26, 28, 29, 32, 34; *APr.* 30ª12, 49ᵇ7; *APo.* 73ᵇ8, 9; 83ᵇ9, 89ª35, 83ª28–30; *Topics* 116ª23, 23–8; 120ᵇ23, 24, 28; 122ᵇ26, 38; 123ª2; 124ª18; 141ª35, 37; *SE* 179ª4, 6; *Physics* 186ª34, ᵇ1; *GC* 330ª26, 27; *Metaph.* Γ4 1007ª32–3, Z4 1030ª4, 5; *EN* 1156ª17.)

[41] In so far as the Having *de re* of necessary properties is grounded in essence, this is connected with the idea that there are *de re* necessities.

anti-Platonic in that the substances of that work, although the bearers of I-predicables, cannot be truly H-predicated of anything at all. A primary substance (πρώτη οὐσία) is an individual τόδε τι,[42] and it is treated as καθ' αὑτὸ λεγόμενον.[43] The only primary substance—indeed the only τόδε τι—in this treatise is the particular (the particular man, the particular horse, etc.). The particular is called what it Is in virtue of itself. The word 'man', for instance, which is used to classify Socrates according to kind, and the definition of man are both L-predicable of him simply in virtue of what he Is—(a) man. He is not called what he Is in virtue of any of the universals that he Has. Furthermore *whatever* man Is, Socrates Is. Anything I-predicable of man is *ipso facto* I-predicable of Socrates as well as man due to the transitivity of Being (FP2).[44]

The only universals in the *Categories* are (i) the natural kinds, the species and the genera to which particulars belong, (ii) their differentiae, and (iii) the various quantities, qualities, and other non-substantial items that are Had by the substances. Aristotle does not yet draw any distinction between species and the corresponding species-form or essence. The essence of the species man is simply the ontological correlate of the definition of man, and as such is identical with the species. An important feature of the earlier doctrine is that non-substantial items can also be subjects for I-predications. The colour white, for instance, Is (a) colour, and hence colour is I-predicable of white. Substances and non-substances alike are endowed with essential natures. *Metaph.* Z4 will modify this claim, arguing that in a primary sense only substances have definitions, and consequently there are essences (in an unqualified sense) only for substances.[45]

In the *Cat.* the notion of 'primary substance' is characterized in terms of the two metaphysical relations 'said of' and 'present in'. The relata are 'beings', or 'things that are' (τὰ ὄντα), and all beings except for primary substances are predicable (either essentially or accidentally) of primary substances.[46] A primary substance, however, is a primary substance in virtue of the fact that it is a subject (ὑποκείμενον) for the other beings that are predicable of it, but is not itself predicable of anything further.[47] It is an ultimate subject for both I-predication and

[42] *Cat.* 1b6-9, 3b10-15.
[43] Not said in so many words. A *Cat.* primary substance is, however, meant to be spoken of καθ' αὑτό in the *APo.* A4 73b5 ff. sense.
[44] *Cat.* 1b10-15.
[45] 1030a17-b13; esp. a28-32, b4-6; see also Z5, 1031a11-14.
[46] 2a11-14, 2a34-2b6, 2b15-17, 2b37-3a1.
[47] Note the διά at 2b15, 17.

and H-predication. In this way we arrive at an answer to the question 'What is it to be a primary substance?'

Aristotle intends individual men, horses, and the like to be the primary substances of the *Cat*., and as is well-known, does not in that work subject such individuals to the hylomorphic analysis that typifies his mature thought on substances in the middle books of the *Metaph*. According to the latter view, a particular man is a composite of matter and form—the potentially living, organized body being the matter, the soul being the actuality, form, and primary substance. The form of a material composite is predicated of its body, thus making it what it Is (a man, a horse, etc.). By way of contrast, although the *Cat*. does make remarks about the individual man, his body, and soul, there is no discussion of the relation between properties of the body, properties of the soul, and properties of the individual man, nor does he address problems concerning the relation between body and soul. Various remarks made require that a man, his body and his soul *all* count as primary substances. This actually precludes hylomorphic analysis.

Anything that can persist through time as numerically one and the same individual while receiving contrary properties must be a primary substance (according to the *Cat*.).[48] One and the same individual man can be pale at one time, dark at another; hot at one time, cold at another; bad at one time, good at another.[49] However, the man's body can be pale at one time, dark at another,[50] so the body must be a primary substance. Further, the soul can be bad at one time, good at another,[51] and hence it must be a primary substance.

A primary substance (but only a primary substance) is a 'this'—an individual not predicable of a substance. Thus an individual man is a 'this', his body is a 'this' and his soul is a 'this'. No 'this' is predicable of a 'this', and so soul is not predicable of body. Also, no substance is ever H-predicable of a 'being'.[52] Where a substance *is* predicable of a subject, both the name and the definition of that substance must apply to the subject in question. Thus there is no room for a substantial form, human soul, that is predicable of the body. Such a form, being substantial, could not be H-predicable of the body. Since it is not true to say of the body that it is a human soul, neither could such a form be essentially predicable of the body.

---

[48] 4^a10–4^b18.   [49] 4^a18–21
[50] See 4^a3–5; also 1^a27–28, 2^a31–32, 2^b1–3.
[51] See 13^a17–31 with 14^a17–18; also 1^a25–27, 1^b1–3.
[52] 3^a7 ff.

So, although the *Cat.* mentions the items that will later play the technical roles of matter and form,[53] this earlier work is incompatible with hylomorphism.

8. PRIMARY SUBSTANCE IN THE 'METAPHYSICS'

An individual man is analysed in the *Metaph.* as a composite of matter and form. In Z3 we find Aristotle stating that the primary subject (or substratum) seems most of all to be substance.[54] He explains that the 'subject' is that of which all other things are said, but is not itself said of anything further.[55] At 1029ᵃ8-9 he deduces from this equation and his definition of subject the conclusion that *substance* is that which is not said of a substratum, but is that of which other things are said.[56] He offers three candidates that might qualify as the subject: matter (ὕλη), form (μορφή), and that which is composed of matter and form (τὸ ἐκ τούτων).[57] Thus once Aristotle envisages the possibility of hylomorphic analysis he must re-examine his earlier claim that the particular is primary substance, for it is no longer clear what the basic subjects are, and it is no longer clear that the *Cat.* characterization of primary substance is adequate.

The matter of a composite apparently satisfies the 'logical subject' condition for primary substance, and Z3 argues that this criterion leads to the view that primary matter is primary substance.[58] Presumably, if our only answer to the question 'What is it to be a primary substance?' is the one given in the *Cat.*, we are committed to the view that matter is the primary subject. Yet matter is neither χωριστόν nor τόδε τι, and hence is not primary substance.[59] Since form is prior to matter, argues Z3, it is prior to the composite (σύνολον), and so the composite is posterior to form.[60] This eventually leads to the view that *form* is primary substance.

---

[53] Water, fire, and such (the inanimate materials of which animals are composed) are recognized members of the ontology (8ᵃ9-10), as well as bodies (both animal bodies and bodies ἁπλῶς, 14ᵃ16, 17) and souls.

[54] Or is thought to be (δοκεῖ): 1029ᵃ1-2; cf. 1028ᵇ34-36.

[55] 1028ᵃ36-37.

[56] See also *Metaph.* Δ8, 1017ᵇ13-14 where he says that bodies and the things composed of them (such as animals) are called substances because they are not predicable of any subject, but other things are predicable of them.

[57] 1029ᵃ2-3. τὸ ἐκ τούτων = τὸ σύνολον (1029ᵃ5).

[58] 1029ᵃ10, 18-19, 26-27. This problem is already latent in *Physics* A—that work alludes to the *Cat.* characterization of primary substance (190ᵃ36-ᵇ1), and calls matter the primary subject (192ᵃ11-12).

[59] 1029ᵃ27-28; cf. *Metaph.* Δ8, 1017ᵇ24-26.   [60] 1029ᵃ5-7.

The matter of which a substantial particular is composed is not itself another substantial individual, not a 'this' in actuality. Although in a sense, a man is composed of inanimate materials (earth, air, fire, and water), the *proximate matter* of a man is a body having organs (more precisely, a set of bodily organs), and this cannot exist separately.[61] The body is the material aspect of a hylomorphic composite, and cannot exist except as such. Socrates's body cannot exist without Socrates.

Call the matter of which something is composed '*that*' (ἐκεῖνο) —for instance, wood, bronze, stone, or bricks. Aristotle insists that a statue that is made of *that* is not itself *that*, but rather is 'thaten' (ἐκείνινον).[62] The statue is wooden, not wood; 'brazen', not bronze. If we call that of which Socrates is composed (say, the set of his bodily organs) '*that*', we may apply this general point as follows. Socrates is not *that* (whatever *that* may be), rather he is *thaten*, or of *that*. If, when pointing at Socrates, I were able to correctly say that this (to which I point) is *that*, then the matter would indeed be a 'this'. However, we cannot correctly say that 'this is *that*', but must say that 'this is *thaten*'. *That*, the matter, cannot be the 'this'.

Suppose for a moment that the body were a 'this'. If it were, it could not be cast in the role of matter. As a 'this', the body would be a separable substantial individual—Socrates's body could, after all, exist without Socrates. As the form that Socrates's body must have in order for Socrates to exist, the soul would be a mere accidental arrangement (or τάξις) of his bodily parts, and would not be a primary substance. (Remember that no substance is accidentally predicable of a 'this'.) So, if Socrates's body were a 'this', Socrates would be an accidental unity of substance and attribute, and would not himself be a substantial individual. Consequently, treating the body as a 'this' is incompatible with treating it as the material aspect of a composite of matter and substantial form. Assuming that Socrates is a 'this', hylomorphism requires that his body is not.

The claim that what makes something a primary substance (and hence a 'this') is that *it is a subject for predicates and not itself a predicable* is inadequate once matter is on the scene. It leaves out the idea that in order for something to be a primary substance (and hence

---

[61] Z15, 1040^{b}5–10 with 1037^{a}6, 9–10 (cf. 1029^{a}27–28); on proximate matter, see H4 (esp. 1044^{b}1–2), and the discussion of potentiality in Θ7 (1049^{a}1 ff.). Matter is potentially, not actually, a 'this' (H1, 1042^{a}27–28).

[62] *Metaph.* Z7, 1033^{a}5–23; see also *Physics* A7, 190^{a}25–26, *GC* B, 329^{a}15–21.

a 'this') *it must Be something or other essentially and in its own right* —it must be καθ' αὐτὸ λεγόμενον. (This is closely connected to AP1.) In the *Metaph*. we find that the particular is now called (on a hylomorphic analysis) what it is called in virtue of a form enforming some matter, and is not (in a strict sense) καθ' αὐτὸ λεγόμενον.

The point of the Z6 thesis is to identify each primary substance with its essence.[63] In *Metaph*. Z a primary substance must be καθ' αὐτὸ λεγόμενον, and the Z6 thesis identifies each καθ' αὐτο λεγόμενον with the essence signified by its definition. The *subject* of the definition is an invisible form (εἶδος), a τόδε τι that is identical with the essence (τὸ τί ἦν εἶναι, or τὸ τί ἐστι) that serves as the predicable. Hence the arguments supporting the Z6 thesis are meant to establish that substance is (as promised in Z1) both τὸ τί ἐστι and τόδε τι.[64]

This thesis can be seen as a fusion of certain *Organon* claims about definition[65] with the idea that each καθ' αὐτὸ λεγόμενον (in the strict sense) is a definable form. The *Organon* doctrine involves the ideas that an essence is the ontological correlate (or signification) of the definiens in a definition, and that definiendum and definiens must signify numerically one and the same thing. With the advent of hylomorphic analysis and the claim that there is a primary or strict sense of I-predication (καθ' αὐτό predication),[66] Aristotle comes to adopt the position that each καθ' αὐτὸ λεγόμενον (in the strict sense) is a definable form —the formal component of a hylomorphic composite.

In *Metaph*. Z a καθ' αὐτὸ λεγόμενον (in the strict sense), and consequently a primary substance, must be a *proper* object of definition. It follows that no *Cat*. primary substance is a *Metaph*. Z substance. However, the mature view retains the idea that a primary substance must be a 'this' (and hence individual). Thus the secondary substances of the *Cat*., although definable, are not the new primary substances, for none is a 'this'.[67] The primary substances we are seeking are individual (or indivisible), yet definable, substantial forms. Just as the *Cat*.

[63] See Z11, 1036ª33-b2. The introduction of the technical notion of matter has forced Aristotle to give up the 'logical subject' criterion for primary substance, and now he characterizes a primary substance as that which is not called what it is called in virtue of one thing being in another, i.e. in a substratum serving as matter (Z11, 1036b3-4).

[64] 1028ª10-15; cf. Z4, 1030ª18-19.

[65] These claims are discussed in my 'On the Origins of Some Aristotelian Theses About Predication', in *How Things Are: Studies in Predication and the History of Philosophy*, ed. by J. Bogen and J. E. McGuire, Reidel, 1974, Sec. IV A.

[66] 1030ª17-b13; esp. ª28-32, b4-6; cf. Z5, 1031ª11-14.

[67] *Cat*. 3b13-18 (and see n. 73).

neither knows of nor has a place for matter, this kind of substantial form differs radically and irreconcilably from the 'beings' that compromise the ontology of that work.

Being a primary substance, a substantial form is a 'this' that is identical with its own essence. Aristotle thinks that Plato's treatment of each item predicable in common of particulars as separable $\tau \acute{o} \delta \epsilon$ $\tau \iota$, rather than a $\tau o \iota \acute{o} \nu \delta \epsilon$, leads to the 'third man'.[68] If the item predicable in common is a separable 'this', then by D8 it is an individual, and hence is H-predicable of all of those items of which it is predicable except itself (see PT2, PT3). If the universal man is a 'this', it is H-predicable of the particular men that participate in it as something they Have in common. The Third Man Argument is designed to show that if the particulars Have a universal man, then both the particulars and the universal Have another man in common, and so on *ad infinitum*.

Strictly speaking, a substantial form is not a universal. It is not predicable of a plurality of separable particulars—rather, it is predicable of matter, and matter is not a 'this' (except potentially).[69] This view requires a distinction between the species and the corresponding species-form.[70] The Being of a particular material composite is explained in terms of its matter Having the form that is responsible for the fact that the matter constitutes that particular.[71] The species to which the particular belongs is a universal composite of matter and substantial form,[72] and is I-predicable of its members. Hence the term 'man' is still (though now in a derivative way) applicable to Socrates in virtue of what he Is, and he is (in a qualified sense) $\kappa \alpha \theta$' $\alpha \dot{\upsilon} \tau \grave{o}$ $\lambda \epsilon \gamma \acute{o} \mu \epsilon \nu o \nu$. He is properly called a man because he Is (a) man.

---

[68] *Metaph.* Z13, 1038b34–1039a2; *SE* 178b36–179a10. There is a fuller discussion of these issues in Sec. III of the paper cited in n. 65.

[69] See n. 61. Also, see my 'No Universal is a Substance: An Interpretation of *Metaphysics* Z13 1038b8–15', *Paideia* (Special Aristotle Issue, 1978), pp. 65–74, esp. Sec. IV, where it is argued that 1038b8–15 is meant to establish that no substance is universal with respect to that of which it is the substance. This does not entail that the substance of a species is not a universal in any sense. A substantial form is not universal with respect to that of which it is the substance, but is still universal with respect to matter. Unlike a species (which must be essentially predicable of, and hence divided among, a plurality of separable particulars), the species-form, although predicable of bodies, is I-predicable of nothing but itself. The species-form in the case of *man* is *human soul* (1035b14–15, 1037a5–6, 28–29), and the definition of human soul applies to neither the particular man nor his body—neither Is (a) soul. The substantial form is essentially predicable of neither, and although universal (with respect to matter), it is also individual.

[70] See n. 3.   [71] Z17, 1041b5–9 with b27–28.

[72] Z10, 1035a27–30 (cf. Z8, 1033b24–26).

The form or substance of the species *man* is that form (i.e. human soul) that makes a human body alive in virtue of the fact that the body Has it, and the word 'man' (as applied to Socrates) signifies the species (a universal composite) that Socrates Is. The word 'man' is applicable to Socrates in virtue of his matter (his body) Having a substantial form, the definition of which does not apply to him at all. The substantial form is strictly speaking a 'this', and Socrates is a 'this' in virtue of the form that his body Has. The species, on the other hand, is not a 'this'. It is a 'such' (τοιόνδε).[73]

The substantial form is the (definable) formal aspect of a particular material composite, and whereas the latter is separable without qualification, the former is separable in account only (definitionally separable).[74] Being separable in this way, its definition (unlike that of the universal *man*, the species) does not apply to composite particulars or signify what any separable particular truly Is *qua* composite. The form in the case of man is the *soul*, and the definition of human soul does not apply to any material composite. Socrates is not *qua* material object a human soul. Hence, although the substantial form is not universal with respect to actual particulars, neither can it be a separable particular itself.

None the less, a substantial form is truly said to Be (what it Is) *just in virtue of itself*. Both its name and the definition of what it essentially Is apply to it solely on the basis of what it Is. The substantial form, not the material particular, is primary substance. This disagreement with the *Cat.* on primary substance is not merely verbal, and as we have just seen is emphatically not over whether the label 'primary substance' should be used for particulars rather than their specific natural kinds. (The primary substances are the forms of the kinds, not the kinds themselves.) The form, being identical with its own essence is simple,[75] though not in the sense that it cannot be defined. It is an individual form, and is not spoken of in virtue of matter Having a form.

According to a hylomorphic theory of this sort, a person lives a human life in virtue of having the capacities assigned to the various parts of human soul, the principle of human life. Soul is that in virtue of which (in the primary sense) we live, think, perceive, etc.[76] However, that in virtue of which *we* do these things is not *something else* that

[73] The phrase 'τόδε τοιόνδε' at Z8, 1035ᵇ24-25, generalizes 'this *man*', and the 'τοιόνδε' picks out the species to which the τόδε belongs, not the species-form.
[74] H1, 1042ᵃ28-31.   [75] Z17, 1041ᵇ9-11.
[76] Not explicit in *Metaph.* Z; but see *de An.* B2, 414ᵃ12-13.

also does them. We think in virtue of the fact that our bodily parts are formed, structured, and organized with that kind of organization that a set of bodily parts must Have in order that one can think. That kind of organization does not itself think when we do. This is why Aristotle argues in the *De Anima* that one need not conclude from the fact that we *say* that the soul grieves, is delighted, is confident, is afraid, is angry, perceives, and thinks, that the soul is actually moved.[77] This, he tells us, is like saying that the soul weaves or builds. It is preferable to say that the man (that is, the material particular) thinks, etc., in virtue of the soul, the *form* of the body.[78] It is important to see that Aristotle is not here advocating linguistic reform, and is not urging that we stop using locutions such as 'the soul thinks'. He certainly feels free to use such locutions (see, for instance, 429^a10-11). His point is that the correct use of such statements does not require the soul to be the subject of change. The particular composite is a subject of change, but as for the soul, 'not only is it false [to say] that the essence of soul is correctly described by those who say that it is what moves (or is capable of moving) itself, but it is an impossibility that movement should even be an attribute of it'.[79]

Since the soul is to be understood as the form of the body,[80] then when we talk about it as though it were itself changing, what we are really talking about is the *formal aspect* of a hylomorphic composite. We do not thereby commit ourselves to the view that the soul is the *subject* of the change. In the case of a candle, there is no object called 'the shape of the candle' that changes when it is true to say that the shape of the candle changes. The subject of change is the candle, not its shape. Likewise, when we talk of the soul (or form of the body) as though *it* were changing, the subject of change is the man.[81]

There is just one such substantial form *per* species. The substance of a species is unique to the species of which it is the substance, and since it is individual, it is not essentially predicable of separable particulars. This view is compatible with the claim that each particular has a particular form, or particular soul, that it shares with no other object, provided that the species-form is not I-predicable of the particular

---

[77] *de An.* A4, 408^b1-5. (As $^b5$ ff. indicates, the complaint is not that thinking, for instance, is an ἐνέργεια rather than a κίνησις.)

[78] 408^b11-15.

[79] *de An.* A3, 405^b31-406^a2 (J. A. Smith translation.)

[80] *de An.* B1, 412^a19-20; cf. *Metaph.* Z10, 1035^b14-16.

[81] Contrast with *Cat.* 4^a10 ff. (Note, however, that whereas the candle acquires a new shape, the man does not acquire a new soul.)

form.[82] Furthermore, since a primary substance must be definable in the strictest sense, and no particular is so-definable, particular forms cannot be primary substances.[83] Since an essence (in the strict sense) is the ontological correlate of a definition (in the strict sense), there cannot be more proper essences than there are proper definitions. If a particular form were a primary substance, it would have to be identical with primary essence, and since there is a one-to-one mapping from such essences to proper definitions it would have to have its own proper definition. Since it has no such definition, it is not a primary substance. Furthermore, if we allow that a particular form does have a particular essence, we still have no reason to *identify* the form with its particular essence. The argument at Z6, 1031^b28-1032^a4 shows that primary definables are the same as their own essence. This provides one with a reason for identifying *human soul* with the essence of human soul, but not for identifying a particular soul with a particular essence. The essentialist ideas explored in the middle books of the *Metaph*. are flexible enough to accommodate particular forms, souls, and essences, but cannot treat them as primary substances, and cannot treat primary substances as universals having them as particular instances.[84]

[82] The discussion of inherited characteristics in *GA* Δ3 could accommodate both particular forms (e.g. one peculiar to just Socrates) and general species-specific forms (one *per* species), but would have to assign to them different explanatory roles. The general form could not play its independent explanatory role if the particular form were an instance of it. Aristotle's metaphysics should be, and is, compatible with this.

[83] Definition is of the universal (Z11, 1036^a28-29), not the particular (Z15, 1040^a5-7).

[84] This paper is an expanded version of portions of my 'Aristotle on the Samenss of Each Things and with its Essence' (Sept. 1980), presented at the Dec., 1980 meeting of the Society for Ancient Greek Philosophy. I am grateful to the National Endowment for the Humanities for their support during the time of the research for this paper. I would like to thank S. Marc Cohen and Alexander Nehamas for their helpful discussions of previous drafts.

17

FITTING FACTS TO EQUATIONS

NANCY CARTWRIGHT

INTRODUCTION

At Paul Grice's seminar on metaphysics in the summer of 1975, we discussed Aristotle's categories. I argued then that the category of quantity was empty; there were no quantities in nature—no attributes with exact numerical values of which it could be said that they were either precisely equal or unequal to each other. I was thinking particularly about physics, and the idea I had was that the real content of our theories in physics is in the detailed causal knowledge they provide of concrete processes in real materials. I thought that these causal realtions would hold only between qualities and not between quantities. Nevertheless, I recognized that real materials are composed of real atoms and molecules with numerically specific masses, and spins, and charges; that atoms and molecules behave in the way that they do because of their masses, spins, and charges; and that our theoretical analyses of the causal processes they are involved in yield precise numerical calculations of other quantities, such as lineshapes in spectroscopy or transport coefficients in statistical mechanics.

Why then did I want to claim that these processes were essentially qualitative? It was because our knowledge about them, while detailed and precise, could not be expressed in simple quantitative equations of the kind that I studied in theoretical physics. The distinction I wanted, it turns out, was not that between the qualitative and the quantitative, but rather the distinction between the tidy and simple mathematical equations of abstract theory, and the intricate and messy descriptions, in either words or formulae, which express our knowledge of what happens in real systems made of real materials, like helium-neon lasers or turbo-jet engines. We may use the fundamental equations of physics to calculate precise quantitative facts about real situations, but abstract fundamental laws are nothing like the complicated, messy laws which describe reality. I no longer want to urge, as I did in the summer seminar, that there are no quantities in nature, but rather that nature is not governed by simple quantitative equations of the kind we write in our fundamental theories.

My basic view is that fundamental equations do not govern objects in reality; they govern only objects in models. The second half of this thesis grew out of another Grice seminar on metaphysics not long after. In the second seminar we talked about pretences, fictions, surrogates, and the like; and Grice asked about various theoretical claims in physics, where should we put the 'as if' operator: helium gas behaves *as if* it is a collection of molecules which interact only on collision, or helium gas is composed of molecules which behave *as if* they interact only on collision, or . . .?

Again, I wanted to make apparently conflicting claims. There are well-known cases in which the 'as if' operator should certainly go all the way in front: the radiating molecules in an ammonia maser behave *as if* they are classical electron oscillators. (We will see more of this in the last chapter.) How closely spaced are the oscillators in the maser cavity? This realistic question is absurd; classical electron oscillators are themselves a mere theoretical construct. What goes on in a real quantum atom is remarkably like the theoretical prescriptions for a classical electron oscillator. The oscillators replicate the behaviour of real atoms; but still, as laser specialist Anthony Siegman reported in his laser engineering class, 'I wouldn't know where to get myself a bagful of them.'[1]

The classical electrons oscillators are undoubted fictions. But, even in cases where the theoretical entities are more robust, I still wanted to put the 'as if' operator all the way in front. For example, a helium-neon laser behaves *as if* it is a collection of three level atoms in inter-action with a single damped mode of a quantized field, coupled to a pumping and damping reservoir. But in doing so, I did not want to deny that the laser cavities contain three level atoms or that a single mode of the electromagnetic field is dominant. I wanted both to acknowledge these existential facts and yet to locate the operator at the very beginning.

It seems now that I had conflicting views about how to treat this kind of case because I was conflating two functions which the operator could serve. On the one hand, putting things to the left of the operator is a sign of our existential commitment. A helium-neon laser *is* a collection

[1] Siegman, Anthony, 'Lasers' (*Electrical Engineering 231*), Stanford University, Autumn Term 1981-2.

of three level atoms . . . But putting things on the right serves a different function. Commonly in physics what appears on the right is just what we need to know to begin our mathematical treatment. The description on the right is the kind of description for which the theory provides an equation. We say that a 'real quantum atom' behaves like a classical electron oscillator; already the theory tells us what equation is obeyed by a classical electron oscillator. Similarly, the long description I gave about of a laser as a collection of three level atoms also tells us a specific equation to write down, in this case an equation called the Fokker–Planck equation; and there are other descriptions of gas lasers which go with other equations. We frequently, for example, treat the laser as a Van der Pol oscillator, and then the appropriate equation would be the one which B. van der Pol developed in 1920 for the triode oscillator.

Contrary to my initial assumption I now see that the two functions of the 'as if' operator are quite distinct. Giving a description to which the theory ties an equation can be relatively independent of expressing existential commitment. Both treatments of the laser which I mentioned assume that the helium-neon laser contains a large number of three level helium atoms mixed with a much greater number of helium atoms, in interaction almost entirely with a single mode of the electromagnetic field. Similarly, when an experimentalist tells us of a single mode of a CW GaAs (gallim arsenide) laser where, 'below threshold the mode emits noise *like a* narrow band black body source; above threshold its noise is *characteristic of* a quieted amplitude stabilized oscillator',[2] he is telling us not that the make-up of the laser has changed but rather that its intensity fluctuations follow from different equations above and below threshold. In these cases what goes on the right of the 'as if' operator does not depend on what we take to be real and what we take to be fictional. Rather it depends on what description we need to know in order to write down the equation which starts our mathematical treatment.

The views I urged in the two seminars go hand-in-hand. It is because the two functions of the 'as if' operator are independent that the fundamental equations of our theories cannot be taken to govern objects in reality. When we use the operator to express existential commitment, we should describe on the left everything we take to be real. From a first, naïve point of view, to serve the second function,

[2] Armstrong, T. A. and Smith, A. W., 'Intensity Fluctuations in a GaAs Laser', *Physical Review Letters*, 14, (1965), p. 68.

we should just move everything from the left of the operator to the right. To get a description from which we can write down an equation, we should simply report what we take to be the case.

But that is not how it works. The theory has a very limited stock of principles for getting from descriptions to equations, and the principles require information of a very particular kind, structured in a very particular way. The descriptions that go on the left—the descriptions that tell us there is—are chosen for their descriptive adequacy. But the 'descriptions' on the right—the descriptions that give rise to equations —must be chosen in large part for their mathematical features. This is chracteristic of mathematical physics. The descriptions that best describe are generally not the ones to which equations attach. This is the thesis that I will develop in the remaining sections of this paper.

1. TWO STAGES OF THEORY ENTRY

Let us begin by discussing bridge principles. On what Fred Suppe has dubbed the 'conventional view of theories',[3] championed by Hempel, Grünbaum, Nagel, and others in the tradition of logical empiricism, the propositions of a theory are of two kinds: internal principles and bridge principles. The internal principles present the content of the theory, the laws that tell us how the entities and processes of the theory behave. The bridge principles are supposed to tie the theory with some kind of observation reports. But with the breakdown of the theory-observation distinction, the bridge principles were required only to link the theory with a vocabulary that was 'antecedently understood'.

The network of internal principles and bridge principles is supposed to secure the deductive character of scientific explanation. To explain why lasers amplify light signals one starts with a description in the antecedent vocabulary of how a laser is constructed. A bridge principle matches this with a description couched in the language of the quantum theory. The internal principles of quantum mechanics predict what should happen in situations meeting this theoretical description, and a second bridge principle carries the results back into a proposition describing the observed amplification. The explanation is deductive because each of the steps is justified by a principle deemed necessary by the theory, either a bridge principle or an internal principle.

[3] In Suppe, Frederick, *The Structure of Scientific Theories*, Urbana, University of Pittsburgh, Autumn 1979.

Recently, however, Hempel has begun to doubt that explanations of this kind are truly deductive.[4] The fault lies with the bridge principles, which are in general far from exceptionless, and hence lack the requisite necessity. A heavy bar attracts iron filings. Is it thus magnetic? Not necessarily; we can never be sure that we have succeeded in ruling out all other explanations. A magnet will, with surety, attract iron filings only if all the attendant circumstances are right. Bridge principles Hempel concludes, do not have the character of universal laws; they hold only for the most part, or when circumstances are sufficiently ideal.

I think the situation is both much better and much worse than Hempel pictures. If the right kinds of descriptions are given to the phenomena under study, the theory will tell us what mathematical description to use and the principles which make this link are as necessary and exceptionless in the theory as the internal principles themselves. But the 'right kind of description' for assigning an equation is seldom, if ever, a 'true description' of the phenomenon studied; and there are few formal principles for getting from 'true descriptions' to the kind of description that entials an equation. There are just rules of thumb, good sense, and, ultimately, the requirement that the equation we end up with must do the job.

Theory entry proceeds in two stages. I imagine that we begin by writing down everything we know about the system under study, a gross exaggeration, but one which will help to make the point. This is the *unprepared description*—it is the description that goes to the left of the 'as if' operator when the operator is used to express existential commitment. The unprepared description contains any information we think relevant, in whatever form we have available. There is no theory-observation distinction here. We write down whatever information we have: we may know that the electrons in the beam are all spin-up because we have been at pains to prepare them that way; or we may write down the engineering specifications for the construction of the end mirrors of a helium-neon laser; and we may also know that the cavity is filled with three-level helium atoms. The unprepared description may well use the language and the concepts of the theory, but it is not constrained by any of the mathematical needs of the theory.

At the first stage of theory entry we prepared the description; we present the phenomena in a way that will bring it into the theory.

[4] Hempel, C. G., in a paper at the conference 'The Limits of Deductivity', University of Pittsburgh, Autumn 1979.

The most apparent need is to write down a description to which the theory matches an equation. But to solve the equations we will have to know what boundary conditions can be used, what approximation procedures can be used, what approximation procedures are valid, and the like. So the prepared descriptions must give information which specifies these as well. For example, we may describe the walls of the laser cavity with their surroundings as a *reservoir* (a system with a large number of resonant modes). This means that the laser has no memory. Formally, when we get to the derivation, we can make a Markov approximation.

The first stage of theory entry is informal. There may be better and worse attempts, and a good deal of practical wisdom helps, but no principles of the theory tell us how we are to prepare the description. We do not look to a bridge principle to tell us what is the right way to take the facts from our antecedent, unprepared description, and to express them in a way that will meet the mathematical needs of the theory. The check on correctness at this stage is not how well we have represented in the theory the facts we know outside the theory, but only how successful the ultimate mathematical treatment will be.

This is in sharp contrast with the second stage of the theory entry, where principles of the theory look at the prepared description and dictate equations, boundry conditions, and approximations. Shall we treat a C W GaAs laser below threshold as a 'narrow band black body source' rather than the 'quieted stabilized oscillator' which models it above threshold? Quantum theory does not answer. But once we have decided to describe it as a narrow band black body source, the principles of the theory tell what equations will govern it. So we do have bridge principles, and the bridge principles are no more nor less universal than any of the other principles. But they govern only the second stage of theory entry. At the first stage there are no theoretical principles at all—only rules of thumb and the prospect of a good prediction.

This of course is a highly idealized description. Theories are always improving and expanding, and an interesting new treatment may offer a totally new bridge principle. But Hempel's original account was equally idealized; it always looked at the theory as it stood after the explanation had been adopted. I propose to think about it in the same way. In the next section I want to illustrate some bridge principles, and illustrate the two stages of theory entry with some examples from quantum mechanics.

2. SOME MODEL BRIDGE PRINCIPLES

If we look at typical formalizations of quantum mechanics,[5] it seems that the fundamental principles do divide into internal principles and bridge principles, as the conventional view of theories maintains. The central internal principle is Schroedinger's equation. The Schroedinger equation tells how systems, subject to various forces, evolve in time. Actually, the forces are not literally mentioned in the equation since quantum mechanics is based on William Hamilton's formulation of classical mechanics, which focuses not on forces, but on energies. In the standard presentation, the Schroedinger equation tells how a quantum system evolves in time when the *Hamiltonian* of the system is known, where the Hamiltonian is a mathematical representation of the kinetic and potential energies for the system. Conservation principles, like the conservation of energy, momentum, or parity, may also appear as internal principles in such a formalization. (On the other hand, they may not, despite the fact that they are of fundamental importance, because these principles can often be derived from other basic principles.)

The second class of principles provide schema for getting into and out of the mathematical language of the theory: states are to be represented by vectors; observable quantities are represented by operators; and the average value of a given quantity in a given state is represented by a certain product involving the appropriate operator and vector. So far, all looks good for the conventional view of theories.

But notice: one may know all of this and not know any quantum mechanics. In a good undergraduate text these two sets of principles are covered in one short chapter. It is true that the Schroedinger equation tells how a quantum system evolves subject to the Hamiltonian; but to do quantum mechanics one has to know how to pick the Hamiltonian. The principles that tell us how to do so are the real bridge principles of quantum mechanics. These give content to the theory, and these are what first-year students spend the bulk of their time learning.

If the conventional view were right, students should be at work learning bridge principles with mathematical formulae on one end and descriptions of real things on the other. Good textbooks for advanced

[5] See, for example, the formalization in Chapter 5, 'Development of the Formalism of Wave Mechanics and its Interpretation', in Albert Messiah's highly respected text, *Quantum Mechanics*, Amsterdam, North-Holland, 1969 or the formal axiomatization in George W. Mackey's *Mathematical Foundations of Quantum Mechanics*, New York, W. A. Benjamin Inc., 1963.

undergraduates would be full of discussions of concrete situations and of the Hamiltonians which describe them. There might be simplifications and idealization for pedagogical purposes; nevertheless, there should be mention of concrete things made of the materials of the real world. This is strikingly absent. Generally there is no word of any material substance. Instead one learns the bridge principles of quantum mechanics by learning a sequence of model Hamiltonians. I call them 'model Hamiltonians' because they fit only highly fictionalized objects. Here is a list of examples. I culled it from two texts, both called *Quantum Mechanics*, one by Albert Messiah[6] and the other by Eugen Merzbacher.[7] This list covers what one would study in just about any good senior level course on quantum mechanics. We learn Hamiltons for

> Free particle motion, including
>> the free particle in one dimension
>> the free particle in three dimensions
>> the particle in a box
> The linear harmonic oscillator
> Piecewise constant potentials, including
>> the square well
>> the potential step
>> the periodic potential
>> the Coulomb potential
> 'the hydrogen atom'
> diatomic molecules
> central potential scattering

and eventually, the foundation of all laser theory,

> the electron in interaction with the electromagnetic field.

There is one real material metnioned in this list—hydrogen. But in fact this case provides a striking illustration of my point, and not a counterexample against it. The Hamiltonian we learn here is not that for any real hydrogen atom. Real hydrogen atoms appear in an environment, in a very cold tank for example, or on a benzene molecule; and the effects of the environment must be reflected in the Hamiltonian. What we study instead is a hypothetically isolated atom. We hope that

---

    [6] Messiah, A., op. cit.
    [7] Merzbacher, Eugen, *Quantum Mechanics*, Second Edition, New York, John Wiley & Sons, 1970.

later we will be able to piece together this Hamiltonian with others to duplicate the circumstances of an atom in its real situation.

But this is not the most striking omission. In his section titled 'The Hydrogen Atom', Messiah proposes a particular Hamiltonian and uses it to provide a solution for the energy spectrum of hydrogen. He says:

This spectrum is just the one predicted by the Old Quantum Theory; its excellent agreement with the experimental spectrum was already pointed out. To be more precise, the theory correctly accounts for the position of the spectral lines but not for their fine structure. Its essential shortcoming is to be a non-relativistic theory ... [Also] the Schroedinger theory does not take the electron spin into account.[8]

These are critical omissions. The discovery of and the account of the fine structure of hydrogen were significant events in quantum mechanics for the reasons Messiah mentions. Fine structure teaches important lessons both about relativity and about the intrinsic spin of the electron.

The passage quoted above appears about three quarters of the way through volume I. About the same distance into volume II, Messiah again has a section called 'The Hydrogen Atom'. There he uses the relativistic theory of the Dirac electron. Even the second treatment is not true to the real hydrogen atom.

Here is what Messiah himself says:

The experimental results on the fine structure of the hydrogen atom and hydrogen-like atoms (notably He+) are in broad agreement with these predictions.

However the agreement is not perfect. The largest discrepancy is observed in the fine structure of the $n = 2$ levels of the hydrogen atom. In the non-relativistic approximation, the three levels $2s_{1/2}$, $2p_{1/2}$, and $2p_{3/2}$ are equal. In the Dirac theory, the levels $2s_{1/2}$, and $2p_{1/2}$ are still equal, while the $2p_{3/2}$ level is slightly lower (the separation is of the order of 10^{-4} eV). The level distance $2p_{3/2} — 2p_{1/2}$ agrees with the theory, but the level $2s_{1/2}$ is lower than the level $2p_{1/2}$, and the distance $2s_{1/2} — 2p_{1/2}$ is equal to about a tenth of the distance $2p_{3/2} - 2p_{1/2}$. This effect is known as the Lamb shift. To explain it, we need a rigorous treatment of the interaction between the electron, the proton and the quantized electromagnetic field; in the Dirac theory one retains only the Coulomb potential which is the main term in that interaction; the Lamb shift represents 'radiative corrections' to this approximation.[9]

[8] Messiah, A., op. cit., p. 419.   [9] Ibid., pp. 932-3.

We know from our earlier discussion that the treatment of these 'radiative corrections' for the hydrogen spectrum is no simple matter.

The last sentences of Messiah's remark is telling. The two sections are both titled 'The Hydrogen Atom' but in neither are we given a Hamiltonian for real hydrogen atoms, even if we abstract from the environment. Instead, we are taught how to write the *Coulumb potential between an electron and a proton*, in the first case non-relativisticly and in the second, relativisticly. Messiah says so himself: 'The simplest system of two bodies with a Coulomb interaction is the hydrogen atom.'[10] 'The hydrogen atom' on our list is just a name for a two body system where only the Coulumb force is relevant. Even if the system stood alone in the universe, we could not strip away the spin from the electron. Even less could we eliminate the electromagnetic field, for it gives rise to the Lamb shift even when no photons are present. This two-body system, which we call 'the hydrogen atom', is a mere mental construct.

Messiah's is, of course an elementary text, intended for seniors or for first-year graduate students. Perhaps we are looking at versions of the theory too elementary? Don't more sophisticated treatments— journal articles, research reports, and the like—provide a wealth of different, more involved bridge principles which link the theory to more realistic descriptions? The answer to this question is *no*. There are some more complicated bridge principles; and of course the theory is always growing, adding both to its internal principles and its bridge principles. But at heart the theory works by piecing together in original ways a small number of familiar principles, adding corrections where necessary. This is how it should work. The aim is to cover a wide variety of different phenomena with a small number of principles, and that includes the bridge principles as well as the internal principles. It is no theory that needs a new Hamiltonian for each new physical circumstance. The explanatory power of quantum theory comes from its ability to deploy a small number of well understood Hamiltonians to cover a wide range of cases. But this explanatory power has its price. If we limit the number of Hamiltonians, that is going to constrain our abilities to represent situations realistically. This is why our prepared descriptions lie.

I claim that in general we will have to distort the true picture of what happens if we want to fit it into the highly constrained structures of our mathematical theories. I think there is a nice analogy that can help us see why this is so. That is the topic of the next section.

[10] Ibid., pp. 000–00.

3. PHYSICS AS THEATRE

I will present first an analogy and then an example. We begin with
Thucydides' views on how to write history:

XXII. As to the speeches that were made by different men, either
when they were about to begin the war or when they were already
engaged therein, it has been difficult to recall with strict accuracy the
words actually spoken, both for me as regards that which I myself
heard, and for those who from various other sources have brought me
reports. Therefore, the speeches are given in the language in which, as it
seemed to me, the several speakers would express, on the subjects under
consideration, the sentiments most befitting the occasion, though at the
same time I have adhered as closely as possible to the general sense of
what was actually said.[11]

Imagine that we want to stage a given historical episode. We are
primarily interested in teaching a moral about the motives and behaviour
of the participants. But we would also like the drama to be as realistic
as possible. In general we will not be able simply to 'rerun' the episodes
over again, but this time on the stage. The original episode would have
to have a remarkable unity of time and space to make that possible.
There are plenty of other constraints as well. These will force us to
make first one distortion, then another to compensate. Here is a trivial
example. Two of the participants had a secret conversation in the
corner of the room. But if the actors whisper together, the audience
will not be able to hear them. So the other characters must be moved
off the stage, and then back on again. In reality everyone stayed in
the same place throughout. In these cases we are in the position of
Thucydides. We cannot replicate what the chracters actually said and
·did. Nor is it essential that we do so. We need only adhere 'as closely
as possible to the general sense of what was actually said'.

Physics is like that. It is important that the models we construct
allow us to draw the right conclusions about the behaviour of the
phenomena and their causes. But it is not essential that the models
accurately describe everyting that actually happens; and in general it
will not be possible for them to do so, and for much the same reasons.
The requirements of the theory constrain what can be literally represented. This does not mean that the right lessons cannot be drawn.
Adjustments are made where literal correctness does not matter very

[11] Thucydides, *The Peloponnesian War*, vol. 1, trans. Charles Forster Smith,
New York, G. P. Putnam's Sons, 1923, p. 39.

much to get the correct effects where we want them; and very often, as in the staging example, one distortion is put right by another. That is why it often seems misleading to say that a particular aspect of a model is false to reality: given the other constraints that is just the way to restore the representation.

Here is a very simple example of how the operation of constraints can cause us to set down a false description in physics. In quantum mechanics free particles are represented by plane waves—functions that look like sines or cosines, stretching to infinity in both directions. This is the representation that is dictated by the Schroedinger equation, given the conventional Hamiltonian for a free particle. So far there need be nothing wrong with a wave like that. But quantum mechanics has another constraint as well: the square of the wave at a point is supposed to represent the probability that the particle is located at that point. So the integral of the square over all the space must equal one. But that is impossible if the wave, like a sine or cosine, goes all the way to infinity.

There are two common solutions to this problem. One is to use a Dirac delta function. These functions are a great help to physics, and generalized function theory now explains how they work. But they side-step rather than solve the problem. Using the delta function is really to give up the requirement that the probabilities themselves integrate to one. Merzbacher, for instance, says 'Since normalization of $\int \psi \star \psi$ to unity is out the question for infinite plane waves, we must decide on an alternative normalization for these functions. A convenient tool in the discussion of such wave functions is the delta function.'[12] I have thus always preferred the second solution.

This solution is called 'box normalization'. In the model we assume that the particle is in a very, very large box, and that the wave disappears entirely at the edges of this box. To get the wave to go to zero we must assume that the potential there—very, very far away from anything we are interested in—is infinite. Here is what Merzbacher has to say in defence of this assumption:

The eigenfunctions (6.2) are not quadratically integrable over all space. It is therefore impossible to speak of absolute probabilities and of expectation values for physical quantities in such a state. One way of avoiding this predicament would be to recognize the fact that physically no particle is ever absolutely free and that there is inevitably some

[12] Merzbacher, E., op. cit., p. 82.

confinement, the enclosure being for instance the wall of an accelerator tube or of the laboratory. V rises to infinity at the boundaries of the enclosure and does then not have the same value everywhere, the eigenfunctions are no longer infinite plane waves, and the eigenvalue spectrum is discrete rather than continuous.[13]

Here is a clear distortion of the truth. The walls may interact with the particle and have some effect on it, but they certainly do not produce an infinite potential.

I think Merzbacher intends us to think of the situation this way. The walls and environment do contain the particle; and in fact the probability is one that the particle will be found in some finite region. The way to get this effect in the model is to set the potential at the walls to infinity. Of course this is not a true description of the potentials that are actually produced by the walls and the environment. But it is not exactly false either. It is just the way to achieve the results in the model that the walls and environment are supposed to achieve in reality. The infinite potential is a good piece of staging.

[13] Ibid., p. 82.

ETHICS

18

DO ONE'S MOTIVES HAVE TO BE PURE?

JUDITH BAKER

Pure gold, without a trace of base metal; honest, unselfish, practical: he took up the Union cause and made himself its champion, as a true Yorkshireman was sure to do, partly because of his Quaker anti-slavery convictions, and partly because it gave him a practical opening in the House. As a new member, he needed a field.

(*The Education of Henry Adams*)

We want our motives to be pure. This demand of ours conflicts with needs that we also think to have moral sanction. Many sceptics think that the ideal of purity of motives does not even make sense. The apparent conflict of the ideal of purity with a common appreciation of the place of sentiments in our practical life prompts many people to deny credibility to the demand that motives be pure. I shall try to show that the idea of purity in motives has some appeal, and that Kant's vision of this purity, despite his sometimes appalling presentation, is a good guideline to understanding the need for such purity. I conclude with a way to reconcile some of the conflicts that arise from taking this vision of purity as an imperative. I do not claim to show that every impure motive is wrong, or to settle every source of the uncertainty of resolving the conflict.

Two questions arise in asking whether one's motives have to be pure. What makes a motive moral? If our action is to have moral value must our motivation be of a special sort, a pure or purified interest in what is right? The second question assumes that we have an idea of what makes motivation moral, but asks whether that motivation can be supported by, or even co-exist with, our more ordinary interests and inclinations. Must we be pure in our single-minded devotion to what is moral? In following conscience may we sometimes be moved by a mixed lot of influences and considerations?

I focus on the second question, whether motives may be mixed without change in the consequent appraisal of the worth of action or agent. My discussion begins with Kant, the most formidable proponent of the view that motives must be pure. Formidable, but somehow unpersuasive. Partly because Kant, at his harshest on this issue, is so unappealing, work needs to be done to see the considerations which prompt him and which might persuade us. The most obvious Kantian arguments for a purified motive do not directly transfer to a demand that the moral motive operate alone. I will maintain, however, that there is a line of argument which can be reconstructed from the moral theory of the *Foundations of the Metaphysis of Morals* and elicited from popular thought which provides support for the ideal of purity.

1. THE KANTIAN PROPOSITION

Two claims, important for the purpose of this paper, are made in chapter one of the *Foundations*: that to have moral worth an action must be done from duty, and that an action done from duty must wholly exclude the influence of inclination. Kant does not distinguish the two questions I separate above, and he does not discuss the possibility of overdetermination of motives. He holds both positions regarding the need for purity. In so far as my action is to have moral worth, there must be a special, conscientious motive which owes nothing to feelings but is the simple recognition of what is one's duty, or what is the law, and I cannot be helped to perform it by any inclination.

There is a history of conflicting readings of this passage. I cannot do justice to it, but here is a short summary. Kant's position is taken to be presented in four examples given in the *Foundations* of individuals who act solely from the motive of duty. Kant has easily dismissed as having no moral worth actions which accord with duty but are performed from self-interest. He then considers whether an action to which we are prompted by a direct inclination can be of moral worth. There is no explicit argument; four examples are presented: an individual through adversities loses his relish for life and wishes for death, but preserves his life through duty; a man's natural sympathy for others is extinguished by his own sorrow and preoccupation with personal need, but he helps others from a sense of duty; a third man is by temperament ill-endowed with fellow-feeling, cold, and indifferent to suffering, but he helps others from a sense of duty; an individual suffering from gout takes care of his own health not from any inclination to happiness but from the thought of duty.

Commentators agree that, by design, none of the men in the examples have any inclination to do the action in question, nor do they take pleasure in its performance. Two examples feature counter-inclinations, a third illustrates a lack of positive inclination, and a variant on the failure of fellow-feeling provides us with a fourth example, somehow over-looked, which is, I think, ambiguous with regard to the question of opposing inclinations. Since differentiation of the two examples of the failure of sympathy may settled some questions about interpretation, I will underline the differences. The first man is the 'friend of mankind', described as 'one of those persons so sympathetically constituted that without any motive of vanity or selfishness they find an inner satisfaction in spreading joy'.[1] When personal sorrow makes him insensible to others' needs he acts solely from duty. The second man is 'by temperament, cold and indifferent to the sufferings of others, perhaps because he is provided with special gifts of patience and fortitude and expects or even requires that others should have the same'.[2]

No one would deny that Kant is lavish in his praise of the individuals portrayed. And perhaps it is the warmth, rather than the fact, of the commendation of people we do not find likeable which accounts for much of the subsequent controversy. In any event, it has seemed to readers that Kant was endorsing all of the following propositions.

1. If an action is to have moral worth one must fight off counter-inclinations. (As in Schiller's parody, one must despise one's friends if one wishes to have moral worth in helping them.)
2. One cannot take satisfaction, or pleasure, in doing what has moral worth.
3. One cannot have affection or sympathy for someone one helps if one's act is to have moral worth.
4. One cannot be helped to perform an action which has moral worth by any inclination.
5. Even if one is motivated to perform an action from a sense of duty, and this motivation by itself would be sufficient for the performance of the action in question, the action has no moral worth if there is another motivation sufficient for performance of the action in question.
6. One cannot be influenced by an inclination to determine to do an action which has moral worth.
7. Only an act done from duty has moral worth: it is moral concern

[1] Immanuel Kant, *Foundations of the Metaphysics of Morals*, translated by Lewis White Beck (Library of Liberal Arts), p. 14.
[2] Ibid., p. 15.

or being motivated by concern to do what is one's duty which makes an action of moral worth.

Philosophers sympathetic to Kant responded by offering an interpretation which would deny that all but the last of the above were consequences of the Kantian examples: Kant was merely trying to isolate that motive which gives an action its distinctive evaluation as being of moral worth.[3] The plausibility of such an interpretation seems to derive from Kant's comparison of his use of examples in the second critique with the chemist's separation of a compound into its elements.[4] But it does not fit the text. Describing the onetime friend of mankind, Kant says

And now suppose him to tear himself, unsolicited by inclination, out of his dead insensibility and to perform this action only from duty and without any inclination—*then*—*for the first time* his action has genuine moral worth.'[5]

To put forth this reading of Kant one must, as a commentator notes, be willing to take the risk of inserting into the above proposition and others like it the qualification that it is the first time we can *know* that an action has moral worth.

Whatever the qualms, in general, of attributing to a philosopher a distinction he has not, but could easily have, made on his own behalf, in this case it is futile. For Kant explicitly, though less dramatically, summarizes his position and says that 'an act done from duty wholly excludes the influence of inclination.'[6]

There is a contemporary replay of opposing interpretations. In a recent article Richard Henson[7] takes the individuals discussed in the *Foundations* to be Kantian exemplars of moral worth, representing the view that the individual who acts from duty has no co-operating motives. But he attempts to make Kant sympathetic by offering two models of moral worth at work in Kant's moral theory. He argues that

---

[3] See, for example, H. J. Paton, *The Categorical Imperative*, Hutchinsons' University Library, p. 47, and Lewis White Beck, introduction, p. xix of Kant, *Foundations*, op. cit. and 'Sir David Ross on Duty and Purpose in Kant', *Phil. and Phen. Research,* 15 (1955), p. 104.

[4] Barbara Herman, 'On the Value of Acting from the Motive of Duty' *The Philosophical Review*, 90, 1981, p. 380 n. cites Beck's discussion of this comparison in his *Commentary on Kant's Critique of Practical Reason*, Chicago, 1960, p. 120 n. Beck refers to Kant's discussion in the *Second Critique*, pp. 92-3.

[5] Kant, *Foundations*, op. cit., p. 14.   [6] Ibid., p. 17.

[7] Richard Henson, 'What Kant Might Have Said: Moral Worth and the Overdetermination of Dutiful Action', *The Philosophical Review*, 88 (1979), 39-54.

we should understand Kant's commendation of the individuals under discussion in terms of the battle-citation model of moral worth. We will then be able to see the point of honouring those who have succeeded against great odds without accepting that it is a moral defect not to display gallantry. This model does not, however, seem to me to be Kant's since Kant, again in his summary, rejects the idea that in an act done from duty the agent must always fight off and overpower counter-inclinations.

Barbara Herman responds[8] with a variant of the idea that Kant's examples are meant to isolate the moral motive. She claims that the absence of inclination in Kant's exemplary individuals is not meant to express a general condition which must be fulfilled in order for an action to have moral worth. An action may be done from duty, have moral worth, even if inclinations are present. The point of their exclusion in the illustrations Kant offers may be seen, she argues, if we attend to the full descriptions of the men portrayed. For these are individuals so constituted that we can assume that they acted solely from inclinations in the past. It is only when they come to have counter-inclinations or to have been made insensible by misfortune that these individuals act from duty. It is of these particular men that Kant concludes that they act from duty 'only when' or 'for the first time' when they have no inclinations.

If Barbara Herman is correct, we cannot generalize on this basis and conclude tht 'if inclinations, no moral worth'. But this reading does not seem adequate for the text. For, without any break, Kant follows the example of the man struck with misfortune by the example of a man poorly endowed by nature with fellow-feeling. And of this creature Kant says that he has the opportunity to give himself 'a far higher worth',[9] by acting not from any inclinations, but from duty alone.

Barbara Herman argues that we should distinguish between the *presence* of inclinations and their *efficacy* in leading to action, and that we should understand Kant to require of action done from duty only that inclinations not be efficacious. They may be present, but they must not, she says, determine an action if it is to have moral worth. Indeed, she claims, this distinction owes much to moral insincerity and the possibility that Kant recognizes, that we may be unsure of our own motivation. Whether or not we think we should distinguish between the presence and the efficacy of inclinations in order to explain what it is

[8] Barbara Herman, op. cit., p. 15.
[9] Kant, *Foundations*, op. cit., p. 15.

for an action to be of moral worth, the text does not support a claim that this is Kant's position. Kant did not make this distinction and we do not know whether he 'failed to notice it' or whether he would have thought the distinction inadequate or mistaken. For the facts which both Kant and ourselves acknowledge, that we may not know the motives we act from and that we may be morally insincere, may be accounted for in more than one way.

A candidate for the attribution of 'mixed motives' might be described as fulfilling any of the following conditions:

a. There are various sources of motivation for the given action. The individual has more than one interest, or more than one concern, which may be expressed in the action. But concerns other than the thought of duty would be present only in what might be called 'dispositional' form. So we might speak of someone concerned about X or sympathetic to X as being disposed to have certain feelings or to want to do certain things for X, but if his concern was dispositionally present he would not 'be in the grip' of feelings.

b. In addition to the moral motive, feelings, sentiments, emotions, which typically lead him to act in certain ways, are non-dispositionally present; but they do not have motivating force on this occasion. They do not tug or push.

c. The feelings and emotions present along with the moral motive *do* have the capacity to move the agent.

To attribute fulfilment of (a) to the agent moved by the thought of duty is sufficient, I think, to account for the possibility of insincerity or lack of self-knowledge. (If I am sympathetically disposed to Mary, then even I feel no waves of emotion I may suspect or expect that my sympathies have motivational pull when I act in ways that affect her. If one is not prepared to believe that a disposition of this sort can have motivational efficacy, but thinks it must be actualized in the form of feelings, one will not, of course, think (a) sufficient.) It is possible to couple the attribution of (a) with a denial that items described in (b) actually exist, or to admit them but reserve the terms 'motivation' and 'inclination' to feelings which do have the capacity to move the agent (items described in (c)). One then has the option of agreeing with Barbara Herman that the presence, but not the efficacy, of items described in (b) or (c) is permitted in action done from duty, or of maintaining that it is not conceivable that one have present an item of co-operative motivating force which is not effective, hence, if actions done from duty exclude the influence of inclinations, items in (c) cannot be present. We can talk about other *possible* supportive motivation, but not actual motivation other than the thought of duty as present at the time one determines the action. Kant held, I said, that an action of moral worth must be motivated solely by the thought of duty. A plain observation is now encrusted with distinctions. I will try to summarize what I take to be Kant's position, as presented in the text. I will refer to my list of alleged consequences of the four examples.

Kant explicitly rejects the first proposition, that to have moral worth an agent must fight off counter-inclinations, and one of the examples features an individual who merely lacks positive inclinations to perform the dutiful action. Kant does not have to accept the second or third propositions, that the individual of moral worth cannot take pleasure in doing what is dutiful or cannot have sympathy for someone she helps if her act is to have moral worth. Kant might have accepted the distinction that inclinations may be present but not efficacious, and rejected (2) and (3). He might have denied the distinction but held that an individual can still be sympathetic, that is, disposed to feelings of compassion. At the time when action done from duty is determined, however, she is not in the grip of feelings. Kant could also have believed that the individual of moral worth gets some satisfaction or pleasure in what she does. For we can attribute to an agent satisfaction or pleasure in performing what is her duty without attributing to her either pleasures of anticipation or the anticipation of pleasure as prompters to act.

What is presupposed in denying (2) and (3) but continuing to maintain the central propositions ((6) and (7)), is a capacity Kant surely would have attributed to the rational agent, namely, the ability to disregard those sources of appeal or interest which would interfere with the proper course of one's deliberation about what to do. Just as the judge may tell the jury to disregard certain facts brought out in testimony, an individual may resolve to disregard those features of the situation which would influence judgement in some unsanctioned manner.

No commentator has disputed (7). Kant consistently claims that only an act done from duty has moral worth. It is being motivated by the thought that it is one's duty to do the action in question which makes the action of moral worth. Moral worth is attributed to individuals in the examples only when inclinations are, at the least, no longer effective. He explicitly denies that actions of moral worth may be influenced by inclinations. So we have ample reason to believe that Kant thought inclinations could not influence the agent in determining to do an action which has moral worth (6).

Would Kant, presented with the possibility of over-determination, have thought an over-determined action could have moral worth? What we know is that Kant did not think inclinations, motivations other than the thought of duty, could be influential in an action of moral worth. If it makes sense to suppose that there is motivation which does not influence action, then Kant could have accepted this kind of over-determination and continued to maintain (6) and (7).

I have left for last the question of (4), whether an inclination may be said to help one to perform an action which has moral worth. There is at least one kind of case which Kant allows for in the *Foundations*. We are said to have an indirect duty to promote our happiness, because if we are happy we will not be susceptible to the temptations to fail to do our duty. A general sense of well-being, positive joys, or delights, all may help. But these are not supportive motives in the form we wish to consider—whether Kant could attribute moral worth to an action for which we have some specific inclination, which does some needed work in getting the action done. Everything we have considered so far shows that Kant denied this possibility, at least in the *Foundations*. I will argue in a later section that there is a possible account of being moved by duty which would allow for supportive motivation and yet satisfy the central requirements of purity of motivation. I present it as a view Kant could accept, not one which is actually present in his work.

2. KANT'S ARGUMENTS

I have maintained that Kant demands both that we have a special moral motive and that it operate alone if our action is to have moral worth. Kant's arguments only support the view that it is a pure, conscientious, motive which confers moral worth on action or agent. None of them directly supports the view that the moral motive must be solitary. The arguments are familiar to Kant's readers: feelings cannot be commanded, but if it is the motivation which makes the act a good one, then the motivation must be what is commanded, as well as the act, so moral motivation cannot consist of a special feeling. If duty is unconditional, individuals cannot be excused from what they are obliged to do, but if duty were prompted by feelings one would be let out if one did not have the feeling in question, hence a sense of duty is not a feeling. Feelings only fortuitously lead to the right action, they cannot, therefore, serve as principles of action or the basis for one's decision of what it is right to do. They are not the right sort of considerations on which to base moral action. And finally, inclinations cannot constitute moral motives because an action which is thought to have moral worth is one which makes us esteem the agent, which is a credit to the individual. Esteem or credit stand in contrast, according to Kant, in other kinds of positive evaluation. The point Kant seems to be making here is that moral worth must be something an individual is able to achieve or give to herself. It stands in contrast to talents or natural temperament which may also be good. The appeal, it seems, is to a distinction between temperament and character, to a distinction between those possibilities for right action and goodness of person which are the function of one's inherited constitition and one's historical advantages, and those which are not. If the capacity for feelings is part of what is given to one, then, on the assumption that motivation is the basis for the attribution of moral worth, moral motivation cannot be a matter of feelings.

Whatever their independent merits, it seems we might accept these arguments without thinking that feelings, in the form of supporting motivation, radically *undermine* the value of the action. We could maintain with Kant that it is the sense of duty which confers or bears the moral value of action, and that feelings do not contribute to the moral worth of an action. But nothing so far indicates why feelings or inclinations which could motivate *preclude* one from acting partly from duty.

The reader may feel that it is only too obvious that Kant's demand for purity is excessively zealous and puritanical; we recognize that there are many considerations which motivate us in ordinary decisions. A job may offer the opportunity to develop one's abilities, and more money. Nothing precludes one from describing the agent as having acted from a desire for both. Nor do we think his appreciation of what money buys undermines whatever value we attribute to him as an individual who wishes to increase his capacities.

It seems to me, however, that the Kantian demand that a sense of duty operates alone can be seen to underlie common moral judgements. A look at a few examples will show the appeal of such a demand and point to an explanation of the principle involved.

Grading

An individual thinks that standards of fair grading require him to give a student a certain grade, which in this case is a good one. Liking the student or liking to give good grades, one feels, cannot be an additional motive which helps the agent in determining the grade if he is to be credited with acting from a sense of fairness. It looks as if the requirements of fairness are what must exclusively determine the action, if it is done from a sense of fairness, and that additional motives are not compatible with the idea of what fairness requires.

Baby-sitting

I promise to exchange baby-sitting. My child is cared for and it is my turn. I recognize that it is right for me to take care of the other child and feel some pull of conscience. But I am not sufficiently moved. I do not make up my mind to undertake the day's task until I am annoyed with the behaviour of my own child and think he might improve with company. It is, I think, difficult to describe me as having acted from the thought that I ought to keep my word.

Bus standing

An old woman has difficulty standing on the bus. I think that the right thing to do is obvious. I should give her my seat. (It is important here that I do not merely think that it a nice, even morally nice, thing to do, or of a sort that in general, I ought to do.) Again, I have some motivation to do it, but I do not. I then notice some resemblance to my aunt, and feelings of kinship prompt me to give her my seat. I think one feels reluctant to say that the thought that it was the right thing to do, even as one of a consortium of motives, moved me to act.

But why not? Even if one has some inclination to make the judgements I have suggested, one may, justifiably, be uneasy if there is no explanation. Why should one deny motivational efficacy to thoughts of fairness and duty just because in the imagined examples they must await support to actually lead to action? The key lies, I think, in the form of the expressed reason or motive. The agent in the above examples is said to think that the action he envisages is morally *required* . . . by need, promise-making, fairness.

Given that it is moral commitment which will make good the claim that the actions are required, it may, none the less, be easier to see the work done by a judgement of what is required if we look at examples which do not exhibit a moral motive. A student is committed to being a philosophy major and has no desire to change his field or the system. He finds that a given course is required by the department. Suppose it is also a course which has some appeal for the student. It does not seem intelligible to say that the student takes the course both because it is required and because it is appealing. Two assumptions are needed to make this example convincing. There is the initial description of the students as being committed to being a philosophy major. (*Requirements* are not decisive if they are not taken to be unconditional, even though commitment and unconditionality, outside of morality certainly, have contextual limitations.) Second, the judgement that the course is required is not a judgement which can be understood simply in terms of the comparative strength of interest in doing what is required. What is common to the moral examples and the philosophy major example is a feature of rational deliberation. This feature helps explain our initially paradoxical claim that we cannot have mixed motives in these cases.

With increased rationality we locate motivational power in the agent's judgement. In so far as we think a person's rational deliberation is successful we think him to operate on the basis of what he thinks justifies his proposed action. The evaluations, reasons, or considerations which figure in deliberation are conceived by the agent to justify to a certain degree, or to have a comparative priority. If we think the person acts as a result of rational deliberation, we think this judgement must be effective. If an individual judges that the reasons he has so far considered are adequate to justify acting, then, in so far as he is rational, he acts on the basis of these reasons. To keep the door open, as it were, to other reasons when he has judged it is time for decision and action is irrational. But if one judges that there are moral considerations which justify doing something, one would be undermining one's own judgement and decision-making to welcome further motivation. And what Kant, or we, seem to take as a fundamental moral intuition is that if one is morally committed, then to think some action is one's duty or the right thing to do *is* to judge that one has reason which is sufficient for action. We are now forced to say of the actions we have been considering so far, of someone acting both from a sense of duty and from some inclination, either that the person was akratic or that the description was incoherent: either the agent was morally committed and, thinking the act the right thing to do judged she had sufficient reason to act, but was not moved (hence we have a case of akrasia with no particularly interesting moral features) or one of the two motivations has been incorrectly described. One who is impressed by the fact, and the need, in ordinary life of the co-operation of factors other than moral concern in actions judged none the less of moral worth, would not be happy to rank these actions with the actions of the akratic.

If I am correct, the demand for purity of motive comes from a central feature of Kant's moral theory. For to judge an action one's duty is not only to judge it necessary; it is to judge it necessary, as motivated by the thought that it *is* necessary.[10] If Kant is correct in his analysis either we are all mistaken in supposing there can be such actions, that we can be so motivated, and so obliged, or, so it seems, the motive of duty must operate alone.

3. RECONSTRUCTIONISM

I hope to have presented the appeal of what at first seems an overly rigorous position, one which insists that recognition of what is the right thing to do (one's duty) must operate on its own in determining our actions. If, however, one finds this persuasive, one must find a way to acommodate the belief that sympathy and benevolence play an important part in moral life, that one is often helped by the capacity for fellow feeling to act as one ought, and that one's undertaking and perseverance in doing what is right may sometimes be supported by the capacity for affection as well as self-assertion, without bringing into question one's moral resolve, or one's capacity for rational action.

In this section I will propose a more generous account of what it is to act from duty, which will allow room for more than the bare recognition that something is right but which will, I hope, escape the objections which have been raised to complex motivation. In the preceding discussion there has been an assumption common to both the supporter and the critic of mixed motives, that in the envisaged situations the various reasons operated in the same way, that is, on the same level, and that one might understand the resultant motivation by simply adding up the combined strength of the motives prompting an action, or, where motives conflict, by vectoring forces. The individual agent is seen as the locus of these pushes and pulls.

---

[10] There is a perhaps illuminating parallel. One might want to say that in so far as one thought a proposition p true one was committed to the following: belief in p is epistemically necessary or required by the thought that it is epistemically required. That this is not otiose is seen in our incredulity regarding an individual who claims to believe q both because the evidence supports q and because q is comforting.

We can be more generous in recognizing varied sources of motivation in action that has moral worth if the agent can be seen to be in control, in control of her own motivation and acting in the name of what is morally required. The strength of the Kantian demand, I will claim, lies not in thinking that a clean wash demands an ever more purified motive, but in demanding that the agent be doing the laundering.

In order to give sense, or aplication, to the idea of the agent being in control of her motives and acting 'in the name of' what is morally required, I will appeal to what I take to be quite ordinary situations.

Jogger

I jog, but I have a hard time getting out in the morning to run, even though I think I ought to, for sound prudential reasons. Jogging contributes to my well-being. Some days I wake up and think the day would be a much better one if I started with a run, but I do not jump into my clothes. Now, reasons both appear and are searched out, marshalled to the side of my belief that I will feel better if I run; 'The sky is particularly beautiful today. It will be beautiful to run by the lake. My clothes are beginning to be tight.' I may appeal to vanity as well as to aesthetic considerations, but the point seems to be this: I think I ought, for prudential reasons, to run, and I will use whatever motivation I can find to get me to do it. The motive of greater well-being does not directly prompt action but works to get other motivation.

Philosopher

A philosopher wants to do some work on a particular problem which has puzzled him for some time, but it is a difficult one, and it is, in any case, not always easy to work. So he arranges to give a paper, knowing he would be too embarrassed to back out or to present something awful. The philosopher, like the jogger, uses knowledge of what moves him to motivate himself.

Host

I may be obliged to entertain a weekend guest, who is boring. In order to fulfil the obligation, as I understand it, to act from concern for him as a person and not merely to perform required tasks, I seek to find in his history something which makes him appealing, or at least engages interest. My interest in him, or liking for him, will then prompt me to do what I judge ought to be motivated by concern for any individual in one's charge.

Lawyer

A woman in full pursuit of her career in corporate law is not interested in family or marriage. She finds, however, that in the practice of corporate law a husband would add to her respectability, or credibility. She thinks, however, that the chances of staying married to anyone she is not fond of are poor. She is careful to cultivate a social life, and finds male acquaintances with qualities she finds amiable. She marries such a man, for whom she has affection.

If these examples are convincing, we will say that the jogger acted from prudence, the philosopher from genuine interest in philosophy, the host from moral concern, and the lawyer from ambition. What is common to these examples is that in each case there is not what might be called a 'heap' of motives but a complex, a structure in which one end dominates others. The dominant motive works, not directly on action, but prompts action by working on other sources of motivation. One might think, at first sight, that there is something in the nature of certain ends which permits the agent to collect motivation; life-long ambition, general well-being, or moral rightness stand in contrast to gluttony or golf, which would not be thought to lead one to collect motivation when the desire to eat or play are absent. But any objective might work; what is crucial is that the agent judges that the objective is of sufficient value for it to be the case that he *ought* to be prompted to action by the thought of it. Just as one may have deliberated and come to the conclusion that a given action is the thing to do but face a problem about means, one may have a problem about motivation, or how to get oneself to do it. It is important to see that a question of how to motivate oneself or keep oneself motivated is like a question of how to obtain the skills necessary for a position or an action. It is not a question of whether there is something more to be said for engaging in a project, something more which would tilt the scale and make one opt for the action in question.

The claim I am making is that one may be deemed to act from the sense of duty as a single, albeit complexly structured, motive, if one judges that a given action is one's duty, thinks that this thought provides one with sufficient reason to perform the action, but finding oneself insufficiently motivated to actually do it, searches out ways of motivating oneself.

I shall conclude by considering two objections to this proposal. A man may be genuinely distressed at his behaviour when angry, morally distressed about what he does. He thinks, for moral reasons, that he ought to check his anger. But becuase he cannot seem to change by himself, he goes to a behaviour modification therapist.[11] The therapist effects an association between the onset of anger and a flood of unpleasant images, which the agent finds too awful to bear. He checks his anger to stop them. Although we may be clear that the individual's motive in going to the therapist is a moral one, it is difficult to think moral concern motivates his later responses. So, one might object, an individual may look for and find motivation which enables him to do what he thinks he ought, because he thinks he ought to do it, yet none the less he may not be thought to act *in the name of* or *from* moral concern.

There are two responses to this example. First, the secondary motivation does not seem to be under the agent's control. Once set up by the therapist the behaviour looks too automatic. We might demand that secondary motivation for acts of moral worth, whether set up for the occasion or cultivated for a general run, be under the agent's continuous control. Second, our attention is drawn to the difference of evaluation of the specific acts of checking anger and the long-term project of changing himself which brings the individual to the therapist. It may be that our interest in character assessment and in determining what are morally good motives leads us to evaluate a slice of life, rather than a specific act, and that what is relevant is the way an individual plans to live during a given period of her life, her projects rather than the acts of a given moment.

I want to turn now to the objection formulated at the end of the last section. Will not the individual who looks for helpful motivation be either akratic or else not fully morally committed? For to judge that moral considerations give him sufficient reason to act, and yet not to act, is to be akratic. But to judge that he ought to act, that there are moral considerations which make an action obligatory, and yet withhold the judgement that he has sufficient reason to act, is to fail to take morality seriously. (It is no doubt difficult in practice to make these distinctions, yet it seems that we want to draw a line between someone who is genuine in his conviction that he ought, morally, to do something, but is somehow unable to get himself to do it (weakness of the will) and someone who *speaks* of what is right or

[11] I am indebted to Charles Marks for the example.

fair but who does not give full weight to his moral concerns, and so cannot be said to judge that moral obligations give him sufficient reason to act.) I argued that a rational being would act on his judgement that he had sufficient reason to perform a certain act, and that thinking an action the morally right thing to do, or what one morally ought to do, committed one to such a judgement. I now want to modify this account, putting to work an idea expounded, in unpublished work, by Paul Grice. It is the view that we should understand the connection between *obligations* and *motivation* in the following way: if John thinks he ought to do some action *a*, then that requires that either John wants to *a* or he thinks that he ought to want to *a*. Since this idea of a disjunction between wanting and the judgement that one ought to want can be regressively applied, if John thinks that he *ought* to want to *a*, then that requires that either he wants to want to *a* or he thinks that he ought to want to do *a*. In principle there is no end to such a regressive analysis. But the idea is that at some point real people will come to a stop and the original judgement of obligation will be cashed out in a desire. But there is no guarantee at what level. This would fit the intuition we have that someone who genuinely believes herself obliged to be motivated must want to do something, while recognizing that there are everyday lapses of sensitivity which may prevent one who thinks she ought to act from wanting to act. In advance we do not know how far we may be from a ground-floor desire to act. But what we will demand is *some* want, and so some chain that leads to action. On this account, we can say equally well of the individual who acts on a second or third order volition to do what is morally required that she acts from the thought that she ought. And what one would expect of an individual who wants to want to do something is precisely a search for (first order) motivation to perform the action.

Suppose we grant that the agent who marshalls motivation to the side of moral concern and the subsequent action are of moral worth. It seems overly rationalistic to think that only a case in which one *actively* seeks out supportive motivation testifies to moral worth or to the moral commitment of an individual. It seems sufficient to require that an individual would, if needed take steps to see that he fulfils his obligations, whether that requires means-taking of the ordinary sort or finding co-operative motivation for himself. And he may find himself with allied interests or inclinations before any such need exists or is perceived, indeed it may be by his own design that support is, in general, at hand. We may, as Kant certainly thought in his later work, have the duty to cultivate natural sympathy to aid practical concern.

4. EPILOGUE

Pure gold, without a trace of base metal; honest, unselfish, practical: he took up the Union cause and made himself its champion, as a true Yorkshireman was sure to do, partly because of his Quaker anti-slavery convictions, and partly because it gave him a practical opening in the House. As a new member, he needed a field.

(*The Education of Henry Adams*)

This paper's limits are set by this quotation. I have not explained how Henry Adams could admire the politician characterized above, nor why we should trust him in his assessment. Yet I think Henry Adams meant us to believe the English politician acted from both sources of motivation, meant us to accept that he was truly admirable, and meant the statement to have its bite. My proposal for a more generous model of moral motivation will not help us here. I argued that what was important for purity of motive was that the agent license the reasons or motives from which he acts. Because he thinks that he ought to be motivated by the recognition of the rightness of an act, he seeks and accepts helpful motivation. But, as I read the quotation above, the politician chose to support the Union, said to himself that this was the area in which he should fight for a good cause, and the reasons for this decision were non-moral. We cannot attribute his extra-moral motivation to the moral motive. My proposal cannot be the whole story of supportive motivation.

If we are to understand the assessment of character made by Adams, we will have to widen the scope of our inquiry. We will have to question the role of the motive of duty within the planning of our lives and not only look at its expression in individual actions, as I have done. To do this will, I think, require an explanation of what it is to be a responsible individual. I have made some use of the idea of an agent's being in control of his motivation, and I suggested, almost in passing, that the push–pull model of motivation has not been adequate in offering us an account of rational agency. It is to be expected that fuller discussion of this question would go hand in hand with the discussion of moral character.

19

GRICE ON HAPPINESS

RICHARD WARNER

Happiness is one of the focal points of Paul Grice's recent work in moral psychology.[1] Like Aristotle, Grice thinks that a detailed and informative account of happiness has a central role to play in the philosophical elucidation of morality, but my concern here is with the account of happiness itself, with Grice's answer to the question, 'What is it to be happy?'—or, more exactly, 'What is it to lead a happy life?'

Right at the outset, it is worth distinguishing this question from the question of what it is to feel happy. To feel happy, one must have a certain sort of *experience*, and one can have an experience of the appropriate sort, one can feel happy, yet not be happy. Suppose one morning I find myself in a euphoric mood; when you remark that you have not seen me so happy in a long time, I paint a bleak picture of my circumstances and prospects. My euphoria is just a brief and unexpected relief from my oppressive sense of failure. I am not happy—in the sense that I am not, over the present stretch of time at least, leading a happy life.

And one can be happy—be leading a happy life—without feeling happy. You might correctly regard yourself as happy even though you are momentarily depressed; you see your depression as a mere transient mood occurring against the background of the successful realization of your most important goals. (This does not, of course, show that one can count as leading a happy life if one *never* feels happy. I will return to this point.)

In what follows, I will use 'is happy' and 'is leading a happy life' interchangeably. This departs somewhat from ordinary usage since one may, for example, use 'Are you happy?' to ask if one feels happy. And there are other uses of 'is happy' I am setting aside—for example 'I am happy with my job' (the truth of which requires neither that I be

---

[1] This work is contained mainly but not exclusively in 'Reflections on Morals' (with Judy Baker), 'Reply to Davidson on "Intending",' and the John Locke Lectures, 'The Conception of Value" (The Carus Lectures, unpublished).

leading a happy life nor that I feel happy). Finally, I will understand both 'is happy' and 'is leading a happy life' as true of a person throughout longer and shorter periods of time. Thus Jones may not have led a happy life for the first two years he lived in New York, may have lived a happy life for the next four years, and then ceased to live a happy life for the next two years. Of course, this does not mean that we cannot ask whether Jones is leading a happy life where the relevant period of time is his entire life—including the eight years in New York; and the answer to the queston may be *yes* even though the eight years in New York include four unhappy years. Taking his life as a whole its unhappy periods may be more than balanced out by its happy periods.

1. A CONDITION OF ADEQUACY

Any proposed answer to the question, 'What is it to be happy?' should provide a basis for explaining—or explaining away—four facts, or apparent facts, about happiness. The answer should explain away any of the proposed facts that it treats as merely apparent—explaining why they are false while accounting for their preanalytic plausibility. The answer should illuminate and explain any of the facts it recognized as genuine. Now while I think all four proposed facts really are genuine facts about happiness, the considerations I offer here are merely intended to make the proposals plausible; I want to leave open the possibility that an adequate account of happiness should reject any or all of the putative facts.

1. The first proposed fact is that a person is happy only if he satisfies enough of his desires.[2]

Reflection on the role of happiness in practical reasoning motivates this requirement. We act so as to satisfy a variety of desires, and one reason we act on the desires that we do is that we think that, in satisfying *those* desires, we will be leading a happy life. We attain happiness, if we do, by satisfying our desires.

And we must satisfy *enough* of our desires—where what counts as enough is a question both of *how many* desires are satisfied, and of *how important* those desires are. The number of desires is relevant

[2] Or, alternatively, realizes enough of his ends. Some philosophers I have talked to have insisted that only the alternative reading is correct. They distinguish between desiring E and having E as an end (which may be true even if I do not desire E), and on their view I must realize enough of my *ends*. Given my purposes here, there is no need to settle this issue.

because a person may be unhappy by virtue of satisfying too few of his desires: Smith succeeds in satisfying the desire for political power which has been his single-minded aim, but despite his success he is unhappy, for he has given up too much—reading, travel, friendship, and so on. None of these things is as important to him as political power, but in giving them up, he has given up satisfying enough of his desires.

But importance also matters. Smith's single-minded pursuit of political power might have made him happy had the desire for it been sufficiently important. Imagine Smith in the midst of his success. He realizes he has given up much, but it does not matter, for in attaining political power he has attained enough of what he wants. The importance of the desire satisfied compensates for the desires whose satisfaction Smith foregoes.

Finally, one must really satisfy enough of one's desires and not merely *think* that one is. To motivate the insistence on this requirement, imagine a man who owns a restaurant. He prides himself on his astute business sense that—in his eyes—has guided the restaurant through difficult times and built it into a success. He also takes great pleasure in the love and respect of his wife and children. Secure in his sense of personal and business success, he regards himself as happy.

In reality, the owner has no business sense whatsoever. The manager really runs the restaurant, but, to preserve his job, he adroitly conceals this fact from the owner. All the employees as well as the owner's wife and children know the true situation. The children regard their father as a buffoon and join with the employees in laughing at him behind his back. His wife is having an affair with the manager.

While the owner thinks he is happy, and while he may feel happy, there is good reason to deny that he is leading a happy life. In support of this point, suppose the owner discovers the truth. Looking back on his deceived state, he regards the happiness he thought he had as a mere illusion. It certainly makes sense for him to regard it as illusory; indeed, it is difficult to see how he could justifiably think otherwise. The best explanation of this point is, I suggest, that happiness requires the actual satisfaction of desires.

2. A person is happy only if he *believes* he is (in the process of) satisfying enough of his desires.[3]

---

[3] There is an ambiguity here which is worth pointing out but which we need not resolve. The second requirement may mean that there is some *particular* collection of desires such that the person believes that in satisfying the desires in

Far from being an apparent fact about happiness, this proposed requirement may seem rather dubious. Cannot a person satisfy enough of his desires yet be so unreflective that he never forms the belief that he is satisfying enough of his desires? And if such a person is possible, why should his being so unreflective exclude him from happiness?

But looked at in another way, the second requirement is not implausible, for it is certainly plausible that the happy person has a certain 'affirmative attitude' toward his life. His way of life appeals to him; he finds it rewarding, and he is firmly emotionally engaged by it. Moreover it is also reasonable to suggest that the happy person has this affirmative attitude because (in part at least) he *sees* that he is satisfying enough of his desires; his perception of his success is part of the explanation of why he finds his way of life so rewarding and appealing.

These considerations may explain the strength of the intuition that to lead a happy life one must realize that one is satisfying enough of one's desires. In one form or another, this intuition is widely shared. Aristotle (as I will argue later) makes such a belief a component of happiness (eudaimonia). Hume makes it clear that, because of the interaction between passion and imagination, one's happiness depends crucially and unavoidably on one's estimate of the extent to which one's desires will be satisfied.[4] Kant defines happiness as 'a rational being's *consciousnnss of* the agreeableness of life which almost without interuption accompanies his whole existence' (my emphasis);[5] he does not define agreeableness. Finally, John Rawls suggests that 'a person is happy . . . during those periods when he is successfully carrying through a rational plan, *and he is with reason confident that his efforts will come to fruition*' (my emphasis).[6]

An account of happiness should either explain away the widespread intuition behind the second requirement or endorse the requirement and explain why it is true.

3. A person is happy only if he not only satisfies enough of his
that collection, he is satisfying enough of his desires. or it may mean that the person believes there is *some collection or other* such that in satisfying the desires in that collection he is satisfying enough of his desires.

[4] David Hume, *A Treatise on Human Nature.*

[5] Immanuel Kant, *The Critique of Practical Reason*, Bobbs-Merrill (trans. Lewis White Beck) 1978, p. 20. This is *one* of the things Kant says about happiness. He tends to say different things in different places.

[6] John Rawls, *A Theory of Justice*, Oxford University Press, 1972, p. 550.

desires but also *enjoys* the experiences and activities that satisfy those desires.[7]

A person certainly does not count as happy if his life is utterly devoid of enjoyment, or if enjoyments are too few and far between. A happy life contains *enough* enjoyment. It is important to note that merely satisfying enough of one's desires does not ensure that one's life contains enough enjoyment, for enjoyment cannot be identified with the mere satisfaction of desire.[8] One may desire—even intensely— to see *Star Wars*; one may even desire to see the movie simply for its own sake, satisfy that desire, yet fail to enjoy seeing the movie. The distinction between desire satisfaction and enjoyment gives the third requirement its point, for a person will not qualify as happy if he fails to experience enjoyment when satisfying his important desires.

For example: Miller is a businessman who believes his happiness consists in becoming president of the company. He satisfies this desire, but he finds his success empty. His problem is not that he wants something else. There is no way of life that he sees as better or more desirable; indeed, in satisfying his desire to be president, he satisfies enough of his desires, for he is in the process of satisfying a group of desires organized around the central desire to be president, and no important desire is absent from this group. Miller's problem, as he is dismayed to discover, is that he does not enjoy the experiences and activities that satisfy these desires. His situation is exactly analogous with the *Star Wars* example except that the divorce between satisfaction and enjoyment occurs throughout the most central part of Miller's life. It does not seem plausible to regard a person in such circumstances as leading a happy life.

The relation between happiness and enjoyment is almost certainly more complex and more important than the discussion so far has indicated, for enjoyment links the concepts of happiness and the self. William James makes this point forcefully in *The Principles of Psychology*. 'I am', James writes,

often confronted by the necessity of standing by one of my empirical selves and relinquishing the rest. Not that I would not, if I could, be both handsome and fat and well dressed, and a great athlete, and make a million a year, be a wit, a *bon-vivant*, and a lady-killer, as well as

[7] The assumption that *experiences and activities* are what one enjoys is not essential, but I think it is correct; see my 'Enjoyment', *Philosophical Review*, vol. 89, no. 4, October 1980.

[8] See 'Enjoyment', pp. 508–11.

a philosopher, a philanthropist, statesman, warrior, and African explorer, as well as a 'tone-poet' and saint. But the thing is simply impossible. The millionaire's work would run counter to the saint's; the *bon-vivant* and the philanthropist would trip each other up; the philosopher and the lady-killer could not well keep house in the same tenement of clay. Such different characters may conceivably at the outset of life be alike *possible* to a man. But to make any one of them actual, the rest must more or less be suppressed. So the seeker of his truest, strongest, deepest self must review the list carefully, and pick out the one on which to stake his salvation. All other selves thereupon become unreal, but the fortunes of this self are real. Its failures are real failures, its triumphs real triumphs, carrying shame and gladness with them.[9]

While James's language is perhaps more picturesque than perspicuous, James's 'standing by one of my empirical selves' does describe a genuine psychological phenomenon, a phenomenon related, as the passage suggests, to enjoyment and happiness.[10]

Another aspect of the relation between enjoyment and happiness is worth noting here; enjoyment ties the notion of being happy to the notion of feeling happy. Suppose you are enjoying the successful realization of an 'empirical self' that you are 'standing by'; then it is appropriate to describe you as feeling happy, and in this sense of 'feel happy', it is reasonable to suggest that one does not count as leading a happy life unless one at least sometimes feels happy. (This is not, of course, to suggest that this is the only sense in which we use 'feel happy'.)

4. A person is happy, is leading a happy life, only if his life is— and is seen by him as being—worthwhile.[11]

An example will be useful here. Suppose Jones supports himself as a part-time computer programmer. He sees this as a mere means which allows him to pursue the activity to which he devotes all the time he possibly can: counting blades of grass. Is Jones leading a happy life? There are three cases to distinguish; in each, we ask Jones what makes his life worthwhile.

[9] William James, *The Principles of Psychology*, Dover, New York, 1950, vol. 1, p. 309–10.
[10] It is frequently suggested (following Harry Frankfurt, 'Freedom of the Will and the Concept of a Person', *Journal of Philosophy*, 14 January 1971) that this phenomenon can be explicated in terms of second-order desires. I do not think this is correct; see Gary Watson, 'Free Agency' *The Journal of Philosophy*, vol. 72, no. 8, 24 April 1975.
[11] The discussion which follows owes much to Andreas Esh_eté.

First case. Jones answers that there is nothing worthwhile about counting blades of grass—unless the mere fact that he likes to do it makes it worthwhile. He just goes in for counting blades of grass, and that is that.

Some may be quite disinclined to count Jones as leading a happy life in this case since his life seems wasted. He wastes his talents and capacities; counting blades of grass hardly employs or develops them, and this waste is not redeemed by the contribution that the activity makes to some significant human concern. But there is disagreement here. Some—notably, Rawls[12]—are willing to count Jones as happy.

Second case. Jones does explain why counting blades of grass is worthwhile; at least, he offers an explanation *he* regards as adequate. He says, 'Well, counting anything is worthwhile, and I happen particularly to enjoy counting blades of grass.' Here, for essentially the same reasons as in the first case, one may be disinclined to count Jones as happy. His answer does not show that his life is not wasted as there is no evident reason we should agree that 'counting anything is worthwhile'.

Of course, this raises the question of what counts as an *adequate* explanation of what makes a life worthwhile, and this in turn raises the question of what it *means* to think a life worthwhile. Any account of happiness that endorses the fourth requirement should answer these questions.

Third case. Jones produces an adequate explanation of what makes counting blades of grass worthwhile. It is not clear that it is possible for Jones to do this; whether it is depends, in part at least, on what counts as an adequate explanation.

Now even if one is sympathetic to the fourth requirement, one may wonder why we should require not only that the happy person's life be worthwhile, but also that the person should *believe* it to be worthwhile. What about a person whose life is worthwhile but who is so unreflective that he never *sees* it as worthwhile? Why should such a person be excluded from counting as happy?

This question is exactly analogous to the question about unreflective people raised by the second requirement, and the answer is essentially the same: namely, that the happy person is characterized by a certain sort of 'affirmative attitude' towards his life. In discussing the second requirement, we said that the happy person finds his life appealing and rewarding because he realizes that he is satisfying enough of his

[12] *A Theory of Justice*, pp. 432–3 and p. 550.

desires. What motivates the fourth requirement is the idea that this 'affirmative attitude' is not just the result of his perception that he is satisfying enough of his desires, but also the product of the perception that his life is worthwhile.

This completes the discussion of the fourth proposed requirements, and at this point one may wonder why we have focused on precisely these four. Why stop with these? Are there not further requirements, some of which may be at least as important as the four we have selected? I think the answer to this question is *no*. It is reasonable to think that the four proposed requirements are jointly sufficient for happiness. Consider someone who meets them all. He is satisfying enough of his desires, and he enjoys the experiences and activities that satisfy these desires; moreover, these experiences and activities, or some of them at least, realize and express one or more 'empirical selves' that he is 'standing by', and he enjoys this self-realization and self-expression. He has an affirmative attitude towards his life; he finds it appealing and rewarding because he sees that he is satisfying enough of his desires, and because he sees that his life is worthwhile. And he is not mistaken in this last conviction. His life is worthwhile.

To meet this description is to be happy; that is certainly not an implausible suggestion.[13] So it is not unreasonable to focus on the four requirements, and to demand that an account of happiness illuminate and explain them (or explain them away).

2. THE ARISTOTELIAN BACKGROUND

How well does Grice's account meet this condition of adequacy? In answering this question I will focus primarily on 'Some Reflections about Ends and Happiness'.[14] Grice begins this paper with a discussion of Aristotle's *Nicomachean Ethics*, and we will follow suit. Grice's account of happiness is a modified version of Aristotle's, and with a sketch of Aristotle's account before us we will be able to see the rationale, extent, and significance of the modifications.

On Aristotle's account, all four proposed requirements turn out to be genuine facts about happiness (eudaimonia),[15] and the simplest way to present the account is to consider each requirement in turn.

[13] Compare Richard Kraut, 'Two Conceptions of Happiness', *The Philosophical Review*, vol. 88, no. 2, April 1979.

[14] This paper is unpublished.

[15] I think Kraut has argued convincingly in 'Two Conceptions of Happiness' that 'happiness' is a good translation of 'eudaimonia'.

First requirement: a person is happy only if he satisfies enough of his desires.

Aristotle certainly thinks that happiness requires the satisfaction of desires. 'Happiness is some kind of activity of the soul in conformity with virtue' (1099ᵃ26),[16] and the activity in question is activity directed toward the satisfaction of desire, for 'virtue is a characteristic involving choice', and 'choice is the starting point of action' (1139ᵃ31) while 'the starting point of choice . . . is desire and reasoning directed toward some end' (1139ᵃ33-34). (This does not mean that all desires one tries to satisfy exist prior to reasoning about what to do; reasoning may lead one to form new desires.[17])

One must really satisfy one's desires and not merely think that one is, for 'virtue is a characteristic which is guided by right reason . . .; and right reason in moral matters is practical wisdom' (1144ᵇ). 'It is a mark of men of practical wisdom to have deliberated well' (1142ᵇ32), and 'excellence in deliberation is correctness in assessing what is conducive to the end, concerning which pracitcal wisdom gives a *true* conviction' (1142ᵇ34, my emphasis).

Finally, one must also satisfy *enough* of one's desires, for 'one swallow does not make a spring, nor does one sunny day; similarly, one day or a short time does not make a man blessed and happy' (1089ᵃ18). In most circumstances, a person satisfies enough of his desires just in case his activity is in conformity with virtue, for such a person 'will not be dislodged from his happiness easily by any misfortune that comes along but only by great and numerous disasters' (1101ᵃ9-11).

One might complain here that Aristotle does not really explain what it is to satisfy enough of one's desires since he does not tell us how to determine when disasters are sufficiently 'great and numerous'. But this complaint is only partially justified. Recall that whether one satisfies enough of one's desires is a question both of how many desires are satisfied and of how important those desires are. Aristotle does tell us how to identify the important desires. Some desires are such that, should one act on them, one's activity will be in conformity with virtue, and some are not. The former are the important ones in the sense that it is only through satisfying those desires that one will be happy.

[16] The translation is Martin Ostwald's (*Nicomachean Ethics*, Bobbs-Merrill, 1962.

[17] See Terry Irwin, 'Aristotle on Reason, Desire and Virtue', *The Journal of Philosophy*, vol. 72, no. 17, 2 October 1975.

Second requirement: a person is happy only if he believes he is satisfying enough of his desires.

Aristotle, as I will argue shortly, holds that the happy person realizes that his activity is in conformity with virtue, so it follows that the happy person believes he is satisfying enough of his desires—since one satisfies enough of one's desires (in most circumstances) just in case one's activity is in conformity with virtue. To see that the happy person realizes his activity is in conformity with virtue, consider what Aristotle says about choice:

Choice is the starting point of action: it is the source of motion but not the end for the sake of which we act. The starting point of choice, however, is desire and reasoning directed toward some end . . . Now thought alone moves nothing; only thought which is directed to some end and concerned with action can do so. And it is this kind of thought also which initiates production. For whoever produces something produces it for an end. The product he makes is not an end in an unqualified sense, but an end only in a particular relation and of a particular operation. Only the goal of action is an end in the unqualified sense: *for the good life is an end, and desire is directed toward this*. Therefore, choice is either intelligence motivated by desire or desire operating through thought, and it is as a combination of these two that man is a starting point of action. (1139^a31–1139^b5, my emphasis)

The good life—happiness—serves as a target at which one aims, and the happy person will use his abilities to perceive and to reason to make sure that he is, and stays, 'on target'. This is why he will believe that his activity is in conformity with virtue.

The target metaphor is Aristotle's. At the beginning of Book VI, Aristotle notes that to act in conformity with virtue, 'we must choose the median, and not excess or deficiency, and the median is what right reason dictates' (1138^b19–21). In this way, virtue provides 'a target on which a rational man keeps his eye as he bends and relaxes his effort to attain it' (1138^b23–24). In this remark, Aristotle is thinking of the target as a particular virtue like courage, but it is one of the points of Book VI that happiness itself serves as such a target. That is, one tries to ensure that one's activity as a whole—the whole pattern of thought, desire, and action—is in conformity with virtue, for it is only with reference to the standard of overall conformity that the person of practical wisdom can determine what counts as the mean between excess and deficiency.[18] So to fail to form beliefs about whether my

[18] Support for this claim can be found in David Wiggins, 'Deliberation

activity as a whole is in conformity with virtue would fail to exhibit practical wisdom (see 1144^{a}23-25 on the difference between practical wisdom and cleverness), and to fail to exhibit practical wisdom is to fail to be in conformity with virtue (1144^{b}31-1145^{a}2) and hence to fail to be happy.

It is necessary then that the happy person believe that his activity is in conformity with virtue; this belief is an essential component of the reason-providing role practical wisdom plays in directing the activities of the happy person.

But this is not the only contribution the belief makes to happiness. Aristotle tells us that 'life is desirable especially for good men, because existence is good and pleasant to them: they are pleased when they are conscious of the presence in them of what is in itself good' (1170^{b}3-5).[19] Courage, honour, health, and truthfulness are examples of things good in themselves, and, of course, so is the highest good—happiness, activity in conformity with virtue. A happy person enjoys seeing the realization in his life of the highest good; this is why life is especially desirable for him.

Third requirement: a person is happy only if he not only satisfies enough of his desires but also *enjoys* the experience and activities that satisfy these desires.

Aristotle assigns enjoyment a central place in his account of happiness, for he holds that

actions which conform to virtue are naturally pleasant, and, as a result, such actions are not only pleasant for those who love the noble but also pleasant in themselves. The life of such men has no further need of pleasure as an added attraction but contains pleasure in itself. (1099^{a}12-17)

Such 'pleasures . . . complete the activities of a perfect or complete and supremely happy man' (1176^{a}26-28).

Aristotle does not link happiness and enjoyment to the self. There is nothing in Aristotle like James's notion of 'standing by one of my empirical selves'. Enjoyment is linked via virtue to character, but Aristotle's notion of character is not at all the same as what James means by an 'empirical self'.

Fourth requirement: a person is happy only if his life is—and is seen by him as being—worthwhile.

and Practical Reason' in Amélie Rorty (ed.), *Essays on Aristotle's Ethics*, esp. pp. 236-7.

[19] See also 1166^{b}11-28.

When discussing courage, Aristotle remarks that 'the closer a man is to having virtue or excellence in its entirety and the happier he is, the more pain death will bring him. Life is more *worth living* for such a man than anyone else, *and he realizes that fact*, and that is painful' (1117^b9-13, my emphasis). The happy person realizes his life is worth living becuase—as we saw in the discussion of the second requirement—he realizes that his activity is in conformity with virtue; and to realize this is to see that one is realizing in one's life intrinisically worthwhile things—courage, honour, health, and so on. And it is clear that Aristotle thinks that courage, honour, and the like are intrinsically worthwhile, intrinsically worthy of choice. As he says, 'Honour, pleasure, intelligence, and all virtue we choose partly for themselves—for we would choose each even if no further advantage would accrue from them' (1097^b1-3). We do not *merely* choose them for themselves because 'we also choose them for the sake of happiness because we assume that it is through them that we will be happy' (1097^b3-5).

Aristotle's account of happiness is attractive for the systematic way it relates virtue, enjoyment, reasoning, and action. Virtue looms large in the account as it has a fourfold function. (1) Virtue plays a role in the explanation of what counts as enough (as we saw in the discussion of the first requirement). (2) Virtue has a reason-providing function in so far as it is a target at which one aims (second requirement). (3) It is also a source of enjoyment (second and third requirements). (4) Conformity to virtue is what makes a person's life worthwhile.

One may feel that virtue looms too large. One may reject—as Bernard Williams does[20]—Aristotle's assumption that there are things that are intrinsically worthwhile, and in light of this rejection one will hardly be inclined to assign an Aristotelian conception of virtue a prominent place in the account of happines. Or, putting aside scepticism about virtue, one may be convinced—along with Aristotle's stoic sucessors as well, of course, as Kant—that one can be happy without being virtuous, and virtuous without being happy.

One would like two things at this point: a way to settle the issue about the role, if any, of virtue in the account of happiness. And, however that issue is settled, a way to preserve what is attractive in Aristotle's account—its systematic connections among enjoyment, reasoning, action, and (perhaps) virtue. There is a way one might

[20] Bernard Williams, 'Internal and External Reasons' in Bernard Williams, *Moral Luck*, Cambridge University Press, 1981. I am assuming that if something is intrinsically worthwhile, there is an external reason to bring it about.

achieve both of these things at once. Suppose we could find a substitute for Aristotle's notion of conformity to virtue—a non-normative
substitute that could be explained without any appeal to value or
worthwhileness. The idea would be to have the substitute notion
discharge at least the first three functions Aristotle assigns to virtue.
The substitute notion would provide a basis for explaining what counts
as enough; it would serve as the target at which one aims, and it would
be linked to enjoyment in ways similar to Aristotle's notion of virtue.
Having developed such a substitute account, we could use it as the
background against which to raise the question of the relation of virtue
to happiness. The hope would be that this procedure would allow an
illuminating and informative treatment of the question.

This is Grice's strategy in 'Some Reflections about Ends and Happiness'.

3. GRICE'S ACCOUNT OF HAPPINESS

Grice's substitute is the notion of a 'set or system of ends suitable for
the direction of life'. Grice writes,

. . . perhaps something can be done with the notion of a set or system
of ends suitable for the direction of life. The leading idea would be of
a system which is maximally stable, one whose employment for the
direction of life would be maximally conducive to its continue employment for the purpose, which would be maximally self-perpetuating.
To put the matter another way, a system of ends would be stable to
the extent to which, though not constitutionally immune from modification, it could accommodate changes of circumstances of vicissitudes
which would impose modification upon other less stable systems.
We might need to supplement the idea of stability by the idea of
flexibility; a system will be flexible in so far as, should modification be
demanded, they are achievable by easy adjustment and evolution;
flounderings, crises, and revolutions will be excluded or at a minimum.
A succession of systems of ends within a person's consciousness could
then be regarded as stages in the development of a single life-scheme,
rather than as the replacement of one life-scheme by another.

It is worth noting in passing that there is a distinctly Aristotelian
echo in the emphasis on stability as an essential component of happiness. Aristotle's remarks that 'no function of man possesses as much
stability as do activities in conformity with virtue' (1100^{b}12-13).

Grice suggests that

the idea that happiness might be . . . partially characterized in something like this kind of way would receive some support if we could
show reason to suppose that features which could plausibly be regarded,
or which *have* been regarded, as characteristic of happiness, are at least
of a satisfactory system of life, are also features conducive to stability.

Grice offers seven features which he regards as very plausible candidates.
I quote at length.

(1) *Feasibility*. An adopted system of ends should be workable; the
more it should turn out that actions and performances dictated by the
system cannot be successfully undertaken, the stronger are the grounds
for modification of the system . . .

(2) *Autonomy* . . . The less reliant one's system of ends is on aids the
availability of which is not within one's control . . . the more stable, or
the more securely stable, it will in general be . . .

(3) *Compatibility of component ends* . . . I think we have to recognize
that, characteristically, an end is such as to be realizable in varying
degrees, and that it would be unrealistic to demand a system in which
the realization of one end was never diminished by the realization of
others. What we in fact may reasonably look for is a *harmony* of ends;
the possibility, that is, with respect to competing ends, of finding
an acceptable balance in the degrees of realization to be expected for
each end . . .

(4) *Comprehensiveness* . . . The comprehensiveness of a system varies
directly with its capacity to yield answers to those practical questions
which should be decided in the light of general principles . . . Deficiency
in comprehensiveness seems to legitimize modification.

(5) *Supportiveness of component ends*. A system's stability will be
increased if the pursuit of some ends enhances the pursuit of others . . .

(6) *Simplicity*. A system's effectiveness as a guide to living will depend,
in part, on how easy it is to determine its deliverances on particular
questions . . .

(7) *Agreeableness*. One form of agreeableness will, unless counteracted,
automatically attach to the attainment of an object of desire, such
attainment being routinely a source of satisfaction. The generation of
satisfaction will, then, not provide an independent ground for preferring one system of ends to another. But other modes of agreeableness,
such as being a source of delight, which are not routinely associated
with the fulfilment of desire, could discriminate independently of other
features relevant to such preferences, between one system and another.

A system the operation of which is specially agreeable would be stable not only *vis-á-vis* rival systems, but also against the weakening effect of incontinence; a disturbing influence is more surely met by a principle in consort with a supporting attraction than by the principle alone.

The simplest way to assess Grice's proposal is to proceed as we did in Aristotle's case and consider each of the four requirements in turn.

First requirement: a person is happy only if he satisfies enough of his desires.[21]

It is not unreasonable to suggest that one satisfies enough of one's desires just in case one pursues a stable and flexible system of ends. Such a system of ends must be 'workable; the more it should turn out that actions and performances dictated by the system cannot be successfully undertaken, the stronger are the grounds for modification of the system' (feasibility). Moreover, the system is not to be excessively reliant on 'aids the availability of which is not within one's control' (autonomy), and 'the pursuit of some ends enhances the pursuit of others' (supportiveness of component ends).

But there is still a difficulty here. Suppose Smith is a political prisoner; he has, for lack of any other alternative, adjusted to prison life to the extent that he pursues a stable and flexible set of ends. But he is not happy, for he is not satisfying enough of his desires, since his most *central and important* desires, his desires for various kinds of political activity, remain unsatisfied, and what counts as enough is determined both by how many desires are satisfied and by how *important* those desires are. The notions of stability and flexibility fail, it seems, to capture the dimension of importance. Aristotle, as we saw, does not face this difficulty since the appeal to virtue allows him to identify what count as the important desires.

One might object that the prisoner example is not convincing since stability requires agreeableness; the operation of Smith's prison system of ends must be agreeable. But surely it will not be—given that Smith is a prisoner. But why not? To be a prisoner is not to be excluded from enjoying reading, writing, contemplation, conversation, conversation, chess, planning one's escape, and so on.

Of course there may be *kinds* of enjoyment that Smith cannot experience; and, if this is true, perhaps we could appeal to it to rule out the prisoner example. In fact, Grice touches on this possibility

[21] Grice talks of ends, not of desires. The distinction does not matter for our purposes.

when he notes that 'Other *modes of* agreeableness, such as being a source of delight, which are not routinely associated with the fulfilment of desire, could discriminate independently of other features relevant to such preferences, between one system and another.' But what are the relevant 'modes of agreeableness', the relevant kinds of enjoyment? We will return to this question below.

Second requirement: a person is happy only if he believes he is satisfying enough of his desires.

On Aristotle's account, this belief plays a reason-providing role and is also a source of enjoyment. It has these same two functions in Grice's account. The first point to note is that a stable and flexible system of ends provides—to revert to Aristotle's metaphor—a target at which one aims. A stable system of ends yields 'answers to those practical questions which should be decided in light of general principles' (comprehensiveness), and the system is easy to use, for its 'effectiveness as a guide to living will depend, in part, on how easy it is to determine its deliverances on particular questions' (simplicity); finally, when there is competiton and conflict among component ends, the system will typically find 'an acceptable balance in the degrees of realization to be expected for each end' (compatibility of component ends).

A person who is guided by such a system of ends will form beliefs about whether he is satisfying enough of his desires. There are two reasons why. First, such a belief is itself an important component of stability. If one believes one is, in pursuing a certain system of ends, satisfying enough of one's desires, one will be all the more likely to continue to pursue those ends. So we should require such a belief as a feature of any maximally stable system of ends. Second, Grice's idea is that in aiming at happiness one is aiming at having a stable and flexible system of ends. If one discovers that one's system is not stable, one should modify it; otherwise, one will fail to achieve happiness. To be alert to the possible need for modification, one must form beliefs about the extent to which one is realizing one's ends, as too serious a lack of success is a sign of instability (as the discussion of feasibility shows). One wants to make sure that one is realizing enough of one's ends (or desires).

We may also suppose that the belief that one is satisfying enough of one's ends (or desires) is a source of enjoyment. Grice does not explicitly discuss the point, but there is no reason why he should reject the idea that enjoyment from this source is one of the modes of agreeableness conducive to stability.

There is an important difference here between Grice and Aristotle, as the following example shows. Imagine that Miller is devoting himself to becoming world chess champion. In aiming at this goal, he pursues a stable and flexible system of ends, but when he succeeds in becoming world champion, he is unhappy, for he fails to enjoy pursuing the system of ends that he pursues as world champion. What he enjoyed was *becoming* world champion; he enjoyed the role of challenger. The analogous situation is impossible on Aristotle's account since 'good men . . . are pleased when they are conscious of the presence in them of what is in itself good'. Miller's problem is that he aims at ends whose realization will not secure his happiness, and this raises the question of whether there is an illuminating and informative way to characterize this defect in Miller's ends. This question does not arise for Aristotle since one is always pursuing a set of ends whose realization will secure one's happiness provided that one's activity is in conformity with virtue. I will return to this question shortly.

Third requirement: a person is happy only if he not only satisfies enough of his desires but also enjoys the experiences and activities that satisfy those desires.

It is clear from Grice's discussion of agreeableness that he endorses this requirement. What Grice does *not* do is link this sort of enjoyment to the self. There are three reasons to do so. First, as the James quote suggests, there are—or at least it is reasonable to suppose there are—important relations between happiness, enjoyment, and the self. Second, by exploiting these relations we could characterize the defect in Miller's system of ends. The self-conception ('empirical self') Miller enjoys realizing is the concetion of himself as the challenger, but what he is aiming at is being champion, and when be becomes champion he fails to enjoy realizing *that* self-conception—being the challenger— whose successful realization leads him to live out a new self-conception, a self-conception whose realization he does not enjoy. We can cite this fact to explain why Miller is unhappy—provided we make enjoying the realization of a self-conception an essential component of happiness.

Third, recall that Grice has difficulty explaining what counts as satisfying enough of one's desires. The problem is that stability and flexibility provide, it seems, no way to identify the desires that it is *important* for one to satisfy. If we link happiness to enjoyment in the way just indicated, we could say that the important desires are desires to realize self-conceptions ('empirical selves') that one is 'standing by', and we could hold (or investigate the possiblity of holding) that the enjoyment of realizing such self-conceptions was an essential part of stability.

Fourth requirement: a person is happy only if his life is—and is seen by him as being—worthwhile.

Grice points out that there are stable and flexible systems of ends that fail to meet this condition. He notes that

we can point to systems of ends which so far as one can tell, might be undifferentiated with respect to stability and the features associated therewith, including agreeableness, yet which intuitively would be by no means equally approvable for the guidance of living; for example, such systems as might be espoused by a hermit, by a monomanical stamp-collector, by an unwavering egotist, and by a well-balanced, kindly country gentleman.

Grice suggests that a condition is needed that 'will differentiate ends or systems of ends in respect of value', and he adds that

here I would seek to explore a road not entirely different from that taken by Aristotle. I would consider the possibility that the idea of happiness in general might be determined by reference to the essential characteristics of a human being (rational animal).

This suggestion occurs at the end of 'Some Reflections about Ends and Happiness', and Grice does not indicate how to 'differentiate ends or systems of ends in respect of value'.

4. SELF AND VALUE

But is it all that clear that we *should* look for a way to 'differentiate ends or systems of ends in respect of value'? Instead, why not drop the fourth requirement altogether? Why insist on any link between happiness and worthwhileness? Of course, dropping the fourth requirement would mean recognizing the blade-of-grass counter as happy—as well as the hermit, the monomanical stamp collector, and the unwavering egotist. But is it so obvious that such lives cannot be happy lives? Grice would certainly resist the suggestion that we dispense with the fourth requirement, for it is important to him that the concept of happiness provide a way to assess ends in respect of value. The explication of happiness is a part of Grice's *moral* psychology; it is to be a cornerstone in the philosophical treatment of the question, 'How ought I to live'?

But this merely motivates an interest in the fourth requirement; what we want is a reason to think it is true. I want to suggest that the key to such a reason lies in the concept of personal identity. The suggestion is twofold: first, that—as Charles Taylor (among others) has argued[22]—an essential part of being a person, of having a personal identity, is organizing one's activities in accord with judgements of value or worthwhileness; second, that to count as satisfying *enough* of one's desires one must have at least some degree of success in realizing what one takes to be worthwile. So if one must satisfy enough of one's desires to count as happy, then it will also be true that one will be happy only if one is, in satisfying those desires, realizing (at least in some cases) ends one regards as worthwhile. Of course, even if this is correct, it provides only a partial defence of the fourth requirement since we will have explained only why a person must *believe* some ends to be worthwile, not why those ends must actually be worthwhile.

I will not argue for the above two claims. My aim is simply to suggest that if we are to understand the relation between happiness and worthwhileness, the notion personal identity should play a far more cetral role in the account of happiness—a role it does not play in either Aristotle's or Grice's accounts. So if we are to pursue Grice's strategy —and it is a promising one—of replacing Aristotle's 'activity in conformity with virtue' with 'suitability for the direction of life', I would suggest that an appeal to the notion of personal identity should play a role in the explication of suitability.[23]

[22] Charles Taylor, 'Responsibility for Self' in Amelie Rorty (ed.), *The Identities of Persons*, University of California Press, 1976.

[23] I am indebted to Andreas Esheté for many helpful discussions of these topics.

THE PUBLICATIONS OF H. P. GRICE

1941 'Personal Identity', *Mind*, vol. 50, Oct. 1941. pp. 330–50.

1956 'In Defence of a Dogma' (with P. F. Strawson), *The Philosophical Review*, vol. 65, April 1956, pp. 141–58.

1957 'Meaning', *The Philosophical Review*, vol. 66, July 1957, pp. 377–88.

1961 'The Causal Theory of Perception', *The Aristotelian Society: Proceedings, Supplementary Volume*, vol. 35, 1961, pp. 121–52.

1962 'Some Remarks About the Senses', in *Analytical Philosophy*, R. J. Butler (ed.), Oxford, Basil Blackwell, 1962, pp. 133–53.

1968 'Utterer's Meaning, Sentence Meaning, and Word-Meaning', *Foundations of Language*, vol. 4, Aug. 1968, pp. 225–42.

1969a 'Utterer's Meaning and Intentions', *The Philosophical Review*, vol. 78, April 1969, pp. 147–77.

1969b 'Vacuous Names', in *Words and Objections: Essays of the Work of W. V. Quine*, D. Davidson and J. Hintikka (eds), Dordrecht, D. Reidel, 1969, pp. 118–45.

1975a 'Logic and Conversation', in *The Logic of Grammar*, D. Davidson and G. Harman (eds), Encino, Dickenson, 1975, pp. 64–75.

1975b 'Method in Philosophical Psychology (From the Banal to the Bizarre)', *Proceedings and Addresses of the American Philosophical Association*, vol. 48, Nov. 1975, pp. 23–53.

1978 'Further Notes on Logic and Conversation', in *Syntax and Semantics: Pragmatics*, vol. 9, P. Cole (ed.), New York, Academic Press, 1978, pp. 113–27.

1981 'Presupposition and Conversational Implicature', in *Radical Pragmatics*, P. Cole (ed.), New York, Academic, 1981, pp. 183–97.

1982 'Meaning Revisited', in *Mutual Knowledge*, N. V. Smith (ed), New York, Academic, 1982, pp. 223–43.

THE MAIN 'UNPUBLICATIONS' OF H. P. GRICE

*Means revised later; article-length pieces indicated by quote marks; book-length pieces, italicised.

1955a (*circa*) 'Aristotle on Pleasure'

1955b (*circa*) 'Can I have A Pain in My Tail'

1958a 'Philosophers Paradoxes'

1958b 'Philosophy in Post-War Oxford'

1961 'Lectures on Negation'

1963 'Philosophy of Life'

1966 'Descartes on Clear and Distinct Perception'

1967 *The William James Lectures*

1969 'Logico-Semantic Paradoxes'

1971a 'Paradoxes of Entailment'

1971b (*circa*) 'Lectures on Formal Semantics'
(Presented at the Summer Institute on Philosophy of Language at the University of California-Irvine, 1971)

1972 'Probability, Desirability, and Mood-Operators'

1973 'The Power Structure of the Soul'
(unfinished; with Judy Baker)

1974 'Reply to Davidson on "Intending"'

1975 'Seminar Papers on the *Nichomachean Ethics*'

1976* *Freedom in Kant*
(with Judy Baker)

1978* 'Hume's Quandry About Personal Identity'
(with John Haugeland)

1979a *The John Locke Lectures*
(Also give as *The Immanuel Kant Lectures*, 1977)

1979b 'Aristotle on the Multiplicity of Being'

1983	*The Conception of Value*
	(Given as *The Carus Lectures*, 1983)
In progress	*Reflections on Morals* (with Judy Baker)
In progress	*Kant's Ethics* (with Judy Baker)

INDEX

DATE DUE